Supply Chain Management

Supply Chain Management

An Introduction to Logistics

2nd edition

Donald Waters

First published in 2003 as *Logistics: An Introduction to Supply Chain
Management*
Reprinted 6 times
Second edition 2009
Published by
PALGRAVE MACMILLAN

Palgrave Macmillan in the UK is an imprint of Macmillan Publishers Limited,
registered in England, company number 785998, of Houndmills, Basingstoke,
Hampshire RG21 6XS.

Palgrave Macmillan in the US is a division of St Martin's Press LLC,
175 Fifth Avenue, New York, NY 10010.

Palgrave Macmillan is the global academic imprint of the above companies
and has companies and representatives throughout the world.

Palgrave® and Macmillan® are registered trademarks in the United States,
the United Kingdom, Europe and other countries.

ISBN-13: 978–0–230–20052–4
ISBN-10: 0–230–20052–4

A catalogue record for this book is available from the British Library.

A catalog record for this book is available from the Library of Congress.

To Dan and Sue

CONTENTS

LIST OF FIGURES

LIST OF TABLES

PREFACE

This is a textbook about supply chain management, which is also called logistics. It describes the way that materials move into an organisation from suppliers, through the operations, and then out to customers. We take a deliberately broad view, looking at every kind of 'organisation', moving every kind of 'material', and making every kind of 'product'.

Every organisation, whether it manufactures goods or provides services, needs a reliable flow of materials. Logistics is an essential function that is best organised as an integrated function, responsible for all aspects of material movement. The way it is managed has a profound impact on customer service, costs – and just about every other measure of performance.

Supply chains are not contained within a single organisation, but they have a unique position in linking external suppliers and customers. No organisations works in isolation, and managers increasingly recognise that they are members of a supply chain whose aim is to satisfy the final customers.

This is a particularly fast-moving field. Developments in operations, communications and technology, global markets, increasing customer service, and a host of other areas are making new demands on logistics. This book gives an up-to-date view of supply chain management and shows how it is responding to these demands.

Approach of the book

This is an introductory book that assumes no previous knowledge of the subject. It can be used by anyone who is meeting the subject for the first time. You might be a student taking a course in business studies, or another subject that needs some knowledge of logistics, or you might read the book to learn more about a central area of management. The book gives a broad description of logistics, covering all the main concepts. It discusses these in enough depth to provide material for a complete course, but it does not get bogged down in too much detail. By concentrating on key issues, we have kept the text to a reasonable length.

The book has a number of features. It:

- is an introductory text and assumes no previous knowledge of logistics or experience of management
- can be used by many types of student, or people studying by themselves
- takes a broad view, covering all types of organisations
- sets logistics within its strategic context
- describes a lot of material, concentrating on topics that you will meet in practice
- develops the contents in a logical order
- is practical, presenting ideas in a straightforward way, avoiding abstract discussions
- illustrates principles by examples drawn from international organisations
- includes a range of features, including chapter aims, examples of logistics in practice, case studies, projects, worked examples, chapter reviews, problems, discussion questions and useful readings
- is written clearly, presenting ideas in an informative and easy style.

Contents

The book follows a logical path through the major decision areas tackled by supply chain managers. An obvious problem is that topics are all related, and decisions are made simultaneously rather than consecutively. In a book we have to take a linear journey through a complex web of material. To make this easier, we have divided the book into three parts. Part I gives an introduction to logistics. It defines key terms, discusses the role of logistics, its aims, importance, trends and the general context of supply chain management.

Part II looks at the design of an effective supply chain. It starts with a logistics strategy that sets the context for all other decisions, and then shows how the strategy is implemented. In particular, it shows how logistics developed into a single, integrated function that now spans global operations. Key decisions in design include the location, number and size of facilities.

Part III shows how materials move through supply chains. It starts by discussing the control of materials, and then looks at specific activities for procurement, inventory management, warehousing, materials management and transport. Logistics managers always look for ways of improving these activities, but they have to work in the context of generally increasing risk.

These three parts describe some of the most important decisions made in any organisation. They include key issues, such as:

- strategic importance of logistics
- globalisation and increasing international competition

- cooperation and integration of supply chains
- trends that put new demands on logistics
- new requirements from e-commerce
- use of new technology and communications
- increasing emphasis on quality and customer service
- environmental concerns
- growing concern over supply chain risk management.

Changes to the second edition

The subject has moved on quickly since the first edition, so this second edition has been completely rewritten and updated. New material has been added, there are new examples of practice, new learning features have been added, references and other sources of material have been expanded, the presentation has been updated, and there is a new glossary of terms. At the same time, some of the less relevant material has been removed.

Each chapter follows a common structure, which is outlined in the following map.

Alongside the book is a new website containing a range of material for students and lecturers. You can access at this at www. palgrave.com\business\waters. If you have any comments, queries, requests or suggestions for the book or associated material, the author and publisher would be very pleased to hear them. You can contact the author at donaldwaters@lineone.net.

Map showing the features included in each chapter

Part
The book is divided into three parts, each describing a different aspect of logistics.
Chapter
There are 15 chapters, each focusing on a specific topic
  Contents
  Giving a list of main sections in the chapter
  Learning objectives
  A bullet list to say what you should learn from the chapter
    Sections
    The main material in each chapter, divided into coherent sections
      Subsections
      Each section is divided into subsections where appropriate
      Key points in boxes
      To highlight definitions and key points
      Tinted Text
      To emphasise key terms

Logistics in practice
Giving examples of real logistics practice (about six per chapter)
Figures and tables
To illustrate points
• **Bullet lists**
To emphasise important lists
Worked examples
To illustrate the calculations in numerical ideas

Chapter review
• Bullet points reviewing the main ideas developed in the chapter

Case study
A description of a real problem, asking you to use some of the ideas from the chapter

Project
A brief description of a project that you can tackle to take the ideas further – this usually involves searching for some additional information about the topic

Problems
Where appropriate, a few numerical problems related to calculations described in the chapter

Discussion questions
About ten questions to encourage you to think a bit more carefully – and collect more information – about topics in the chapter

References
A list of sources for information and quotations

Further reading
Some suggestions for books on the subject

LIST OF IDEAS IN PRACTICE

Each chapter includes a number of 'ideas in practice', which describe some real aspect of logistics. These include examples from the following organisations:

Chapter 1

Tesco
Listerine's Supply Chain
Wal-Mart
Augulla Limited
Konigshaven Schlesser

Chapter 2

Concerns about Supply Chains
First Great Western
Zara
Pharmaceutical Supply Chain
Formats for Online Grocery Shopping
Deutsche Post World Net

Chapter 3

Czeskava–Imhof
The Emirates Group
Bjorg–Aichesson Pharmaceuticals
The Schenker Group
Aluminium Drinks Cans
David Hamilton Pharmaceuticals

Chapter 4

Bjorn Friderikson Car Rentals
Sainsbury's

PART I

An overview of supply chain management

This book gives a comprehensive review of logistics. It shows how managers control the movement and storage of products on their journey from original suppliers through to final customers.

The book is divided into three parts. The first part introduces the broad concept of supply chain management. It defines some key terms and discusses ideas that are developed in the rest of the book. The second part of the book considers the design of supply chains, and the third part describes the activities needed to move materials along the chains.

There are two chapters in this first part:

- Chapter 1 reviews the broad context of logistics and defines some key terms. It discusses the role of supply chain management, its aims, importance and key activities.

- Chapter 2 shows how logistics has evolved from a series of isolated activities into a single, integrated function. It is an area where ideas are changing quickly, so the chapter considers some current trends.

LOGISTICS AND SUPPLY CHAINS

Contents

LEARNING OBJECTIVES

After reading this chapter you should be able to:

- understand the broad role of logistics

- see how logistics support the operations of an organisation

- describe the role and structure of supply chains

- discuss the overall aims of logistics

- understand how logistics contribute to organisational performance

- appreciate the balance between customer service and costs

- list the activities within logistics and understand the relationships between them

- recognise the importance of logistics to every organisation.

Role of logistics

Every organisation has to move materials. Manufacturers have factories that collect raw materials from suppliers and deliver finished goods to customers; retail shops have deliveries from wholesalers; a television news service collects reports from around the world and delivers them to viewers. Most of us live in towns and cities and eat food brought in from the country. When you order books from a website, a courier delivers them to your door, and when you buy a mobile phone it has probably travelled around the world to reach you. Every time you buy, rent, lease, hire or borrow anything at all, someone has to collect it and deliver it to your door. Logistics is the function responsible for this movement.

Logistics
the function responsible for all aspects of the movement and storage of materials on their journey from original suppliers through to final customers

> • **Logistics** is the function responsible for all aspects of the movement and storage of materials on their journey from original suppliers through to final customers.

On a national scale, logistics needs a huge amount of effort. China has become 'the factory of the world' and exports US$100 billion of goods a month, while the internal trade of goods within the European Union (EU) is worth more than US$2 trillion a year – and all of this has to be moved between strings of suppliers and customers. A rule of thumb says that logistics accounts for 10–20% of gross domestic product (GDP), so the USA's GDP of US$13 trillion[1] might include US$2 trillion for logistics. The 30 members of the Organisation for Economic Co-operation and Development (OECD) have a combined GDP of US$40 trillion[2] and might spend US$6 trillion on logistics.

Despite this effort, we hardly notice logistics as it goes about its business – but sometimes you might notice the lorries driving down a motorway, visit a shopping mall, drive through a trading estate, see a container ship unloading, fly from an airport, or have a parcel delivered by a courier service. These are the visible signs of a huge industry that employs millions of people and costs billions of dollars a year. In this book, we describe this complex function, seeing exactly what it involves and how it can be managed.

Logistics support operations

Product
the combination of goods and services that an organisation supplies to its customers

Every organisation delivers products to its customers. Traditionally, these products are described as either goods or services. Then manufacturers like Sony, Ford and Guinness make tangible goods, while the BBC, Qantas and Vodafone provide intangible services. But this view is misleading, and it is more realistic to describe every product as a complex package that contains a mixture of both goods and service. For example, Toyota manufactures cars, but they also give services through warranties, after-sales guarantees, repairs and finance packages. McDonald's provides a combination of goods (burgers, cutlery, packaging, etc.)

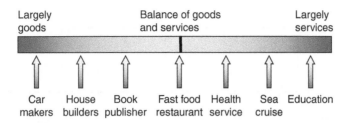

Figure 1.1 Spectrum of products

and services (when they prepare food, sell it and clean the restaurant). Then we can describe a product package as lying on the spectrum (shown in Figure 1.1). At one end of this spectrum are products that are predominantly goods, such as cars, domestic appliances, clothes and furniture; at the other end are products that are predominantly services, such as insurance, banking, education and telephone services. In the middle are products with a more even balance, such as restaurant meals, hospitals and some websites.

Product package
view of a product as a complex mixture of goods and services, including logistics

At the heart of an organisation are the operations that create and deliver the products. These operations take a variety of inputs and convert them into desired outputs, as shown in Figure 1.2. The inputs include raw materials, components, people, equipment, information, money and other resources. Operations are the manufacturing, serving, transporting, selling, training, and so on. The main outputs are goods and services. For instance, The Golden Lion restaurant takes inputs of food, chefs, kitchen, waiters and dining area; its operations include food preparation, cooking and serving; the main outputs are meals, service, customer satisfaction, and so on.

Operations
all the activities that create an organisations's products

Logistics manages the flow of inputs from suppliers, the movement of materials through different operations within the organisation, and the flow of materials out to customers (as shown in Figure 1.3).

Moving materials into the organisation from suppliers is called inbound or inward logistics; moving materials out to customers is outbound or outward

Inbound or inward logistics
move materials into an organisation from suppliers

Outbound or outward logistics
move materials from an organisation out to customers

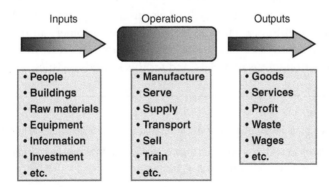

Figure 1.2 Operations transform inputs to desired outputs

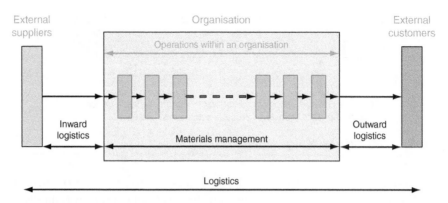

Figure 1.3 The flow of materials controlled by logistics

logistics; moving materials within the organisation (often described as collecting from internal suppliers and delivering to internal customers) is materials management.

Materials management
controls the movement of materials within an organisation

Materials

We have outlined the role of logistics in moving materials – but what exactly do we mean by materials? Sometimes this is obvious, for example, when a power station brings coal from a mine, a farmer takes potatoes to a market, or a computer manufacturer delivers PCs to a warehouse. With tangible goods it is easy to see the role of logistics, and even organisations providing the most intangible services move some goods around (perhaps paperwork or consumables).

Materials
anything that is moved into, through, or out of an organisation

Often the flow of materials is less clear, for example, when a television company delivers entertainment to its viewers, a telephone company provides a communications service, an internet service provider (ISP) gives access to the Web, or a research company creates knowledge. A broad view of materials also includes these intangibles. Then logistics is responsible for moving both tangible goods and intangible services – and this might include materials, components, finished products, people, information, paperwork, messages, knowledge, consumables, energy, money, and anything else needed by operations. A television company uses logistics to transmit programmes to customers, in the same way that an oil company uses logistics to deliver petrol. The clear message is that every organisation moves materials, and for this it needs logistics.

> **To summarise:**
> - A **product** is the mixture of goods and services that an organisation passes to its customers.
> - **Materials** are all the things needed to make a product, and these can be both tangible (such as raw materials) and intangible (such as information).
> - **Logistics** is responsible for moving and storing all the materials.

It can be difficult to imagine the effort put into logistics, but next time you go into a supermarket, think how difficult it would be to get everything delivered to the shelves. Then imagine a company like Tesco that has to keep all the shelves filled in its 4000 stores around the world.

LOGISTICS IN PRACTICE – TESCO

Tesco is one of the world's leading retailers, with more than 4000 stores and sales of £50 billion a year. They have a long-term strategy of continuing growth, based on their aspiration to: 'Strive every day to do the best we can for our customers.' For this they concentrate on four areas – growth in the core UK business, strong international expansion, to be as strong in non-foods as in foods, and to follow customers into new retailing services.

To support its operations it has a huge, efficient logistics network that spans the world. This continually evolves to meet changing customer demands, 'Following the customer – as customers' shopping habits change, we change and respond by providing new products and services.' You can see this effect in their UK stores. In the 1970s most of Tesco's sales were in fairly small supermarkets in town centres. Over the next 20 years they closed many of these smaller stores to focus on larger, out-of-town developments. More recently, they added smaller Express and Metro formats, so by 2008 they had 2.5 million square metres of sales area with four main formats to meet varying needs:

- 150 Extras with more than 6000 square metres and selling a complete range of household products
- 450 Superstores with 2000–5000 square metres and focusing on food
- 200 Metro stores with 700–1500 square metres selling a smaller range of food and ready meals
- 550 Express stores with up to 300 square metres giving a local service of 7000 lines.

The food range continues to expand, adding own brand, 'Finest', 'organic', 'fair trade', 'Healthy Living', 'Free From', and so on. Alongside food, the company now sells household goods – and continues its diversification into finance, insurance, telephone and Internet services, petrol stations, pharmacies, healthcare, and so on. Operations within the stores have also changed, with the growth of 24-hour opening, self-service checkouts, shelf-ready packaging, Clubcard and on-line shopping. Tesco has moved heavily into e-commerce, which has transformed many aspects of their logistics, including a web-based home delivery service with sales of more than a billion pounds a year.

Question

- What do you think that Tesco's logistics tries to achieve? What are likely to be the main problems?

(*Source*: Company annual reports and website www.tesco.com)

Supply chains

So far we have described the movement of materials through a single organisation. But no organisation works in isolation, and each one acts as a customer
when it buys materials from its own suppliers, and then it acts as a supplier
when it delivers materials to its own customers. For instance, a wholesaler acts
as a customer when buying goods from manufacturers, and then as a supplier
when selling goods to retailers. A manufacturer buys raw materials from suppliers, assembles these into finished products, and sells them to wholesalers. As
a result, most products move through a series of organisations as they travel
between original suppliers and final customers. Milk moves through a farm,
tanker collection, dairy, bottling plant, distributor and supermarket before we
buy it. A toothbrush starts its journey with a company extracting crude oil, and
then it passes through pipelines, refineries, chemical works, plastics companies,
manufacturers, importers, wholesalers and retailers before finishing in your bath-
room. A sheet of paper moves through a string of organisations before it reaches
your desk (illustrated in Figure 1.4).

People use different names for these chains of activities and organisations.
When they emphasise the operations, they refer to the process; when they
emphasise marketing, they call it a logistics channel; when they look at the
value added, they call it a value chain;[3] when they see how customer demands

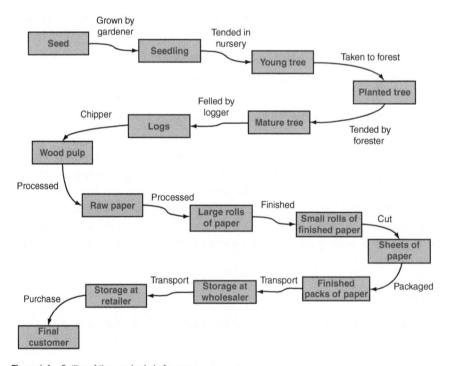

Figure 1.4   Outline of the supply chain for paper

are satisfied, they call it a demand chain. Here we are emphasising the movement of materials and use the most common term of supply chain.

> • A **supply chain** consists of the series of activities and organisations that materials move through on their journey from initial suppliers to final customers.

Supply chain
consists of the series of activities and organisations that materials move through on their journey from initial suppliers to final customers

Basic structure

Every product has its own unique supply chain, and this can be both long and complicated. A supply chain in Cadbury starts with cocoa beans growing on farms and ends when hungry customers buy bars of chocolate. A supply chain for Levi jeans starts with someone growing a field of cotton and ends when you buy them in a shop. The supply chain describes the total journey of materials as they move 'from dirt to dirt'.[4] Along this journey, materials may move through farmers, miners, processors, raw materials suppliers, agents, component makers, manufacturers, assemblers, finishers, packers, logistics centres, warehouses, third-party operators, transport companies, wholesalers, retailers, and a whole range of other operations.

The simplest view of a supply chain has a single product moving through a series of organisations, each of which somehow adds value to the product. Taking one organisation's point of view, activities in front of it (moving materials inwards) are called upstream; those after the organisation (moving materials outwards) are called downstream.

The upstream activities are divided into tiers of suppliers (shown in Figure 1.5). A supplier that sends materials directly to the operations is a first-tier supplier; one that send materials to a first-tier supplier is a second-tier supplier; one that sends materials to second-tier supplier is a third-tier supplier, and so on back to the original sources. Customers are also divided into tiers. One that gets

Upstream
in front of an organisation and moving materials inwards from original suppliers

Downstream
after an organisation and moving materials outwards to final customers

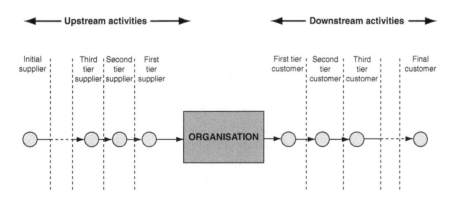

Figure 1.5 Activities in a simple supply chain

a product directly from the operations is a first-tier customer; one that gets a product from a first-tier customer is a second-tier customer; one that gets a product from a second-tier customer is a third-tier customer, and so on to the final customers.

This view of a supply chain seems reasonable, but you soon meet problems with the definition of boundaries. For instance, the supply chain for bread starts with wheat growing in a field. But the grain farmer might buy seed from a merchant, who in turn buys electricity to power their facilities – and you could extend the chain backwards almost endlessly. In the same way, there may not be a clear end to the chain, as logistics is increasingly seen as extending beyond the final customer to include the eventual disposal of products. For instance, the European Waste Electrical and Electronic Equipment (WEEE) Directive[5] became law in 2003 and sets collection, recycling and recovery targets for all types of electrical goods. In particular, it says that suppliers should have some responsibility for eventual disposal of their products so that, 'Users of electrical and electronic equipment from private households should have the possibility of returning WEEE at least free of charge.' The broad calls to 'reduce, reuse and recycle'[6] mean that logistics is increasingly concerned with the collection and return of materials as well as with its original delivery.

The boundaries around a supply chain are rather fuzzy and we have to draw an arbitrary line to define our primary interest, and say that anything outside this is of secondary interest. But there is another complication as our linear model of a simple series of organisations is not really accurate. Virtually every organisation gets materials from many different suppliers and sells products to many different customers. So each sees supply chains converging on its operations as raw materials move in through the tiers of suppliers, and then diverging as products move out through tiers of customers. For instance, a manufacturer might see sub-assembly works as first-tier suppliers, component makers as second-tier suppliers, material suppliers as third-tier suppliers; and it might see wholesalers as first-tier customers, retailers as second-tier customers, and end-users as third-tier customers (as illustrated in Figure 1.6).

Most supply chains follow this general pattern, but each product has its own unique chain and they come in a huge variety of different shapes and sizes. An everyday object like a shirt or blouse has a long journey from the farm growing cotton through to the final customer – and it also has different chains merging as buttons, polyester, dyes, packaging and other materials join the main process. When you buy a computer, many upstream strands merge as Intel provide the processor, Matshita the DVD drive, Agfa the scanner, Hewlett-Packard the printer, Microsoft the operating system, and so on.

After the operations, parallel marketing channels mean that supply chains also diverge into separate downstream strands, with the same product following different routes to different types of customer. For instance, car component makers

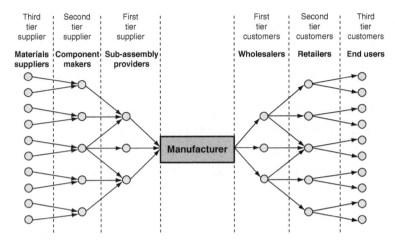

Figure 1.6   Typical supply chain around a manufacturer

sell to car assembly plants, wholesalers, garages, retail shops, car owners, and anyone else interested in buying their products.

LOGISTICS IN PRACTICE – LISTERINE'S SUPPLY CHAIN

Listerine was first formulated in 1879 as a surgical antiseptic, and has been used by dentists for oral care since 1895. In 1914 it became the first over-the-counter antiseptic mouthwash. The original formula has a notoriously strong flavour, but it was almost 80 years before new variations were introduced. Then in 1992 Cool Mint Listerine was introduced, followed by FreshBurst in 2003 – and now there are eight different versions, marketed under the slogan 'Kills germs that cause bad breath'.

The ownership of Listerine has changed several times. Most recently it was owned by Pfizer's consumer healthcare division until this was taken over by Johnson and Johnson in December 2006.

We can summarise the main elements in Listerine's supply chain as follows (illustrated in Figure 1.7):

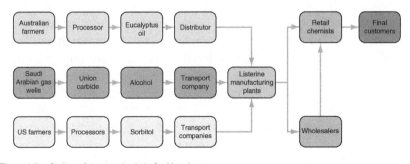

Figure 1.7   Outline of the supply chain for Listerine

LOGISTICS IN PRACTICE – LISTERINE'S SUPPLY CHAIN (CONTINUED)

- Australian farmers grow eucalyptus, harvest the leaves and send them to a processing company to extract oil.

- The eucalyptus oil is then sold to distributors and on to one of Johnson and Johnson's manufacturing plants (perhaps a Warner Lambert factory in Texas).

- Natural gas is drilled in Saudi Arabia.

- Union Carbide buys liquid gas and processes it into alcohol, which is shipped to the manufacturing plant.

- Farmers in the US mid-West harvest corn.

- This is processed to make Sorbitol which both sweetens and adds bulk to the mouthwash.

- Sorbitol is sent to manufacturing plant.

- The manufacturing plant collects ingredients and does all the operations needed to produce Listerine.

- The mouthwash is packed and sent to wholesalers, or directly to retail chemists.

Questions

- How typical do you think Listerine's supply chain is?

- Would it be useful to add more details to the description of the chain? What might these include?

(*Sources*: Website at www.listerine.com, 2008; Kalakota, R. and Robinson, M. (1999) *e-Business, roadmap for success*, Addison Wesley, Reading, MA)

Networks and webs

Our picture of supply chains is getting more complicated, with various mergers and divisions along their length. The reality is even more complex, as each chain can have more complex movements, such as loops where materials are returned. Most importantly, each organisation works with many – often thousands – of different products, each of which has its own supply chain. For instance, the French company Carrefour is Europe's largest retailer and comes at the end of tens of thousands of supply chains; Mittal's steel is used by countless other companies, Dell's computers are used for huge amounts of information transfer. This leads to Peck's[7] view of a rather nebulous 'flow of materials, goods and information (including money), that pass within and between organisations, linked by a range of tangible and intangible facilitators, including relationships, processes, activities, and integrated information systems'.

Because of the complexity, some people argue that the term 'supply chain' gives too simple a view and they prefer to talk about a **supply network** or **supply web**. In reality, these terms still describe the same structure and functions, and differences are largely a matter of definition. In this book we stick to the usual name of supply chain, and recognise that it refers to a complex pattern of movements and relationships.

Of course, you might ask why supply chains become so complicated and wonder if there is some way of simplifying them, rather like farm shops selling vegetables directly to consumers. But the truth is that short supply chains are not necessarily the most efficient. For instance, suppose the whole population of a town decides to buy vegetables directly from a farm shop. Then everyone in the town has to travel separately to the farm and back. It clearly makes sense to have a transport company collect the vegetables from the farm and deliver them to a central location in the town – like a supermarket. If the transport company delivers to one town, it can easily deliver to other nearby towns, perhaps stopping at a depot to organise local deliveries. This depot might store vegetables when the supply is plentiful and keep them for times of shortage. When the vegetables are being stored, the depot can add value by cleaning and preparing them. Continuing with this kind of argument, you can infer long supply chains develop. Bringing even basic products to your door is a complicated process, and it really is better to involve more steps and organisations.

Essentially, a new element should be added to a supply chain whenever it gives a net benefit – which means that it either adds value by doing work that customers are prepared to pay for, or else it reduces costs. The following worked example suggests the type of calculation needed for this.

WORKED EXAMPLE

Sterling Chemicals deliver products directly from their main plant to customers. Business is growing and they can use a specialised warehouse as an intermediary. With the following estimated costs (in euros) for each batch of chemicals, would this be a sensible move?

Plant logistics costs	Current system	With warehouse
Storage and handling	1,000	100
Packaging	350	0
Stock holding	100	50
Transport to warehouse	0	350
Transport to customer	1,600	200
Fixed costs	6,000	4,000
Administration	150	100
Warehouse costs	Current system	With warehouse
Storage and handling	0	300
Packaging	0	250
Stock holding	0	150
Fixed costs	0	4,500
Administration	0	150

WORKED EXAMPLE   (CONTINUED)

Answer

Adding the logistics costs shows that the total for the current system is €9200 a batch, which is clearly cheaper than using a warehouse costing €10,150 a batch. So the Sterling should not immediately use a warehouse. However, the figures also show the breakdown between fixed and variable costs.

Current system: Fixed costs €6000   variable cost €3200
With warehouse: Fixed costs €8500   variable cost €1650

The variable cost is lower with a warehouse, suggesting that this is more attractive for higher volumes. As Sterling's business is growing, the company could move in this direction at some point in the future.

An interesting point is that adding extra elements to a supply chain does not necessarily make it more complicated, and can actually simplify movements. For instance, imagine four factories sending products directly to eight customers, as shown in Figure 1.8. Here logistics managers have to organise 32 different delivery routes, but if the factories use a central wholesaler, the number of routes is cut to 12.

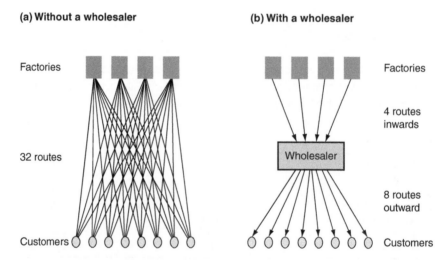

Figure 1.8   Adding a wholesaler simplifies material flows

Aims of logistics

We have said that logistics is responsible for the flow of materials through a supply chain, so it is also described as supply chain management. Some people argue that logistics is somewhat narrower and concentrates on the movements within a single organisation, while supply chain management takes a broader view of the whole chain. But again this is largely an argument over semantics rather than a real difference. Here we stick to the convention that the two terms refer to exactly the same function. This view is supported by the Chartered Institute of Logistics and Transport who give the following definitions:[8]

- '**Logistics** is the time-related positioning of resources, or the strategic management of the total supply-chain.'
- 'The **supply-chain** is a sequence of events intended to satisfy a customer.'

These definitions are deliberately broad and can include virtually everything that an organisation does. Imagine a car assembly plant, where each car passes along a series of operations. In principle, each time a car moves one step along the production line it can be described in terms of logistics moving materials, but it is usually considered in terms of production or operations management. This points to a basic interaction between logistics (moving materials to the point where they are needed) and operations management (working on the products). There can be no clear boundary between these two functions, and there is no point in drawing artificial boundaries around the activities to be included in each.

In this context, you might also hear people talk about logistics management, business logistics, distribution, physical distribution, supply management, materials management, merchandising, and a series of other terms. These are usually alternatives for the more general 'logistics', but you have to be careful as they sometimes refer to specific parts of the supply chain or slightly different activities.

Essential purpose

Supply chains exist to overcome gaps between suppliers and customers. They permit operations that are best done – or can only be done – in locations that are some distance away from customers or suppliers. Supply chains are needed to bridge the gap between coffee bean growers in South America and their customers in North America, and between natural gas wells in Siberia and customers in Europe, coal mines and power stations, food in the country and people in cities, and so on.

Overcoming physical distance is only one purpose of supply chains, as they allow for any kind of mismatch between supply and demand. For instance, the demand for sugar is more or less stable throughout the year, but the supply varies with the harvesting of sugar cane and beet. When there is excess supply, stocks build up in the supply chain and these stocks are used after the harvests finish. So in general, supply chains exist to overcome any kind of gap between customers and suppliers. Alderson discussed this idea in 1954[9] and we can extend his ideas to suggest that they overcome:

1. *space gaps*, with suppliers physically separate from customers (for example, bauxite is mined in Australia but is used by distant manufacturers)

2. *time gaps*, when there is a difference between the time a product become available and the time when customers want to buy it (for example, whisky is distilled in Scotland and then stored for at least three years while it matures)

3. *quantity gap*, between the amounts available from suppliers and the demand from customers (for example, publishers print books in large batches to reduce their operating costs, but each customer usually buys a single copy)

4. *variety gap*, when customers want a wider variety of products than is available from a single supplier (for example, each music company has contracts with particular singers, but we buy CDs from retailers who stock a broader range)

5. *information gap*, when customers do not know about the availability or source of products, and suppliers do not know about potential customers (for example, some countries have no McDonald's restaurants because the supply chains have not yet penetrated the markets).

Customer service

Logistics managers want to overcome these gaps as efficiently as possible – but what exactly do we mean by 'efficiently'? There are several answers to this, and managers may define it in terms of fast deliveries, low costs, little wastage, quick response, high productivity, low stocks, no damage, few mistakes, high staff morale, and so on. Although these are all worthy goals, they are really measures of performance rather than aims. To find the real aim of logistics, we must relate it to the wider objectives of the organisation.

An organisation usually states its overriding aims in a corporate strategy, and this typically refers to profitability, return on investment, share value, sales, customer base, and so on. The key point is that every organisation achieves its aims by supplying products to customers, and its success ultimately depends on achieving customer satisfaction. If an organisation does not satisfy its customers it will not survive for long, let alone achieve any of its aims.

This gives the context for logistics, and allows us to phrase the overriding aim of logistics in terms of providing customer service. To put it simply, managers should organise logistics in the best way to achieve customer satisfaction.

We have to be careful here, as any organisation can give outstanding customer service if it allocates enough resources. But resources cost money and higher customer service almost inevitably comes at a higher price. If you want to travel to a nearby town you might hire a chauffeur-driven limousine (giving high service and price), or catch a bus (giving lower service and price). The problem is that customers will only pay a certain amount for a product, so a more realistic aim for logistics is to find the best balance between service and cost. It might aim at providing a specific level of customer service for the lowest cost or, alternatively, maximising the service that is given for a specific cost.

- An overriding **aim of logistics** is to help the organisation achieve customer satisfaction.
- Higher customer service needs more resources that come with higher costs,
- A realistic aim is to provide the best balance of customer service and costs.

People often summarise the aims of logistics as getting, 'the right materials, in the right quantity, at the right place, at the right time, from the right source, with the right quality, at the right price' (which Bowersox[10] characterises as the 'Seven Rs'). No one can argue with this but, of course, it depends on what we mean by 'right'. This is defined by customers who, in different circumstances, can demand very different things. For instance, when you post a letter, you sometimes want it delivered quickly – in which case the 'right' delivery is the fastest. Sometimes you want it delivered as cheaply as possible, or with high security, at a specified time, with a receipt, to a specified person, and so on. Logistics must deal with these varying demands, with the essential point that it must give a service that customers are prepared to pay for. This is usually phrased in terms of logistics 'adding value' – which means that its costs are less than the perceived benefits that it brings.

Managers often describe the added value of logistics as a utility. When products are available at the place they are needed, logistics is said to have added place utility; when products are delivered at the time they are needed, logistics has added time utility; when products are delivered to the right people, logistics has increased ownership utility. Then we might phrase the aim of logistics in terms of maximising added value or achieving the highest possible utility. To achieve this, managers have to make two types of decision. The first type concerns design, when managers take a strategic view and devise the best structure for their supply chains. We look at different aspects of supply chain design in Chapters 3–9. The second type of decision concerns the flow of materials through this chain. We look at ways of getting an efficient flow of materials in Chapters 10–15. Summarising these two types of decision, Harrington[11] says that, 'logistics is both the glue that holds the materials/product pipeline together and the grease that speeds product flow along it'.

Utility
a measure of added value

Place utility
value added by having products available at the place they are needed

Time utility
value added by having products available at the time they are needed

Ownership utility
value added by having products delivered to the right people

LOGISTICS IN PRACTICE – WAL-MART

In 1962 Sam Walton opened a discount store in Rogers, Arkansas. He started with the idea that, 'The secret of successful retailing is to give your customers what they want' and this includes 'a wide assortment of good quality merchandise; the lowest possible prices; guaranteed satisfaction with what you buy; friendly knowledgeable service; convenient hours; free parking;

LOGISTICS IN PRACTICE – WAL-MART   (CONTINUED)

a pleasant shopping experience'. Sam called his store Wal-Mart, and was so successful that his chain grew quickly. In 1983 he opened a Sam's Club warehouse for members, and in 1988 the first 'Supercenter' selling groceries. During the 1980s Wal-Mart became the leading retailer in the USA, and started its international expansion. Early moves into Mexico, Puerto Rico and Canada were followed by South America, Asia and Europe – with most of the later expansion from buying local companies (such as ASDA in the UK and Interspar in Germany).

Wal-Mart is a classic example of how to manage rapid growth without changing the company's underlying values – in this case 'the basic value was, and is, customer service'. This is emphasised from the front door of each store, where someone greets each customer and tells them about special offers and promotions. Wal-Mart is now the world's largest retailer and in 2007 had 6700 stores, serving 176 million customers a week, employing 1.9 million staff – or 'associates' – and a turnover of US$345 billion.

A large Wal-Mart store stocks 120,000 different items, each of which has its own supply chain. Not surprisingly, the company needs a huge logistics effort, with 61,000 suppliers delivering $4 billion dollars' worth of goods a week. In the mainland USA products move through a hundred distribution centres, and on to 1000 Wal-Mart stores, 2300 Supercentres, 600 Sam's Clubs and 120 Neighbourhood Markets.

Efficient logistics plays a large part in Wal-Mart's success, and it uses the 'industry's most efficient and sophisticated distribution system'. This includes high levels of automation, sophisticated communications, utilisation of resources, and guaranteed availability of products. The logistics costs are so high that small improvements can have a considerable effect on profit. For instance, improving fuel consumption in their fleet of 7000 trucks by one mile a gallon would save more than US$50 million a year. In 2006 installing auxiliary power units in trucks that made overnight stops (meaning that the main engine could be turned off for longer) saved 10 million gallons of diesel fuel a year, US$25 million and 100,000 tonnes of carbon dioxide emissions.

Question

- Are logistics always as complicated as they are in Wal-Mart?

(*Sources*: Wal-Mart reports and websites at www.walmart.com, www.walmartstores.com and www.walmartfacts.com)

Activities of logistics

Logistics is a broad function which consists of a series of related activities. You can imagine these by following some materials on their way through an organisation, when you would typically see the following:

- *Procurement or purchasing*. The flow of materials into an organisation is usually initiated by a purchase order sent to a supplier. To prepare this a purchasing, or procurement, department finds suitable suppliers, negotiates terms and conditions, organises delivery, arranges insurance and payment, and does everything needed to get materials into the organisation. In the past, this was a clerical job that processed the transactions of orders, but this is now largely automated and procurement focuses on its role as the main link with upstream activities. We describe procurement in Chapter 10.

- *Inward transport or traffic* moves materials from suppliers to an organisation's receiving area. For this, managers have to choose the type of transport (road, rail, air, etc.), find the best transport operator, design a route, make sure that all safety and legal requirements are met, ensure deliveries on time, keep costs low, and so on. We describe transport in Chapter 13.

- *Receiving* makes sure that materials delivered match an order, acknowledges receipt, unloads delivery vehicles, inspects materials for damage, and sorts them.

- *Warehousing or stores* moves materials from the receiving area into storage and makes sure that they are available when needed. Warehousing also looks after stored materials, giving the right conditions, treatment and packaging to keep them in good condition. This is particularly important with, say, frozen food, drugs, alcohol in bond, chemicals, animals, and dangerous goods. We describe warehousing in Chapter 12.

- *Stock control* sets the policies for inventory. It considers the materials to store, overall investment, customer service, stock levels, order sizes, order timing, and so on. We describe stock management in more detail in Chapter 11.

- *Material handling* is the general term for moving materials within an organisation. Every time that materials are moved around operations, it uses materials handling, whose aim is to give efficient movements, with short journeys, using appropriate equipment, with little damage, and using special packaging and handling where needed. We describe materials handling in Chapter 12.

- *Order picking* finds and removes materials from stores. Typically, materials needed for a customer order are located, identified, checked, removed from racks, consolidated into a single load and moved to a departure area for loading onto delivery vehicles.

- *Packaging* wraps materials to make sure that they are properly protected during movements so that damage is kept to a minimum.

- *Outward transport* takes materials from the departure area and delivers them to customers (with concerns that are similar to inward transport).

- *Physical distribution* is a general term for the activities that deliver finished goods to customers, including outward transport. It is often aligned with marketing and forms an important link with downstream activities.

Physical distribution
a general term for the activities that deliver finished goods to customers

* *Recycling, returns and waste disposal*. Even when products have been delivered to customers, the work of logistics may not be finished. Sometimes there are problems with delivered materials and they have to be collected and brought back (perhaps because they were faulty, or too many were delivered, or they were the wrong type). Sometimes associated materials such as pallets, delivery boxes, cable reels and containers are returned to suppliers for reuse. Sometimes materials are brought back for recycling, such as metals, glass, paper, plastics and oils. Other materials cannot be recycled but are returned for safe disposal, such as dangerous chemicals. Activities that return materials back to an organisation are called reverse logistics (compared with forward logistics that made the original deliveries).

Reverse logistics
returns materials back to an organisation after they have been delivered to customers

Forward logistics
makes deliveries out to customers

* *Location*. Logistics activities are usually spread over many locations. For instance, stocks of finished goods can be held at the end of production, moved to nearby warehouses, sent to regional depots, put into stores near to customers, passed on to third parties, or a range of alternatives. Managers have to find the best locations for each activity, and consider related questions about the size and number of facilities. These decisions define the underlying structure of the supply chain, and we discuss them in Chapter 7.

* *Communication*. Alongside the physical flow of materials is the associated flow of information. This links all parts of the supply chain, passing information about products, customer demand, materials, movements, schedules, stock levels, availability, problems, costs, service levels, and so on. Coordinating the flow of information is always difficult, and logistics managers often describe themselves as processing information rather than moving goods. This view led Christopher to say that, 'Supply chain competitiveness is based upon the value-added exchange of information.'[12] The Council of Supply Chain Management Professionals highlights the combination of materials and information flow in their definition:

> Logistics management (is the function) that plans, implements and controls the efficient, effective forward and reverse flow and storage of goods, services and related information between the point of origin and the point of consumption in order to meet customers' requirements.[13]

LaLonde et al.[14] run regular surveys that show the activities most commonly included in logistics, and in 2007 these were transport (93% of replies), warehousing (86%), inventory management (75%), procurement (67%), forecasting (65%) and customer service (63%). In different circumstances, many other activities can be included in logistics, such as production scheduling, overseas liaison, third-party operations, information processing, and so on. The important point is not to compile a list of activities and draw boundaries around them, but to recognise that logistics includes many activities that must all work together to give efficient flows of materials. When we bring these activities together, we get the following general features of supply chains:

- Logistics managers make all decisions about the design of supply chains and the subsequent flow of materials.
- Materials flow through a series of activities and organisations.
- The forward flows start at initial suppliers and end with final customers, with reverse logistic moving materials backwards.
- Each organisation in the supply chain is a customer when buying materials, and is a supplier when selling its products.
- There are different kinds of relationships between suppliers and customers .
- There are always costs of logistics and these must be controlled and related to the levels of service given.
- Each element in the supply chain somehow adds value to the products.
- Alongside the flow of materials are associated flows of money and information.
- Stocks are formed whenever materials stop moving.
- There are inherent risks in supply chains, and things do not always go according to plan.

LOGISTICS IN PRACTICE – AUGULLA LIMITED

Augulla Limited makes a range of basic clothes in its Mumbai factory. Typical products are plain white T-shirts, underwear and shorts. The process is fairly straightforward, but Pradhir Augulla, the company's chairman, is disappointed by long delays in the supply chain. When he investigated these, he found that it takes an average of 365 days to move one product from an initial purchase of fibres on the open commodity market to purchase by final customers.

- Start of the supply chain with fibre available on the open commodity market:

  - Store fibre in commodity warehouses   (140 days)
  - Buy fibre and move to spinners   (11 days)
  - At spinners:

    - store raw fibre   (21 days)
    - spin to form yarn   (13 days)
    - store yarn as finished goods   (11 days)
  - Buy yarn and move to knitters   (8 days)
  - At knitters

    - store yarn   (6 days)
    - knit to form fabric   (9 days)
    - store work in progress as grey stock   (12 days)
    - dye standard colour and finish fabric   (7 days)
    - store fabrics as finished goods   (8 days)

LOGISTICS IN PRACTICE – AUGULLA LIMITED   (CONTINUED)

- Buy fabric and move to Augulla Limited   (7 days)
- At Augulla Limited

  - store fabric   (12 days)
  - cut to form components   (5 days)
  - store buffer of components   (6 days)
  - sew components to form garments   (14 days)
  - store garments as finished goods   (18 days)

- Deliver to regional distribution centre and store   (21 days)
- Deliver to local wholesaler and store   (17 days)
- Deliver to retail shop and store   (19 days)

- End of supply chain when customer buys garment from shop.

The main operations of spinning, knitting, dyeing, cutting and sewing take 48 days, and it seems that the various aspects of logistics take another 317 days. Pradhir Augulla is convinced that the supply chain can be more efficient, and has considered buying other companies to give more vertical integration and improve flows.

Question

- Much of the time in this supply chain seems to be used for storage and transport. Do you think this is common?

(*Source*: Pradhir Augula and company records)

Importance of logistics

Logistics is an essential function in every organisation. It is easiest to imagine in a manufacturer, with forklift trucks unloading pallets from lorries and moving them around warehouses – but the same principles apply in any other organisation. When a rock band goes on tour they carry huge amounts of equipment. Procurement buys everything that is needed on the tour, transport pack it and move it to the next destination, receiving make sure that everything arrives safely, warehousing keeps things safe until they are needed, materials handling moves things between trucks and the stage, location decides where to perform. The same types of decision are made with even the most intangible service, and an insurance company decides what kind of branch network to have, where to locate offices, who to buy telephone and other services from, how to deliver information to customers, and so on. Christopher[15] supports this view, saying that, 'Logistics has always been a central and essential feature of all economic activity.' Shapiro and Heskett[16] agree, saying that, 'There are few aspects of human activity

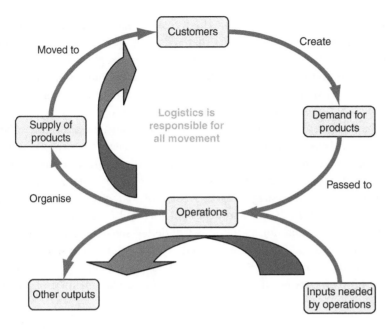

Figure 1.9 Essential role of logistics in meeting demand

that do not ultimately depend on the flow of goods from point of origin to point of consumption.' Bowersox et al.[17] say that, 'It is difficult to visualise accomplishing any marketing, manufacturing or . . . commerce without logistics.' To put it simply, without logistics, no materials move, no operations can be done, nothing is made, no products are delivered, and no customers are served.

Figure 1.9 suggests the role of logistics is an essential part of every trade. Customers generate demand for products, which operations create using necessary resources – and logistics move everything around this loop.

Not only is logistics essential, but it is also expensive. Unfortunately, it is difficult to say exactly how expensive, because normal accounting conventions do not separate logistics costs from other operating expenditure, and there is always disagreement about the activities to include. As a result, very few organisations can put precise figures on their logistics costs, and many have almost no idea of the amounts involved. One obvious point, though, is that expenditure on logistics varies widely between different industries. Building materials, such as sand and gravel, have very high logistics costs compared with, say, jewellery, pharmaceuticals and cosmetics.

We have already mentioned the rule of thumb that logistics accounts for 10–20% of GDP, but you have to interpret such figures carefully. Malone[18] suggests that the actual cost of US logistics reached US$1.2 trillion by 2005, accounting for 10% of GDP – but this estimate focuses on transport, which only accounts for 60% of total logistics costs.[19] The UK government says that 11% of the GDP comes from wholesale and retail trades and another 4% from transport and storage,[20] suggesting that overall logistics costs are much higher.

These national figures translate into high costs for each company, and although they differ in detail, everyone agrees that logistics is very expensive. Whether it is getting more expensive is open to debate. Some people say that fuel, land, safety, environmental protection and employee costs are rising and making logistics more expensive. They argue that this is a long-term trend that will inevitably continue. An opposing view says that improvements to logistics are more than compensating for price rises. This says that new and more efficient methods – such as lower stocks, more efficient vehicles, fewer empty journeys, e-business, lower overheads, and so on – mean that logistics costs are falling as a proportion of product value. The Council of Supply Chain Professionals[21] reports a mixed picture suggesting that the cost of logistics in the USA more than doubled over the 20 years to 2006, but then fell from 16% to 9% of GDP. This is probably a common pattern, as Childerley suggests that in 1980 logistics accounted for 32.5% of the UK's GDP,[22] but is now considerably lower. A broader survey in Europe[23] suggests that logistics costs fell from an average of 14.3% of sales revenue in 1987 to 7.5% in 2003, but then began rising again.

LOGISTICS IN PRACTICE – KONIGSHAVEN SCHLESSER

Konigshaven Schlessar is a food wholesaler, delivering to supermarkets in southern Denmark and Northern Germany. Its accounting system does not separate logistics costs, so the managers of one warehouse did some calculations to identify areas that need special attention. They used some estimates, opinions and simplifications, but feel that they have a reasonable starting point for further analyses. The following figures show the costs incurred for each €100,000 of net sales.

a. Cost of sales   €58,000
   – cost of purchasing products that are sold on to customers, including administration of the purchasing office

b. Transport inwards   €3,000
   – cost of bringing goods from suppliers and delivering them to the warehouse

c. Other costs of delivery to warehouse   €4,000
   – a general category that covers all other costs associated with supplier relations

d. Warehousing and handling   €6,000
   – cost of receiving materials, checking, sorting, moving to the warehouse and storing

e. Stock financing   €1,000
   – cost of financing stock, including debt charges

f. Sales force   €12,000
   – including salaries and all other costs of the sales office

| g. Special promotions | €3,000 |
| – including presentations, visits and samples | |

| h. Delivery to customers | €5,000 |
| – cost of taking goods out of the warehouse and delivering to customers | |

| i. Debt financing | €2,500 |
| – cost of financing plant and equipment | |

| j. Information processing | €2,000 |
| – including all aspects of order processing | |

| k. Returns and recycling | €500 |
| – cost of recovering pallets and any other materials returned to the warehouse | |

These figures are open to interpretation, but an initial estimate is that transport (b+c+h) accounts for 12% of sales and warehousing (d + e) a further 7%. Several other costs might be included in logistics, including some purchasing, sales, information processing and recycling.

Question

- If logistics is so important, why is it difficult to find the costs?

(*Source*: Company annual reports and internal memos)

Effects on financial performance

As an expensive function, logistics has a clear impact on an organisation's financial performance. In the example of Konigshaven Schlessar you can see that any savings in logistics costs give an immediate increase in profit. In this light, the Institute of Supply Management estimate that every 1% saved in materials delivery cost gives the same benefit as a 5% increase in sales.[24]

You can see the financial importance of logistics from a company's return on assets (ROA), which is defined as the pre-tax profit divided by the value of assets employed.

$$\text{Return on assets} = \frac{\text{profits earned}}{\text{assets employed}}$$

This gives a measure of how well an organisation's resources are used, and higher values usually suggest better performance.

Assets are described as either current (cash, accounts receivable, stocks, etc.) or fixed (property, plant, equipment, etc.). Both of these depend on logistics. For instance, improving the flow of materials reduces the amount of stock held, and this lowers the value of current assets. Similarly, improving the utilisation of facilities and equipment reduces the amount needed, thereby reducing fixed assets.

We can expand the basic equation to look at the effects of logistics on ROA summarised in Figure 1.10:

$$\text{ROA} = \frac{\text{units sold} \times \text{selling price} \times \text{profit margin}}{\text{current assets} + \text{fixed assets}}$$

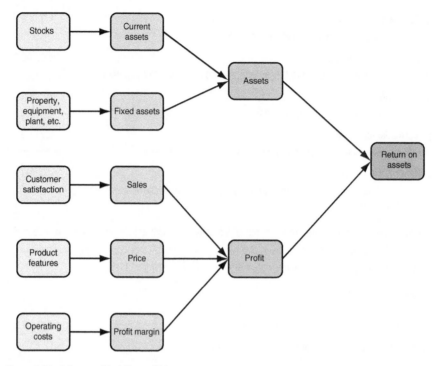

Figure 1.10   Influence of logistics on ROA

1. *Current assets.* More efficient logistics reduces the current assets, primarily through lower stock levels. Then lower investment in stock can free up cash for more productive purposes and reduce the need for borrowing.

2. *Fixed assets.* Its warehouses, transport fleets, materials handling equipment and other facilities, mean that logistics is a heavy user of fixed assets. Using these more efficiently can bring considerable savings.

3. *Sales.* By supplying a more attractive product, or delivering them efficiently to improve customer service, logistics can increase sales and give higher market share.

4. *Profit margin.* More efficient logistics reduce operating costs and directly increase profit margins.

5. *Price.* Logistics can improve the perceived value of products – perhaps making them more readily available, enabling faster delivery, or shortening lead times. This increased value can allow premium prices.

Good logistics can reduce assets and increase profits, both of which lead to a higher ROA (as illustrated in the following worked example). Using similar reasoning we can show the effects on other financial measures, such as share price, liquidity, investment, borrowing, and so on.

WORKED EXAMPLE

Mitchell Company has sales of £10 million a year. Its stocks amount to 25% of sales, with annual holding costs of 20% of the value held. Operating costs (excluding the cost of stocks) are £7.5 million a year and other assets are valued at £20 million. What is the current return on assets? How does this change if stock levels are reduced to 20% of sales?

Answer

- Taking costs over a year, the current position is:

Cost of stock	=	amount of stock × holding cost		
	=	10 million × 0.25 × 0.2	=	£0.5 million a year
Total costs	=	operating cost + cost of stock		
	=	7.5 million + 0.5 million	=	£8 million a year
Profit	=	sales − total costs		
	=	10 million − 8 million	=	£2 million a year
Total assets	=	other assets + stock		
	=	20 million + 10 million × 0.25	=	£22.5 million
Return on assets	=	profit / total assets		
	=	2 million / 22.5 million	=	0.089 or 8.9%

- With stock reduced to 20% of sales:

Cost of stocks	=	10 million × 0.2 × 0.2	=	£0.4 million year
Total costs	=	7.5 million + 0.4 million	=	£7.9 million a year
Profit	=	10 million − 7.9 million	=	£2.1 million a year
Total assets	=	20 million + 10 million × 0.20	=	£22 million
Return on assets	=	2.1 million / 22 million	=	0.095 or 9.5%

Reducing stocks gives lower operating costs, higher profit and a significant increase in ROA.

Other aspects of performance

Managers are largely judged by their financial performance, so they tend to focus on costs. But logistics also has an impact on other measures of performance. We have already mentioned this in terms of customer service, where the level of support given by logistics directly affects satisfaction with products. Then companies like FedEx and Amazon.com prosper by having efficient logistics that can promise deliveries within a specified, short time. In the same way, logistics affects measures like the waiting time for delivery, amount of damage, availability of products, and so on. It also affects less easily measured values, such as ethical standards and relations with suppliers and customers.

We could start listing the measures of organisational performance and show how logistics contributes to each of them, but the message should already be clear. Logistics affects virtually every aspect of an organisation's performance, from the aspirational values it espouses through to the lead time for delivering its products. This is based on its awkward combination of being essential, expensive and spanning most of the organisation's operations. As Bowersox et al.[17] say, 'No other area of business operations involves the complexity or spans the geography of logistics.' Novich[25] points out that, 'Poor logistics are the cause of roughly 50% of all customer complaints.' So the lesson is obvious – a well-run supply chain can give a huge competitive advantage and help achieve success; a badly run one leads to dissatisfied customers and commercial failure. With this in mind, we can summarise the importance of logistics by saying that it:

- is essential, as all organisations, even those offering intangible services, rely on the movement of materials
- has strategic importance with decisions affecting long-term performance and even survival
- is expensive, with costs often forming a large part of turnover
- has effects on most operations within an organisation
- directly affects profits, lead time, reliability and other measures of organisational performance
- forms links with upstream suppliers, developing mutually beneficial, long-term trading relationships
- forms links with downstream customers, contributing to customer satisfaction and added value
- determines the best locations and sizes of facilities
- gives public exposure and familiarity with visible locations, advertising on trucks, corporate citizenship, and so on.
- is inherently risky, with widespread safety, health, economic and environmental concerns
- prohibits or discourages some operations, such as moving excessive loads or dangerous goods
- can encourage growth of other organisations such as suppliers and intermediaries offering specialised services.

The following chapters describe current thinking about this central function.

Chapter review

- Every organisation supplies products that satisfy customer demand. Creating and delivering these products needs an efficient flow of materials.
- Logistics is the function responsible for all aspects of the movement and storage of materials. It moves materials into organisations from suppliers,

through operations, and out to customers. This is an essential function in every organisation, even those providing intangible services.

- No organisation works in isolation, and each forms a link in broader supply chains. A supply chain consists of the series of related activities and organisations that a product moves through on its journey from initial suppliers through to final customers.

- Each product has its own supply chain, so they come in many different forms. Nonetheless, there is an underlying pattern, with each organisation seeing materials converging through tiers of suppliers, and products diverging through tiers of customers.

- A fundamental aim of logistics is to help achieve customer satisfaction. However, there is a limit to the amount that customers will pay for any service, so a realistic aim looks for the best balance between customer service and cost.

- Logistics is best viewed as a single function, but it consists of a series of related activities. These range from procurement to initiate the flow of materials into an organisation, through to physical distribution to deliver products to customers.

- Logistics is always expensive, so it is in the awkward position of being essential, expensive and spanning most of the organisation's operations.

- The way that supply chains are organised affects costs, profits, relations with suppliers and customers, customer service, and virtually every other aspect of performance. As such, it plays a significant role in the success or failure of every organisation.

CASE STUDY – ACE DAIRIES

Roger Smitheram has run Ace Dairies for 16 years, providing a home delivery service for milk, dairy products and related goods. His product is a combination of goods (the items he delivers) and services (the delivery and associated jobs he does for customers).

At the heart of operations is an information system that contains details of Roger's 500 customers, including their regular orders, special orders, where to deliver, how they pay, and so on. Each day the system calculates the likely sales of all products for the following days. Roger adds some margin of safety, allows for known events (such as local fairs or holidays) and passes his order to Unigate Dairy in Totnes, Devon.

The Unigate dairy is 150 km away and acts as a wholesaler for local dairies and milkmen in Wales and the southwest of England. On the evening after it receives Ace's order, the dairy delivers it to a holding depot in Camborne. Later it moves the order a further 10 km to a cold store in Hayle. At 05:30 the following morning Roger collects his order from the cold store and starts delivering to customers. This normally takes until 13:30 in the afternoon, but on Fridays he spends more time collecting money and often finishes after 17:00.

CASE STUDY – ACE DAIRIES   (CONTINUED)

There are several specific problems facing Ace Dairies. For example, there is some variation in daily demand – particularly during holiday periods – so Roger has to carry spare stock. He cannot carry too much, as dairy products have a short life and anything not delivered quickly is thrown away. Roger aims at keeping this waste down to 2% of sales. There are also problems maintaining a service during holidays, when traffic congestion causes delays, and when Unigate has difficulties with their deliveries. However, Roger's main concern is maintaining his sales over the long term. Demand for doorstep deliveries is steadily declining as people buy more milk at supermarkets. The number of milkmen in Hayle has declined from ten in 1987 to two in 2008. Most of Roger's customers have been with him for many years, but he generates new custom by canvassing, delivering leaflets, special offers, carrying a range of other products, introducing new services, and so on.

Questions

- Describe the supply chain for milk.
- Where does Ace Dairies fit into this? What specific activities form the logistics in Ace Dairies?
- What are the main problems that Ace Dairies has with logistics?

(*Source*: Roger Smitheram and internal reports)

Project – useful websites

You can find a huge amount of information about logistics on Websites. Many of these give limited views, typically to advertise their own services, but others give more general information and advice. For instance, there is a surprising number of online logistics magazines such as:

    www.loginstitute.ca – Logistics Quarterly from the Logistics Institute

    www.logisticsit.com – manufacturing and logistics IT

    www.logistics-mag.com – magazine for logistics planning

    www.scdigest.com – supply chain digest

    www.sdcexec.com – supply and demand chain executive

    www.supplychainstyandard.com – incorporating the journal of the European Logistics Association

Search the Web and see what sites are useful for logistics. The following sites published by major organisations concerned with supply chain management give useful starting points.

    www.ciltuk.org.uk – Chartered Institute of Logistics and Transport (UK)

    www.cips.org – Chartered Institute of Purchasing and Supply

    www.cscmp.org – Council for Supply Chain Management Professionals (USA)

    www.elalog.org – European Logistics Association

    www.fta.org.uk – Freight Transport Association

    www.im.ws – Institute for Supply Management

    www.lmi.org – Logistics Management Institute

    www.lscms.org – Logistics and Supply Chain Management Society

    www.supply-chain.org – Supply Chain Council

    www.infochain.org – Canadian Association of Logistics Management

Discussion questions

1.1 Is it true that every organisation has to move materials to support its operations? Give examples from different types of organisation to support your views.

1.2 How important is logistics to the national economy? How has this changed over time?

1.3 Organisations are only really interested in making products that they can sell to customers. Provided they have reliable first-tier supplies and transport for products to first-tier customers, logistics is irrelevant. Do you think this is true?

1.4 Very few organisations deal with the final customer for a product. Most work upstream and form one step of the supply chain, often passing materials to internal customers within the same organisation. How does the type of customer affect the organisation of logistics and the measures of customer satisfaction?

1.5 The cost of logistics varies widely from organisation to organisation. What factors affect these costs? Are the costs fixed or can they be controlled?

1.6 How can you measure customer service or satisfaction, and why is it important?

1.7 How can a company find the best balance between service level and costs?

1.8 Is it really true that logistics affects all aspects of an organisation's performance?

1.9 'Logistics is a part of every product package.' What does this mean, and is it true?

1.10 In 1996 a survey by Deloitte & Touche in Canada[26] found that 98% of respondents described logistics as either 'critical' or 'very important' to their company. The survey also emphasised the rate of change in the area, with over 90% of organisations either currently improving their supply chain or planning improvements within the next two years. Do you think that these findings are still valid?

References

1. United Nations Statistics Division (2008) Industrial Statistics Yearbook, UN, New York and Website at www.unstats.un.org.
2. Organisation of Economic Co-operation and Development (2008) Annual National Accounts, EOCD, Paris and Website at www.oecd.org.
3. Porter, M.E. (1985) Competitive advantage, Free Press, New York.
4. Cooper, M.C., Lambert, D.M. and Pagh, J.D. (1997) Supply chain management, International Journal of Logistics Management, 8(1), 2.
5. European Community (2002) WEEE Directive 2002/96/EC, Brussels.
6. International Standards Organisation (2007) ISO 14000: environmental management, ISO, Geneva.
7. Peck, H. (2006) Supply chain vulnerability, risk and resilience, in Global Logistics (5th edition), Waters D. (editor), Kogan Page, London.
8. Chartered Institute of Logistics and Transport (1998–2007) Members' Directory, CILT, London and Website at www.ciltuk.org.uk.
9. Alderson, W. (1954) Factors governing the development of marketing channels, in Clewett R.M. (editor) Marketing channels for manufactured products, Richard D. Irwin, Homewood, IL.
10. Bowersox, D.J. et al. (1992) Logistical excellence, Digital Press, Burlington, VT.
11. Harrington, L. (1996) Untapped savings abound, Industry Week, 245(14), 53–58.
12. Christopher, M. (1996) Emerging issues in supply chain management, Proceeding of the Logistics Academic Network Inaugural Workshop, Warwick.
13. The Council of Supply Chain Management Professionals (formerly The Council of Logistics Management), promotional material and Website at www.cscmp.org.
14. LaLonde, B.J., Ginter, J.L. and Stock, J.R. (2007) The Ohio State University 2007 survey of career patterns in logistics and Website at www.cscmp.org.
15. Christopher, M. (1986) The strategy of distribution management, Heinemann, Oxford.
16. Shapiro, R.D. and Heskett, J.L. (1985) Logistics strategy, West Publishing, St Paul.
17. Bowersox, D.J., Closs, D.J. and Cooper, M.B. (2007) Supply chain logistics management (2nd edition), McGraw-Hill, New York, NY.
18. Malone, R. (2006) Logistics costs soar, Forbes.com, 18 July 2006.

19. Federal Highway Administration (2005) Freight management and operations, U.S. Department of Transport, Washington, DC.
20. Office for National Statistics (2008) Annual abstract of statistics, HMSO, London.
21. Council of Supply Chain Management Professionals (2007) 18th Annual State of Logistics Report, CSCMP, Oak Ridge, IL.
22. Childerley, A. (1980) The importance of logistics in the UK economy, International Journal of Physical Distribution and Materials Management, 10(8), 185–92.
23. A.T. Kearney Ltd (2004) Excellence in logistics, European Logistics Association, Brussels.
24. Institute for Supply Management Website at www.im.ws.
25. Novich, N.S. (1990) Leading-edge distribution strategies, The Journal of Business Strategy, November/December, 48–53.
26. Factor, R. (1996) Logistics trends, Materials Management and Distribution, June, 17–21.

Further reading

There are a number of books on logistics, and you might find the following useful.

Bowersox D.J., Closs D.J. and Cooper M.B. (2007) Supply chain logistics management (2nd edition), McGraw-Hill, New York, NY.

Chopril S. and Meindl P. (2007) Supply chain management (3rd edition) Pearson Education, Upper Saddle River, NJ.

Christopher M. (2005) Logistics and supply chain management (3rd edition), FT Prentice Hall, Harlow, Essex.

Coyle J.J., Bardi E.J. and Langley C.J. (2002) The Management of business logistics (7th edition), South Western College Publishing, St Paul, MN.

Gattorna J.L. (2006) Living supply chains, FT Prentice Hall, Harlow, Essex.

Grant D., Lambert D.M., Stock J.R. and Ellram L.M. (2006) Fundamentals of logistics management – European Edition, McGraw-Hill, Maidenhead, Berks.

Handfield R.B. and Nichols E.L. (2008) Introduction to supply chain management (2nd edition), Prentice Hall, Englewood Cliffs, NJ.

Harrison A. and van Hoek R. (2007) Logistics management and strategy (3rd edition), FT Prentice Hall, Harlow, Essex.

Hill J.E. and Fredenhall L.D. (2001) Basics of supply chain management, St Lucie Press, Philadelphia, PA.

Rushton A., Croucher P. and Baker P. (2006) The handbook of logistics and distribution management, Kogan Page, London.

Simchi-Levi D., Kaminsky P. and Simchi-Levi E. (2007) Designing and managing the supply chain, McGraw Hill, New York.

Waters D. (2007) Global logistics (5th edition), Kogan Page, London.

2

DEVELOPMENT OF LOGISTICS

Contents

LEARNING OBJECTIVES

After reading this chapter you should be able to:

- review the development of logistics
- discuss the pressures that force logistics to change
- outline ways in which managers respond to these pressures
- consider the move towards increasing customer service
- appreciate the ideas behind lean and agile logistics
- describe the effects of improved technology and communications in logistics
- list ways in which logistics is responding to changes in the business environment
- describe some new types of logistics operations.

Early logistics

There is no single point that marks the origin of logistics, and it has been evolving ever since people have wanted to move things. Its profile was raised by military campaigns, illustrated by Napoleon's remark that 'An army marches on its stomach', and Eisenhower's comment that, 'battles campaigns and even wars have been won or lost primarily because of logistics'. Taylor[1] described the surprising effects of railway timetables on the origins of the First World War. However, we do not want to dwell on the history of logistics, but want to show how the modern subject has developed. For this we need only look at changes in the recent past.

The last chapter showed how logistics is an important function in every organisation. Despite this importance, managers have not always given it much attention, preferring instead to concentrate on making products and giving little thought to the associated supply chains. Materials were clearly needed, but their movement and storage were simply unavoidable chores that raised the overheads of doing business.

In the 1920s some people began to look more carefully at the transport of finished goods.[2-4] But their work did not have much impact and in 1962 Drucker could still describe logistics as 'the economy's dark continent'[5] and say that this formed 'the most sadly neglected, most promising area of ... business'. By the early 1970s economic pressures on business grew and as firms searched for greater efficiencies they realised that logistics was not just a technical irritant, but a core function where they could make considerable savings. Since then it has become one of the most dynamic areas of business, continually introducing new methods and allowing new types of operation. For instance, Internet trading is only possible because logistics managers designed new methods for collecting orders and delivering packages quickly to customers. Similarly, China became a manufacturing centre only because of new shipping operations that gave low cost transport to their export markets; the price of food has remained relatively low because supermarkets use efficient supply chains; and shops are full of different products that they can get delivered from global suppliers.

Pressures to improve logistics

The main reason for the changing role of logistics was the recognition that it was expensive. In 1955 Unilever's annual report[6] said that a delay of one day in the flow of its products would need an additional £5 million of working capital (equivalent to around £100 million in 2010). They also found that it took 13 man hours to produce a ton of washing powder, but 19 man hours to distribute it. By the 1970s[7,8] and 1980s[9-12] surveys were suggesting that the movement and storage of materials typically accounted for 15–20% of revenue. This was a revelation, as the fragmented nature of logistics, along with prevailing accounting conventions, effectively hid the costs for most firms. In 1994 Hill[13] could still say that, 'many distributors are unaware of the costs of the distribution service they provide'. However, the foundations were laid and as logistics evolved into a coherent function the costs became clearer. Many companies started doing calculations like those in the following worked example.

WORKED EXAMPLE

JL Francisco & Partners run a wholesale fruit business around Rio del Plata. In normal circumstances the company makes a gross profit of 5% of sales. A consultant's report recently suggested that 22% of their operating costs are due to logistics, and that improved efficiency might reduce this by 10%. How much extra profit would this generate? If they do not improve logistics, how much would sales have to rise to get the same increase in profit?

Answer

If we take notional sales of $100, then the gross profit is 5% or $5. This means that operating costs amount to $100 - 5 = \$95$. At present, 22% of this, or $95 \times 0.22 = \$20.90$, is due to logistics.

If the company can reduce the cost of logistics by 10%, it would save $20.90 \times 0.1 = \$2.09$. Assuming that there are no changes to the selling price or other costs, this gives a direct increase in profit. A 10% reduction in the cost of logistics raises profit from $5 to $7.09 – or an increase of 42%.

Without reducing the cost of logistics, the company would have to increase sales by 42% to get the same increase in profit.

Other pressures for change

Apart from costs, there have been other pressures to improve logistics performance, such as increasing competition, more informed customers, technological developments, deregulation, and so on. The following list suggests some of the main pressures for change,[14] and logistics managers have to respond to these, or else lose out to more agile competitors.

Changing management attitudes

- recognition that logistics is an essential function which must be managed carefully
- realisation that decisions about the supply chain have a strategic impact

- identification of the high costs of logistics – with improvements bringing significant benefits
- increasing concerns about risks and vulnerability of extended supply chains
- a movement away from confrontational relationships and towards cooperation through alliances, partnerships, collaboration and other arrangements. (We develop this theme in Chapter 5.)

Changes in the nature of markets

- broad demands for faster deliveries, with materials moving quickly, giving shorter lead times
- fiercer competition forcing organisations to grab every opportunity to improve operations
- global operations meaning that new competitors are continually entering established markets
- movement of power in supply chains downstream to retailers and customers
- concentration of ownership meaning that a few large companies get economies of scale and dominate many industries (as you can see in the retail sector that is dominated by chains such as Wal-Mart, Tesco, Toys-R-Us and McDonald's)
- other changes in retail markets, such as 24-hour opening, home deliveries, out-of-town shopping malls, retail parks, telephone and online shopping.

Changes in the nature of customers

- growing emphasis on customer satisfaction – and recognition that this depends on logistics
- more knowledgeable customers who use technology to compare products from widely dispersed suppliers
- more demanding customers who want higher quality, lower costs, faster delivery and generally better service.

Changes in business operations

- new types of operations – such as just-in-time, lean operations, time compression, flexible manufacturing, mass customisation and virtual operations – which need new services from logistics
- improved communications allowing electronic data interchange (EDI), electronic fund transfer (EFT), e-commerce, radio frequency identification (RFID), improved contacts with trading partners, point-of-sales-data (POS), global positioning, satellite navigation, and so on
- broader effects of technology giving improved vehicle design, automated warehouses, driverless vehicles, new materials for packaging, and so on

- Organisations focusing on their core operations and outsourcing peripheral activities to third parties (with services like transport and warehousing increasingly outsourced)

- many organisations adopting a process focus, moving their focus away from a certain product and towards the whole process of satisfying customer demand.

Changing views of society

- Changing attitudes towards transport, with growing concerns about road congestion, air pollution, environmental damage, waste disposal, road construction, safety, and a host of other green issues.

- Traditionally, governments controlled transport, either by public ownership or regulation, but since the 1970s there has been widespread deregulation of the industry.

This seems like a long list, but it really only begins to describe the pressures for change. There are many others, including uncertain market conditions, price inflation, political change, shortage of skilled staff, fluctuating exchange rates, new customer demands, industrial disagreements, potential accidents, wars, change of ownership – and many more. The result is that logistics managers are under constant pressure to change. They cannot sit back and enjoy the status quo, as more entrepreneurial competitors will change their own operations to gain an advantage. Even when a company has the best logistics available, this is only temporary, as competitors are always improving their own operations and will soon catch up and overtake.

So the question is, how do managers respond to these pressures, and how is logistics changing? We start to answer this in the rest of the chapter. As logistics managers face many common pressures, it is not surprising that they often adopt similar solutions. This creates obvious trends in the industry, such as increasing globalisation, growth of e-business, outsourcing, reducing stock levels, and so on. We can review some of the most obvious trends, starting with an increased emphasis on customer satisfaction.

LOGISTICS IN PRACTICE – CONCERNS ABOUT SUPPLY CHAINS

In 2001 Warwick Business School's Operations Management Group ran a survey to identify concerns about the supply chain. Interestingly, customer satisfaction did not appear explicitly in the survey, with the most common management worries reported as:

Factor	% of respondents
Costs	100%
Integration of the supply chain	86%
Globalisation	71%
Procurement	57%

> ## LOGISTICS IN PRACTICE – CONCERNS ABOUT SUPPLY CHAINS (CONTINUED)
>
> Managers did not seem to be making much progress, even in areas they were concerned about. For instance, integration was clearly considered important, with 70% of respondents saying that more integration was needed to reduce costs. However, few organisations reported any real progress in this direction, and almost none had achieved widespread integration. Managers typically (in 88% of organisations) said that they could not increase integration because of difficulties in merging systems and consolidating electronic data links. Similarly, many managers regarded e-business as the major challenge – and opportunity – facing business. Yet less than 40% felt that e-procurement was a strategic issue, and only 36% included it in a written strategy.
>
> ### Question
>
> - Are you surprised by this survey result? What factors would you expect logistics managers to be most concerned about?
>
> (*Sources*: Anon. (2001) *Logistics and Transport Focus* 3(1), 48–9 and www.lefevre.co.uk)

Customer satisfaction

Customer satisfaction depends on logistics meeting, and preferably exceeding, customer expectations

Customer satisfaction is clearly one of the driving forces of logistics. The basic requirement is that customers get products delivered with the level of service that they expect. A more ambitious target is to give a better level of service than expected, hopefully leaving customers completely satisfied.

> - **Customer satisfaction** depends on logistics meeting – and preferably exceeding – customer expectations.

It is in everyone's interest to achieve customer satisfaction, so that customers have the deliveries they want and suppliers can look forward to repeat business. Unfortunately, it is more difficult to get agreement on how to achieve this satisfaction, as customers judge logistics by the product availability, reliability of deliveries, total travel time travelled, total distance travelled, delivery cost, information available, order tracking, on-time deliveries, mistakes in deliveries, complaints, frequency of delivery service, loss and damage, vehicle utilisation, consistency – and a whole series of other factors. Each of these can be important, and customers usually judge a service by a mixture of different ones, perhaps assigning a different weight to each. For instance, a company with a strategy of cost minimisation will put a lot of weight on the cost of logistics, but will also consider the lead time to make a delivery, reliability, damage, mistakes, and other relevant factors.

Different views of service

Some aspects of service can be directly measured, and then it is relatively easy to define a Customer service.

Customer service
a measure (or set of measures), that show how well logistics is performing

> • **Customer service** is a measure (or set of measures), which show how well logistics is performing.

If a shop has a particular product on its shelves for 95% of the time, managers have a clear measure of customer service. But other factors cannot be directly measured and rely on judgement, such as courtesy of staff, ease of ordering, flexibility, and delivery conditions. These are more difficult to include in a service measure, but they are still important.

People often assume that customer satisfaction and service are the same, and although they are related they are essentially different. Service uses objective measures to show how well logistics is performing; satisfaction is more subjective and takes a customer's perspective. This illustrates a divergence between:

- an **internal** view of suppliers, who largely consider a service in terms of cost and efficiency
- an **external** view of customers, who judge a service by how pleased they are with the result.

You can see the difference when airline executives want resources used fully with higher seat occupancy (an internal view), and passengers prefer low seat occupancy so they have room to move about (an external view). The problem is that when managers focus on the internal view they get a very efficient service, but one that customers do not like; and when they focus on the external view customers like the service, but it is inefficient. So logistics managers always have to look for trade-offs between the two – and this returns to the balance between cost and service that we mentioned in Chapter 1. This is a particularly important theme as it introduces two schools of thought, which are described as lean (with efficient operations using few resources) and agile (with flexible operations to ensure customer satisfaction). We return to this theme later in this chapter, but notice that in the past managers emphasised the internal view (suggesting that their view of an efficient service should be acceptable to customers) and now they take more notice of customer opinions (recognising that in a competitive environment they have to aim for customer satisfaction). The result is a trend towards increasing customer satisfaction, which is achieved through better customer service (illustrated in Figure 2.1).

Lean
an approach that aims at removing all waste

Agile
a flexible approach that aims that aims at removing all waste

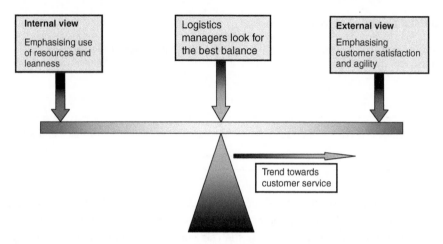

Figure 2.1   Logistics managers always balance competing aims

---

LOGISTICS IN PRACTICE – FIRST GREAT WESTERN

The emphasis on customer satisfaction is by no means universal, and you can find many examples where it fails. For instance, commuters on the UK's First Great Western trains were dissatisfied with the service, which they described as unreliable, overcrowded, late and using old rolling stock. First Great Western did not seem to respond to these complaints, but raised the price of fares by 10% to make them 'the most expensive in Europe'.[15] Commuters planned a 'fare strike' on 28 January 2008, wore cow masks to show that they were being treated like cattle, and printed their own 'Worst Late Western' tickets.

Not many people actually joined the fare strike (which could attract harsh penalties) but First Great Western did apologise saying that it, 'accepts that it has failed to deliver an appropriate level of service and is taking steps to improve its service'.[16] At the same time it agreed to freeze fares and double the compensation for late services.

Question

- Can you find other examples of logistics failing to give customer satisfaction?

(*Sources*: BBC News, 28 January 2008; www.news.sky.com; www.firstgreatwestern.co.uk)

Customer service is largely determined at the interface between a supplier and its customers, and is based around the common activities that link the two. These common activities include dealing with enquiries, negotiating terms, order processing, transport, billing, warranty claims, and all the others jobs where they meet. LaLonde and Zinszer[17] say that the essential feature of customer service is that 'each of the parties to the transaction or contract is better off at the completion of the transaction than they were before the transaction took place'. More recently Grant et al.[18] described it as a 'measure of how well the logistics system is performing in providing time and place utility for a product or service'.

In 1976 LaLonde and Zinszer[17] put the elements of customer service into three categories:

1. *Pre-transaction activities* – include everything that is done before an actual commercial transaction to set the scene. They might include the place of logistics within an organisational structure, status of logistics and its ability to affect operations, openness of an organisation to customers, flexibility of systems for dealing with customers, quality of sales staff, management services available, attitudes towards risk, and so on. These are usually defined by the organisation's long-term strategies and they provide the environment for customer transactions.

2. *Transaction activities* – include everything that forms part of the commercial transaction. These are relatively short-term interactions, with three main elements for:

   - taking and processing of orders (including assessment of customer requirements, checking product availability, credit checks, financial terms)

   - ensuring product availability (through inventory systems, substitute products, warehouse handling systems, emergency orders, and so on)

   - delivery of materials (including types of transport, lead time, special deliveries, transhipment, order tracing, and so on).

3. *Post-transaction activities* – include all the activities that occur after a customer has received a delivery, such as invoicing, unpacking, installation and testing of complicated items, maintenance, service and repairs. If things go wrong these include systems for dealing with complaints, and the increasingly important area of reverse logistics.

These three elements form part of every product package – meaning that logistics positively contributes to customers' view of a product. You see this effect with something you buy from a website. The ability of logistics to deliver quickly contributes to your opinion of the product, and you are likely to view a product that is delivered within a day as better than the same product with delivery taking six weeks. So logistics contributes to the product package to give a competitive advantage, which Jobber[19] describes as, 'the achievement of corporate goals through meeting and exceeding customer needs better than the competition'.

Aspects of customer service

We know that customer service can be measured in many ways, and return to this theme in Chapter 14. However, it is worth mentioning two particularly important ways that logistics affect the product package: through costs and lead times.

It is in virtually everyone's interests to keep logistics costs as low as possible, so that suppliers' products remain competitively priced and customers pay as little as possible. But low costs have broader effects, as they mean that new operations become feasible. For instance, low transport costs mean that a firm can sell its products over a wider geographical area, and cheap parcel delivery means that a manufacturer can sell products directly to customers, rather than using the traditional route through wholesalers and retailers.

Lead time
the total time between ordering materials and having them delivered and available for use

The lead time is defined as the total time between ordering materials and having them delivered and available for use. Again, it is normally in everyone's interest to make this as short as possible. When customers decide to buy something, they want it delivered as soon as possible; suppliers want to keep customers happy with fast service, and not have products hanging around in supply chains and raising storage costs.

Mass customisation
a production method that combines the benefits of mass production with the flexibility of customised products

The lead time is particularly important for products that are customised to specific requirements. Here lead times are traditionally longer, but companies can use new technologies to speed things up. For instance, mass customisation combines the benefits of mass production with the flexibility of customised products, and it relies on flexible supply chains that can respond quickly to varying conditions. Dell computers made a lot of progress with mass customisation, and instead of building standard computers and selling them through retailers, they waited until a customer placed an order on their website and then build a computer with the exact specifications requested. Efficient logistics make sure that raw materials were always available for manufacturing, and then delivered the finished machine quickly to the customer. Unfortunately, competition in the computer market forced Dell to move away from this strategy and since 2007 they have used more traditional methods. On the other hand, research into the '3DayCar Programme' suggests that the motor industry could become more flexible with 80% of cars in the UK built to order.[20, 21]

These two factors of costs and lead time are both important, and they represent two schools of thought for logistics. Low cost is clearly aligned with efficiency and leanness, while short lead times are aligned with customer service and agility.

Lean and agile

Lean logistics
an approach that aims to remove all waste from supply chains

Lean logistics always aims at a more efficient flow of materials, typically looking for faster deliveries, lower stock levels, less handling, fewer movements, and lower costs.[22, 23] It focuses on removing all waste from supply chains. For this, its characteristic approach is to analyse current operations in the chain, and then systematically remove all the wasted effort, movement, materials, time and other resources. This seems a simple idea, and you might assume that it is standard practice. To a certain extent you would be right, but leanness is more than a causal look around to find obvious improvements, and it is a relentless search throughout the whole organisation to identify all waste and design new methods for eliminating it. The result can be dramatic improvements in performance.

The alternative view says that leanness is too absorbed in its search for efficiencies and can inadvertently reduce customer service. The argument is that customer service is paramount and organisations should be willing to sacrifice some efficiency if it leads to greater customer satisfaction. In particular, agile logistics should be flexible enough to give a customised service and respond quickly to changing demands.[24]

It is easy to assume that there is conflict between these two movements. To some extent this is true, but the two themes are not really mutually exclusive and managers can design logistics that are both lean and agile.[25,26] For instance, using a website to collect customer orders can both reduce costs and increase customer satisfaction; reducing the length of a supply chain can make the movement of materials both faster and more flexible; using a specialised delivery service can increase both leanness and agility. Indeed, we might see the low costs achieved by leanness as a way of increasing customer satisfaction. This is an important theme that needs more attention, and we return to it in Chapter 3.

Agile logistics
a flexible approach, which aims at customer satisfaction

LOGISTICS IN PRACTICE – ZARA

The Spanish company Inditex is one of the world's largest producers of fashion clothing. It was founded in 1975 and grew dramatically to more than 4000 stores in 70 countries and a turnover of €10 billion by 2008. This success in a highly competitive market has been achieved with virtually no marketing, but by focusing on customers to the extent that, 'Our customers are the basis and reason for our group's existence.' A key part of this appears with their combination of lean and flexible logistics.

The fashion industry traditionally works to four distinct seasons a year. Production schedules typically have clothes designed in one season, produced in the second, and sold in the third – giving a total lead time of up to nine months.

At the start of each season shops have to be full of products in the new styles, meaning that they have high stocks of clothes that were made in the previous season, and wholesalers have high stocks of the same products to re-supply shops at short notice. Unfortunately, if demand for a product is particularly high, there are shortages as manufacturers have already moved on to next season's designs; and if demand is unexpectedly low the supply chain is already full of the product, so the only option is to get rid of it in end of season sales.

Zara has abandoned this seasonal pattern and has moved to flexible operations that allow continuous reviews with, 'Our own and our suppliers' production . . . [are] able to focus on trend changes happening inside each season.' In other words, they continuously monitor changes in fashion and have agile operations that can bring new products to stores in five or six weeks and sometimes in less than two weeks. The company makes 85% of products in the season they are sold, it changes 75% of products every three or four weeks, and creates 10,000 new products a year. Customers know that new products are continuously arriving, so it is worth making frequent visits – and by closely matching the supply to their demands Zara does not have to discount old stock in end of season sales.

Zara's process for getting goods in stores so quickly begins with its Design Department, which collects information about trends from company electronic point-of-sales (EPOS) returns, fashion

Electronic point-of-sales
system for automatically recording and transmitting information about sales from cash terminals

shows, competitors' stores, university campuses, pubs, clubs, and anywhere else they can. These ideas are worked into designs within days. They cannot get a rapid response by shipping products through extended supply chains, so at a time when most fashion companies have moved manufacturing to the Far East, Zara says that this would give unacceptable delays in its major markets of Europe and the Americas. Instead, it manufactures three-quarters of garments in quick-response facilities in Europe (about half in Spain). These move quickly through logistics centres in Spain, giving at least two deliveries a week to all stores. The company does import about a quarter of its garments from low-cost centres in Asia, but these are standard garments with a longer shelf life where cost is a more important factor.

Question

● Can you find other examples of companies that combine lean and agile logistics?

(*Sources*: Website at www.inditex.com and www.zara.com)

Improving communications

Another clear trend in logistics – as in almost every other aspect of life – has been the increased use of technology. This appears in many forms, but probably the greatest impact comes with better communications. In the recent past managers would send materials on journeys and effectively lose sight of them until they appeared at their destination. Now they continuously monitor progress and can make adjustments during the journey.

You can see the effects of improved communications in the way that companies place orders. When a company wants to buy something, it typically has to generate a description of the products, a purchase order, order confirmation, contract terms, shipping papers, financial arrangements, delivery details, special conditions, invoices, and so on. In the past, all of these – and mountains of other paperwork – had to be printed and posted between organisations. This could make even a simple transaction seem complicated and very time-consuming. Telephones help with some transactions but, as Sam Goldwyn pointed out: 'a verbal contract isn't worth the paper it's written on'.

New technology in the past few years has revolutionised the way that orders are placed. Some progress came with fax (or facsimile) machines that send electronic copies of document between distant locations in seconds rather than days. But early fax machines only transmitted printed documents, so a document could

Electronic data interchange
uses standard formats to allow remote computers to exchange data without going through any intermediaries

EDI
Electronic data interchange

be produced by computer, printed, fed into a fax machine, transmitted over telephone lines to another fax machine, printed, and the information entered onto another computer.

By the 1990s the obvious next step had arrived with electronic data interchange (EDI), which introduced standard formats to allow remote computers to exchange data without going through any intermediaries. Early users were supermarkets, who linked their stock control systems directly to suppliers' order processing systems. This means that their checkouts can record sales of each item when scanning its bar code, and when stocks become low the system automatically sends a message asking for another delivery. This use of EPOS data results in less paperwork, lower transaction costs, faster communications, fewer errors, more integrated systems, and closer business relations.

By 1997 it was estimated that 2000 companies in the UK regularly used EDI for trade with suppliers.[27] Over the next few years electronic trading became more widespread and sophisticated. The mushrooming of email and was followed by of e-business, e-commerce, e-shops, e-auctions – and soon 'e-anything'. With purchasing this developed into e-purchasing or e-procurement (which we discuss in Chapter 10). This comes in many forms, all based on the direct exchange of data between supplier's and customer's computers. Two main versions are B2B (business-to-business, where one business buys materials directly from another business) and B2C (business-to-customer, where a final customer buys from a business).

Two associated technologies have developed to support e-business. The first is item coding, which gives every item a unique identifying tag. Early versions of this tag – and still the most common – are bar codes that can be read automatically as an item moves along its journey. Then logistics systems know where all items are at any time, and automatic handling equipment can move, sort, consolidate, pack and deliver them. A more recent development is radio frequency identification (RFID), which is not a passive label, but is an active transmitter. When it receives an enquiry, a RFID tag transmits a range of information about the product, its location, status, and so on.

The second technology to support e-business is electronic fund transfer (EFT), which automatically transfers money between bank accounts. When the receipt of materials is acknowledged, EFT automatically debits the customer's bank account and credits the supplier's. Now there is a closed loop, with EDI to place orders, item coding to track the movement, and EFT to arrange payment.

EPOS
electronic point of sales

e-purchasing
purchasing products using the Internet

e-procurement
acquiring products using the Internet

B2B
trade that is business-to-business

B2C
trade that is business-to-customer

Item coding
gives every item a unique identifying tag so that its movements can be traced

Radio frequency identification
an active transmitter used for identifying items

RFID
radio frequency identification

Electronic fund transfer
automatically transfers money between bank accounts

EFT
Electronic fund transfer

e-business

We need hardly say that Internet trading has grown enormously in recent years. In 1998 there was some trading, but the future was clearly signalled when General Motors and Wal-Mart announced that they would only buy from suppliers through e-procurement. By 2002 around 83% of UK suppliers were using electronic catalogues for B2B[28] and the worldwide value of B2B trade was over US$2 trillion.[29] However, it is difficult to put a reliable value on e-business as there are so many variations. Is it a transaction where every stage is completed through the Internet, one that is initiated by a website, or one where even a single activity is done over the Internet? Figure 2.2 shows two views of the early growth of global electronic trade[30, 31] and this is likely to continue for the foreseeable future.

The important point about e-business is that it does not just improve the speed of purchasing by using standard formats for instant communication between systems, but it allows completely new types of operations. For instance, companies

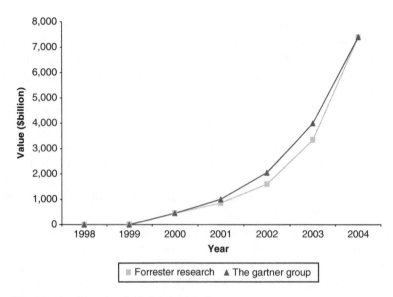

Figure 2.2   Estimates of the value of global electronic trade

can reduce the length of supply chains be dealing directly with upstream suppliers, and B2C allows final customer to skip tiers of suppliers. In many ways it has moved the effort of logistics from physical materials to information, 'replacing inventory by information'. For example, organisations traditionally held spare stock to allow for uncertain demand, but e-business removes this by reducing the uncertainty in demand by monitoring real-time information about sales, and locating replacement supplies that can be used to cover any emergencies.

Early on-line catalogues – effectively e-shops – have developed in several ways. Early moves were to e-auctions, where customers bid against each other for products. The best known of these is eBay, with 276 million registered users trading goods worth $60 billion in 2007.[32] Searching through the websites of individual suppliers takes some time, so new services appeared to automatically compare offerings from different sites, and report on the options (in the way that Confused.com compares quotes from many car insurance companies). A similar approach appears in 'third-party marketplaces', where suppliers list both their own products and those available from competitors – and if you buy from the competitor, the site charges them a transaction fee. You can see this in Amazon.com, which lists all available copies of a book and you can choose to buy either from Amazon or from another supplier.

Although less familiar, the value of B2B is far greater than that of B2C. It started with direct links between two companies and then grew into more sophisticated formats, starting with buying exchanges. These have companies – usually major manufacturers – creating their own, private networks for dealing with suppliers, and they only trade with members of this network. In the motor industry, General Motors, Ford and DaimlerChrysler initially formed their own trading networks. However, they dealt with common suppliers and it was easier to merge the separate networks into a single exchange, with pooled information making it easier to plan their own production and supplies.[33] Buying exchanges evolved into e-marketplaces, which are large websites that allow easier interactions businesses. Essentially, they help buyers find suppliers, and help suppliers find new buyers.

e-business continues to expand, but a major concern is security and the possibility that unauthorised people can access information and illegally transfer money. Despite continuing developments in security, fraud and identity theft are continuing problems. Perhaps the most familiar way of dealing with these are through intermediaries like PayPal, who separate the buyer from the seller and provide a secure third party to organise transfers of money and information.

LOGISTICS IN PRACTICE – PHARMACEUTICAL SUPPLY CHAIN

A common criticism of e-business is that it automates existing transactions but does not take the opportunity to design entirely new operations. An example of this is the way that prescription medicines are handled.

Traditionally, to get a prescription medicine, a patient goes to their doctor, who examines them and writes a paper prescription for medicine. The patient takes the prescription to a pharmacist who exchanges it for the medicine. There is a huge number of medicines and they can be expensive, so pharmacists only keep a limited stock. If they do not have the requested medicine, they order it from a wholesaler who typically makes several deliveries a day. Then the patient returns some time later to pick it up. Figure 2.3 shows the main elements of this supply chain.

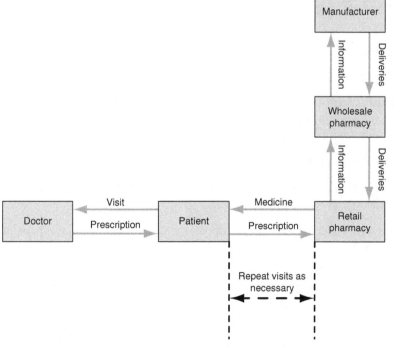

Figure 2.3   Part of the traditional supply chain for pharmaceuticals

---

LOGISTICS IN PRACTICE – PHARMACEUTICAL SUPPLY CHAIN (CONTINUED)

The usual approach of improving this involves making some adjustments, such as using e-mails for repeat prescriptions, adding pharmacies to doctors' premises, and starting a prescription collection and delivery services. But e-business allows a more efficient alternative shown in Figure 2.4. Here a patient goes to their doctor who examines them, uses an electronic link to the manufacturer, and gets the medicine delivered directly to the patient's home.

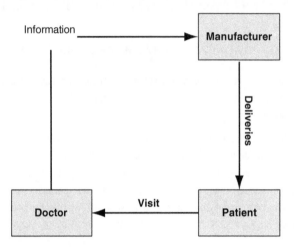

Figure 2.4 Simplified supply chain for medicine

Question

• What are the benefits of the new system? Does it have any disadvantages?

(*Source*: Duncan, R. (2007) Internet traders can increase profitability by reshaping their supply chains, in Waters, D. (editor) Global Logistics, Kogan Page, London.)

Effects of e-business

We have already mentioned some of the common benefits of e-business, and a reasonable list includes the following:

• *Less paperwork*. The essential feature of e-business is that it replaces paper transactions by electronic ones – resulting in less paper, fewer manual operations, fewer mistakes, faster transactions, more information available, and so on.

• *Shorter supply chains*. e-business allows upstream organisations to trade directly with downstream customers, bypassing layers of intermediaries.

• *Improved communications*. Organisations within the supply chain can communicate directly, avoiding the traditional restriction that routes information only from one tier of organisations to the next.

- *Transaction recording.* Most routine transactions can be done automatically, becoming much faster and more reliable. For instance, automated purchasing does away with all of the traditional steps in submitting a purchase order.

- *Convenient timing.* A major advantage of e-business is that it is available at any time, and customers are not limited to fixed opening times. Suppliers who work with both e-business and traditional stores generally notice that their e-business trade is greater at times when their stores are closed.

- *Convenient location.* Purchases can be made from any location that has a computer, so neither customers nor suppliers have to travel to specific locations for the transaction. This is particularly useful for small suppliers who can dramatically expand their geographical coverage.

- *Lead time.* The effect here can differ widely. It takes much longer to get a delivery of goods from a remote supplier than it takes to visit a local store, so there may be no point in using the Internet for small, routine or urgent orders. On the other hand, some items – particularly software, DVDs, music and reports – can be downloaded from websites and their delivery is much faster.

- *Type of facilities.* Unlike traditional businesses that are typically located near to customers or key suppliers, e-businesses can work anywhere that has good communications and transport links. So they generally aim for economies of scale and use large facilities in low cost areas.

- *Range of products.* Large facilities allow e-business suppliers to hold a much larger range of products than traditional stores. For instance, the stock of books at Amazon.com is measured in millions, while that in a regular bookshop is measured in thousands.

- *Transport.* e-business needs rapid delivery of small quantities – often individual packages – to customers. This is inherently less efficient that traditional transport, which concentrates goods into fewer, large deliveries, and it probably accounts for a reduction in the efficiency of national vehicle fleets.[34]

- *Stock.* By using large, central facilities and improving the flow of materials in shorter supply chains, e-businesses can generally work with lower stocks of each item.

- *Order tracking.* Internet orders can seem to disappear as soon as they are placed, and only reappear when goods are delivered. This effect is reduced by tracking systems that show the location of goods and state of an order at any time. For instance, FedEx tracks all of its 7 million shipments a day, so that it can give online reports on the exact location and condition of each.[35]

- *Flexible pricing.* Online suppliers can change their prices and terms to reflect real-time conditions. Airlines take advantage of this, and when there are spare seats on a flight they offer last-minute bargains – meaning that you can see prices on their websites changing quickly in response to current supply and demand.

- *Goods return.* Sometimes goods have to be returned to suppliers, particularly with online orders where customers have no chance to examine goods before they buy them. It is more difficult and expensive to return items, as there is no store for customers to visit, and they have to make alternative arrangements for collection. A criticism of online supermarkets is that deliveries have substitute products when those ordered are unavailable, and customers sometimes feel that the substitutes are unacceptable.

- *Operating costs.* Efficient operations allow e-businesses to give lower costs, but this is not inevitable as high transport charges and slow delivery can increase prices. Price is only one factor in the decision to use e-business and other factors may be more important.

LOGISTICS IN PRACTICE – FORMATS FOR ONLINE GROCERY SHOPPING

Although e-business is growing quickly, online grocery shopping has had mixed success. Some firms have enjoyed dramatic success, while others have closed after a short period of trading.

In principle, online grocery shopping is a convenient way of avoiding visits to supermarkets, by using a website to place orders and arrange a home delivery. Some people are attracted to this because of the convenience, speed, price, product variety, service – and the whole experience of buying groceries while avoiding the crowds, queues, stress and inconvenience of bricks-and-mortar shops.

On the other hand, people are not attracted to online grocers when they want to see, touch and smell food before they buy it, are worried by security and privacy, cannot deal with deliveries at inconvenient times, and would miss the whole experience of visiting shops.

There are three ways of organising online groceries.

1. Pure online grocers do not have stores, but use warehouses to fulfil customer orders. This has the advantage of offering a wide range of items, economies of scale, and efficient operations – but the disadvantages of high investment, high transport costs, little brand recognition or established reputation. Early entrants in the USA such as Webvan, Homegrocer, Streamline and Shoplink all hit problems with this format and went out of business.

2. They can use the warehouse system of an established retailer, in the way that the UK's Ocado and Waitrose or the USA's Peapod and Royal Ahold work. Then online customers order directly from the same warehouses as the supermarkets, with the online operations working in parallel with existing supply chains. This gives the benefits of using a recognised brand name, while sharing common facilities.

3. Local stores can to fulfil orders. Customer orders are sent to local supermarkets, which pick items from their shelves and use a small van for deliveries. This has the advantages of using an established reputation and local operations, and is the format used by Tesco, the UK's leading online grocer.

All three formats have strengths and weaknesses, but the store-based one is currently most successful. In 2007 Tesco met 250,000 online orders each week, with a value of more than £1 billion. All three formats also illustrate an essential point of e-business, which is that communications are not the main problem. It is easy to build a good-looking website and use it to collect orders. The difficult part is the physical collection of goods and their delivery to customers.

Question

• Can you give other examples of e-business dramatically changing the way that a traditional business works?

(*Sources*: Tanskanen, K., Jola, Y.R., and Holmstrom, J. (2002) The way to profitable Internet grocery retailing, *International Journal of Retail and Distribution Management*, 28(1), 17–26; Kempiak, M. and Fox, M.A. (2002) *Online Grocery Shopping*, www.firstmonday.org; and websites www.tesco.co.uk,www.fmi.org)

Responding to changes in the business environment

We have reviewed two areas where logistics is changing quickly – greater customer satisfaction and improving communications. In later chapters we discuss the origins and consequences of other trends, but here we only want to show that logistics is a dynamic area that is moving quickly. Practices that were standard only a few years ago are no longer acceptable (such as only delivering fresh fruit that is locally in season) or feasible (such as frequent postal deliveries).

To prepare for later discussion we review some other types of changes. Some of these are relatively minor adjustments, while others change the whole way of doing logistics. The changes are not all independent and their effects combine to move logistics in certain directions. For instance, new technology, postponement, cross-docking and outsourcing all combine to give lower stocks. In this section we mention some ways in which managers are responding to changes in the business environment, and the next section reviews some new types of operation.

• **Cooperation and integration.** Organisations within a particular supply chain increasingly recognise that they share an overriding objective – which is to satisfy their final customers. If any single member of the supply chain fails, then customers are unhappy and are likely to move their business elsewhere, meaning that all other members of the chain suffer. So members should cooperate to make sure that they all work together to satisfy final customers. This is an important point, as it means that competitors are not other organisations within the *same* supply chain, but are organisations in *other* supply chains. Christopher[36] summarises this view by saying that 'supply chains compete, not companies'. We discuss this trend towards integration of supply chains in Chapter 5.

- **Globalisation**. Improved communications and better transport mean that physical distances are becoming less significance, and international trade continues to grow. Organisations have become global in outlook – buying, storing, manufacturing, moving and distributing materials in a single, worldwide market. Leontiades[37] says that, 'One of the most important phenomena of the 20th century has been the international expansion of industry. Today, virtually all major firms have a significant and growing presence in business outside their country of origin.' By 2007 around \$12 trillion of merchandise was moved around the world each year, with \$1.5 trillion of commercial services.[38] We return to this question of globalisation in Chapter 6.

Outsourcing
has organisations concentrating on their core operations and outsourcing peripheral activities to third parties

Third-party logistics
outsources logistics to specialised third-party providers

3PL
third-party logistics

- Outsourcing. More organisations are realising that they can benefit from concentrating on their core operations and outsourcing peripheral activities to specialists. These peripheral activities might be anything from cleaning and catering through to accounting, legal services and information processing. It is particularly common for organisations to outsource some of their logistics to specialist service providers – perhaps starting with transport, extending to warehousing, and then on to other tasks in the logistics. This use of third-party logistics (3PL) can give the benefits of lower fixed costs, expert services, combined work to give economies of scale, flexible capacity, lower exposure to risk, increased geographical coverage and guaranteed service levels. Sometimes the administration of several 3PL contracts gets so complicated that another company is used to manage it – giving fourth-party logistics (4PL).

  McKinnon says that, 'Outsourcing has been one of the dominant business trends of the 1980s and 1990s.'[39] Almost 60% of Fortune 500 firms outsource some logistics.[40] In the EU the outsourced logistics market was valued at €176 billion by 2004, and this was set to rise to 45% of all logistics expenditure by 2008.[41] Armstrong and Associates[42] put the value of global third-party logistics in 2006 at US\$391 billion, of which Europe accounted for US\$139 billion and the USA a further US\$114 billion.

- **Using fewer suppliers**. Traditionally, organisations have used a large number of suppliers to encourage competition, ensure that they get the best deal, and guarantee continuing deliveries if one supplier runs into difficulties. However, increasing cooperation within a supply chain – particularly strategic alliances – encourages organisations to look for a small number of the best suppliers and work exclusively with them. Rank Xerox illustrated this effect, when they reduced their suppliers from 5000 to 300, while Ford moved from 4000 to 350.[43]

- **Concentration of ownership**. Large companies achieve economies of scale and can organise efficient operations, so a few large companies often dominate industries. There are, for example, many shops and transport companies – but the biggest ones continue to grow at the expense of smaller ones. The result is a continuing concentration of ownership, which you can see in many logistics sectors ranging from food wholesalers to cruise lines.

- **Movement of power to retailers**. Historically, most power in supply chains was with manufacturers, in the way that Toyota is still the focal organisation in its supply of cars. Several trends – including the outsourcing of manufacturing to low cost regions and global sourcing – have promoted the movement of power in supply chains. In particular, retailers are often the key player because of their link with final customers.

- **Increasing environmental concerns**. There is growing concern about air and water pollution, climate change, energy consumption, urban development, waste disposal, population growth and other aspects of environmental damage. It is fair to say that logistics does not have a good reputation for environmental protection – demonstrated by the emissions from heavy lorries, noisy and inefficient vehicles, use of green-field sites for warehouses, calls for new road building, use of extensive packaging, oil spillage from tankers, low resource utilisation, and so on. On the positive side, logistics is moving towards greener practices, through its general operations as well as expansion into reverse logistics. There is a growing recognition that careful management can combine environmental protection with lower costs and more business opportunities.

- **Risk management**. As supply chains become longer, there is inevitably more chance of disruption from both natural and organisational damage. Managers are increasingly aware that they have to assess risk and plan their actions either to avoid it, or to mitigate the effects.[44] This is an increasingly important area that is discussed in Chapter 15.

New logistics operations

In recent years, logistics managers have designed many new types of operation to improve performance. There are far too many of these changes to give a complete list, but we can illustrate their scope with some examples.

- Postponement. Traditionally, manufacturers move finished goods out of production and store them in the distribution system until they are needed. When there are many variations of a product, this can result in high stocks of similar products. Postponement moves almost finished products into the chain, and delays finishing or customisation until the last possible moment. You can imagine this with 'package-to-order', where a company keeps a product in stock, but only puts it in a box written in the appropriate language when it is about to ship an order.

  Manufacturers of electrical equipment, such as Phillips and Hewlett-Packard, used to build into their products the transformers and plugs needed for different markets. Then they had to keep separate stocks of products destined for each country. Now they make the transformer and cables as separate, external units. This means that they only keep stocks of the basic, standard products, and

Postponement
moves almost-finished products into the distribution system and delays final modifications or customisation until the last possible moment

customise them for different markets by adding the proper transformers and plugs at the last minute. This results in much lower stocks. In the same way, Benetton used to dye yarn different colours, knit sweaters and keep stocks of each colour to meet varying demand. Now they knit sweaters with undyed yarn, keep much smaller stocks of these, and dye the finished sweaters to meet actual orders.

- **Factory gate pricing.** One way to coordinate the flow of materials in a supply chain is for a key player to take over the management of logistics. With factory gate pricing, a single organisation takes responsibility for movements from the factory gate through to the final customer. As retailers are increasing their power, they have considerable expertise in logistics, want more control over movements, and are likely to take this responsibility.

- **Cross-docking.** Traditional warehouses move materials into storage, keep them until needed, and then move them out to meet demand. Cross-docking coordinates the supply and delivery, so that goods arrive at the receiving area and are transferred straight away to a loading area, where they are put onto delivery vehicles. This dramatically reduces stock levels and associated administration. There are two basic forms of cross-docking. In the first, packages are moved directly from arriving vehicles and onto departing ones, so they only need a simple transfer point. In the second form, there is some work done, typically with materials arriving in larger containers which are opened, divided into smaller quantities, sorted, consolidated into deliveries for specific customers and transferred to delivery vehicles. The key point is that neither form has goods actually kept in storage.

  Cross-docking can develop to the point where there is no need for the warehouse. Any stock is kept within vehicles, giving 'stock on wheels'. A related arrangement uses drop-shipping, where wholesalers do not keep stock themselves, but coordinate the movement of materials directly from upstream suppliers to downstream customers.

- **Direct delivery.** More customers are buying through the Web, or finding other ways of trading with upstream suppliers, such as mail order or telephone shopping. This 'disintermediation' has the benefits of reducing lead times, reducing costs to customers, having manufacturers talking directly to their final customers, and allowing customers access to a wider range of products.

- **Other stock reduction methods.** Keeping stock is expensive, so organisations continually look for ways of reducing the amount stored in supply chains. There are many ways of doing this, either with better inventory management or adopting just-in-time operations to coordinate activities. Another approach has vendor managed inventory, where suppliers manage both their own stocks and those held further down the supply chain. We return to these themes in Chapters 9 and 11.

Factory gate pricing has a single organisation, often a major retailer, taking responsibility for delivering products from the factory gate through to the final customer

Cross-docking coordinates the supply and delivery of materials so that they arrive at a warehouse receiving area and are transferred straight away to the loading area, where they are put onto delivery vehicles

Drop-shipping has wholesalers keeping no stocks themselves, but coordinating the movement of materials directly from upstream suppliers to downstream customers

Vendor managed inventory has suppliers managing both their own stocks and those held further down the supply chain

- **Small deliveries**. Some operations – such as just-in-time, e-business and direct deliveries – inevitably lead to smaller, more frequent deliveries. This suggests a movement away from transport in large trucks and towards smaller deliveries. As these are inherently less efficient, logistics managers have to find ways of improving their performance, such as round-the-clock deliveries to unattended destinations, better planning of deliveries, and higher vehicle utilisation. The new requirements have also spurred the growth of couriers and parcel delivery services such as FedEx, TNT, UPS and DHL.

- **Increasing vehicle utilisation**. For a variety of reasons – including unbalanced demand, composition of the vehicle fleet, characteristics of the vehicles and loads, poor coordination, and so on – vehicles spend a proportion of their time travelling empty or partially loaded. This is clearly wasteful, and methods for reducing it include backhauls (where delivery vehicles find loads for their return journeys), reverse logistics (returning goods for repair, reuse or recycling), freight forwarding (where loads from several companies are combined), and more efficient schedules (perhaps with regular routes). To some extent these measures counteract the move to smaller loads, but after continuous improvements for almost half a century, the overall productivity of the UK's transport fleet peaked in 1999 and is now stable or even falling.[45]

LOGISTICS IN PRACTICE – DEUTSCHE POST WORLD NET

Deutsche Post World Net has moved a long way from its origins as the German state postal service. It has been a private company since 2000, and through a series of mergers and takeovers now describes itself as 'the world's leading logistics group'. It works in 220 countries, employs 500,000 people and has an annual turnover of €60 billion. The company is organised into four divisions:

1. mail service – based on Deutsche Post's origins

2. express delivery – centred on DHL, which merged with Deutsche Post in 2000

3. logistics services – best known through DHL, Danzas, Air Express International, and so on

4. financial services – through Postbank, the largest retail bank in Germany.

The company say that, 'Logistics is making quantum leaps in the areas of cost reduction, high speed customer service, and delivery quality.' It bases this view on key developments, which it identifies as:

- globalisation of production and trade – increasing world-wide trade, opening new opportunities

- transition to a post-industrial society – with the growth of the service sector

- time-based competition – and the need to react quickly to customers in an 'on-demand' world

- growing environmental sensitivity – with recycling leading to a 'circular economy' of production and return

- structured processes – with success through integrated supply chains

- deregulation and privatisation – of public services in transport and communications

---

LOGISTICS IN PRACTICE – DEUTSCHE POST WORLD NET (CONTINUED)

- focus on shareholder value – through concentration on core competencies and outsourcing
- advances in technology – with continually improving communications.

Question

- What other trends do you think Deutsche Post World Net might have mentioned?

(*Sources*: Deutsch Post World Net (2007) Annual Report. Bonn: DPWN; website at www.dpwn.de)

Chapter review

- Logistics has been around for as long as people have wanted to move things. However, it was given little attention by business until the 1970s. Then changing economic conditions forced managers to recognise it as an important function where they can make significant savings, improve customer service, and help achieve organisational objectives.

- In recent years, logistics has become one of the most dynamic areas of business. Managers face many pressures for change, ranging from more demanding customers through to environmental protection.

- Logistics managers have responded to the pressures, and developed new methods and types of operation. Often they adopt similar responses and form obvious trends in the industry.

- A major trend is towards increasing customer service. Logistics forms a part of every product package, which means that firms can use it to gain a competitive advantage.

- Increasing customer service illustrates a major theme of logistics, which is towards agility (with flexible operations that strive for customer satisfaction). The other theme is towards leanness (and more efficient use of resources). In reality, these two themes are not mutually exclusive, and managers can simultaneously make progress in both directions.

- Another clear trend in logistics is its use of technology. This often appears as e-business, which allows both improvements to existing operations and entirely new ones.

- Other trends in logistics originate with changes in the business environment. These include integration of supply chains, globalisation, outsourcing, use of fewer suppliers, concentration of ownership, movement of power, increasing environmental concerns and risk management.

- Yet other trends reflect new types of operation, including postponement, factory gate pricing, cross-docking, direct delivery, other stock reduction methods, small deliveries, and increasing vehicle utilisation.

CASE STUDY – SINTHAL Y MANGULLO

Sinthal y Mangullo (SyM) are major food wholesalers in southern Europe, dealing with more than 20 million transactions a month. Their business can be summarised as buying food products from suppliers, storing the products until needed – and then picking, sorting, consolidating and delivering loads to meet customer demand. The main suppliers are different types of food manufacturers, while the main customers are retail supermarkets.

There is intense competition among food retailers, and this is driving retail prices down – a trend that is encouraged by the growing numbers of very large stores, hypermarkets and chains of heavy price discounters. In these conditions, all firms are looking for ways to reduce costs, and are actively trying to find more savings in their supply chains. In particular, retailers are putting intense pressure on wholesalers to trim their margins. When this does not work, large chains of retailers increasingly get supplies directly from manufacturers.

SyM emphasise that their service improves overall choice and efficiency. Rather than having large numbers of small deliveries between manufacturers and stores, the wholesaler consolidates deliveries from different manufacturers into more efficient full-truck loads. They also use standard equipment to reduce the amount of handling needed in stores, provide frequent deliveries, schedule all deliveries for convenient time slots, take care of negotiations with different manufacturers, and reduce problems with pollution, fuel consumption and congestion. SyM also emphasise the support services they can provide, such as information analysis, product promotions, repackaging and vendor managed inventory. A typical service would collect data automatically from a retailer's POS systems and use this to forecast demands, compare performance with industry standards, identify areas that need attention, automatically generate orders for replenishment, manage stocks, arrange deliveries, and pass marketing information back to manufacturers.

SyM is organised into three operational divisions. The warehouse division is responsible for materials storage and movement within four major logistics centres and ten smaller, local warehouses. The transport division is responsible for moving goods into, and between, storage facilities, and then out to customers. The information division is responsible for the central system that controls all transactions within the company.

Questions

- What pressures is SyM facing? Are these the same as all food wholesalers?
- What can the company do to respond to these pressures?
- How do you think their operations have changed in recent years?

Project – supply partnerships

Supermarkets are intensively competitive and are continuously looking for ways of reducing costs. As a result, they have designed some of the most sophisticated and innovative supply chains. The purpose of this project is to explore and describe the logistics within a successful supermarket chain.

To start this project you have to identify a successful supermarket chain, where you have several national and international options. Then describe the details of its logistics. To collect information for this you might start looking in company websites, annual reports, newspapers, logistics journals, consultants' websites, and a host of other places – including visits to local sites.

The current operations can raise a series of question. Why are logistics done in this way? How do they differ from logistics of competitors? What specific benefits do they bring? Are there any problems with logistics? How might these problems be overcome? How can the costs be reduced?

The end result should be a report giving a detailed description and analysis of a successful logistics system.

Discussion questions

2.1   People say that logistics is now changing so quickly that it is going through a revolution. Is there evidence to support this view?

2.2   What are the main factors encouraging logistics to change?

2.3   How is logistics responding to the pressures to change? What changes do you think there will be in the next decade?

2.4   What exactly is meant by 'customer satisfaction', and how is it achieved?

2.5   How have attitudes towards customer service changed in recent years, and why are they now considered so important?

2.6   Logistics are either lean or agile. What does this mean, and is it true?

2.7   Logistics managers often describe themselves as processors of information rather than movers of goods. To what extent is this true? How has the situation changed in recent years?

2.8   Why do traditional companies find it so difficult to compete against e-companies?

2.9   Some people argue that globalisation has been the largest single driver of change in logistics. Do you think this is true?

2.10 In 1996 a survey of Canadian logistics companies[46, 47] listed the main benefits expected from outsourcing logistics as follows. Are these benefits likely to be different in other countries, or to have changed in Canada over the past few years?

Factor	% of companies
Reduce total cost	79
Focus on core competency	67
Improve financial performance	66
Improve customer service	53
Improve flexibility	53
Access to new technology or systems	41
Enhance competitiveness	41
Increase capacity	37
Provide alternative logistics channels	29
Increase market share	21
Broader market coverage	20

References

1. Taylor, A.J.P. (1969) War by time-table, Macdonald and Jane's, London.
2. Shaw, A.W. (1916) An approach to business problems, Harvard University Press, Cambridge, MA.
3. Clark, F.E. (1922) Principles of marketing, Macmillan, New York.
4. Borsodi, R. (1927) The distribution age, D. Appleton, New York.
5. Drucker, P. (1962) The economy's dark continent, Fortune, April, 4, 103.
6. Unilever (1955) Annual report, Unilever Ltd, London.
7. Ray, D. (1976) Distribution costing, International Journal of Physical Distribution and Materials Management, 6(2), 73–107.
8. Little, W.I. (1977) The cellular flow logistics costing system, International Journal of Physical Distribution and Materials Management, 7(6), 305–329.
9. Firth, D., Denham, F.R., Griffin, K.R., Heffernan, J. et al. (1980) (editors) Distribution Management Handbook, McGraw Hill, London.
10. Ray, D., Gattorna, J., and Allen, M. (1980) Handbook of distribution costing and control, International Journal of Physical Distribution and Materials Management, 10(5), 211–429.
11. McKibbin, B.N. (1982) Centre for Physical Distribution Management national survey of distribution costs, FOCUS on Physical Distribution, 1(1), 16–18.
12. Delaney, R.V. (1986) Managerial and financial challenges facing transport leaders, Transportation Quarterly, 40(1), 35.
13. Hill, G.V. (1994) Assessing the cost of customer service, in Logistics and Distribution Planning (2nd edition), Cooper, J. (editor), Kogan Page, London.
14. Waters, D. (2007) Trends in the supply chain, in Global logistics (5th edition), Waters, D. (editor), Kogan Page, London.
15. www.news.sky.com (2008) Rail passengers stage fare protest, 28 January 2008.
16. www.firstgreatwestern.co.uk (2008) First Great Western response to fares protest, 28 January 2008.
17. LaLonde, B. and Zinszer, P.H. (1976) Customer Service; meaning and measurement, National Council of Physical Distribution Management, Chicago, IL.
18. Grant, D., Lambert, D.M., Stock, J.R. and Ellram, L.M. (2006) Fundamentals of Logistics Management – European edition, McGraw-Hill, Maidenhead, Berks.
19. Jobber, D. (2004) Principles and Practice of Marketing (4th edition), McGraw-Hill, Maidenhead, Kent.
20. Holweg, M., Judge, B. and Williams, G. (2001) The 3DayCar challenge: cars to customer orders, Logistics and Transport Focus, 3(9), 36–44.
21. 3DayCar Programme (2001) website at www.cf.ac.uk/3DayCar.
22. Jones, D., Hines, P. and Rich, N. (1997) Lean logistics, International Journal of Physical Distribution and Logistics Management, 27(3/4), 153–173.
23. Womack, J. and Jones, D. (1996) Lean thinking, Simon and Schuster, New York.
24. Christopher, M. (1999) Global logistics: The role of agility, Logistics and Transport Focus, 1(1).
25. Rowley, J. (2001) Lean and agile, Logistics and Transport Focus, 3(6), 52–57.
26. Evans, B. and Powell, M. (2000) A pragmatic view of lean and agile, Logistics and Transport Focus, 2(10), 26–32.
27. Stafford-Jones, A. (1997) Electronic commerce: the future with EDI, Logistics Focus, 5(9), 9–10.
28. MRO Software (2001) Supplying the Goods, MRO Software, London.
29. The Gartner Group (2001) website at www.gartner.com.
30. Forrester (2006) Report on eBusiness, Forrester Research Paper, Cambridge, MA.
31. Gartner (2006) Worldwide B2B Internet Commerce, The Gartner Group, Stamford CT.
32. Website at www.ebay.com.
33. Simson, R., Werner, F. and White, G. (2000) Big three carmakers plan net exchange, The Wall Street Journal, 28 February, 2000.
34. McKinnon, A.C. (2007) Road transport optimisation, in Global Logistics (5th edition), Waters, D. (editor), Kogan Page, London.
35. Website at www.fedex.com.
36. Christopher, M (1996) Emerging issues in supply chain management. Proceeding of the Logistics Academic Network Inaugural Workshop, Warwick.
37. Leontiades, J.E. (1985) Multinational Business Strategy, D.C. Heath & Co., Lexington, MA.

38. World Trade Organization (2008) International Trade Statistics, WTO, Geneva and website at www.wto.org.
39. McKinnon, A.C. (1999) The outsourcing of logistical activities, Global Logistics and Distribution Planning (3rd edition), Waters, D. (editor), Kogan Page, London.
40. Eye for Transport (2005) Survey of outsourcing; the latest trends in using 3PL providers, www.eyefortransport.com.
41. Datamonitor (2004) European Logistics Market Maps 2004, Datamonitor, London.
42. Armstrong and Associates Inc. (2007) US and Global 3PL Financial Results 2006, www.3plogistics.com.
43. Lamming, R. (1993) Beyond Partnership: Strategies for Innovation and Lean Supply, Prentice Hall, London.
44. Waters, D. (2007) Supply Chain Risk Management, Kogan Page, London.
45. Department for Transport (2006) Transport Statistics Great Britain, HMSO. London.
46. Deloitte & Touche Consulting Group (1996) Canadian Trends in Supply Chain Management and Logistics Service Outsourcing, Deloitte & Touche, Toronto.
47. Factor, R. (1996) Logistics trends, Material Management and Distribution, June, 17–21.

PART II

BUILDING EFFECTIVE SUPPLY CHAINS

This book is divided into three parts. The first part introduced the ideas underlying logistics and supply chain management. This made the point that managers have to design the structure of their supply chains, and then control the movement of materials through them. This second part of the book looks at the design of supply chains. It shows how managers can define structures that give efficient operations and achieve long-term objectives. The third part of the book discusses the movement of materials through these chains.

There are six chapters in this second part, each of which describes a different aspect of design:

- Chapter 3 shows how a logistics strategy sets the context for other decisions, emphasising the strategic significance of logistics and the strategic choices available.

- Chapter 4 discusses the implementation of this strategy and approaches to change.

- Chapter 5 shows how the separate activities within supply chains can be integrated into an efficient whole.

- Chapter 6 discusses the increasingly important area of global – or international – logistics.

- Chapter 7 shows how the shape of the supply chain is set by the location and number of facilities.

- Chapter 8 considers the planning of capacity along a supply chain.

LOGISTICS STRATEGY

Contents

LEARNING OBJECTIVES

After reading this chapter you should be able to:

- describe the features of strategic decisions
- review the strategic importance of logistics
- discuss the contents of a logistics strategy
- understand how a logistics strategy fits into an organisation's decisions
- describe an approach to designing a strategy
- appreciate the need for a strategic focus
- discuss lean and agile strategies
- review a range of other strategies.

Levels of decision

Some decisions are very important to an organisation, with consequences felt over many years. Other decisions are less important, with consequences felt over days or even hours. We can use their importance to classify decisions as follows:

- **Strategic decisions** are most important and set the overall direction of the organisation; they have effects over the long term, involve many resources and are the most risky.

- **Tactical decisions** implement the strategies over the medium term; they look at more detail, involve fewer resources and some risk.

- **Operational decisions** are the most detailed and concern activities over the short term; they involve few resources and little risk.

A traditional view has senior managers making the strategic decisions that set their organisation on its course. These strategic decisions give the objectives, constraints and context for the tactical decisions made by middle managers. These, in turn, set the objectives, constraints and context for operational decisions made by junior managers. In essence, strategic decisions show what the organisation wants to do, tactical decisions show how to do it, and operational decisions actually do it.

This traditional view is reasonably accurate, but new styles of management and improved technology have encouraged changes. Now you rarely see such a strict hierarchy, even among conventionally rigid organisations like the armed forces. Most decisions are discussed, negotiated and agreed rather than simply passed down. There is also a growing recognition that the best people to make decisions are those most closely involved, even when they are relatively junior. This leads to empowerment (which devolves decisions to the lowest possible level) and delayering (to remove unnecessary layers of management).

Strategic decisions

The long-term strategic decisions also occur at different levels (illustrated in Figure 3.1). We can describe these as:[1]

- **Mission or vision** – a precise statement that gives the overall purpose and aims of an organisation. This shows what the organisation wants to do, its responsibilities, values, measure of long-term success, and so on.

- **Corporate strategy** – shows how a whole diversified corporation will achieve its mission. This typically describes the industries and markets to work in, level of diversification, amount of vertical integration, relationships between business units, plans for growth, and so on.

- **Business strategy** – shows how each business within a diversified corporation contributes to the corporate strategy. This typically shows the type of products to make, customers to serve, geographical coverage, innovation, competitive advantages, and so on.

- **Functional strategy** – shows how each function within a business will contribute to the business strategy. This typically shows the long-term plans for each function (logistics, finance, marketing, operations, human resources, and so on).

With this picture, a logistics strategy shows how logistics will help a business achieve its long-term goals. If a company's business strategy is to make products at the lowest possible cost, the logistics strategy shows how logistics will reduce their costs to a minimum; if a business strategy specifies rapid customer service, the logistics strategy shows how it will get fast deliveries; if the business strategy includes strategic alliances with suppliers, the logistics strategy shows how these alliances will be achieved.

Strategy
sets the long-term direction of an organisation

In its turn, a logistics strategy sets the context for all tactical and operational decisions within logistics. If the logistics strategy is to reduce logistics costs to a

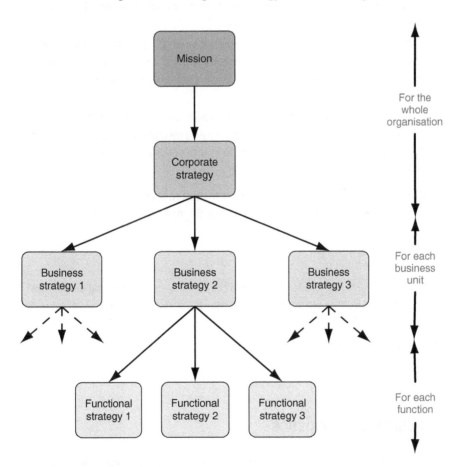

Figure 3.1 Types of strategic decision

minimum, all lower decisions will be made with this in mind, and constantly look for ways of reducing costs.

IDEAS IN PRACTICE – CZESKAVA–IMHOF

Czeskava–Imhof (C-I) is a joint enterprise between four industrial companies in Eastern Europe, and provides a specialised transport and distribution service for its owners. Within the company, managers define several layers of strategic decision. In principle, these strategies are designed during a series of annual planning meetings. However, the principles were agreed some years ago and now they only need review and adjustment. This is done every six months, in virtual meetings arranged to collect opinions from a wide spectrum of managers.

The strategy has many parts, but one thread through the different layers can be summarised as follows:

- *mission of C-I* – to provide outstanding logistics services for its owners
- *corporate strategy* of C-I – to provide services that meet the logistics demands of the corporate owners
- *business strategy of the Polish division* – to provide the most efficient logistics service possible within Poland in terms of customer satisfaction, return on investment, costs and a number of key performance indicators; to expand both the range of services offered and geographical area covered
- *logistics strategy within the Polish division* – to provide the industry's most efficient delivery service within Poland; to have transport and warehousing operations that ensure a combination of low costs and high customer service; and to continuously look for new ways of improving performance.

There are parallel threads down through the layers of strategy, each ending in a set of strategic aims for a particular function. These aims lay the foundations for lower tactical and operational decisions.

Question

- Czeskava–Imhof is a specialised logistics company, so it is not surprising that the strategies concentrate on logistics performance. Do you think the strategies in other types of company would be similar?

(*Source*: Company records)

Strategic role of logistics

Our next move is to describe the details of a logistics strategy but, before we start, we should review the arguments for logistics actually having a strategic impact.

In Chapters 1 and 2 we saw that logistics is essential in every organisation, even those supplying intangible services. It is concerned with major decisions that have a clear strategic impact, such as the size and location of facilities, levels of customer satisfaction, design of product packages, and relations with other organisations. We showed that logistics is a major user of resources, including warehousing and transport; it has an impact on organisational performance, including profit, return on assets and other financial measures; it affects lead time, perceived product value, reliability and other measures of customer service; it gives public exposure, and is a key part of marketing. It has inherent risks and raises questions about safety, environmental issues, sustainability; it encourages some kinds of operations and prohibits others.

The evidence for logistics having a strategic impact seems undeniable. You can find more support for this in company mission statements. It is not surprising that logistics companies refer to the supply chain in their missions, and Hanson Logistics of the USA say:

> Hanson Logistics will prosper and grow as the Midwest preferred provider of logistics and refrigerated storage solutions.[2]

FedEx say that:

> FedEx will produce superior financial returns for shareholders by providing high value-added supply chain, transportation, business and related information services through focussed operating companies.[3]

Even companies with less direct links to logistics acknowledge their importance. Amsino is a leading manufacturer of products for the healthcare industry, and their mission includes the view that:

> We believe that complete customer satisfaction in all areas of our operations – product design and development, engineering and technical support, manufacturing, quality control and inspection, shipping and logistics, sales, marketing, customer service – is the key to our success and future growth.[4]

Kiran Pondy Chems Limited is a chemicals manufacturer in Chennai, India and their mission includes the following aim:

> To create an infrastructure and logistics to widen our customers' needs – and to be a fair trade partner in business.[5]

Retailers depend on their ability to manage supply chains, which is implicit in Sainsbury's objectives that include:

> To provide unrivalled value to our customers in the quality of the goods we sell, in the competitiveness of our prices and in the range of choice we offer.
>
> To achieve efficiency of operation, convenience and customer service in our stores...[6]

The long-term survival of every organisation depends on the flow of materials through its supply chains, and the strategic importance of logistics stems from the basic truth that without logistics there can be no operations, no products – and no organisation.

In Chapter 2 we mentioned that managers have only recognised the strategic role of logistics quite recently. Many now view this recognition as one of the most significant developments in business, as it fundamentally changes their view of the supply chain. In particular, logistics moves to the centre of decision making and is integrated with other decision areas. The formal route for achieving this is through a logistics strategy.

Contents of a logistics strategy

A logistics strategy contains everything related to the long-term direction of logistics within an organisation.

Logistics strategy consists of all the long-term goals, plans, policies, culture, resources, decisions and actions that relate to the management of an organisation's supply chains

> - A logistics strategy consists of all the long-term goals, plans, policies, culture, resources, decisions and actions that relate to the management of an organisation's supply chains.

This definition suggests a broad scope and that – in common with all other strategies – a logistics strategy is a complex mixture of parts. Some of these are formally stated in policy documents, others are inferred from other published documents, and others are assumed (perhaps emerging from the corporate culture). The overall strategies are complex and come in so many forms that it is difficult to suggest even a general list of contents. However, having given that warning, you might find that logistics strategies commonly contain elements like the following:[7,8]

- a summary statement, giving an overview of the logistics strategy and how this relates to other strategies and parts of the organisation
- the underlying beliefs and culture of logistics, ethical standpoints, priorities, and so on
- the aims of logistics, identifying the customers, markets, suppliers, services provided, performance targets, and so on
- a description of how the logistics function will achieve these aims, describing the type of activities, changes needed to current practices and how these changes will be managed
- policies about supply chain structure, including ownership, geographical coverage, number and size of facilities, length and breadth of chains
- policies about the movement of materials, including control systems, technology used, measures of performance, and so on
- a description of how the separate activities of logistics will contribute to the strategy and how they will be organised

- resources needed to achieve the strategy, how these are managed, together with projections of costs and financial performance
- a description of the way that this strategy affects the rest of the business.

Whatever the details of its contents, a logistics strategy forms a link between the more abstract, higher strategies and the detailed operations of the supply chain. While the corporate and business strategies describe broad aims, the logistics strategy concerns the actual movement of materials needed to achieve them. The business strategy of UPS calls for 'outstanding service to its customers', and this translates into a logistics strategy that creates a very fast parcel delivery service to almost any point in the world.

Logistics managers do not simply respond to the higher strategies, but they actively contribute to their design. They review their operations and the performance that they can realistically achieve, and this forms one of the inputs for the design of higher strategies (as shown in Figure 3.2). For UPS the recognition that it can actually get efficient logistics allows it to have a business strategy of aiming at outstanding service; if it could not guarantee efficient logistics then a business strategy of outstanding service would make no sense.

An interesting question asks how much logistics contributes to the design of higher strategies. In practice this varies considerably. At one end of a spectrum (shown in Figure 3.3) are organisations where logistics is not a core issue, and its managers contribute little to the higher strategies. Logistics managers simply

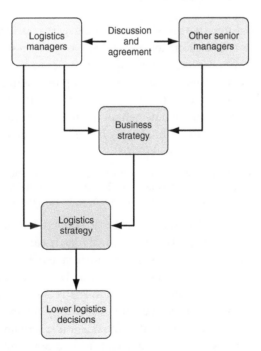

Figure 3.2 Role of logistics managers in strategic decisions

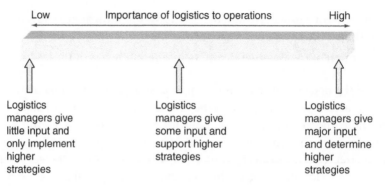

Figure 3.3   Logistics managers give different amounts of input to higher strategies

accept the strategies designed by others, and design their own operations to make sure they can be achieved. For instance, logistics is not a core function for a firm of accountants, so it has little input to the business strategy. At the other end of the spectrum are organisations whose primary business is logistics, and then its managers really dictate the higher strategies. For example, the Channel Tunnel offers a unique logistics service, and its higher strategies are based on its logistics operations. Most organisations come in between these two extremes, with logistics – along with all other functions – offering some input to strategic design.

Designing a logistics strategy

The design of a logistics strategy starts with managers considering what their logistics must achieve in the long term, and then designing a strategy to achieve it. In essence, they want the long-term shape of logistics to give the best possible support to the business strategy. This suggests a long-term aim for logistics, and managers might summarise this in a logistics mission. In the same way that an organisation's mission is a simple statement of its underlying aims, a logistics mission states the long-term aims of the supply chain, and it might say something like:

Logistics' mission states the underlying long-term aims for the supply chain

> Our mission is to help the business achieve its long-term goals by providing the best possible logistics support. We provide a flexible, efficient, reliable and cost-effective service that satisfies the demands of our customers, both internal and external.[8]

Logistics missions are useful for setting the broad context, but they are much less common than organisational mission statements. They can also suffer from the same weaknesses, with managers making very broad statements of ambition, such as being 'acknowledged leaders', 'the best', 'world class', and so on. Smith[9] says that such flowery statements fail in three ways. Firstly, they are over-ambitious, setting targets that the organisations cannot realistically achieve. Secondly, they are so vague that no-one can tell whether the mission is actually being achieved or not. Thirdly, they miss the opportunity of using a powerful tool that really could help logistics managers with their other decisions.

IDEAS IN PRACTICE – THE EMIRATES GROUP

The Emirates Group was founded in 1985 in Dubai. It is best known for its rapidly growing airline, Emirates, which generate most of its $1.5 billion annual profit. Logistics in the group is guided by the following mission statement.[10]

> Procurement & Logistics' mission is to provide an innovative and responsive service which positively supports the Group in a commercially astute manner. This will be achieved through shared objectives with both suppliers and departments, securing the lowest total cost of acquisition and/or ownership and through continuous improvement, the adoption of best practices and beneficial supplier relationships.

Question

- What are the advantages of a written logistics mission?

- With such benefits, why does every organisation not have a logistics mission?

(*Sources*: The Emirates Group (2008) Annual report, Dubai; websites at www.ekgroup.com and www.procurement.ekgroup.com)

Strategic fit

Starting with a logistics mission – even one that is not formally written down – the next step is to develop this into a full strategy. Unfortunately, the way to do this is not so clear. There is no standard procedure for designing a strategy, and there is no single best strategy for any particular circumstances. Gooderham says,[11] 'No one "right" way to develop and implement strategy exists.' But he adds that, 'The key to successful planning is to get the best fit between the chosen tools and techniques, the organisation's current culture, capabilities and business environment and the desired outcome.' This usually means finding ways to match what the organisation is good at with what customers want – often described as achieving strategic fit.

In practice, managers have to balance three factors (shown in Figure 3.4):

Strategic fit
means that there is a good balance between higher strategies, organisational strengths and external environment

1. *Higher strategies*, which set the organisation's broad goals and the context for all logistics decisions. The logistics strategy must support the mission, corporate and business strategies. For example, when a business strategy calls for high customer service, the logistics strategy must show how logistics will achieve this.

2. The *business environment* consists of the factors that are external to the logistics function and over which it has no control. These include:

   - *customers* – their expectations, attitudes, demographics

   - *market conditions* – size, location, stability

   - *technology* – current availability, likely developments, rate of innovation

   - *economic climate* – gross domestic product, rate of growth, inflation

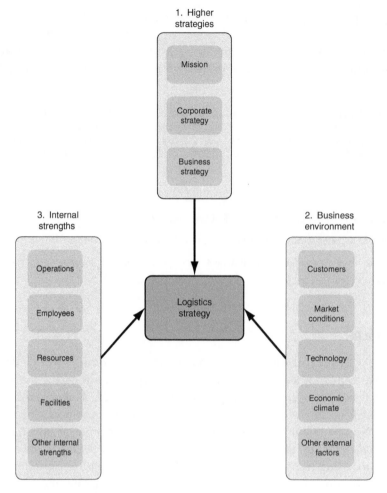

Figure 3.4   Factors in the design of a logistics strategy

- *legal restraints* – trade restrictions, liability and employment laws
- *competitors* – number, ease of entry to the market, strengths
- *shareholders* – their target return on investments, objectives, profit needed
- *interest groups* – their objectives, strengths, amount of support
- *social conditions* – customers' lifestyles, changing demands, significant trends
- *political conditions* – stability, amount of governmental control, external relations.

3. *Internal strengths* are the activities that logistics does particularly well. In 1957 Selznick[12] established the principle that an organisation can only succeed by developing distinctive capabilities – which are key activities that it does better than competitors. So logistics managers must develop distinctive capabilities

to set them apart from competitors. These take many forms, but are largely based on the use of assets such as:

- *customers* – their demands, loyalty, relationships
- *suppliers* – their services, flexibility, partnerships
- *operations* – types, quality, reputation, flexibility
- *employees* – skills, expertise, knowledge, loyalty
- *facilities* – types, locations, capacity, age, reliability
- *finances* – costs, cash flow, overheads
- *technology* – currently used, systems, updates, special types
- *innovation* – in services, operations, systems
- *organisation* – structure, relationships, flexibility.

The business environment and distinctive competence essentially show where an organisation is now, and the higher strategies show where it wants to be in the future. The logistics strategy shows how to move from one to the other.

Adding details to the design

Although there is no standard method for designing a strategy, a reasonable general approach has the following eight steps:[1]

Step 1. *Assess the current logistics strategy.* Apart from entirely new operations, there must be some logistics strategy in place, even if it is implicit rather than formally recorded. So an obvious starting point is to analyse the current strategy and see how well it is working, concentrating on:

a. the contents of the current strategy – including the purpose, goals and objectives, how these are achieved, types of operations, level of strategic fit, distinctive capabilities, and so on.

b. apparent problems with the current strategy – which are the symptoms that something is wrong, such as unmet performance targets, missing trends in the environment, being difficult to implement, giving poor use of resources, falling behind competitors, giving low customer satisfaction, and so on

c. real problems with the strategy – which are the real faults that should be addressed, such as needing skills that the organisation does not have, not developing logistics capabilities, giving no real competitive advantage, being inflexible and slow to change, not fitting in with other strategies, and so on

d. amount of adjustment – describing the effort needed to overcome problems with the current strategy (bearing in mind that it is a major task to implement a new strategy, so it is almost always better to adjust and rework the current one).

Step 2. ***Define the aims of logistics***. These are set by the higher strategies, so managers:

   a. analyse the business strategy – and other strategies – from a logistics viewpoint, and then define the overall purpose and aims of logistics, and phrase these as a logistics mission

   b. expand the logistics mission into a series of specific strategic goals to show exactly what the supply chain must achieve

   c. translate these goals into more precise – preferably quantitative – objectives.

Step 3. ***Analyse the business environment from a logistics perspective***. The environment consists of a complex picture of business, competitive, economic, political, technological, cultural, historical and social factors, all of which interact and are constantly changing. A logistics environmental scan analyses this emphasising:

   a. circumstances within the organisation, but outside logistics (such as finance, marketing, HR, etc.)

   b. conditions in the organisation's external environment, including its industry, markets, competition, stakeholders, economy, regulation, constraints, etc.

   c. opportunities – being factors that logistics can exploit to gain some kind of advantage

   d. threats – being factors that might harm logistics.

Environmental scan analyses the business environment in which the logistics work

Step 4. ***Analyse the current logistics***. This needs a logistics audit, which systematically collects information about existing logistics and typically includes:

   a. details of all current logistics activities, practices, capabilities, technology, and so on

   b. analyses of the success of logistics in satisfying organisational needs

   c. areas for key logistics decisions, such as customer service levels, outsourcing, investment, transport modes, locations, and so on

   d. use of resources, with capacities, costs, measures of performance

   e. benchmarks for logistics, comparing performance with industry leaders

   f. changes needed to adopt the industry's best practices

   g. strengths – being factors that can develop into distinctive capabilities

   h. weaknesses – being factors that have to be improved.

Logistics audit systematic collection of information about existing logistics activities, procedures, costs, resources, utilisation, performance, and all other relevant details

Step 5. ***List alternative new logistics strategies***. There is never a single right strategy, so managers may generate a number of feasible alternatives by:

   a. considering an ideal future state for logistics

b. generating a set of alternative logistics strategies that would move towards this ideal

   c. considering the resources needed by each strategy

   d. assessing the likely performance of each strategy in different conditions.

Step 6. *Compare these alternative strategies and choose the best, based on*:

   a. which strategy contributes most to achieving logistics' aims

   b. which performs better in terms of customer satisfaction, resource utilisation, logistics' excellence and distinctive capabilities

   c. how much the organisation's capabilities and resources limit the alternatives that are feasible

   d. how management preferences, standards, views on risk, opinions, and so on, limit the alternatives.

Step 7. *Add details to the chosen strategy, defining the logistics infrastructure*:

   a. describing the broad features of logistics

   b. designing the structure of supply chains in terms of length, breadth, location of facilities, capacity, technology used, and so on

   c. defining the best organisational structure, controls and systems for logistics

   d. setting performance targets to measure progress

   e. designing any other features included in the logistics strategy.

Step 8. *Implement the strategy*. Where managers translate the designed strategy into actual operations by:

   a. planning the implementation, including changes to organisational structure, methods and systems

   b. initiating the process for getting new ideas, methods and goals introduced throughout the logistics function

   c. initiating the design and implementation of new operations

   d. setting targets for all levels of logistics

   e. monitoring actual performance to make sure that they achieve the planned results

   f. controlling the strategy, looking for improvements and making adjustments to reflect changing conditions.

This procedure is summarised in Figure 3.5. You can see that it is based on a balance of the three factors – higher strategies (from step 2), the business environment (from step 3) and internal strengths (from step 4). The procedure is undoubtedly daunting, but it still only gives some general advice, and is nowhere near a complete recipe. At the very least, strategy design is an iterative search with managers repeatedly considering solutions until they find one that is broadly acceptable.

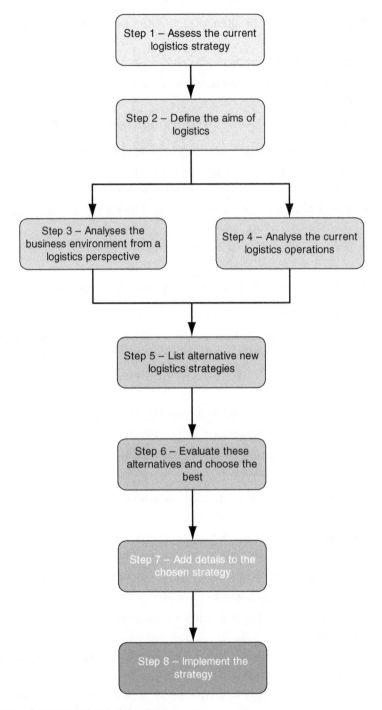

Figure 3.5   Steps in designing a logistics strategy

Top-down or bottom-up

This traditional approach to strategy design assumes that senior managers design a logistics strategy and then pass it down to lower levels for implementation. When this happens it is called top-down design. This has several advantages, such as giving a structured procedure, having clearly identifiable managers responsible for the strategy and its consequences, using people with the most experience, encouraging a long-term view, and so on. But we suggested earlier that this rigid approach is no longer accepted, as it has inherent weaknesses.[13] In particular, senior managers may not understand the complexities of prevailing conditions, they lack necessary skills and knowledge, are remote from actual operations, make unrealistic assumptions, assume that strategy design is an end in itself, their solutions lack ownership and acceptance, and so on.

Top-down design has senior managers designing a logistics strategy and then passing it down to lower levels for implementation

The alternative to top-down design is a bottom-up emergence. This assumes that senior managers do not design a strategy, but it emerges over time from the actions of managers lower down the organisation. These lower managers continually respond to actual conditions, making practical decisions to cope with new problems as they arise – and their decisions follow a pattern that develops a strength and, over time, this emerges as a strategy. Imagine a fairly junior logistics manager who is under pressure to supply an order quickly, and finds a way of saving some time. The new method may improve customer service and be more convenient, so the manager repeats it for future deliveries. Over time, others follow his example and the fast service becomes a key feature of logistics. Eventually, its importance is recognised and it emerges as part of the logistics strategy – not because senior managers decided to move in this direction, but because the capabilities filtered up from lower levels.

Bottom-up emergence assumes that senior managers do not design a strategy in a single step, but that it emerges over time from the actions of managers lower down the organisation

In reality, a logistics strategy usually needs a combination of both top-down design and bottom-up emerging. The exact contribution of each depends on many factors, particularly the corporate culture.

SWOT analysis

The results from the environmental scan are often summarised as a set of opportunities and threats, while the results from the logistics audit are summarised as a set of strengths and weaknesses. Bringing these four together gives a SWOT analysis, which considers:

SWOT analysis analyses internal strengths and weaknesses, and external opportunities and threats

- *Strengths* – what logistics does well, giving features it should build on
- *Weaknesses* – problem areas for logistics that should be improved
- *Opportunities* – openings that can help logistics and should be developed
- *Threats* – hazards that can damage logistics and should be avoided.

SWOT analyses are used to identify and evaluate strategic options. For example, a SWOT analysis by Synergistic Logistical Services[8] listed their strengths as expertise, innovation and local contacts; weaknesses as small size, local operations and

gaps in experience; opportunities from the increasing use of information technology, growing interest in logistics, and service-based local economy; threats
from larger competitors, high overheads and a possible take-over. Based on this,
the company designed a strategy based on moderate growth within its current
core market.

LOGISTICS IN PRACTICE – BJORG–AICHESSON PHARMACEUTICALS

Bjorg–Aichesson Pharmaceutical (BAP) is a biotechnology company that develops and markets
specialised drugs for Alzheimer's disease. It is a relatively small, specialised company that
competes directly against giant internationals, and its success comes from focusing on a niche
market.

Last year, BAP was concerned that a major competitor was introducing a treatment that was
similar to their own best-selling product. As part of their response, BAP planned to adjust their
logistics strategy to improve customer service. In particular, they planned regional warehouses in
major markets of northern Europe that could guarantee delivery to any customer within half a day.
To make sure that this was a sensible move, the company ran a survey of 80 major customers.
The following table shows the importance that customers gave to certain factors on a scale of 1
(not important) to 5 (very important).

Factor	Average response
Same-day delivery	3.1
Next-day delivery	4.8
Delivered when promised	2.7
Products delivered from stock	3.4
Cost of products	1.3
No errors in delivered products	2.8
No errors in paperwork	1.5
Ease of order entry	1.7
Ease of payment	1.4
Ease of access to customer relations	2.1
Knowledge of customer relations	2.5

Customers clearly consider the delivery time to be very important, but most seemed satisfied
with a next-day delivery. A more disturbing finding was the perception that BAP did not share
information with customers, and did not publish details of product availability, lead times, possible
shortages, and so on.

Based on this information, BAP adjusted its proposed strategy. It would still aim for the industry's best logistics performance, but could do this by guaranteeing same-day delivery for 70% of
products (compared with competitors who only guaranteed same-day delivery for about 40% of
products) and next-day delivery for everything else. This would need fewer warehouses, so the
planned expansion was cancelled with a saving of $2 million a year. The company also improved

its communications, publishing more material on its websites and encouraging contacts with customers through an expanded Customer Relationship Management department.

Question

- Do you think that BAP should have gone ahead with their original plans to provide even better customer service?

(*Source*: Internal company reports)

Strategic focus

When managers design a strategy, it would seem reasonable for them to aim at doing everything well – giving low costs, good customer service, fast delivery, low stocks, flexibility, using high technology, and so on. Unfortunately, this is simply impossible – and managers always have to look for balances and compromises. For instance, a company cannot simultaneously minimise its investment in stock, and still keep everything in store to guarantee availability; it cannot give the fastest delivery, while minimising the costs of transport; it cannot collect materials from remote locations, and guarantee short lead times. So managers have to design strategies that concentrate on their most pressing needs – in other words, they focus on some aspect of performance. For instance, Ryanair focuses on cost giving a cheap service; FedEx focuses on delivery speed; Diamond Limousines focuses on comfort; Securicor on security. This does not mean that they ignore other measures, but it shows where they put their priorities.

> **(Strategic) Focus**
> an aspect of performance
> that an organisation's
> strategy concentrates on

Deciding where to put the focus is one of the key skills of managers. Initial suggestions follow the traditional view of marketing that organisations compete through the 'four Ps' – product, place, promotion and price – and logistics should focus on some aspect of these. A broader view says that customers are concerned with cost, quality, service level, reliability, availability, flexibility, delivery speed, location, sourcing, supplier relations, environmental impact, recycling, and a whole range of other things. Organisations could gain a competitive advantage by focusing on any of these – or in differing circumstances almost any facet of logistics.

LOGISTICS IN PRACTICE – THE SCHENKER GROUP

The Schenker Group was founded in Vienna in 1872, and has been working internationally ever since. The group now has 1500 offices in 150 countries, employing 55,000 people, with annual sales of more than €13 billion.

Schenker is one of the world's leading suppliers of integrated logistics services. To put it simply, they, 'provide support to trade and industry in the global exchange of goods'.[14] For this they have integrated road and rail operations with regularly scheduled routes throughout Europe, global air and shipping operations, a network of logistics centres, and supply chain design services. Overall, they can meet the transport needs of virtually every customer, with a seamless movement of products and information through global supply chains.

One of Schenker's strengths is its strategic focus on customer service. This is made clear in their mission, which says that they, 'help our customers make decisions regarding their supply chain that will produce extraordinary results'. This creates a corporate culture that is 'customer oriented' – and they were the first full service logistics company in the US to achieve ISO 9000 certification. Their American office opened in 1947, and in answer to the question, 'Why choose Schenker?' their first answer is that they are, 'Dedicated to total customer satisfaction'.[15]

All operations focus on customer satisfaction, and the company has clear policies for achieving this, such as:

> We will service our customers in an innovative, proactive manner. We will always be aware of how our service impacts their business.

The reasoning behind this focus is clear, when Schenker say that, 'Our customers are our future. Without them – there is no future.'

Question

- How does this strategy of customer satisfaction affect Schenker's approach to logistics on a tactical and operational level?

(*Sources*: Promotional material and websites at www.schenker.com and www.schenkerusa.com)

Generic strategies

Each organisation designs its own logistics strategy, but they often move along similar lines. For instance, the logistics strategies of Ford and Volkswagen are broadly similar, as are the strategies of Lufthansa and Air France. In reality, firms often use some variation on common, generic strategies – perhaps low costs, or quick service. Michael Porter[16] said that there are essentially three generic strategies:

- *Cost leadership* makes the same, or comparable, products as competitors, but at a lower price.
- *Product differentiation* makes products that customers cannot get from other sources.
- *Market niche* specialises in some way, perhaps dealing with a limited part of the market, offering a specialised service, and so on.

The Post Office is a cost leader that delivers all kinds of mail to every possible location as efficiently as possible with low unit costs; UPS uses product differentiation to offer a specialised express package delivery service; Mammoet has a niche strategy of delivering very heavy loads to customers.

The third approach of delivering a niche service calls for specialisation, offering services to a market that is somehow limited. For most firms this option is too restricting and the choice is essentially between focusing on low costs and offering customers a novel service. As you saw in Chapter 2, for logistics this is usually phrased in terms of a lean strategy (giving low costs) or an agile strategy (giving high customer service).

Lean and agile strategies

No organisation can completely avoid the cost of logistics, so the next best option is to make them as small as possible. There are really three variations on this cost objective:

- *lowest costs* – where cost is a dominant factor and managers want the lowest costs possible
- *competitive costs* – where cost is relatively important and managers want them to be competitive, but they use other factors to gain a competitive advantage
- *acceptable costs* – where cost is not a major factor, such as transporting luxury goods, hazardous materials, pharmaceuticals, works of art, and so on.

A lean strategy is most aligned with the first of these, using efficient operations to get low costs. As Porter[17] says, 'Cost is generated by performing activities, and cost advantage arises from performing particular activities more efficiently than competitors.'

However, leanness does not only mean minimising costs. The essence of leanness is that it maintains customer service while using fewer resources – so a greengrocer could minimise its inventory costs by having no stock, but it would not be lean as there is no customer service. In fact, leanness is reluctant to work with costs, as results depend so heavily on the accounting conventions used. It is notoriously difficult to allocate overheads fairly, and redistributing them can radically change the apparent costs of logistics without affecting performance. So a reasonable objective for leanness is to maintain acceptable levels of customer service while using as few resources as possible.

> - The aim of a **lean strategy** is to maintain acceptable customer service while using fewer resources – people, facilities, time, stock, equipment, and so on.
> - It achieves this by remorselessly eliminating waste from supply chains.

Managers have always tried to reduce waste, so leanness has a long history. However, the formal methods of systematically removing waste really started in the motor industry, led by Toyota.[18, 19] Initially, it concentrated on removing waste from manufacturing processes – giving 'lean production' – but soon expanded to broader 'lean operations' in a 'lean enterprise'.

The basic approach of leanness is to examine all the operations used to deliver a final product, identify those that add no value for the customer, and then set about removing them. Womack and Jones[19–21] found that it was common for factories to have less than 5% of activities positively adding value, 35% not adding value but still necessary, and 60% adding no value and unnecessary. The aim of leanness is to eliminate the 60% of non-value adding activities – and then to finds ways of reducing waste in the remaining activities.

Early work identified seven major areas of waste (numbered 1 to 7 below)[22] and we can add some others to give the following list:

1. *overproduction* – making units that are not currently needed and giving excess stocks of finished goods

2. *waiting* – with resources sitting idly waiting for operations to start or finish, materials to arrive, equipment to be repaired, and so on

3. *transportation* – moving materials over too long distances between suppliers and customers

4. *poor process* – with unnecessary, complicated, or time-consuming operations

5. *work in progress* – with materials held up and moving slowly through supply chains

6. *movement* – with products making unnecessary, long, or inconvenient movements during operations

7. *product defects* – with resources wasted as poor quality units are scrapped, repaired, reworked or returned to an earlier part of the process

8. *overbuying* – giving high stocks of raw materials that are not immediately needed

9. *spare capacity* –that lies idle and gives low utilisation and productivity

10. *waste of human resources* – not using people to their full potential

11. *bureaucracy* – giving too many layers of management, slow decisions, inefficient flows of information, and so on

12. *excessive overheads* – with various fixed costs adding an unnecessary burden to operations.

The obvious message is that managers should examine these areas and see if they can eliminate any waste. There is plenty of scope here, as Robert Townsend says that, 'All organisations are at least 50% waste – waste people, waste effort, waste space and waste time.'[23]

LOGISTICS IN PRACTICE – ALUMINIUM DRINKS CANS

If you buy a can of cola (or any soft drink) from a supermarket in the UK, its supply chain is surprisingly long. It has four main strands that merge at the drink manufacturer before moving on to the supermarket:

Strand 1. starts with corn growing on a farm, moving through processing into syrup and on to the drink manufacturer

Strand 2. starts with a field of sugar beet, moving through processing into sugar and on to the manufacturer

Strand 3. starts with a bauxite mine, moving through processing into aluminium, which is formed into cans

Strand 4. starts with fir forests, moving through processing into cardboard and then into packaging

These are the four main strands – for syrup, sugar, cans and packaging – but there are other parts, such as phosphorus that comes from mines in Idaho before being processed to food-grade quality, and caffeine that is added to the syrup.

Perhaps surprisingly, the longest chain is not the drink, but the can that it comes in. This chain starts in Australia with the mining of bauxite, which is moved by road to a chemical reduction mill that takes half an hour to purify each tonne of bauxite into half a tonne of aluminium oxide. This is stored until a shipload is collected, and then it travels on a giant ore carrier to Sweden or Norway, where cheap hydroelectricity reduces the cost of smelting. The journey to Scandinavia takes a month, and after arrival the ore usually sits at the smelter for another two months. Actual smelting takes two hours to turn each tonne of aluminium oxide into half a tonne of aluminium. This is formed into ingots 10 metres long, which are cured for two weeks before being shipped to roller mills in Germany or Sweden. There ingots are heated to 500°C, rolled down to a thickness of 2–3 mm, formed into 10-tonne coils, and put into storage. The coils are then sent to a cold rolling mill where they are rolled down to the final thickness. The result is shipped to the UK, where it is punched, formed into cans, which are washed, dried, painted with a base coat, and given their final coat of paint (including product information). The cans are then lacquered, flanged, sprayed inside with a protective coating, inspected, palletised and stored. When needed, they are shipped to a bottling plant, where they are washed, cleaned, filled with cola, sealed and put into cardboard cartons. Then they are stored, palletised again, shipped to a regional distribution centre, and then quickly delivered to a supermarket where they are usually sold within three days.

Moving from the bauxite mine to the supermarket takes 319 days, most of which is transport and storage – while actual processing might take as little as three hours. During its journey, the aluminium is picked up and put down 30 times, and moves through 14 different types of storage.

Questions

- Why do you think aluminium cans spend so much time in their supply chain?

- How can manufacturers set about reducing this time?

(*Source*: Womack, J., Jones, D. and Roos, D. (1990) The Machine that changed the world, Harper Perennial, New York)

Agile strategy

Some people say that lean logistics work best with large-scale mass production where efficiency and cost are dominant factors, but the principles do not transfer so successfully to other types of supply chain. They argue that waste is always important but it is not necessarily a dominant factor, particularly when there are variable and uncertain conditions. Then it is more important to maintain customer service and be responsive to rapid changes. This leads to the alternative strategy of 'agility'. As Christopher says,[24] when 'turbulent and volatile markets are becoming the norm...the key to survival in these changed conditions is through "agility", in particular by the creation of responsive supply chains'.

The supporters of agility say that leanness puts too much emphasis on costs, and cannot deal with changing conditions, increasing competition, or more sophisticated and demanding customers. Suppose that demand for a product is steady at 100 units a week. Then a lean strategy will remove all the waste and have just enough capacity to deliver these 100 units. But if the demand suddenly rises to 110 units, the lean operations have no slack and cannot meet the new demand, and customers are lost.

Christopher[24] notes the paradox of lean assembly plants being very efficient at making cars in 12 hours or less, 'yet inventory of finished vehicles can be as high as 2 months of sales – and still the customer has to wait for weeks or even months to get the car of his or her choice!'

- An **agile** supply chain gives high customer service by responding quickly to changing conditions.
- Its key feature is flexibility and speed of response.

In practice, there are two main aspects of agility. Firstly, there is the speed of reaction; agile logistics keep a close check on customer demand and react quickly to changes. Secondly, there is the ability to tailor logistics to each customer's needs, giving a unique service that satisfies the requirements of each individual. So while leanness is largely associated with mass production, agility is more likely in smaller operations with more variable products.

Organisations with an agile strategy put so much emphasis on customer satisfaction that they are said to have a customer focus, and they typically:

Customer focus means that organisations have a strategy that includes an emphasis on customer satisfaction

- are sensitive to market conditions and know exactly what customers want
- aim for customer satisfaction
- offer a wide range of products, with make-to-order or mass-customisation
- have variable demand that is less predictable

- base operations on actual customer demands rather than forecasts
- cooperate with supply chain partners to share information and ensure that final customer demands are met
- ensure that all operations are flexible enough to respond quickly to changing conditions
- design logistics to meet, or exceed, likely demands
- have an open organisation that allows customer easy access
- routinely ensure, perhaps through after-sales-checks, that customers remain satisfied
- look outwards and keep in touch with customers, potential customers, competitors, and so on.

One clear benefit of agility is that satisfied customers are much more likely to return with repeat business – with a rule of thumb saying that it is five times as expensive to attract a new customer as to retain an existing one. Satisfied customers also attract new business, as they recommend a good service to four or five other people – compared with dissatisfied customers who warn a dozen potential customers about a bad experience.

Like leanness, agility is a broad concept rather than a particular programme, and it can be easier to describe the benefits rather than the ways of achieving it. But there is agreement that agility needs a major change of viewpoint, including, 'a business-wide capability that embraces organisational structures, information systems, logistics processes, and, in particular, mindsets'.[24] In reality, there are many ways of increasing agility, including postponement, alliances with suppliers, just-in-time operations, negotiated performance – and on to flexible manufacturing. Generally, the most important step in achieving agility is to increase cooperation among all members of a supply chain. Then the whole chain can become responsive to customer needs, as discussed in Chapter 5.

On the other hand, the greatest obstacle to agility is probably long lead times from suppliers. If a firm's suppliers take a long time to deliver materials, it is very difficult to provide a fast service to their own customers.

Lean versus agile

At first sight the aims of lean and agile operations seem contradictory. Leanness tries to maximise efficiency and sees customer service as a constraint; agility tries to maximise customer service and sees resource as a constraint. Leanness needs standard operations that reduce flexibility, while agility needs extra resources that lower efficiency. Some significant differences are summarised in the following table:

Factor	Lean logistics	Agile logistics
Objective	Efficient operations	Flexibility to meet different and changing demands
Focus	Elimination of all waste	Customer satisfaction
Constraint	Customer service	Cost and efficiency
Products	Standard, predefined	Variable, customer defined
Change	Little with long-term stability	Rapid and frequent, reacting to changing circumstances
Measures of performance	Productivity, utilisation, efficiency, cost	Service level, lead time, satisfaction, repeat business
Type of work	Uniform, standard	Variable, more local control
Control	Formal planning cycles	Less structured with empowered staff
Product finish	According to schedule	Late, with postponement

In practice, there is no clear distinction between the two strategies. When a supplier improves EDI links with its customers, it can both reduce costs and increase customer service – becoming both leaner and more agile. Similarly, when a manufacturer sells its products through a website, or a wholesaler introduces cross-docking they become both leaner and more agile. Both strategies accept that customer satisfaction and low costs are dominant themes, but they give each a different weight.

In fact, the two strategies often come to similar conclusions. For example, both recommend reducing the number of suppliers and working with the most reliable – and both demand more integration, shared information, simpler chains, removal of non-value adding elements, guaranteed quality, using actual demand to pull materials through the chain, and so on. Purists could even argue that leanness is essential for good customer service and is, therefore, an aspect of agility.

To put it simply, both strategies move an organisation towards operations that are generally accepted as 'good practice' in logistics. They can certainly work together, and there is no need to choose one strategy at the expense of the other. As Evans and Powell[25] conclude, 'lean and agile are not mutually exclusive, they both have their merits, but also limitations, especially if an individual aspect is taken, in isolation, to the extreme'. A common arrangement has each strategy dominate a different part of a chain. For instance, leanness might dominate in manufacturing, while agility dominates downstream operations.

Other strategies

Supporters of leanness and agility say that both have moved beyond their origins and developed into broader management philosophies. This encourages the supporters to claim that their philosophy includes virtually every aspect of good management. Low stocks, say, or short lead times become cornerstones of both leanness and agility. A consequence is that there are many possible strategic foci, but virtually all of them can claim to be a part of leanness or agility – or indeed both. Nonetheless, we review some of the most common strategies, starting with cooperation among members of a supply chain.

Strategic alliances and partnerships

By its nature, logistics depends on good working relations with suppliers and customers, and an organisation can put so much emphasis on these relationships that they form the basis of its logistics strategy. In particular, they look for the long-term benefits that come with alliances and partnerships. This is an important theme that we develop in Chapter 5.

Time-reduction strategies

Time is obviously important for logistics, and the simplest time-based strategy aims at a guaranteed fast delivery of products. This is achieved by a combination of eliminating activities that add no value, and speeding up the core activities that actually add value. This is often described as time compression.

Time compression is a type of lean strategy that concentrates on eliminating wasted time in the supply chain. Many developments here are based on just-in-time operations (described in Chapter 9). These organise all operations to occur at exactly the time they are needed – they are not done too early (which would leave materials waiting until they are actually needed) and they are not done too late (which would give poor customer service). Instead, they give very efficient flows of materials, by coordinating each task to occur at exactly the right time.[26]

We have already mentioned that even the most efficient, automated processes have products spending most of their time waiting for something to happen. In 1990 the ground-breaking study by Womack, Jones and Roos[19] found that value-adding activities accounted for only 5% of the time spent in supplying a product, and later Beesley[27,28] could say that, 'In typical UK manufacturing supply chains at least 95% of the process time is accounted as non-value adding.'

Ironically, when managers look for improvements in the supply chain they typically concentrate on improving the 5% of value-adding operations and ignore the 95% of non-value adding ones. Firms that start looking at the 95% of wasted time can soon find significant benefits. For example, H&R Johnson reduced their customer lead time from two weeks to two days,[28] GKN Hardy Spicer reduced the time for inbound logistics by 85% and Massey Ferguson reduced their process time by 20%. To achieve such reductions, Carter et al.[29] identified seven options:

1. *simplification* – making core operations simpler
2. *integration* – to improve information and material flows
3. *standardisation* – using standard procedures and materials

Time compression
a strategy based on the reduction of the time taken for activities in the supply chain, largely by removing things that add no value

4. *concurrent operations* – moving away from serial operations to do more tasks in parallel

5. *variance control* – to reduce variation, ensure high quality and avoid waste

6. *automation* – to improve effectiveness and efficiency

7. *resource planning* – to remove bottlenecks and ensure a smooth flow of materials.

Successful time-compression gives a number of related benefits that include lower costs (by having less stock in the supply chain, less expediting, etc.), improved cash flow (by not having to wait so long for payments), less risk (by reducing the number of changes to orders, eliminating obsolete stock, etc.) and simpler operations (by eliminating delays and unnecessary stores).

But faster deliveries do not necessarily mean more satisfied customers, and they can actually reduce the service quality. For instance, a delivery company might speed up order processing, but then make more mistakes; an airline might reduce turn-around time, with passengers feeling rushed and uncomfortable; a shipping line might speed up its ships by stopping in fewer ports. In reality, fast service is only one aspect of time-based strategies, and there are several variations. For instance, most managers prefer slightly slower deliveries when they are less variable and more reliable. So alternative strategies can reduce the variability in timing, always deliver at the specified time, increase the proportion of value-adding time, and so on.

Increasing productivity strategies

Managers generally want to increase productivity, but some emphasise it to the extent that it becomes a strategic focus. Logistics facilities often have high fixed costs, and using them at full capacity spreads the costs over more units. If you use a delivery truck for seven journeys a week rather than six, its productivity rises and its unit delivery costs fall.

Again, this is an aspect of a lean strategy that concentrates on reducing the wastage of under-used resources. This leads to a slightly different view from, say, reducing costs. Imagine a warehouse that is working at 60% of capacity. To improve its productivity a lean approach would look for ways of removing the 40% spare capacity – perhaps by selling or renting out spare space. A high productivity strategy is more likely to accept the present capacity, and start looking for alternative uses for the excess, such as bringing in another set of operations. Similarly, a transport fleet with spare capacity might start to carry materials for other organisations (whereas a pure lean strategy would reduce its size).

Although this seems a straightforward aim, different measures of productivity can give conflicting advice, and raising some measures inevitably lowers others (an effect that we discuss in Chapter 14). In reality, managers are likely to disagree about the measures of productivity to improve, the amount of improvement achievable, and the best way of achieving it.

Material management strategies

Not surprisingly, a common focus for logistics strategies is to get an efficient movement of materials through supply chains. This generally means a smooth flow without interruptions. The problem with any breaks in the flow is that materials accumulate as stocks of work in progress, and these can be surprisingly expensive. So this strategy is closely aligned to strategies for reducing inventory costs – and is again aligned with leanness.

The traditional way of reducing stock uses quantitative models to calculate optimal stock levels and corresponding order sizes. These methods (discussed in Chapter 11) remained the standard means of controlling the flow of materials for almost a century. Then new alternatives appeared for certain types of operation, and in the 1960s material requirements planning (described in Chapter 9) appeared as a way of relating the supply of materials directly to production plans. In the 1970s another alternative grew under the general name of just-in-time (also described Chapter 9).

Value-added strategies

We have described supply chains in terms of a series of activities, each of which adds value to the final product. So a reasonable strategy has an organisation adding as much value as possible during its part of the supply chain. Logistics adds more value by increasing time, place or ownership utility – and this strategy concentrates on doing things in ways that customers perceive as adding more utility. This means either doing current activities better, or add new activities. For instance, a transport firm may add extra work in sorting and packaging of goods, and an equipment delivery service may also install, test, give instructions on use, remove old machines, offer maintenance contracts, and so on. Of course, the key point is that customers must perceive these extra jobs as really adding value, and they must be prepared to pay the extra costs.

Diversification and specialisation strategies

These strategies consider the range of services offered by logistics. Some organisations have strategies of diversification, offering the widest range of services and satisfying as many customers as possible. This is the approach of a department store which sells every product you can imagine. Other organisations have a strategy of specialising in a very narrow range of services, but being the best provider in their chosen area. They target a few customers and provide a service that cannot be found anywhere else – like a bespoke tailor. In the same way, some transport companies have a strategy of diversification and set out to offer a complete service, perhaps moving everything from letters through to specialised oversize loads. Others have a strategy of specialisation in, say, small packages, high security or tanker deliveries.

Growth strategies

Many logistics operations get substantial economies of scale, and larger operations can give both lower costs and better service. A common strategy is based on growth to attain these economies. There are several ways of achieving growth, such as taking over competitors, expanding the geographical area covered, diversifying into more logistics activities, moving different types of materials, or simply increasing market share.

Environmental protection strategies

More organisations are including environmental protection in their strategies. For instance, The Body Shop emphasises its ethical standards, and in logistics this means fair trade, reusable containers, recycling materials and ethical relationships with other organisations. There are good reasons for organisations to adopt similar policies of environmental protection, and a survey of UK companies in 1993 suggested that most were already aware of environmental pressures – mainly from EU and government regulations.[30] However, the survey found that companies only change policies and practices when they see significant cost savings. At the time the main environmental concerns were identified as waste and packaging disposal (25% of respondents), noise and emission (23%), public perception of HGVs (15%), fuel use (12%) and road congestion (11%).

Since then, organisations have come under increasing pressure to 'go green' both from customers and from more formal regulations. For instance, the European Waste Electrical and Electronic Equipment (WEEE) Directive[31] became law in 2003 and sets collection, recycling and recovery targets for all types of electrical goods. On a broader front, the ISO 14000 family of standards gives guidance for environmental management systems – emphasising the call to 'reduce, reuse and recycle'[32] and firms are increasingly having to monitor their emissions of carbon dioxide and environmental impact. But managers tend to see these pressures as threats, and miss the opportunities created. Hart[33] points out that organisations that do not recognise the strategic benefits of environmental protection are missing the 'biggest opportunities in the history of commerce' with Porritt et al. reporting that the output of 'environmental industries' will rise from $280 billion in 1999 to $640 billion in 2010, creating half million jobs in the European Union.[34] A strategy of environmental protection can improve an organisation's performance in a whole range of ways, including less energy waste with better insulation of buildings, increasing fuel efficiency, reducing distances travelled, avoiding congestion, travelling outside peak hours, reusing packaging, and so on.[35]

Human resource strategies

Many organisations claim that, 'our most valuable asset is our people'. Unfortunately, the truth is that firms often treat their employees very badly. When it is time to reduce costs most companies immediately start sacking people – thereby getting rid of their most valuable assets, while keeping the office furniture, equipment and other peripherals. Harvey-Jones[36] said, 'There is practically no area of business where the difference between rhetoric and actuality is greater than in the handling of people.'

A strategy based on human resource management develops employees and uses their abilities to the full. One way of achieving this is to reward people for supporting the organisation, so that the aims of employees coincide with the aims of the organisation and everyone pulls in the same direction. Starting points for this might be profit sharing, bonus payments, rewards for suggestions, merit pay increments, and so on. But not all rewards involve money, and you can see many schemes for recognising 'the employee of the month', or something similar. Other rewards are less specific and have organisations treating employees with courtesy, respect and consideration. One aspect of this might be empowerment, where decisions are devolved to the lowest possible level and people control, and have responsibility for, their own work. This allows them to use their own judgement, skills and experience for the benefit of the organisation.

LOGISTICS IN PRACTICE – DAVID HAMILTON PHARMACEUTICALS

When people go to pick up medicines (or over-the-counter products) from retail pharmacies, they expect them to either be in stock or available very quickly. But there are many drugs, they are expensive, and they go out of date – so pharmacies do not carry a full range. Instead they use wholesalers who guarantee a fast delivery.

David Hamilton Pharmaceuticals (DHP) is a typical wholesaler. When they receive an order before 11.30 they deliver it before 15.00 the same day, with later orders delivered before 10.00 the following day. Most pharmacies deliver their orders (by telephone or electronically) between 09.00 and 11.30, DHP picks and assembles the orders between 11.30 and 13.30, and delivers between 13.30 and 15.00.

The daily surge of work at DHP means that they have to receive and process 1000 orders from their regular customers, assemble 30,000 items (with an average of 30 items an order), plan the routes and schedules of 50 delivery vans, pack orders and load the vans, and make sure that each van delivers to its 20 customers within the prescribed time slot. In addition, there is all the associated administration, morning deliveries to arrange before 10.00, emergency deliveries, reminder calls to pharmacies who do not submit expected orders, late orders, returned goods, orders to suppliers, stock levels to be controlled, narcotics control, security arrangements, and a string of other jobs.

A lot of work is done during the daily peaks, and this is managed within a context of DHP's objectives to:

- focus on customers
- improve sales efficiency and performance

LOGISTICS IN PRACTICE – DAVID HAMILTON PHARMACEUTICALS (CONTINUED)

- ensure 'right-first-time' deliveries
- reduce lead times throughout supply chains
- reduce inventory costs.

Question

- How would you describe the strategic priorities at DHP?

(*Source*: Company reports; Reisman, L. (2002) Pharmaceutical industry wholesale and distribution, Logistics and Transport Focus, 4(4), 36–41)

Chapter review

- Strategic decisions are high level, long term, use many resources and have major consequences for the whole organisation. They set the overall direction of an organisation and give the context for lower decisions.

- There are several levels of strategic decision. We described these as a mission or vision followed by corporate, business and functional strategies. A logistics strategy is one of the functional strategies.

- The strategic importance of logistics is clear from its role as an essential function, its long-term effect on organisational performance (and even survival), its major use of resources, its inclusion in mission statements, its involvement in important decisions, and so on.

- A logistics strategy consists of all the long-term goals, plans, policies, culture, resources, decisions and actions that relate to the management of an organisation's supply chains. There is a huge variety of different formats.

- The design of a logistics strategy can start with a logistic mission. This is expanded to give a strategy that balances the needs of higher strategies, internal strengths and the external environment. There is no single best method for strategic design, but we described a useful approach in eight steps.

- Traditional top-down design has weaknesses, and a logistics strategy is more likely to develop from a combination of top-down design and bottom-up emerging.

- Ideally, an organisation would do everything perfectly, but in reality it has to focus on aspects of performance that are particularly important. In different circumstances, almost any aspect of logistics can have a strategic importance.

- As organisations move in similar directions, their logistics strategies are often variations on generic ones. Common generic strategies focus on leanness (using the fewest possible resources) and agility (achieving customer satisfaction).

- There are many other possible strategies that might focus on alliances, time, productivity, environmental factors, and so on. There is no 'best' strategy for any particular circumstances.

CASE STUDY – HESSINGEN HERB FARM

Conrad and Elizabeth Kole moved into Hessingen Farm in 1988. Over the past few years their income from milk and traditional crops has dropped because of lower market prices. They have supplemented this income from other sources, including the conversion of old barns into holiday homes.

Eight years ago Elizabeth took over a small field and started growing herbs. She sold a small range of these to local people who wanted fresh, organic produce for cooking. Passing tourists would also buy an unusual souvenir, and the herb business began to prosper. Five years ago Elizabeth started growing more unusual herbs, expanded her growing area into a second field and opened a visitors' centre. People now came to look at the growing and preparation of herbs, and taste samples in various foods. Three years ago Elizabeth introduced a new range of herb products. This was a major expansion, converting some of the farm buildings into a 'herb kitchen' and making products for cooking (sauces, dressings and marinades), perfumes (posies, pot-pourris and sachets of dried herbs) and what she called 'healthy stuff' (herb mixtures traditionally said to have beneficial effects).

The farm is now widely advertised as a tourist attraction. The website is particularly useful, as Elizabeth uses it to collect orders. She now delivers 100 parcels a week to regular locals (up to 50 km away) and posts 200 parcels to more distant customers.

Herbs started as a small business to generate additional income for the farm, but have now become its main activity. Elizabeth is considering another expansion. She could expand the product range even further and move all the processing to an industrial estate 15 km away. Supporting this would need sales around ten times the current postal sales. Elizabeth plans to generate these by introducing a mail order catalogue and increasing use of the website.

Questions

- How does Elizabeth currently organise her logistics? What do you think are her aims and priorities?
- What would be the effect of the expansion on logistics? What problems would Elizabeth face, and what options does she have to overcome them?

Project – mission and strategy

Many organisations refer, either explicitly or implicitly, to logistics in their mission. You can find statements about the role of logistics published in corporate strategies, objectives, aims, publicity and related documents. Search through the documents published by different types of organisation, and see how they mention the strategic role of logistics. Can you identify different attitudes to logistics in different kinds of industry? Are there differences between different companies in the same industry?

It is more difficult to get information about functional strategies – specifically logistics strategies. But see if you can find some interesting examples of logistics strategies and missions.

Discussion questions

3.1 Is logistics really a strategic function with a long-term affect on organisational performance?

3.2 What is a logistics strategy?

3.3 What is meant by 'strategic fit' and how can a logistics manager try to get it?

3.4 Some managers argue that there is no point in publishing logistics strategies, as everyone knows that they deliver products to customers. Do you find such arguments convincing?

3.5 There should never be a top-down design of strategy, as senior managers never know enough about day-to-day operations to design realistic strategies. Do you think this is true?

3.6 When customers judge products, they include factors like availability, lead time and after-sales service – and these are part of logistics. So does logistics really form a part of the product package?

3.7 What are the options for a logistics strategy? What factors affect an organisation's choice?

3.8 There is only one 'best' logistics strategy in any circumstances, and managers should look for this. Do you think this is true?

3.9 Can logistics really be both lean and agile at the same time?

3.10 How can a supply chain become agile?

References

1. Waters, D. (2007) Operations strategy, Thomson Learning, London.
2. Website at www.hansonlogisticsgroup.com.
3. Website at www.fedex.com.
4. Website at www.amsino.com.
5. Website at www.kiranindia.com.
6. J. Sainsbury company annual reports and website at www.j-sainsbury.co.uk
7. Murray, R.E. (1980) Strategic distribution planning, Proceedings of the Eighteenth Annual Conference of the National Council of Physical Distribution Management.
8. Waters, D. (2007) A review of logistics strategy, Institute of European Logistics, Geneva.
9. Smith, R.J. (2000) The logistics mission, Members' Directory, pp. 22–27, The Institute for Logistics and Transport, Corby.
10. Website at www.procurement.ekgroup.com
11. Gooderham, G. (1998) Debunking the myths of strategic planning, CMA magazine, May.
12. Selznick, P. (1957) Leadership in administration, Harper and Rowe, New York.
13. Hamel, G. and Prahalad, C. (1994) Competing for the future, Harvard Business School Press, Boston MA.
14. Website at www.schenker.com.
15. Website at www.schenkerusa.com.
16. Porter, M.E. (1985) Competitive advantage, Free Press, New York.
17. Porter, M.E. (1996) What is strategy, Harvard Business Review November-December, pp. 61–79.
18. Ohno, T. (1988) Toyota production system, Productivity Press, New York.
19. Womack, J., Jones, D. and Roos, D. (1990) The machine that changed the world, Harper Perennial, New York.
20. Womack, J. and Jones, D. (1994) From lean production to the lean enterprise, Harvard Business Review, February–March.
21. Womack, J. and Jones, D. (1996) Beyond Toyota: how to root out waste and pursue perfection, Harvard Business Review, September–October.
22. Monden, Y. (1983) Toyota production system, Industrial Engineering and Management Press, Atlanta, GA.
23. Townsend, R. (1970) Up the organisation, Coronet Books, London.
24. Christopher, M. (2000) The agile supply chain, Industrial Marketing Management, 29, 37–44.
25. Evans, B. and Powell, M. (2000) Synergistic thinking: a pragmatic view of 'lean' and 'agile', Logistics and Transport Focus, 2(10), 26–32.

26. Waters, D. (2002) Operations management, FT Prentice Hall, Harlow, Essex.

27. Beesley, A. (1995) Time compression – new source of competitiveness in the supply chain, Logistics Focus, 3(5), 24–25.

28. Beesley, A. (2007) Time compression in the supply chain, in Global logistics (5th edition), Waters, D. (editor), Kogan Page, London.

29. Carter, R., Melnyk, P.L. and Handfield, S.A. (1994) Identifying sources of cycle time reduction, Quorum Books, Texas.

30. Szymankiewicz, J. (1993) Going green – the logistics dilemma, Focus on Logistics and Distribution Management, 12(5), 36–41.

31. European Community (2002) European Waste Electrical and Electronic Equipment Directive 2002/96/EC, Brussels.

32. International Standards Organisation (2007) ISO 14000: environmental management, ISO, Geneva.

33. Hart, S.L. (1997) Beyond greening, Harvard Business Review, January–February, p. 71.

34. Porritt, J. et al. (1999) A new vision for business, Committee of Enquiry into a New Vision for Business, London.

35. McIntyre, K. (2007) Delivering sustainability through supply chain management, in Global Logistics (5th edition), Waters, D. (editor), Kogan Page, London.

36. Harvey-Jones, J. (1994) All together now, Heinemann, London.

IMPLEMENTING THE STRATEGY

Contents

LEARNING OBJECTIVES

After reading this chapter you should be able to:

- understand the meaning of logistics strategy implementation

- appreciate the difficulties of implementation

- consider the type of decisions involved in strategy implementation

- discuss the elements of a logistics infrastructure

- consider alternative organisational structures

- discuss the structure of a supply chain

- consider related questions about location, ownership and capacity

- recognise the importance of change in logistics

- discuss the management of change.

Relating a strategy to lower decisions

Chapter 3 discussed the design of a logistics strategy, which contains all of the long-term goals, plans, policies, culture, resources, decisions and actions relating to an organisation's supply chain. But even the best designed strategy is no use unless it is actually used, so in this chapter we look at the steps needed to implement a strategy. This means taking the plans and ideas described in the strategy and translating them into actions.

- A **strategy** shows the long-term aspirations and intent for logistics – implementing the strategy makes sure that these are realised.
- Implementation **translates strategic plans into positive actions.**

Implementation
translates strategic plans
into positive actions

Cascade of decisions

A logistics strategy sets the context for all other logistics decisions. This means that managers have to examine the strategy and see how it affects their own decisions. In their jobs they might search for answers to questions like:

- What is the best shape for the supply chain?
- Should we change our warehouse and transport operations?
- What is the best way to schedule activities in the supply chain?
- How much stock should we hold?
- Do we need more facilities?
- Do we have, or can we train, people with the necessary skills?
- What are the impacts on staff, facilities, organisation, technology, and so on?

These – and the huge number of other decisions needed for logistics – are not strategic, but they are more detailed tactical and operational decisions. So managers look to the logistics strategy for guidance when they make more detailed, lower-level decisions. For instance, a strategy of selling products through a website would affect managers' medium-term, tactical decisions about warehousing, investment in stock, transport, materials handling, recruiting and training, customer service, and so on. These tactical decisions, in turn, affect short-term, operational decisions about resource scheduling, inventory control, expediting, vehicle routes, and so on.

You can see that this gives a mechanism for implementing strategy, with decisions moving progressively downwards through layers of management, and each layer adding progressively more details. Managers at each level look at the aims and requirements set by managers above them, and they decide the actions they must take to achieve these. These actions define their own aims and requirements, which are passed down to managers below. When this is repeated through the

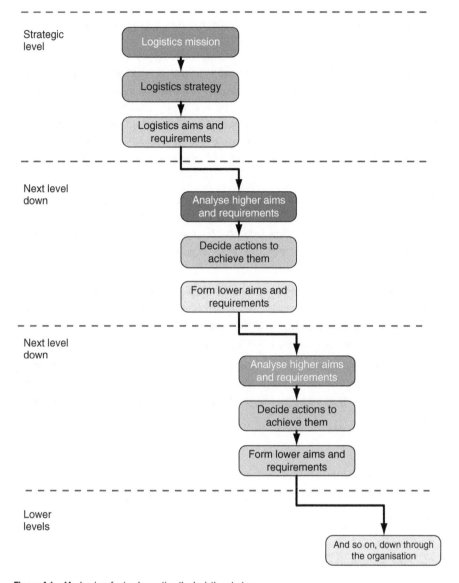

Figure 4.1 Mechanism for implementing the logistics strategy

different levels of management it gives a mechanism for cascading decisions down from the strategy, as illustrated in Figure 4.1.

Suppose that senior managers set a strategy of selling in a certain market. Then the next layer of managers would make a decision to open a local warehouse – followed by a series of increasingly detailed decisions about the type of products to be stored, suppliers to use, how much of an item to keep in stock, how to monitor demand for the item, how much to order this week, where to put the order when it is delivered, and so on. Eventually, this cascade of decisions moves down to the most detailed level, and defines all aspects of logistics.

OPERATIONS IN PRACTICE – BJORN FRIDERIKSON CAR RENTALS

When Bjorn Friderikson Car Rentals (BFCR) started a business in Stockholm, there were already many competitors in the market. In general, the major international companies tended to compete by service, including Hertz ('Call the world's No. 1'), Avis ('We try harder'), Eurodollar ('Rent from the best'), Europcar ('All around – a better service'), Ford ('A big name in rental'), Thrifty ('World class service at your doorstep'). The smaller, local companies tended to compete on price, such as Economy ('The lowest prices around'), Capital ('Competitive rates, best value'), and Harald ('Lowest rates in town').

BFCR decided that they would compete with a strategy that combined a good, personal service with a reasonable price. They obviously could not provide the scale of service offered by the international companies, but they learned a lot from their operations. For example, they automated administration, so that repeat customers can pass a plastic card through a reader and pick up a car immediately.

At the same time, BFCR recognised that private customers were very interested in price, so they looked at the operations of smaller companies to see how they could reduce operating costs. Now they do not use expensive locations like airport arrival lounges, keep their cars for rather longer, buy more basic models, and have more flexible pricing.

BFCR effectively benchmarked their operations against international companies when looking at the quality of service, and local companies when looking for low costs. The important point is that the company's strategy showed what it wanted to achieve, and then lower decision show how to achieve this.

Question

- What kinds of decisions would be needed to implement BFCR's strategy?

(*Source*: Friderikson, C. (2007) Benchmarking Car Rentals. Scandinavian Operations Group, Copenhagen)

Difficulties with implementation

The iterative expansion of a logistics strategy can be surprisingly difficult. You can imagine this when a strategy is poorly designed and lower managers have to translate vague concepts like 'global leadership' into actual operations. But it can also be difficult to implement a good strategy that has been properly designed. For instance, a strategy of good customer service seems sensible, and it might be translated into a target of delivering all orders within two working days. But now managers have to design the detailed operations that achieve this – and this is where the difficulties might appear. It may simply be impossible to achieve the target, or it might only be achievable at very high cost or with too much strain on the supply chain.

There are two options at this point. Firstly, managers can say that the strategy has been carefully designed, and everyone must work harder or find new, innovative ways of achieving the targets. This builds on the belief that strategic managers have done their job properly and set goals that are intentionally demanding (forcing the organisation to perform as well as it can), but achievable (so that it can actually be implemented). Secondly, managers can say that the practical difficulties are too great, and that there was a mistake in designing an unrealistic strategy. This is more worrying, as it means that the strategic managers did not do their job properly, and all their work has been wasted. It seems obvious that managers should design a strategy that can actually be implemented, with long-term plans leading smoothly to realistic tactical and operational decisions. But the underlying problem – especially in organisations with rigid hierarchies – is that one group of senior managers designs the strategies, and a different group of more junior managers implements them. The two groups have different objectives, goals, information, experience and skills. Even with good communications, senior managers are remote from operations, and typically see financial ratios, but with little knowledge of the operations that achieved them. At the same time, people working with the detailed bustle of day-to-day activities have little time for corporate ideals – and the lofty aim of 'being acknowledged world leaders' has no consequence for someone who is rushing to make an overdue delivery.

Continuing this line of reasoning, we can suggest the following list of common problems with implementing logistics strategies:

- People who design the strategies are not responsible for their implementation.
- People who implement the strategies have little interest in them and, at best, pay lip-service to their aims.
- The strategy is badly designed – perhaps having aims that are too vague or a mistaken focus.
- The strategy is designed without enough knowledge, information or input from the broad organisation.
- It is impossible to translate hazy strategic aims into actual, real operations.
- The strategy does not take enough account of constraints on operations.
- The strategy is over-ambitious or unrealistic.
- Enthusiasm for the strategies declines over time.

One surprisingly common mistake is to go through all the steps of designing a logistics strategy and then starting to think about its implementation. The result often cannot be implemented – and an obvious way of avoiding this is to consider implementation all the way through the design. This needs widespread participation in the design process, particularly from those most closely involved with its implementation. Some other factors that help to design a strategy that can be used are:

- an organisational structure that is flexible and allows innovation
- formal procedures for translating the strategy into reasonable decisions at lower levels

- efficient information systems
- open communications, which encourage the free exchange of ideas
- acceptance that strategies are not fixed, but continue to evolve over time
- control systems to monitor progress
- convincing everyone that the strategy is beneficial, so they are willing to work towards its success
- developing an organisational culture that supports the strategy.

LOGISTICS IN PRACTICE – SAINSBURY'S

Sainsbury's is a major supermarket with annual sales of £19 billion. In common with all supermarkets, it would like to have all products on its shelves all the time, but realistically it achieves an average availability of around 96%. This means that 96% of customers who look for a product are likely to find it on the shelves. This seems good, but it means that a person who wants 12 items has only a 61% chance of finding them all in stock.

This illustrates one practical problem of implementing the company's strategic aim of complete customer satisfaction. Sainsbury's continuously works to improve the implementation of its strategies and, during one study, identified some fundamental problems, including:

- commercial strategies that were making supply chains increasingly complex
- supply chain strategies that were not aligned to customer demands
- business processes that were not integrated but worked in isolation
- technology that was not used to its full potential
- management strategies that failed to produce motivated, focused, creative, and organised teams.

Such problem can best be overcome by increasing cooperation, and although this is growing, it is far from universal within the company. For instance, the logistics function is likely to design operations that 'maximise its own performance at the expense of operational effectiveness in the stores'. With planning, 'there was a disconnect between the aspirations of the planners and the capability of the stores to implement'.

Question

- Why do you think logistics strategies are so difficult to implement?

(Sources: Green, M. (2004) Availability on the shelf, Focus on Logistics and Transport, 6(10), 22–7; Green M. (2006) The last 50 metres, Focus on Logistics and Transport, 8(4), 29–32, website at www.sainsbury.co.uk)

Areas for strategic decisions

As lower managers add details to a logistics strategy, their scope seems to spread out. A mission gives a particular focus; lower decisions look at the functions of procurement, packaging, warehousing, transport, location, and so on; following levels look at broader aspects of each of these functions, and so on down the organisation (illustrated in Figure 4.2). So you might ask about the types of concern that are specifically raised within a strategy. For instance, is a strategy likely to refer to customer service levels, or are these set at lower levels; does it make decisions about purchasing or are these operational details?

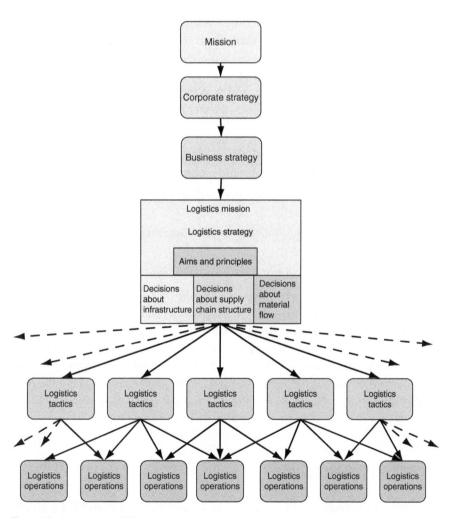

Figure 4.2   Increasing detail of decision in logistics

A traditional view is summarised by Ballou[1] who says that a strategy needs to concentrate on four areas; customer service, facility location, inventory policy and transport. This is a fairly restricted view – rather like Chopra and Meindl's[2] 'six drivers' of facilities, inventory, transportation, information, sourcing and pricing. Helming and Zonnenberg[3] give a more inclusive view by suggesting decisions in five areas: supply chain configuration, enabling practices, strategic relationships, organisation and application of information technology. They also emphasise the importance of implementation by saying, 'Companies hurl staggering sums of money and human resources at their supply chain infrastructure, only to fail at implementing their supply chain strategy.'

An even broader view says that, depending on circumstances, any decision areas might be mentioned in a logistics strategy and we should consider them all from procurement through to final delivery. Inventory might be an operational detail when deciding how much to order today, but it is tactical when deciding how much to invest in stock this year, and it becomes strategic when deciding whether to build a new warehouse or ship directly from production. Customer service involves operational decisions to schedule deliveries to a customer, tactical when organising the transport fleet, and strategic when designing supply chains. However, we can classify areas that are likely to have a strategic impact into five general types:

1. *purpose and aims* – showing what logistics is trying to achieve
2. *principles* – stating organisational standards, ethics, beliefs, culture, and so on
3. *logistics infrastructure* – giving the organisational structure and systems used to achieve the principles
4. *structure of supply chains* – defining the elements it contains and their relationships
5. *the flow of materials through supply chains* – saying how the flows are controlled.

In Chapter 3 we discussed the purpose and aims of logistics, and this sets the scene for the others. The principles describe the beliefs of the firm and the way that it does business. The last three give the tools needed to achieve the aims. So an aim of high customer service is achieved while adhering to the business principles of the firm, and is followed by decisions about an appropriate infrastructure, decisions about the supply chain structure, and decisions about the flow of materials through the chain. The important point is that all of these decisions are strategic and show how logistics will work in the long term.

Logistics infrastructure

A key task in implementing a strategy is to define who is responsible for all the remaining activities – in other words, to build an organisation that is capable of achieving the aims. This starts with an appropriate structure for the logistics function, with clearly defined responsibilities. It also adds the systems, human resources, culture and resources that support this structure. Together, these form the logistics infrastructure.

Logistics infrastructure consists of the organisational structure and the systems, human resources, culture and resources to support it

> • A **logistics infrastructure** consists of the organisational structure and the systems, human resources, culture and resources to support it.

Organisational structure

When designing an infrastructure, managers have to consider:

- how logistics fits into the broad organisation
- the design of an internal structure for logistics
- internal policies, methods – and general culture – that support the strategy
- allocation of budgets and resources to activities that are most important for strategic success
- motivation of people to pursue strategic targets
- integration of logistics activities
- design of information, communication, financial, control and other support systems
- leadership needed to drive the strategy forward.

At the heart of such decisions is an appropriate organisational structure.

> • An **organisational structure** divides a whole organisation into distinct parts, and defines the relationships between each part.

The structure shows who has responsibility for what, who has authority over whom, and who reports to whom. The result is described in an organisational chart that shows the place of logistics within the broader organisation, how it is related to other functions, and how it is organised internally. This structure also determines the broad nature of internal systems. For instance, information, financial and control systems must be designed to fit into, and support, the designed structure.

We can outline a procedure for designing an organisational structure, which starts by identifying the key types of activities in logistics and combining these into coherent groups. These form the organisational building blocks. Now assign responsibility for each building block to one person, and decide how much authority to delegate to lower levels. Then establish the means of coordinating different blocks, usually by having related blocks report to a single, senior manager. This gives the skeleton for the structure, which is expanded by adding the details.

Five concerns in this design are:[4]

1. *Defining the units* – dividing logistics activities into coherent parts, each of which has a prominent place in the organisation chart.

2. *Formality* – defining the extent to which formal rules and procedures govern decisions and working relationships. Very formal organisations have rigid procedures, so people know what to do in any circumstances – but they can be slow to act, bureaucratic, inflexible and not innovative. In practice, it is often the informal systems which exist in even the most rigid structure that ensure things get done.

3. *Centralisation* – refers to the location of authority and control within an organisation – and particularly the extent to which decision making is kept within the higher levels of the hierarchy. In highly centralised organisations, a few top managers are responsible for all decisions. This assumes that managers are promoted for their ability to make decisions, so centralised decision making puts decisions in the hands of the most capable. Decentralised organisations give lower-level managers more autonomy, with the assumption that they have more specialised knowledge, more incentives to do better job, and can react quickly.

4. *Specialisation* – or the extent to which an organisation's activities are separated into distinct functions. A highly specialised organisation puts each type of specialist (perhaps accountants or lawyers) into a group that performs a narrow range of activities and acts as a consultant when needed. A less specialised organisation forms diverse groups with a variety of different skills.

5. *Rigidity* – the extent to which organisational relationships remain unchanged over time. A rigid organisation does not change over long periods, which gives the advantage of stability, predictability and established procedures, but the disadvantages of inflexibility and lack of response to changing conditions.

Types of structure

Decisions about these define the relationships between units, but logistics is organised in a huge number of different ways and there is certainly no single, best arrangement. A small organisation might have one person looking after everything. A medium-sized organisation might have a small logistics department with different sections for purchasing, transport, stock control, distribution, and so on. A large organisation might have a distinct logistics division employing thousands of people. Sometimes all the activities are organised in a single department reporting to a logistics director; sometimes they are part of a larger department such as marketing or production; sometimes they are spread out in small pockets throughout a firm; sometimes they are contracted out to third-party suppliers.

Each activity might be in a distinct unit, or there might be cross-functional task forces, special project teams, self-contained work teams, contact managers, relationship managers, and many other adjustments. Although there is no standard pattern, the following organisational structures are most common.

- *Functional organisation* – a traditional view, where units are defined by the function that they perform, illustrated in Figure 4.3. This gives different divisions for procurement, transport, warehousing, and so on, and each manager reports to a more senior manager within the same function. The benefits of this include: stable groups that work well together, pooling expertise and sharing knowledge, being easy to administer, with clear authority, no duplication of effort and continuity. On the other hand, it has the disadvantages of encouraging a 'silo mentality' where each function concentrates on its own work rather than the broader good of the organisation, developing bureaucratic procedures that become aims in themselves, and diverting attention away from customer satisfaction.

- *Product organisation* – where each group is responsible for the logistics of a particular type of product, as illustrated in Figure 4.4. This has the advantages of concentrating specialised knowledge about each product, developing and retaining special expertise, giving clear authority and simplified communications. Its main strength is a focus on the delivery of products to satisfy customers.[5] But it can also duplicate effort, have people reporting to managers with no knowledge of their functional skills, no one with responsibility for an entire function, unclear loyalties, and difficulty in transferring skills between products. Variations on this theme divide logistics (and the broader organisation) not by product, but by geographical area, project, brand, or some other division based on the use of resources.

- *Hybrid organisation* – which combines aspects of both functional and product structures. There are many forms of hybrid structure, which makes it the most widespread type in practice. One common format has an overall functional structure, but one major product is so important that it is worth having a distinct group to look after it. Then the units are based on a mixture of functions and products. Another common format has a functional structure at the top of the organisation, but a product structure lower down – or the reverse, with a product structure at the top of the organisation, changing to a functional structure lower down.

- *Matrix organisations* – are a type of hybrid, where a functional organisation is overlaid by a product organisation, as shown in Figure 4.5. You can imagine this in an organisation that works with a number of key products, and then purchasing people, say, work both within a purchasing department and also on a specific product. Again, this structure comes in many different varieties, based on different types of division and allocation of authority. It has the advantages of focusing on key operations, being flexible and adapting to needs, allowing easy transfer of skills and easier information flows. On the other hand, there

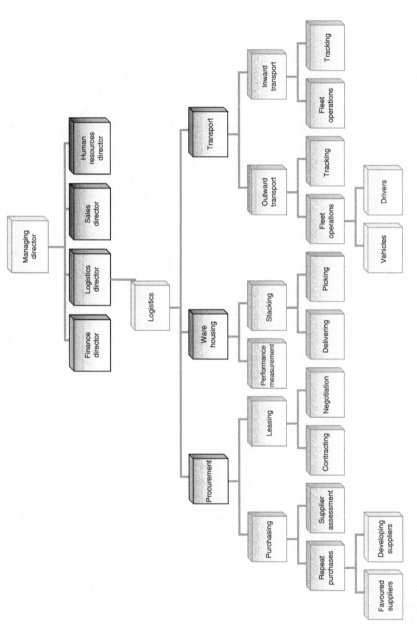

Figure 4.3   Example of a functional organisation structure

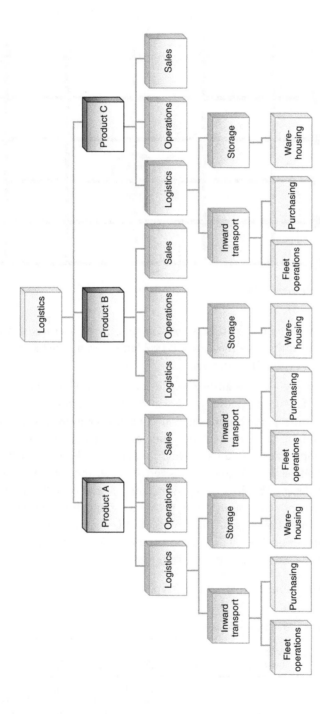

Figure 4.4 Example of a product organisation structure

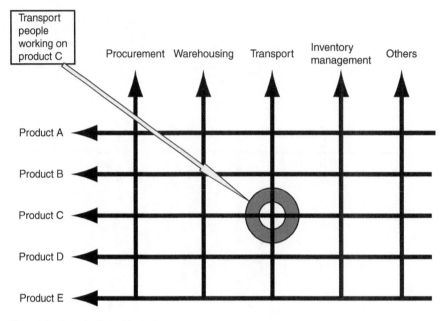

Figure 4.5   Example of a matrix structure

are problems with built-in conflicts, extra management overheads, complex authority relationships, and the inherent problems of everyone having at least two bosses with conflicting interests.

- *Self-managed groups* – where authority is delegated down to groups working within the organisation. Traditional organisational structures are based on a hierarchy, with reporting upwards and control downwards. Self-managed groups have almost all of the decisions and control delegated to lower levels, with each group working, to a large extent, independently. This structure has the benefit of encouraging expertise, it is very flexible, and delegates authority to appropriate levels. The disadvantages include a loss of overall coordination and control, difficult communications, problems with defining authority, reconciling different objectives of the groups, and general complexity. Because of the practical difficulties, it is more common to find self-managed groups working within a more formal overall structure.

Table 4.1 compares some features of these types of structure.

Table 4.1   Properties of different organisational structures

| | | *Factor* | | | | | |
		Centralisation	Specialisation	Efficiency	Cost	Flexibility	Relationships
Type of	Functional	High	High	Medium	High	Low	Formal
structure	Product	High	Low	Medium	High	Medium	Formal
	Matrix	Medium	Medium	Low	Medium	Medium	Medium
	Self-managed	Low	High	High	Low	High	Informal

Managers should design an organisational structure that best achieves their aims – giving the best match between strategy and structure. There is certainly no single best structure for all conditions, and the usual practice is to choose a basic design, modify it as necessary, and then supplement it with coordinating communication and control mechanisms. In practice, small single business organisations usually have a centralised, functional structure; organisations with broad geographic coverage typically have regional operating divisions; most larger organisations have some form of hybrid structure. There is probably some trend towards decentralised structures with devolved authority and self-managed groups. These groups are becoming smaller and leaner, with fewer managers, more technology, and more open communications.[6,7]

Supporting the structure

After designing the organisational structure, the next step is to add the systems to support it – for accounts, communications, information, order processing, customer relations and other basic operations. There may also be specialised systems, such as reservation systems in airlines, parcel tracking in logistics companies, maintenance systems for service companies, patient care in health services, and so on.

Most of these systems are based on the collection of data, its analysis and presentation of results around the organisation. They obviously come in a huge variety of forms ranging from 'post-it' stickers through to artificial intelligence systems with automated decisions. However, their essential structure consist of hardware that collects and delivers information, rules and procedures for deciding what information is delivered to each person, and statements of how they should respond to the information.

Now, if we add the formal and informal aspects of people's behaviour that also support the structure, we have the elements shown in Figure 4.6.

Different organisational structures use systems and delegate authority in different ways. Traditional structures tend to keep most authority at the top of the organisation, whereas more recent self-managed groups devolve decisions to the lowest possible level. Current thinking emphasises the contribution of people to organisational success, with studies by Pfeffer and Veiga[8,9] illustrating the benefits of good HRM in American industry, and similar findings reported by the DTI for the UK[10] and Blimes et al. for Germany.[11]

The message from these, and subsequent, studies is that we all respond better to motivation than discipline – the carrot works better than the stick in getting what Joynson described as 'extraordinary efforts from ordinary people'.[12] This idea of motivation is difficult to define, but a person is motivated if they keep working hard to achieve an appropriate goal. In other words:

- Motivated people work hard.
- They persevere and continue their efforts for as long as needed.
- They are effective and work towards an appropriate goal.

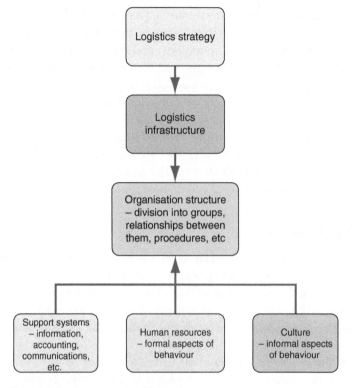

Figure 4.6 Elements in forming an operations infrastructure

Of course, the key question is how to get people motivated. There has been a huge amount of work in trying to answer to this, often following the classical studies of Maslow's hierarchy of needs[13] and Hertzberg's internal and external motivators.[14] But there is still no agreement about a best approach, beyond general advice such as Brown et al.'s[15] emphasis on:

- *commitment to people* – recognising that employees are a key strategic resource and having clear policies about employees, job security, selection of employees and rewards
- *shared purpose* – through strategic leadership, distribution of information, participation in decision making and employee ownership
- *enabling structures* – including the organisational structure, communications, devolved management and informal structures
- *learning and development* – with a commitment to training, upgrading skills, continuous improvement and broader organisational learning
- *involvement* – with team working, removal of internal boundaries, participation and recognition of stakeholder needs.

When these are practised over the long term, they become a part of the organisation's broader culture. Unfortunately, it is difficult to say exactly what we mean by an organisational culture, except that it broadly defines the values, norms, beliefs and assumptions that influence the way that people within an organisation think and behave; it defines the shared, basic assumptions about the organisation, work, principles, human relationships, beliefs, aims, ethics, and so on. The concept of a corporate culture may be vague, but it forms a framework that affects all aspects of logistics. It shows 'how we do things' and determines the way that people work, how they feel about the organisation, how they treat customers, how they deal with other people in the organisation, their ethical standards, and every other aspect of their work.

Structure of a supply chain

A single organisation sees a supply chain as tiers of suppliers feeding materials from original sources into its operations, and then tiers of customers moving materials out to final customers (as shown in Figure 4.7).

In practice, there are many variations on this basic model. Some supply chains have few tiers of customers and suppliers, while others have many; some chains have very simple flows of materials, while others have complex and convoluted networks. Different types of products clearly need different structures in their supply chain – and you can imagine that building sand needs a very different type of chain from a mobile phone. Factors that determine the best structure for a supply chain include the product's complexity, number of components,

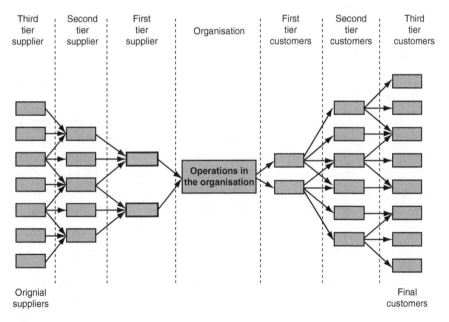

Figure 4.7   Structure of a supply chain

technology, value, bulk, perishability, availability and profitability. Sand has low value, is bulky and is readily available – so it needs a short, simple supply chain with suppliers as close as possible to final customer. Mobile phones are small, expensive and are assembled from many components in specialised factories – so they have longer, more complex chains.

Logistics managers have to consider the product and all other factors before designing a supply chain. In particular, they are aiming for the benefits that come from a well-designed chain, which include:

- operations sited in the best locations, regardless of the locations of suppliers and customers
- core operations concentrated in large facilities, giving economies of scale
- simpler transport with fewer, larger deliveries, reducing costs
- large orders with suppliers, giving lower unit costs and price discounts
- storage of materials to overcome mismatches between supply and demand
- materials stored at appropriate points to give short lead times
- lower stocks, as reliable suppliers guarantee deliveries
- known locations for customers to find products
- aggregation of stocks from many suppliers, giving customers a broader choice of products
- convenient locations for essential activities like sorting and consolidating loads
- postponement increasing flexibility to change and customise products
- repeated operations that become practised and routine.

Alternative structures

The underlying structure of a supply chain is defined by its length and breadth (illustrated in Figure 4.8).

(Supply chain) length is the number of tiers, or intermediaries, that materials flow through between source and destination

- Supply chain length – is the number of tiers, or intermediaries that materials flow through between source and destination. Some supply chains are very short, for example, when a producer sells directly to final customers. And other supply chains are very long, perhaps with intermediaries connecting several stages of manufacturing and distribution through a series of logistics centres, transport operators, agents, freight forwarders, brokers and agents.

(Supply chain) breadth is the number of parallel routes that materials can flow through, or the number of organisations in each tier

- Supply chain breadth – is the number of parallel routes that materials flow through, or the number of organisations in each tier. Cadbury has a broad supply chain, which means that it has many routes out to customers, and you can buy their chocolate in a huge number of retailers; Thorntons has a narrower chain, with most of their chocolate selling through their own shops; Pigalle et Fils has a very narrow chain as they sell their chocolate in a single shop in Belgium.

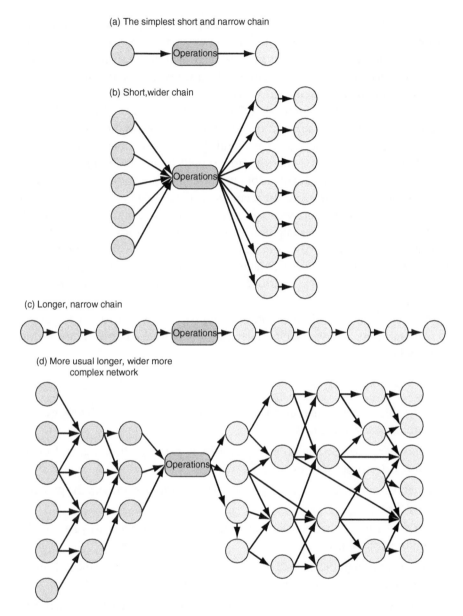

Figure 4.8   Alternate shapes of supply chains

On top of this basic structure are a series of related features that include the types of organisations in the chain, the activities that each does, the size of facilities, their locations, capacity, the relationships between them, and so on. Together these describe the overall structure of the supply chain.

The best shape for a supply chain depends on individual circumstances. It largely depends on the type of product, but also the logistics strategy. For instance, a company that focuses on fast service will use a chain with facilities close to final customers, so that it can make quick deliveries; a company that focuses on low costs will centralise all operations in a few, large facilities that give economies of scale. Other factors that affect the supply chain structure include the type of customer demand, economic climate, availability of logistics services, culture, rate of innovation, competition, market and financial arrangements. Three particularly important factors are the amount of control that an organisation wants over its logistics, the quality of service offered and the cost. A manufacturer delivering directly to customers has a short, narrow supply chain (like Figure 4.8a). This gives a lot of control over logistics, but it may be difficult to achieve either high customer service or low costs. Broadening the chain (Figure 4.8b) gives higher customer service, but it increases costs and reduces the manufacturer's control. Making the supply chain long and narrow (Figure 4.8c) uses the expertise of intermediaries to reduce costs, but the manufacturer loses control and the customer service does not improve. Making the supply chain both long and broad (Figure 4.8d) removes most control from the manufacturer, but customers get good service.

The shape of the distribution part of a supply chain is particularly important to manufacturers, and we can list some commonly used patterns (illustrated in Figure 4.9).

1. direct shipping from manufacturer to customers, probably from storage at the manufacturing site (M–C)

2. shipping to a consolidation point for sorting, packing, finishing, and so on, before delivering to customers (M–P–C)

3. shipping from manufacturer to retailers where customers pick up the products (M–R–C)

4. shipping through wholesalers and retailers for customers to pick up the products (M–W–R–C)

5. shipping through the manufacturer's branches (possibly with some finishing), and then retailers for customer pick up (M–B–R–C)

6. shipping through the manufacturer's branches, and then wholesalers and retailers for customer pick up (M–B–W–R–C).

There are many variations on each of these patterns including having retailers deliver products to customers with options 3 to 6, including other agents at various points, involving other manufacturers or industrial users in the chain, having more consolidation points for organising deliveries, and using more levels of warehousing and storage points. Each of these formats comes with a variety of different options for ownership and control.

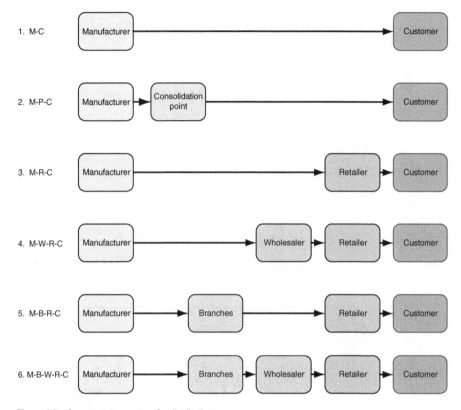

Figure 4.9   Some common patters for distribution

LOGISTICS IN PRACTICE – SHOERIGHT LIMITED

ShoeRight Limited is a manufacturer of shoes in Lahore, India. Figure 4.10 shows part of their supply chain, describing the distribution of shoes to final customers. This has finished shoes passing
to a logistics centre which either prepares them for the domestic market or sends them to a ship-
per for export. For the domestic market shoes are passed to the final customer either by direct
sales (mail order, websites or factory shops), or to a distributor who passes them to general retailers (specialised shoe shops, clothes shops, supermarkets, large multiple retailers, small multiple
retailers or mixed retailers), or to specialist retailers (such as shopping clubs, discount stores, retail
warehouses, and door-to-door sales). Then there are other intermediaries, such as wholesalers,
buying groups, agents, brokers, or cooperatives. Superimposed on the chain are specialised services such as transport, warehousing, finance, freight forwarders, and so on. The whole picture
becomes very complicated, and a pair of shoes can pass through a surprisingly large number of
hands before it reaches the final customer.

LOGISTICS IN PRACTICE – SHOERIGHT LIMITED (CONTINUED)

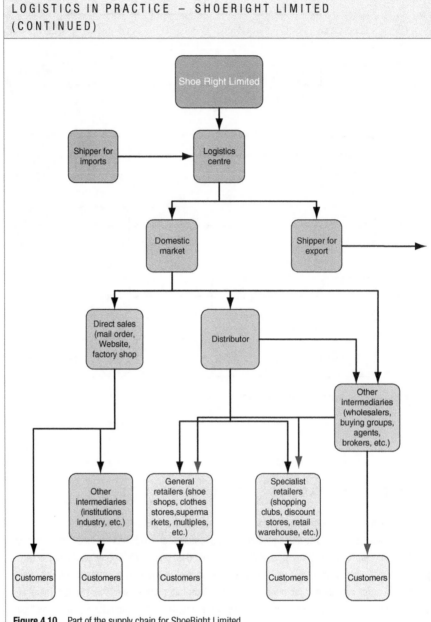

Figure 4.10 Part of the supply chain for ShoeRight Limited

Question

- Is the distribution chain at ShoeRight unusually long or complicated?

(*Source*: Company records)

Location of facilities

The general structure of a supply chain defines the number of participants, including wholesalers, warehouses and logistics centres. A related question asks where each facility should be located. As usual with logistics, this depends on many factors. As a starting point, a logistics strategy might define the geographical areas in which it operates, and this limits the feasible locations of facilities. More specifically, when an organisation has a strategy of fast delivery, it will use local warehouses that are physically close to customers; when it wants low costs, it will concentrate stocks in large, centralised warehouses that are inevitably some distance away from customers; if it exports a lot of products it might use warehouses near to ports or rail terminals; if it manufactures products, it will probably keep a stock of finished goods near the factory.

The location of facilities has a clear effect on logistics performance, so this is an area that managers should consider very carefully. The effect is also long term, as once a facility is opened it is difficult to close it down or move it. We look at the question of location in Chapter 7, but an important point is that location is not an isolated decision. It leads to a series of related decisions about the work done in each location, size of each facility, level of technology used, layout of resources, customers to serve from each location, and so on.

Ownership and outsourcing

Another key decision for supply chain structure concerns its ownership. Supply chains usually span many organisations, but all members have the common objective of satisfying final customers – and this means that they should cooperate to gain mutual benefits. This cooperation appears in many forms, ranging from informal arrangements, through strategic alliances and partnerships, and on to outright ownership. It seems reasonable to suggest that cooperation is easiest when one organisation owns much of the chain, and it becomes more difficult when many diverse organisations are involved, each with its own aims and objectives. So one pressure on logistics is for organisations to move towards greater vertical integration, and control more of the chain.

However, we have already discussed an opposing pressure, which has organisations concentrating on their core activities and passing peripheral ones to third-party providers. The theory is that specialist companies can do some activities more efficiently, so it is better to use these rather than do the work internally. Rowley summarises the benefits this brings by saying that, 'The results of successful outsourcing are service improvement, cost reduction and quality enhancement.'[16] Of course, there are disadvantages to be set against this, such as less flexibility to respond to unusual circumstances, more complicated communications, conflicting objectives, and less control over quality, costs, price.[17]

As we saw in Chapter 2, the move towards outsourcing is prevailing. But this is not always the best option, and the decision to outsource is really a special type of make-or-buy decision. Sometimes it is better to keep logistics within

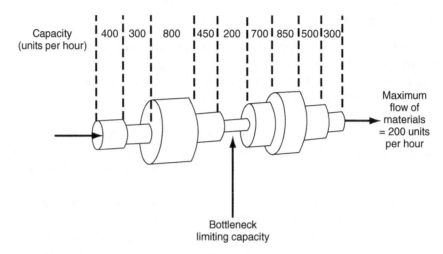

Figure 4.11   Capacity of a supply chain is set by the bottleneck

the organisation, and at other times it is better to use a specialist. Later in the book we look at these arrangements for warehousing (Chapter 12) and transport (Chapter 13).

Capacity

A third feature of supply chain structure concerns its capacity. Every chain has a fixed capacity, which is the largest amount of materials that can flow through it in a given time. A lorry might have a capacity of 25 tonnes that it can carry on a single journey, an airline has a capacity of 450 passengers on a flight, a warehouse can unload 210 lorries a week, or a retail shop can serve 120 customers an hour. Not all parts of a chain have the same capacity, so the overall capacity is set by the part with the smallest individual capacity. This forms the bottleneck. If wholesaling forms the bottleneck with a capacity of 200 units of a product an hour, this sets the capacity of the whole supply chain – even if other parts have a much higher capacity (as illustrated in Figure 4.11).

Bottleneck
the part of a supply chain that limits throughput because it has the smallest individual capacity

To get a smooth flow of materials through the supply chain, managers have to make sure that each part has an appropriate capacity. We consider this problem of capacity planning in Chapter 8.

LOGISTICS IN PRACTICE – RALSTON ENERGY SYSTEMS

The main products of Eveready Battery Co. (EBC) are its leading brand range of batteries and torches. To support these, it runs manufacturing plants in America, Europe and Asia – with distribution branches in almost every country of the world.

Until 1998 Ralston Energy Systems s.r.o. (RES) was an affiliate of EBC working in the Czech Republic. There it ran two warehouses, with part of its supply chain shown in Figure 4.12). The

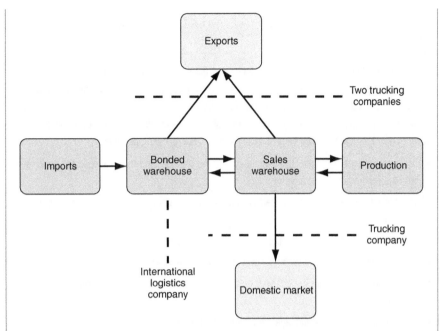

Figure 4.12   Summary of logistics at Ralston Energy s.r.o.

first warehouse was bonded and used to store imported materials, most of which were transferred to the RES main site in Prague, while some were re-exported. This warehouse was 50 km from Prague and was run under contract by a specialised international logistics company. The second warehouse was a 'sales warehouse' run by RES on their main site. This organised the distribution of products made in Prague, which were either destined for the domestic Czech market, or exported. Transport from this warehouse was organised by a local company that gave a good and flexible service. Two other trucking companies were involved in export and import operations, and the sales warehouse was about three times the size of the bonded warehouse.

This structure had a number of weaknesses:

- The sales warehouse was leased from a company that, two years previously, had become a competitor of RES. The company did not feel that it was appropriate to store finished goods in a competitor's facilities.

- The sales warehouse had become too small, and RES was having to store finished goods in the manufacturing plant.

- The sales warehouse had poor arrangements for loading and unloading trucks, which resulted in significant time delays.

- All goods imported into the Czech Republic were sent to the bonded warehouse, and were then moved by weekly transport to the manufacturing plant.

- Local distributors charged high rates for each truck load delivered.

LOGISTICS IN PRACTICE – RALSTON ENERGY SYSTEMS (CONTINUED)

RES looked for improvements to their logistics and the solution was to outsource it all to a third party. They negotiated an agreement to run the bonded warehouse with a new operator, who also took over distribution from the sales warehouse and effectively took over the sales warehouse. There were various problems and disruptions for about eight months, and then everything settled down to give a much improved service, which brought the following benefits:

- flexible warehousing space; RES expanded into the Ukraine, and the new operator could deal with their increased requirements

- variable warehousing costs – based on the volumes actually stored, without the substantial fixed costs

- variable distribution costs – again based on the amounts actually moved

- increased service quality – with new methods and procedures

- associated services from the operator – such as labelling, display rack assembly, preparation of promotional bundles

- saving overhead costs of management in the warehouse

- extending operating times

- removing the conflict of interest with a competitor-owned warehouse

- managing remote stock in Slovenia from the same facilities.

Question

- Could RES have got more benefits by designing a new structure for their supply chain?

(*Source*: Internal company reports)

Managing change

Managers design a logistics strategy – and the consequent supply chains – based on a range of prevailing internal and external factors. But these factors are constantly changing. Within the organisation there are continuous changes to employees, goals, products, facilities, plans, processes, costs, suppliers, customers, and so on. Externally there are changes to customers, markets, economic conditions, competitors, technology, suppliers, and so on. An obvious consequence is that logistics has to evolve over time. Managers cannot design a strategy, implement it, and then sit back with their job finished. Instead, they have to keep adjusting the strategy and the way that it works.

Unfortunately, this presents a problem, as most of us do not really like changes. We might claim to welcome change, as it stops us getting bored and offers new opportunities – but the truth is that changes need a lot of effort, forcing us to abandon old and familiar practices, to learn new skills, new ways of doing things, new procedures, and to form new relationships. Change moves us away from a reasonably predictable future to one with uncertainty and risk. The result is a certain inertia that resists change, and at an organisational level encourages firms to stick to old practices and continue with current operations. Unfortunately, such inflexible organisations then lose out to more dynamic competitors who are willing to improve their own operations. Some signs that an organisation is not changing to meet new circumstances include:

- low sales and falling market share, as old products are overtaken by new ones from competitors
- rising numbers of customer complaints, particularly about quality and delivery dates
- reliance on a few customers, especially with long-term, fixed price contracts
- old-fashioned attitudes, products and operations
- poor industrial relations, with low employee morale and high staff turnover
- poor communications within the organisation and with trading partners
- too much, inflexible top management with no new appointments
- inward-looking managers who are out of touch with operations, suppliers and customers.

Change is a normal part of business and those who do not respond are inevitably overtaken by competitors. To be more positive, we should welcome change as it creates opportunities, improves work conditions, introduces better practices, improves performance, and gives more interesting, better paid and secure jobs. This welcoming attitude does not happen by chance, but it needs careful management. In many organisations this needs a champion, or change manager, who generates enthusiasm for change, has the vision to see how the organisation can improve, and the ability to lead initiatives that move in the right direction. This can be a traumatic journey through stages that can typically be characterised as:[18, 19]

Change manager generates enthusiasm for change within an organisation

1. *denial* – where people deny that there is a need for change
2. *defence* – defending the current way of doing things and criticising new proposals
3. *discarding* – beginning to move away from the old ways and towards the new ones
4. *adoption* – using the new ways and accepting that they bring benefits
5. *integration* – assuming the new ways are normal and using them naturally.

This process must be managed to convince people who have to work in new ways that the changes are both essential and beneficial.

Rate of change

An important feature of change is the rate at which it occurs. Some organisations change very quickly, such as Intel, which works at the frontiers of technology and is continually developing new products. Others change very slowly, and even make a virtue out of stability, such as Morgan sports cars whose basic design originated in the 1930s.

Major changes can be very disruptive, so organisations generally prefer a series of small adjustments. This iterative approach gives continuous improvement, which is often described by the Japanese name of kaizen. The small, incremental changes have the benefit of being easily absorbed without major disruption – and there is little risk of things going seriously wrong, as the small changes can easily be reversed if they turn out to be mistakes. Over time, the series of adjustments gather momentum, and introducing small improvements becomes part of normal work. In the long term the repeated, iterative adjustment can build up to give dramatic improvements.

Of course, managers say that they continuously look for improvements – but most of their methods are fairly informal. Kaizen is a more positive approach that deliberately goes out to examine operations and find improvement. Brown et al.[15] suggest that organisations move from the informal approach to the more formal procedures of Kaizen through a series of five levels. Then, Level 1 is the natural or background approach where managers informally look around to see if they can identify improvements. Level 2 has a more structured approach that uses formal methods, such as a plan-do-check-act cycle. Level 3 links formal methods of improvement to strategic goals, giving a more coordinated approach. Level 4 adds devolved responsibility so that individuals can experiment and develop their own innovative ideas. Level 5 is a notional end point where everyone is experimenting, learning, sharing ideas and involved in innovative improvements.

Suggestions for iterative improvements come from many sources, such as customers, competitors or suggestion boxes. Sometimes there is a more formal arrangement, such as the plan-do-check-act cycle that we just mentioned. This has a team of people who positively look for improvements to logistics using the cycle:

- **plan** – looking at the existing logistics, collecting information, discussing alternatives, and suggesting a plan for improvement
- **do** – where the plan is implemented, and data is collected on subsequent performance
- **check** – which analyses the performance data to see if the expected improvements actually appeared
- **act** – if there are real improvements the new arrangements are made permanent, but if there are no improvements, lessons are learnt and the new arrangements are not adopted.

Continuous improvement
a series of small adjustments to give iterative improvements

Kaizen
continuous improvement

Plan-do-check-act cycle
approach to finding continuous improvements

Figure 4.13 Plan-do-check-act cycle for process improvement

The team is continuously looking for improvements, so at this point they return to the beginning of the cycle, and consider more changes (illustrated in Figure 4.13).

LOGISTICS IN PRACTICE – HOTPOINT

Hotpoint is a major supplier of domestic appliances, owned by GE. Before 1990 it worked as an independent company, but was not responding quickly enough to changing conditions. It distributed its own finished products, but the operations were inefficient and costs were rising rapidly. The company decided to overhaul its distribution, with the aims of:

- reducing costs
- increasing customer service, which had fallen to unsatisfactory levels
- strengthening the management team
- renegotiating pay and conditions for staff
- introducing systems to measure and monitor performance
- reducing the amount of damage to products in transit
- designing a distribution strategy for the next five years.

As a starting point, the company designed a mission for distribution, which was, 'To deliver Hotpoint goods to the customer; when expected and agreed; in the manner expected; in good condition; at an acceptable cost to the company.' This laid the foundation for a new culture, based on customer satisfaction and competitive performance. It took a huge effort of communication, negotiation and training, as a result of which logistics slowly improved, with progress monitored by benchmarking companies like TNT, Exel and TDG.

An important factor for Hotpoint was control over the supply chain. It put a lot of emphasis on its home delivery service, where retailers take orders and Hotpoint deliver appliances directly to customers. This allowed drivers to make sure the appliances are in good condition, installed properly and working. Hotpoint aimed for a high quality service, with guaranteed delivery in a specified time slot, removal of packaging, collection of old appliances for recycling, and so on.

To achieve this service, Hotpoint designed a wide and short distribution network, with satellite depots around the country giving daily deliveries to towns and regular visits to rural areas. These

---

depots are largely stockless, being fed each day with their requirements. They are also used for the distribution of parts sent from the national distribution centre at Peterborough.

The new arrangements set the scene for logistics over the next decade. During this period the supply chain grew in importance, and become more responsive. Lead times were reduced, more frequent deliveries were made, stocks were lowered by 50%, operating costs were significantly reduced, customer service was increased, and staff morale improved. The company won a Motor Transport Award for 'Excellence'. Changes made throughout the 1990s moved the distribution system from 'a sleeping dinosaur to a cost effective and customer-driven entity'.

Question

• Can you find other examples of supply chains that have dramatically improved performance?

(*Sources*: Grange C. (1999) The long and winding road, Logistics and Transport Focus 1(4), 36–41; Grange, C. (1999) The long and winding road. Presentation to the Institute of Logistics and Transport Annual Conference, and www.hotpoint.co.uk)

Business process reengineering

Continuous improvement is the standard approach for most organisations, but critics say that continually tinkering with a process gives an impression of uncertainty and lack of leadership. It might also move the process in the wrong direction, as a small change might block the way for much bigger gains in another direction. The major criticism, however, is that incremental changes do not get to the root of problems. If you have a fundamentally bad process, then making small adjustments only tinker with the details and still leave you with a bad process.

The alternative approach is not to adjust existing supply chains, but to start from scratch and design a completely new set of operations. This gives an opportunity to create a dramatically improved – and even the best possible – logistics. The best known approach of this kind is business process reengineering (BPR), which Hammer and Champy[20] define as follows:

Business process reengineering
the fundamental redesign of business processes to achieve dramatic improvements

---

• **Business process reengineering** is the fundamental rethinking and radical redesign of business processes to achieve dramatic improvements in critical, contemporary measures of performance, such as cost, quality, service and speed.

The idea behind reengineering is that you do not look for improvements in current operations, but you start with a blank sheet of paper and design a new process from scratch. This is rather like running an old car. You can tinker with it and keep it going a bit longer, but the reengineering solution is to buy a new car. If you have a poor logistics system, you should not waste time tinkering to find small improvements, but should throw away the whole system and design a new one from scratch.

BPR is a general approach to change rather than a formal procedure, so it does not have any specific procedures. In fact, it does not really involve any new methods – and some people see it as a restatement of Juran's 'breakthrough theory'.[21] However, it consolidates several related ideas, and some of its main principles for the supply chain are that:

- A supply chain should be designed across functions and allow work to flow naturally, concentrating on the whole supply chain rather than the separate parts.
- Managers should strive for dramatic improvements in performance by radically rethinking and redesigning the supply chain.
- Improved information technology is fundamental to reengineering as it allows radical new solutions.
- All activities that do not add value should be eliminated.
- Activities should be done where they make most sense – for instance, information processing becomes a part of logistics rather than a separate function.
- Decisions should be made where the work is done, and by those doing the work.
- You do not have to be an expert to help redesign a supply chain, and being an outsider without preconceived ideas often helps.
- Always see things from the customer's point of view.

Continuous improvement and BPR give completely different approaches, with features summarised in Table 4.2. But it is important to recognise that BPR does

Table 4.2 A comparison of continuous improvement and reengineering

	Continuous improvement	Reengineering
Size of change	Minor	Major
Effect	Adjustment to exiting operations	Dramatic change with new process
Timescale	Short term and continuous	Long term and disruptive
People involved	Everyone	A few champions
Rate of change	Gradual	Abrupt
Theory	Maintain and improve	Scrap and rebuild
Investment	Low, but higher maintenance	High, but lower maintenance
Primary direction	Bottom-up emerging	Top-down design
Risk	Low	High
Correcting mistakes	Easy	Very difficult
Technology	Continues existing levels	Uses the latest technology

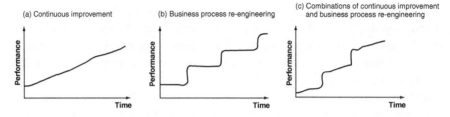

Figure 4.14   Rate of performance improvement

not replace continuous improvement. It is possible to have a series of radical improvements, and still introduce smaller continuous improvements (illustrated in Figure 4.14).

LOGISTICS IN PRACTICE – ACCOUNTS PAYABLE AT FORD

In reality, organisations have mixed experiences with BPR. Some have reported outstanding results – like the early work in the IBM Credit Corporation, which increased output by a factor of 100. But around three-quarters of organisations fail to get the improvements they hope for.[22]

An early classic study by Hammer and Champy was based in the Accounts Payable Department of Ford of America in 1988. At the time it employed 500 people with a standard accounting system where:

1. The purchasing department sent a purchase order to the supplier and a copy to the Accounts Payable Department.

2. The supplier shipped the goods ordered and sent an invoice to Accounts Payable.

3. When the goods arrived at Ford, they were checked and sent to stores. A description of the goods arriving was sent to Accounts Payable.

4. Accounts Payable now had three descriptions of the goods – from the purchasing department, supplier and arrivals. If these matched they paid the invoice.

5. Sometimes the paperwork did not match, and problems had to be sorted out. This took a lot of effort, often lasting several weeks.

Ford could have improved this system, and estimated that they might save 25% of staffing costs. Instead they chose a more radical solution and reengineered the whole system. At the centre of this was their purchasing database, so for the new system:

1. The purchasing department sent a purchase order to a supplier and updated the database.

2. The supplier shipped the goods.

3. When the goods arrived at Ford they were checked against outstanding orders on the database.

4. If the details match, the goods were accepted, the database was updated to show that they have arrived, and the supplier was paid.

5. If the details did not match, the goods were not accepted and were sent back to the supplier.

Suppliers soon learned that the new system would not allow any mistakes in deliveries, and they were quickly eliminated. The streamlined system reduced Ford's accounts payable department to 125 people, giving a 400% increase in productivity.

Question

- Why do you think that reengineering does not always work?

(*Source*: Hammer, M. and Champy, J. (1993) Reengineering the corporation, Harper Collins, New York)

Chapter review

- A logistics strategy sets the overall direction of logistics within an organisation – but to be of any use it has to be implemented. This means that the strategic plans are translated into positive actions.

- The mechanism for implementing a strategy has decisions cascading down through an organisation, with more details added to the plans at each level.

- Unless the strategy is designed properly, implementation can be difficult or impossible. To avoid this, managers should consider implementation during the design of the strategy and they should involve the people responsible for the implementation.

- Strategic decisions for logistics cover different types of question, and we can classify these as affecting aims, principles, infrastructure, supply chain structure and flow of materials.

- A logistics infrastructure consists of the organisational structure and the systems, human resources, culture and resources to support it.

- A key part of the infrastructure concerns the organisational structure. There are many forms for this, often based on functional, product, hybrid, matrix structures or self-managed groups.

- Another important question concerns the structure of the supply chain. This is largely defined by its length (the number of tiers of suppliers and customers) and breadth (the number of organisations in each tier). Related questions concern the type of organisations, the activities that each does, the size of facilities, their locations, the relationships between them, relationships between members, ownership, capacity, and so on.

- Supply chains continually evolve to keep up with changing conditions. These changes can be difficult, and need careful management.

- An important question about change concerns the rate at which it occurs. Continuous improvement uses a series of small adjustments to build up a momentum for change over time. Business process reengineering looks for more radical changes.

CASE STUDY – PASSENGER INTERCHANGE

Road congestion is increasing in most major cities. Some of this is due to commercial vehicles, but by far the majority is due to private cars. There are several ways of controlling the numbers of vehicles using certain areas. These include prohibition of cars in pedestrian areas, restricted entry, limits on parking, traffic calming schemes, and so on. A relatively new approach has road-user charging, where cars pay a fee to use a particular length of road – like the London congestion charge. Automated collection systems allow different fees for different types of vehicle, with fees changing with time or prevailing traffic conditions.

Often, the most effective way of reducing traffic congestion is to improve public transport. These services must be attractive to people who judge it by a wide range of factors including convenience, cost, timing, reliability, comfort, crowding, handling of luggage, availability of food, toilets, safety, facilities in waiting areas, availability of escalators, and so on.

Buses are often the most flexible form of public transport, with the total time for a journey depending on:

- joining time, which is the time needed to get to a bus stop
- waiting time, until the bus arrives
- journey time, to actually do the travelling
- leaving time, to get from the bus to the final destination.

Transport policies can reduce these times by a combination of frequent services, well-planned routes, and bus priority schemes. But there is often a problem when people have to change buses, or transfer between buses and other types of transport, including cars, planes, trains, ferries and trams. Then there are additional times for moving between one type of transport and the next, and waiting for the next part of the service. These can be minimised by an integrated transport system with frequent, connecting services at passenger interchanges.

Passenger interchanges are not necessarily popular, and most people prefer a straight through journey between two points, even if this is less frequent than an integrated service with interchanges. The main reason is that interchanges increase the complexity of journeys, give more opportunities for things to go wrong, and generally increase uncertainty; and experience suggests that starting part of a journey does not guarantee that it will all finish successfully.

Major cities clearly have sophisticated systems of passenger interchanges, and they are spreading into smaller towns, such as Montpellier in France. In the ten years to 2001 the population of Montpellier grew by more then 8.4%, raising it from the 22nd largest town in France to the eighth. It has good transport links with the port of Sete, an airport, inland waterways, main road networks and a fast rail link to Paris. In 2001 public transport was enhanced with a 15-km tram-line connecting major sites in the town centre with other transport links. At the same time, buses were rerouted to connect to the tram, cycling was encouraged for short distances, park-and-ride services were improved, and journeys were generally made easier. As a result, there has been an increase in the use of public transport, a reduction in the number of cars in the town centre, and improved air quality. In 2006, a second line added a further 20-km route, with forecasts of 52,000 passengers a day, and a 23-km third line is still being planned.

Questions

- Are the problems of moving people significantly different from the problems of moving goods or services?

- What are the benefits of public transport over private transport? Should public transport be encouraged, and if so how?

- What are the benefits of integrated public transport systems?

(*Sources*: Hellewell, D.S. (2000) Improving passenger interchange, *Logistics and Transport Focus*, 2(6), 32–6; Gemmell, C. (2001) An integrated public transport system, *Logistics and Transport Focus*, 3(3), 36–42; DTI (1998) A new deal for transport (White Paper, Cmnd 3950), HMSO.)

Project – structure of a supply chain

Take a familiar product – such as a type of drink, a brand of shoe, a DVD or a mobile phone – and describe its supply chain. Discuss the structure of this chain, emphasising its length and breadth. What other features are important in the structure?

The supply chain you describe has a certain structure designed by logistics managers. Why do you think they chose this particular structure? What alternative could they have chosen? What would be the benefits and disadvantages of these?

The product you have chosen probably has direct competitors. Do they have the same type of supply chains? What are the key differences?

Discussion questions

4.1 What exactly is meant by 'implementing the logistics strategy'?

4.2 It is often more difficult to implement a logistics strategy that to design one, so most logistics plan fail in the practice rather than the theory. What exactly does this mean – and is it necessarily true?

4.3 What can an organisation do to improve the implementation of its logistics strategy?

4.4 What exactly is a logistics infrastructure?

4.5 Apart from showing who reports to whom, what else does an organisational structure show?

4.6 What determines the best shape for a supply chain?

4.7 When a company outsources logistics it loses control over the operations, employs someone who is unfamiliar with the work of the organisation and has completely different aims and culture, and pays enough to give the third-party provider a healthy profit. Does this seem like a sensible move?

4.8 What sets the capacity of a supply chain?

4.9 Supply chains are not usually designed from scratch, but evolve over time. Does this create any particular problems?

4.10 Reengineering might be attractive in principle, but in reality it is difficult, expensive, risky – and unlikely to get the expected benefits. If this is true, why do organisations still consider radical changes?

References

1. Ballou, R.H. (1981) Reformulating a logistics strategy, International Journal of Physical Distribution and Materials Management, 11(8), 71–83.
2. Chopra, S. and Meindl, P. (2007) Supply chain management (3rd edition), Pearson Education, Upper Saddle River, NJ.
3. Helming, W. and Zonnenberg, J.P. (2000) The five fulcrum points of a supply chain strategy, Supply Chain and Logistics Journal, Winter.
4. Hosmer, L.T. (1982) Strategic management, Prentice Hall, Englewood Cliffs, NJ.
5. Keen, P.G.W. (1997) The process edge, Harvard Business School Press, Boston, MA.
6. Mohrman, S.A., Galbraith, J.R. and Lawler, E.E. (1998) Tomorrow's organisation, Jossey-Bass Wiley, San Francisco, CA.
7. Volberda, H.W. (1999) Building the flexible firm, Oxford University Press, Oxford.
8. Pfeffer, J. (1998) The human equation, Harvard Business School Press, Boston, MA.
9. Pfeffer, J. and Veiga, J. (1999) Putting people first for organisaional success, Academy of Management Executive, 13(2), 37–48.
10. DTI (1997) Competitiveness through partnerships with people, Department of Trade and Industry, HMSO, London.
11. Blimes, L., Wetzker, K. and Xhonneux, P. (1997) Value in human resurces, Financial Times (10 February).
12. Joynson, S. (1994) Sid's heroes – uplifting business performance and the human spirit, BBC Books, London.
13. Maslow, A. (1954) Motivation and personality, Harper, New York.
14. Hertzberg, F. (1966) Work and the nature of man, World Publishing, Cleveland, OH.
15. Brown, S., Lamming, R., Bessant, J. and Jones, P. (2004) Strategic operations management (2nd edition), Butterworth Heinemann, Oxford.
16. Rowley, J. (2001) Outsourcing across borders in Europe, Logistics and Transport Focus, 3(1), 54–6.
17. Wentworth, F. (2003) Outsourcing services: the case against, Logistics and Transport Focus, 5(2), 57–9.
18. Cubitt, B. (2000) Change: the final frontier?, Logistics and Transport Focus, 2(3), 39–42.
19. Carnall, C. (1991) Managing change, Routledge, London.
20. Hammer, M. and Champy, J. (1993) Reengineering the corporation, Harper Collins, New York, NY.
21. Juran, J.M. (1988) Juran on planning for quality, Free Press, New York, NY.
22. Hammer, M. (1996) Beyond reengineering, HarperCollins, New York.

INTEGRATED SUPPLY CHAINS

Contents

LEARNING OBJECTIVES

After reading this chapter you should be able to:

- appreciate the problems of considering logistics functions in isolation

- discuss the benefits of creating a single, integrated logistics function

- outline the steps needed for internal integration

- discuss the benefits of external integration along supply chains

- review the difficulties of achieving this external integration

- describe different types of external integration.

Problems with fragmented logistics

In the last two chapters we have developed the idea of a logistics strategy and the way that managers implement it to give the structure of supply chains. Figure 5.1 summarises the view of logistics within a single organisation, where a series of related activities add value to the final product. These activities have traditionally been managed separately, so that an organisation might have distinct departments for purchasing, transport, warehousing, inventory management, distribution, and so on.

Unfortunately, dividing up logistics in this way creates a number of problems. When dealing with a particular product, purchasing might look for the most reliable suppliers, inventory management for low unit costs, warehousing for fast stock turnover, materials management for easy handling, transport for full vehicle loads, and so on. These aims are all worthy, but problems soon appear when the separate aims of each activity come into conflict. For example, purchasing can reduce its administrative costs by sending fewer, larger orders to suppliers – but this increases stock levels and raises the amount of money tied up in the warehouse. Similarly, warehousing might save money by reducing the stock of raw materials – but this results in more frequent shortages that raise the costs of expediting and transport for emergency deliveries. Using sea transport rather than air freight reduces transport costs – but increases the amount of stock held in the supply chain. In reality, the different activities of logistics are very closely related, and actions in one inevitably affect the others.

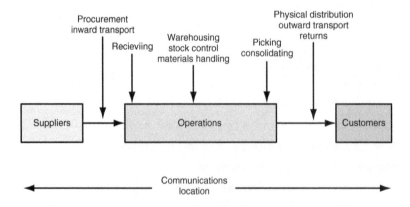

Figure 5.1   Summary of logistics' activities

LOGISTICS IN PRACTICE – RP TURNER CORPORATION

RP Turner Corporation makes pipeline valves for the oil industry in western Canada. It buys materials from Japan, the USA and eastern Canada, manufactures valves in Edmonton, Alberta and ships the finished products to oil fields in the north.

The company grew by emphasising the high quality of its products, which work reliably in the harsh weather conditions of the Arctic. Transport to remote customers is expensive, and the company continually looks for ways of reducing its costs. At one time the separate functions of logistics worked more or less independently, and the three main departments – Marketing, Production and Finance – were in different locations. Production was in Edmonton, as the nearest major city to the oil fields; Marketing was in Calgary, near to oil company headquarters; Finance (including procurement) was in Vancouver, near the port and financial centre. This meant that Production was 1000 km away from Finance, 500 km away from Marketing and over 2000 km from delivery points.

The company rewarded each department for different types of performance and, not surprisingly, they had different priorities.

○ **Marketing wanted:**

- high stocks of finished goods to satisfy customer demands quickly
- a wide range of finished goods always held in stock
- locations near to customers to allow delivery with short lead times
- production to vary output in response to customer orders
- emphasis on an efficient distribution system
- optimistic sales forecast to make sure that production is geared up for actual demand.

○ **Production wanted:**

- high stocks of raw materials and work in progress to safeguard operations
- a narrow range of finished goods to give long production runs
- locations near to suppliers so that they can get raw materials quickly
- stable production to give efficient operations
- emphasis on the efficient movement of materials through operations
- realistic sales forecasts that allow efficient planning.

○ **Finance wanted:**

- low stocks everywhere
- few locations to give economies of scale and minimise overall costs
- large batch sizes to reduce unit costs
- make-to-order operations
- pessimistic sales forecasts that discourage under-used facilities.

Despite good communications, the company realised that its operations were too widely dispersed. Eventually, they centralised operations at its main plant in Edmonton. This brought the functions physically close together, and the different departments developed a unified view of the supply chain that improved both efficiency and customer service.

Question

- What were the disadvantages of considering each activity of logistics as independent?

(*Source*: Ray Turner and internal company reports)

There are inevitably problems when logistics is divided into separate functions. In principle, all the functions should coordinate their efforts to achieve the overriding strategy, but when they are organised as distinct entities this is an aspiration rather than a realistic aim. Each develops its own operations, goals, and ways of achieving them – and both their formal and informal procedures diverge. The result has each function moving in a different direction, and there is duplicated effort and wasted resources. You can imagine this effect on a wholesaler who has one fleet of vehicles run by materials management to bring materials in from suppliers, and a separate fleet run by distribution to deliver the same goods out to customers. This might work, but there is clearly duplicated effort and wasted resources in managing two separate vehicle fleets. Another organisation might have three stocks – raw materials, work in progress and finished goods – each run by different departments and using different standards and systems.

A fragmented supply chain also makes it difficult to coordinate the flow of information through different systems. Suppose a production department knows that it is running short of a material and needs a new delivery. This information should pass seamlessly to purchasing, but if it has to pass from one system to another there is more chance of errors, uncertainty, delays and inefficiency. These in turn increase the chances of late deliveries, emergency orders, expediting and shortages.

In general, fragmenting logistics into different parts has disadvantages that include:

- setting different, often conflicting, objectives within an organisation
- duplicating effort and reducing productivity
- giving worse communications and information flows between the parts
- reducing coordination between the parts – leading to lower efficiency, higher costs and worse customer service
- being unresponsive, as each member of the chain has to identify changes and then start planning their reaction
- increasing uncertainty and delays along the supply chain
- increasing variability along the chain
- making planning more difficult
- introducing unnecessary buffers between the parts, such as stocks of work-in-progress, spare transport and duplicated administrative procedures
- obscuring important information, such as the total cost of logistics
- giving logistics a low status within an organisation.

The benefit of integration is that it overcomes these weaknesses – in other words, it sets common objectives, reduces effort, improves information flows, improves efficiency, is responsive to change, reduces uncertainty and variability, makes planning easier, eliminates the need for buffers, highlights important information and raises the status of logistics as a function.

Bringing activities together

The way to avoid problems with fragmented supply chains is to bring the activities together and consider logistics not as a series of distinct tasks, but as a single integrated function. Then all the parts work together to get the best overall result for the organisation – and for its customers. This is why Sheehy, former Chairman of BAT, could say, 'I believe that a well designed, integrated logistics system is a vital prerequisite for commercial success.'[1] We can summarise our argument as follows:

- Integrating logistics within an organisation has all the related activities working together as a single function.

- This is responsible for all storage and movement of materials throughout the organisation.

- It tackles problems from the viewpoint of the whole organisation, and looks for the greatest overall benefit.

Integrating logistics
has all the related activities of logistics working together as a single function

An early driver of logistics integration came in the 1960s when organisations began to analyse the total logistics cost, which we can define as:

Total logistics cost = transport cost + warehouse cost + stock holding cost

+ packaging cost + information processing cost

+ other logistics overheads

Total logistics cost
total cost of all logistics activities

The traditional view considered each of these cost elements as independent, so reducing, say, the transport cost automatically lowers the total cost. But we know that the activities are not really independent, and the interactions between activities mean that reducing one cost might significantly increase another. A reduction in one cost might give an overall increase in the cost of logistics, and conversely, increasing the amount spent on some activities can reduce the total logistics cost. Lewis et al.[2] gave an early example of this, when they found that it was cheaper to switch from road transport to air. Air freight itself was much more expensive than road transport, but faster delivery eliminated the need for local stocks and warehouses, thereby giving considerable overall savings

The real boost for integrated logistics came with advanced information and control systems. These allow managers to collect, store, analyse, distribute and present all the information needed by logistics ranging from its strategic aims down to details of each transaction. Integration became a realistic possibility when EDI meant that this information could be exchanged between remote sites and different parts of an organisation. As technology has improved, this exchange has become easier. Really, the practical transfer of information has become easier, but there remain the organisational and other objections to distributing private information in an age where 'information is power'.

Steps in integration

We can summarise the effects of integration in three important observations:

1. The overall performance of the system is important, and not the performance of individual parts.
2. The separate activities need not be working optimally to get this best overall performance.
3. There are trade-offs between the different activities.

These show the main thrust of logistics, which is to get an efficient function. Historically, managers would concentrate on getting each part of logistics to be efficient, and were disappointed when the overall result was not very good. But looking at each part separately ignores the interactions. The only way to get efficient logistics is to take a holistic view of the whole function and, surprisingly, the best overall results may be achieved when some activities do not seem to be as efficient as possible. For instance, having apparently spare capacity in some operations can reduce the need for stocks in others, or spending more on some stocks can reduce the needs of transport.

Bringing the separate activities together to give an integrated view of logistics is difficult. There are many activities involved, with different types of operation, using different systems, with different aims, which are geographically dispersed. The usual approach has integration developing over time. One department might slowly take over all aspects of ordering and receiving raw materials. Another department might slowly take over all aspects of delivering finished products to customers. Some organisations are tempted to stop when they reach this stage, and they work with two functions: materials management, aligned with production and looking after the inwards flow of raw materials and their movement through operations; and physical distribution, aligned with marketing and looking at the outward flow of finished goods. However, this still leaves an artificial break in what is essentially a continuous function. The obvious step is to combine the two into a single function responsible for all material movement into, through and out of the organisation.

This completes the **internal integration** of an organisation's logistics, and moves it from a low priority, fragmented function that is dispersed throughout a firm, to a concentrated, strategic, integrated one. It may be easier to see this change in seven stages:

Stage 1. separate logistics activities are not given much attention or considered important

Stage 2. recognition that the separate activities of logistics are important for the success of the organisation

Stage 3. making improvements to the separate functions, trying to ensure that each is as efficient as possible

Stage 4. realising the benefits of internal cooperation, with a systems view leading to internal integration that combines the separate activities

Stage 5. developing a logistics strategy, to set the long-term direction of logistics

Stage 6. benchmarking to compare logistics' performance, learn from others' experiences, identify best practices, find areas that need improvement, and show how to achieve the improvements

Stage 7. continuous improvement, accepting that further changes are inevitable and always searching for better ways of organising logistics.

The first four stages show the move towards integrated logistics, and the last three stages show how the resulting function can be continually improved. Stage 5 emphasises a strategic view to guide the new function over the long term; Stage 6 looks at other organisations for comparisons and lessons; and Stage 7 recognises that logistics must continually evolve.

Difficulties of achieving internal integration

The practical difficulties of achieving these stages vary from organisation to organisation, but the following list suggests some common ones.

- *Finding a sponsor.* Perhaps the obvious difficulty is finding someone with the knowledge, enthusiasm, ability and authority to carry through the necessary changes. This needs a senior manager who acts as a champion or sponsor, with the necessary power to start the process. Once initiated, people should see the benefits of integration, and changes can gather momentum and percolate through the organisation.

- *Changing practices.* Most people feel comfortable with established practices and do not want to change. They do not necessarily welcome change, and there is inevitably some resistance to new practices, methods, skills, knowledge, relationships, and so on.

- *Organisation.* Most firms are organised into departments, each of which does one type of activity – such as purchasing, transport, inventory management, warehousing. This means that everyone in a department focuses on the central activity, and all other kinds of work are largely irrelevant. The implication is that when two departments are asked to merge, they feel that they have little in common – and would have to divert attention away from their central activity. The result is the 'silo mentality' that stifles inter-departmental cooperation.

- *Cultural changes*. A departmental organisation is essentially based on a culture of self-interest and conflict, where each can benefit at the expense of others. You can see this effect at discussions of annual budgets, where limited funds are shared between all departments and each can only increase its own share by having other reduce theirs. This has to be replaced by a culture where individuals work together, developing effective teams and cooperating for the common good. It is notoriously difficult to introduce such cultural changes.

- *Rewards*. Traditional goals, performance measures and rewards are largely based on departmental achievement. This does not encourage integration, which needs rewards that are based on the broad success of logistics in achieving its goals.

- *Information systems*. Despite the theoretical ease of transferring information, systems have traditionally been built to support the specialised needs of each departments and – especially with remaining legacy systems – are not integrated. An integrated logistics function needs new information flows that cross departmental borders. As Bowersox et al.[3] say, 'Supply chain information systems are the thread that links logistics activities into an integrated process.'

- *Hoarding of resources*. There is always a temptation for each department to hoard resources – perhaps stock, cash or information – to safeguard their own position and act as a buffer against unexpected events. This hoarding of resources by individual departments reduces the performance of the whole.

Despite such problems, internal integration of logistics is an essential step towards more efficient operations. But it is not the end of the story. Once an organisation has efficient, integrated and strategic logistics, it can start looking at integration along more of the supply chain.

LOGISTICS IN PRACTICE – SUPPLY CHAIN MANAGEMENT SOFTWARE

A single integrated information system is essential for integrated logistics. However, these systems come with different levels of sophistication. We can describe five levels of sophistication:

1. At the basic level the systems simply record the huge amount of transactional data that is needed for logistics.

2. The next level of sophistication adds measures of performance – including costs, productivity, utilisation, customer service – that managers need to control their operations.

3. The third level adds tools to help managers with their planning and decision making – typically models for inventory management, routing, location decisions, and so on.

4. The fourth level gives the support that managers need for strategic planning and long-term development of the supply chain.

5. The final level includes automation where some types of decision are devolved to the system.

A lot of commercial software is available at each of these levels. For example, International Business Systems (IBS) is one of the largest vendors of software for supply chain management. The company was formed in 1969, is listed on the Stockholm Stock Exchange, works internationally with subsidiaries in 22 countries, has more than 5000 clients, and employs 2000 people.

IBS software products include a range of modules based on core activities – such as procurement, inventory management, warehouse management, distribution, customer relationship management, finance, manufacturing, and business intelligence. Within these modules are different components for order processing, forecasting, sales analysis, Internet trading, bar coding, vendor managed inventory, spare-part handling, after-sales support, project management, and the host of other jobs.

The important point is that the modules come together to form an integrated system to improve overall performance. Then they 'automate and optimise business processes throughout the supply chain'. This is assisted by Enterprise Application Integration software that seamlessly brings all parts of the system together to look after the complete, 'flow of goods and information in such a way that you give better customer service and achieve shorter lead times, with less capital tied up, thereby releasing resources for more profitable activities'.

Question

- What are the basic requirements of software before any supply chain integration can occur?

(*Sources*: website at www.ibsuk.com and promotional material)

Integration along supply chains

We have described the benefits of integrating logistics within an organisation, but can extend the arguments to suggest the same benefits for integrating logistics along more of a supply chain. If organisations within a supply chain only look at their own operations, there are unnecessary boundaries between them that disrupt the flow of materials and increase costs. In the way that internal integration removes these boundaries within an organisation, **external integration** removes them in the longer chain. Now, as well as internal departments cooperating to improve organisational performance, external firms also cooperate to improve performance in the whole chain.

This effectively gives three levels of integration. The first has logistics as a separate activity within an organisation; the second has internal integration to bring them together into a single function; the third has external integration, where organisations look beyond their own operations and integrate more

(a) Separate functions within an organisation

(b) Integration within the organisation

(c) Integration along the supply chain

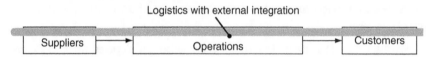

Figure 5.2   Three levels of logistics integration

of the supply chain (as illustrated in Figure 5.2). The lowest levels are characterised by arm's-length relationships between supply chain partners, while the third level has cooperation that might be formalised in strategic alliances and partnerships.

External integration is difficult and develops over time. You can imagine this starting with two companies reducing transport costs by coordinating their flows of materials. Over time, the integration may progress from the coordination of physical movements, to information flows, control over material movements, and then to the design and working of the infrastructure.[4]

The key point about integration is that all organisations in the same supply chain have the same overall objective, which is to satisfy their final customers. Essentially, all members want to sell more products to final customers – thereby giving extra benefits that can be shared by members of the chain. If any part of the supply chain fails to work towards this, then the whole supply chain suffers. As Christopher[5] says, 'supply chains compete, not companies'. So competitors are not other companies in the same supply chain, but companies in other supply chains. The aim of an integrated supply chain is to improve overall efficiency and reduce overall costs, rather than have each organisation working independently and pushing costs and inefficiencies to other parts of the chain.

- Organisations within the same supply chain should **cooperate** to get final customer satisfaction.
- They should not compete with each other, but with organisations in other supply chains.

Bullwhip effect

Forrester[6] described an important effect of a fragmented supply chain, which has become known as demand amplification, or the bullwhip effect. Imagine a retailer who notices that in one week demand for a product rises by five units. When it is time to place the next order, the retailer assumes that demand is rising, and orders ten extra units to make sure there is enough stock. The local wholesaler sees demand rise by ten units, so it assumes that demand is rising and orders an extra 20 units to meet the growth. The regional wholesaler sees demand rise by 20 units, so it orders another 30 units. As this movement travels through the supply chain, a relatively small change in final demand is amplified into a major variation for early suppliers. You can see this effect in the following worked example.

WORKED EXAMPLE

In a simple supply chain, each organisation holds one week's demand in stock. In other words, each buys enough materials from its suppliers to make its closing stock at the end of the week equal to the demand during the week. Demand for a product has been steady at 100 units a week. One week, demand from final customers is five units higher than usual. Assuming that deliveries are very fast, how does this affect movements in the supply chain?

Answer

The spreadsheet in Figure 5.3 shows this for the first week when demand of 100 units moves through the supply chain. For each tier, you can see:

- demand – which equals the amount bought by the next tier of customers
- opening stock at the beginning of the week – which equals its closing stock in the previous week
- closing stock at the end of the week – which inventory policies set as equal to the demand in the week
- number of units bought – which equals demand plus any change in stock:

$$\text{buys} = \text{demand met} + (\text{closing stock} - \text{opening stock})$$

In week 1 everything is going smoothly, with the usual 100 units flowing down the supply chain. Then in week 2 customer demand goes up to 105 units. The retailer must buy 105 units to meet this demand, plus an additional 5 units to raise its closing stock to 105. So it buys 110 units from the local wholesaler. The local wholesaler has to supply this 110 units, plus an additional 10 units to raise its closing stock to 110 units – so it buys 120 units from the regional wholesaler. The regional wholesaler has to supply this 120 units, plus another 20 units to raise its closing stock to 120 – so it buys 140 units from the manufacturer. The manufacturer makes 180 units to give a closing stock of 180 units.

WORKED EXAMPLE (CONTINUED)

Week		1	2	3	4	5	6
Customer							
	Demand	100	105	100	100	100	100
Retailer							
	Demand	100	105	100	100	100	100
	Opening stock	100	100	105	100	100	100
	Closing stock	100	105	100	100	100	100
	Buys	100	110	95	100	100	100
Local wholesaler							
	Demand	100	110	95	100	100	100
	Opening stock	100	100	110	95	100	100
	Closing stock	100	110	95	100	100	100
	Buys	100	120	80	105	100	100
Regional wholesaler							
	Demand	100	120	80	105	100	100
	Opening stock	100	100	120	80	105	100
	Closing stock	100	120	80	105	100	100
	Buys	100	140	40	130	95	100
Manufacturer							
	Demand	100	140	40	130	95	100
	Opening stock	100	100	140	100	130	95
	Closing stock	100	140	100	130	95	100
	Makes	100	180	0	160	60	105

Figure 5.3   Showing the effects of demand amplification

In week 3 we get the reverse effect as customer demand returns to 100 units. The retailer now reduces closing stock to 100 units, so it only has to buy 95 units from the local wholesaler. The local wholesaler reduces its closing stock by 15, so it only has to buy 80 from the regional wholesaler. The regional wholesaler reduces its closing stock by 40, so it only buys 40 from the manufacturer. The manufacturer would like to reduce its closing stock by 100 units, but its demand is only 40 units so it stops production and meets all demand from stock.

A variation in customer demand of five units in one week has made manufacturing vary by 180 units a week, with an effect continuing for several more weeks.

Benefits of external integration

This worked example clearly suggests the problems when each part of a supply chain works independently. The way to overcome such problems is for each member of the supply chain to cooperate with the others and pass on relevant information. If the manufacturer had known that demand only varied by five units, it would only have adjusted production by five units rather than 180. Christopher again notices this effect and says that, 'Most opportunities for cost reduction and/or value enhancement lie at the interface between supply chain partners.'[7]

We can give further illustrations of the benefit of integration. Imagine the logistics at Confederated Bottlers who used to deliver bottles from their main plant in Elizabethville to a brewery in Johnston, 115 miles away. The brewery filled the bottles and took them to a distribution centre 20 miles outside Elizabethville. Both companies used their own trucks to deliver products, returning empty. Eventually, they formed a joint transport company that used the same trucks for both deliveries – taking empty bottles on one direction and full bottles on the return. Not surprisingly, the transport costs almost halved.

Now consider the stocks held in a disjointed supply chain. Stocks are held to give a buffer against unexpected events, with any uncertainty encouraging firms to hold higher stocks to give themselves a greater margin of safety. These stocks increase costs and make the chain slow to react to changing conditions; for instance, when customers demand new products, all the stocks of old products in the supply chain have to be sold on before the new ones appear. But when members of a supply chain exchange information, the level of uncertainty declines and stocks can be reduced – giving lower costs and greater agility.

We could continue giving examples of the benefits of external integration, but it is becoming clear that these include:

- common objectives for all parts of the supply chain, and genuine cooperation to achieve these objectives
- shared information to highlight important events, and reduce uncertainty, errors and delays
- improved material flow, with coordination giving faster and more reliable movements
- lower costs – due to balanced operations, lower stocks, less expediting, removal of duplicated activities, elimination of activities that waste time or do not add value, and so on
- better customer service, with shorter lead times, faster deliveries and more customisation
- improved broader performance – with more accurate forecasts, better planning, higher productivity of resources, rational priorities, and so on
- more flexibility, with organisations reacting faster to changing conditions
- standardised procedures, becoming routine and well-practiced, with less duplication of effort, information, planning, and so on
- replenishment and movements triggered by actual demands rather than forecasts

Organisations started to move towards external integration in the 1990s[8] and a survey by PE Consulting in 1997[9] found that 57% of companies had some form of integration in their supply chains. More than 90% of companies expected further integration within three years, with a quarter looking for 'fully integrated' systems (although it was not clear what they meant by this).

However, we have to give a word of warning here. The benefits of external integration are clear, and the move towards greater integration might appear inevitable. But this is not always the best model and neither integration nor discrete, arm's-length relationships are intrinsically better. It is often more effective to have elements of both, in the way that Dell has strong single-supplier relationships with Intel for its processors and Microsoft for operating systems, but more distant relations with vendors of other components. Even when integration would offer clear benefits, there can be many practical difficulties. For instance, organisations may simply not trust other members of the supply chain enough to share sensitive information. When there is enough trust, there can be problems with different aims, priorities, competition, data exchange, appropriate systems, skills, security, the complexity of systems, and so on. Chopra and Meindl[10] classify obstacles to integration as:

- incentive – where different parts of the chain have different aims and are rewarded for different types of performance
- information processing – caused by imperfection in the data or means of transmission
- operational – as members have different types of operations that are often incompatible
- pricing – which distorts demand (such as quantity discounts or promotions)
- behaviour – with different cultures and ways of doing things.

The difficulties of achieving integration explain why a survey in 2003 by Poirier and Quinn[11] found that most organisations were still working on internal integration and were moving towards external integration – but only 10% had made any significant progress. They conclude that, 'Only a comparatively small percentage of companies have evolved to the more advanced stages of supply chain management.' Christopher[12] ran a similar survey and found that, 'all interviewees agreed that end-to-end management of an organisation's complex and unstable supply chain network (particularly up-stream into the supplier base), would be an improbable if not impossible task'.

LOGISTICS IN PRACTICE – PERMAN FRERE

Perman Frere is a small manufacturer based in Brussels. It exports most of its products and has a finished goods warehouse near the port of Ostende. Van Rijn is one of its customers, also based in Brussels. It imports most of its materials and has a raw materials warehouse near the port of Rotterdam.

The two companies have traded for many years and in 2007 they started looking for ways of increasing cooperation. It was soon obvious that they could make some minor adjustments to improve logistics. As an example, some parts were made by Perman Frere in Brussels, sent to their warehouse in Ostende, delivered to van Rijn's warehouse in Rotterdam, and then brought back to van Rijn's plant in Brussels. It was fairly easy to organise deliveries directly between the companies in Brussels. This gave a much shorter journey, reduced transport and handling costs, removed excess stocks, simplified administration, and reduced the lead time from five days to three hours. They also coordinated deliveries to towns in northern France, with one vehicle delivering products from both companies.

Both companies benefited from these changes. When they were introduced people in both companies said that they had been aware of the problems for a long time, but could not find any mechanism for overcoming them.

Question

- Is it likely that many supply chains could be made more efficient by increasing integration?

(*Sources*: Georges Perman and internal company reports)

Achieving integration

As each member of a supply chain is owned and managed by a different legal entity – with its own interests, aims, operations, culture, and so on – it is not surprising that external integration can be difficult. An initial step has members of the supply chain recognising that they share the same overriding aim of satisfying final customers. This might seem obvious, but it means that trading partners have to overcome the traditional adversarial view. When an organisation pays money to its suppliers, people assume that one can only benefit at the expense of the other. If the organisation gets a good deal, it automatically means that the supplier is losing out: if the supplier makes a good profit, it means that the organisation pays too much. This adversarial attitude has major drawbacks. Suppliers often set rigid conditions, and as they have no guarantee of repeat business they see no point in developing relationships and try to make as much profit from each sale as possible. At the same time, organisations have no loyalty, and they shop around to get the best deal and remind suppliers of the competition. Each is concerned only with their own objectives and will – when convenient to themselves – change specifications and conditions at short notice. The result is uncertainty about the number and size of orders, constantly changing suppliers and customers, changing products and conditions, different times between orders, no guarantee of repeat orders and changing costs.

To avoid these problems, organisations have to recognise that it is in their own long-term interest to replace conflict by agreement. This may need a major change of culture, with some specific adjustments suggested in Table 5.1.

Table 5.1   Different views with conflict and cooperation

Factor	Conflict	Cooperation
Profit	One organisation profits at the expense of the other	Both share rewards
Price	As high/low as possible	Agreed at reasonable level
Relationship	One is dominant	Equal partners
Trust	Little	Considerable
Timeframe	Single order	Long term
Communication	Limited and formal	Widespread and open with shared systems
Information	Secretive	Open and shared
Control	Intensive policing	Delegation and empowerment
Quality	Blame for faults	Solving shared problems
Contract	Rigid	Flexible
Focuson	Own operations	Customers

Customer relationship management
covers all aspects of the ways that companies manage their relationships with downstream customers

CRM
Customer relationship management

Supplier relationship management
covers all aspects of the ways that companies manage their relationships with upstream suppliers

SRM
Supplier relationship management

Cooperation brings trading partners together, and this trend is associated with a growth of customer relationship management (CRM) – and to a lesser extent supplier relationship management (SRM) (illustrated in Figure 5.4).

SRM and CRM are very similar in principle, so we will consider them together in terms of CRM. This is a broad term, which covers all aspects of the ways that companies manage their relationships with downstream customers. The principle is that when customers have a bad experience dealing with a company, they move to another supplier; CRM aims to improve the experience to retain customers and ensure repeat business. A standard view says that this needs three types of activity:

- support systems that allow sales departments to improve the service their representatives give to customers
- direct communications with customers that do not involve sales people, such as websites or EDI
- analysis of customer and sales data.

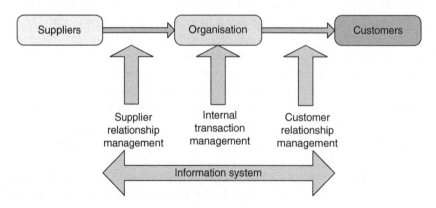

Figure 5.4   Role of customer/supplier relationship management

At the heart of CRM systems are the databases and software to support these activities. To be more specific the systems are primarily aimed at marketing (doing the planning to identify target customers, products to offer, prices, details of campaigns, and so on), sales (such as dealing with the pre-sales arrangements, actual purchases, order processing, delivery) and service (which focus on the level of customer service, achievement of performance targets, warranties, and so on).

LOGISTICS IN PRACTICE – REXAM

Rexam is a leading consumer packaging company. It offers a broad range of packaging products and services, and is the world's largest producer of beverage cans.

In 1996 Rexam Pharmaceutical Packaging and Grafica Zannini formed a joint venture called GZ Rexam with the aim of supplying packaging to the pharmaceutical industry in Europe. This is an important area, as pharmaceutical companies occasionally have product recalls costing several million pounds each – but more than 50% of these recalls are caused by faults in printed material.

John Stevenson, the Sales and Marketing Director of Rexam, says that, 'The days of the conventional supply chain where everyone existed as an independent entity . . . are no longer.' He quotes three reasons for partnerships:

- Lower costs – due to better coordination, elimination of duplicated effort, less bureaucracy, quantity discounts, economies of scale. GZ Rexam estimates that it can save up to 60% of packaging costs through partnerships.

- Shorter lead times – from improved coordination, procedures and administration. With Eli Lilly they reduced lead times from six to two weeks, with just-in-time deliveries for specific orders.

- Higher quality – with uniform standards, collaboration in quality initiatives, less reliance on inspections and a commitment to long-term improvements.

Rexam regularly forms joint ventures as a way of expanding the business, such as their move into China with Rexam Beverage Can Zhao Oing as a joint venture with the Hua Xing Investment Limited. Similarly, in 2006 it announced a move into India, by opening a beverage can plant in a joint venture with the Hindustan Tin Works. And in 2007 it formed a joint venture with Envases Universales to build a new beverage can plant in Guatemala, with a capacity of a billion cans a year.

Question

- Will companies always benefit from the closer relations that come with external integration?

(*Sources*: Stevenson, J. (1999) Partnering – improving the supply chain, Logistics Focus, 7(2) 9–11 and website at www.rexam.com)

Types of cooperation

When trading partners recognise that there are benefits from closer collaboration, there are several ways they can arrange this. Of course, they can simply carry on doing business with each other. If an organisation has a good experience with a supplier, it will usually continue to use them and over some period will develop a valuable working relationship. This is probably how you buy things, regularly going back to your favourite shops. But the key point is that there is no commitment, and you are free to change your mind at any time. Japanese companies take this approach further forming Keiretsu – which are groups of organisations that routinely work together, but without any kind of formal partnerships.[13]

Such informal arrangements have the advantage of being flexible and non-binding, but they have the disadvantage that either party can end the cooperation without warning, at any time that suits them. For this reason, many organisations prefer a more formal arrangement, typically with a written agreement or contract setting out the obligations of each party. These are common when organisations see themselves as working together for some time. For example, an electricity company might agree to supply power at a fixed price for the next three years, provided a customer buys some minimum quantity. More formal agreements have the advantage of showing the details of the commitment, so that each side knows exactly what it has to do. On the other hand, they have the disadvantage of losing flexibility and imposing rigid conditions.

Unfortunately, even written agreements do not guarantee performance, as one side can still break a written contract. For instance, in 2001, electricity suppliers in California realised that their long-term contracts with customers specified prices that were too low to cover the rising costs of generation, so the suppliers ignored their contractual obligations and switched off supplies, causing widespread power cuts. Nonetheless, formal agreements should significantly reduce uncertainty. These agreements come in several forms, starting with an exchange of relevant information.

Sharing information

We have already seen that sharing basic information can improve supply chain efficiency. Passing information along a supply chain can reduce uncertainty and smooth the flow of materials. On a broader front, small companies can pool information about their requirements for materials, and make joint purchases to get the same quantity discounts as larger companies. They can also combine loads to reduce transport costs, in the way that freight forwarders combine loads from different companies. Shared information can also lead to agreement about standard package sizes to ease material handling, lists of preferred suppliers, special marketing promotions that affect demand, ethical standard for purchasing, and so on.

EDI makes this kind of data sharing easy, and it is generally the first formal level of cooperation. In practice, its most common form has a retailer passing back point of sales (POS) information to suppliers. Then upstream suppliers know actual demands with certainty, and they can plan and adjust their own operations to meet these in the best possible way. This result where one organisation can see what is happening in other parts of the supply chain is called visibility.

If we think about the benefits of visibility, we can suggests another level of cooperation, where organisations do not only share the sales data, but also forecasts of future demand and plans to meet this. In other words, rather than have each organisation separately forecasting and planning its operations, they cooperate to design a single efficient set of forecasts and plans for key logistics activities. When this is combined with automatic purchasing, the process is known as collaborative planning, forecasting and replenishment (CPFR). This was developed by Wal-Mart in the mid 1990s[14] and its growth has largely been concentrated among retailers. Voluntary Inter-industry Commerce Solutions (VICS) have been developing standards for CPFR, with their first report published in 1998.[15,16] Many organisation have reported considerable benefits from such collaboration.

The next stages of cooperation do not stop at planning, but set shared goals and incentives for achieving them. As organisations move closer together, there comes a point where it may be beneficial to move on to longer-term arrangements, such as an alliance or partnership.

Strategic alliances

When an organisation and a supplier are working well together, they may both feel that they are getting the best possible results and neither could benefit from trading with other partners. Then they might look for a long-term relationship which guarantees that their mutual benefits continue. This is the basis of a strategic alliance or partnership.

> • A strategic alliance is a formal, long-term relationship between two or more organisations to pursue a set of agreed goals, or achieve a specified business need.
>
> • The organisations remain independent, but work closely together to achieve their mutual aims.

Figure 5.5 shows the main thrust of such arrangements. Traditional arrangements are adversarial, with distinct organisations coming together temporarily in adversarial arrangements with little sharing of information or common ground. As the organisations increase cooperation they increase visibility and have more shared activities and goals. With alliances, they develop a long-term relationship that moves both organisations in the same direction.

Ellram and Krause[17] prefer the term supplier partnering, which they define as 'an ongoing relationship between firms, which involves a commitment over an

Visibility
has shared information to allow one organisation to see what is happening in other parts of the supply chain

CPFR
collaborative planning, forecasting and replenishment

Strategic alliance
a long-term relationship between organisations that brings mutual benefits as the pursue common goals

Partnership
a long term, mutually beneficial trading relationship between two organisations

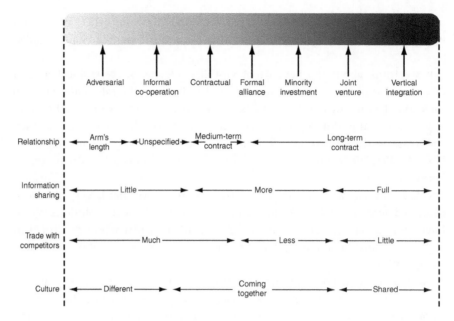

Figure 5.5   Spectrum of relationships for co-operation

extended time period, and a mutual sharing of information and the risks and rewards of the relationship'.Whatever we call them, the main features of formal alliances are:

- organisations working closely together at all levels
- senior managers and everyone in the organisations supporting the alliance
- shared business culture, goals and objectives
- openness and mutual trust
- long-term commitment
- shared information, expertise, planning and systems
- flexibility and willingness to solve shared problems
- continuous improvements in all aspects of operations
- joint development of products and processes
- guaranteed reliable and high quality goods and services
- agreement on costs and profits to give fair and competitive pricing
- increasing business between partners.

These arrangements are now common, and you often hear statements like 'Abbey National treats its suppliers as partners.'[18] The supplier knows that it has repeat business for a long time, and can invest in improvements to products and operations; the organisation knows that it has guaranteed – and continually improving – supplies. Other benefits include shared products, technology, capital, intellectual property, markets, management skills, and so on.

Partnerships can lead to fundamental changes in operations. For example, the stability of a partnership might encourage suppliers to specialise in one type of product. Then they might give such commitment to the alliance that they reduce their product range, make a few products as efficiently as possible, and concentrate on giving a small number of customers a very high quality service. They can share information with customers without the threat that this will be used to obtain some form of trading advantage. At the same time, customers reduce their number of suppliers, as they no longer need to look around to get the best deals. Japanese companies were among the first to develop strategic alliances, and at the time when Toyota had formed partnerships with its 250 suppliers, General Motors was still working separately with 4000 suppliers.

Forming alliances

A useful starting point for creating alliances is to analyse operations and see if alliances would be useful – in other words, assess the value of such a relationship. Clearly, there would be few benefits from an alliance if a firm only buys a few materials, or constantly changes its operations, or is sensitive about confidentiality, or cannot find reliable suppliers. But many organisations could benefit, and they should start looking at possible arrangements. Typically, their efforts start with a project team to identify benefits, objectives, timetables, resource implications, technology, terms, and so on. This is the first stage in defining the scope of a relationship. The second stage is to identify potential partners and assess their likely performance. In particular, firms need to know their potential partner's strengths and weaknesses, management styles, motives, culture, resources, problems that must be overcome, and so on. Perhaps the key points here are to see whether the organisation would be willing to form an alliance, and whether it could actually be a partner in a successful relationship. The third stage compares the potential partners, selects the best and starts contract negotiations. When these are successful it is time to start the alliance, work with it, continually monitor progress, and make adjustments and improvements.

LOGISTICS IN PRACTICE – PETRO-CANADA

Petro-Canada (PC) is one of Canada's largest oil and gas companies, whose aim is to develop responsibly energy resources. It has 5000 employees around the world, production of 400,000 barrels of oil a day, and profits of more than $1 billion a year. It is involved in all oil operations from upstream exploration in sites around the world, to downstream retail operations that supply 16% of Canada's oil products through 1600 petrol stations. The Canadian government founded PC to compete with international companies in 1975, but it began privatisation in 1991 and sold its last shares in 2004.

LOGISTICS IN PRACTICE – PETRO-CANADA (CONTINUED)

In the 1990s PC started to form strategic alliances with its major suppliers. It was looking for ways of reducing costs, and supplier partnerships were a clear option for a company that spent over $2 billion a year on materials other than oil. To find the best way of forming strategic alliances, PC benchmarked other companies who reported a history of successful partnerships, including Motorola and Dow Chemicals. In practice, growing pressure to improve performance meant that PC had to get results quickly, and they quickly developed their own approach. This had targets of reducing costs to by 15% in a first phase, and eventually 25%.

An early step for PC was the realisation that it needed guaranteed product quality, so it consolidated its use of Total Quality Management (TQM) and included this as a requirement for suppliers. This was important because Deming's '14 principles'[19] advise organisations not to buy products on the basis of cost alone, but to include a range of factors such as quality, reliability, timing, features and trust.

After setting the context, PC started talking to prospective partners. It chose these from companies that it currently did most business with, and those whose products were critical. There were already long-standing, informal relationships with many of these, and PC considered extending these to more formal alliances. Important considerations were that the suppliers were committed to high quality, emphasised customer satisfaction, and had the potential to become 'the best of the best'.

Now it had a set of potential partners, the next stage was to form joint development teams to move forward with more detailed planning and execution (as well as getting some quick returns and generating enthusiasm for the alliance).

PC's approach to developing partnerships can be summarised in eight steps:

1. Prepare the organisation for alliances with research, training, systems and practices.

2. Assess the risk and benefits of partnerships, setting aims and targets.

3. Benchmark other partnership arrangements.

4. Select qualified suppliers.

5. Form joint teams to manage the initiative and move it forward.

6. Confirm the partnership's principles, commitments, relationships and obligations.

7. Formalise the terms and conditions.

8. Continue training and improving.

Question

• What do you think are the most important steps in forming a strategic alliance?

(*Sources*: Internal company reports and website at www.petro-canada.ca)

Forming a partnership is only the first step, and it needs a lot of effort to get it working successfully – and keep it working over the long term. Some specific factors that contribute to a successful partnership include a high level of achieved service, real cost savings, a growing amount of business, increasing profits, joint projects, merging of cultures, and so on. Rowley[20] gives a broader list of key success factors including management commitment, a contract specifying costs and responsibilities, agreed performance indicators, agreed objectives, shared culture and joint information systems.

In this context Lambert et al.[21] describe three key elements of alliances: drivers, which are the reason for forming alliances, facilitators in the environment that support this move, and components, which are the joint activities that constitute the alliance.

- *Drivers*, which are the compelling reasons for forming partnerships, such as increased efficiency, cost reduction, improved customer service, profit growth, or security. Both partners must believe that they will get such benefits over the long term, but they may not look for the same benefits, or equal ones.

- *Facilitators*, which are the supportive corporate factors that encourage partnerships, such as compatibility of operations, similar management styles, common aims, mutual skills, openness of communications, and so on. Without this support an alliance cannot develop, even when there are strong drivers.

- *Components*, which are the joint activities and operations used to build and sustain the relationship, such as communication channels, joint planning, shared risk and rewards, and investment. Components turn the ideas of an alliance into reality, through actual operations and results.

Drivers and facilitators are the means for forming an alliance, while the components keep it going. After this, the alliance delivers results, and if these meet expectations the alliance continues. However, it is always possible to get disappointing returns, and when either party is unsatisfied the alliance will not last. This is an important point, as alliances may bring considerable benefits in some circumstance, but they are certainly not always the best answer. At a practical level, some purchases are so small, or materials are so cheap, that the effort needed to maintain an alliance is not worth while; sometimes managers do not want to lose control or share information; sometimes an organisation may not be able to find a partner willing to make the necessary commitment; organisational structures or cultures may be too different; it may be impossible to reach the necessary level of trust; there may be nobody with the necessary skills and enthusiasm to support an alliance, and so on. Several years after starting its supplier partnership initiative, Petro-Canada still bought 20–40% of materials through traditional supplier-customer relationships.

However, alliances are still growing in popularity. As Ewer[22] says, we have 'the powerful combination of improved technology, which can enable better partnering, a growing consensus that partnering enabled by e-B2B is essential, and a growing public profile for partnering issues in general'.

Vertical integration

Some people suggest that there is a difference between strategic alliances (which are long-term contractual relationships), and partnerships (which they say involve some kind of shared ownership). This is not a generally accepted distinction, but it does suggest that when an organisation wants to go beyond partnerships, it has to own more of the supply chain. A common arrangement for this has one company taking a minority share in another. Then it has some say in their operations, but it does not necessarily control them. A manufacturer, for example, might take a minority share in a wholesaler, to get some influence in the way that its products are distributed; or a retailer may take a minority share in a transport company to influence its delivery policies.

Joint venture
where two (usually) companies put up funds to start a third company with shared ownership

Another option is for two organisations to start a joint venture, where they both put up funds to start a third company with shared ownership. Perhaps a manufacturer and supplier might together form a transport company for moving materials between the two. This gives a mechanism for exerting control over the third party, while sharing the risks and benefits.

Vertical integration
the amount of a supply chain that is owned by one organisation

However, the most common arrangement has one organisation simply buying another, adjacent member of the supply chain. This increases its level of vertical integration.

- **Vertical integration** describes the amount of a supply chain that is owned by one organisation.

If an organisation buys materials from outside suppliers and sells products to external customers, it does not own much of the supply chain and has little vertical integration (as shown in Figure 5.6). If the organisation owns its sources of initial supply, does most of the value adding operations, and distributes products through to final customers, it owns a lot of the supply chain and is highly vertically integrated (like Petro-Canada that we mentioned above).

Backward integration
when an organisation owns a lot of the upstream operations in a supply chain

When the organisation owns a lot of the supply side or upstream activities it has backward integration; when it owns a lot of the distribution network or downstream activities it has forward integration.

Forward integration
when an organisation owns a lot of the downstream operations in a supply chain

In some circumstances vertical integration is the best way of getting different parts of the supply chain to work together. For instance, when Ford of America was growing quickly the only way that it could guarantee supplies was to own everything from steel mills through to distributor networks and repair shops. This reduces uncertainty, makes sure that all operations are synchronised, can lower costs, gives opportunities for more value adding and profit, has common aims, and so on. But most organisations do not have so much integration and they focus on a narrower set of their own strengths – in the way that Ford now focuses on the actual assembly of cars. The drawbacks with vertical integration are that it is very expensive, leads to huge diversified organisations that spread their resources

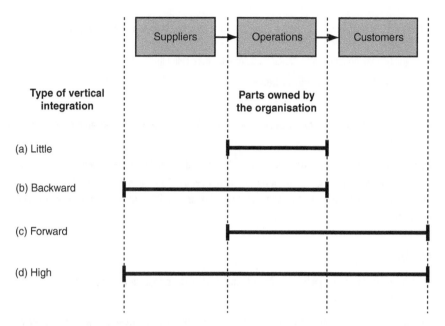

Figure 5.6 Different levels of vertical integration

too thinly, needs to combine specialised skills that one organisation does not have, becomes too bureaucratic, and has less flexibility to respond to changing conditions. So vertical integration is not necessarily desirable – and realistically it is often impossible for even the biggest organisation to own much of their supply chains. For instance, Heinz is a huge company, but it could not – and would not want to – buy all the farmers, processors, steel mills, canners, wholesalers, retailers and other organisations in the supply chain for their baked beans.

LOGISTICS IN PRACTICE – ELLIS AND EVERARD

By 2000 Ellis and Everard had become a major distributor of chemicals, particularly bulk liquids. Its continuing growth made it Europe's fourth largest chemical distributor, with a turnover of £600 million and employing 2000 people.

The company had been actively developing long-term alliances with its trading partners for many years, and it was considered a leader in the field. It had partnerships forward with customers (such as Merck, 3M and Sterling organics) and backward with suppliers (such as ICI, Solvay Interox and Junbunzlauer). Around 95% of its supplies, and 6% of customer demand were met through partnerships. Chris Whincup, Director of Sales, said that, 'Partnerships make our lives simpler, and as such more productive and effective.'

Among the benefits Ellis and Everard gained from partnerships were:

- faster decision making
- higher sales and easier introduction of new products

- stability, making long-term planning easier and more reliable
- removal of unproductive administration
- on-time payments from customers
- easier introduction of new initiatives, such as EDI for stock levels and automatic delivery scheduling

However, companies in the industry were finding that they could get more benefits from even closer integration, and this was achieved through a series of mergers and acquisitions. In 2001 the Dutch company Royal Vopak bought Ellis and Everard for £310 million, and merged the two companies.

Question

- What benefits do companies get from formal partnerships that they cannot get from normal, good trading relationships?

(*Sources*: Company annual reports, websites at www.pslcbi.com, www.vopak.com and www.icis.com)

Chapter review

- Traditionally, logistics has been organised as a series of distinct activities. This inevitably leads to conflicts and inefficiencies. A better approach develops a single integrated function that is responsible for all aspects of logistics within an organisation.
- Integration only became feasible when technology allowed the widespread sharing of information.
- Internal integration brings considerable benefits, but it is difficult to achieve and involves major changes within an organisation. These changes usually involve a series of stages that progressively merge operations. Most companies have moved in this direction.
- There are also benefits of extending integration to more organisations in the supply chain – giving external integration. This creases a smooth, seamless flow of materials and removes barriers throughout the chain. Not surprisingly, this can be difficult to achieve in practice.
- In practice, there are several ways of organising external integration, ranging from informal agreements to vertical integration. The most popular has some form of strategic alliance or partnership.

CASE STUDY – FRIEDLAND TIMBERS ASA.

Johann Klassen is the Managing Director of Friedland Timbers asa., which makes specialised wood products for the construction industry. He has recently been worried by late deliveries to some important customers. The industry is very competitive, and Johann knows that customers will go to other suppliers if he cannot guarantee deliveries. The marketing manager is particularly upset because he has worked with these customers for a long time, and promised deliveries that were not made.

Johann asked the production manager for an explanation. She told him that, 'Our own suppliers were late in delivering certain types of wood. This shortage of a key raw material disrupted our production plans. We cannot be blamed for this. If anyone in the company is to blame, it is the warehouse manager who does not keep enough stocks of raw materials to cover for late deliveries.'

Johann then went to the warehouse manager to see what was happening. 'There can't be anything wrong here', he was told. 'Stocks have been climbing for the past year, and last month they were at an all time high. In part, this is a deliberate decision, as I want to improve service levels to production. In part, though, stocks seem to have just drifted upwards. Now we have high stocks of most items, but there are still occasional shortages. These high stocks are causing me problems with space, and are stretching my budget. I think that the blame lies in purchasing, who do not order the amounts that we request.'

Johann found that stocks of some materials were drifting upwards because purchasing were buying unusually large quantities. At the same time, they were delaying purchases of other materials, and this led to shortages. The purchasing manager explained to Johann, 'Can I remind you that eight months ago you instructed me to reduce materials costs? I am doing this by taking advantage of the discounts given by suppliers for larger orders. Often I order more than requested under the assumption that we will need the material at some stage, so I get a discount and the material is already in stock when we need it. Sometimes keeping things in stock would take too much space or be too expensive, so then I might delay an order until I can combine it with others to get bigger discounts.'

Johann thought that he was near the source of his problems, and might ask for the purchasing policies to be reviewed. Then he talked to the transport manager who was not so sure. 'It is much more efficient for me to bring larger quantities into the company', he said. 'If you reduce the average order size, the transport costs will go up. Our budget is already being squeezed, as we have to pay for expensive express deliveries of materials that production classify as urgent. If you lower the order size, there will be more shortages, more express deliveries and even higher costs.'

Johann talked to some major suppliers to see if they could somehow improve the flow of materials into the company. Unhappily, while he was talking to one company, they raised the question of late payments. Friedland's had a stated policy of immediate payment of invoices, so he asked the accounting section for an explanation. He was given the unwelcome news that, 'The company's inventory and transport costs are so high that we are short of cash. We are delaying payments to improve our cash flow and avoid using expensive overdraft facilities.'

CASE STUDY – FRIEDLAND TIMBERS ASA.   (CONTINUED)

Later that day Johann found that the late customer deliveries which had started his investigation, were actually caused by poor sales forecasts by the marketing department. They had seriously underestimated demand, and planned production was too low. All the employees at FT were doing their best, but many things seemed to be going wrong.

Questions

- Why do all the logistics costs at Friedland seem to be rising at the same time?
- What do you think are their basic problems?
- What would you recommend Johann do?

Project – supply partnerships

You can find the details of a product's supply chain by following it backwards and identifying the main suppliers at each stage. Find a product whose supply chain is easy to study, such as petrol, a telephone service, cars, a restaurant chain, or a computer game. Describe the main features of this supply chain.

If you have chosen even a simple product, are you surprised at how quickly its supply chain grows? What alternatives shapes might the supply chain have? Have all competing products actually chosen the same shape for their chains?

How much integration is there in the chain? Would logistics be better with more integration? How could this be achieved?

Discussion questions

5.1   When logistics is divided into separate functions, each has its own objectives. Is this necessarily a bad thing, or can there be positive benefits?

5.2   An integrated supply chain is a convenient notion, but it does not reflect real operations. An organisation is only really concerned with its own customers and suppliers, and does not have time to consider other organisations further along the chain. Do you think that this is true?

5.3   Integration depends on the sharing of information. Why should one company be willing to give its confidential information to another?

5.4   Why do large fluctuations in supply and demand appear when customers do not talk to their suppliers? Is this inevitable, or are there ways of reducing the variations?

5.5   What are the benefits of supply chain integration?

5.6   When Christopher[5] says that 'supply chains compete, not companies', what exactly does he mean?

5.7   Decker and van Goor[4] say that integration in the supply chain can be at the level of:

- physical movement
- shared information
- integrated control
- integrated infrastructure.

What do they mean by this?

5.8   An organisation makes money by paying its suppliers less and charging its customers more. Does this seem a reasonable basis for cooperation? What can be done to improve things?

5.9 What is the best level of integration for a supply chain?

5.10 Some people say that all the recent developments in logistics can be summarised as 'integration'. Do you think this is true?

References

1. Sheehy, P. (1988) Quality – the springboard to success, Focus on Physical Distribution and Logistics Management, 7(8), 3–9.
2. Lewis, H.T., Culliton, J.W. and Steel, J.D. (1956) The role of air freight in physical distribution, Harvard Business School, Boston, MA.
3. Bowersox, D.J., Closs, D.J. and Cooper, M.B. (2007) Supply chain logistics management (2nd edition), McGraw-Hill, Boston, MA.
4. Decker, H. and van Goor, A. (1998) Applying activity-based costing to supply chain management, Proceedings of the 1998 Logistics Research Network Conference, School of Management, Cranfield University.
5. Christopher, M. (1996) Emerging issues in supply chain management, Proceeding of the Logistics Academic Network Inaugural Workshop, Warwick University.
6. Forrester, J. (1961) Industrial dynamics, MIT Press, Boston, MA.
7. Christopher, M. (1999) Global logistics: the role of agility, Logistics and Transport Focus, 1(1).
8. Guinipero, L.C. and Brand, R.R. (1996) Purchasing's role in supply chain management, The International Journal of Logistics Management, 7(1), 29–37.
9. P-E Consulting (1997) Efficient customer response – supply chain management for the new millennium? P-E Consulting, Surrey.
10. Chopra, S. and Meindl, P. (2007) Supply chain management (3rd edition), Pearson Education, Upper Saddle River, NJ.
11. Poirier, C.C. and Quinn, F.J. (2003) A survey of supply chain progress, Supply Chain Management Review, September/October.
12. Christopher, M. (2002) Supply chain vulnerability: final report on behalf of DTLR, DTI and Home Office, School of Management, Cranfield University.
13. Miwa, Y. and Ramseyer, J.M. (2006) The fable of the keiretsu, University of Chicago Press, Chicago, IL.
14. Haag, S., Cummings, M., McCubbrey, D., Pinsonneault, A. and Dnovan, R. (2006) Management information systems, McGraw-Hill Ryerson, Toronto.
15. Voluntary Inter-industry Commerce Solutions (1998) CPFR Committee, VICS, Lawrenceville, NJ.
16. VICS website at www.vics.org.
17. Ellram, L.M. and Krause, D.R. (1994) Supplier partnerships in manufacturing versus non-manufacturing firms, The International Journal of Logistics Management, 5(1), 43–53.
18. Abbey National (2007) website at www.abbeynational.plc.uk.
19. Deming, W.E. (1986) Out of the crisis, MIT Press, Cambridge, MA.
20. Rowley, J. (2001) Outsourcing across borders in Europe, Logistics and transport Focus, 3(1), 54–6.
21. Lambert, D.M., Emmelhainz, M.A. and Gardner, J.T. (1996) Developing and implementing supply chain partnerships, International Journal of Logistics Management, 7(2), 1–17.
22. Ewer, G.A. (2001) View point, Logistics and Transport Focus, 3(2), 2.

6

GLOBAL LOGISTICS

Contents

LEARNING OBJECTIVES

After reading this chapter you should be able to:

- appreciate the importance of international trade and its impact on logistics

- discuss the factors that encourage international trade

- review the different ways that organisations can move into a new market

- describe ways that international operations can be organised

- consider some options for global supply chains

- review the geographic areas of main economic activity

- discuss the difficulties of international logistics.

International trade

In Chapter 5 we developed the idea of an integrated logistics function, with coordinated activities that move materials from initial suppliers through to final customers. But the suppliers and customers are increasingly found in different parts of the world, and supply chains cross borders to become international – and even global. Sometimes this move to international business is almost accidental, as a firm finds that it can buy materials more cheaply in a foreign market, or sell products more profitably. At other times the move is part of a well-defined strategy to develop global operations. Whatever the incentive, there is no doubt that international trade continues to grow at a remarkable rate. Leontiades[1] notes that, 'One of the most important phenomena of the 20th century has been the international expansion of industry. Today, virtually all major firms have a significant and growing presence in business outside their country of origin.'

Figure 6.1 shows the growth of world exports of manufactured goods over a ten-year period in billions of dollars.[2] There is a clear upward trend, with the value of exports having doubled in a decade. Some of this effect might be due to rising prices, but Figure 6.2 shows how the total volume of goods exported is consistently rising.[2] It is interesting to see that this rise is also considerably higher than the growth of GDP, suggesting that a higher proportion of goods are being traded internationally.

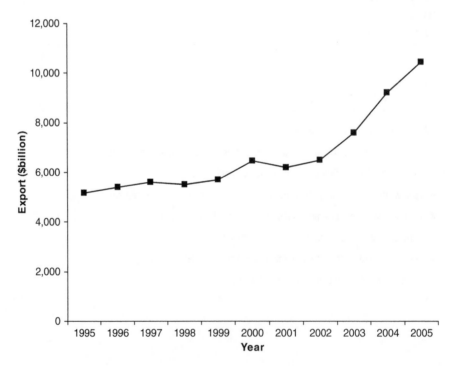

Figure 6.1   Value of world exports ($billion)

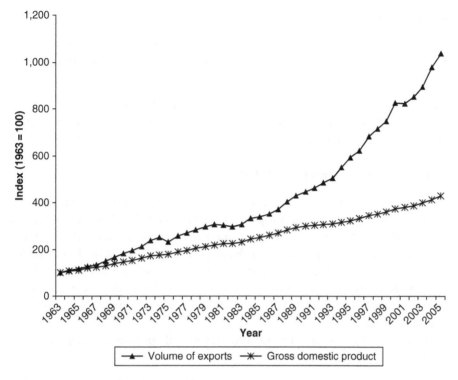

Figure 6.2 Comparing the growth of international trade with GDP

- International logistics occur when supply chains cross national frontiers.
- This brings benefits and is an increasingly common feature of logistics.

International logistics
occur when supply chains
cross national frontiers

All international trade is based on the recognition that an organisation can buy things from a supplier in one country, use logistics to move them, and then sell them at a profit in another country. Efficient communications, transport, financial arrangements, and trading agreements allow materials to be moved long distances at relatively low cost; then international logistics adds value by increasing place – and possibly ownership – utility. Some of the benefits of international operations include:

- purchase of products and materials at lower prices
- access to low-cost operations
- geographic expansion into new areas and markets
- positive response to increasing competition in home markets
- expansion or consolidation of operations to get economies of scale

- improvement in profit margins
- encouragement of innovation and diversification into new products
- a new market for products that are near the end of their life cycles in domestic markets.

The International Monetary Fund valued international trade at US$16 trillion in 2007 – which is around a quarter of all trade and is forecast to continue growing at 7–11% for the foreseeable future.[3]

Factors that encourage international trade

With rare exceptions, governments are keen to encourage international trade as a way of improving national prosperity. Over the years they have signed many agreements on trade, and formed international organisations like the Organisation for Economic Co-operation and Development (OECD) and the World Trade Organization (WTO). Most significantly, they have built free-trade areas, such as the European Union (EU), North America Free Trade Association (NAFTA), Association of South-East Asian Nations (ASEAN), Mercosur in South America and the African Union.

Many other factors have encouraged this growth in international trade, as suggested by the following list.

- *Growing prosperity*. As countries and geographical regions become more prosperous they demand greater volumes of products. The scale of growth often cannot be met by local suppliers.

- *Demand for foreign products*. Customers travel, watch television, surf the Web, see films, and use telephones to see different types of product that are available in other areas. This creates demand for new products that are specifically made by foreign companies.

- *Convergence of market demands*. Centralised manufacturing only works if different markets accept the same products – or at least products with minor differences in the finishing. There is clear evidence for a convergence in tastes – which Ohmae call 'Californianisation'[4] – and this allows Coca-Cola, McDonald's, Toyota and Sony and all other multinationals to sell the same products in virtually any country.

- *Removal of trade barriers*. A major force towards global free trade was the General Agreement on Tariffs and Trades (GATT), which stipulated that all its members should be treated equally. Countries in several regions have taken this idea further to create free trade areas that ease trade restrictions and reduce tariffs. This is one reason why the amounts collected as tariffs fell from 20% of trade in the 1950s, to 7% and the beginning of the 1990s, and 3% by 2000.[5,6]

- *Manufacturers' economies of scale*. Significant changes in manufacturing mean that many operations are more efficient with stable, large-scale production.

The best size for facilities is often larger than the demand from a single market. Hence centralised production, with its economies of scale and lower unit costs, can make produce that are cheaper than locally produced ones.

- *Integration of the supply chain.* Integration of the supply chain works towards a smooth movement of goods from initial suppliers through to final customers. This only becomes possible when national frontiers are transparent, and the same organisation works on both sides of the border.

- *More demands on suppliers.* Customers are putting greater demands on suppliers – including new products, low prices, fast delivery, just-in-time operations, total quality and customisation. Local suppliers may not be able to meet these demands, and organisations may have to look further afield to find the best sources.

- *Improved communications.* The Web, Internet, e-business, EDI, mobile phones, and other growing channels of communication have meant that physical separation is less relevant – and it is almost as easy to do business with a partner on the other side of the world as it is to visit the next town.

- *Changing practices in logistics.* Developments in logistics make long-distance trade easier. For instance, containerisation made the movement of goods easier, faster, cheaper and more reliable. Postponement allows products to finish manufacture at a later point in the supply chain, giving more customisation and flexibility in meeting demands. Inter-modal facilities make it easier to move goods between transport modes; larger ships can transport more goods; and so on.

- *Specialised support has grown.* Historically, when companies wanted to do business abroad, they had to do all the work themselves. Now a major industry has grown providing specialised intermediaries to do all the routine chores associated with exporting, international transport, trade credit, foreign exchange, customs clearance, and so on.

- *Cheap transport.* The overall result from many of the above effects is that the cost of transport has declined. For instance, bulk carriers reduce the cost of transporting a tonne of iron ore from Brazil to Sweden to less than $3, while container ships reduce the cost of moving a bottle of whisky from Scotland to Japan to $0.20 (a cost that has halved in the past ten years).[7]

LOGISTICS IN PRACTICE – EUROPEANISATION OF LOGISTICS

A single market was created within the European Union in 1993, with further expansions creating a market of 450 million people and gross regional product of €12 trillion. This has had a considerable effect on logistics and wider operations. The amount of trade within the European Union has continued to grow, with more companies working internationally, and seeing the whole of the Union as their market.

LOGISTICS IN PRACTICE – EUROPEANISATION OF LOGISTICS (CONTINUED)

Some specific changes are contributing to the 'Europeanisation' of business.

- Regulations are increasingly developed at EU rather than national level.

- There is an overall movement to deregulate and liberalise services, including those of logistics.

- Companies are integrating their operations in different countries, using common processes and logistics practices.

- There is rationalisation of supply chains, with half of companies reducing the number of facilities they use.

- Rationalisation has lowered the costs of stock, warehousing and materials.

- There has been a significant increase in the number of warehouses serving more than one country – and a clear trend towards pan-European logistics centres.

- Service levels are continuing to rise to meet more demanding international customers.

- Opportunities for cost reduction and enhanced customer service have raised the profile of logistics as a core function.

- EDI has become an essential part of logistics.

Questions

- As Europe moves towards a single logistics market, what effect will this have on the long-term operations?

(*Sources*: Hefflinger, T (2002) European logistics, THCo, Brussels; O'Sullivan D. (1995) Logistics in Europe, Logistics Focus, 4(6), 9–11)

Effect at an organisational level

It is easy to talk about world trade expanding by 7.4% in 2008, but such aggregate effects come from thousands of individual organisations deciding to expand their operations into new areas. The motor industry is probably the best example of this, with the main car manufacturers being among the largest international traders. They buy materials and components from suppliers around the world, collect everything in a relatively small number of assembly plants, and then ship finished cars out to customers, who again might be anywhere in the world. This system works because of the huge economies of scale for car assembly, and the ability of logistic to move materials quickly and cheaply through international supply chains. The extra cost of moving materials is relatively small compared with the total cost of production. This is an important point – that international trade is only feasible when transport adds a relatively small cost. The cost of transport is usually related to the weight and size being moved, so this limits international trade to materials whose value is high in relation to their size and weight. Some products, such as computers and wine, are expensive and small – so there is a major international trade; other products, such as bricks and soft drinks, have a low value relative to their weight and it would be too expensive to move them far. This effect of value to size or weight is measured by the value density.

Value density
the ratio of a product's
value to its weight or size

• The **value density** is the ratio of a product's value to its weight or size.

Low value density means that it would be too expensive to move products long distances, so demand is likely to be met by domestic suppliers – and these are typically smaller suppliers who serve local needs. High value density means that logistics adds a small amount to the cost, and this encourages a few large suppliers to work globally. This is the reason why the telephone you use is made by one of a handful of manufacturers and has travelled around the world before it got to you, while the bread you eat was made locally by a relatively small baker.

Of course, value density is only one factor that affects the feasibility of international operations. Another important issue centres on brand, and a well-known name such as Perrier or Evian can make international operations more attractive by compensating for low value density by charging premium prices. In the same way, beer has a low value density, but some brands have established names that allow them to meet international demand from a few large breweries. The stage in a product's life cycle is also important. Near the beginning of the life cycle profits are high and availability, measured by lead times, is more important than cost.

Clearly, some products are more suited to international trade than others. Factors that encourage local suppliers, rather than international ones, are products that:

• have relatively low value, or value density

• deteriorate or have a short shelf life

• are sensitive to cultural and other differences

• allow differentiation between competitors, perhaps with brand loyalty

• need high customer contact or personal service

• do not emphasise cost but focus on other features

• give limited economies of scale in production

• generate social or political pressures to produce locally

• have uneven development of markets.

As logistics has become more efficient, products with lower value density are being moved further. Manufactured goods are now routinely shipped from China, and even low cost items are moved long distances. This can be controversial. For instance, basic foodstuffs are flown long distances to give customers a continuous supply of out-of-season products – but this comes at a cost to local farmers who cannot compete with low cost production areas. Even coal, which has a very low value density, is moved around the world rather than using local mines – with the resultant closure of national mining industries.

LOGISTICS IN PRACTICE – AIRBUS A380

When products move from one country to another you can imagine some steps in a typical supply chain – perhaps a manufacturer making a product, national transport moving the product to a port, port operators storing the product until a ship arrives and then loading it, shippers moving the product to a delivery port, port operators unloading the product, and national transport moving it to the customer. The real picture might add several other steps to store the product at various points, arrange sorting and load consolidation, package it, move it though customs, arrange transfers between transport modes, switch operators, and a host of related activities.

Even an apparently simple journey can be complicated, as illustrated by the Airbus A380, which is the largest commercial airliner ever built. It is assembled in Toulouse, France – but its parts have a longer journey, as you can see from the wings.

1. Bauxite is mined in western Australia, followed by initial processing.
2. The ore is shipped by road, train and bulk ore carrier to a smelting plant in Texas, USA where it is formed into ingots.
3. The ingots are moved up the Mississippi and formed into plates in the world's largest aluminium mill at Davenport, Iowa (the only mill large enough to handle the plates).
4. Plates are moved on special, extendable trucks to Baltimore, Maryland.
5. They are shipped to the world's largest wing assembly plant in Broughton, North Wales.
6. After completion, a 96-wheel trailer carries the wings 1.6 km to the river.
7. A specially designed barge takes them 26 km down river to the port of Mostyn.
8. A specially designed cargo ship takes them to the port at Bordeaux, France.
9. A barge carries the wings 100 km up the Garonne River to the village of Langon.
10. A convoy of special trucks moves the wings 240 km to Toulouse, travelling at less than 20 km/hr and with adjacent roads closed.

Other parts may also have long journeys, so you can see that each finished plane involves a hugely complicated, international effort.

Question

- Is it possible to simplify supply chains like that of the A380?

(*Source*: CILT (2005) A380 – the world's biggest passenger aircraft, CILT World, The Chartered Institute of Logistics and Transport (Sept/Oct), 11; www.airbus.com)

Organising for international trade

Virtually all major companies work internationally. We know the advantages of working internationally, but what actually triggers the expansion from their home market? In reality, there are many factors in this decision, ranging from the serious (perhaps forecasts for long-term economic growth in overseas markets) through to the trivial (maybe senior managers want to do some travelling). Hopefully, the serious considerations carry more weight in this difficult decision that needs a clear understanding of the benefits and problems. In particular, the incentive for international operations comes from a business strategy that includes a theme of global expansion. Only when higher strategies set the scene can logistics move towards global trading. But this raises the question of how to actually start international operations.

If you think of a company starting to work in a new country, you probably imagine it building factories, logistics centres, shops, or whatever facilities it needs. This is certainly one option, and on a world scale about half of the trade between industrialised countries is accounted for by trade between subsidiaries of the same company.[8] About a third of US exports are sent by American companies to their overseas subsidiaries, and another third is from foreign manufacturers sending products back to their home market.

However, in principle, a company can continue working normally in its home market and pass all dealings with a new market on to a third party. Then the company only has to deal with this third party – called an **export distributor** – which effectively runs all operations in the new market. This kind of arrangement is usually too limiting, but it does show that there are different ways of entering new markets.

Ways of reaching foreign markets

Imagine a manufacturer that wants to sell products in a new, international market. There are essentially six possible arrangements, with the following list in order of increasing investment and risk:

1. *Licensing or franchising.* Here the manufacturer passes all operations to a local company and allows it to make equivalent products. In return for a fee or royalties, the manufacturer allows the local company to use its processes, designs, operations, trademarks, brands, knowledge, or other skills that it passes across. The licensee is responsible for operations in the new market, and the manufacturer retains some control through negotiated conditions for quality, testing, materials, sales, and so on.

   This arrangement has the advantages of needing little capital, having low risks, using the licensee's knowledge of local conditions, reducing costs by using existing facilities and skills, and avoiding local import tariffs and quotas. The most frequent disadvantages are lack of the manufacturer's control over products sold in its name, limited returns to the manufacturer, and the development of a potential new competitor.

2. *Exporting finished goods.* Here the manufacturer continues making products in its own facilities, but uses local companies to distribute them. There are several variations on this theme, which include local marketing, trading companies, freight forwarding, distribution, and other intermediaries who provide an export service.

   The benefits of exporting are that it still uses the expertise of local companies and existing facilities – but now with support from expert intermediaries who handle the trading and import arrangements. As there is no local manufacturing, the domestic company needs less investment, and the exporter can achieve economies of scale. On the other hand, exports contributes least to the local economy, so governments often add tariffs, import quotas, currency restrictions, or some other constraints. The success of a product also depend on the skills of export intermediaries, over which neither the manufacturer nor the domestic company have much control. So a manufacturer runs the risk of increasing production to satisfy a demand that largely depends on the success of other organisations.

3. *Setting up a local sales and distribution network.* In this variation, products are still exported to meet local demand but the manufacturer increases its control of the supply chain by replacing the local distribution company with its own subsidiary.

   This gives the manufacturer more control of distribution, which it runs itself – but for this it needs a greater investment in the country and more knowledge of local conditions. In particular, it must know enough about local markets and logistic – or be able to attract enough people with the necessary knowledge and skills.

4. *Exporting parts and using local assembly and finishing.* This moves into the area of partnerships, where the manufacturer develops a closer supplier-customer relationship with a local assembler. Essentially the manufacturer exports product kits, which a local firm assembles.

   This needs significant facilities in the local market, which bring the advantage of using more local knowledge and skills. Local operations might be cheaper, and so reduce costs, and there is certainly a chance to reduce transport costs. Perhaps more importantly, this approach adds some local value, but the limited local content of such 'screwdriver' operations mean that they are not necessarily popular with host countries, and are often seen as a means of gaining skills that can be developed for future opportunities. At the same time, the manufacturer loses control over key assembly operations, which depend on the local assembler. An option here is to start in a small way, perhaps with postponement to customise products for the local market, and if this is a success, to keep adding more local operations.

5. *Joint venture with a local company.* With this option the manufacturer might want to open full production in the new market, but it does not have the

necessary finance, resources, skills, or some other key requirement. Then it might look for a joint venture with a local company – where they start a new company, which is jointly owned by the two.

This has the advantages of less risk and investment than full local production, while still allowing the manufacturer considerable control over operations. Often this is the only realistic way of entering a new market that restricts foreign ownership.

6. *Full local production*. This is the extreme case, where the manufacturer opens full production facilities within the new market, to make and distribute its products. Opening full production can be very expensive and time consuming. When Nissan, Toyota and Mazda wanted a presence in the European Union, they spent billions of euros and years of preparation opening new plants. This is also the approach adopted by the retailers Lidl and IKEA. Often companies ease the organisation and commitment by setting up a local subsidiary. Then, if problems arise, there is some separation between the local company and its parent. A faster way of getting a significant presence is to buy a company that is already working locally. If a firm already works successfully in a market, a larger company can buy it, inject cash and build on its assets. This is how Wal-Mart moved into the UK by buying Asda, which was already third biggest supermarket group in the country.

The essential feature of local production is that the manufacturer retains control over all operations, and it reduces transport, operating costs and the effort needed to import goods. On the other hand it has the disadvantages of needing greater investment and long-term commitment, and it is vulnerable to changes in local conditions and exchange rates.

Organisations might like the control, potential profits, avoidance of tariffs and import quotas that come with full production facilities. On the other hand, few can afford the investment and risk, or manage the complex and uncertain operations. The best choice depends on many factors, such as the firm's strategic aims, capital available, attitude towards risk, target return on investment, timescale, local knowledge, transport costs, tariffs, trade restrictions, available workforce and cultural differences. Then they might do some calculations to compare options, like those illustrated in the following worked example. This might lead to a more cautious approach, typically expanding their foreign operations in a series of steps. In effect, they move down the list, slowly increasing their investment and only moving on when each previous stage has proved successful.

WORKED EXAMPLE

Warwick Supplies is planning to expand its European network. It is considering a number of options, each of which has a fixed annual payment (for rent, electricity, and other overheads) and a variable cost that depends on throughput (handling, depreciation, staff, etc.). The following table shows a simplified view of these costs.

WORKED EXAMPLE   (CONTINUED)

Alternative	Fixed Cost	Variable Cost
A. exporting from existing facilities	€800,000	€900
B. using a local distributor	€2,400,000	€700
C. open a facility for local finishing	€9,000,000	€520
D. open limited production facilities	€8,000,000	€360
E. open larger production facilities	€12,000,000	€440

Alternately, Warwick can avoid entering the market by licensing a local manufacturer to make the product in return for a royalty of 2% of sales. What options might the company consider if it is planning to sell about 10,000 units a year with a profit margin of 10%?

Answer

We have a limited amount of financial information, and can use this for a break-even analysis, as illustrated in Figure 6.3. This shows the ranges over which each option has lowest costs. You can see that alternatives C and E are never cheapest. This leaves a choice between alternatives A, B and D.

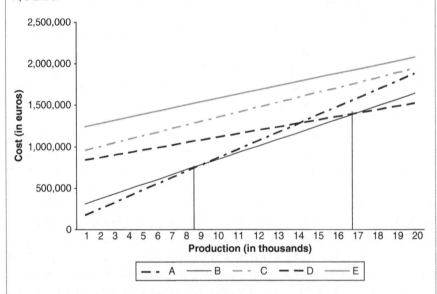

Figure 6.3   Break even analysis for location of Warwick Supplies

- Alternative A is the cheapest for throughput, X, from 0 until:

$$800,000 + 900X = 2,400,000 + 700X \text{ or } X = 8000$$

- After this alternative B is cheapest until:

$$2,400,000 + 700X = 8,000,000 + 360X \text{ or } X = 16,471$$

- After this point D remains the cheapest.

With production of 10,000 units a year, alternative B, using a local distributor, is cheapest with costs of $(2,400,000 + 10,000 \times 700 =)$ €9.4 million. Alternative A, exporting directly with existing facilities is not much more expensive at $(800,000 + 10,000 \times 900 =)$ €9.8 million, and is probably easier to organise.

Option B has an average cost of $(€9,400,000/10, 000 =)$ €940 a unit, and adding a profit margin of 10% gives a selling price of $940 \times 1.1 = $ €1034, and total profit of €940,000. Using the same selling price, if Warwick negotiates a royalty of 2% of sales, they get a profit of only $1034 \times 0.02 \times 10,000 = $ €206,800.

Of course, these figures only give the starting point for a decision. Now Warwick has to look at the more detailed costs, its aims, longer-term plans, amount of control it want, and a whole series of other factors.

LOGISTICS IN PRACTICE – RENFIELD PHARMACEUTICALS

Renfield Pharmaceuticals is a specialised branch of a major Swiss pharmaceutical company, whose main products are for the treatment of hypertension and kidney damage. It works in many parts of the world, and uses a standard procedure for organising its expansion – while limiting its risks in less successful markets. This procedure can be summarised in five steps.

1. Export to local trading companies and independent distributors. This usually gives limited sales, but it allows a convenient way of testing the market. If the market looks attractive, Renfield moves on to the next step.

2. Send a team of field representatives. These work with the local distributors, collect orders directly for Renfield, and talk extensively to actual and potential customers. Their experience of local conditions allows them to make recommendations for the next step of expansion.

3. Set up a local distribution network. Occasionally Renfield buys local companies that have been distributing their products. But usually they start up their own marketing and logistics organisation, which works in parallel with local companies. Over time, preferential trading terms allow the Renfield subsidiary to take a dominant position in the market. It always uses local employees and resources, but there is strong control from Renfield headquarters.

4. If the subsidiary distribution company develops a sizeable and profitable market, Renfield considers opening production facilities. In the first instance this is usually a packaging plant. Ingredients are sent in bulk from other Renfield plants, and the local plant arranges final production, packaging and labelling before passing products to the distribution company.

5. After a reasonable period of successful and profitable operations, if forecast demand continues to grow, Renfield considers larger production facilities. These typically concentrate on one or two of the company's main products, together with limited production of associated material. The mix of products and size of facilities depends on the country's population, economic conditions, trade and monetary restrictions, education levels, raw materials, and so on. Products from these facilities are exported to test new markets – and the process of expansion continues.

> **LOGISTICS IN PRACTICE – RENFIELD PHARMACEUTICALS (CONTINUED)**
>
> **Question**
>
> - What are the benefits of Renfield's slow development of a market, rather than a more forceful entry?
>
> (*Source*: Company reports)

Global operations

We know that international trade does not necessarily mean that a firm has to work internationally itself. As we saw in the last section, it can use various intermediaries to deal with its foreign operations. But someone has to move goods over frontiers, even if it is left to a transport company, and this leads to the inevitable principle that international trade means international companies. These companies have to deal with the different conditions and regulations that they meet in each country. Sometimes these can be dramatically different on either side of an international border. A company has to find the most appropriate organisational structure for dealing with these variations, and for this it has four main options. Some people use these terms in slightly different ways, but we can differentiate:

National companies only work within their home market

1. *National companies* – which only work within their home market. If they want a presence in international markets, they export to marketing organisations in foreign countries, perhaps offering factory-gate prices.

International companies have facilities in different countries, but they are centred on one home country

2. *International companies* – which have facilities in different countries, but are centred on one home country. The headquarters (and often the main operations) are located in this home country, with subsidiaries in all other areas. The headquarters controls the activities of all subsidiaries.

Multinational companies form a more loosely linked, largely independent set of companies working in different geographical regions

3. *Multinational companies* – which work more widely and form a more loosely linked, largely independent set of companies working in different geographical regions. This arrangement is often described as a multi-domestic organisation, with no rigid control from a central headquarters. The separate divisions have more flexibility to adjust operations and products to local needs.

Global companies see the world as a single market

4. *Global companies* – see the world as a single market. They make standard products for shipment anywhere in the world, using the locations where they can work most effectively and efficiently. The main feature of global organisations is that they coordinate all their activities as if they supply a single market. Coca-Cola, for example, make the same products around the world, with all operations coordinated to meet demand as efficiently as possible.

These descriptions may be misleading as they suggest that organisations choose a single best organisation and use it for all their operations. In reality, firms always have to be flexible enough to respond to local conditions, practices and demands. This generally needs a looser structure that includes aspects of the different types of operation, but gives a unified culture for the overall organisation. Then a company might work 'globally' in Europe and 'internationally' in Africa. Such flexible structures are sometimes described as 'transnational'.

There is a trend for more companies, especially the biggest, to see themselves as working globally. Levitt[9] summarises the features of these by saying that, 'The multinational corporation operates in a number of countries and adjusts its products and prices in each – at high relative costs. The global corporation operates with resolute certainty – at low relative costs – as if the entire world (or major regions of it) were a single entity; it sells the same things in the same way everywhere.' In a similar way, Christopher[10] says, 'Whereas the emphasis in multi-national marketing has been to tailor products and marketing strategies to meet perceived local needs, the thrust of global marketing is to seek to satisfy common demands worldwide.' The principle of global organisations is that, 'the customer in Bogota is little different from his counterpart in Birmingham'[11] and can be satisfied by the same products. Table 6.1 suggests some differences in viewpoint.

Benefits of global operations

There are clear advantages in working globally, from both a logistics and operations point of view. Global organisations limit the range of products, concentrate research and development, ensure economies of scale, remove duplicated functions, simplify management structures, simplify the product design function, use standard processes, generate widespread expertise in products, give a unified marketing view, and so on. They coordinate all activities to make sure they are done in the best way and in the best places – to provide efficient and seamless operations. For instance, if a global company has a shortage of products in Sri Lanka, it can ship stocks from Brazil; if costs rise in Poland, it can move production to China; if demand falls in India, it can divert products to Australia.

Table 6.1 Some features of global operations

	Domestic/export	International/ multinational	Global
Product	Variations on domestic product	Tailored to local markets	Single product in all markets
Product range	Fairly narrow for domestic needs	Wide for different needs	Narrow
Marketing to	Specific customers	National markets	All regions
Operating costs	High	Medium	Low
Logistics providers	Third party and intermediaries	Subordinate firms	Appropriate parts of the organisation
Management	Centralised	Diverse	Coordinated
Information	Based in home country	Diverse	Integrated

The benefits are so clear that it seems sensible for organisations to move in this direction, but there are practical problems that make this difficult. For instance, people in Sri Lanka may simply not like the same products as people in Brazil. Some other barriers and problems to global operations include the following:[12]

- Although companies may act 'globally' in limited areas, true global operations need so many resources that they are limited to very large companies.
- Customers in different countries and regions may demand different types of products.
- Products have some specific features, which mean that they are not suitable for global operations.
- Global products of any kind are not viewed favourably by some customers, who might reject them on principle.
- Organisations lack the human and technical resources needed to work and compete globally.
- Organisations many not be able to build the right structures or design strategies that work globally.
- Managers in different regions have fundamentally different objectives for themselves and the organisation.
- There are other cultural and economic differences that make coordination too difficult.
- Each region and country has different infrastructure, facilities and capabilities that make common operations impossible.

These factors, along with many others, make it impossible for most organisations to have global operations. Many firms start with this in mind, but hit problems – often very simple ones like products that offend local tastes, lack of transport to move goods to their final destination, or poor finances.

Global supply chains

Whatever organisational structure is chosen, logistics managers have to design supply chains to actually move materials around the world. They have to ask questions about the structure of the chain: Is it better to concentrate logistics operations in a single centre or have more dispersed facilities? There is no single best model for global supply chains, so each organisation has to find its own solution that comes closest to satisfying all its needs. The result is that global supply chains come in a huge variety of forms. Nonetheless, they do have common features, and the following list outlines six options:

- *Outsource logistics.* As we have seen, the simplest way for organisations to enter international markets is to license local firms to use their designs, brand name, operations, specialised knowledge, and so on. This effectively passes all responsibility to a local firm and means that the licensing firm does not get involved with any global logistics. This may not seem like a strategy for global logistics but, of course, it is a viable option – accepting that other organisations can do the logistics better than the licensee.

- *Global operations with limited needs for logistics.* Not all global organisations need global – or even complex – supply chains. For instance, McDonald's works globally, but practicalities demand that it does not have an extended supply chains to move products around the world. Most of its suppliers are sourced locally, supply chains are short, and its customers are local. This means that even a huge organisation working globally in thousands of locations can have relatively simple supply chains.

- *Concentrating production and sourcing in one area and then selling globally.* This is an exporting strategy that gives logistics the relatively straightforward job of moving materials from local suppliers into the organisation – but then a complex job of distributing finished products from a single location to international customers. The manufacturer is a pure exporter with global marketing and distribution rather than global operations. This model is also the most vulnerable to external pressures, as it is widely seen as concentrating economic benefits in the centre.

- *Concentrating production in one centre, but buying materials and selling products globally.* Again this is an exporting strategy, but now with global sourcing collecting materials from anywhere in the world, followed by global marketing to sell products to customers in any location. This gives the most difficult logistics where both the inward and outward flows are complicated. However, it is more popular with host countries as it spreads the economic benefits more widely, even though the main value adding activities are still concentrated in one location.

- *Postponement to move the finishing of production down the supply chain.* This is aligned to a strategy of local assembly, typically with limited facilities for finishing products. This adds some local value, but all components are generally imported from main production centres. So there is a complex problem with inbound logistics to the main production centres, then a relatively straightforward movement to local finishers, followed by fairly straightforward distribution to customers. When the finishing is done by local firms, they almost invariably use their local knowledge to organise the distribution to customers as well.

- *Operating as a local company, with local suppliers and customers.* This is aligned to a strategy of full local production – typically for a multinational company. Then both inward and outward logistics are easier, as they are organised relatively locally. This is the most popular approach with host countries as it develops local skills and brings economic benefit – but it means that operations are vulnerable to changing local conditions. It also means that the independent parts lose much of the benefits of size, so the local firms are likely to look for growth that allows them to export – and this increases the complexity of supply chains.

LOGISTICS IN PRACTICE – TRIFAST

TR Fastenings was formed in 1973, and in 1976 opened its first manufacturing plant in Uckfield, Surrey. Since then it has grown into 'a worldwide manufacturer and distributor of industrial fasteners and components'. Trifast now supply more than 100,000 different products that range from tiny screws for microelectronics through to large bolts for agricultural machines. It focuses on 'fastening solutions' that dramatically reduce their customers' assembly times.

Trifast faces fierce competition, and it meets this by developing new products, offering new services, efficient operations, sophisticated logistics and a policy of expansion. For instance, they have a strong R&D department that works closely with customers to develop new products; they are world leaders in vendor managed inventory, and direct deliveries to production.

Typically, Trifast will visit a manufacturer, analyse their products, design the type of fasteners needed, and then supply them. They only make 16% of the fasteners themselves, with the remainder sourced from 2000 suppliers – so their main job is to source and manage the supply. They are constantly looking for additional services and diversification. For instance, while they are managing the supply of fasteners, they can easily arrange the supply of associated parts, such as springs, plastic ties and pulleys. Then they do some work on these, assembling parts into components – or kitting. This adds value for Trifast, and brings benefits to manufacturers, who have a guaranteed supply of materials, but only deal with one supplier.

To maintain competitiveness, Trifast has looked for opportunities to expand, starting in the 1990s with moves into the growing manufacturing centres of Asia. The company had considered opening distribution centres and supplying these from its factory in the UK, but the stocks needed were too high. Instead it bought manufacturing companies in Singapore (Formac Technologies) and Malaysia to form the hub of its new operations. Then they bought companies in Ireland, Norway and Sweden, and established new companies in France and Hungary. The move to America came with the purchases of a west coast distributor. Trifast describes itself as 'acquisitive' and continues to buy suitable companies that expand its geographical coverage, market sector, product range, or revenue. For instance, in 2005 it bought Serco-Ryan, the UK's fourth largest fastener company. Now there are six manufacturing plants in China, Singapore, Malaysia, Taiwan and the UK, with 30 distribution sites in 16 countries. Their revenue from 5000 customers in 57 countries is more than £130 million, 78% of which come from Europe, 19% from Asia and 3% come from the Americas.

Trifast moves goods from its own manufacturing plants and suppliers into main warehouse hubs, and then either to smaller satellite warehouses or directly to customers using 3PL. This system allows them to deliver quickly to customers in any part of the world, while keeping stocks down to 12 weeks demand.

Question

• Should Trifast continue its policy of global expansion, and how can it achieve this?

(*Sources*: Company annual reports; Lawless, J. (1998) Challenges of going global, The Sunday Times, 26 April; website at www.trifast.com)

Location of international trade

Global operations – and to a large extent international trade in general – assume that the world is a single market that is homogenous enough for it to use common operations. But this is patently not true, and there are few similarities between selling in, say, Tokyo and Kolwezi. There are differences in terrain, climate, infra-structure, population density, economic strength, political systems, cultures, and just about everything else. Global trade is really an ideal – and in practice it tries to find enough markets that shares features. A few products come close to this – with Coca-Cola selling in more than 200 countries and territories. But even international icons like McDonald's only trade in half this numbers – and the international activities of most firms are focused in a handful of neighbouring countries.

The single factor that has most effect on trade is the economic strength of a country or region. In general terms, stronger economies:

* move more materials, as they can afford to consume more products
* have more efficient logistics, due to better infrastructure, systems and support.

You can see that there is a cycle here, with greater prosperity allowing efficient logistics – and efficient logistics actively contributing to prosperity. So the cycle has more efficient logistics that lower the costs of delivered products, encour-age sales, increase trade, open new markets, increase economic growth and employment – and generally increase prosperity, which allows more investment in infrastructure and systems, economies of scale, and generally more efficient logistics. This effect was noticed by Adam Smith in 1776 when he wrote, 'Roads, canals and navigable rivers . . . [are] the greatest of all improvements.'[12] This gives a clear reason for organisations like the World Bank to support infrastructure and trade projects that break into this cycle.[13]

Porter's review of the reasons why nations are prosperous concluded that, 'a nation's ability to upgrade its existing advantages to the next level of technology and productivity is the key to its international success'.[14,15] He described four important factors in this upgrade:

1. *factor condition* – the key factors that affect a country's ability to host industry (such as resources, education and infrastructure) and create a competitive advantage
2. *demand conditions* – related to customer demand in the local economy, including the market size, types of demand, buyer sophistication, marketing
3. *supporting industries* – which include the availability, competitiveness and effi-ciency of commercial services like banking, insurance, legal services – and logistics
4. *company strategy, structure and competition* – which give the market structure and features of domestic competition.

This is clearly a simplified view, but it begins to suggest the enormous range of factors that affect a nation's economic strength. The result is the observed fact that different countries have different trading features that need different types of logistics.

Major markets

Until a few years ago, the world's major economies were the USA, Japan, Germany and the UK. Now there have been changes with the arrival of China and India, as illustrated in Table 6.2.[16]

The economies of China and India have been growing at around 10% a year for some time, fuelled by their exports. Several other countries have achieved this kind of rapid development, with Japan being a classic example. In the 1950s Japan was still suffering from the effects of the Second World War, with outdated industry, insufficient capacity and old-fashioned products. But by the 1960s its 'economic miracle' was under way as it developed new industrial methods and high quality products aimed specifically at export markets. These strategies were clearly successful, and Japan soon came to dominate international markets such as motorcycles, cameras, steel, computers and cars, and grew into the world's second largest economy. This success was founded on a combination of new operations, and efficient logistics that could support the export-led growth. Over time, Japan's domestic economy grew, and its industry moved away from exporting to become multinational and then global.

Perhaps surprisingly, Japan's logistics were slower to develop than their manufacturing. The logistics Industry has been dominated by small

Table 6.2 GDP of major countries and trading areas

GDP (US$ trillion)

1. Countries	
USA	13.1
China	10.2
Japan	4.2
India	4.2
Germany	2.6
UK	1.9
France	1.9
Italy	1.8
Russia	1.7
Brazil	1.7
2. Free Trade Areas	
NAFTA	15.4
EU	13.1
3. World	
All countries	66.0

operations – perhaps based on historical government preferences, and the system of keiretsu, which forms many informal relationships. The resulting supply chains have many intermediaries, and they tend to be both long and complex.

Other countries followed Japan's lead, particularly the 'Asian Tiger' economies of Singapore, Taiwan, South Korea and Hong Kong. The whole area of the Pacific Rim – which actually refers to countries in the south-east of the Pacific – realised that they could become more prosperous through international trade. Most recently, China has followed the same route, developing its manufacturing industry to become 'the world's factory', concentrating on exports for growth. China has now overtaken Japan as the world's second largest economy, and is moving up to challenge the USA. India is now following China, and has moved into a period of rapid growth to become the world's fourth largest economy.

Experience clearly shows that economic growth comes from increasing trade, but historically many artificial barriers have been raised to limit the free movement of products. Typically, one country will protect a domestic industry by prohibiting or taxing imports, and then trading partners will retaliate by imposing their own restrictions. In recent years, there have been enormous moves to remove these barriers. The most common arrangements are bilateral agreements, where two countries look for closer cooperation and mutually beneficial trading arrangements. But there have been several more widespread agreements notably the European Union (EU) and North America Free Trade Agreement (NAFTA). The benefit of these agreements comes in forms like the tripling of Mexican trade with the USA in the 12 years after NAFTA came into effect in 1994, and the doubling of Poland's exports in the five years after joining the EU in 2002.

The EU has expanded, from its original six members in 1951 to 27 members in 2007. This creates a single market with a population of 490 million people and a gross regional product of US$13.1 trillion. In many ways, the economies of EU countries are converging – helped by the removal of trade barriers and the move towards the euro as a standard currency (adopted by 12 members in 1999, with Slovenia joining in 2007). However, there are still widespread differences between markets – illustrated by separate languages, culture, laws and geography. The GDP per capita ranges between US$7000 and US$69,000,[16] and this is considerably lower in new members than in the older ones. This difference between newer and older members is also clear from a logistics perspective, with recent members having relatively poor infrastructures, particularly roads, transport links, banking, telecommunications and trading arrangements.

NAFTA was established in 1992 as an agreement between the USA, Canada and Mexico. This is a much looser union than the EU, focusing on trade, but without the underlying trend towards political and social harmonisation. The three members have a combined GDP of US$15.4 trillion which, in principle, makes it the world's largest free trade area. However, it is dominated by the USA which has 85% of production. Supporters say that it is rapidly helping the Mexican economy to catch up with the USA and Canada; critics say that it allows

American companies to use cheap labour in Mexico to replace expensive labour in their home markets.

The third largest free trade areas is the Association of Southeast Asian Nations (ASEAN) which was formed by Indonesia, Thailand, Philippines, Malaysia, Vietnam, Singapore, Myanmar, Cambodia, Laos and Brunei. The total GDP is closer to $2 trillion,[17] and this is more variable and prone to political instability.

Many other agreements are listed by the World Trade Organization,[18] such as the Common Market for Central and Southern Africa, Greater Arab Free Trade Area, Central American Common Market, South Asia Free Trade Agreement, and a surprisingly large number of others.

Differences in logistics

We might characterise NAFTA countries as having generally good logistics infrastructure, long transport distances, relatively low population densities, high costs, only three languages and two international borders. The EU is geographically much smaller, has generally good (but variable) infrastructure, higher population density – but there is much more variation in the 27 countries that it comprises. South-east Asia is characterised by high populations, lower GDP per capita, worse infrastructure, but low costs. It is immediately clear that firms cannot simply move the same logistics methods from one area to another – and international logistics are different from national logistics. Some common features that make international logistics different include the following:

- Longer distances are travelled, increasing both transport costs and delivery times.
- There are more changes between transport modes and carriers, giving complex routing.
- There are more disruptions, such as international borders, or waiting for transport.
- Order sizes are larger to compensate for the difficulties and cost of transport.
- Demands are more erratic, and affected by many factors.
- There are more intermediaries, such as freight forwarders and customs agents.
- The intermediaries and distances involved make relations with customers and trading partners more difficult and remote.
- Communications are more difficult at a distance, and across language and cultural barriers.
- Financial arrangements, conditions and terms of trade vary and are unfamiliar.
- Organisations have less experience with international logistics, so they are working in areas where they have less expertise'.

- Documentation, regulation, laws, legal systems, government policies, and so on, are more complicated and less familiar.
- There are more risks from failures, accidents, incidents, problems, and so on.

These differences – and many others that might be encountered – suggest that global logistics is inevitably more complex and difficult. So it is worth listing some common problems with global logistics.

Problems with global logistics

International logistics are inevitably complicated, and present a whole new range of problems for managers. If you imagine a simple transaction, where an organisation buys materials in one country, and arranges for them to be delivered to another country, you can begin to see the complications. It is not just a question of sending someone to pick up the materials and transport them. The transaction also involves international banks to arrange finances and exchange currencies, one government's regulations on exports and another government's regulations on imports, customs clearance with duties and taxes, transport operations in both countries, some mechanism for transferring materials between transport operators and across borders, translators for documents written in different languages, lawyers to check the contracts and conditions, insurance, and so on. There is a surprising number of people involved in even a small transaction – and a surprising number of possible difficulties.

Some of the difficulties are practical, such as physically moving materials across a frontier and organising transport over longer distances; some are cultural, such as speaking new languages and meeting different customer demands; some are economic, such as obtaining local currency to pay local taxes and tariffs. As the EU moved towards a single market, it identified three types of problem that are due to:

- **physical barriers** – such as natural features, international borders, customs procedures
- **technical barriers** – such as different communications infrastructure, safety standards
- **fiscal barriers** – such as tax regimes, rates of value-added tax and excise duty.

We can add some details to this list and illustrate some typical problems that managers face with international logistics.

- *Political and legal systems.* The types of government and legal systems give significantly different trading conditions in different countries. Practices that are accepted in one country may be unacceptable – and even illegal – in a neighbouring country. You can imagine an example of this before the two parts of Germany were reunited in 1990, when stepping from West Germany to East Germany meant a change from a free market economy with systems aligned to western Europe (including private transport) to a centrally planned economy with systems aligned to the east (including nationalised transport).

- *Economic conditions.* Often aligned with political systems are the economic conditions, with significant differences in prosperity, disposable income and spending habits. Again, these can change very rapidly by, say, crossing the border between the USA and Mexico or between North and South Korea.

- *Technology available.* Logistics companies often need sophisticated technologies for e-commerce, satellite location, in-cab navigation, real-time routing, package tracking, and a whole range of other activities. Of course, this does not mean that every logistics company uses the highest technology available – or that the technology is available in every location. Most of the world does not have access to, does not need, or cannot afford the latest technology. In many areas the movement of goods still depends on manual effort and bullock carts, with a lorry as the most advanced technology available.

- *Infrastructure.* The quality of infrastructure varies widely, with particular differences between developed and industrialising regions. For instance, it is normal practice to use containers in many regions, but there are few large container ports in the whole of Africa. Similarly, India has one of the world's largest road networks, but of the 3.5 million kilometres of roads less than half is paved and 40% of villages are not connected by all-weather roads.[19]

- *Social systems and culture.* It is usually easier to trade with someone who has similar culture, habits, expectations, language, and so on. And it is easier for a company working in Belgium to open new facilities in France than, say, Iran. You might assume that these differences are only important if dealing with widely separate locations – but many people who live very close together seem to have very little in common, while other people who live far apart seem to be closely related.

- *Finance.* There can be many difficulties with finance, particularly when banking systems are not well developed. Some countries do not allow their currency to be exported; the value of some currencies fluctuates wildly or falls quickly; some banking systems are inefficient; sometime exchanging money is difficult; credit and debit cards do not work; interest rates are high; local tax regimes are difficult to work with, and so on. A different type of problem arises with customs duties and tariffs for materials entering a country (which we mention in the following section).

- *Competition in logistics.* Historically, many countries felt that transport was a sufficiently important national resource to need close control or even government ownership. The result was a small, tightly regulated industry with little or no competition. This is far less frequent now, following widespread privatisation and deregulation. But you can still see the effects in, for example, national airlines. The amount of competition in logistics still varies widely and ranges between intense, market-driven competition through to state run monopolies.

- *Geography.* Transport is normally easier in straight lines over flat terrain. So crossing the American prairies is easy, but problems grow in the Rockies to the West. Physical barriers hinder transport and these can include seas, mountain ranges, desserts, jungles, rivers, cities, national parks and many other obstacles.

- *Customs.* It is often the practical details that make the movement of materials across international frontiers time-consuming and irritating – and you hear of deliveries that are held up for days, simply because the driver cannot speak the same language as the customs people. In the days of the Soviet Union, it used to take two or three days for a lorry to cross the border between Poland and Germany – since Poland joined the EU this delay has been eliminated.

- *Documentation.* Traditionally, it has taken a lot of paperwork to move goods internationally. Much of this is now handled electronically, and free trade areas have removed the need for most administration – but there can still be problems, largely when each country sets its own regulations and requirements. Any mistakes in documentation can cause a lot of misunderstanding and long delays. Surveys[20] typically suggest the main problems met by exporters are:

Main problem	Percentage of exporters
export documentation	23
transportation costs	20
high import duties	17
cannot find foreign representatives with enough knowledge	16
delay in transfer of funds	13
currency fluctuations	12
language barrier	10
difficult to service products	10

The most common documents needed to move goods internationally are:

- *Certificate of origin* – shows the country in which the goods were produced, to assess tariffs, comply with government restrictions on trade, and allow statistical recording.

- *Commercial invoice* – is written by the supplier to describe the materials carried and the terms of trade. This allows goods to move through customs, and is the invoice that must be paid by the customer.

- *Packing list* – gives the detailed contents of each package in the shipment, and is used by customs and in any insurance claims.

- *Bill of lading (or waybill)* – is issued by the shipping company (or other transport operator) and is a contract for carrying materials, defining legal responsibilities, and is used to transfer ownership to named parties.

○ *Commercial letter of credit* – is a contract between the customer and a bank, which transfers responsibility for paying for materials to the bank.

○ *Bill of exchange* – is a means of arranging payment for materials, by requesting the customer's bank to collect and transfer payment to the supplier's bank. When this is done the ownership of materials (and related documents) are transferred to the customer.

○ Insurance certificate – explains the type of insurance cover for the materials.

LOGISTICS IN PRACTICE – BORDER CROSSINGS

Crossing international borders can be very time consuming. Lorries driving across the European Union might cross most borders without even slowing down, but when they hit the Belarus border they may be delayed for days rather than hours. You can see some of the reasons for this when considering the border between Mexico and the USA.

NAFTA was signed between the USA, Canada and Mexico in 1994. This liberalised trade, it allowed Mexico to protect local trucking companies by prohibiting USA and Canadian firms from operating within Mexico for ten years. Until this condition ran out, companies moving materials from the USA to Mexico had to follow a strange ritual at the border. This had a US carrier delivering goods in a trailer to a point close to the border. This company had lower rates than its Mexican counterpart, but it could not transport materials in Mexico, or even move them through the border. So a cartage agent took over the paperwork and organised the trailer's move through customs and across the border. There a Mexican carrier picked up the trailer, and completed the onward the journey to customer. Later the Mexican carrier returned the empty trailer to a point near the border, where a cartage agent again moved it through customs and across into the USA, and a US haulier could pick it up and return it.

Such systems are not unusual, and they cause many delays. In extreme cases, governments may simply close borders, meaning that nothing can move across. However, the most common cause of delays is queries over paperwork. Customs agents can sort most of these out fairly quickly, but EDI gives an opportunity for faster processing – and particularly with pre-clearance. Here a firm sends a message ahead to a customs point that its vehicle is soon arriving at a border. The message gives details of materials carried, owners, destination, value, contact points, and any other relevant information. If all goes smoothly, customs clearance is agreed before the vehicle arrives, and it can continue its journey with little interruption. This is particularly useful for marine transport, where most deliveries are cleared by customs before they arrive at a port.

Question

- If free trade areas are so beneficial, why are border controls not reduced to give a free movement of goods?

(*Source*: Helfont, G. (2002) Customs clearance in NAFTA, Logistics Forum; Anon. (1994) Clearing customs, Materials Management and Distribution, November, 24)

International frontiers

As you can see from the last example, many problems of global logistics actually occur at borders, at the point when goods are trying to leave one country and enter another. On the whole, entering a new country is more difficult than leaving an old one (and you hear occasional stories of people leaving one country, moving across the border and then being refuse entry to the next country – and when they turn around to return to the country they left, being refused permission to re-enter). Each border can mean different conditions and restrictions on movement – and tariffs to be paid. Even paying the tariffs is not always easy, as there can be a range of different taxes, duties and rates in the calculations. For instance, materials entering the European Union might have to pay customs duty, excise duty, import VAT, countervailing duties, anti-dumping duty, common agricultural policy levies, and compensatory interest. These tariffs are not levied at fixed rates, and in 2000 Grainger[21] quoted the duty on a television tube entering the EU as 14% from Malaysia, 9.8% from Thailand, 7.3% from South Africa and 0% from Poland (which was not then a member).

If materials cross a series of frontiers they might, in principle, have to pay these costs at each, but countries rarely charge duties of materials that are simply moving through, meaning that duty only becomes payable at the final destination. To allow normal operations, ports are normally declared as duty free zones, which means that duty only becomes payable when materials leave the port. These zones can be extended to duty free warehouses or larger areas around container ports, where goods are stored until they are taken to final customers. Free trade areas like the EU extend this idea, as duty is only paid when materials enter the union – which is seen as the final market – and inside the area there is free movement.

Sometimes duty really is charged on goods in transit. For instance, in 2007 Belarus announced that it would charge a duty of US$6.50 for every barrel of oil moving through a pipeline across the country from Russia to Western Europe.[22] Their argument was that both Russia and Western Europe benefited from the pipeline across their country, but Belarus gain no economic benefit at all. However, this illustrates the point that not everybody is in favour of removing barriers at international borders or encouraging trade. Some people argue that there should be strict controls to:

- prevent goods that are considered undesirable from entering a country
- protect domestic producers from foreign competition
- generate revenue for the host country
- collect statistics on trade.

Supply chain intermediaries

Not surprisingly in such a complex field, a range of intermediaries has grown to help arrange international logistics. These fall into two main types:

1. *Firms that operate facilities within the supply chain* – These are firms that actually move the materials such as international transport operators, shipping lines, port operators, export packers, public warehouse operators, and so on.

2. *SERVICES that help administer movements* – These are firms that do not actually move materials themselves but somehow assist the smooth flow of materials. For instance, a customs house broker makes sure that documentation is correct and facilitates the movement of materials through customs; and international freight forwarders consolidate loads and are experts in arranging international deliveries.

Most of these intermediaries are involved in transporting goods, so we consider them again in Chapter 13.

Chapter review

- Many factors encourage international trade, ranging from growing international prosperity to the formation of free trade areas, like the European Union.

- As a result of these factors, international trade continues to grow quickly. All such trade depends on efficient logistics to move materials quickly and cheaply around the world.

- The continuing growth of aggregate global trade is a result of individual decisions in thousands of organisations, who see the benefits of expanding into new, international markets.

- An organisation does not necessarily have to work internationally itself to have a presence in oversees markets. In particular, it has six options that range from licensing and exporting, through limited local facilities, and on to full local production.

- International operations inevitably mean that some organisations must work in different countries. There are several ways these can be organised, including international, multinational and global. There is a general trend towards global operations, which see the world as a single integrated market.

- Each type of operation has different requirements of the supply chain. There are many different models, but global supply chains often have common features.

- Despite the view of global markets, there are considerable differences between countries and areas. One of the main factors affecting logistics is the relative strength of an economy. Here there is a cycle with economic strength allowing efficient logistics, which in turn encourage further economic growth.

- Traditionally governments have built barriers that disrupt the free movement of materials, but increasing these barriers have been removed in free trade areas such as the EU and NAFTA.

- There can be many problems for international logistics. These come in different forms, but they are generally a result of physical, technical or fiscal barriers. Many problems appear at international borders, where intermediaries can help smooth journeys.

CASE STUDY – O'DAID GROUP

Sean O'Daid runs part of a family business in Cork, Ireland, producing a range of natural conditioners for gardens. The main product is peat. This is dug from local bogs owned by the company, dried, shredded to give a uniform texture, treated to remove unwanted material and then compressed for packing into 25 kg and 50 kg bags. These are delivered throughout Ireland, but highest sales are in the south around Cork, and east around Dublin.

Over the past 20 years, trade has varied, depending on the state of the economy and enthusiasm for gardening (which is often affected by television programmes). A more serious problem is the environmental damage done by peat extraction, which is encouraging gardeners to look for environmentally friendly alternatives. O'Daid Garden Products is a small company, but they extract more that 10,000 tonnes of peat a year. Continuing at this rate of extraction, their accessible reserves will last about a century. Sean summarises this situation by saying, 'we have lots of peat in the ground, but demand is certainly falling, and is likely to go even lower. We are actively developing new materials as alternatives to peat, but these are more expensive and will probably be more attractive in the longer term. In the medium term we want to exploit our existing reserves, and get a smooth transition to the new products. In particular, we want to increase current peat production, and start exporting to the UK and rest of Europe.'

Sandra O'Daid runs another part of the family business. She imports materials to make a range of high-value Celtic jewellery, which she exports to 42 countries around the world. Her materials are largely gemstones and precious metals from Southern Africa and Australia. Her main exports are to the countries around the Pacific Rim, particularly Singapore and Australia. Last year sales from her traditional customers fell slightly, and she started looking for sales in the Middle East and South America.

Questions

- How would you compare the logistics requirements of these two parts of the family business? What problems are they each likely to face? How can these be overcome?

- Do you think that expanding internationally is a reasonable strategy for Sean? Can he learn anything from Sandra's experience?

Project – parcel transport

Suppose that you want to send a parcel of books weighing 100 kg from Copenhagen, Denmark to Lima, Peru. How would you set about finding the options available for making the move?

What do you think is the best route? Describe in detail the journey of your package, and list the people involved in each stage. What specific problems would you meet?

Rather than acting as an individual, imagine that you work for a major publisher that wants to send 100 kg of books a week in Peru. How would this affect your approach to logistics?

Discussion questions

6.1   What are the main differences between logistics within a single country and logistics that span a number of different countries? What are the specific problems of working internationally?

6.2   By their nature, all supply chains must be international. Do you think this is true?

6.3   Is it always best to locate factories in areas that give lowest production costs?

6.4   Some regions of the world present particularly difficult problems for logistics. What regions do you think are most difficult to work in, and why?

6.5   Companies adopt many patterns for ownership and operations when they work internationally. What are the most successful patterns?

6.6   Global operations are a simplistic ideal that can never work in practice. Do you think this is true?

6.7   Where are the world's largest free trade areas? Do they really allow free trade between members? What benefits do these bring?

6.8   If free trade is such a good idea, why do countries not simply remove all their duties and tariffs on trade?

6.9   If you were delivering a truckload of materials through a series of international borders, what problems might you expect to meet. How could you reduce or avoid these?

6.10 Why are companies moving towards global operations? What are the implications for logistics?

References

1. Leontiades, J.E. (1985) Multinational business strategy, D.C. Heath & Co., Lexington, MA.
2. World Trade Organization (2008) International trade statistics, WTO, Geneva and Website at www.wto.org.
3. IMF (2008) World economic outlook, International Monetary Fund, Washington.
4. Ohmae, K. (1985) Triad Power – the coming shape of global competition, Free Press, New York.
5. Grainger, A. (2000) Globalisation – implications for supply chains, Logistics and Transport Focus, 2(2), 46–7.
6. Anon (1998) World trade systems at 50, Financial Times, 18 May.
7. Eurostat (2007) Transport statistics, European Commission, Brussels, and Website at www.eurostat.ec.europa.eu.
8. Julius, D.A. (1990) Global companies and public policy, Royal Institute of International Affairs, London.
9. Levitt, T. (1983) The globalization of markets, Harvard Business Review, May/June.
10. Christopher, M. (1989) Customer service strategies for international markets, Council of Logistics Management International Conference, Oak Brook, IL.
11. Jain, S. (1989) Standardisation of international marketing strategies, Journal of Marketing, 53, January.
12. Smith, A. (1776) The wealth of nations, London.
13. Website at www.worldbank.org.
14. Porter, M. (1990) Why nations triumph, Fortune, 12 March, pp. 54–60.
15. Porter, M. (2000) The competitiveness advantage of nations, Free Press, New York.
16. CIA (2007) The world factbook, Central Intelligence Agency, Washington, DC and www.cia.gov.
17. Website at www.aseansec.org.
18. Website at www.wto.org.
19. Planning Commission (2002) Indian economic road map: the next five years 2002–2007, Government of India, New Delhi.
20. Waters, D. (2007) Problems with global logistics, Richmond Associates, New York.
21. Grainger, A. (2000) Customs and international supply chain issues, Logistics and Transport Focus, 2(9), 40–3.
22. Heintz, J. (2007) Belarus files case against Russian company, The Associated Press, www.abcnews.go.com.

7

LOCATING FACILITIES

Contents

LEARNING OBJECTIVES

After reading this chapter you should be able to:

- understand the scope and importance of location decisions

- discuss factors that affect the choice of location

- review some current trends in business location

- describe a hierarchical approach to facility location

- discuss important factors in the choice of region to work in

- understand infinite set approaches to location, illustrated by the centre of gravity

- compare locations using costing and scoring models

- appreciate the use of network models for locating facilities, illustrated by the median and covering problems.

Location decisions

In Chapter 6 we looked at some aspects of global logistics, and the reasons why products are increasingly moved around the world. This raises questions about the location for operations and related facilities. Organisations have to make decisions about locating their facilities every time they start new operations, whether it is Toyota building a new assembly line, Carrefour opening a new store, CEVA Logistics deciding where to build a warehouse, or Pfizer moving into new markets.

Facilities location
finds the best geographic
locations for different
elements in a supply chain

> • Facilities location **finds the best geographic locations for different elements in a supply chain.**

In practice, location decisions are needed whenever there are major changes. For instance, manufacturing costs are now lower in China, so many companies are moving their manufacturing plants; in the same way, call centres are locating in Mumbai, India; financial services in London; high technology companies in Silicon Valley; oil wells in Siberia, and so on. The reasons for such moves include:

- the end of a lease or tenure on existing premises
- expansion of the organisation into new geographical areas
- changes in the locations or requirements of customers or suppliers
- changes to operations, such as just-in-time production or an electricity company moving from coal generators to gas
- reorganisations, perhaps reducing the number of tiers in a supply chain
- improved facilities, perhaps introducing new technology
- changes to transport, such as a switch from rail to road
- changes to the transport network, such as the opening of the Channel Tunnel or the road bridge between Sweden and Denmark
- mergers, acquisitions or changes of ownership that give duplicate facilities.

Importance of location decisions

In Chapter 4 we showed how the length and breadth of a supply chain defined its essential shape, and now location decisions show where each element is sited. By implication, this also considers the number of facilities, their sizes and relationships. Location decisions are important because they affect an organisation's performance over many years. A company might invest millions of dollars in opening new facilities, and if it makes a mistake and chooses a poor site it cannot simply close down and move somewhere better. Working in the wrong place may be expensive, but moving to a new site may cost even more.

As you can imagine, choosing the best location is an old problem, which people have been working on for many years. Early villages were built in good growing areas, settlements grew near to river crossings, and castles were built on promontories. Then when industry arrived, weavers set up near water power, steel mills were built near iron ore deposits and coal mines, ports appeared near deep water inlets, and so on. In the nineteenth century Von Thünen[1] did some formal analyses for the value of crops at different locations in terms of the costs of land and transporting the crops to market. In the twentieth century analysts such as Weber[2] built on this work to consider a wide range of location problems.

The underlying message behind location decisions is that choosing the right site does not guarantee success, but choosing the wrong site certainly guarantees failure. Nissan opened a highly successful assembly plant in Washington in the north-east of England – and they put a lot of effort into choosing this site, which became Europe's most productive car plant. But if they had chosen a poor location, they could have had low productivity, unreliable suppliers, poor materials, low quality products and high costs. This reasoning shows why nightclubs do not open in residential areas filled with retired people, big petrol stations avoid country lanes where there is no passing traffic, factories stay away from city centre with their high costs, and railway stations are usually near to town centres.

This seems obvious, but you can find many examples of organisations working in the wrong place – and often going out of business. Sometimes, it is not obvious that a location is poor, and you might see an attractive site near a town centre where a string of cafes or clothes shops open and quickly close down. At other times, organisations forget that location decisions are for the long term and are tempted by short-term benefits, such as development grants, temporary rent reductions, or tax breaks. Such sweeteners can be attractive, but they rarely form the basis of good long-term decisions. Unfortunately, over the long term, conditions can change, and you can see examples of organisations making the right decisions. But circumstances change – such as garages that were in good locations before a new by-pass opened, small shops that worked well before a new supermarket arrived, or mines where the ore reserves were exhausted.

Alternatives to locating new facilities

Location decisions are always difficult, and you might think that one way of avoiding them is to stay in the same place. However, this is still a location decision, as it assumes the current site is the best – and it is certainly better than moving operations somewhere else. In practice, when an organisation wants to change its facilities – either expand, move or contract – it has three alternatives:

1. expand or change operations at an existing site
2. open additional facilities at another site, while maintaining operations at the existing site (perhaps modified in some way)
3. close down existing operations and move all operations to a new site.

As a rule of thumb, around 45% of companies expand on the same site; this is the most conservative option that involves least risk and can give economies of scale. The rule of thumb also suggests that 45% of companies open additional facilities. The remaining 10% of companies close down existing operations and move; this is the most radical option, which is often disruptive and has very high costs.

Even when new facilities are clearly needed, there are different ways of managing them – as we mentioned in Chapter 6. For instance, a manufacturer that wants to expand into a new market can consider the following:

1. licensing or franchise operations, which requires no new facilities

2. exporting finished goods from existing facilities, which may need expansion of existing production facilities

3. Local sales and distribution, which might need expansion of existing production facilities and then opening a distribution system in the new market

4. Local assembly and finishing, which might need some adjustments to existing facilities, with new production and distribution facilities in the new market

5. Joint venture/full local production, which is the most radical alternative and means that major new production and distribution facilities are needed in the new market.

Trends in location

When organisations look at their operations and business environment, it is not surprising that they often see similar conditions – and come to similar choices about locations. This is the reason that certain regions, countries, towns or trading estates become popular, as many organisations recognise independently that they are the best place to locate. For instance, many logistics companies in the UK build facilities around Birmingham, as the city within easiest reach of the main centres of population.

On a broader front, we have already mentioned some trends in location, such as the obvious growth of China as a manufacturing centre. Many factories are opening there to serve the export trade, so they are largely located near to ports along the eastern coastline. As areas in China – particularly around Hong Kong and Shanghai – become more industrial their operating costs rise, and now factories are moving inland to less developed areas. Other areas that have seen rapid industrial development are south-east Asia (following the lead of Japan, Singapore, Taiwan, South Korea and China as global traders), central Europe (for increasing trade with the EU) and the Maquiladoras factories on Mexico's northern border (to serve the USA).

Apart from the growing popularity of specific regions and areas, there are other types of trend in location, such as a growing number of out-of-town shopping malls, supermarkets and retail estates. This, together with the growth of e-business, means that traditional high streets often find it difficult to compete, and are in a relative decline. At the same time, the move towards shorter supply chains means that layers of intermediaries are disappearing and logistics is concentrated into fewer facilities that serve wider areas. An obvious example is the EU, where companies can replace small, national warehouses by a single European logistics centre. At a lower level, the growth of just-in-time operations has seen many suppliers moving physically closer to manufacturers, e-businesses looking for the economies of scale that come with centralisation, and services moving into cities to be close to the growing populations.

This movement of population is interesting, as many aspects of logistics ultimately depend on the distribution of populations. So they are affected by major movements of people from, say, central to Western Europe, from central to North America, and from Southern Asia to Europe. Alongside these are less dramatic moves of, say, rural dwellers into cities – and corresponding moves of many city dwellers into the countryside.

The important point about these trends is that they all emerge from individual organisations choosing the best locations for their operations. They do formal analyses and reach similar conclusions. The following example outlines the approach to one location decision, which determines the expenditure of billions of dollars.

LOGISTICS IN PRACTICE – LOCATION OF THE 2012 OLYMPIC GAMES

The Olympic Games take place every four years in a different location. Although the cost of hosting them runs into billions of dollars, it is widely felt that they bring long-term gains. This brings competition to run the games, so the International Olympic Committee (IOC) has a formal procedure for choosing each location. This procedure itself costs each applicant millions of dollars and requires several years of preparation.

Nine 'applicant cities' submitted bids for the 2012 Olympic Games – Havana (Cuba), Istanbul (Turkey), Leipzig (Germany), London (United Kingdom), Madrid (Spain), Moscow (Russian Federation), New York (USA), Paris (France) and Rio de Janeiro (Brazil). The International Olympic Committee (IOC) examined each city's ability to host the games, and evaluate the strengths and weaknesses of their plans. There were two phases in this evaluation. The first phase lasted about ten months, during which the applicant cities answered 25 questions that gave an overview of their proposals. A working group of IOC administration members and external experts did a technical assessment of the answers, looking at areas such as government support, public opinion, general infrastructure, security, venues, accommodation and transport. The IOC Executive Board then chose a shortlist of cities to be accepted as 'candidate cities'.

In May 2004 five candidate cities were announced as London, Madrid, Moscow, New York and Paris. The second phase of the selection procedure called for detailed plans within six months. These were studied and analysed by the IOC Evaluation Commission, which visited each city and evaluated the bids' performance in a number of areas that are critical to the successful organisation of the games.

A hierarchy of decisions

Location decisions are always difficult. Managers have to consider many different factors – and there are serious consequences for making mistakes. Some of the factors in location decisions can be measured – or at least estimated – such as operating costs, wage rates, taxes, currency exchange rates, economic growth, number of competitors, distances from customers and suppliers, development grants, population and reliability of supplies. Other factors are non-quantifiable, such as business strategies, quality of infrastructure, political stability, social attitudes, industrial relations, legal system, culture, lifestyle, climate, and so on. To include all of these factors, managers need a hierarchy of decisions. At the top of this are broad decisions about the geographic regions to work in. Then come more local decisions about countries or areas within this region. Then they look more closely at alternative cities and towns within this area. Finally, they consider different sites within a preferred town (as shown in Figure 7.1). For instance, in 2005 the clothes retailer C&A decided to expand their retail network into central Europe. They looked at various countries and decided to open branches in Poland. Then they looked at cities within Poland and decided to open a branch in Warsaw. After looking at available sites, they opened a store in the city centre opposite the Cultural Palace.[3]

We can include this hierarchy in a general approach that coordinates location decisions with other decisions about the supply chain, particularly fitting it into the logistics strategy.

1. *Review the aims of a supply chain.* A logistics strategy and other plans specify the goals to be achieved by location decisions. This gives the context and requirements of any location.

2. *Do a logistics audit*, to describe the current logistics system, including the location of facilities, connecting network, measures of performance, and industry benchmarks. This shows how well the current supply chain is achieving its requirements.

3. *Identify mismatches*, between goals (from Step 1) and actual performance (from Step 2).

4. *Examine alternatives for overcoming the mismatch*, looking to see how and where the structure of the supply chain can be improved. This step considers the effects of alternative supply chain configurations including general locations for facilities. This might identify the best areas for locations.

5. *Make location decisions*. Having considered the general features of a supply chain in Step 4, this step considers alternative sites that are available and chooses the best. This adds most detail, moving from areas down to choosing a specific site.

6. *Confirm the location*, making sure that the location identified in Step 5 really is best, and adding details of the facilities to be built or changed, capacities, resources available, and so on.

7. *Implement and monitor the solutions*, doing whatever is needed to execute the changes and continuing to check performance.

This procedure emphasises that the hierarchy of location decisions must fit into the broader logistics strategy. If the logistics strategy calls for short delivery times, then facilities must be in locations that can achieve these; if the strategy calls for

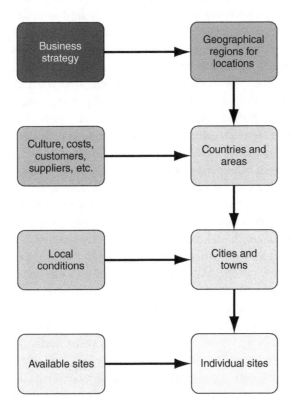

Figure 7.1 Hierarchy of decisions for locations

low costs, facilities will probably be centralised to get economies of scale. The main decisions about locations are made in Steps 4 and 5, and these set the overall shape of the supply chain, which should be designed to achieve the broader organisational aims. In particular, Step 4 gives decisions in principle along the lines of, 'We need a warehouse in the Benelux countries.' Then Step 5 considers the sites that are actually available and identifies the best. Step 6 adds commercial and other details needed to finalise the choice of site. Unfortunately, this procedure is rarely as easy as it seems, and it usually needs a lot of iteration through the steps before it gives a satisfactory solution.

Choosing a geographical region

The broadest decisions about geographical regions and countries come from the business strategy. For instance, an organisation with a strategy of global operations or expansion must continually look for new locations, while other strategies might specify operations in a particular market, or close to suppliers. Such strategies led Toyota to open plants in the USA to be near to the major car market, and Exxon operate in the Middle East to be near to sources of oil. These two examples illustrate one view of location, which is to choose a site that is near to either customers or suppliers. Unfortunately, it is rarely possible to be close to both suppliers and customers, so managers have to find some kind of balance.

Another problem is added when organisations want low operating costs, as these often come at sites that are some way from both customers and suppliers. Then firms have to make sure that lower operating costs are not swamped by higher logistics costs. For example, large, efficient steel mills in Japan, Taiwan and South Korea have low operating costs – but importing coal, oil and iron ore, and then moving finished steel to customers is so expensive that their delivered price is high. Similarly, SAB Miller brew very good beer in South Africa, but little of it is imported to Europe because of the high transportation costs.

Managers have to balance operating and logistics costs, recognising that areas with low operating costs do not always give the lowest total costs. This balance is more difficult than it seems. People often assume that low wage areas inevitably give low operating costs, but this is not always true. For a start, there may be a string of additional costs ranging from unexpected employment taxes through to constraints on currency exchange. Then low wages might be accompanied by very low productivity – and there is no point in halving wage rates if productivity is cut by three-quarters. This is particularly relevant for automated processes where wages form a very small part of overall costs. It makes little sense for a high-tech company to move away from its main markets and support services to work in a low wage economy when wages amount to only 2% of its costs.

The problem of balancing operating and logistics costs is made more difficult by the rapid variations in both – perhaps caused by moving exchange rates, taxes, inflation or oil prices. In 1980 the Tandy Corporation decided to move production of its latest computer to South Korea to take advantage of low operating costs. Then rising shipping costs, long lead times for the sea voyage to the USA, changing value of the dollar and more automation in the process, encouraged them to reconsider their location. In 1987, they moved back to Fort Worth, Texas and reduced costs by 7.5%. This is the argument that Dell used to justify a new plant in North Carolina, where a spokesman reported that, 'The cost of moving a PC around is much more than the labour cost of building one, so we locate close to customers.'

LOGISTICS IN PRACTICE – MILLICRA ELECTRONIC COMPONENTS

Millicra Electronic Components grew as a supplier of parts to the US motor industry. Until 1997 their operations were based in Pittsburgh and Detroit, and their main customers were assembly plants around Detroit. Although their processes were largely automated, their costs were high by world standards, and they worked in an intensively competitive market where cost reduction was a priority.

In 1998 the main US car manufacturers – General Motors, Ford and Chrysler – were all planning assembly plants in the Philippines. These would meet the rapidly growing domestic market, which was currently dominated by Japanese manufacturers (Toyota 22%, Mitsubishi 21%, Honda 12% and Nissan 11%) and they would give a low cost production base for export to other countries in the region.

Millicra made a decision to join the car makers in the Philippines. Rather than spread production over three sites, they decided to close their plants in America, giving the advantages of:

- production costs that were much lower in the Philippines than in America
- they could get economies of scale from a single location
- they could introduce the latest methods and technology
- they would be near a growing market, with easy transport back to their existing customers
- the Philippine government gave a six-year income tax holiday and other tax breaks
- there was a pool of cheap labour ready for training.

The company allowed six months to open their new plant, and another six months to sort out problems and get things running smoothly. Then they laid off all the staff at their US plants, with only one experienced manager accepting the company offer of a job in the Philippines. Millicra found it fairly easy to recruit staff in Manila, but language and cultural problems became more obvious when they started training. It was surprisingly difficult to implement new procedures, and there were a series of problems with supervision, training and working practices. Overall, productivity was lower than expected and costs were considerably higher.

LOGISTICS IN PRACTICE – MILLICRA ELECTRONIC COMPONENTS   (CONTINUED)

There were also problems with transport, with shipping costs rising and increasing the cost of importing components and delivering finished products to the US. The long sea journeys increased risk and uncertainty, tied up stock in the supply chain and slowed responses to both customers and suppliers.

By 2001 Millicra's old customers in the USA had formed alliances with new local suppliers, and general economic conditions meant that local demand around the Philippines was lower than forecast. Millicra could see no end to their problems, and ceased trading in August 2001. However, the US management felt that there were still opportunities and they formed a new company in 2002, again working in Detroit.

Question

- Can you find other examples of companies moving to low cost areas and subsequently returning to their original locations?

(*Sources*: Marozzi, J. (1998) Chrysler and GM follow Ford's path to Philippines, Financial Times, 17 April; Scarborough, J. (2007) Coming home, Detroit Financial Review, 14 November)

Important factors when choosing a region

We have mentioned the location of suppliers and customers and the operating costs, but many factors might make one region more attractive than another.[4, 5] Traditional economic theory takes a rather passive view and says that a region's attractiveness comes from the inherent features of land, labour, location, local population size and natural resources. This has been refined to more positive views, such as Porter's,[6, 7] which we mentioned in the last chapter as describing the attractiveness in terms of factor conditions (key factors that encourage production), demand conditions (related to customers in the local economy), supporting industries (typically commercial services) and company strategy, structure and competition (the general state of competitiveness).

In practice, the attractiveness of a region is judged by more specific features, with the following list including the most common. Managers should consider these, and all the other relevant factors, before making a strategic decision to use locations in a particular region. Cushman & Wakefield considered 15 factors when considering the location of distribution centres in Europe and concluded that Belgium was ranked first, followed by France, the Netherlands and the Czech Republic.[8]

- *Location of customers and markets*. Service providers often need personal contact with their customers, so they have to be physically close – which is why you find shops, busses, libraries, restaurants, solicitors and banks in the centre of towns. Similar arguments hold for manufactured goods that have a low value density – which is why you also find local bakers, brewers, dairies and egg producers. Being close to customers allows firms to reduce delivery costs and give high levels of service.

- *Location of suppliers and materials.* Manufacturers are more likely to locate near to supplies of raw materials, particularly if these are heavy or bulky. This is why power stations are close to coal mines, steel works are close to iron ore, and pulp mills are near to timber forests. Some operations have to be close to perishable materials, which is why fruit and vegetable processors are close to farms, and frozen seafood companies are near fishing ports.

- *Location of competitors.* This can make a location less attractive when competitors offer similar products and are aggressively fighting for a larger share of a fixed market. This means that you rarely find two hospitals next door to each other. On the other hand, it can make a location more attractive when a cluster of similar organisations attract new customers and consolidate expertise. You often see the results when a cluster of banks open in a commercial centre, or nightclubs open in the same street.

- *Infrastructure and availability of transport.* It is essential to have appropriate transport to move materials. Often this means access to a good road network, but it might also mean links to rail, air, sea or pipelines – or intermodal terminals.

- *Culture.* It is easier to expand into an area that has a similar language, culture, laws and costs, than to expand into a completely foreign area. Then a company currently operating in Belgium would find it easier to expand into France than, say, Korea. The decision to build Disneyland Europe near Paris is an interesting example of a very successful American company that had initial problems with a new location in Europe.

- *Government attitudes.* National and local government policies can seriously affect attractiveness. Some governments do not welcome foreign investment, usually because they want to control foreign influences; and investment in, for instance, Myanmar fell when a less welcoming government came to power. But most governments give incentives to attract companies to an area. This can be aimed at encouraging certain types of industry (particularly high technology, finance, oil or leisure companies) while restricting access to others (perhaps nuclear, chemical or polluting industries).

- *Direct costs.* These are the costs of operations, including wages, materials, overheads, utilities, transport, interest rates, construction, and so on. Clearly, the most attractive locations offer a combination of low direct costs and high performance. Unfortunately, lower costs often mean lower productivity, so managers look for a balance – which might encourage them to accept high costs as a means of getting related benefits.

- *Indirect costs.* These include local taxes, currency exchange rate variations, restrictions on exporting funds, inflation, and charges on the payroll such as social insurance, pension and social costs. These can also appear as controls on local operations and ownership, typically insisting that a local company has a controlling interest in a joint venture.

- *Social attitudes*. Some countries put more emphasis on social welfare than others – and they might have higher union membership, protective legislation and emphasis on individual rather than corporate benefits. Other regions do not necessarily admire high productivity and there might be higher absenteeism and staff turnover. These – together with skills, education levels, unemployment rates and related factors – are often summarised in terms of a 'labour climate'.

- *Quality of life*. It is difficult to measure, or even describe, a region's quality of life – but it essentially shows how much people like living there. This typically depends on a range of factors like climate, housing, health care, education, cost of living, crime, the environment, public transport, recreation facilities, state of the arts, and so on. An attractive quality of life means that it is easier to recruit and retain employees, as well as suppliers and customers.

- *Local control*. We saw in Chapter 6 that there are differences between international, multinational and global operations. If you go into a McDonald's restaurant anywhere in the world you will see virtually identical operations. It is easier to control operations in this way, but it loses the benefit of local knowledge and practices. Other organisations blend into the local environment and adapt their operations so they are more familiar to their host countries.

- *Organisational strategy*. Apart from all the rational factors, an organisation – or more realistically its senior managers – might simply prefer some locations to others.

LOGISTICS IN PRACTICE – MCDONALD'S CORPORATION

McDonald's is almost an emblem of globalisation, with one of the world's best known brands and images. It has 450,000 employees in 120 countries, serving 55 million customers each day, so there are few companies with greater experience of locating in new markets. But they still have problems in some locations. For instance, some French people complained at the very notion of fast food; in 2002 Hindus found that French fries contained traces of beef extract; and any anti-American sentiments are inevitably channelled towards McDonald's.

Some of the problems with entering a new market emerged in 1990 when the world's largest McDonald restaurant with 700 seats opened in Pushkin Square, Moscow. This branch is operated jointly by McDonald's of Canada and local Russian companies, with negotiations having started 20 years previously with the Soviet Union.

The inside of the restaurant is exactly as you would expect, with the standard menu, colour scheme and decor, staff training, levels of cleanliness and cooking. Everything follows the standard McDonald's pattern, but this was only achieved after considerable effort. As well as the initial political problems, there were serious practical difficulties. When the restaurant opened, beef was not readily available in Moscow and the quality was variable. So McDonald's had to import breeding cattle and start a beef farm to supply the restaurant. Potatoes were plentiful, but they were the wrong type to make McDonald's fries; so seed potatoes were imported and grown. Russian cheese was not suitable for cheeseburgers, so a dairy plant was opened to make the right processed cheese. Staff were not used to McDonald's standards, and they needed special training – but the company could be selective as 27,000 people answered a single 'help wanted' advertisement.

When it opened the Pushkin Square branch was an immediate success, and 30,000 customers formed a queue half a mile long outside – and it is still the world's busiest branch. There are now more than a hundred outlets in Russia serving a quarter of a million customers a day, and in 2006 the company was named as 'The best employer in Russia'.

(*Sources*: www.mcdonalds.com; Cockburn, P. (2000), Big Mac, big trouble, The Independent, 14 November)

Models for location

After making a decision about the geographical region, an organisation has to look in more detail at areas and then individual sites. There are many analyses to help with this decision, usually based on some kind investigation of costs. One approach that is *not* recommended is personal preference. Managers often seem to be subjective and choose sites they like – perhaps in the town where they live or grew up in, or where they spend their holidays. These decisions may be successful, but they are unreliable and often lead to very poor choices – because you like spending your holidays in a particular town, it does not mean that this is the best location for a business.

There are two distinct approaches to location decisions:

1. infinite set approach – which uses geometric arguments to find the best location, assuming that there are no restrictions on site availability
2. feasible set approach – where there are only a small number of feasible sites that managers have to compare and choose the best.

Infinite set approach
uses geometric arguments to find the best location, assuming that there are no restrictions on site availability

Feasible set approach
where there are only a small number of feasible sites so that managers have to compare and choose the best

An infinite set approach finds the best location in principle, and then managers can look for an available site nearby; a feasible set approach compares sites that are currently available and chooses the best. These approaches are often used together, with an infinite set approach homing in on the best area to locate, in principle, and then a feasible set approach comparing available sites nearby.

Infinite set approaches

Many different approaches can look for the best location in principle[9] and we can illustrate their general approach by finding the centre of gravity of demand. This method was formalised in the 1940s, when Hoover[10] described three basic policies. Managers can locate a facility near to customers, or they can locate it near to suppliers, or they can compromise and put it somewhere in between (as illustrated in Figure 7.2).

A location near to customers gives fast customer service and low costs for transport out to customers – but long journeys in from suppliers. Conversely, a location near to suppliers moves products quickly into the supply chain and gives low costs for inward transport – but now there are long journeys out to customers. If we add the two transport costs together we typically get the graph shown in Figure 7.3. This suggests that a compromise location somewhere between customers and suppliers balances the costs and gives the lowest total.

A way of finding this compromise location calculates the centre of gravity of supply and demand.[11] This looks at the map coordinates (X, Y) of each customer

Centre of gravity
the centre of supply and demand defined as the point (X_0, Y_0), where $X_0 = \sum XW / \sum W$ and $Y_0 = \sum YW / \sum W$

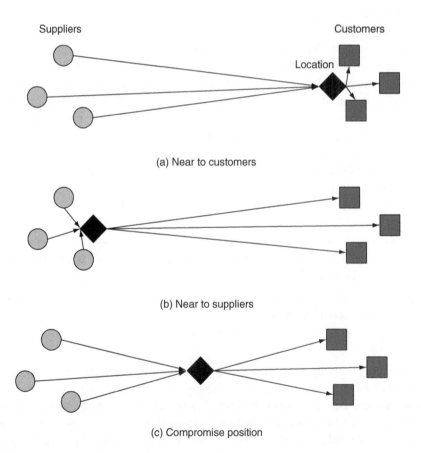

(a) Near to customers

(b) Near to suppliers

(c) Compromise position

Figure 7.2   Alternative policies for location

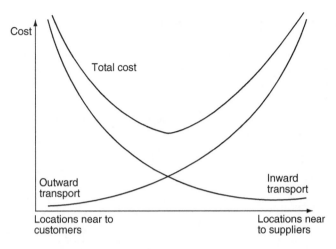

Figure 7.3 Variation in transport cost with location

and supplier and finds the weighted average of them. In particular, it calculates the centre of gravity (X_0, Y_0) from:

$$X_0 = \frac{\sum X_i W_i}{\sum W_i} \qquad Y_0 = \frac{\sum Y_i W_i}{\sum W_i}$$

Where: (X_0, Y_0) are the coordinates of the centre of gravity
(X_i, Y_i) are coordinates of each customer and supplier, i
W_i is expected demand at customer i, or expected supply from supplier i

We can illustrate this calculation by a small example.

WORKED EXAMPLE

Van Hendrick Industries is building a central logistics centre to collect components from three suppliers, and send finished goods to six regional warehouses. The map coordinates for these and the weights to be moved are shown in Figure 7.4. Where is the centre of gravity of demand?

Answer

Figure 7.4 shows a spreadsheet with the location of customers and suppliers, along with the calculation for the centre of gravity. You can see that columns E and F calculate $X_i W_i$ and $Y_i W_i$ respectively, with the sums given in cells E18 and F18. Dividing each of these by the total weight given in cell D18 gives the calculations:

$$X_0 = \frac{\sum X_i W_i}{\sum W_i} = \frac{16,380}{360} = 45.5$$

$$Y_0 = \frac{\sum Y_i W_i}{\sum W_i} = \frac{18,108}{360} = 50.3$$

which confirms the result given in the spreadsheet.

WORKED EXAMPLE   (CONTINUED)

	A	B	C	D	E	F
1	**Centre of gravity**					
2						
3						
4		**X**	**Y**	**Weight**	**X*Weight**	**Y*Weight**
5	**Supplier**					
6	S1	91	8	40	3640	320
7	S2	93	35	60	5580	2100
8	S3	3	86	80	240	6880
9						
10	**Warehouse**					
11	W1	83	26	24	1992	624
12	W2	89	54	16	1424	864
13	W3	63	87	22	1386	1914
14	W4	11	85	38	418	3230
15	W5	9	16	52	468	832
16	W6	44	48	28	1232	1344
17						
18	**Totals**			**360**	**16380**	**18108**
19						
20	**Centre of**			**X =**	**45.5**	
21	**Gravity**			**Y =**	**50.3**	

Figure 7.4   Calculation of centre of gravity

A good place to start looking for locations is around (45.5,50.3). As this is very close to warehouse 6 it is probably better to expand on this site rather than look for an entirely new location (as shown in Figure 7.5).

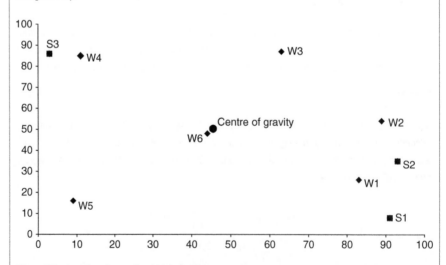

Figure 7.5   Locations for van Hendrick Industries

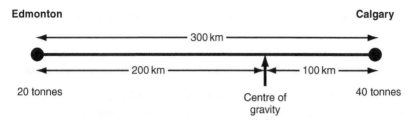

Figure 7.6 A weakness of the centre of gravity location

The centre of gravity often gives a reasonable location, but you have to be a bit careful. We can easily show this by considering a location decision in Alberta, Canada. Suppose that you want a warehouse to deliver 20 tonnes of materials a day to Edmonton and 40 tonnes a day to Calgary. These two cities are connected by a straight road 300 km long (as shown in Figure 7.6). If the costs of getting deliveries from suppliers are the same regardless of location, where would you build a warehouse?

Taking the coordinates of Edmonton as (0,0) and those of Calgary as (300,0), the centre of gravity is:

$$X_0 = \frac{(40 \times 300 + 20 \times 0)}{60} = 200$$

$$Y_0 = (40 \times 0 + 20 \times 0) = 0$$

So the centre of gravity is at (200,0) or 200 km from Edmonton. A warehouse here would have to move $200 \times 20 = 4000$ tonne-kilometres to Edmonton and $100 \times 40 = 4000$ tonne-kilometres to Edmonton, giving a total of 8000 tonne-kilometres. But if you built the warehouse in Calgary, you would only have to move $20 \times 300 = 6000$ tonne-kilometres to Edmonton. This suggests a rule of thumb, which says that a good location is in the centre of highest demand.

Adjusting the centre of gravity

We can improve the basic centre of gravity model in many ways, such as using actual road distances rather than map coordinates for the calculation. Often the speed of delivery is more important that the distance, so we can replace distance by travel time, or we can use some more direct measure of cost. Another approach uses an iterative calculation, which keeps searching for a better location near to the centre of gravity. For instance, we might try an initial location and then iteratively improve it using the equations[12]:

$$x^{n+1} = \frac{\sum W_i X_i / d_i}{\sum W_i / d_i}$$

$$y^{n+1} = \frac{\sum W_i Y_i / d_i}{\sum W_i / d_i}$$

where: x^{n+1} and y^{n+1} are the next iterated values for the facility coordinates
X_i and Y_i are the coordinates of customers and suppliers
W_i = weight moved to or from location i
d_i = distance from the previous iterated location of the facility to location i

Beyond this we have to use a more sophisticated optimising model, usually based on linear programming. These look for a theoretical optimal solution, but they are much more complicated. The extra effort may not be worth while, as more complex models do not guarantee better results, and the answers are still based on a series of approximations and assumptions. For instance, a company will rarely know in advance the exact locations of its customers or the amounts they will buy. Just as importantly, the models cannot include all the real complications or any non-quantifiable factors.

Regardless of how sophisticated the model, all infinite set approaches have the weakness that their suggested locations may not be practical. For instance, there may be no suitable site available anywhere near the solution, or available sites may be too expensive, or further development may be prohibited, or there may be no roads or workforce, or the solution might be at the top of a mountain or in the sea.

LOGISTICS IN PRACTICE – WAREHOUSE LOCATIONS IN THE USA

We can often use the population of an area as a surrogate for demand. The population of Stockholm is three times the population of Oslo, so we can assume that the demand for a wide range of products is also three times as large. Then we can look at the population distribution, and use the centre of gravity of population to approximate the centre of gravity of demand.

In the UK the centre of gravity of population is near to Birmingham, and this might be a useful place to start looking for a facility. In the USA the centre of gravity of population is at Bloomington, Indiana.

We can go further with this approach and find the best locations for more facilities. For instance, in continental USA the following locations give shortest lead times to customers.

Number of facilities	Best locations	Average lead time (days)
1	Bloomington, IN	2.3
2	Ashland, KY; Palmdale, CA	1.5
3	Allentown, PA; Palmdale, CA; McKenzie, TN	1.3
4	Lancaster, PA; Palmdale, CA; Chicago, IL; Meridian, MS	1.2
5	Summit, NJ; Palmdale, CA; Chicago, IL Dallas, TX; Macon, GA	1.1
6	Summit, NJ; Pasadena, CA; Chicago, IL; Dallas, TX; Macon, GA; Tacoma, WA	1.1

With nine facilities, the average lead time is 1.04 days, and at this point there is little benefit in adding a tenth location.

Question

• Where would the best locations be for facilities in Europe?

(*Sources*: Chicago Consulting (2008) Ten best warehouse networks. Chicago, IL: Chicago Consulting; Anon. (1998) Are you putting goods in the right location? Purchasing 124(6), 115; website at www.chicago-consulting.com)

Feasible set approaches

Feasible set approaches consider a small number of sites that actually are available, compare them, and identify the best. An obvious analysis for this calculates the total cost of working from each location. In practice, the costs of running a facility may be largely fixed regardless of its location, and then instead of looking at all the costs we can concentrate on the variable ones. Then we might find that:

$$
\begin{array}{llll}
\text{Total variable} & \text{Variable} & \text{Inward} & \text{Outward} \\
\text{cost of using} & = \text{operating} & + \text{transport} & + \text{transport} \\
\text{a location} & \text{cost} & \text{cost} & \text{cost}
\end{array}
$$

Unfortunately, even this is difficult, as we have already said that managers cannot know the real costs before they actually open a facility. For example, how can they know the cost of outward transport when they do not know exactly who their customers will be, where they are located, or how much they will buy? Even with good forecasts, demands and costs change over time and the analysis soon become outdated.

On the other hand, the strength of cost calculations is that they are useful for comparisons, even when they do not necessarily show the real costs that will be incurred. If the analysis shows that one location costs £5000 a week, while another costs £10,000, this gives a useful comparison, even if the figures are only surrogate measures rather than accurate forecasts.

WORKED EXAMPLE

Bannerman Industries want to build a depot to serve seven major customers located at coordinates (100,110), (120,130), (220,150), (180,210), (140,170), (130,180) and (170,80). Average weekly demands, in vehicle loads, are 20, 5, 9, 12, 24, 11 and 8, respectively. Three alternative locations are available at (120,90), (160,70) and (180,130). Which is the best site if operating and inward transport costs are the same for each?

WORKED EXAMPLE   (CONTINUED)

Answer

Figure 7.7 shows a sketch of the locations for customers (1–7) and possible depots (A–C). We only have a limited amount of information for comparisons, so we may as well make the calculations as easy as possible. For a start, we can assume that operating costs and inward transport costs are about the same for each location, so we do not need to consider them. We do not know the exact costs of delivering to each customer, but we can assume that the transport cost is proportional to the distance moved. In fact, we can use another shortcut here and assume that the transport cost is proportional to the rectilinear distance between points, where this is defined as:

Rectilinear distance between two points is the difference in x coordinates plus the difference in y coordinates

Rectilinear distance = Difference in X coordinates + Difference in Y coordinates

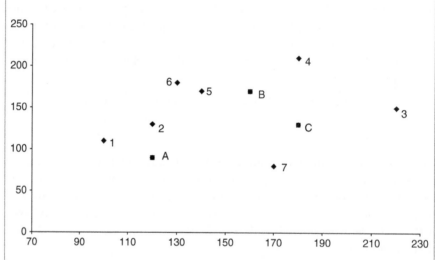

Figure 7.7   Locations for Bannerman Industries

Customer		Site A		Site B		Site C	
	Load	Distance	Distance * Load	Distance	Distance * Load	Distance	Distance * Load
1	20	40	800	120	2400	100	2000
2	5	40	200	80	400	60	300
3	9	160	1440	80	720	60	540
4	12	180	2160	60	720	80	960
5	24	100	2400	20	480	80	1920
6	11	100	1100	40	440	100	1100
7	8	60	480	100	800	60	480
Totals			8580		5960		7300

Figure 7.8   Comparison of three sites

Then the rectilinear distance from site A to customer 1 is:

difference in X coordinates + difference in Y coordinate $= (120 - 100) + (110 - 90)$

$$= 20 + 20 = 40$$

Now rather than using costs we can compare locations using the surrogate measure of total load $\times$ rectilinear distance moved. Figure 7.8 shows these calculations, and as the best location gives lowest values, site B is clearly the best.

Number of facilities

We can use a variation of the costing model to consider a related question, which asks how many facilities to use. The principle here is that each additional facility gives a smaller benefit. You can see this effect with the US warehouses described above, where moving from one location to two gave a significant improvement in the service, but moving from nine to ten made almost no difference. This suggests that there is some optimal number of facilities, beyond which the extra costs are greater than the likely benefits. We can find this optimal number using the following argument.

- When an organisation concentrates activities in a few key locations – such as main logistics centres – inward transport consists of a few large deliveries and the cost is low. However, the facilities are, on average, further away from customers, and the outward transport costs are high (as illustrated in Figure 7.9a). This option generally gives lower customer service, and is used when cost is a major consideration.

- When there is a large number of facilities – such as retail shops – inward transport consists of small deliveries to more destinations and the cost is high. However, facilities are, on average, nearer to customers, so they have the benefits of higher customer service and lower outward transport cost (as illustrated in Figure 7.9b).

- Operating costs also vary with facility size, with larger facilities generally more efficient and giving economies of scale. (But remember that larger facilities do not necessarily give economies of scale, and there can be real 'diseconomies' caused by higher cost of supervision, coordination, communication, and so on.)

If we plot these transport and operating costs against the number of facilities, we typically get the pattern shown in Figure 7.10. Adding the three costs gives a U-shaped curve with a minimum that corresponds to the optimal number of facilities. This suggests the best number of facilities, but managers have to consider a whole range of other factors before making such an important decision, such as management overheads, communications, fixed costs, employment effects, customer service, information flows, and so on.

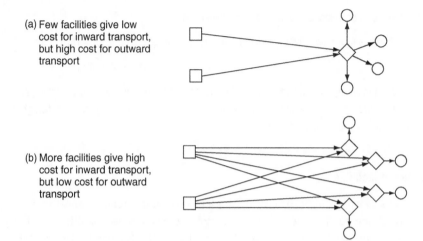

(a) Few facilities give low cost for inward transport, but high cost for outward transport

(b) More facilities give high cost for inward transport, but low cost for outward transport

Figure 7.9   Variation in transport cost with the number of facilities

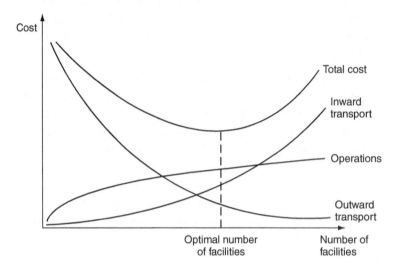

Figure 7.10   Finding the optimal number of facilities

Scoring models

Costing models can give useful comparisons, but they have weaknesses, including the difficulty of finding accurate costs, data that depends on accounting conventions, costs that vary over time, customer locations not being known in advance, order sizes not known in advance, factors that cannot be costed, and so on. Because of these, it is often better to use some other measures for comparison. The most common alternative is a scoring model.

Scoring models focus on the different factors that are important for locations, but which cannot easily be costed or quantified. For example, a location with an attractive lifestyle would certainly benefit employees, reduce employee turnover

Scoring model
assigns a range of factors, weighted scores to compare locations

and assist in recruiting – but it is impossible to give a realistic measure of lifestyle. This is a common problem and Andel[13] say that, 'More often than not, the decision on site selection is based upon factors you can't always put in a matrix or express quantitatively.'

We have already seen the type of factor that is important in selecting a region to work in, and can develop similar lists for the more detailed decisions. For instance, Gooley[14] says that the important factors are infrastructure, proximity of suppliers and customers, political and tax considerations, and international trade conditions. A more detailed list of factors includes:

- **In the country and area**

  - availability, skills and productivity of the workforce
  - local and national government policies, regulations, grants and attitudes
  - political stability
  - economic strength and trends
  - climate and attractiveness of locations
  - quality of life – including health, education, welfare and culture
  - location of major suppliers and markets
  - infrastructure – particularly transport and communications
  - culture and attitudes of people.

- **In the city or town**

  - population and population trends
  - availability of sites and development issues
  - number, size and location of competitors
  - local regulations and restrictions on operations
  - community feelings
  - local services, including transport and utilities.

- **In the site**

  - amount and type of passing traffic
  - ease of access and parking
  - access to public transport
  - organisations working nearby
  - total costs of the site
  - potential for expansion or changes.

Although we cannot quantify these factors directly, we can move in this direction by awarding each a score. You see this approach with hotels, where it is difficult to measure their quality, but the best are awarded five stars and lower quality ones have fewer stars. This idea of assigning subjective scores is the basis of scoring models. These need the following five steps:

Step 1. Decide the most important factors for location decisions.

Step 2. Give each factor a maximum possible score that shows its importance.

Step 3. Consider each location in turn and give it an actual score for each factor, up to the maximum.

Step 4. Add the total score for each location and find the highest.

Step 5. Discuss the result and make a final decision.

WORKED EXAMPLE

Williams-Practar considered five possible locations for a new warehouse to distribute their musical instruments throughout South-east Asia. After many discussions they compiled a list of important factors, their maximum scores, and actual scores for each site. What is the relative importance of each factor? Which site would you recommend?

Factor	Maximum score	A	B	C	D	E
Climate	12	9	6	10	7	5
Infrastructure	20	14	12	14	7	13
Accessibility	10	6	8	7	9	9
Construction cost	7	5	1	4	3	1
Community attitude	8	6	8	7	3	8
Government views	5	2	1	3	5	3
Closeness to suppliers	15	10	9	12	13	10
Closeness to customers	20	12	9	16	17	10
Availability of workforce	5	1	2	4	5	3

Answer

The most important factors are those with highest maximum scores, which are the infrastructure and closeness to customers, with 20 points each. The closeness of suppliers is a bit less important with up to 15 points, and then come climate, accessibility and community attitude.

Adding the scores for each location gives:

Location	A	B	C	D	E
Total scores	65	56	77	69	62

These scores suggest that location C is the best. The company should now consider all other relevant information before coming to a final decision.

Important factors in scoring models

We have just listed some factors that might be included in such models, but the details of these and their relative importance depends on the circumstances. For instance, a manufacturer might aim for economies of scale by building a large factory near to raw materials, and its decision is dominated by:

- availability of a large site
- closeness of suppliers and services
- quality of infrastructure
- availability of a workforce with appropriate skills
- labour relations and community attitudes
- environment and quality of life for employees
- government policies towards industry.

On the other hand, services may use smaller locations that are near to customers, and their decisions put more weight on:

- population density
- socioeconomic characteristics of the nearby population
- location of competitors and other services
- location of other attractions such as retail shops
- convenience for passing traffic and public transport
- ease of access and convenient parking
- visibility of site.

The objectives in locating factories and services are clearly different, which is why town centres have shops but no factories, and industrial estates have factories but no shops.

LOGISTICS IN PRACTICE – INTEL IN COSTA RICA

Deloitte & Touche Fantus developed a list of factors that high tech industries consider in their location decisions. This includes:

- *Essential factors*:
  - skilled and educated workforce
  - proximity of research institutions
  - attractive quality of life
  - access to venture capital.
- *Important factors*:
  - reasonable cost of doing business
  - established technology industry
  - adequate infrastructure
  - favourable business climate and regulations.

LOGISTICS IN PRACTICE – INTEL IN COSTA RICA
(CONTINUED)

- *Desirable factors*:

    ○ established suppliers and partners

    ○ community incentives.

One company that considered such factors in a key location decision was Intel. This American corporation was founded in 1968 and is now the world's leading producer of semiconductor devices. They are best known for computer chips, but they make 450 products with annual sales of $35 billion. In the mid-1990s the company was planning a new expansion, and was considering a location in Costa Rica. To encourage Intel, the Costa Rican government offered eight years free of income tax, followed by four years at half rate, duty free import of materials, and unrestricted movement of money into and out of the country. In addition, they granted licences to foreign airlines to increase the number of international flights, built a new power sub-station for the site, reduced the cost of electricity by 28%, and reduced the liability for corporation tax.

Intel decided to locate a $300 million semiconductor testing and assembly plant near San Jose, and by 2000 this employed 2000 people. A spokesman for Intel said that, 'When we are considering a site we use a multifaceted set of criteria. Incentives are part of this.'

Question

- What factors are generally important for the location of high tech industries?

(*Sources:* Anon. (2000) Wall Street Journal Special Report. 25 September; Multilateral Investment Guarantee Agency (2008) Foreign Direct Investment Survey. Washington: World Bank and websites at www.iinteractive.wsj.com and www.miga.org)

Combining the two approaches

We have outlined several models for location, but these are by no means the only ones and a huge amount of work has been done in this area. Useful models range from simple rules of thumb (such as, 'locate near to similar firms that is already working successfully') through to complex optimisation methods (such as mathematical programming). But these methods need not work in isolation and they can be combined to give more thorough views. For instance, we could use an infinite set approach to find the best general area, followed by a finite set approach to compare available sites in the area. A formal procedure for this has the following five steps:

Step 1. Identify the features needed in a new location, determined by the business and logistics strategies, structure of the supply chain, aims, customers, and other relevant factors. Look for global regions that can best supply these.

Step 2. Within the identified region, use an infinite set approach – such as the centre of gravity or similar model – to find the best area for locations.

Step 3. Search around this area to find a feasible set of available locations.

Step 4. Use a feasible set approach – such as a costing model or scoring model – to compare these alternatives.

Step 5. Discuss all available information and come to a decision.

Locating facilities is always difficult, and it is important enough for organisations to look at every available analysis before reaching a conclusion.

Network models

Sometimes it is difficult to relate the models we have described so far to actual road layout and geographical features. But another type of model specifically considers the road layout. There is a huge variety of models, but we can illustrate their approach by two standard ones, known as the single median problem and the covering problem.

Single median problem

Imagine a cluster of towns connected by a network of road. There are demands for some product in each town, and you want to locate a depot to deliver to these towns. An interesting result here is that the best location is always in one of the towns.[15] So we only have to compare locations in each town and identify the best.

Suppose that you want to find the location with the shortest average travel distance to all customers. This is called the single median problem. To find the single median you form a matrix of the shortest distances between each pair of towns. Now the average of each column in the matrix shows the average distance from one town to all the others. So the column with the lowest average identifies the single median.

Single median problem finds the location with the shortest average travel distance to a set of customers

---

WORKED EXAMPLE

Ian Bruce delivers goods to eight towns, with locations shown in Figure 7.11. Which location minimises the average delivery distance?

Answer

We start by building a matrix to show the distances between each pair of town, as shown in Figure 7.12.

This shows that DI is an average of 11.3 from the other towns, and as this is the lowest, DI is the single median.

When there are different amounts to be delivered at each town, we should weight the distances by the amount moved. If the figures by each town in Figure 7.11 show the amount to be delivered, how does the affect the single median?

Instead of finding the average distances in each column, we have to multiply these by the weights shown in column B of Figure 7.13. Taking one column, say C: this shows the distance from AL

WORKED EXAMPLE   (CONTINUED)

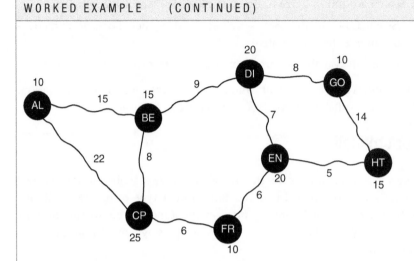

Figure 7.11   A map of Ian Bruce's single median problem

Single median calculation

	AL	BE	CP	DI	EN	FR	GO	HT
AL	0	15	22	24	31	28	32	36
BE	15	0	8	9	16	14	17	21
CP	22	8	0	17	12	6	25	17
DI	24	9	17	0	7	13	8	12
EN	31	16	12	7	0	6	15	5
FR	28	14	6	13	6	0	21	11
GO	32	17	25	8	15	21	0	14
HT	36	21	17	12	5	11	14	0
Totals	188	100	107	90	92	99	132	116
Average	23.5	12.5	13.4	11.3	11.5	12.4	16.5	14.5.

⇧
Lowest

Figure 7.12   Single median calculations for Ian Bruce

to each other town, and multiplying this by the corresponding weight in column B gives the weight-distance between AL and each other town. Adding these down the column gives the total weight-distance for a logistics centre in AL, shown in Row 14.

$$Weight - distance\ of\ a\ centre\ at\ AL = (10 \times 0) + (15 \times 15) + (25 \times 22) + (20 \times 24)$$

$$+ (20 \times 31) + (10 \times 28) + (10 \times 32) + (15 \times 36)$$

$$= 3015$$

Dividing this by the number of deliveries, eight, gives the average weight-distance. Repeating this calculation for each of the other town gives the results in Row 15, with EN now the lowest.

	A	B	C	D	E	F	G	H	I	J
1	Weighted single median calculation									
2										
3										
4		Weight	AL	BE	CP	DI	EN	FR	GO	HT
5	AL	10	0	15	22	24	31	28	32	36
6	BE	15	15	0	8	9	16	14	17	21
7	CP	25	22	8	0	17	12	6	25	17
8	DI	20	24	9	17	0	7	13	8	12
9	EN	20	31	16	12	7	0	6	15	5
10	FR	10	28	14	6	13	6	0	21	11
11	GO	10	32	17	25	8	15	21	0	14
12	HT	15	36	21	17	12	5	11	14	0
13										
14	Totals	125	3015	1475	1485	1330	1275	1395	2080	1690
15	Average	15.6	376.9	184.4	185.6	166.3	159.4	174.4	260.0	211.3
16							↑			
17										
18							Lowest			

Figure 7.13   Weighted Single median problem

Covering problem

Sometimes the average distance or time to a facility is less important that the maximum. Classic examples of this are fire engines and ambulances, which try to respond to emergencies within a maximum time. In the same way, suppliers might guarantee deliveries within a specified period. This is the basis of the covering problem.

There are two versions of the covering problem. In the first version, an organisation wants the single location that gives the best service to all towns – in other words, it wants the lowest value for the maximum time needed to reach any town. A company might find that a warehouse in Vienna could reach any of its customers within 12 hours, while a warehouse in Prague could reach any customer within ten hours. Then Prague is clearly better. To solve this type of problem we simply compare the longest journey times from each location, and choose the location with the shortest.

The second version of the covering problem specifies a level of service that must be achieved, such as a delivery guaranteed within five hours. The problem is then to find the number of facilities needed to achieve this. As with all such problems we do not need to worry about the calculations, as a lot of software does this automatically.

Covering problem
finds the location with the best maximum delivery lead time

WORKED EXAMPLE

Figure 7.14 shows part of a road network, with the travel time (in minutes) shown on each link. Where would you locate a depot to give best customer service? How many depots would be needed to give a maximum journey of 15 minutes?

Answer

Figure 7.15 shows the results from a simple spreadsheet add-on that solves lots of types of routing problem. This finds the best single location as C, which has a maximum journey of 25 minutes. If this is too much, facilities at A and I will reduce the maximum journey to 15 minutes.

WORKED EXAMPLE   (CONTINUED)

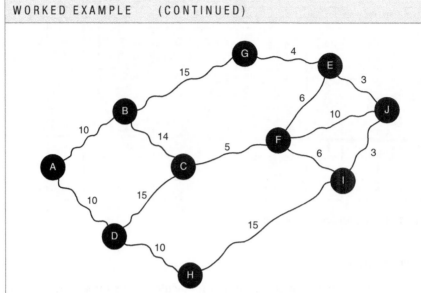

Figure 7.14   Road network showing travel times between locations

Covering problem

Distance matrix

	A	B	C	D	E	F	G	H	I	J
A	0	10	24	10	29	29	25	20	35	32
B	10	0	14	20	19	19	15	30	25	22
C	24	14	0	15	11	5	15	25	11	14
D	10	20	15	0	26	20	30	10	25	29
E	29	19	11	26	0	6	4	23	8	3
F	29	19	5	20	6	0	10	21	6	10
G	25	15	15	30	4	10	0	27	12	7
H	20	30	25	10	23	21	27	0	15	20
I	35	25	11	25	8	6	12	15	0	5
J	32	22	14	29	3	10	7	20	5	0
Maximum	35	30	25	30	29	29	30	30	35	32

Single location	C
Maximum time	25

Two locations   Service assignment

	A	I
A	0	
B	10	
C		11
D	10	
E		8
F		6
G		12
H		15
I		0
J		5
Maximum time	10	15

Figure 7.15   Solution to the covering problem

Chapter review

- Location decisions find the best geographical sites for the facilities in a supply chain. These are important, strategic decisions that largely define the features of the supply chain and have long-term effects on an organisation's performance.

- A location decision is needed whenever there are major changes to an organisation's operations. The choice of best location depends on many different factors.

- Organisations often face similar problems with locations, and come to similar conclusions. This leads to a series of trends in location. Some of these are major, such as the growth of China as a manufacturing centre, while others are smaller in scope, such as the move of rural populations into cities.

- There is a hierarchy of location decisions, which starts with a decision about the geographic region to work in. This is followed by decisions about the best country and area, then the best city, and eventually the best site.

- Location decisions start with a choice of geographical region. The most attractive depends on many factors, ranging from the location of customers to the personal preferences of managers.

- There are two types of model for location decisions. Infinite set approaches use geometrical arguments to show where the best location would be in principle. This gives a starting point for identifying actual sites. We illustrated this with the centre of gravity method.

- Finite set approaches compare a limited number of feasible locations and find the best. We illustrated this by costing and scoring models.

- Sometimes it is better to consider location in the context of a network of towns and roads. There are many models for solving problems on networks, which we illustrated by the median and covering problems.

CASE STUDY – BRENNER REFRIGERATION SALES

John Brenner had worked for the same domestic appliance retailer for over 20 years when he saw an advertisement from a central European manufacturer, which wanted to sell its brand of appliances in the UK. John answered the advertisement and spent a year preparing and negotiating with the manufacturer.

The manufacturer was not keen to have all their distribution done by a new and untried company. In the end, John agreed to set up a company called Brenner Refrigeration Sales, and the manufacturers agreed to give him exclusive rights to distribute their products throughout the UK for two years. The agreement will be reviewed after a year and renegotiated after two years.

John invited three other directors to join the company. Their first problem is to find a location for the head office and main logistics centre. This centre will receive appliances directly from the manufacturer, and deliver them to retailers around the country. The directors realise that their future success depends on this site, but are finding it difficult to agree on a location.

CASE STUDY – BRENNER REFRIGERATION SALES (CONTINUED)

They have considered passing the problem to a management consultant, with estimated costs of £50,000 for an initial report and £125,000 for a more detailed study. Alternatively, the directors could solve the problem themselves. The following summary reviews their initial discussions:

- Stefan Maior worked as a service repairman for many years before being promoted to Service Manager. He is now 54 years old and is looking for an opportunity to make some money for his retirement. Gordon argues that the location should be in Leeds. The appliances could be shipped to Liverpool or Hull, and then brought to Leeds by train. Leeds has a good transport system and it is a major population centre. Two of the directors live in Leeds and they understand local conditions.

- Pradesh Gupta has a degree in Mechanical Engineering, and worked as an economic consultant in central Europe. He knows the manufacturer and is impressed by their progressive attitudes. Pradesh is critical of Stefan's approach as being old-fashioned and relying more on where he feels at home than on sound business criteria. He says that the sale of appliances is likely to depend on the population so they should identify the main centres of population in the UK, estimate sales in each of these, and then do some analyses to find the best location.

- Fiona McGregor worked in a retail bank, specialising in consumer loans. She is now 32 years old and is ambitiously looking for a long-term career that is both challenging and financially rewarding. She does not like the idea of only opening a logistics centre, but says that they should become more directly involved in sales to final customers. They should consider a head office – probably in London – a central receiving area near to a port, and showrooms around Britain. The fastest way of doing this is to take over an existing retailer, or several retailers, to give coverage throughout the country.

- John Brenner says that Fiona McGregor's scheme is too ambitious, while the other two put the convenience of the company above the customers. He says there is only one way to sell appliances and that is to give customers a product they want in a location they can get to. John's idea is to open a logistics centre to serve retailers, combined with a cash-and-carry warehouse for sales direct to customers, typically generated through the company website or direct marketing. To find the best location, they can see where successful distributors already work, and open facilities nearby.

The time for a decision is now running short. The directors are concerned that if they delay any longer the manufacturer will consider them indecisive, and give a harsh review at the end of the first year. To build entirely new premises would take more than a year. Alternatively, they could find existing premises that are empty, or they could rent temporary premises until the company finds more suitable, permanent premises.

Questions

- If you were a director of Brenner Refrigeration Sales, what would you do now?
- What kind of facilities does Brenner need? What factors are important for their location?
- What location, or locations, would you recommend?

Project – poor locations

Unfortunately, it is quite easy to find examples of companies that open facilities in the wrong location. Historically, ports were built on rivers that silted up and the Victorians built railway stations in open spaces to serve planned towns that never appeared. More recently, container ports were built too far up river so that the largest ships cannot reach them and factories were built to get development grants which soon disappeared (like the Hillman car plant outside Glasgow).

Find an example of an organisation that has made a mistake in locating some kind of facilities, and say why their decisions went wrong. This does not have to be a major development, and you might find a local shop that has changed hands surprisingly often, or a factory on an industrial estate that hardly opened before it closed down.

Problems

7.1 Mai Lao Industries manufacture 70 tonnes of goods a week in factory A and 50 tonnes a week in factory B. The map coordinates of these factories are (14,11) and (54,48), respectively. Goods are delivered to fourteen main customers whose average weekly requirements and coordinates are shown below. The company wants to improve its customer service and decides to open a logistics centre. There are four possible locations located at (20,8), (61,19), (29,32) and (50,22). Assuming that each logistics centre has the same operating costs, which location is best?

Customer	Demand	Coordinates	Customer	Demand	Coordinates
1	4	(11,16)	8	16	(12,69)
2	11	(30,9)	9	2	(27,38)
3	8	(43,27)	10	4	(51,6)
4	7	(54,52)	11	6	(43,16)
5	17	(29,62)	12	3	(54,16)
6	10	(11,51)	13	12	(12,60)
7	15	(8,10)	14	18	(12,3)

7.2 A new electronics factory is planned in an area that is encouraging industrial growth. There are five possible sites. A management team is considering these sites and has suggested the important factors, relative weights and site scores shown below. What is the relative importance of each factor? Which site appears best?

Factor	Maximum score	Scores for sites				
		A	B	C	D	E
Government grants	10	2	4	8	8	5
Community attitude	12	8	7	5	10	5
Availability of engineers	15	10	8	8	10	5
Experienced workforce	20	20	15	15	10	15
Nearby suppliers	8	4	3	6	3	2
Education centres	5	5	4	1	1	5
Housing	5	2	3	5	3	2

7.3 Find the centre of gravity of the data in question 7.1. What would be the transport cost of a distribution centre located there? Can you find a cheaper solution?

7.4 An assembly plant is planned to take components from four suppliers and send finished goods to eight regional warehouses. The locations of these and the amounts supplied or demanded are shown in the following table. Where would you start looking for a site for the assembly plant?

Location	X, Y coordinates	Supply/demand
Supplier 1	(7,80)	140
Supplier 2	(85,35)	80
Supplier 3	(9,81)	120
Supplier 4	(11,62)	70
Warehouse 1	(12,42)	45
Warehouse 2	(60,9)	65
Warehouse 3	(92,94)	25
Warehouse 4	(8,79)	45
Warehouse 5	(10,83)	60
Warehouse 6	(59,91)	35
Warehouse 7	(83,49)	50
Warehouse 8	(85,30)	85

7.5 Pierre Malpasse is opening a logistics centre for his French clothing operations. If the likely demand is proportional to the population, where should he start looking for locations?

7.6 Figure 7.16 shows part of a road network and population of eight towns. Where would you start looking for a location for a new warehouse?

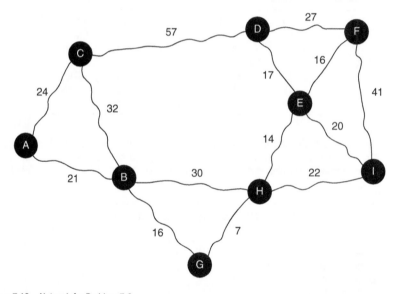

Figure 7.16   Network for Problem 7.6

Discussion questions

7.1   If a company chooses a poor site it can always move to a better one. Such changes are an essential part of business. Do you agree with this?

7.2   Which areas of the world currently have the fastest economic growth? Why? Is this likely to change over the next 20 years?

7.3   What are the most important factors in choosing a region or country to work in?

7.4   A city often has restaurants congregating in one area. Why do businesses form such clusters of similar firms, when each could separate and move away from the competition?

7.5   What costs should you consider when making a location decision? Is cost always an important factor? Are costs distorted by government grants and incentives?

7.6   Mathematical models for location take a simplified view – they make assumptions, approximate values, and only include a few factors that are most easily quantified. How useful are they for real decisions?

7.7   What is the basic difference between infinite set and feasible set approaches to location? Can they be used together?

7.8   What features would you expect to see in computer software that helps with location decisions? Do a survey of relevant packages to see how they work and the kind of analyses included.

7.9   What kinds of problem are solved by network models?

7.10 How has improving technology helped with making business location decisions?

References

1. Von Thünen, J. (1862) The isolated state, Beziehung auf landwirtschaft und nationalökonomie, Hamburg.
2. Weber, A. (1928) Theory of location in industries, University of Chicago Press, Chicago, IL.
3. Website at www.c-and-a.com.
4. McQuaid, R.W. (2004) The importance of transport in business location decisions, Department of Transport, London.
5. McCann, P. (2001) Urban and regional economics, Oxford University Press, Oxford.
6. Porter, M. (1990) Why nations triumph, Fortune, March 12, 1990, pp. 54–60.
7. Porter, M. (2000) The competitiveness advantage of nations, Free Press, New York.
8. Cushman & Wakefield/Healey & Baker (2006) European distribution, C&W/H&B, London and website at www.cushmanwakefield.com.
9. Website at www.mathematik.uni-kl.de/~lola/.
10. Hoover, E.M. (1948) The location of economic activity, McGraw-Hill, New York.
11. Haley, K.B. (1963) Siting of depots, International Journal of Production research, 2, 41–45.
12. Eilon S., Watson-Gandy C.D.T. and Christofides N. (1971) Distribution management, Griffin, London.
13. Andel, T. (1996) Site location tools, Transport and Distribution, June, pp. 77–81.
14. Gooley, T.B. (1998) The geography of logistics, Logistics management Distribution Report, 37(1), 63–66.
15. Ahituv, N. and Berman, O. (1988) Operations management of distributed service networks, Plenum Press, New York.

Further reading

Church, R.L. and Murray, A.T. (2008) Business site selection, location analysis and GIT, John Wiley, Chichester.

Drezner, Z. and Hamacher, H.W. (2007) Facility location: applications and theory, Springer-Verlag, Berlin.

Harrington, J.W. and Warf, B. (1995) Industrial location: principles and practice, Routledge, London.

Hayter R. (1997) The dynamics of industrial location, John Wiley, Chichester.

Mucchielli, J.L. and Mayer, T. (2004) Multinational firms' location and the new economic geography, Edward Elgar Publishing, Cheltenham, Glos.

Salvaneschi, L. (2002) Location, location, location: how to select the best site for your business (2nd edition), Oasis Press, OR.

Schiller, R. (2001) Dynamics of property location, Routledge, London.

Schriederjans, M.J. (1999) International facility acquisition and location analysis, Quorum Books, Westport, CT.

Sule, D.R. (2001) Logistics of facility location and allocation, Marcel Dekker, New York.

Waters, C.D.J. (2007) Global logistics and distribution planning (5th edition), Kogan Page, London.

CAPACITY MANAGEMENT

Contents

LEARNING OBJECTIVES

After reading this chapter you should be able to:

- outline the levels of planning in logistics

- discuss the meaning of capacity

- assess the overall capacity of a supply chain

- describe a standard approach to capacity planning

- describe some methods for adjusting capacity over the long, medium and short term

- discuss systematic changes in capacity over time

- consider the expansion of capacity plans to give medium-term aggregate plans and master schedules.

LOGISTICS IN PRACTICE – EU WORKING TIME DIRECTIVE

The EU's Working Time Directive came into effect in 2005, and this reduced the amount of time that people could work from 55 hours a week to 48. Because of their irregular workloads, lorry drives can work up to 60 hours in a single week, provided that they do not exceed an average of 48 hours in any four-month period.

This effectively reduced the supply of drivers, and hence the capacity of transport fleets. The only way around this is to employ more drivers – but these come at higher costs, especially when there is already a shortage of skilled drivers. The Freight Transport Association estimated that the industry would need another 44,000 drivers, while the Road Haulage Association estimated the annual cost at almost £4 billion.

Lex Transfleet ran a survey to analyse the effects, and found that a typical transport company – with a turnover of £4.5 million, employing 30 people, and running 25 lorries – expected to make 12% more journeys, employ 7 more drivers and buy 2 more vehicles.

Question

- Does restricting the capacity of operations always increase their costs?

(*Sources*: Rowley, J. (2003) Working time directive, *Logistics and Transport Focus*, 5(6), 15–17; website at www.lextransfleet.co.uk)

Strategic plans

Chapter 7 discussed the location of facilities in a supply chain, and touched on closely related questions about the number and size of facilities. Managers may decide to build a single logistics centre, and then they not only have to decide where to put it, but also how big it has to be. Alternatively, they may decide to build a number of local warehouses, and again they have to decide not only where to put them, but how big each one will be.

- Three related decisions about facilities are:
  - *the number* – how many facilities to use
  - *the locations* – where to put them
  - *the size* – how big each one is.

Of course, using more locations means that each one is smaller. The other general rule discussed in the last chapter is that large, centralised facilities have lower costs for inward transport and economies of scale giving lower operating cost, but these are balanced by higher costs for outward transport and worse customer service. More dispersed facilities have higher costs for inward transport and less efficient operations, but lower costs for outward transport and better customer service. Adding the costs of inward transport, operations and outward transport gives an estimate of the total cost of using facilities. If we plot this against the number of facilities we get a U-shaped curve, with a minimum that identifies an optimal number of locations. Managers should only move away from this minimum if they are convinced that the benefits – perhaps better customer service or increasing economies of scale – are worth the additional costs.

WORKED EXAMPLE

Thomson Automatic is planning a new distribution system and has estimated the costs (in consistent units) for transport and operations shown below. What do these tell you?

Number of facilities

Number of locations	Inward transport	Operating costs	Outward transport	Total cost	
1	120	11	9	140	
2	75	26	10	111	
3	52	35	12	99	
4	37	41	14	92	
5	26	47	17	90	Minimum
6	20	53	22	95	
7	17	59	27	103	
8	14	64	35	113	
9	12	68	45	125	
10	10	70	58	138	

Answer

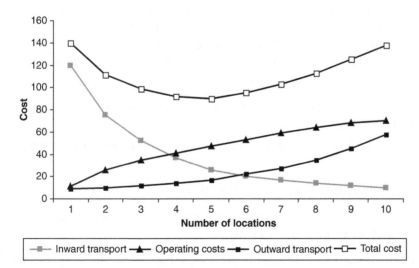

Figure 8.1 Graph of costs for different numbers of locations

WORKED EXAMPLE   (CONTINUED)

If you add the total costs for each number of locations and draw a graph of the result you get the result shown in Figure 8.1. This shows that the total cost is U-shaped, with a minimum corresponding to five warehouses. If the company uses either more or fewer locations its costs will be higher.

These three decisions form a central part of supply chain planning. They are strategic, with long-term effects, and lead to more detailed plans for the use of facilities. This is an important point, as all activities in a supply chain have to be planned. Managers have to prepare timetables to show when activities are performed. For instance, plans for customer delivery show when each one is to be visited, purchase plans give a schedule for buying materials, warehouse plans give schedules for activities. Plans show what an organisation is doing at any specific point of time, and this means that it can face the future with confidence. Without this planning a firm does not know what will happen in the future, so they work from minute to minute, with no continuity – and in constant danger of meeting unexpected conditions and descending into chaos.

We have already shown the broad approach to planning a supply chain, which starts with a logistics strategy to give the context and overall aims. Then a cascade of decisions downwards progressively adds more details to the plans and gives more immediate goals. So senior managers translate the logistics strategy into long-term plans; middle managers add details to get the medium-term, tactical plans; then junior managers add more details to give short-term, operational schedules. This gives the standard approach to planning illustrated in Figure 8.2.

The logistics strategy sets the scene for all planning decisions about logistics, and leads to the three strategic decisions about facility plans (which, to be pedantic, actually form a part of the logistics strategy). These lead to tactical decisions, and in the same way that there are different types of strategic plans, there are also different types of tactical plans. People use different names for these, but the most common for supply chains are:

Aggregate plans
tactical decisions that give summarised plans for related activities, typically by month at each location

- aggregate plans – tactical plans that summarise related activities, typically by month at each location

Master schedules
tactical plans that give schedules for each activity, typically by week

- master schedules – tactical plans that give timetables for each activity, typically by week.

Underneath these tactical plans are the operational schedules:

short-term schedules
operational plans that show detailed timetables for all jobs and resources, typically by day

- short-term schedules – operational plans that give detailed timetables for all jobs and resources, typically by day.

Details of planning are different in every organisation, but the key point is that each level of decision sets the context and goals for lower levels, and as the plans move down the organisation more details are continually added. In this

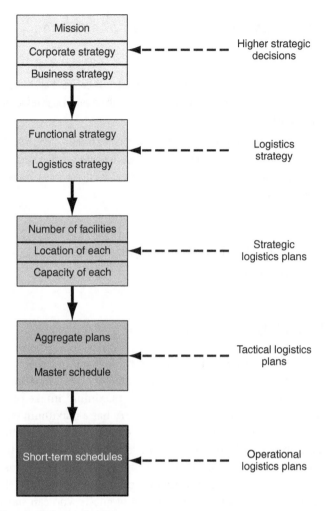

Figure 8.2   Hierarchy of planning decisions

chapter we concentrate on high-level capacity plans, and discuss other levels of planning in Chapter 9.

LOGISTICS IN PRACTICE – M-TRAIN CORPORATION

You can see the general hierarchy of planning in the M-Train Corporation, which runs a train service around the city of Madison and the surrounding commuter belt. Their plans start with a business strategy, which states that the company's aim is to provide efficient public transport around Madison. This aim is expanded in a logistics strategy, which shows how the company run a network of train services, largely for commuters moving between the city centre and surrounding areas.

Medium-term plans start with the routes the company will serve and the type of service they will offer. The company forecasts demand for their services over the medium term, and then makes

---

LOGISTICS IN PRACTICE – M-TRAIN CORPORATION
(CONTINUED)

sure it has enough capacity to meet this. In other words, it buys enough trains, hires and trains enough staff to operate them, and generally makes sure that there are enough resources available over the next year or two.

The medium-term plans are expanded to give timetables for their trains – giving basic information about when trains will arrive at each station. The final stage in planning is to expand these timetables into detailed operating schedules for individual trains, drivers, inspectors, materials, and all the other resources needed to run the service.

Question

- Why is it necessary for M-Train to put so much effort into planning?

(*Source*: Company publicity)

Planning capacity

The capacity of any operation is its maximum throughput in a specified time. All operations have some limit on their capacity: a factory has a maximum number of units it can make a week, a university has a maximum intake of students; a train has a maximum number of seats, and a lorry has a maximum weight it can carry. Sometimes the stated capacity makes an explicit reference to time, such as a maximum number of customers that can be served in a day. Even when it is not mentioned explicitly, every measure of capacity refers to time. For instance, the number of seats on a bus sets the capacity for a particular journey and the number of rooms in a hotel sets the maximum number of guests who can stay each day.

Sometimes the capacity seems obvious – such as the number of seats on a plane or volume of a tanker. At other times the capacity is not so clear. How, for example, can you find the capacity of a supermarket, airport or train network? The usual answer has a surrogate measure, such as the maximum number of customers per square metre of floor space in a shopping mall, or the minimum distance between planes. These measures come from discussion and agreement rather than any physical ceiling – in the way that the maximum number of children in a classroom is set by government policy rather than physical limits of the building.

Capacity is an important concept for logistics, as it defines the maximum flow through the supply chain in a given time.

Capacity
of a supply chain is its maximum throughput in a given time

- The capacity of a supply chain is its maximum throughput in a given time.
- It sets the maximum amount of product that can be delivered to final customers.

Most organisations do not like to work at full capacity, as this put too much pressure on both resources and people. Instead, they work at a lower level that they can reasonably sustain over time. We allow for this disparity by defining different kinds of capacity. If you imagine a supply chain that is working in ideal conditions with no disruptions or problems of any kind, then the maximum throughput is its designed capacity. In reality, you seldom find such ideal conditions, and a more realistic measure is the effective capacity. This is the maximum throughput that can be sustained under normal conditions, and allows for disruptions, variations in performance, breakdowns, maintenance periods, holidays, sickness, and so on. Then below this is the throughput actually achieved.

Designed capacity
the maximum possible throughput in ideal conditions

Effective capacity
the maximum realistic throughput in normal conditions

- **Designed capacity** is the maximum possible throughput in ideal conditions.
- **Effective capacity** is the maximum realistic throughput in normal conditions.
- **Actual throughput** is normally lower than effective capacity.

A transport operation might have a designed capacity of 1200 containers a week. It might achieve this for short periods, but taking into account disruptions and other effects its sustainable, effective capacity is 1000 containers a week. Last month their actual throughput averaged 850 containers a week.

Bottlenecks

A supply chain does not have a constant capacity along its length, but each operation has a different capacity. If the supply chain is well designed the variation in capacity is small and the supply chain is said to be 'balanced'. But there can be wide variation along an unbalanced chain. However much the capacity varies, there must be some point that limits the overall throughput of the chain – and this forms a bottleneck (illustrated in Figure 8.3). If you want to move some materials from Johannesburg to Amsterdam, you might find a bottleneck at the docks in Cape Town; a traveller might notice a bottleneck at an airport terminal; a transport company might find a bottleneck in the road network through a town.

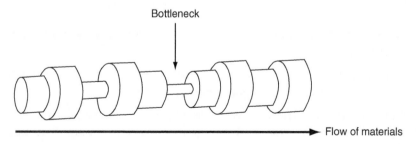

Figure 8.3 The bottleneck in a supply chain limits overall capacity

Bottleneck
the part of a supply chain that limits throughput because it has the smallest individual capacity

- A bottleneck is formed by the resources or facilities that limit the overall throughput of the chain.

WORKED EXAMPLE

The main bottling plant at J&R Softdrinks has a capacity of 80,000 litres a day, and works a seven-day week. It fills standard bottles of 750 ml, and these are passed to a packing area, which can make up to 20,000 cases a day with 12 bottles each, and works a five-day week. The cases are taken to warehouses by a transport company whose 8 lorries can each carry 300 cases, and make up to 4 trips a day for 7 days a week. There are two main warehouses, each of which can handle up to 30,000 cases a week. Local deliveries are made from the warehouses by a fleet of small vans that can handle everything passed to them by the warehouse. What is the capacity of this part of the distribution system? How can J&R increase the capacity?

Answer

We have information about five parts of the supply chain and can find the capacity of each part in consistent units – say bottles a week.

- The bottling plant has a capacity of 80,000 litres a day, or:

$$7 \times 80,000/0.75 = 746,666 \text{ bottles a week}$$

- The packing area has a capacity of 20,000 cases a day, or:

$$5 \times 12 \times 20,000 = 1,200,000 \text{ bottles a week}$$

- The transport company's lorries can handle 300 cases on each journey, so their capacity is:

$$7 \times 4 \times 8 \times 300 \times 12 = 806,400 \text{ bottles a week}$$

- Each warehouse can handle 30,000 cases a week, giving a combined capacity of:

$$2 \times 30,000 \times 12 = 720,000 \text{ bottles a week}$$

- We only know that the capacity of the delivery vans is greater than the capacity of the warehouses.

The capacity of this part of the supply chain is the smallest of these separate capacities, and this is 720,000 bottles a week in the warehouses (shown in Figure 8.4).

J&R can only increase capacity by expanding the warehouses. Improving other parts of the supply chain will have no effect at all – except increasing spare capacity. If the capacity in warehousing is increased, another bottleneck will limit throughput, this time in the bottling plant.

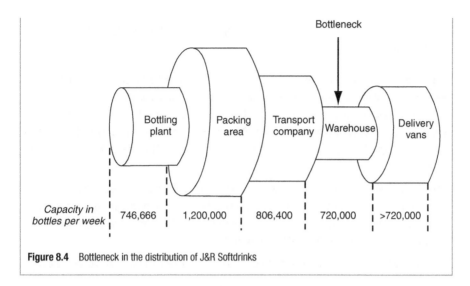

Figure 8.4   Bottleneck in the distribution of J&R Softdrinks

The bottleneck limits the overall capacity of a supply chain, which means that this part is working at full capacity.[1, 2] Everywhere else could handle more, so it has unused, spare capacity. The more unbalanced a chain is, the more unused capacity it has away from the bottleneck.

The only way to increase overall capacity is by adding more capacity at the bottleneck. In the last worked example, J&R Softdrinks can only increase overall capacity by increasing the amount of warehousing; any increase at other points would only give more spare, unused facilities and reduced utilisation. This seems obvious, but you often see companies missing the point – for example, transport companies recruit more managers to give leadership, when they are actually short of drivers; bus stations increase the size of waiting rooms, when congestion in arrival bays is limiting the number of buses; manufacturers increase their market-ing effort, when they cannot deliver enough products to meet existing demand; airlines introduce bigger aeroplanes when passenger terminals are already over-crowded. You see an irritating example of this when you are waiting a long time to be served – perhaps in a bank – but can clearly see non-serving staff who are hanging around and apparently doing nothing useful.

LOGISTICS IN PRACTICE – THE GLOBAL CAR INDUSTRY

If all car manufacturers worked a standard two-shift, the global capacity for motor vehicle pro-duction in 2000 would have been 79.2 million units. Actual production was 58.8 million units, so there was an apparent overcapacity of 20.4 million units. This suggests an average utilisation of production facilities of 58.8/79.2 = 74%. This is very bad news for an industry that must generally achieve utilisation well over 80% to be profitable, and many commentators described the severe problems facing the industry.

LOGISTICS IN PRACTICE – THE GLOBAL CAR INDUSTRY (CONTINUED)

But things were not really this bad. The installed capacity ranges from modern, state-of-the-art, flexible manufacturing plants, to out-of-date lines for assembling kits of parts. It also ranges from giant new production complexes, to small, obsolete plants. The old, obsolete and mothballed factories account for about 7 million units, leaving $79.2 - 7 = 72.2$ million units of real production. But this is the designed capacity, and the effective capacity is about 90% of this, or $72.2 \times 0.9 = 65$ million units.

The forecast demand is also uncertain and, historically, actual demand has been up to 20% more than forecasts. Companies allow for this uncertainty by having some contingency plans for capacity, usually around 7.5%. So with a forecast demand of 58.8 million, a reasonable capacity for the industry would be $58.8 \times 1.075 = 63.2$ million units.

This suggests that the real overcapacity is closer to $65 - 63.2 = 1.8$ million units or only 2.8%.

Question

- Do you think that commentators were really worried about over-supply in the car industry – or did they see an opportunity to create dramatic headlines?

(*Sources*: Pemberton, M. (2005) Overcapacity – myth or reality, Autolligence Weekly Insight, London (6 May); Jowit, J. (1999) Overcapacity costing car sector $130 billion, Financial Times (19 January); websites at www.autelligence.com; justauto.com)

Matching capacity and demand

Capacity planning has to match the available capacity of facilities to the demands put on them. Any mismatch can be expensive. If capacity is less than demand, bottlenecks limit the movement of materials, some demand cannot be met and customer service declines; if capacity is greater than demand, all materials can be moved, but there is spare capacity and resources are under-used. You can see these effects in shops. When you go into some shops there are not enough people serving and you have to wait. The capacity of the shop is less than demand, and you probably go to a competitor where the queues are shorter. Other shops have a lot of people waiting to serve customers – so there are no queues, but the cost of paying these under-used people increases your bill.

The standard approach to capacity planning aims at matching available capacity to forecast demand. This uses forecasts to calculate the resources needed over a particular period, compares these with the resources actually available, and then considers ways of overcoming differences. To be more specific, it comprises the following six steps:

Step 1. examines forecast demand and translates this into a capacity needed
Step 2. finds the capacity available in present facilities

Step 3. identifies mismatches between capacity needed and that available

Step 4. suggests alternative plans for overcoming any mismatch

Step 5. compares these plans and chooses the best

Step 6. implements the best plan and monitors actual performance.

The following example shows how this can work:

WORKED EXAMPLE

Anne Jenkins delivers an average of 100 computers a week to schools in South Wales. The systems have customised software installed, which takes an hour to test before delivery. The testing is done by two people, who achieve an average efficiency of 75%, and say that they are currently under pressure. They work a single eight-hour shift five days a week, but could move to double shifts or work overtime at weekends. How many testers should Anne employ?

Answer

Following the six steps in the standard procedure:

Step 1. *Find the capacity needed*: we know this to be 100 units a week.

Step 2. *Find the capacity available*: each tester is available for $8 \times 5 = 40$ hours a week. Average efficiency is 75%, so their useful time is $40 \times 0.75 = 30$ hours a week. Each computer takes 1 hour to test, so each tester can finish 30 systems a week. There are two testers so the available capacity is $2 \times 30 = 60$ units a week.

Step 3. *Identify mismatches*: Anne needs a capacity of 100 units a week, and currently can handle 60 units a week, so there is a shortage of 40 units a week.

Step 4. *Suggest plans for overcoming the mismatch*. There are several ways of doing this.

- Working a single shift on weekdays would need $100/30 = 3.33$ testers. If Anne only employs full-time testers, she has to round this up to 4. Then the utilisation of each would be $3.33/4 = 0.83$ or 83%.

- Employing three testers full time, and one tester part time for 1/3 time would meet the total demand with 100% utilisation.

- Using overtime at the weekends would need 3 full-time testers who are willing to finish 10 tests at the weekend (working $10/0.75 = 13.3$ hours).

With more information we could continue along these lines, suggesting alternative plans, adding allowances for holidays, problems, varying demand, and so on.

Step 5. *Choose the best*: Anne would now have a reasonable set of alternative plans and could complete her capacity planning by comparing them and choosing the best.

Step 6. *Implement the best*: The final step in the procedure implements the best solution and monitors performance to make sure that it works properly.

Resource requirements planning
a standard approach to matching available resources to forecast demand

This standard approach to capacity planning can be extended to all types of planning, and it is often called resource requirement planning. But taking the steps in a straightforward sequence does not usually work. There can be a huge number of possible plans, and it is often impossible to list them all let alone consider them in detail. At the same time, there are also so many competing objectives and non-quantifiable variables, that it is difficult to find any plan that satisfies everyone, let alone identify the 'best'. A more realistic view suggests that managers only consider a few reasonable plans and look at these in more

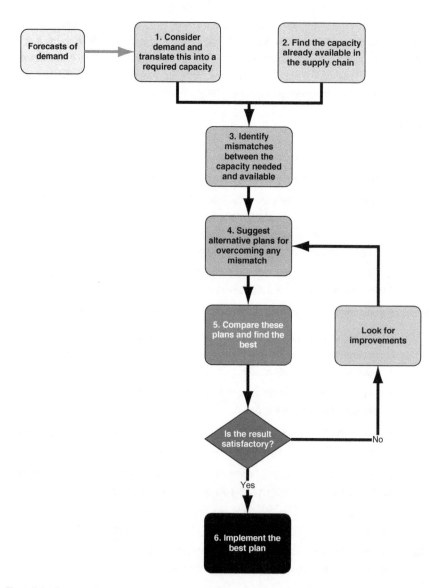

Figure 8.5   Procedure for capacity planning

detail. In essence, they give superficial consideration to a long list of options, but quickly home in on a shortlist of feasible ones, and then choose the one that satisfies most of the requirements. This generally appears as an iterative procedure, where managers design an initial plan and see how closely it gets to achieving their objectives. If the plan performs badly, they modify it to find improvements, in effect, repeating steps 4 and 5 until they reach a reasonable solution (as shown in Figure 8.5).

Finding alternative plans

There are several problems with this planning procedure. For instance, we rarely know what demand will actually be in the future, so we have to use forecasts. Unfortunately, these can be wrong, so the whole procedure is based on uncertain values. Another problem is finding the capacity. Supply chains are very complicated, so it may be difficult to identify the real bottlenecks and their constraints. A third problem is that capacity varies over time, and we return to this later in the chapter. Yet another problem is generating alternative plans, let alone evaluating them and getting agreement about their quality.

Looking at the last problem, there are several ways of generating alternative plans, including:[3]

1. **Haggling and negotiating**. Real conditions are so complex that formal analyses are often of little use. Then the best option might be to get people to negotiate and agree a plan. This may not be in any way 'optimal' – or even good – but it should have the support of everyone concerned.

2. **Intuitive or heuristic methods**. These use simple rules that seem to give good result, such as general guidance to 'add ten percent extra capacity to cover uncertainty'.

3. **Adjust previous plans**. Very few operations start entirely from scratch, so an obvious way of planning capacity is look at the current operations, identify any problems or changes to circumstances, and make adjustments to improve things. This has the benefit of being relatively easy and giving stable operations.

4. **Spreadsheets**. One of the most popular approaches to planning uses spreadsheets. Information can be presented in a variety of formats to show the consequences of a plan, and then managers can quickly adjust features to try a new solution – effectively doing a series of 'what-if' analyses.

5. **Graphical methods**. Planners often find it easier to work with some kind of graphs or diagrams. A popular format uses a graph of cumulative demand over time, and the corresponding line of cumulative supply. The aim is to get the cumulative supply line nearly straight – giving constant throughput – and as close as possible to the cumulative demand line (as shown in Figure 8.6).

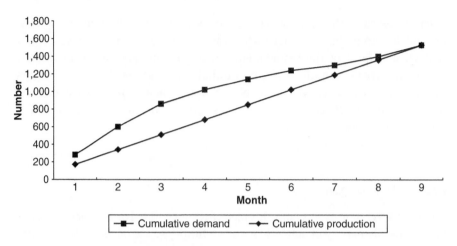

Figure 8.6   Graphical approach to capacity planning

6. **Simulation**. This gives a dynamic view of a supply chain, and follows operations through a series of typical periods. Suppose you want some information about a logistics network; you could simply stand and watch the network for some time to see what happens. Unfortunately, this takes a long time and things may not work normally while you are watching. An alternative is to simulate the process, using a computer model of the network. Once this model has been designed, managers can simulate any number of situations, adjusting features and seeing how various options would work.

7. **Expert systems and artificial intelligence**. These include managers' knowledge and judgement in an automated procedure, using specialised systems to try and make computers duplicate some of the skills of human planners. Essentially, skills, expertise, decisions and rules used by experts are collected in a knowledge base, and then a user passes a problem to an inference engine, which chooses the knowledge needed to find a solution.

8. **Mathematical programming and other mathematical models**. The previous approaches rely on human judgement (even when automated in expert systems) but the mathematical analyses look for an objective optimal solution that gives the best possible performance. The most common approach uses mathematical programming. Unfortunately, this can be very complicated and it cannot deal with subjective and non-quantifiable factors.

The most appropriate method depends on several factors, the most obvious being the balance between the cost of planning and the expected benefits. If you are moving huge quantities of oil in tankers and pipelines, costs are high and it is worth putting a lot of effort into a sophisticated model that guarantees good results. On the other hand, a small business is unlikely to have the necessary resources and will use a simple method to give reasonable results with a lot less effort.

LOGISTICS IN PRACTICE – INDIAN ROAD NETWORK

The Indian government states that 'An efficient transport system is a pre-requisite for sustained economic development.' It identifies the benefits as encouraging economic growth, helping the development of backward regions and integrating them into the mainstream economy, increasing business productivity, enhancing international competitiveness and promoting national integration.

India has one of the largest road networks in the world, with 4 million km of road that handles 60% of freight and 80% of passenger traffic. The network is classified into three categories:

- National highways – that cover the country for medium and long-distance inter-city traffic. Forming only 2% of the road network, these carry 40% of the traffic.

- State highways and major district roads – that provide links between the national highways, towns, tourist centres, industrial areas, minor ports, and generally link rural and urban areas. These comprises 20% of the total road length and carry 40% of the traffic.

- Other district roads and village roads. These link villages and are the routes for agricultural products to markets, forming a key element in rural development.

As India becomes more prosperous, the population of motor vehicles is growing very quickly – a lot faster than the road network, which is showing clear signs of stress:

- Only 47% of the network is paved.

- High-density corridors linking cities and ports are crowded and working at more than designed capacity.

- Almost half the national highways are under severe strain due to high traffic volumes.

- Only 5% of national highways have four lanes, and 80% have two lanes: there is an urgent need to upgrade 14,000 km to provide four lanes and a further 10,000 km to provide two lanes.

- Trucks travel an average of only 200 km a day, compared with the 350–400 km they could manage with less congestion.

- Road maintenance is inadequate, with only 20% of paved roads described as being in good condition.

- 40% of villages are not connected by all-weather roads.

Substantial investment is needed in the roads to increase capacity and allow for future growth. The government continues to give high priority to the road network, and in recent years has widened more than 14,000 km of national highways to 4/6 lanes, upgraded large sections of state highways to national highways, expanded village roads to connect all villages with populations of more than 500, extensively improved surfaces, bridges and culverts, and has a continuing programme of major projects.

Question

- Does the capacity of road networks have a real impact on national economies?

(*Source: Planning Commission (2002), Indian economic road map: the next five years 2002–2007, Government of India, New Delhi*)

Adjusting capacity

Imagine an airline using planes with 360 seats to fly passengers between London and New York. While the demand is between zero and 360 passengers, the airline can meet all demand with a single flight. But when demand goes over 360 passengers it has a choice either of losing customers or putting on a second flight. It would be wasteful to put on a flight for a handful of extra passengers, so the airline will wait and accept the loss of some customers. In practice, it is likely to wait until demand would almost fill another plane before considering a second flight. The essential problem for the airline – and with almost every other problem of capacity – is that demand comes in small quantities and can take almost any value, while capacity only comes in large, discrete amounts. Typically, a firm can only increase capacity by opening another shop, using another vehicle, building another warehouse, employing another person, opening a new road, and so on.

This inherent difference between patterns of supply and demand means that there is rarely an exact match between them. Things become even more complicated as both demand and capacity vary over time. So the best that managers can do is look for a reasonable match that is generally acceptable, and then make short-term adjustments to cover any immediate problems.

Matching capacity and demand

Suppose that the throughput of a supply chain rises steadily over time. Capacity should be increased at some point, but the increase will come as a discrete step. There is no way of exactly matching the discrete capacity to a continuous demand, so there are three alternatives (shown in Figure 8.7).

(a) **Capacity more or less matches demand** – meaning that there is sometimes spare capacity and sometimes a shortage. This gives a relatively balanced performance that avoids the problems of both excess capacity and too many lost customers.

(b) **Capacity leads demand** – so that there is always enough capacity to meet all demand. This maximises revenue and customer satisfaction – and there is a capacity cushion to allow for unexpected circumstances. But it needs more investment, utilisation is lower, unit costs are higher – and there is a risk of having resources that are never used if the long-term forecasts are too optimistic.

(c) **Capacity lags demand** – with more capacity added only when the extra facilities would be heavily – preferably fully – used. This delays and reduces investment, ensures high utilisation, and gives low unit costs. But it restricts throughput, loses customers, causes delays, lowers customer satisfaction, and has no flexibility to deal with unexpected conditions.

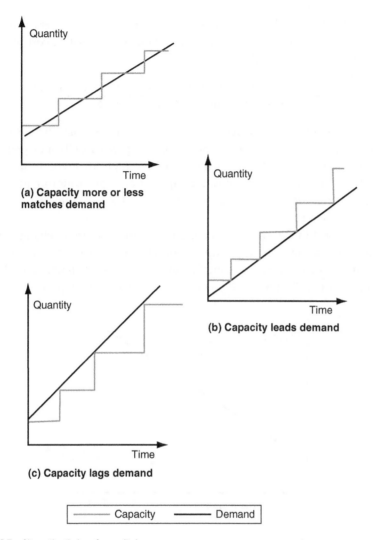

Figure 8.7   Alternative timing of capacity increases

Each of these options is best in different circumstances. Factors that encourage an early increase in capacity include high cost of shortages, low cost of spare capacity, widely variable demand, high profit margins, varying efficiency, and capacity increases that are relatively small. On the other hand, the main factor that encourages a delay is the capital cost, and the knowledge that resource would not be fully used until some point in the future. The capacity of a large furniture shop, such as MFI, is largely set by the number of sales people. The nature of demand and relative costs, mean that the shop is likely to increase capacity early and make sure that there are always enough staff to serve customers. On the other hand, new motorways are expensive and controversial, so expansions are delayed for as long as possible and new roads are crowded as soon as they open.

Some analyses can help with this decision, particularly in the costing of alternatives. Hayes and Wheelwright[4] suggest looking at the relative cost of excess capacity and shortage, calculating:

$$\frac{\text{Cost of a unit of capacity shortage} - \text{cost of a unit of excess capacity}}{\text{Cost of a unit of capacity shortage}}$$

When the cost of excess capacity is high, this ratio is small, which can be interpreted as meaning that there should be no spare capacity and preferably a shortage. When the cost of capacity shortage is high, this ratio is large, suggesting that there should be a positive capacity cushion. Unfortunately, such calculations often depend on measuring the cost of lost customers, and this is notoriously difficult.

Another aspect in the decision to change concerns the size of changes. Extra capacity may come in discrete quantities, but is it better to keep increasing capacity in relatively small steps, or to combine several of these into fewer, much bigger jumps (as shown in Figure 8.8). If you want to hire five new people over the next

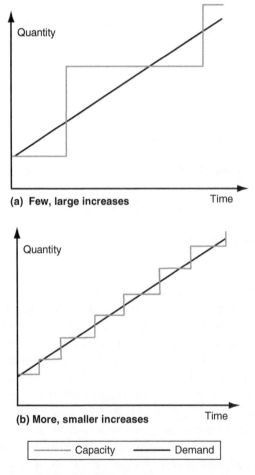

Figure 8.8 Alternative sizes of capacity increases

few months, should you add them one at a time when needed – or would it be better to have one big campaign to recruit all five at the same time?

There can be benefits to both of these approaches. The benefits from a few large increases include longer periods without disruptions, bigger expansions give lower costs per unit of expansion, less risk of not meeting unexpected demand, earlier economies of scale, incentives to encourage more demand, and gaining a lead over competitors. On the other hand, the advantages of more, smaller expansions include a closer match to demand, less serious disruptions, capital not being tied up in unused facilities, higher utilisation of resources, less risk if demand changes or does not reach expected levels, and expansions being timed more carefully.

Short-term adjustments to capacity

Capacity planning is largely a strategic function. Managers can increase the capacity of a supply chain by opening a warehouse, designing a new process, opening new offices, or moving to a new location. They can reduce excess capacity by closing warehouses, shutting down a plant, or transferring facilities to other products. These are strategic decisions with long-term consequences. But capacity can also be adjusted in the shorter term by leasing extra space, working overtime, employing temporary staff, or sub-contracting some work. These are clearly tactical and operational decisions.

A fairer picture of capacity planning says that the context is set at the strategic level, but superimposed on this are medium and short-term adjustments. Tactical decisions affect capacity over the medium term and typically adjust the number of people employed, responses to seasonal changes, amount of sub-contracting, leasing additional resources, etc. Operational decisions affect capacity over the short term and typically look at employees' work schedules, amount of overtime, dealing with urgent problems, and so on.

There are really two ways of making these adjustments:

- supply management – which adjusts the available capacity to match known demand
- demand management – which adjusts the demand to match available capacity.

Supply management
adjusts available capacity to match known demand

Demand management
adjusts demand to match available capacity

Imagine a wholesaler's warehouse that sees a temporary increase in business when a construction site opens nearby. The wholesaler can use supply management and rent extra space for the duration of the construction project – or it can use demand management to limit demand to match existing capacity, perhaps by raising prices. In practice, supply management is more usual, and this is achieved as follows:

- Change the work pattern to match demand, with overtime and undertime to make final adjustments
- Hire or fire full-time staff

- Employ part-time or temporary staff to cover peak demands
- Cross-train employees, so that each can move to the job that is most urgent
- Use outside contractors
- Rent or lease extra facilities
- Adjust the speed of working
- Reschedule maintenance periods or other backroom activities
- Make customers do some work, such as using automatic banking or ticket machines, or packing their own bags in a supermarket
- Redesign operations to make them more efficient.

These adjustments cannot be done too often or too severely, as they affect employees, operations and customers. For instance, a company cannot change work schedules every few days as this would be unacceptable to employees, and frequent changes to working hours would confuse customers.

The alternative is demand management, and although this seems strange, it is surprisingly common. For instance, restaurants charge high prices to restrict numbers, professional institutions put up barriers to entry, and doctors insist on appointments. More generally firms can:

- vary the price (provided they remain high enough to cover costs, but low enough to be competitive)
- only serve customers who have specific qualifications
- offer incentives to change demand patterns, such as free samples, discounts or off-peak rates
- change the marketing effort
- change related products to encourage substitution
- vary the lead time
- use a reservation or appointment system
- use stocks to cushion demand.

LOGISTICS IN PRACTICE – PORT OF GUAYMAS

In 1995 CANAMEX was inaugurated as a major trade corridor to connect Canada, the USA and Mexico. This travels from the North down through Tucson, Arizona 65 miles south to Nogales on the US/Mexican border, 280 miles to Guaymas on Mexico's West coasts, and then continues southwards.

Guaymas is a small port, that used to move petrochemicals and bulk cargoes, but throughput declined from 5.7 million tons in 1996 to 2.9 million tons in 2004[5] and utilisation fell to 10% of capacity. However, the port's position on CANAMEX allows rapid transport to a larger area, particularly up to Tucson. It could be well placed to take advantage of the increasing north–south trade through NAFTA, and the increasing east – west trade between Asia and the USA. This is particularly useful as the main Californian ports of Long Beach and Los Angeles are getting increasingly congested, with delays of up to 21 days.

The possible development of Guaymas as a container port raised the question of whether the transport links have enough capacity. These included the port of Guaymas itself, the road to Nogales, Mariposa port of entry on the border, road link to Tucson, terminal at Tucson. In parallel with this was a rail link from Guaymas, through Nogales, and on to Tucson.

Interestingly, the main bottleneck was identified as the Mariposa port of entry, followed by railway inspections on the US side of the border and then the port of Guaymas.[6] The capacity of the route was estimated at 175,000 TEU a year if container services are available on both road and rail links – but this falls to 104,000 TEU a year if no railway container service is available, and 120,000 TEU a year with no road service. In all cases, facilities at the border formed the bottlenecks.

By 2008 the Mexican government deepened Guaymas port from 36 feet to 42 feet, and invested $200 million into a new road link connecting Guaymas to western Arizona. The US government is adding two high-speed lanes at border crossing, and is planning a $70 million expansion of the Mariposa port of entry by 2010.[7] By 2008 three new terminals were opened at Guaymas – one for cruise ships, another for the world's largest steel maker, Arcelor Mittal, and a third for the Australian mining company BHP Billiton. Plans are still progressing for new container facilities.

Question

• Is it easy to identify a supply chain's bottleneck or measure its capacity?

(*Sources*: Hawley, C. (2005) For Arizona, Mexican port promises new opportunity, The Arizona Republic, September 14; Villalobos, J.R. et al. (2006) Logistics capacity study of the Guaymas-Tucson corridor, Arizona Department of Transportation, Phoenix, AZ; Rico G. (2008) The port growth a boost for Tucson, Arizona Daily Star, 18 April).

Systematic changes to capacity

So far we have assumed that capacity is constant over time. But the effective capacity of a supply chain can change quickly due to staff illness, interruptions, break-downs, accidents, weather, enthusiasm of employees, and so on. Even when there is no change to the operations, the capacity can vary quite widely. For instance, a group of people moving heavy goods around a warehouse might start on Monday morning fresh and productive – but at the end of an eight-hour shift on Friday they are tired and need a break, so their effective capacity is much lower.

The capacity of a supply chain is affected by both random effects and more systematic ones. Among the systematic changes is the well-known learning curve, which shows that the more often you repeat something, the easier it becomes and the faster you can do it (as shown in Figure 8.9). The usual shape for a learning

Learning curve
which shows that the more often you repeat something, the easier it becomes and the faster you can do it

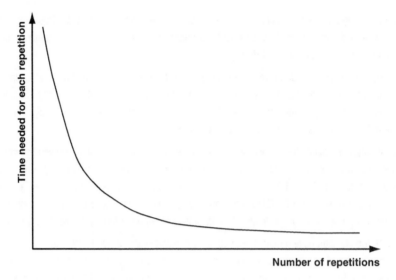

Figure 8.9   Typical shape of a learning curve

curve has the time taken to do some activity falling by a fixed proportion – typically around 10% – every time the number of repetitions is doubled. If you take 10 minutes to do a job for the first time, the second time takes only 90% of the time, or 9 minutes; the fourth time takes 90% of the time for the second repetition or 8.1 minutes, and so on. The following table shows the times for repetitions with this '90% learning curve'.

Number of repetitions	Time for the last (minutes)
1	10.0
2	9.0
4	8.1
8	7.29
16	6.56
32	5.90
64	5.31
128	4.78

Another reason for systematic changes to capacity is the effect of ageing equipment and facilities. As equipment gets older its effective capacity declines as it breaks down more often, develops more faults, gives lower quality, slows down, and generally wears out. Sometimes the changes are slow, like the fuel consumption of a car, which rises steadily with age. Sometimes the change is very fast, like a bolt, which suddenly breaks. The overall effect, though, is a systematic decline in effective capacity with age. But this declining performance is by no means inevitable, and there are many things – ranging from mobile telephones to teapots – whose performance stays much the same for long periods. Even if

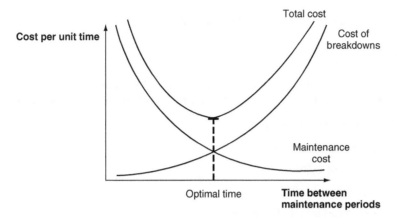

Figure 8.10 Identifying the optimal time between maintenance

performance does decline, there are ways of slowing its effects, such as preventive maintenance and replacement policies.

With preventive maintenance, equipment is inspected and vulnerable parts are replaced after a certain period of use. By replacing bits that are worn – or are most likely to wear – the equipment is restored to give continuing, satisfactory performance. The next question asks how often we should undertake this maintenance. If we do it too often, the equipment runs efficiently but the maintenance costs are too high; if we do not do it often enough, the maintenance costs are low but the equipment still breaks down. One way of finding the best compromise is to add together the costs of maintenance and expected failure. Then, plotting the total cost against the frequency of maintenance, we get a U-shaped curve with a distinct minimum that defines the best time between maintenance periods (illustrated in Figure 8.10).

WORKED EXAMPLE

Juanita Princepio has recorded the costs of an automatic guided vehicle (AGV) that moves materials around an assembly hall. The longer the AGV works without maintenance, the higher are the expected failure costs (shown below). The maintenance also affects the resale value, giving a varying capital charge. Preventive maintenance can be done at a cost of £1000 and this restores the AGV to its new condition. What is the best time between maintenance periods?

Months since maintenance	0	1	2	3	4	5
Cost of breakdowns in month	0	50	150	200	1600	3000
Capital charge	100	200	400	500	800	1200

WORKED EXAMPLE   (CONTINUED)

Answer

We can find the total monthly cost of running the AGV over some period by adding the total costs of maintenance, capital and breakdowns, and dividing this by the number of months it worked.

- If the AGV is maintained every month:

  ○ Breakdowns cost nothing.

  ○ Capital costs £100.

  ○ Maintenance costs £1000.

  ○ The total cost is £1100 for the month.

- If the AGV is maintained every two months:

  ○ Breakdowns cost nothing in the first month, plus £50 in the second month

  ○ Capital charge is £100 in the first month, plus £200 in the second month

  ○ Maintenance costs £1000.

  ○ The total cost is £1350 every two months, or £675 per month.

- If the AGV is maintained every three months:

  ○ Breakdowns cost £0 in the first month, plus £50 in the second month, plus £150 in the third month.

  ○ Capital charge is £100 in the first month, plus £200 in the second month, plus £400 in the third month.

  ○ Maintenance is £1000

  ○ The total is £1900 for three months or £633 a month.

Repeating this gives the following values, which suggest a minimum cost of £633 a month when maintenance is done every three months.

Months between maintenance	1	2	3	4	5	6
Maintenance cost	1000	1000	1000	1000	1000	1000
Cumulative cost of breakdowns	0	50	200	400	2000	5000
Cumulative capital charge	100	300	700	1200	2000	3200
Total cost	1100	1350	1900	2600	5000	9200
Average cost per month	1100	675	633	650	1000	1533

Even with regular maintenance there comes a point when repairs are too expensive and it is cheaper to buy new equipment. These replacement decisions can be expensive when building, say, a new logistic centre, ship, or shopping mall. Like maintenance, managers have to compromise on the timing of replacement – too frequently results in efficient operations but high replacement costs; too rarely gives low replacement costs but high operating and failure costs. So there is an optimal time for replacement, and we can find this by extending the analysis for preventive maintenance. In other words, we add the total cost of operating equipment over a number of years and divide this by the age at replacement to give an average annual cost. This might show that the optimal policy is to replace delivery vans every five years, or replace computer systems every three years.

One drawback with planned replacement is that equipment is routinely replaced when it appears to be working well – in the way that computer equipment is replaced when it still looks new. Replacement inevitably causes some disruption while people get used to new equipment, so it can be difficult to persuade them that this really is better than waiting until the old equipment stops working.

LOGISTICS IN PRACTICE – CAPACITY OF HEATHROW AIRPORT

BAA run seven airports in the UK, including the three London airports at Heathrow, Gatwick and Stansted. In the year to 2007 these three airports handled 126 million passengers, an increase of 1.3% over the previous year. But this figure understates the growth of demand, as Heathrow has been working at full capacity for many years, can handle no more passengers or flights, and the number of destinations served has fallen by 20% in recent years. Actual demand in the south-east of England continues to rise and is forecast to double over the next 15 years.

London Heathrow is the world's biggest international airport, and handles 68 million passengers a year. This remained constant for 2007, while Gatwick grew by 5% to 34 million passengers and Stansted grew by 7% to 24 million passengers.

The problem for BAA is that the UK's major international hub airport is clearly working at full capacity, and despite a continuing programme of airport expansion, BAA has to limit demand. This diverts passengers to other airports, and opens opportunities for BAA's competitors, particularly on the European mainland. To increase terminal capacity BAA opened a fifth terminal in 2008 after a public enquiry lasting four years and construction costing £4.5 billion spread over six years. It is also redeveloping terminals 1, 2 and 3 and together with £1 million a day spent on general upgrades this should increase terminal capacity to 85 million passengers a year. At the same time, transport connections are being improved by a better express rail link to Paddington, a second express rail link to St Pancras, improved access roads, and extension to the London Underground. The airport currently employs 68,000 people and this will rise to 84,000 after these changes.

Perhaps the most difficult problem to overcome is runway capacity. There is a minimum allowed time between landings and take-offs, and because of its closeness to residential areas there are restrictions on flights during the night. These limit the number of plane movements on the two runways to 480,000 a year. There are continuing discussions about reducing the gap between planes, and larger aircraft (particularly the 800-seat A380) put more passengers in each time slot. Currently one runway is used for landings and the second for take-offs, but mixing the two could increase utilisation and allow 540,000 movements a year. A more radical plan was announced in 2007 to consider a third runway, which would increase capacity to more than 700,000 movements. Realistically, the congestion at Heathrow is likely to continue for the foreseeable future. All airport

> ### LOGISTICS IN PRACTICE – CAPACITY OF HEATHROW AIRPORT (CONTINUED)
>
> expansion plans are controversial. Noise restrictions mean that the mixed use of runways could not be completed until after 2015, and even if a third runway is approved it would only become available at some point after 2020. In the meantime, other airports are expanding. Gatwick spent £500 million increasing its capacity from 27 million to 30 million passengers, and is currently expanding up to 40 million. Stansted handles 25 million passengers a year and is one of Europe's fastest growing airports. The renamed London Luton Airport is looking at continuous expansion to 30 million passengers by 2030. And the small London City Airport handles 2.5 million passengers a year.
>
> #### Question
>
> - If capacity is such a problem at Heathrow, why does BAA not simply expand the facilities?
>
> (*Sources*: Department for Transport (2007) Adding capacity at Heathrow Airport, HMSO, London; Ellson, C.(1998) London's airports set for expansion, The Times, 30 April; Skapinker M. (1999), BAA plans to expand capacity at Gatwick, Financial Times, 31 May and website www.future-heathrow.com)

Associated plans

We have now discussed capacity planning, but this is not an end in itself, and the next stage is to show how the available capacity is used. In particular, managers have to design tactical aggregate plans and master schedules, which give medium-term timetables for activities. These lead to the most detailed level of planning, which designs operational schedules for all resources.

Tactical plans

Aggregate planning takes medium-term forecasts of demand and uses this to design plans for each type of activity for, typically, each of the next few months. Suppose that Proctor Transport forecasts demand of 800 tonnes of materials to be delivered to Scandinavia over the next year. Capacity plans make sure that they have enough resources to deliver this. Then aggregate plans give an outline timetable for the deliveries, perhaps with deliveries of 100 tonnes a month between January and August. Aggregate plans only look at families of activities and not at the details, so they might show the number of cases moved through a logistics centre, but do not break this down into types of case or contents.

> - **Aggregate planning** makes the tactical decisions that translate forecast demand and available capacity into schedules for families of activities.

Aggregate plans try to meet forecast demand, while using supply chain capacity as efficiently as possible. Typically, they aim at low costs, high customer service, stable throughput, full utilisation of resources, or some other objectives. To achieve this, they adjust variables like the number of people employed, hours worked, amount of stock, amount subcontracted, resources available, demand, and so on. Essentially, aggregate planners look for answers to questions such as:

- Should we keep throughput at a constant level, or change it to meet varying demand?
- How should we use stocks to meet changing demand?
- Should we vary the size of the workforce?
- Can we change patterns of work?
- Should we use subcontractors or outside suppliers to cover peak demands?
- Can we allow shortages, perhaps with late delivery?
- Can we smooth the demand?

At the end of the aggregate planning, an organisation has schedules for its major types of activity, typically for each month, at each location. The next stage is to add more detail, and this is done in the master schedules.

A master schedule 'disaggregates' the aggregate plan and shows the planned activities for, typically, each week over then next few weeks. The aggregate plan of Proctor Transport might show deliveries of 100 tonnes to Scandinavia next month. Then the master schedule gives more details, perhaps showing two deliveries of 9 tonnes to Denmark in week one, three deliveries of 7 tonnes to Sweden in week two, and so on.

- The **master schedule** gives a timetable for activities, typically for each week.
- Its aim is to achieve the activities described in aggregate plans as efficiently as possible.

For both types of tactical plan we can use the general procedure described above as resource requirement planning. Remember that this has six steps to find the resources needed, find the resources available, identify mismatches, find ways of overcoming the mismatch, compare options and find the best, and implement the best plan. We can show how this is used for tactical planning in the following example:

WORKED EXAMPLE

A&B Coaches plan their capacity in terms of 'coach-days'. They classify their business as either 'full day', which are long-distance journeys, or 'half day' which are shorter runs. Forecasts show expected annual demands for the next two years to average 400,000 full-day passengers and 750,000 half-day passengers.

WORKED EXAMPLE   (CONTINUED)

A&B have 61 coaches, each with an effective capacity of 40 passengers a day for 300 days a year. Breakdowns and other unexpected problems reduce efficiency to 90%. They employ 86 drivers who work an average of 220 days a year, but illness and other absences reduce their efficiency to 85%.

If there is a shortage of coaches the company can buy extra ones for €220,000 or hire them for €100 a day. If there is a shortage of drivers they can recruit extra ones at a cost of €40,000 a year, or hire them from an agency for €220 a day.

How can the company approach its tactical planning?

Answer

The company can use the six-step procedure outlined above.

Step 1. *Find the resources needed.*

- 400,000 full-day passengers are equivalent to 400,000/40 = 10,000 coach days a year, or 10,000/300 = 33.33 coaches.

- 750,000 half-day passengers are equivalent to 750,000/(40 × 300 × 2) = 31.25 coaches.

- Adding these two gives the total demand as 64.58 coaches. Each coach needs 300/220 drivers, so the company needs a total of 88.06 drivers.

Step 2. *Find the resources available.*

- The company has 61 coaches, but the efficiency of 90% gives an availability of 61 × 0.9 = 54.9 coaches.

- There are 86 drivers, but an efficiency of 85% reduces this to 86 × 0.85 = 73.1 drivers.

Step 3. *Identify mismatches.*

Without details of the timing, we can only take overall figures. There is a total shortage of 64.58 − 54.9 = 9.68 coaches and 88.06 − 73.1 = 14.96 drivers.

Step 4. *Suggest plans for overcoming the mismatch.*

Assuming that A&B do not want to reduce demand, they can either buy or hire coaches, and employ drivers or hire them from an agency. The only information we have about these alternatives are some costs.

- To buy 10 coaches would cost €2,200,000. To hire coaches to make up the shortage would cost 9.68 × 300 × 200 = €580,800 a year. There is, of course, the alternative of buying some coaches and hiring others

- To hire 15 drivers would cost €600,000 a year, while using temporary drivers from an agency would cost 14.96 × 220 × 220 = €724,064 a year. There is also the option of hiring some drivers and making up shortages from an agency.

Step 5. *Choose the best.*

We do not have enough information to make the final decisions, and we have only outlined a couple of alternatives. With more options and analyses we might suggest a solution along the lines of buying eight coaches and making up shortages by renting others, and hiring 12 drivers and making up the shortage from the agency.

Step 6. *Implement the best.*

When A&B have finalised their decision they can implement them, which means turning the ideas into actions. A part of this is to add more details to the plans, moving to aggregate plans for types of journeys each month. Then they might choose the number of southern European journeys each month for the next six months, the number of Scandinavian journeys, and so on. The next stage of planning would break down the aggregate plans into master schedules of journeys typically each week. These might show the number of journeys to Denmark in the first week, the number of journeys to Italy in the third week, and so on. The final step in planning would add the operational detail to the master schedule, and show what each coach, driver, and all other resources are doing at any point.

Remember that this approach has many practical difficulties, such as the way of generating and comparing alternatives. There are usually so many possible plans that we cannot even list them all, let alone compare their merits – and there are so many competing objectives and non-quantifiable factors, that it is difficult to find any plan that satisfies everyone, let alone identify the best.

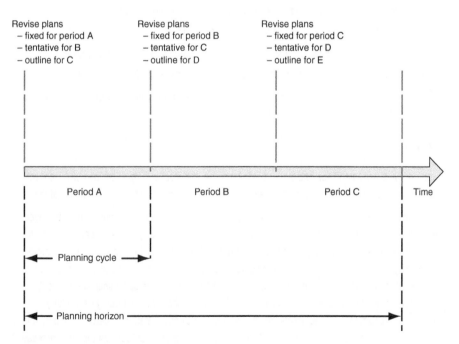

Figure 8.11 Revision of plans during cycles

An important point about planning is that it is never finished. It is continuous, and as plans for one period are finalised and implemented, planning moves on to the next period. The usual way of organising this is to work on plans for several periods at the same time; plans for the near future are fixed, while those for the more distant future are still tentative. Planning is then done in cycles. In one cycle an organisation might finalise plans for the next period and make provisional plans for the following period, and outline plans for the period after that. This gives the pattern of planning shown in Figure 8.11.

WORKED EXAMPLE

Hucek Transport in Prague designs aggregate plans for each of the next six months. They start with forecasts of monthly demands for transport, and at the beginning of 2008 had the following information for one type of transport.

Month	January	February	March	April	May	June
Forecast demand	80	100	125	130	150	75

These figures show nominal 'truck journeys', and there are associated costs for:

- spare transport that is not used = €1000 a unit held at the month end
- shortage of transport = €10,000 a unit at the month end
- cost of moving an employee to this function from other jobs = €1000 per employee
- cost of moving an employee from this function to other jobs = €700 per employee.

At the beginning of the year 16 people were employed, each of whom can make 5 journeys a month. How can the company set about planning its transport?

Answer

They know the demand for one type of transport, so can design aggregate plans. A common approach uses a spreadsheet to do the calculations, and Figure 8.12 show an initial part of this.

The initial production plan is shown in row 8, and simply starts with a supply, set at the average demand over the six months (110). This needs six more employees, so there are costs for transferring people into the function in the first month. Each month there is either excess supply or shortage, which is calculated from the cumulative supply minus the cumulative demand. Lines 10 and 11 show that there is excess supply in months 1 to 4 followed by shortage in month 5. The costs for these are shown in rows 12 and 14, with the shortage cost being particularly high. The next step would be to adjust the initial plan and try to find a better fit between supply and demand – and the move is to reduce availability of vehicles in the first four months, and increase it in month 5. Managers can keep making adjustments until they get a reasonable solution.

	A	B	C	D	E	F	G	H	I
1	Hucek Transport								
2									
3	Aggregate plan								
4									
5	Month		1	2	3	4	5	6	Total
6	Forecast demand		80	100	125	130	150	75	660
7	Cumulative forecast demand		80	180	305	435	585	660	660
8	Supply rate		110	110	110	110	110	110	660
9	Cumulative supply		110	220	330	440	550	660	660
10	Unused supply		30	40	25	5	0	0	100
11	Shortage of supply		0	0	0	0	35	0	35
12	Cost of unused supply		30,000	40,000	25,000	5000	0	0	100,000
13	(Line 7 x €1000)								
14	Cost of shortage		0	0	0	0	350,000	0	350,000
15	(Line 8 x €10,000)								
16	Number of employees		22	22	22	22	22	22	
17	Cost of moving employees		6000	0	0	0	0	0	6000
18	Total cost		36,000	40,000	25,000	5000	350,000	0	456,000
19	(Line 9 + Line 11 + line 14)								
20									
21									
22	Master schedule								
23									
24	Month	1				2			
25	Week	1	2	3	4	1	2	3	4
26	Vehicles A	5	5	6	6	6	6	5	5
27	Vehicles B	11	14	12	11	15	12	15	14
28	Vehicles C	11	9	9	11	6	10	7	9
29	Weekly total	27	28	27	28	27	28	27	28
30	Monthly total				110				110

Figure 8.12 Spreadsheet for planning in Piotr Hucek

When the aggregate plan is finalised, managers can move on to design a master schedule, which shows the supply of vehicles of each type by week. The lower part of Figure 8.12 shows the start of this for the initial plan. To provide 110 units each month, three types of vehicle are used, with the supply shown for each week. The key point is that the total monthly supply specified in the master schedule must equal the supply in the aggregate plan. Then adjusting the aggregate plan would lead to corresponding changes to the master schedule. The final stage of planning would break down the master schedule into short-term timetables for all resources.

Chapter review

- A supply chain needs planning at different levels. Strategic plans give the general shape of the chain, and these are expanded into lower levels.
- Among the strategic plans for supply chains are the number of facilities to use, their locations and sizes. These are closely related, and lead to the tactical and operational plans that manage the flow of materials.
- The capacity of a supply chain is the maximum amount that it can deliver to final customers in a given time. Complex chains mean that this is difficult to measure, and there is a difference between designed and effective capacity.
- The capacity of a whole supply chain is set by the bottleneck. Overall capacity can only be increased by putting more resources into the bottleneck.

- Capacity planning matches the available capacity and demand. A standard procedure – generally called resource requirements planning – iteratively searches for an acceptable solution.

- Other practical questions affect capacity decisions, such as the timing and size of any changes.

- Capacity decisions are generally strategic, but managers also have to make shorter-term adjustments to deal with changing conditions. For this they can either use supply or demand management.

- Effective capacity can vary over time, either due to random effects or systematic changes. Among the systematic changes are learning curves and ageing.

- Tactical plans show how the available capacity is used. In particular, the long-term capacity plans can be expanded to give aggregate plans (giving medium-term timetables for families of activities) and master schedules (show more detailed timetables for each type of activity). These can then be expanded to give short-term schedules.

CASE STUDY – PRIMAL AUTOPARTS

Primal Autoparts is a supplier of car parts to customers in south-western USA. It sources these from its own manufacturing plant and from other manufacturers in China and the Pacific Rim. It plans to extend its operations to include customers in north-western USA and the western provinces of Canada. George Havering is a senior partner for Mayer, Jones and Armanti, and has been given the job of designing realistic alternatives for Primal's additional logistics requirements. Whatever alternative he suggests must be integrated with the existing distribution system.

George's problem is that he does not know much about Primal's existing operations. He knows that after the manufacture and import of parts, they primarily work as wholesalers, keeping stocks in warehouses until delivered to customers. Their customers are largely mechanics working in repair workshops, who have to repair cars as quickly as possible, and need parts delivered at very short notice. Primal must give at least overnight delivery, with parts available at the start of the next working day – and ideally they would give shorter lead times with several deliveries a day. This is not helped by the variable demand for most parts, which can include seasonality (such as radiators that are vulnerable during severe winters).

George feels that his best approach is to study the existing distribution system and look for ways of expanding it. At present, Primal's main warehouse is in San Francisco, with smaller depots in Los Angeles, Phoenix and Salt Lake City. The largest parts they supply are bodies, which can easily be carried by road, rail or air. Most of their distribution is done by road, with some use of rail for imported materials and air freight for emergency deliveries. The company is hoping that the move into new areas will expand its business by at least 75%, but George feels that this is optimistic as the largest population centres in western states are clustered in the south. But perhaps Primal can use their existing skills and resources to serve a wider customer base, and spread their fixed costs.

Questions

- If you were George Havering, how would you start your study? What steps would you follow, and what would you aim to put in your report to Primal?

- What type of logistics systems might you consider? How would you compare these alternatives?

- What information would you need for this study, and how would you collect it?

Project – network planning

Consider an organisation that has a well-established logistics network. You might take a local company or a national one such as a supermarket, airline, or car manufacturer. Describe the main features of the network. Where are the bottlenecks that limit capacity?

Is the supply chain balanced, or does the capacity vary widely? How do you think these capacities of the main elements in the supply chain were chosen?

Problems

8.1 A ski lift at Mont Pernache has pairs of chairs pulled on a continuous wire from the bottom of a ski run to the top. One pair of chairs is timed to arrive at the bottom of the slope every six seconds. If the lift works 10 hours a day for 120 days a year, what is its designed capacity? On a typical day 15% of users need help getting on the lift, and they cause average delays of 12 seconds. A further 25% of people using the lift are alone, and only one chair of the pair is used. How can you describe the performance of the lift?

8.2 A purchasing department sends out about 100 routine orders a day. Each person in the department can send deal with three orders an hour, but has to do associated paperwork that takes an average of 40 minutes an order. Each person also loses about 20% of their time doing other things. The standard working day is from 0900 to 1600 five days a week, with an hour off for lunch. How many employees do you think the department should employ?

8.3 The fixed cost of a warehouse is €220,000 a year, and the capacity can be increased by using more equipment at a cost of €110,000 each unit. The total output of the operation, measured in some consistent units, is:

Equipment	1	2	3	4	5	6	7	8
Output	55	125	230	310	375	435	460	470

How would you get the lowest unit cost?

8.4 Winston Logistics estimate that periodic maintenance of facilities costs 100,000. If they do not do this maintenance, the breakdown costs rise as shown below. How often should they maintain the plant?

Time since last maintenance (years)	0	1	2	3	4	5
Annual cost of breakdowns ($000)	0	10	40	80	150	240

8.5   If it takes twenty minutes to do a job the first time, how long will it take to do the job after 250 repetitions with a 90% learning curve?

8.6   A warehouse has to meet the demand for a product shown below. Each unit of stock remaining at the end of a month has a notional holding cost of 20. If there are shortages, 20% of orders are lost with a cost of 200 a unit, and the rest are met by late deliveries with a cost of 50 a unit. A production department sends the product to the warehouse. Designed capacity of this department is 400 units a month, but utilisation seldom exceeds 80%. Every time the production rate is changed it costs 15,000. How would you set about designing an aggregate plan for the product?

Month	1	2	3	4	5	6	7	8
Aggregate demand	310	280	260	300	360	250	160	100

Discussion questions

8.1   To what extent are location decisions and capacity plans related?

8.2   Capacity is the most important decision in the design of a supply chain, as it affects the amount of materials that can be moved. Do you find this argument convincing?

8.3   You often see notices at the entrance to bars, pubs, clubs, halls and other buildings with messages along the lines of, 'The capacity of this facility of 300 people.' What does this really mean?

8.4   Is it possible to measure the capacity of an entire supply chain?

8.5   All plans are based on forecasts. These inevitably contain errors – so the resulting plans are inaccurate at best and often useless. What do you think of this view?

8.6   How would you set about planning the capacity of a supply chain?

8.7   No company would seriously consider limiting the amount of customer demand, and they would always raise capacity instead. Do you think this is true?

8.8   What type of decisions would managers need when considering the expansion of facilities?

8.9   Why does capacity change over time?

8.10 Formal planning is useful for manufacturers, but they cannot be used for logistics. Do you think this is true?

References

1. Goldratt, M. and Cox, J. (1986) The goal, North Press River Press, Boston, MA.
2. Schmenner, R.W. and Swink, M. (1998) On theory in operations management, Journal of Operations Management, 17, 97–113.
3. Waters, D. (2001) Operations management, Financial Times/Prentice Hall, London.
4. Hayes, R.H. and Wheelwright, S.C. (1984) Restoring our competitive edge, John Wiley, New York.
5. Hawley, C. (2005) For Arizona, Mexican port promises new opportunity, The Arizona Republic, 14 September.
6. Villalobos, J.R., Maltz, A., Ahumada, O., Trevino, G., Sanchez, O. and Garcia, H.C. (2006) Logistics capacity study of the Guaymas-Tucson corridor, Arizona Department of Transportation, Phoenix, AZ.
7. Rico, G. (2008) The Port growth a boost for Tucson, Arizona Daily Star, 18 April.

Further reading

Comel, J.G. and Edson, N.W. (1998) Gaining control: capacity management and scheduling (2nd edition), John Wiley, San Francisco, CA.

Jackson, H.K. and Frigon, N.L. (1998) Fulfilling customer needs, John Wiley and Sons, San Francisco, CA.

Klammer, T.P. and Klammer, T. (1996) Capacity management and improvement, Irwin, Homewood, IL.

Levinson, W.A. (2007) Beyond the theory of constraints, Productivity Press, New York.

McNair, C.J. and Vangermeersch, R. (1998) Total capacity management, St. Lucie Press, Boca Raton, FL.

Plenert, G. and Kirchmier, B. (2000) Finite capacity scheduling, John Wiley and Sons, San Francisco, CA.

Proud, J.F. (1999) Master scheduling (3rd edition), John Wiley and Sons, San Francisco, CA.

YuLee, R.T. (2002) Essentials of capacity management, John Wiley and Sons, Chichester.

PART III

MOVING MATERIALS THROUGH SUPPLY CHAINS

This book is divided into three parts. The first part introduced the ideas of logistics and supply chain management. The second part discussed the design of effective supply chains. This is the third part, which focuses on the movement of materials through the chains. This broadly covers the area of materials management. More specifically, it describes the different activities that work together to make sure that a reliable supply of products reaches the final customers.

There are seven chapters in this part, each of which describes an important function of logistics:

- Chapter 9 shows how the flow of materials is controlled in supply chains.
- Chapter 10 looks at the procurement of materials, which initiates the flow.
- Chapter 11 considers the stocks of materials that accumulate when materials stop moving.
- Chapter 12 discusses warehousing and handling of materials.
- Chapter 13 describes the transport used to move materials.
- Chapter 14 looks at the measurement and improvement of performance.
- Chapter 15 discusses the increasing concerns about risk to supply chains.

CONTROLLING THE FLOW OF MATERIALS

Contents

LEARNING OBJECTIVES

After reading this chapter you should be able to:

- appreciate alternative approaches to planning in supply chains

- describe the traditional approach of expanding strategic plans into tactical plans and short-term schedules

- understand how short-term schedules control the flow of materials in a supply chain

- describe the distinctive approach of material requirements planning

- discuss the benefits and problems with MRP

- understand how MRP can be extended both within an organisation and along supply chains

- describe the principles of just-in-time (JIT) operations

- understand the use of kanbans for controlling JIT

- discuss the benefits and disadvantages of JIT

- understand how JIT is extended along supply chains.

Traditional planning

Chapter 8 described the traditional approach to planning logistics, which takes the logistics strategy and progressively adds more details to get lower-level plans. This moves down through long-term capacity plans, through medium-term aggregate plans and master schedules, and on to short-term schedules. The short-term schedules give detailed timetables for all jobs and resources, typically for each day.

The aim of a supply chain is to deliver materials at the right time to the point they are needed. The importance of short-term schedules is that they give the timetables for making these deliveries. However, the schedules do not just show the times of deliveries, but organise all the other resources, including equipment, people, materials, facilities and all other resources. When 'Sam the Fridge' goes out on his daily run to repair customer appliances, his short-term schedules show the times he is due at each customer, and the resources he needs, including vans, assistants, tools, spare parts, and so on.

Short-term schedules
operational plans that show detailed timetables for all jobs and resources, typically by day

> • Short-term schedules give detailed timetables for jobs, people, materials, equipment and all other resources in a supply chain.

These schedules say exactly when materials are needed, so managers can use them to make sure that they are ordered, purchased and delivered at the right time. Then the schedules give a means of controlling the flow of materials through supply chains. Managers know when tasks have to be done, so they do everything needed to make sure that things actually occur at the specified times – effectively controlling the associated flows through their supply chains. When Sam the Fridge arrives at a customer's door, managers have made sure that all materials have moved through their supply chains and are ready for use. If Sam has to go away and wait for a part to be delivered, it means that managers have failed in this job.

Designing short-term schedules

The aim of these short-term schedules is to organise the resources needed for the master schedule, giving low costs, high utilisations, and other measure of performance. Managers do this by adding details to the master schedule. This is one of the most common jobs in every organisation. Whenever you go to work, fit an appointment into your diary, travel somewhere, go shopping, cook a meal, or almost any other job, you have designed a short-term schedule. When you get up in the morning and go to bed at night – and virtually every job in between – you are working to a schedule.

Scheduling is such a common problem that you might think it is easy – but really it is surprisingly difficult. To start with there are so many possible schedules to consider. Imagine that you have ten jobs that you must finish today. You can choose the first job as any one of the ten; then you can pick the second job as any of the remaining nine, the third job can be any one of the remaining eight, and so on. So the total number of ways that you can organise the jobs is:

$$10 \times 9 \times 8 \times 7 \times 6 \times 5 \times 4 \times 3 \times 2 \times 1 = 3,628,800$$

An apparently simple scheduling jobs is very difficult to solve, and Eilon[1] noted that this type of problem 'has become famous for its ease of statement and great difficulty of solution'. When a company has to schedule hundreds or thousands of jobs, there is a huge number of possible sequences. Each of these is somehow better or worse, and they give a different level of performance. Some will perform better with some measures, but worse with others – so managers have to balance each type of performance, and take into account all the complications that appear in real problems.

Imagine a typical scheduling problem where a set of jobs is waiting to use some equipment. The master schedule shows when jobs have to be finished, so you want to organise them in the most efficient way. The available methods are again those listed in Chapter 8, and range from negotiation through to mathematical programming. In practice, the more complicated methods are usually too difficult and time-consuming for short-term schedules, so most organisations almost invariably use simple methods. Decisions have to be made quickly and implemented in the near future, so there is rarely enough time for sophisticated analyses. The most common approach has experienced people using their knowledge to design reasonable schedules. When you make an appointment with a doctor, this is the method used to give you to a particular time-slot.

In practice, people often use scheduling rules, which are simple rules that experience suggests give reasonable results. You see examples of scheduling rules in banks, which schedule customer service in the order 'first-come-first-served', or hospitals, which schedule emergency care in the order 'most urgent first'. Schedulers use many such rules for their specific needs. We can illustrate these with four common ones. For this, imagine that you have a number of jobs waiting to use a piece of equipment. Reasonable suggestions would take jobs in the order:

Scheduling rules
simple rules, which experience suggests give reasonable results for scheduling problems

1. **First come, first served**. This is the most obvious rule and simply takes jobs in the order they arrive. It assumes no priority, urgency, or any other measure of relative importance. It is perceived as fair, but has the drawback that urgent jobs can be delayed while less urgent ones are being processed.
2. **Most urgent job first**. This rule assigns an importance, or urgency, to each job and they are processed in order of decreasing urgency. The benefit of this rule is that more important jobs have higher priority – but this means that jobs with low priority can be stuck at the end of a queue for a long time.

3. **Shortest job first**. A useful objective is to minimise the average time spent in the system, where:

$$\text{time in the system} = \text{processing time} + \text{waiting time}$$

If a patient needs four days' treatment in a hospital but waits in the queue for 60 days, their time in the system is 64 days. Taking the jobs in order of increasing duration minimises the average time spent in the system. This allows smaller jobs to move on quickly, but longer jobs can spend a long time waiting.

4. **Earliest due date first**. This sorts jobs into order of delivery date, and the ones that are due earliest are processed first. This has the benefit of minimising the maximum lateness of jobs.

When you have a set of jobs like this, the total time to do the work is fixed regardless of the order in which you take them (assuming the time to transfer from one job to the next is constant). But the order of doing jobs changes other measures of performance, and it is these that can be most important.

WORKED EXAMPLE

A master schedule of Zambrucci Move shows that the following six jobs have to be done by a heavy lift crane. What would be a reasonable schedule for the crane?

Jobs	A	B	C	D	E	F
Duration in days	12	8	4	16	2	10
Target completion (days from now)	12	40	44	48	4	20
Importance/urgency	2	4	1	3	6	5

Answer

The simplest way of tackling this problem uses a decision rule, like the four mentioned.

1. First come, first served gives the schedule:

Job	Duration	Start	Finish
A	12	0	12
B	8	6	20
C	4	10	24
D	16	12	40
E	2	20	42
F	10	21	52

The jobs are finished by day 52. Every sequence of jobs will give this same completion time, but they will perform differently when judged by other measures.

2. Shortest first gives the schedule:

Job	Duration	Start	Finish
E	2	0	2
C	4	2	6
B	8	6	14
F	10	14	24
A	12	24	36
D	16	36	52

This minimises the average time in the system (which is the same as the average finish time). Here this is $134/6 = 22.3$ days, compared with $190/6 = 31.7$ days for 'first come, first served'. By day 36 this schedule has finished five jobs, while the previous schedule had only finished three.

3. Most urgent first. Here the company has used some notional scale of importance to give the schedule:

Job	Duration	Start	Finish
C	4	0	4
A	12	4	16
D	16	16	32
B	8	32	40
F	10	40	50
E	2	50	52

4. In order of due date, gives the schedule:

Job	Duration	Start	Finish	Due date	Lateness
E	2	0	2	4	0
A	12	2	14	12	2
F	10	14	24	20	4
B	8	24	32	40	0
C	4	32	36	44	0
D	16	36	52	48	4

This minimises the maximum lateness. Here the maximum lateness is 4 days for jobs D and F, and an average lateness of $10/6 = 1.7$ days.

Whichever the company uses, they can use the results to schedule all activities and control the associated movements through supply chains.

LOGISTICS IN PRACTICE – SCHEDULING AT MUMBAI TAXIS (CONTINUED)

Mumbai Taxis have a fleet of 210 cars working around greater Mumbai, India. They employ 260 full-time drivers, and a varying number of part-time drivers. Usually there are around 100 of these, but at busy times there can be up to 200. Their aim is to keep the taxis on the roads for as many hours as possible each day.

The taxis are maintained in the company's garage. This has five bays, 11 full-time mechanics, five part-time mechanics and seven apprentices. Mumbai also employ 14 controllers who take telephone calls from customers, schedule the work, and pass instructions on to taxis. The controllers keep a continuous check on the location and work of each taxi.

You can already see that Mumbai do a range of scheduling. They start by scheduling the hours worked by cars, so that there are always enough taxis on the road to meet likely customer demand. Then they schedule the drivers to make sure that each car has a driver when needed. The controllers design routes for each car, starting with customers who make advance bookings and a list of regular customers who have block bookings. These routes are continually modified as customers telephone in with new orders (which are assigned to the nearest car with free time), and the cars pick up passengers who hail them on the streets.

As well as scheduling the cars, drivers and routes, the controllers design schedules for the maintenance and repair of cars, mechanics' time, other internal work in the garage, work for external customers of the garage, hours worked by all staff, purchase of parts and materials, cleaning and maintaining the building, staff training, and all other operations of the business.

Question

- Do all logistics involve such complex scheduling problems?

(*Sources*: Waters, D. and Chandrasekar, J. (2007) Updating the schedules Western Operations Seminar, Toronto, Canada; Company reports)

Other approaches to planning

We have outlined the traditional approach to planning, but in recent years two alternatives have appeared:

1. **material requirements planning**, which 'explodes' a master schedule to give the schedule of materials needed
2. **just-in-time operations**, which use a 'pull' system to get materials to arrive at exactly the time they are needed.

Material requirements planning

The traditional approach to planning has some drawbacks. For instance, it is rigid and slow to react to changing conditions – and when a customer wants an urgent delivery, we cannot really tell them to wait until we fit it into the next planning cycle. A more fundamental concern is its reliance on forecasts. The initial capacity plans are based on long-term forecasts for logistics. Then managers design plans to meet these forecasts – but there is the obvious difficulty that forecasts tend to be wrong. To get round this, managers keep updating their forecasts and making adjustments to plans. For example, when moving from capacity plans to tactical plans, they make medium-term forecasts and adjust their plans as necessary. When they move on to operational schedules they do some short-term forecasting and again look for adjustments.

An assumption underlying the whole of this approach is that overall demand for a product is made up of individual demands from many separate customers, each of whom acts independently. Demand from one customer is not related to demand from any other customer, or to demand for different products – so there is independent demand. There may be variations, but they tend to counteract each other and we can get reliable forecasts of the underlying patterns. But sometimes demand is clearly not independent and demand for one product clearly depends on demand for another. For instance, when a manufacturer assembles products from a number of components, demands for each of the components are clearly related – and linked through the master schedule. This gives dependent demand.

With dependent demand we can use another approach to planning, which finds the demand for one product from the known demand for another. This might seem rather difficult, but you can imagine it with manufacturers who have a fixed master schedule. Then they can relate demand for all the components, parts and other materials needed back to their fixed production schedule. This approach is known as material requirements planning (MRP) and was widely publicised by Orlicky from the 1970s.[2,3]

> - **Material requirements planning** uses the master schedule, along with other relevant information, to plan the supply of materials.

Independent demand
means that demand from one customer is not related to demand from any other customer

Dependent demand
means that demand for different products (or from different customers) are somehow related

Material requirements planning
uses the master schedule and other relevant information to plan the supply of materials

MRP
material requirements planning

You can see the differences between traditional planning and MRP in the way that restaurant chefs plan the ingredients for a week's meals. With the traditional approach, the chefs see what ingredients they used in previous weeks, use these past demands to forecast future demands, and then make sure they have enough ingredients to cover these forecast demands. With the alternative MRP approach, chefs look at the meals they are going to cook each day, analyse them to see what ingredients they need, and then order the ingredients to arrive at the right time.

An important difference between the two approaches is the pattern of material stocks. With independent demand systems, stocks are kept high enough to cover likely demand. These stocks decline during operations, but are soon replaced to give the pattern shown in Figure 9.1a. With MRP, stocks are directly linked to production – so they are generally low, with deliveries made just before operations

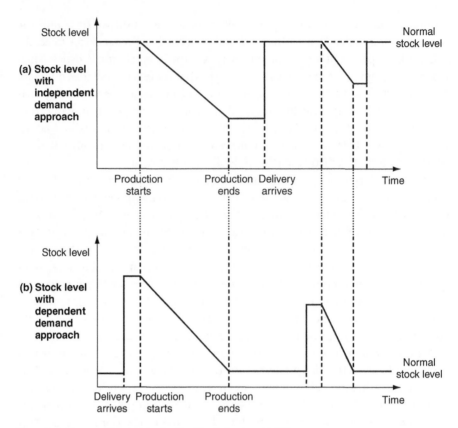

Figure 9.1 Comparing the stock levels of traditional planning and MRP

start. The stock is then used during production and declines to its normal, low level, as shown in Figure 9.1b.

The MRP approach

For its distinctive approach, MRP uses a lot of information about schedules, products, materials and suppliers. This comes from three main sources:

- *master schedule*, which shows the number of every product to be made in each period
- *bill of materials*, which gives an ordered list of the materials needed to make each product
- *inventory records*, which show the materials available and related details.

A master schedule shows a timetable for products to be made – and a bill of materials shows the parts needed for each product. By combining the two, managers can get a timetable for materials needed. Inventory records show the materials available, so they can design a timetable for ordering any materials needed.

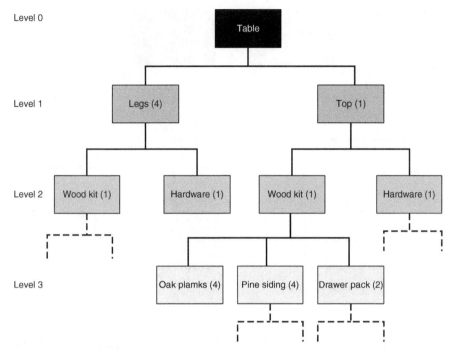

Level 0 — Table

Level 1 — Legs (4), Top (1)

Level 2 — Wood kit (1), Hardware (1), Wood kit (1), Hardware (1)

Level 3 — Oak plamks (4), Pine siding (4), Drawer pack (2)

Figure 9.2 Part of a bill of materials for a table

Suppose that a company assembles tables from a top and four legs. Then each top is made from a wood kit and hardware; the wood kit has four oak planks, side panels, and so on. Figure 9.2 shows the start of the bill of materials for the table. Here every item has a 'level' number that shows where it fits into the process, so the finished product is level 0; level 1 items are used directly to make the level 0 item, level 2 items are used to make the level 1 items, and so on. Figures in brackets show the numbers needed to make each unit.

A full bill of materials keeps going down through different levels until it reaches materials that the organisation always buys in from suppliers – and by this time there might be hundreds or thousands of different materials.

Suppose that our table maker has a master schedule which specifies 10 tables assembled in February. It obviously needs 10 tops and 40 legs ready for assembly at the beginning of February. These are the gross requirements, but the company may not have to order them all as there might already be some in stock or in an outstanding order that is due to arrive shortly. If we subtract these from the gross requirements, we get the net requirements. The company needs 40 table legs by the beginning of February, but if it already has 8 in stock and an order of 10 arriving in January, the net requirement is $40 - 8 - 10 = 22$.

Net requirements = gross requirements – current stock – stock on order

Now we know the quantities of materials to order and the time these should arrive, so the next step is to find the time to place orders. For this we need

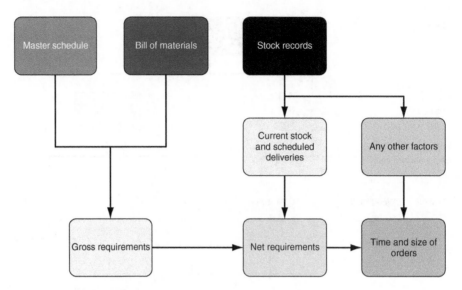

Figure 9.3   Summary of MRP calculations

the lead times – and we place orders this lead time before materials are actually needed. If the company buys table legs from a supplier who gives a lead time of four weeks, it should place an order at the beginning of January.

This procedure gives the initial order pattern, and then the company has to add any other relevant information, such as minimum order sizes, discounts, minimum stock levels, variation in lead time, and so on. The result is a detailed timetable for placing orders (with the calculations summarised in Figure 9.3).

The MRP procedure now continues down through the levels of the bill of materials. The demand for table tops (level 1) sets the demand for wood kits and legs (level 2); these in turn set the demands for oak planks, drawer kits, etc. (level 3). Then the overall procedure has the following steps:

- *Step 1*. Use the master schedule to find gross requirements of level 0 materials.
- *Step 2*. Subtract any stock on hand and orders arriving to give the net requirements for level 0 materials. Use the lead time and any other relevant information to give the size and timing of operations to meet these net requirements.
- *Step 3*. Take the next level of materials. Use the bill of materials to translate the net requirements from the last level into gross requirements for this level.
- *Step 4*. Take each material in turn and:

  ○ subtract the stock on hand and scheduled deliveries to find the net material requirements
  ○ use the lead time and any other relevant information to give the size and timing of operations.

- *Step 5. If there are more levels of materials, go back to step 3 and continue with lower levels of materials.*

- Otherwise, make any adjustments and finalise the timetable.

WORKED EXAMPLE

Semple-Brown assemble kitchen tables using bought-in parts of four legs and a top. These have lead times of two and three weeks, respectively, and assembly takes a week. The company receive orders for 20 tables to be delivered in week 5 of a planning cycle and 40 tables in week 7. It has current stocks of 2 complete tables, 40 legs and 22 tops. When should it order parts? If the company assembled table tops from kits of components, how would it schedule these?

Answer

The orders give the following schedule for finished tables – shown as the gross requirements for level 0 items. Subtracting the current stock of finished tables gives the net requirements. Then allowing a week for assembly gives the start times.

Level 0 – kitchen tables							
Week	1	2	3	4	5	6	7
Gross requirements					20		40
Opening stock	2	2	2	2	2		
Net requirements					18		40
Start assembly				18		40	
Scheduled completion					18		40

The 'scheduled completion' show the number of units that become available in a week, which is the number started the lead time earlier.

The bill of materials for this example is the first two levels in Figure 9.2. We can use this, together with the production plans, to find gross requirements for level 1 items – which are legs and tops. In week 4 there is a net requirement of 18 tables, which translates into a gross requirement of $18 \times 4 = 72$ legs and $18 \times 1 = 18$ tops. Similarly, the net requirements of 40 tables in week 6 translates into gross requirements of $40 \times 4 = 160$ legs, and $4 - \times 1 = 40$ tops. Then the gross requirements for level 1 materials are:

- legs: $18 \times 4 = 72$ in week 4, and $40 \times 4 = 160$ in week 6

- tops: 18 in week 4, and 40 in week 6.

Subtracting the stock on hand from these gross requirements gives the net requirements. To make sure the parts arrive on time, they must be ordered in the lead time in advance – which is two weeks for legs and three weeks for tops. This gives the following schedule for level 1 materials.

WORKED EXAMPLE   (CONTINUED)

Level 1 – legs

Week	1	2	3	4	5	6	7
Gross requirements				72		160	
Opening stock	40	40	40	40			
Net requirements				32		160	
Place order			32	160			
Scheduled deliveries				32		160	

Level 1 – tops

Week	1	2	3	4	5	6	7
Gross requirements				18		40	
Opening stock	22	22	22	22	4	4	
Net requirements						36	
Place order			36				
Scheduled deliveries						36	

There are no more levels of materials, so we can finalise the timetable of events as:

- week 2: order 32 legs
- week 3: order 36 tops
- week 4: order 160 legs and assemble 18 tables
- week 6: assemble 40 tables

If the company made table tops, the parts would form level 2 materials. Then it would continue the MRP procedure, finding the gross requirements for table kits from the net requirements for tables, and so on.

Benefits of MRP

The obvious point about MRP is that it relates the supply of materials to actual, known demand – so it does not need stocks to cover uncertainty or forecast error. Associated benefits include:

- lower stock levels, with supply of materials matched to known demand
- savings in capital investment for warehouses, materials handling, and so on
- higher stock turnover, with no obsolescence
- better customer service, with no delays caused by material shortages
- more reliable and faster delivery times
- less time spent on expediting and emergency orders
- more accurate and timely information.

MRP can also give early warning of potential problems and shortages. If the MRP schedules show that some materials will arrive too late, the organisation can expedite the deliveries or change production plans. In this way MRP improves the wider performance of the organisation – measured in terms of equipment utilisation, productivity, customer service, response to market conditions, and so on.

Disadvantages of MRP

There are also some problems with MRP, the most obvious being that it can only be used when an organisation has a master schedule that is designed far enough in advance, that is accurate, shows what actually happens, and does not have frequent changes.

MRP also needs a bill of materials, information about current stocks, orders outstanding, lead times, and other information about suppliers. Some organisations simply do not record this information – but more find that their information does not have enough detail, is in the wrong format, is not accurate enough, or cannot be transferred between systems. Accuracy is particularly important, as there is a huge amount of data processing, with any errors magnified through the repeated calculations. This suggests another weakness of MRP, which is its inflexibility. It does not hold any stocks in reserve, so the only materials available are those needed by the specified master schedule making short-term adjustments impossible. Some general disadvantages of MRP include:

- it must have a reliable, fixed master schedule prepared some time in advance
- it needs a lot of other detailed and accurate information
- integrated systems must allow the transfer of information
- MRP systems become very large and complex
- inflexibility does not allow short-term adjustments
- the order sizes suggested by MRP can be inefficient
- MRP may not recognise capacity and other constraints
- It can be expensive and time consuming to implement.

LOGISTICS IN PRACTICE – BRITISH AIRWAYS

British Airways (BA) is one of the world's largest airlines, carrying 40 million passengers and a million tonnes of cargo each year to 550 destinations. They are a 'full service' airline, which means that each passenger flight needs a lot of materials delivered reliably before the start. For instance, it serves 60 million meals a year to passengers. These are now provided by third parties (including Gate Gourmet at Heathrow and Alpha Catering Services at Gatwick) as BA sold their catering operations to focus on core activities. But BA is still responsible for the non-food items, such as crockery, wine, dry foods and cutlery. A typical Boeing 747 flight carries around 45,000 of these items.

The airline industry has intense competitions and BA continuously looks for ways of reducing costs. As part of this, BA Catering reviewed its efficiency, services and costs, reduced the length of supply chains, and managed links with supply chain partners more positively. It also introduced MRP for several million items from 300 suppliers. Passenger bookings provide the master schedule, and these are used to coordinate the airlines stock levels and deliveries. By matching supply to known demand – thereby eliminating waste and reducing stocks – BA saves £4 million a year. The company's original investment in MRP was repaid within the first year.

But lower costs are only one benefit of the system. Less storage space is needed at airports, lead times are reduced, there is less waste, control of materials is improved, shortages are reduced, and so on. More reliable information is available, and by recording every item demanded by every route, flight and even customer, BA has a means of significantly increasing customer service.

Question

- Although it was developed for manufacturers, how has MRP been adopted in services?

(*Sources*: website at www.ba.com; Collinge, P. and Reynolds, P. (1997) Food for thought, Logistics Focus, 5(9), 2–8, Jones, C. (1998) Making the missing link, Logistics Focus 6(7), 2–6)

Extending the scope of MRP

There are many ways of extending the basic MRP approach. For example, the suggested order sizes may be small, so it may be cheaper and more convenient to combine several of these into a few larger orders. There are several ways of doing this, generally using a simple batching rule.[4]

Another improvement comes when the same material is used for different products, and then we combine the demands from all products to give the overall gross requirement. Similarly, when several materials are ordered from the same supplier, it makes sense to combine them all into a single order.

A more significant extension to MRP adds feedback. When MRP generates a schedule for ordering materials there is usually has some variation over time. But we saw in Chapter 5, that any variation can be magnified in the supply chain to give widely varying demands for upstream suppliers. It may be difficult to deal with this varying demand, particularly during peaks, so MRP is used to anticipate such problems during the planning stage, and then to adjust orders or capacity to remove any problems. In other words, we introduce feedback from MRP to capacity planning, giving **closed-loop MRP**. (This procedure is summarised in Figure 9.4.)

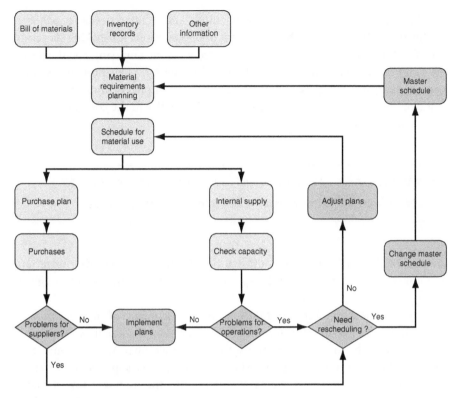

Figure 9.4   A closed-loop MRP system

MRP II, ERP and DRP

You can see how closed-loop MRP (sometimes called capacity requirements planning) extends the MRP approach further into the organisation – initially, MRP schedules the delivery of materials, and then it is used in capacity planning. But it does not stop there. Materials are only one resource, and organisations have to schedule all the others, including people, equipment, facilities, finances, transport, and so on. Surely, we can use the same MRP approach to schedule these as well. This thinking has led to a major extension of MRP into manufacturing resources planning, or MRP II.

Imagine a company that uses MRP to get a timetable for purchasing materials and the internal operations to make components and assemble them into products. It knows when the components have to be ready, so it knows when to start making them. In other words, MRP is used to design production plans for components. But we can use the production plans for components to get timetables for the equipment used, people working on it, raw materials, and all other resources. We know when materials have to be delivered, so we can schedule inward transport, drivers, quality checks, and so on. Continuing with this thinking, we can build an integrated system to 'explode' the master schedule and give timetables

Manufacturing resources planning
is an integrated system for synchronising functions within an organisation by connecting the schedules back to the master schedule

MRP II
manufacturing resources planning

for all the jobs, equipment, operators, machines, and facilities needed to achieve it. Effectively, MRP would schedule all internal operations for making its products. But there is no need to stop at production, as the company could extend the approach to associated costing, finance, marketing, sales, human resource management, and so on. Eventually it would get a completely integrated system that would use the master schedule to drive all activities in the company. This is the aim of MRP II.

- **MRP II** gives an integrated system for synchronising functions within an organisation.
- It links schedules for all operations and resources back to the master schedule.

Even MRP II is still not the end of the story. With the trend towards integration of supply chains, we can extend the approach to trading partners – and this gives enterprise resource planning (ERP).

Enterprise resource planning
extends the MRP approach to other organisations in the supply chain

ERP
Enterprise resource planning

Suppose a manufacturer uses MRP to find the schedule of material orders. It can then use EDI to transfer this information to its suppliers. Then the suppliers can use these requirements to drive their own MRP systems and schedule their own operations. In principle, the first-tier suppliers could then link second-tier suppliers to the MRP system, and the messages would move backwards through the supply chain to integrate all planning (as illustrated in Figure 9.5).

Linking the schedules of different firms in a supply chain can give very efficient operations. There are no late deliveries or shortages as all flows are coordinated, no accumulated stocks of work in progress, and materials move smoothly through the whole chain. The whole process would be based on the free flow of information through internal systems, EDI, the Internet and all the tools of e-business – moving towards 'virtual enterprise resource allocation'.[5] However, we have to say that this approach has serious practical difficulties. It is difficult to get the level of trust and commitment between organisations for them to share so much information, let alone agree to common planning. More specifically, the resulting systems are so complex and difficult to install that companies ask if the returns are worth the effort.

A specific problem is that MRP tends to be inflexible, so a whole organisation run in this way would arguably be cumbersome, unwieldy, and slow to respond to changing conditions. Extending this to a whole supply chain could give a rigid monolith that would be unable to cope with real and changing conditions.

Many organisations have moved towards MRP II and ERP, but because of the practical difficulties they tend to stop a long way before full implementation. Nonetheless, many companies describe their systems as ERP when they make even a small move beyond MRP.

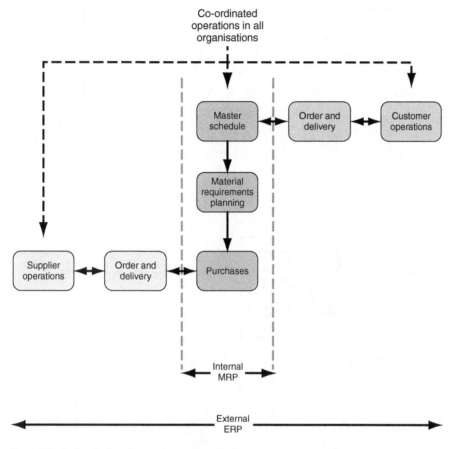

Figure 9.5   Scehmatic view of enterprise resource planning

In practice, a common option is to stop the expansion at distribution requirements planning (DRP), which is used to plan logistics. In particular, DRP plans
outward logistics, in a similar way to MRP controlling inward logistics (as
illustrated in Figure 9.6).

However, there is a fundamental difference between MRP and DRP. The principle feature of MRP is that it is driven by a master schedule – but there is no
master schedule for customer demand, so DRP is driven by detailed forecasts of
final demand at each customer. These are combined to give the demand at the
previous tier of customers; then these are combined to give the demand at the
previous tier, and so on back to the firm itself. The result is a picture of the requirements at every stage of distribution from the firm out to its final customers, and
this gives the schedule for distribution. Of course, the weakness of DRP is that it
again depends on forecasts.

**Distribution requirements
planning**
uses the MRP approach to
plan logistics

DRP
distribution requirements
planning

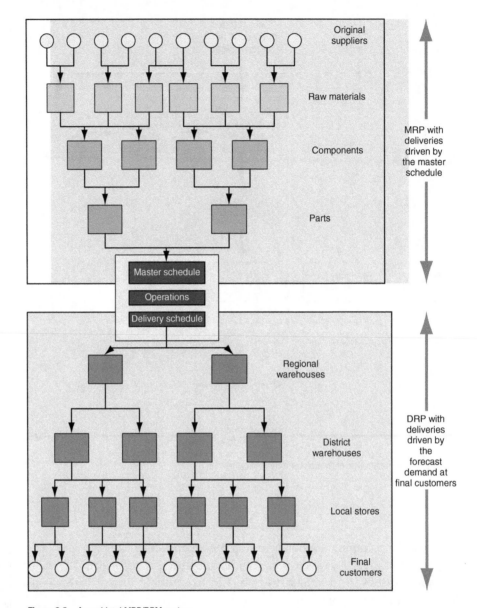

Figure 9.6   A combined MRP/DRM system

LOGISTICS IN PRACTICE – SAP AG

ERP software has been available since the 1990s and the market has grown very quickly. Estimates of world sales value vary widely, but it probably reached $10 billion a year before 2000.

SAP was founded in Walldorf, Germany in 1972 by five former IBM employees. It has now grown to become the world's largest business software company, employing 43,000 people in more than 50 countries. It is the leading supplier of ERP systems, with more than 30% of the total market.

But, in common with almost all suppliers, their systems are used to coordinate functions within a single organisation, rather than include more of the supply chain.

SAP ERP is based on an integrated suite of programs that 'automate and streamline marketing, sales, service, and other core operations'. More specifically, the current version of my SAP ERP has modules for:

- self-services – supplying managers with a range of information
- performance management – giving measurements and statistics
- financials – giving a broad view of financial performance
- human capital management – dealing with aspects of the workforce
- procurement and logistics execution – looking after the movement of materials
- product development and manufacturing – ensuring a supply of products
- sales and service – organising the sales effort
- corporate services – for managing assets.

A large system might cost $15 million to install, with 15% of this for software, 15% for hardware, 45% for professional services and 25% for internal staff costs. The time to get a system working might range from 18 months to over 30 months. Peter Burris[6] of META Group reviews this effort with the comment, 'To say that implementing (ERP) requires an enormous commitment is an understatement. They are expensive, time-consuming, and require change in virtually every department in the enterprise.'

Question

- What features would you expect to find in ERP software?

(*Sources*: websites at www.sap.com and www.metagroup.com; Brace, G. and Rzevski, G. (1998) Elephants rarely pirouette, Logistics Focus, 6(9), 14–18; Anon (1999) ERM solutions and their value, Meta Group, Stamford, CT)

Principles of just-in-time

Both traditional planning and MRP control the flow of materials by designing schedules. Just-in-time (JIT) offers another approach, which does not use rigid plans, but gives a ways of organising all activities to occur at exactly the time they are needed. They are not done too early (which would leave materials hanging around until they are actually needed) and they are not done too late (which would give poor customer service). You can see this effect when you order a taxi to collect you at 08:00. If the taxi arrives at 07:30, you are not ready and it wastes time sitting and waiting; if it arrives at 08:30 you are not happy and will not use the service again. When the taxi arrives at 08:00 – just in time for your trip – it does not waste time waiting, and you are pleased with the service.

Just-in-time (JIT) organises all activities to occur at exactly the time they are needed

JIT seems an obvious idea, but companies like Toyota[7, 8] spent years developing useable methods through the 1970s. These can have a dramatic effect on the way that materials are organised, which we can illustrate by stock levels. The main purpose of stock is to give a safety buffer between operations. It allows operations to continue normally when a delivery is delayed, some equipment breaks down, demand is unexpectedly high, or some other unexpected incident occurs. The standard view of managers is that some hiccups are inevitable in supply, so stocks are essential to guarantee smooth operations. With more chance of problems, firms need higher stocks. So the traditional approach is to keep stocks that are high enough to cover any likely difficulties (we discuss the analyses for this in Chapter 11). Unfortunately, when conditions are uncertain – such as widely varying demand or uncertain supply – the corresponding stock levels can be very high, as are the associated costs. MRP reduces the amount of stock by using the master schedule to match the arrival of materials more closely to demand. In practice, batching rules and uncertainty add some stocks, but the principle is clear – the more closely we can match the supply of materials to demand, the less stock we need to carry. So the principle of JIT is that it goes to the next step and delivers materials directly to operations at the exact time they are needed. It aims at matching the supply of materials exactly to demand – thereby eliminating the need for any stocks at all (as illustrated in Figure 9.7).

- **Just-in-time** operations organise materials to arrive just as they are needed.
- By coordinating supply and demand, they eliminate stocks of raw materials and work in progress.

You can see an example of just-in-time operations with the fuel in a lawnmower. When a lawnmower has a petrol engine, there is a mismatch between the fuel supply that you buy from a garage, and demand when you actually mow the lawn. You allow for this mismatch by keeping stocks of fuel in the petrol tank and spare can. This is the traditional approach to inventory control, with stocks that are high enough to cover likely demand. But when a lawnmower has an electric motor, the supply of electricity exactly matches demand and there are no stocks of fuel. This is the just-in-time approach.

So what happens when there really is a mismatch between supply and demand? What does a supermarket do when it sells loaves of bread one at a time, but gets them delivered by the truckload? The traditional answer is to hold enough stock to cover the mismatch – the supermarket puts the truckload of bread on its shelves until it is sold or goes stale. JIT looks for ways of overcoming the mismatch – such as using smaller delivery vehicles, or opening a small bakery on the premises. This demonstrates JIT's approach, which positively looks for improvements to solve

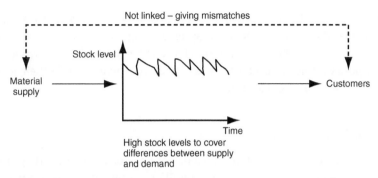

(a) Traditional method of stock control

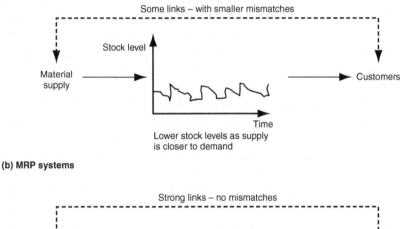

(b) MRP systems

(c) JIT approach

Figure 9.7 Stock levels with different types of control

problems rather than accept current bad practice. With stocks, its argument goes as follows:

- Stocks are held to cover short-term mismatches between supply and demand.

- These stocks serve no useful purpose – they only exist because poor coordination does not match the supply of materials to the demand.

- As long as stocks are held, there are no obvious problems and no incentive for managers to improve things.

- So operations continue to be poorly managed, with problems hidden by stocks.

- The real answer is to improve operations, find the reasons for differences between supply and demand, and then take whatever action is needed to overcome them.

This argument is so convincing that almost every organisation now uses some elements of JIT, whether it is a shop organising a delivery of products to arrive when its stock is about to run out, a bus company scheduling a service to arrive at a port in time to meet a ferry, or commuters who arrange their journeys to arrive at work at the right time.

Demand pull

It is easy to say that operations must be done at exactly the time they are needed, but we need some way of arranging this. JIT is successful because it gives a method for achieving this by 'pulling' materials through the operations.

In a traditional process and MRP, each operation has a timetable of work that must be finished at a given time. Finished items are then 'pushed' through to the next operation. But this ignores what the next operation is actually doing. It might be working on something completely different, or be waiting for a different item to arrive. Whatever is happening, the new material is added to a stock of work in progress to wait until the second operation is ready to work on it. The result is high stocks of work in progress and interruptions to the flow of materials.

JIT uses another approach to 'pull' materials through a process. When one operation finishes work on a product, it passes a message back to the preceding operation to say that it needs another unit to work on. The preceding operation only passes materials forward when it gets this request. This means that earlier operations do not **push** work forward, but later operations **pull** it through. You can see the difference in a take-away sandwich bar. With the traditional push system, someone makes a batch of sandwiches and delivers them to the counter where they sit until a customer buys them. With a JIT pull system, a customer asks for a particular type of sandwich, and this is specially made and delivered – thereby eliminating the stocks of work in progress.

In reality, there is inevitably some lead time between operations requesting material and having it arrive, so messages are passed backwards this lead time before they are actually needed. The materials are usually delivered in small batches rather than individually, so JIT still has some stock of work in progress, but these are as small as possible.

LOGISTICS IN PRACTICE – SCANDINAVIAN HEALTH PRODUCTS

Scandinavian Health Products (SHP) sell a range of 310 products to customers in northern Europe. They deliver products by post, with orders received by e-mail, telephone, fax and post. Their main products are vitamin pills, mineral supplements, oil capsules, herb extracts and a range of other natural products that foster good health.

Operations in SHP are organised into four sections:

- At the beginning of each day the Receipt section looks at all new orders, checks the details and sends orders down to the warehouse.

- The Warehouse section looks at each order, collects the products requested in a box and passes this to the Finishing section.
- The Finishing section checks the contents of each box against the order, checks the bill, adds some promotional material and seals the box.
- The Transport section consolidates and wraps the boxes, and at 4 o'clock each afternoon they take the day's orders to a national parcel delivery service which guarantees delivery by the following morning.

This process should work smoothly, but the Finishing section used to complain that they had to work late, and orders often missed the post. The logistics manager identified the problem as the trolleys used to move boxes between the warehouse and finishing. These trolleys carried over a hundred boxes. People in the Warehouse section loaded up a trolley, and when it was full they used a forklift truck to push it through to the Finishing section.

On most days the Warehouse section cleared their orders just before going home, and pushed two or three trolleys through to the Finishing section just before the four o'clock deadline. So the Finishing section got a surge of work that they could not complete in time to get to the Transport section and make the overnight delivery.

The logistics manager found a simple solution to the problem, which is based on JIT principles. He reorganised the working day so that people in the Finishing section started and finished work 15 minutes later than those in the warehouse. Rather than wait for trolleys to be delivered, they collect them whenever they run out of work. The big trolleys were replaced by small ones that only carry five boxes and which can be pushed by hand. People in the Warehouse section make sure that there are always one or two trolleys filled and waiting for the Finishing section to collect.

Question

- When you walk around normally, can you see many simple examples of JIT operations?

(*Source*: Brandt, K. (2007) Update on JIT, Practice seminar, Logistics Quest, Oslo)

Kanbans

Another requirement for JIT is the means of passing a message back to previous operations, and the simplest way of arranging this has materials moved in containers. When a second stage needs some materials from the preceding stage, it simply passes an empty container back as a signal to fill it with materials and return it (as shown in Figure 9.8).

This method is not reliable enough for most operations, so the usual alternative uses kanbans (where 'kanban' is the Japanese for a card, or some kind of visible record).

Kanban
card that control the flow of materials through JIT operations

- **Kanbans** are cards that control the flow of materials through JIT operations.
- They organise the 'pull' of materials through a process.

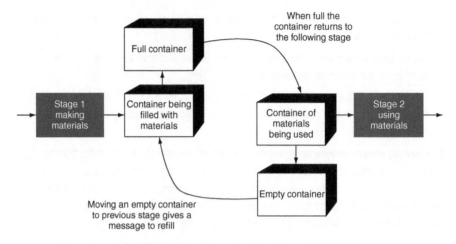

Figure 9.8   The simplest type of message for JIT

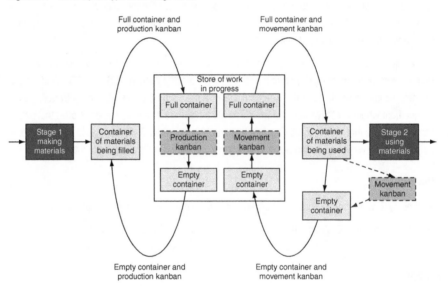

Figure 9.9   A traditional system using two types of kanban

There are many ways of using kanbans, with paper messages increasingly replaced by electronic ones. But the traditional system (illustrated in Figure 9.9) uses two types of card, a *production kanban* and a *movement kanban*.

- All material is stored and moved in small, standard containers – with different containers for each material.

- A container can only be moved when it has a movement kanban attached to it.

- When one stage needs more materials (meaning that it has enough stock to last the lead time) a movement kanban is put on an empty container. This gives permission to take the container to a small stock of work in progress.

- A full container is found in this stock, which has a production kanban attached.

- The production kanban is removed and put on a post. This gives a signal for the preceding stage to make enough to replace the container of materials.

- The movement kanban is put on the full container, giving permission to move it back to the operation.

This system is very simple to administer, but the kanbans allow a rigid control of all movements and they eliminate stocks of work in progress. In reality, there must be some stock, but this is as small as possible. It is kept between operations in containers with production kanbans attached, so the actual amount is fixed by the number of production kanbans and the size of each container. In practice, the size of each container is small – typically 10% of a day's needs – and set as the smallest reasonable batch that can be supplied. The aim of JIT is to work with minimum stocks and, therefore, a minimum feasible number of kanbans.

Wider effects of JIT

JIT certainly reduces stock levels, but it is much more than this. It has evolved into a management philosophy that changes the way an organisation looks at all its operations. Its supporters described it as 'a way of eliminating waste', or, 'a way of enforced problem solving'. In this wider sense, JIT sees an organisation as having a series of problems that hinder efficient operations, such as long lead times, unreliable deliveries, constrained capacity, equipment breakdowns, defective materials, interruptions, overly complex systems, and so on. Managers overcome these problems by holding large stocks, buying extra capacity, keeping back-up equipment, employing 'troubleshooters', and so on. But these methods only hide the symptoms of problems – and a much better approach is to identify the underlying problems and solve them.

This approach sounds simple, but it leads to a number of changes in viewpoint.

- *Stocks*. As we have seen, organisations hold stocks to cover short-term differences between supply and demand. JIT assumes that these stocks serve no real purpose – so managers should find the reasons for the mismatch between supply and demand, and then take the actions needed to remove it.

- *Stability*. Every time a process switches from making one product to making another, there are delays, disruptions and costs. JIT says that these changes are wasteful and should be eliminated. In other words, it wants a stable environment where a process makes large numbers of a standard product, at a fixed rate, for a long time.

- *Automation*. A stable environment encourages lower costs by using specialised automation. This suggests that JIT is most useful for high volume, mass production, typically in balanced assembly lines.

- *Suppliers*. Deliveries are made directly to the assembly line at the time they are needed. So JIT relies totally on its suppliers, who must be able to adapt to this kind of operation – supporting the view of customers and suppliers working closely together in long-term partnerships pursuing common objectives.

- *Batch size.* Operations tend to prefer large batches, as they reduce set-up costs and disruptions. But if demand is low, products made in large batches simply sit in stock for a long time. JIT looks for ways of reducing batches to the smallest practical size – with a theoretical target of making individual units.

- *Reorder costs.* If small batches are used the administrative costs – described as a reorder or delivery cost – can be high. So managers should look for ways of reducing these to the lowest possible levels.

- *Lead times.* Long lead times encourage high stocks, which are needed to cover uncertainty until the next delivery. JIT needs short lead times from responsive suppliers – and it encourages suppliers to build facilities that are physically close.

- *Quality.* Organisations traditionally allow some arbitrary level of acceptable quality, such as 'one defect in a hundred units'. But JIT does not have any stocks to give safety cover, so any defective materials would interrupt production. This means that materials must be totally reliable and free from defects (supporting the view of Total Quality Management).

- *Reliability.* Quality also extends to operations, which should allow continuous, uninterrupted production. This means that operations should be completely reliable, without problems from, say, defective equipment.

- *Employees.* If something goes wrong, people working on the process must be able to find the cause, take the action needed to correct the fault, and make sure that it does not happen again. This needs a skilled and flexible workforce that is committed to the success of the organisation.

- *Relations.* Some organisations still experience friction between 'managers' and 'workers'. JIT argues that this is a meaningless distinction, as the welfare of everyone depends on the success of the organisation. All employees should be treated fairly and equitably.

We could continue with these arguments, but it is already clear that JIT is not just a way of minimising stocks. By coordinating activities, it aims at increased efficiency by eliminating waste. This is the aim of a lean strategy, and JIT is certainly the source of much lean thinking. It is probably true to say that JIT expanded and evolved into leanness.

LOGISTICS IN PRACTICE – GUY LA ROCHELLE INTERNATIONAL

Guy La Rochelle International is one of Europe's leading manufacturers of cosmetics and toiletries. It has a major production plant near Lyon that employs more than 700 people.

One of the problems with La Rochelle's market is the speed at which customers' tastes change. To meet these changing demands, maintain market share and remain competitive, La Rochelle has to be very flexible. In recent years, it has improved its response to customers and reduced costs by introducing just-in-time manufacturing. Now it has small batch sizes, short production runs, low stocks, fast changeover between products, reliable delivery from suppliers, efficient shipment of goods to customers, and fast response to changing customers' tastes. Customers are guaranteed products that have been made within the past few days and have not spent weeks sitting on a warehouse shelf.

When La Rochelle reduced its stock of lipstick by $1 million it saved $250,000 a year. Their Baby Soft bath oil changed from a production run of 60,000 units over 30 days, to 6000 units over 3 days; the run of 200,000 units of lipstick over 65 days has changed to 30,000 units over 10 days. Typical response times include daily deliveries from suppliers, and guaranteed deliveries to customers the day after they transmit orders.

The conversion to JIT is well supported by La Rochelle employees, each of whom has been trained with a variety of skills, works in teams, and is well rewarded.

Question

- How is JIT related to leanness?

(*Source*: Company reports)

Benefits and disadvantages of JIT

We introduced JIT as a way of lowering stocks, and organisations report reductions of up to 90%.[9] This gives related benefits, such as 40% less space being needed and 15% saved in procurement, less investment in stocks, and so on. In general, JIT gives the following benefits:

- emphasis on solving problems in the process rather than accepting them
- lower stocks of raw materials and work in progress
- shorter lead times with faster throughput of products
- increased productivity, equipment capacity and utilisation
- simplified planning and scheduling
- less paperwork
- improved quality of products with less scrap and wastage
- better morale and participation of the workforce
- better relations with suppliers.

However, JIT only works well in certain types of organisation and in certain conditions. The most successful users are large-scale assembly plants that make virtually identical products in a continuous process – such as car assembly plants.

They get the benefits, but there are also some increased costs. For instance, ensuring continuous operations might need more maintenance and better support; reducing set-up times might need more sophisticated, flexible equipment; small batches can increase production costs; more skilled employees bring higher training costs and wage bills; facilities that must respond quickly to changing demand need spare capacity. It is fair to say that the benefits of JIT do not come without an initial investment. Then some specific problems met by users include:

- high risks of introducing completely new systems and operations
- initial investment and cost of implementation
- long time needed to get significant improvements
- reliance on perfect quality of materials from suppliers
- inability of suppliers to adapt to JIT methods
- need for stable production when demand is highly variable or seasonal
- reduced flexibility to meet specific, or changing, customer demands
- difficulty of reducing set-up times and associated costs
- lack of commitment within the organisation
- lack of cooperation and trust between employees
- problems linking JIT to other information systems, such as accounts
- need to change the layout of facilities
- increased stress in workforce
- inability of some people to accept devolved responsibilities.

Many of these can be summarised as an inability of JIT to deal with unforeseen circumstances, and a fairly simple accident can interrupt supplies and stop production. In 2001 in the UK protests over high costs of fuel caused some interruptions to supplies and blocked delivery vehicles.[10] Manufacturers using JIT had to stop work immediately, while those with higher stocks continued working normally through the problems.

LOGISTICS IN PRACTICE – HARLEY DAVIDSON

In the 1960s many countries had domestic manufacturers of motorcycles who met most of the local demand. These included Harley-Davidson in America, BSA in Britain and BMW in Germany. But in the 1970s the industry changed dramatically, and many well-established companies went out of business. Their problem was the sudden new competition from the Japanese companies of Honda, Yamaha, Suzuki and Kawasaki.

These four companies could supply motorcycles anywhere in the world with higher quality and lower cost than local manufacturers. In 1978 Harley-Davidson in America tried – but failed – to prove that the Japanese companies were dumping motorcycles on the market at less than the cost of manufacture. During these hearings it was shown that the Japanese companies' had operating costs that were 30% lower than Harley-Davidson's. One of the main reasons was their use of JIT.

Harley-Davidson recognised that it could only compete by using the same methods, and adopted JIT in 1982. They stuck to their 'materials as needed' programme – their version of JIT– through initial difficulties and are now thriving in a competitive market. In a five-year period Harley-Davidson reduced machine set-up times by 75%, warranty and scrap costs by 60%, and work in progress stocks by $22 million – and productivity rose by 30%. Harley Davidson is now a strong company with sales rising from 60,000 machines in 1990 to 350,000 in 2006.

Other companies that lead the move towards JIT had similarly dramatic results. The Xerox Corporation reduced the number of suppliers from 5000 to 300, stocks by more than 80%, material costs by 40%; and defects were virtually eliminated. Similarly, the IBM plant at Raleigh reduced the space it needed from 5000 square metres to 1000 square metres; Hewlett-Packard reduced stocks at its Sunnyvale plant by 85%; General Motors cut the distance moved by components at its Flint works from 2500 metres to 45 metres; General Electric cut the defects at its Louisville plant by 51%.

Question

- Does JIT inevitably bring benefits?

(*Source*: Schonberger, R.J. (1986) World class manufacturing, Free Press, New York; www.harley-davidson.com)

Extending JIT along the supply chain

JIT forces suppliers to change the way they work. The easiest way to meet these requirements – which also reinforces the idea of integration along supply chains – is to adopt JIT methods themselves. So there is pressure for first-tier suppliers to start using JIT. But then the first-tier suppliers put pressure on the second-tier suppliers to adopt JIT, and ideally the whole supply chain starts working together with the same principles and types of operations. This extension of JIT along the supply chain is known by a variety of names, particularly quick response and efficient consumer response (ECR).

- **Efficient consumer response** links operations in the supply chain, so that materials are pulled through tiers of suppliers.
- It extends JIT principles to tiers of suppliers

Quick response
a form of efficient customer response that links organisations to pull materials through supply chains

Efficient consumer response
connects operations in the supply chain, so that materials are pulled through tiers of suppliers

ECR
efficient customer response

Early work on ECR was done in the fashion industry, whose traditional planning around four seasons gave severe problems with stocks. At the start of, say, the summer season shops had to be full of new products in the latest styles to give customers choice and tempt them to buy something new. The shops needed high stocks and wholesalers needed high stocks to re-supply them at short notice. To make sure that these stocks were in place, manufacturing was done some time before the start of the season. Then clothes for the summer season were designed in autumn and made in spring. If demand for an item was unexpectedly high, there would be shortages as manufacturers had already moved on to making their autumn and winter collections. If demand was low, stocks were already in the supply chain and they could only be removed by end-of-season discounts. The industry recognised that it could get huge savings by smoothing its operations – and the way to do this is not to have huge stocks sitting in the supply chain, but to respond quickly to customer demands with flexible manufacturing and fast movement of products through to customers. The way they organised this was through JIT, linking information systems to pull products through the supply chain. When a retailer sells an item, their cash register automatically sends a message to the wholesaler requesting a replacement. In turn, the wholesaler's system sends a message to the regional logistics centre asking for a delivery, and they send a message back to the manufacturer. The manufacturer is not bogged down in making unwanted items that are later sold at discounts, but its flexible operations respond quickly to demand and replace garments that have actually been sold.

ECR has grown since the mid-1990s, and when you buy a packet of biscuits in a supermarket the till automatically sends a message back to the supplier, the supplier's system sends a message to its own supplier, and so on back through the chain. This extends the benefits of JIT to the whole supply chain. So it brings lower stocks, better customer service, lower costs, more responsive operations, improved space utilisation, less paperwork, and so on. An early system appeared in 1985 when the US retailer J.C. Penney formed an ECR partnership with Burlington (a fabric manufacturer) and Lanier Clothing (a garment maker). This move increased sales by 22% and reduced stocks by 50%.[11] Later Quaker Oats reported a threefold increase in stock turnover, 65% lower stocks and 77% reduction in paperwork.[12] Integrated Systems Solutions reported 3–4% increase in service level, 40–50% reduction in stock and 2–3 times increase in stock turnover.[13]

Introducing ECR

Like JIT itself, ECR can only be used in certain circumstances. For instance, a supply chain that starts with potatoes would have difficulties, as they are grown in a particular season and farmers cannot suddenly grow a crop at short notice. Another problem comes with the length of the supply chain, as longer chains are inevitably more difficult to coordinate. If the supply chain crosses a difficult international border, or includes an area where productivity is low, or hits other problems, the delays become unacceptable and ECR cannot work.

ECR also depends on close cooperation with trading partners, and a single organisation that does not want to be involved can interrupt the flow. However, when firms want to cooperate there must be a workable mechanism for control. JIT does this with kanbans; ECR needs EDI between trading partners – and hence 'electronic kanbans' that trigger deliveries and all the associated accounting and production tasks. This level of cooperation is only possible with some level of transparency (allowing supply chain members to see what is happening along the chain), understanding (of the operations, conditions and constraints on other members), and flexibility (to deliver requirements at short notice). Some organisations take the integration further and pass all responsibility for managing stocks over to a supplier, through vendor managed inventory. Then the supplier is responsible for stocks at their customers, monitoring levels, checking availability, organising deliveries and all other aspects of inventory control that ensure materials are available when needed.

There is no point in having an efficient control system if the physical delivery of materials is slow – so ECR also needs fast transport. We have already noted Beesley's comment[14, 15] that, 'In typical UK manufacturing supply chains at least 95% of the process time is accounted as non-value adding', so the movement of materials should be made more efficient by removing non-value adding steps. In particular, managers should look for ways of reducing any time spent in storage, with Karabyus and Croza[11] saying that, 'product should never be warehoused or stored, but should continually be in movement, with the least possible number of handling steps'. Cross-docking is one way of achieving this, with the supply and demand for material coordinated so that they never go into storage but are transferred from an arrival bay directly to a departure bay. Luton[16] positively says that, 'Efficient consumer response requires cross-docking' and he suggests a target of turning over stock at least daily.

ECR certainly offers huge potential, but no one suggests that it is easy to achieve. It needs major changes to operations and to whole supply chains. Because of this, progress has been relatively slow. By 1997 virtually no organisations had full a ERC system,[17] but there was a lot of interest. Szymankiewicz said that, 'If the massive increase in ECR activity predicted . . . becomes a reality, it will become the main catalyst for developments in supply-chain thinking . . . ECR could well become the basis for supply-chain management.'[18] There has been a lot of movement in this direction, but there is still a lot of work to do.

Chapter review

- Planning is needed to give a timetable for logistics to move materials. There are essentially three ways of generating these plans – traditional planning, material requirements planning and just-in-time operations.

- Traditional planning starts with decisions about capacity, and progressively adds more details. Aggregate plans show timetables for families of activities over the medium term; master schedules give more details of individual activities; short-term schedules give detailed timetables for all resources.

- Logistics managers take the timetable of activities and turn these into schedules for all the activities in logistics. These give a basic means of controlling the flows of materials.

- There are many ways of producing schedules, ranging from negotiation through to mathematical programming. The simplest methods, such as scheduling rules, are by far the most common.

- The traditional approach to planning is based on forecasts of independent demand. When actual demand is known, we can use approaches based on dependent demand.

- Material requirements planning is a dependent demand system which 'explodes' a master schedule to give timetables for the delivery of materials. By relating deliveries to actual requirements, MRP can both reduce costs and improve customer service.

- There are several extensions to MRP, such as closed-loop MRP, which gives feedback for capacity planning. In particular, MRP II extends the idea of MRP to other functions, and DRP includes distribution. ERP forms links with other members of the supply chain to coordinate material flows, but this is very difficult to achieve in practice.

- Just-in-time organises operations to occur at exactly the time they are needed. It does this by pulling materials through a supply chain (rather than the traditional push). This movement is controlled by kanbans.

- JIT eliminates stocks by matching the supply of materials to the demand. But the approach has grown into a drive to eliminate waste from an organisation (forming the basis of lean operations). It introduces a new way of thinking that solves problems rather than hides them.

- Efficient consumer response extends the ideas of JIT along supply chains, to give coordinated flows of materials.

CASE STUDY – SELMENICCHA INC.

SelMenicCha Inc. has one main plant in the Indian state of Tamil Nadu that makes a range of plastic injection moulded components. These are sold to more than 100 manufacturers. Recently they have been changing their operations in response to a major customer, The Sunit Instrument Company. Sunit make parts that are eventually used by car manufacturers. Most of its business is with other Indian companies, but an expansion strategy has led it to deliver more widely, and it recently won a contract to supply a major European company. This means that it has to adapt its own operations, and in particular introduce total quality management and just-in-time operations.

Although SelMenicCha is several tiers up the supply chain, it is affected and also has to adjust operations to meet more demanding standards. Jaydeep Julami is the production manager at SelMenicCha, and is considering the changes he has to make. The company makes 60 main products and 280 minor ones, and the plant works a single shift for five days a week. Their current production planning is based on a regular six-week cycle. The first 15 days of this cycle are spent making the main products, and the next 15 days making minor ones. This schedule was designed to reduce the disruption of changing production from one product to another. Each change usually takes less than an hour, but could take up to four hours if things go wrong.

A dashboard instrument casing is typical of SelMenicCha's main products. Annual demand is around 200,000 units, which the company makes in batches of 25,000 and sends to a store of finished goods. When customers order the panel, there is a minimum order quantity of 10,000. Most orders are met from stock, but if SelMenicCha do not have enough stock they occasionally reschedule production. This gives a week's delay, as well as upsetting the schedules of other products.

Transport is arranged by a local company, who pick the parts up from SelMenicCha and deliver them to customers. Within India, the transport company uses rail and road transport – along with their own warehouses – to make deliveries in three to four weeks. Export orders are generally shipped from the nearest port of Chennai, with a lead time that depends on the final destination.

Jaydeep was reading an article about Hewlett-Packard's introduction of JIT. This said that they introduced JIT in seven stages:

1. Design an efficient mass production process.

2. Implement total quality management.

3. Stabilise production quantities.

4. Introduce kanbans.

5. Work with suppliers.

6. Continually reduce stocks.

7. Improve product designs.

Hewlett-Packard's experience might be useful in SelMenicCha's plant. Jaydeep knew roughly what was involved, but was certainly not confident that he could get JIT to work.

Questions

- Describe in detail the steps that Hewlett-Packard used to introduce JIT.

- From the limited information available, do you think that SelMenicCha should consider JIT? What benefits could they get?

- How might they set about introducing JIT?

Project – planning in practice

One of the main differences between MRP and JIT is their reliance on computer systems. MRP needs specialised software – often growing into huge integrated systems. Do a survey to see what programs you can find for MRP and compare their features. A useful starting point is to search for software suppliers' websites and see how they describe their products. Do those advertising ERP systems really deliver these, or are they more limited extensions to MRP?

JIT looks for simple systems and assumes that complex MRP systems are largely wasted. Do you think this is true? Restaurants use a simple form of kanban when waiters pass messages back to cooks, telling them what to prepare. What other examples of JIT pull can you find?

Discussion questions

9.1   What decisions are needed for tactical and operational planning for logistics?

9.2   How do short-term schedules control the flow of materials through supply chains?

9.3   By definition, 'optimal schedules' are best. So why are organisations satisfied with worse schedules that come from, say, scheduling rules?

9.4   MRP was developed to plan the supply of parts at manufacturers, so it cannot really be used in other types of organisation. Do you think this is true?

9.5   MRP II may be a good idea in theory, but it is difficult to plan logistics, let alone finance and marketing, from a master schedule. Any working system would be so unwieldy that they could never work properly; and even if they did work, operations would be too inflexible to cope with agile competitors. What do you think of these views?

9.6   What are the main difficulties of using ERP?

9.7   What are the most significant changes that JIT brings to logistics in an organisation?

9.8   What happens if an organisation wants to introduce JIT, but finds that its suppliers cannot cope with the small batches and frequent deliveries?

9.9   If you were in hospital and need a blood transfusion, would you choose the transfusion service that uses traditional system of holding stocks of blood, or a just-in-time system? What does this tell you about JIT in other organisations?

9.10   ECR does not eliminate stock from the supply chain, but simply passes it on to someone else. Do you think this is true?

References

1. Eilon, S., Watson-Gandy, C.D.T. and Christofides, N. (1971) Distribution management, Griffin, London.
2. Orlicky, J. (1975) Materials requirement planning, McGraw-Hill, New York.
3. Plosl, G. (1995) Orlicky's material requirements planning (2nd edition) McGraw-Hill, New York.
4. Waters, C.D.J. (2003) Inventory control and management (2nd edition), John Wiley and Sons, Chichester.
5. Brace, G. and Rzevski, G. (1998) Elephants rarely pirouette, Logistics Focus, 6(9), 14–18.
6. Burris P. (1999) Study dispels common myths about ERP/ERM, Press release by META Group, 1 January.
7. Monden, Y. (1994) Toyota production system (2nd edition), Chapman and Hall, London.
8. Shingo, S. (1981) Study of Toyota production system from industrial engineering viewpoint, Japanese Management Association, Tokyo.
9. Hay, E.J. (1988) The just-in-time breakthrough, John Wiley and Sons, New York.
10. Waters, D. (2007) Supply chain risk management, Kogan Page, London.
11. Karabyus, A. and Croza, M. (1995) The keys to the kingdom, Materials Management and Distribution, May, 21–22.
12. Boden, J. (1995) A movable feast, Materials Management and Distribution, November, 23–26.
13. Margulis, R.A. (1995) Grocers enter the era of ECR, Materials Management and Distribution, February, 32–33.
14. Beesley, A. (1995) Time compression – new source of competitiveness in the supply chain, Logistics Focus, 3(5), 24–25.
15. Beesley, A. (2007) Time compression in the supply chain, in Waters D., Global logistics (5th edition), Kogan Page, London.
16. Luton, D. (1995) Efficient consumer response requires cross-docking, Materials Management and Distribution, April, 15.
17. P-E Consulting (1997) Efficient customer response, P-E Consulting/Institute of Logistics, Surrey.
18. Szymankiewicz, J. (1997) Efficient customer response, Logistics Focus, 5(9), 16–22.

Further reading

Hermann, J.W. (2006) Handbook of production scheduling, Springer-Verlag, New York.

Hutchins, D. (2005) Just in time (3rd edition), Jaico Publishing House, London.

Kupanhy, L. (2007) JIT/lean methods and Japanese management, iUniverse.com Louis R.S. (2006) Custom kanban, Productivity Press, Cambridge, MA.

Luscombe, M. (1993) MRP II: integrating the business, Butterworth-Heinemann, London.

Productivity development team (1998) Just-in-time for operators Productivity Press, New York.

Proud, J.F. (2007) Master scheduling (3rd edition), John Wiley and Sons, New York.

Ptak, C.A. (1996) MRP and beyond, McGraw-Hill, New York.

Sule, D.R. (2007) Production planning and industrial scheduling (2nd edition), CRC Press, Boca Raton, FL.

Takeda, H. (2006) The synchronised production system, Kogan Page, London.

Vollman, T.E., Berry, W.L. and Whybark, D.C. (1996) Manufacturing planning and control systems (4th edition), Richard Irwin, Homewood, IL.

Waters, D. (2001) Operations management (2nd edition), Financial Times/Prentice Hall, London.

Waters, D. (2003) Inventory control and management (2nd edition), John Wiley and Sons, Chichester.

Wight, O. (1996) Manufacturing resource planning: MRP II, John Wiley and Sons, New York.

10

PROCUREMENT

Contents

LEARNING OBJECTIVES

After reading this chapter you should be able to:

- discuss role of purchasing and procurement
- appreciate the importance of procurement
- describe the activities done by procurement
- choose a suitable supplier for materials
- list the steps needed to procure materials
- discuss developments in e-procurement and its advantages
- review some different arrangement for purchasing.

Purchasing and procurement

In Chapter 9 we looked at ways of controlling the movement of materials. In particular, we said that the main options use a series of schedules (with traditional planning and MRP) or by kanbans (with JIT). These control the internal flows, and can be extended along supply chains. Whatever system is used, there must be some trigger to initiate the actual flow of materials from one organisation to another. With ERP this is provided by a kanban, but more generally it comes from a purchase order. This is a message that an organisation sends to a supplier, saying, 'We have negotiated and agreed terms, so send us materials and we will pay.'

Purchase orders initiate the actual flow of materials from a vendor to a purchaser

> • **Purchase orders** initiate the actual flow of materials from a vendor to a purchaser.

Purchasing is the function responsible for buying all the materials needed by an organisation

Purchasing is the function responsible for buying all the materials needed by an organisation. Essentially, this means that it sends out the purchase orders – but this is only one step that comes after the main job of preparing the way for the orders. In practice, many transactions are not simple purchases, but they may include rental, leasing, contracting, exchange, gifts, borrowing, and so on. It is really more accurate to talk about the 'acquisition of materials' or the more common term of procurement.

Procurement is responsible for acquiring all the materials needed by an organisation

> • **Procurement** is responsible for acquiring all the materials needed by an organisation.
> • It consists of the related activities that get goods, services and other materials from suppliers and into the organisation.

People often assume that 'procurement' is the same as 'purchasing' – but strictly speaking there is a difference. Purchasing describes the actual buying, while procurement has a broader meaning that can include different types of acquisition (purchasing, rental, contracting, and so on) as well as the associated work of selecting suppliers, negotiating, agreeing terms, expediting, monitoring supplier performance, arranging delivery, organising transport, checking arrivals, clearing payment, and so on. Procurement arranges the change of ownership of materials, organises the delivery, and does all the related administration. Another function – usually transport – actually delivers them, so procurement is largely concerned with processing information. At every point in the supply chain, procurement passes messages backwards to describe what customers want, and it passes messages forwards to say what suppliers have available.

Importance of procurement

Every organisation needs a reliable supply of materials, and as procurement is responsible for organising this supply it is an essential function within every organisation. More specifically, it forms an essential link between vendors and purchasers, and provides the mechanism that triggers the movement of materials. If it is done badly, materials do not arrive, or the wrong materials are delivered, in the wrong quantities, at the wrong time, with poor quality, at too high price, low customer service, and so on. Successful procurement does not ensure an organisation's success, but you can find many example where poor procurement has led to inevitable failure.

We can mention one example of procurement problems when Coca-Cola found contamination in a Belgian bottling plant.[1] Their chief scientist said that the major problem was due to quality lapses at the plant that allowed contaminated carbon dioxide to enter final products. Coca-Cola did not test the gas when it arrived, assuming that the supply was pure; the supplier did not test the gas, as Coca-Cola had never asked for a certificate of analysis verifying the quality. Tests were not specified in the purchase contracts, so the vendor and purchaser each assumed that the other was checking the quality.

Not only is procurement essential, but it is also responsible for a lot of expenditure. Surveys in the USA[2] suggest that 50% of the cost of goods in a typical manufacturer is spent on material, while other estimates suggest this is as high as 70%.[3] The exact figure varies from organisation to organisation, and the definitions used. The wage bill of a service provider might account for 80% of its costs, with overheads and materials forming the other 20%.[4] But if the company uses staff on short-term contracts, procurement may also be responsible for the administration of recruitment, and this considerably raises the costs. A rule of thumb suggests that materials generally account for 60–70% of corporate expenditure. This figure is consistently rising, as raw materials become relatively more expensive, and manufacturers are outsourcing more of their operations.

Whatever the exact figure, procurement is responsible for much of a company's spending, so a relatively small improvement can give substantial benefits. Suppose that a company buys raw materials for €60, spends €40 on operations and then sells the product for €110. It clearly makes a profit of $110 - (60 + 40) = €10$ a unit. Now suppose that procurement negotiates a 5% discount on materials. Materials now cost $60 \times 0.95 = €57$, and with the same selling price the €3 saving goes straight to profit. The profit on each unit now jumps to €13, so a 5% decrease in material costs raises profit by 30%. Using this calculation Philips Electronics found that a 2% reduction in their purchasing expenditure increased their return on assets by almost 16%.[5]

WORKED EXAMPLE

Last year Miroslaw Limited had total sales in Poland of Ł108 million. Their direct costs were Ł58 million for materials, Ł27 million for employees and Ł12 million for overheads. What is the effect of reducing the cost of materials by 1%? If material costs are not reduced, how much would sales have to increase, or overheads fall, to get the same effect?

WORKED EXAMPLE   (CONTINUED)

Answer

- The actual profit last year was $108 - (58 + 27 + 12) = £11$ million.

- If the cost of materials drops by 1%, it falls to $58 \times 0.99 = £57.42$ million, saving £0.58 million. The profit rises to $108 - (57.42 + 27 + 12) = £11.58$ million. A 1% decrease in material costs increases profits by 5.3%. Profit as a percentage of sales rises from 10.2 to 10.7%.

- If material costs do not change, and assuming that other costs remain the same proportion of sales value, then sales would have to rise by 5.3% to £114 to get the same increase in profit.

- To get the same extra profit the fixed costs would have to fall by £0.58 million or 4.8%.

Like logistics itself, procurement was not given much attention until quite recently. It used to be considered little more than a clerical job, buying materials as they were requested. In recent years there has been wider recognition of its importance, and now procurement is now considered an important management function in its own right. This trend has been encouraged by changing patterns of procurement – with greater outsourcing, various patterns of e-business, alliances reducing the number of suppliers, more demanding customers – and the greater role of logistics in general.

Organisation of procurement

The way that procurement is organised clearly depends on the type and size of the organisation. In a small organisation, a single buyer might be responsible for all purchases, policy and administration. A medium-sized organisation might have a department with buyers, expeditors, storekeepers, and clerks. A large organisation might have hundreds of people coordinating huge amounts of purchases.

Usually procurement is organised as a single department to get the benefits of **centralised purchasing**. These benefits include:

- consolidation of all orders for the same, and similar, materials to get quantity discounts

- coordinating associated activities to reduce costs of transport, stockholding and administration

- eliminating duplicated effort and haphazard practices

- having a single point of contact for suppliers and giving them consistent information and service

- developing specialised skills and improving procurement operations

- allowing other people to concentrate on their own work without diverting into purchasing

- concentrating responsibility for procurement, making management control easier.

These benefits can be considerable, but centralised purchasing has its critics. If you work in an office in Leeds, it seems nonsensical to contact your purchasing department in Milton Keynes (450 km away) to buy materials from a supplier in Bradford (20 km away). An alternative view says that organisations which work over a wide geographical should also consider local purchasing. Local offices are likely to have better knowledge of local conditions and culture, better relations with suppliers, more flexible operations, lower transport costs, and so on. The benefits from local contacts might more than offset the costs of less centralisation. In practice, most organisations use a combination of centralised purchases (typically for larger items) and local (typically for smaller items).

LOGISTICS IN PRACTICE – SEARS ROEBUCK

You can get a feel for the importance of procurement from the example of Sears Roebuck in the first half of the twentieth century, when isolated farmers in the US Prairies found it difficult to buy ordinary goods.

Sears Roebuck is a major retailer in the United States. It was founded in 1886 and now has annual revenues of over $40 billion. Much of its early growth came from delivering goods to remote farmers in the Prairies, where it introduced a new way of buying that gave farmers the same access to products as the rest of the population. In 1913 it printed a catalogue containing 1500 pages, with thousands of items ranging from boxes of matches to complete houses. People in any location could post orders for items in the catalogue – or send them to company agents – and have goods delivered by post or train. The customers were always satisfied, as the company gave a comprehensive guarantee on their catalogue cover: 'If for any reason whatsoever you were dissatisfied with any article purchased from us, we expect you to return it to us at our expense. We will then exchange it for exactly what you want or will return your money, including any transportation charges you have paid.' The company has always maintained this tradition, and still advertise, 'Satisfaction guaranteed or your money back.'

Of course, mail order businesses have become common, and evolved into telephone sales and then ordering from websites. This type of business has important features for logistics, including the following:[6]

- Suppliers have direct contact with customers.

- This direct contact allows more precise ordering.

- An efficient system for exchanging information is essential.

- Orders are smaller than normal.

LOGISTICS IN PRACTICE – SEARS ROEBUCK   (CONTINUED)

- Customers are more demanding and want better service.

- Transport is more complicated.

Question

- Can you find other examples to show the importance of procurement?

(*Sources*: Promotional material, company reports and website at www.sears.com)

Activities in procurement

The aim of procurement is to ensure that an organisation has the materials that its operations need. This generally means guaranteed deliveries of high quality products from reliable suppliers. So procurement managers consider questions about what to buy, how much to buy, when to buy, from whom buy, at what price, with what quality, with what conditions, and so on. Typically, this involves the following activities:

- *Identifying users' needs for materials*. Procurement usually starts with a user within the organisation identifying a need for materials and passing the details to the procurement department. Then the department has to examine the request to purchase, and examine the materials, costs, budgets, approvals and other factors needed to start the procedure.

- *Describing the materials*. The procurement department has to get a clear idea of the materials needed, including technical details and costs. This means that they must work closely with user departments, understand their needs and get an accurate view of the materials.

- *Deciding whether to acquire the materials*. Not all requests for purchases are actually justified, so procurement have to ask whether there is a better alternative, such as making the materials internally, using alternative materials that are already in stock, or simply not buying the materials.

- *Deciding the type of purchase*. When a decision is made to use outside suppliers, there are several ways of organising the acquisition (such as purchase, renting, leasing, e-purchases, blanket orders, and so on) and procurement have to find the best.

- *Reviewing market conditions*. This considers the general shape of the market for the materials to see how competitive it is, supply conditions, lead times, availability, likely difficulties, new products, and so on.

- *Forming a long list of suppliers*. There is a widely variable number of suppliers for any product, so procurement should examine the market and draw up a long list of potential suppliers they could use.

- *Forming a short list of suppliers.* This long list will then be screened to get a reasonable number – typically four or five – of the most suitable suppliers.

- *Evaluating the short list.* The next task is to do a more detailed check on the remaining suppliers, getting bids for the materials, finding delivery conditions, finalising costs, and so on.

- *Choosing the supplier.* All aspects of the short list of suppliers' performance are then compared before doing final negotiations and choosing the best. This identifies the single supplier that is best able to deliver materials with acceptable quality, at the time and place needed, with reasonable costs and conditions, while satisfying any other requirements.

- *Ordering the materials.* The order is then awarded, confirming details, noting the effects on stock levels, costs, arranging deliveries, and so on.

- *Recording the arrival.* This ensures that the materials are delivered as expected and according to conditions. Payment can then be arranged and the transaction is largely completed.

- *Expediting.* Sometimes there are problems with materials or deliveries, and some follow-up actions are needed. Typically a delivery is delayed and procurement has to negotiate with the supplier to sort things out and make the delay as short as possible.

- *Reviewing the purchase.* Lessons can always be learnt, so procurement should review the purchase process, see what went well and badly, how the supplier performed, and consider a range of related questions.

This list shows typical activities for procurement, but the details of any single transaction vary with conditions. It would not be worth going through this type of procedure to buy a few envelopes, but if you want to buy a computer you will probably do more of the steps. When a company wants to buy a new oil tanker it adds many other analyses, particularly about design, financing and delivery.

Make or buy decision

Notice the important point that procurement does not always buy the materials requested. On closer examination, there may be no need for the materials, or there are already alternatives in use. Another option is to make the materials internally, rather than buy them, especially when an order is repeated often enough. This gives a standard **make-or-buy** decision. The standard setting for this has a manufacturer deciding which of its components it makes itself, and which it buys from suppliers. But it is a common problem – for instance, should a company use a firm of accountants or hire its own staff; should a television company make its own programmes or buy them from other companies; should a company run its own catering or use specialist providers – and, in more general terms, should a company use third-party providers to outsource operations or is it better to keep them internal.

So the simplest form of the make-or-buy decision asks whether it is cheaper to make a certain item or to buy it. The argument in favour of outsourcing – the 'buy' side of the 'make-or-buy' decision – is that efficient operations and economies of scale often mean that specialised suppliers can deliver products efficiently at the lowest possible prices. The providers give the benefits of specialisation, access to greater expertise, lower stock levels, reduced risk, flexibility, and so on. On the other hand, internal operations can be more reliable, give greater control over supply, tailor products, have short lead times, use spare resources, protect designs, keep value-adding operations, and increase the size of the company. In practice, the three main considerations in such decisions are:

- *financial factors* – particularly the total acquisition costs
- *operational factors* – relating to capacity, responsiveness, flexibility, reliability, and so on
- *strategic factors* – relating to the long-term implications of the decision.

As there is a considerable move towards outsourcing, the arguments in its favour are clearly more convincing.

Considering the increasing number of materials that are bought in, a much simplified view says with the three core tasks of procurement defining what you want, identifying a supplier and negotiate the terms. The aim is to find the combination of products and suppliers that best satisfies your needs. We discuss these two key tasks of choosing suppliers and actually purchasing in the next section.

LOGISTICS IN PRACTICE – CN RAILWAY

Canadian National Railways (CN) is Canada's major railway company, with 16,000 miles of track and 23,000 employees. It has continuously improved procurement, which at the beginning of the 1990s employed 1400 people in 60 locations. In recent years they had used alliances and volume purchasing to reduce the cost of materials by up to 35%. Bob Gallant, head of supply management, said that, 'Purchasing is one of the most powerful ways to enhance economic performance.'

Then they moved from their traditional approach of buying each material from the best supplier, negotiating for the lowest price, and found that they could get lower overall costs by purchasing from a few main distributors. For instance, in 1994 they stopped dealing individually with 500 suppliers in Western Canada and formed an alliance with Acklands, a major distributor who became responsible for coordinating these supplies. CN replaced 6000 annual invoices by a single monthly bill and reduced costs by C$1.2 million a year.

They chose Acklands as it could provide 'a total package', and had similar views to CN and management commitment. The transition to new procurement and changing culture was not easy, with the most difficult part convincing people that they were aiming for the lowest overall cost, rather than the cheapest immediate price.

By 1995 CN had reduced its Supply Management Department to 280 people in 25 locations, the total cost of materials purchased by C$14 million and stocks by C$4 million. The following year they looked for reductions of C$40 million in costs and C$34 million in stock, with similar improvements in 1997.

In 2000 CN changed the systems again moving to e-procurement to integrate and simplify procurement from its 35 strategic suppliers. CN's ERP system now process 100,000 orders annually, and has reduced the administration costs from C$50 each to C$4. The number of core staff has now fallen to 135. Other benefits include greater accuracy of information, greater transparency, lower stocks, and more volume discounts.

Question

- Do you think that it is common for a major corporation to keep changing its procurement system?

(*Sources*: Anon. (1996) Buying power, Materials Management and Distibution, February, 43–5; Stern, G.W. (2001) How CN cut $10 million inprocurement costs, www.cfo.com; www.accenture.com)

Choosing a supplier

Arguably, the most important part of procurement is finding the right supplier – and the general advice is that a poor supplier causes more problems than poor materials. Imagine that you are working on a project and want to buy some important materials – perhaps some prefabricated components for a construction project. You will look for two factors: firstly, a product design that satisfies your needs – and this comes from the internal user department; secondly, a supplier who can guarantee to deliver the product as designed. There is no point in having a well-designed product, if the supplier cannot actually deliver it, so procurement must identify a supplier who can do the work, guarantee high quality, stick to delivery schedules, and meet all other requirements. To put it simply, procurement has to find a well-qualified supplier, and this means one that:

- is financially secure with good long-term prospects
- can develop and wants to maintain long-term relationships
- has the ability and capacity to supply the materials requested
- is experienced and has expertise in their products
- only sends materials of guaranteed high quality
- delivers reliably, on time with short lead times
- accurately delivers materials ordered
- quotes acceptable prices

- offers good financial terms and total cost of acquisition
- is flexible to customer needs and changes to orders
- has a good reputation in the industry
- has a history of successful supply in the past
- uses convenient and easy procurement systems.

In different circumstances, many other factors might be important, such as convenient location, ability to deal with variable demand, regular delivery runs, specialised transport, and so on.

Most organisations have a list of approved suppliers who have given good service in the past, or who are otherwise known to be reliable. If there is no acceptable supplier on file, procurement managers have to search for one. For low-value items they probably look in catalogues, trade journals, or through business contacts. More expensive items need a thorough search, and this can be very time consuming. We have hinted at the procedure for identifying a qualified supplier in the list of procurement activities, and can list a reasonable set of steps explicitly:

1. Review market conditions to get a clear view of the conditions of supply.
2. Build a long list of qualified suppliers who can deliver the materials.
3. Compare organisations on this long list and eliminate those who are, for any reason, less desirable.
4. Continue eliminating organisations until you have a short list (usually four or five) of the most promising suppliers.
5. Prepare an enquiry, or request for quotation, and send it to the short list.
6. Receive bids from the short list.
7. Do a preliminary evaluation of bids and eliminate those with major problems.
8. Do a technical evaluation to see if the products meet all specifications.
9. Do a commercial evaluation to compare the costs and other conditions.
10. Arrange a pre-award meeting to discuss bids with the remaining suppliers.
11. Discuss and negotiate specific conditions that have to be met.
12. Choose a preferred supplier that is most likely to win the order.
13. Arrange a pre-commitment meeting to sort out any last-minute details
14. Finalise details and award an order to the preferred supplier.

Often the steps are concluded within a procurement department but sometimes, perhaps with government work, procurement has to be more open and visibly fair. Then all potential suppliers must have an opportunity to submit quotations, and rather than focusing on a short list, managers have to widely advertise for quotations. Then they have to use an established – and often published – procedure to compare all the bids submitted and choose the one that best meets

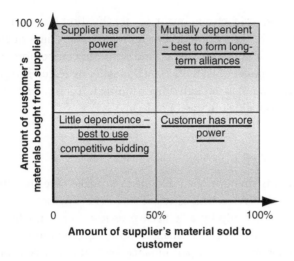

Figure 10.1 Relative power of a customer and a supplier

the prescribed criteria. This is called open tender. A variation reduces the administrative effort by putting some qualifications on suppliers – perhaps based on experience, size or financial status – and this gives a limited tender.

As you can see, we are talking about purchasers selecting vendors, and assume that suppliers are happy to serve all the customers they can find. This is usually true, but sometimes suppliers have more power and effectively choose their customers. A supplier with a monopoly, or near monopoly, of some material might limit supplies to artificially raise prices. People often describe OPEC as controlling the oil market and limiting production to ensure high prices. Even when a shortage is temporary, suppliers choose the customers they will supply, perhaps giving preference to larger customers, those who pay more, or those who have long-term agreements. In these cases the supplier has more power, as shown in Figure 10.1. This suggests that vendors have more power when a small part of their output constitutes a major part of a customer's demand. Conversely, customers have more power when a small part of their procurement constitutes a major part of a supplier's output. When a vendor and purchaser do a lot of their business with each other, they are mutually reliant, and they have an incentive to continue working together and form long-term alliances. When both a vendor and purchaser do little business together, there is no incentive to develop such a relationship.[6]

From a vendor's perspective there are three key steps in the purchasing procedure:

1. to get on the long list, and for this they must offer the type of materials wanted

2. to qualify for the short list, which means that they have features that puts them among the best competitors

3. to win the order, which means that they have specific features that make them the best supplier on the short list.

Cost might be a typical factor in qualifying for the short list, with suppliers who are too expensive being automatically eliminated; then high quality might be the winning factor that makes them stand out from competitors. To succeed in the long term, a supplier must have enough qualifying features to get them onto most short lists – and then enough order winning features to make sure that they actually win a reasonable number of orders.

Monitoring performance

Supplier rating
has a customer monitoring the performance of a supplier

Vendor rating
has a customer monitoring the performance of a vendor

Most organisations monitor their suppliers' to make sure that they continue to give satisfactory service. This is called supplier rating or vendor rating. This might be done informally by a subjective review – or it might use measures for virtually every aspect of performance. Most organisations use a compromise that gives a reasonable view of performance, but with an acceptable amount of effort. They typically use a checklist of important factors to see if the supplier meets an acceptable standard in each of these. The checklist might ask whether deliveries have been made on time, if the quality is high enough, if the price is still competitive, if there have been complaints, and so on. When a supplier does not meet any criterion, the customer may discuss performance with the vendor, ask for specific improvements, and then look for ways of achieving these improvements. It takes time to find a good supplier, so a customer should only start looking for a new one as a last resort.

A more useful approach to rating gives the supplier a score for different aspects of performance. For instance, a firm might give a supplier a score out of ten for on-time delivery and if, over time, the score drifts down below eight the firm can start discussing ways of improvement. Unfortunately, such scoring models can be difficult to use, as everyone has to agree the most important factors to measure, the importance of each, the actual performance, and the lowest acceptable performance. Real results are likely to come from a combination of discussion and agreement, rather than more precise measurement.

LOGISTICS IN PRACTICE – SUPPLIER RATING

Philips Semiconductors plant in Stadskanaal, the Netherlands uses just-in-time operations on its automated assembly lines, so materials have to be delivered to the plant at exactly the right time and with the right quality. Over 65% of the plant's cost is materials, and Philips put exacting demands on its suppliers, typically tolerating a few defects per million parts, and demanding annual decreases in price. To monitor performance, Philips use a Supplier Rating System which measures five criteria each month:

1. delivery performance: an acceptable standard is 99.5% of deliveries on time, with an average of two deliveries a week

2. quality: with an acceptable standard of less than 3 parts per million defective

3. price: expected to fall by 7% a year

4. responsiveness: with supplier feedback within two hours for critical problems

5. audit score: compiled by Philips audit system.

FedEx uses a similar approach to give scores to suppliers' performance for:

1. on-time delivery performance

2. cycle time improvement

3. quality

4. service

5. financial stability

6. cost

7. diverse supplier development

8. other relevant features.

Question

• What factors do you think are most important when rating a supplier?

(*Sources*: Philips Semiconductors, Stadskanaal, Purchasing annual report, 1998; www.philips. com; www.fedex.com)

Number of suppliers

○ An important question for procurement concerns the best number of suppliers to use. We saw above that Canadian National Railway reduced its costs by using fewer suppliers, and in Chapter 5 we saw how the trend towards alliances and partnerships reduce the number of suppliers. In the extreme, a firm might move to single suppliers where it buys each material, or related materials, from only a single supplier. The argument for single sourcing is that it allows trading partners to develop mutually beneficial relationships over the long term, and typically brings benefits like:

Single sourcing
has an organisation acquiring each material, or related materials, from only a single supplier

• a stronger relationship between customers and suppliers, often formalised in alliances or partnerships

• commitment of all parties to the success of the relationship

• discussions that lead to better performance

• economies of scales and price discounts with larger orders

• easier communications, reduced administration and simpler procedures for regular orders

• less variation in materials and their supply

• greater ease in maintaining confidentiality of requirements, conditions, and so on.

There is a strong trend towards the use of fewer suppliers, so there is little doubt that these benefits are convincing. However, the alternative view is that a firm becomes too vulnerable when it relies on a single supplier, and it can become vulnerable to events over which it has no control. To avoid this, some organisations have a policy of buying the same materials from a number of competing suppliers. They might use rules of thumb like, 'never let a manufacturer account for more than 20% of total revenue; never let a customer absorb more than 50% of total resources'.[7] The advantages of multi-sourcing include the following:

- Competition between suppliers reduces prices.
- There is less chance of disrupted supplies, as problems can be avoided by switching suppliers.
- It is easier to deal with varying demands.
- Involving more organisations can give access to wider knowledge and information.
- It is more likely to encourage innovation.
- It does not rely on trusting one external organisation.

Multi-sourcing gives one way of avoiding potential problems, but an alternative uses forward buying. This makes an arrangement now, for a number of deliveries phased over different points in the future. This guarantees supplies over some period in the future and minimises the effects of possible disruptions. Because the purchases are at fixed costs, it also reduces the risks from price rises. Of course, things can still go wrong. A company that signs a long-term contract can still go out of business, or a warehouse can burn down, but the chances of a problem are much smaller.

LOGISTICS IN PRACTICE – LAND ROVER

Land Rover is known for its multi-terrain vehicles, and has been owned at some point by Rover, British Leyland, British Aerospace, BMW, Ford, and more recently by Tata Motors. In common with all car makers, the company actively reduced its supply base, and UPF-Thompson became the sole source of chassis frames for its best-selling model, the Discovery. Unfortunately, UPF lost money on other ventures into foreign markets and went bankrupt at the end of 2001. To find a new supplier would take Land Rover up to nine months, during which time it would lay off its 1400 workers at Solihull, UK, with a further 10,000 people working for suppliers also losing their jobs.

KPMG were appointed receivers for UPF and demanded a payment of £35 million from Land Rover to continue supplies. They justified this claim by saying that they were legally obliged to recover money for creditors, and the sole supplier agreement was a valuable asset. Land Rover refused to pay, questioning the legality of the claim and saying that the demand would make customers liable for suppliers' debts.

Eventually, Land Rover paid £10–£20 million of UPF's debt and took effective control of the company. This gave a continuing supply of chassis frames, and allowed them time to review longer-term options.

Question

- Bearing in mind Land Rover's experience of the risks of single sourcing, why are so many companies moving in this direction?

(*Sources*: Business credit news at www.creditman.co.uk, 9 December 2001; Waters, D. (2007) Supply chain risk management, Kogan Page, London)

Steps in procurement

Once they have chosen a supplier, managers have to set about the actual procedure of procurement. Imagine that you want to buy something expensive, like a new computer, and have identified the features you want and a preferred supplier. Now you actually have to buy it. The procurement function in an organisation works in exactly the same way, and follows a specified procedure for each purchase. This procedure is different in every organisation – and it varies with the type of thing being purchased. You would not expect an organisation such as the US army, which buys millions of items a day, to work in the same way as the directors of Real Madrid football club when they acquire a new striker – and the US army would not approach its decision to buy pencils in the same way as its decision to buy helicopters.

Despite the inevitable differences in detail, we can give a general approach to procurement. In practice, the procedure for buying often includes the selection of the supplier, which we discussed above. So the following description includes elements of supplier selection, which shows how the jobs are interrelated.

We know that procurement starts with a user identifying a need for materials (Step 1 and 2 below), moves through supplier selection (Steps 2 to 4) and then arranges the purchase (Steps 4 to 8). The whole procedure finishes when materials are delivered and paid for. This typical procedure has the following steps (illustrated in Figure 10.2), and is traditionally based on a series of key documents (which are in bold in the description).

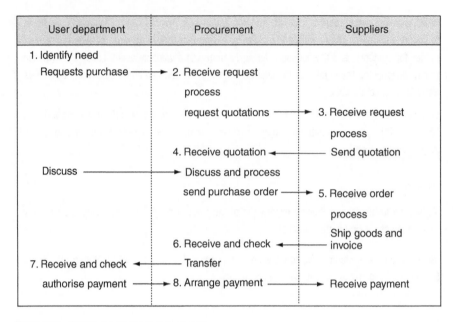

Figure 10.2   Steps in a typical procurement cycle

1. *A user department*:

   • identifies a need for purchased materials
   • prepares **specifications** to describe the details
   • checks departmental budgets and gets clearance to purchase
   • prepares and sends a **purchase request** to procurement.

2. *Then procurement*:

   • receive, verify and check the purchase request
   • examine the material requested, looking at current stocks, alternative products, make-or-buy options, and so on – and after discussions with the user department confirm the decision to purchase
   • form a long list and then short list of possible suppliers, from regular suppliers, lists of preferred suppliers, or those known to meet requirements
   • send a **request for quotations** to this short list.

3. *Then each supplier*:

   • examines the request for quotations
   • checks the customer's status, credit, and so on
   • sees how it could best satisfy the order
   • sends a **quotation** back to the organisation, giving details of products, prices and conditions.

4. *Then procurement*:

- examine the quotations and do commercial evaluations
- discuss technical aspects with the user department
- check budget details and clearance to purchase
- choose the best supplier, based on the details supplied
- discuss, negotiate and finalise **terms and conditions** with the supplier
- issue a **purchase order** for the materials (with terms and conditions attached).

5. *Then the chosen supplier*:

- receives, acknowledges and processes the purchase order
- organises all operations needed to supply the materials
- ships materials together with a **shipping advice**
- sends an **invoice**.

6. *Then procurement*:

- acknowledge the delivery
- do any necessary follow-up and expediting
- receive, inspect and accept the materials
- notify the user department of **materials received**.

7. *Then the user department*:

- receives and checks the materials
- authorises transfer from budgets
- updates inventory records
- uses the materials as needed.

8. *Then procurement*:

- arrange payment of the supplier's invoice.

The first three steps sort out the materials and supplier, and then the crucial point comes with the issue of a purchase order in Step 4. At this point the organisation agrees to buy specified materials from a supplier, and the supplier agrees to deliver them. The purchase order becomes a legal contract between two trading partners, which both of them have to stick to. It is also the trigger that keeps materials moving along the supply chain.

This procedure seems complicated, but if you buy something expensive it is worth the effort to make sure that everything is clearly defined and there are no misunderstandings. For major purchases there are more complicated procedures to fix product specifications, negotiate terms, sort out finances, and so on. On the other hand, it is clearly not worth going through this whole procedure for small purchases. In 2001 Allen was quoting figures of $115 to $150[8] to process a simple order, and a rule of thumb suggests this is now around £80. This is too expensive for low-value items, where the procurement would cost more than the materials. So managers should match the effort put into procurement to the value of the materials bought, and for cheap things this means the simplest automatic or ad hoc procedures. If you are buying pencils, the shop next door is probably as good as any other supplier. Normally, an organisation should put little effort into procurement when:

- it is buying low-value materials
- there is only one qualified supplier
- there is already a successful arrangement with a supplier
- there is not enough time for extended negotiations
- the organisation has a policy of selecting specific types of supplier.

Apart from its cost, another problem with the formal procedure is the time it takes. Paul Sigarro buys material to make designer dresses for l'Haute Vision in Stockholm, and it normally takes one day for the materials to be flown in from the supplier in Nice. But the formalities of organising this delivery take up to five weeks.[9] This effect was recognised by a survey in the USA in 1976,[10] which found the following average times for processing orders in manufacturers:

Stage in procurement	Average days
From customer placing order, to supplier receiving it	1.9
From supplier receiving order, to finishing administration	2.1
From supplier finishing administration, to shipping order	2.2
From supplier shipping order, to customer receiving it	4.1
Total	**10.3**

A traditional, paper-based system took an average of 10.3 days for a customer to get materials delivered from a manufacturer's stock. If there were problems – such as shortages, customised products that need additional work, special transport or delivery arrangements, difficult negotiations of conditions, or any other difficulties – this time would be considerably longer. Despite huge improvements in technology, these times have not necessarily fallen significantly. For instance, if you buy a new car you may be surprised at the time you have to wait for it to be delivered. Similarly, when you buy furniture from IKEA, you can take it home with you – but if you buy it from another shop you may be surprised at having to wait for the delivery to arrive in months rather than weeks.

A lot of work has been done to reduce both the cost and time for procurement. For instance, **blanket orders** use a single order to cover al the deliveries of materials over some specified time in the future. **Value analysis** uses a team of people from different functional areas to find substitute materials that are lower in price but equally as good as the original. Single sourcing and other long-term arrangements eliminate the need to identify suppliers and negotiate terms. But these adjustments do not really tackle the underlying problems of time, cost and unreliability. With traditional paper-based procurement, staff typically spend a third of their time dealing with problems that occur when the procedures fail in some way.[11, 12]

We can summarise the weaknesses of traditional paper-based procurement as:

- taking a long time to go through the whole procedure
- relying on a lot of forms and paperwork that move around different locations
- needing a lot of people to complete, analyse, process, store and generally deal with all the paper
- having other people to supervise, manage and control the administrative procedures
- errors that are inevitably introduced by so many documents and people
- not having information readily available when it is needed
- not giving attention to related systems, such as stock control.

A major step in improving procurement obviously came with electronic purchasing. EDI laid the foundations for automated procurement in the 1980s. There are now many variations on automated procurement, all of which are considered under the general heading of **e-procurement**.

e-procurement

The essence of e-procurement is that trading partners somehow link their information systems. At a basic level, this might involve procurement managers transmitting orders through their supplier's website. At a more sophisticated level ECR links systems and when it is time to place another order for materials a message is automatically passed back to the supplier, who responds by automatically arranging a delivery. Surveys[11, 12] suggest that by 2002 over 60% of UK companies used e-procurement, and 80% of European managers soon expected to use it extensively.

When a major software company moved to e-procurement it estimated the following costs (in € per transaction), with the system giving a return on investment of 400% a year.

Process step	Original cost	Cost with e-procurement
1. Create detailed requirement	17.2	9.3
2. Approval process	5.5	2.7
3. Check requirements	20.2	0
4. Order processing	54.4	6.8
5. Receiving	10.3	2.9
6. Internal delivery	35.0	13.0
7. Payment process	23.6	0.6
Total	**166.2**	**35.3**

Although the cost savings are significant, e-procurement does more than this and brings the advantages of:

- allowing instant access to suppliers anywhere in the world
- creating a transparent market where products and terms are readily available
- automating procurement with standard procedures
- greatly reducing the time needed for transactions
- reducing costs, typically by 12–15%
- convenient access to markets that are always available
- outsourcing some procurement activities to suppliers or third parties
- integrating seamlessly with suppliers' information systems.

The two main types of e-procurement are described as B2B (where one business buys materials from another business) and B2C (when a final customer buys from a business). Other options include B2G (business to government), C2C (consumer to consumer) and even B2E (business to employee).

Most of us are familiar with B2C transactions, where we buy books, music, software or travel from websites. The predominant format has online catalogues and ordering forms, and between 1999 and 2002 the number of people using these in the UK rose from 2 million to 6 million[13] – and continued to rise until it reached half the population. However, forecasts that the majority of shopping would soon be done through the Internet were mistaken and by 2007 'e-tailing' probably accounted for 5% of retail sales. It is difficult to get reliable figures for e-business – in part because there are so many different forms of shopping that might be included – but B2C is likely to continue growing strongly.

Of course, a problem with B2C is that people do not necessarily like e-procurement. If you want to buy a book, you can use various websites and get it delivered within a few days. But it may be better to go to your nearest bookshop, examine a copy, decide if you really want it, and then bring it home immediately. People often want to see and touch what they are buying, rather than just read about it. This effect is clear in the USA, where 1% of car purchases are made through the Web, but before buying 75% of people do online searches to compare prices and specifications.[13]

C2C transactions are growing largely through online auctions, where customers bid against each other for products. The best known of these is eBay, with 276 million registered users trading goods worth $60 billion in 2007.[14]

In terms of volume, B2B is much more important that B2C – because a supply chain might include many B2B transactions before a final B2C one. In 1998 the future of B2B was clearly signalled when General Motors and Wal-Mart announced that they would only buy from suppliers through e-procurement.

By 2002 around 83% of UK suppliers were using electronic catalogues[15] and the value of B2B passed a trillion dollars and continued to rise strongly.

B2B started with direct links between two companies and then more tools helped formats, starting with buying exchanges. These have major companies creating their own, private networks for dealing with suppliers, and they only trade with members of this network. We mentioned in Chapter 2 that General Motors, Ford and DaimlerChrysler initially formed their own trading networks, but merged them when they recognised that they dealt with common suppliers and it was easier to work with a single market.[16] Buying exchanges evolved into **e-marketplaces**, which are large websites that allow easier interactions – and transactions generally – between two businesses. Essentially, they help buyers find suppliers, help suppliers find new buyers, make B2B transactions faster, easier and cheaper, manage all the payments and transactions. Such marketplaces can specialise in specific industries, or work across industries but specialise in specific types of products. Another distinction has vertical marketplaces for transactions within the same supply chains, and horizontal marketplaces which work across different supply chains. Some major companies set up their own e-marketplaces, and any business that wants to work with them has to use it. This also allows reverse auctions, where a company publishes its requirements in the e-marketplace and asks suppliers to bid. The supplier that gives the best bid before the end of the specified auction time wins the contract.

An obvious comment about e-procurement is that it may organise the procedures for procurement very efficiently – but this does not necessarily improve the physical flow of materials. There is no point in having an impressive website to collect orders, but then have a poor delivery system. As Doerflinger et al. say, 'The real barrier to (B2B) entry is the back-end – fulfilment – not the Website itself.'[17] So to get the benefits of e-business, organisations have to redesign their logistics to give appropriate responses. This is in line with Merrill Lynch's view[18] that e-business brings:

- continuing growth in the use of the Internet for procurement
- changing patterns of logistics to meet new needs
- new buying patterns – but probably not much extra business
- improved customer service by, for example, home delivery services.

LOGISTICS IN PRACTICE – AMAZON.COM

The traditional way of buying books is to visit a bookshop, or perhaps join a book club. In 1995 Jeff Bezos went a step further and started an online book retailing business from his garage. His mission was 'to use the Internet to transform book buying into the fastest, easiest, and most enjoyable shopping experience possible'. His aim of stocking every book in print soon made Amazon.com the world's largest book retailer. In its first full year of operation its sales were

---

LOGISTICS IN PRACTICE – AMAZON.COM   (CONTINUED)

$15.7 million, and rose by 34% a month. Stock was turning over 150 times a year, compared with three or four times in a normal bookshop. To develop their logistics, Amazon looked at the best practices and recruited the vice-president of logistics (and 15 other staff) from Wal-Mart.

At the heart of Amazon's operations is a sophisticated system to guide customers through the steps of making their purchases. This system records customer orders, gets the payment, and arranges delivery. But it does far more than this and can search for material in different ways, list similar books and other people's purchases, recommend books, give reviews from other readers, pass on information from authors and publishers, tell you about new books that are being released, send newsletters, let you track an order, and a whole range of other functions.

Amazon use their efficient operations give low overheads, so they get substantial economies of scale, and use their size to negotiate discounts from publishers. As a result, they can give discounts of up to 50% on the publishers' price of best sellers. This combination of customer service, wide choice, efficient delivery and low costs has seen the business grow very quickly. At the launch of J.K. Rowling's *Harry Potter and the Deathly Hallows* in 2007, Amazon sold 2.5 million copies.

They have expanded beyond their original operations in Seattle, with major operations in the UK, Germany, France, Austria, Canada, Japan and China. They have also expanded beyond books – firstly into associated areas of CDs and videos, and then into toys, games, garden furniture, gifts, hardware, kitchen equipment, shoes, auctions – and just about everything else. They stock millions of products – estimates suggest 20 million but it is really too complicated to say. Their UK branch probably lists 1.2 million British books, 250,000 US books, 220,000 CDs and 25,000 DVDs. Sales for 2007 were almost $15 billion, an increase of 35% in the year.

Question

- Can you suggest ways for Amazon.com to improve its procurement procedures or logistics?

(*Sources*: Company annual reports and Website at www.amazon.com; Kotha, S. (1998) Competing on the Internet, European Management Journal, April)

Order processing

We have been looking at procurement largely from the customer's point of view, but the receipt of an order needs a response from the supplier, and this also has some kind of procedure. Typically, a supplier has to check if the materials are in stock, order more from its own suppliers, make parts – and all the other steps needed to prepare materials and ship them to customers. Figure 10.3 outlines this procedure. The time taken clearly depends on all sorts of factors and might range from a few minutes for things already in stock to years for major items that have to be designed and built.

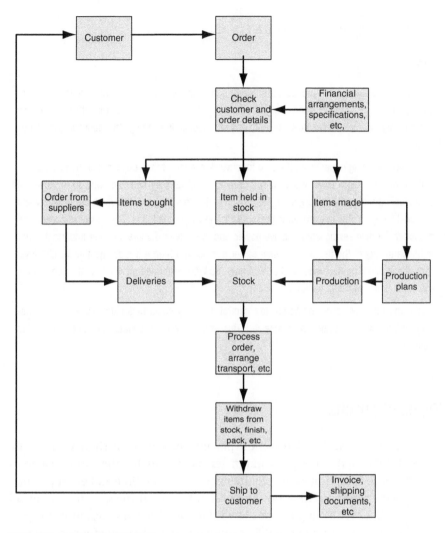

Figure 10.3   Typical order processing

WORKED EXAMPLE

Woodfield Electrical record the following average times (in days) for one of their suppliers. Where could they start looking for improvements?

1. Placing order	1
2. Transmitting it to the supplier	0
3. Order processing	3
4. Production finishing	8
5. Order assembly and packing	2
6. Transport	7
7. Receiving and checking	1

WORKED EXAMPLE   (CONTINUED)

Answer

The two longest steps are production finishing and transport, so it is logical to start looking for savings here. But Woodfield only really control Steps 1, 2 and 7 – where it is difficult to reduce times below the current two days. The only way of reducing time is to get the supplier to do things faster.

Production finishing depends on the amount of work needed at the supplier, and their schedules. If there really is eight days' work, then it is fixed – unless they can find ways to improve the operations. If there is less work but it has to wait to fit into schedules, there is more flexibility and Woodfield may be able to exert some pressure for improved scheduling. Their success depends on the nature of their relationship, relative power, and many other factors. Another important factor is the variability of the times. It is much easier to deal with Step 4 if it always takes eight days, rather than find it ranges between 4 and 64 days. So Woodfield need more information about both the mean times and their variances.

Again, the transport is out of Woodfield's control, but they could negotiate to use faster transport, or take over the transport themselves. This would give more control over a key step in the delivery.

Types of purchase

We have already said that the effort put into procurement should match the value of the materials bought – and in general, the higher the cost of materials and the more complicated the requirements, the more time and effort procurement needs. Many organisations formalise this into set rules, perhaps using ad hoc procedures for buying routine, low-value supplies, a simple, automatic procedure for purchases up to £20,000, a more rigorous procedure for purchases up to £150,000, and special analyses for bigger purchases. But it may be better to consider the importance of materials rather than their price, and Van de Vliet[19] shows how 3M describe the following:

- *Non-critical materials*, with low profits and little risk to supply: these need basic, simple procedures for purchasing.
- *Bottleneck materials*, with low profits but more risk to supply: these need long-term contracts with alternative sources to avoid potential problems.
- *Strategic materials*, with higher profits: these need more formal relationships with suppliers over the long term, possibly developing into alliances and partnerships.

Once such rules are established, managers can use supplier rating to monitor the results, make sure that things are going well, purchases are actually made as expected, the effort is reasonable in relation to the costs and importance – and that the procedure is not failing in some way.

This approach of using different procurement procedures for different types of product is illustrated in the distinction between repeat orders and new ones. If a supplier has given good service over some extended time, purchasers can avoid most of the steps in procurement and simply send a repeat order. This is a routine message that effectively says, 'Send another order like the last one.' A variation on this has blanket orders, where a single order is placed to cover deliveries over some period in the future. This reduces the amount of administration and has the same effects as forward buying.

Other variations are in the precise type of acquisition. Managers talk about 'placing an order' for goods, but 'signing a contract' for services and 'leasing' equipment. To a large extent, these are different ways of saying the same things – that materials are acquired. However, there are significant legal differences. For example, with hire purchase the materials remain the property of the supplier until they are fully paid for; with debt financing the ownership may pass to the organisation providing the funds; with commercial debt the purchaser may get ownership, but use the materials as security – only with cash payments can a purchaser ensure that it actually owns the products.

A specific type of procurement has **contracts**, which describe an agreement between an organisation and a supplier that says exactly what each will do. Organisations often use contracts instead of purchase orders for services (such as a contract for the supply of electricity) or for a specific piece of work (such as a construction company's contract to build a length of road). Related to this are **sub-contracts**. These appear when a supplier signs a contract with an organisation, but it does not do all the work itself, and passes some on to another firm – or sub-contractor. Then, there are two agreements – the contract between the organisation and the supplier, and the sub-contract between the supplier and sub-contractor. For big projects, there can be several more layers of sub-contracting.

Another important variation gives leases and rental agreements. These again give the terms and conditions of acquiring materials, but they are generally used for buildings or equipment that is returned to the owner after some period of use. For example, you can rent or lease a car, and when you have finished with it you return it to the owner.

Comparing terms

The different types of purchase all become more complicated when you look into the legal details of each – not just ownership but also rights and responsibilities. Imagine the scene by the side of a railway where there has been an accident involving a passenger train. In a privatised industry, discussions start immediately about whether the blame might lie with the train operator, the company that owns the track, the company that maintains the track, the company that owns the rolling stock, the company that supplies the crew, the company that built the track, the company that maintains the signals, or a host of other involved parties. There are so many different ways of purchasing – together with different terms and conditions – that it is difficult to compare them. You see this problem when buying a commodity, such as electricity or a telephone and internet service. In principle, it seems fairly easy to choose the best supplier as the one that gives the lowest price. But there are so many different options that it is difficult to identify this lowest price.

In general, there are four ways of setting a price for materials:

1. **Price lists**, where suppliers quote fixed prices. When you go into a supermarket, the prices displayed are fixed. These may appear as published price lists, and everyone pays the same fixed price.

2. **Special quotations**, where suppliers quote appropriate prices to each customer. Customers ask for a price – usually for non-standard items – and the supplier returns a price and conditions that it is willing to offer to the customer. Typically, larger customers are offered a standard rate of discount.

3. **Negotiation**, when there is some flexibility in price and conditions. Then a supplier might quote a price, but will negotiate if it can get some benefit such as repeat orders. Similarly, customers can negotiate if they want special conditions, such as fast delivery.

4. **Commodity pricing.** For commodities such as oil, coffee, gold and wheat, market forces set the going rate that is used by all suppliers.

The acquisition cost is clearly important, but it is not in an organisation's long-term interest to force suppliers to give unrealistically low prices. If a powerful customer forces a supplier to offer an unrealistic price, the supplier will make a loss and eventually go out of business. Apart from the obvious effect of removing the supplier next time the customer wants to buy something, this gives a bad reputation and makes other suppliers reluctant to deal.

Even when a price is agreed there can be a whole host of other conditions. For instance, who pays for transport to the final location and who accepts the risks for the journey? Several standard conditions are used for delivery (shown in Figure 10.4). For historical reasons these are phrased in terms of shipping, but they are now considered in a more general context, so that a 'port' can be any depot or convenient location, and a 'ship' can be any type of transport.

- **Ex-works or factory gate.** The purchaser accepts materials 'at the factory gate' and takes over all responsibility for transport, documentation, customs clearance, insurance, risk, and so on. This type of contract works best when the purchaser has more experience than the supplier of moving materials through the relevant area. If neither has enough experience, they can sub-contract the movement to third-party specialists.

- **Free alongside (FAS).** Here the supplier moves materials to a specified port and delivers them 'alongside a ship'. Then the customer takes over the loading onto a vessel and movement onward.

- **Free on board (FOB).** This is a variation of FAS, where the supplier also takes care of the loading onto a vessel, and then the customer is responsible for onward transport. This might seem like a small adjustment to FAS, but loading might involve heavy lifts, risk of damage, or use of lighters (which are small vessels used to move materials out to a larger vessel moored in deeper water).

- **Delivered ex ship.** Where the goods are available on the ship (or quayside) but the customer has to arrange for customs clearance, duty, and so on.

- **Cost and freight (C&F).** The supplier arranges transport to an agreed point, but the customer accepts any risk and arranges insurance for the journey.

- **Cost, insurance and freight (CIF).** Where the supplier delivers to an agreed point, and also arranges insurance for the journey.

- **Delivered.** Where the supplier is responsible for all aspects of the transport up to delivery at the customer, or some other agreed point.

Since these terms have become more widely used, some people have begun to use them in slightly different ways. For instance, they might use FAS to describe delivery to a supermarket delivery bay (leaving the supermarket to unload) while FOB means delivery to the supermarket stockroom. As always, when you hear people using these terms you should understand exactly how they are using them.

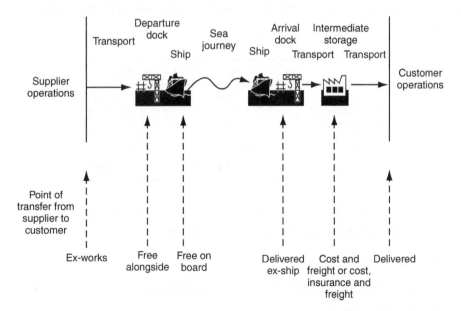

Figure 10.4   Some arrangements for delivery

The choice of pricing can have an impact on broader operations. For example, with delivered prices buyers know in advance exactly how much the goods will cost, and they do not have to get involved with administering transport. But this leaves control of transport with the seller, who may have different priorities – perhaps choosing the lowest cost carrier rather than the most reliable. Power in many supply chains is moving towards the final retailers, and they are increasingly organising their own deliveries through integrated transport. They have considerable expertise in managing deliveries, and their ability to consolidate loads gives fast and efficient operations. The result is a clear trend towards factory gate pricing.

LOGISTICS IN PRACTICE – TT&G/PESCHIMOL

TT&G/Peschimol (TP) make prefabricated buildings for use in the Russian and Canadian Arctic, where they are used in oil companies' exploration camps. More than 60% of TP's operating costs are spent on procurement, so they look for the best possible deals.

The company's purchasing policies were designed at a time when it was more difficult to get guaranteed supplies, especially in Russia, so they tended to make most of their own components. Recently, supplies have become more reliable, and TP now outsource most of their component supplies and only assemble the final buildings. For many components, they have moved towards single sourcing through a set of preferred suppliers. Although they have not analysed the costs of this arrangement, there have been significant reductions in procurement times. For example, the following table compares some times for current partnering and the previous competitive bidding.

	Partnering	*Bidding*
Bid review	1–2 weeks	4–6 weeks
Drawing preparation	4–5 weeks	7–10 weeks
Drawing approval	1 week	2–3 weeks
Manufacturing time	10–12 weeks	18–24 weeks
Test time	1 week	2–3 weeks
Total	**17–21 weeks**	**33–46 weeks**

Transport is expensive, but the oil companies have a lot of experience at setting up remote camps, so TP always negotiate with purchasers and give factory gate prices.

Question

- In what circumstances would other types of pricing be appropriate?

(*Source*: Company reports)

Chapter review

- The actual flow of material through a supply chain is generally triggered by a purchase order. This is prepared by the purchasing function. In practice, there are other options to purchasing, which are included in the broader term of procurement.

- Procurement is responsible for acquiring all the materials needed by an organisation. It consists of all the activities needed to organise an inward flow of materials.

- Procurement is an essential function in every organisation. It is often responsible for the greatest part of expenditure, and a small improvement can bring significant benefits.

- Procurement does a series of activities that range from identifying users' needs for materials, through the ordering process to recoding the arrival of the materials and analysing the procurement process. Details of the approach depend largely on the type of materials bought.

- The core elements of procurement are deciding what to buy, finding a supplier and buying the materials. Choosing a supplier is particularly important, and we outlined a standard procedure for this. After choosing a vendor, supplier rating monitors their performance over time.

- Traditional approaches to procurement can be expensive, slow and prone to errors. In many circumstances e-procurement offers a better alternative and brings a range of benefits. Many types of e-procurement have developed, and these are all continuing to grow rapidly.

- Different types of purchase need different conditions, with the amount of effort generally related to the product value or its importance. There are so many different types of purchase and conditions that it is surprisingly difficult to compare them.

CASE STUDY – HARALD PIETERSSON

For many years Harald Pietersson worked in the Norwegian port of Bergen. In 2005 he had his 60th birthday and took early retirement. He had a number of projects he wanted to work on, including making wooden children's toys, buying and selling mechanical toys, and writing a history of Norse influences on Russian culture.

Harald found a surprising demand for his wooden and mechanical toys, but he seemed to have less success with his books. He finished his first book in 2006 and published it through Norgeldt, a specialist publisher in Oslo. It sold 300 copies in the first year, and Harald began work on a second book on the links between Norse mythology and Russian folklore. He had considerable expertise in this field and Harald planned to write a series of books. Obviously, they would not have broad appeal, but there was a steady demand in this specialised market, and Norgeldt seemed happy to consider new proposals.

CASE STUDY – HARALD PIETERSSON   (CONTINUED)

A clear problem was that Norgeldt only really worked in Norway and Sweden, where they estimated a continuing demand for Harald's books at around 200 copies a year. But Harald was not really happy with this as he felt that the publisher was not reaching the large Scandinavian populations in the USA, Canada, Australia and other countries, and there were almost no sales in Russia.

Harald was not expecting a great return from his books, but he was disappointed by his royalty cheques. His book retailed for 1000 NKr, but his royalties were calculated at 6% of the publisher's selling price, which depended on the discounts offered, but was usually less than 700 NKr. He could change publisher, but was unlikely to get any interest from the major, international companies. He could also approach a 'vanity publisher' who would charge a fee for publishing the book, but return more of the income generated.

Alternatively, Harald could set up a website to advertise his books more widely – and by selling books directly to customers he could bypass the retailer and distribution network. He could go further and also bypass the publisher, either producing the book himself, or avoiding a paper version and allowing customers to pay a fee to access an electronic version. Such a website could also be used to market his wooden and mechanical toys. Perhaps it would be easier to use an established e-market place or e-auction site, at least to test likely sales.

Questions

- Harald clearly has to think hard about the way he sells and distributes books. What options do you think he has? What would be the benefits and problems with each?

- What route would you recommend him to follow?

Project – how to buy

Imagine that you want to buy something expensive, such as a car. Describe the steps you would follow in making the purchase.

With the three core tasks of procurement being defining what you want, identifying a supplier and negotiating the terms, how would you set about each of these?

Now compare your approach with a company making a similar purchase. How would their approach depend on circumstances? Is it difficult to get information about the procedure that a company actually uses for procurement? Why?

Discussion questions

10.1   Is there really a difference between purchasing and procurement?

10.2   People often say that you should get four or five quotations, even for repeat orders, as this encourages competition and keeps prices low. Other people say that you should form an alliance with one supplier so that you understand each other's needs and can work closely together. Which of these views do you find more persuasive?

10.3   What exactly do procurement departments do?

10.4   What features would make an ideal supplier?

10.5   Outsourcing decisions are not strategic but the result of simple 'make-or-buy' analyses. What does this mean, and is it true?

10.6   Forward purchasing has many advantages – as demonstrated by the huge markets in financial futures. What are these benefits? If these are so obvious, why do many organisations buy just-in-time?

10.7   Is it fair to say that the effort put into procurement should be related to the value of materials bought?

10.8   Do you think an organisation should always negotiate hard with suppliers to get the cheapest prices and best conditions it can?

10.9   There is a lot of talk about the benefits of purchasing through the Internet. What are these?

10.10 In 2000 The Trading and Standards Institute in London made test purchases from 102 retail websites. There were problems with 37% of these, 38% arrived later than promised and 17% did not arrive at all.[20] What does this tell you about e-procurement?

References

1. Deogun, N. (1999) Anatomy of a recall: how Coke's controls fizzled out in Europe, The Wall Street Journal, 29 June, p. A1.
2. Industry Week (2007) Census of manufacturers, Penton Media, Cleveland, OH and website at www.industryweek.com.
3. Lysons, K. (2000) purchasing and supply chain management (5th edition) FT/Prentice Hall, Harlow, Essex.
4. Ackerman, K.B. and Brewer, A.M. (2001) Warehousing: a key link in the supply chain, Chapter 14 in Handbook of logistics and supply chain management, Brewer, A.M., Button, K.J. and Hensher, D.A. (editors), Pergamon, Oxford.
5. Philips Electronics (1999) Purchasing becoming supply chain management, Quality Matters, January, Issue 94.
6. Scott, C. and Westbrook, R. (1991) New strategic tool for supply chain management, International Journal of Physical Distribution and Logistics Management, 21(1), 23–33.
7. Perry, R. (1998) Quoted in Lawless J., Challenges of going global, The Sunday Times, 26 April.
8. Allen, S. (2001) Leveraging procurement: the quiet e-business, Logistics and transport Focus, 3(4), 29–30.
9. Sigarro, P. (2007) Speeding up procurement – an update, Logistics Discussion Seminar, Marseilles.
10. LaLonde, B.J. and Zinszer, P.H. (1976) Customer service, National Council of Physical Distribution Management, Chicago.
11. Cummings, N. (2002) UK leading the world in e-procurement, OR Newsletter, 9 March.
12. Website at www.barclaysb2b.com.
13. Rushe, D. (2001) www.basketcase, The Sunday Times, 2 September, 5.
14. Website at www.ebay.com.
15. MRO Software (2001) Supplying the goods, MRO Software, London.
16. Simson, R., Werner, F. and White, G. (2000) Big three carmakers plan net exchange, The Wall Street Journal, 28 February 2000.
17. Doerflinger, T.M., Gerharty, M. and Kerschner, E.M. (1999) The information revolution wars, Paine-Webber Newsletter, New York.
18. Merrill Lynch (1999) e-commerce: virtually there, Merrill Lynch, New York.
19. Van de Vliet, A. (1996) When the gaggling has to stop, Management Today, June, pp. 56–60.
20. Website at www.tradingstandards.gov.uk.

Further reading

Arnold, J.R.T (1996) Introduction to materials management (2nd edition) Prentice Hall, Englewood Cliffs, NJ.

Axelsson, B. and Wynstra, F. (2002) Buying business services, John Wiley and Sons, Chichester.

Baily, P., Farmer, D., Jessop, D. and Jones, D. (1998) Purchasing principles and management (7th edition), Pitman, London.

Day, M. (2002) Handbook of purchasing management (3rd edition), Gower Publishing, London.

Gattorna, J.L and Walters, D.W. (1996) Managing the supply chain, Palgrave, Basingstoke, Hampshire.

Leenders, M.R., Fearon, H.E., Flynn, A.E. and Johnson, P.F. (2002) Purchasing and supply management (12th edition), McGraw-Hill Irwin, Burr Ridge, IL.

Lysons, K. (2000) Purchasing and supply chain management (5th edition), FT Prentice Hall, Harlow.

Monczka, R., Trent, R. and Handfield, R. (2005) Purchasing and supply chain management (3rd edition), South Western, Mason, OH.

Saunders, M. (1997) Strategic purchasing and supply chain management (2nd edition), FT Prentice Hall, London.

Van Weele, A.J. (2002) Purchasing and supply chain management (3rd edition) Thomson Learning, London.

11

INVENTORY MANAGEMENT

Contents

LEARNING OBJECTIVES

After reading this chapter you should be able to:

- understand why organisations hold stocks

- analyse the costs of holding stock

- calculate economic order quantities

- do calculations for lead times, costs and cycle lengths

- discuss service levels and do related calculations for safety stock

- describe periodic review systems and calculate target stock levels

- do ABC analyses of inventories.

Reasons for holding stock

In Chapter 10 we saw how procurement triggers the flow of materials through a supply chain. Ideally, materials move smoothly and continuously, controlled by the methods we described in Chapter 9. But in reality, there are always delays when materials stop moving. Whenever materials wait in the supply chain, they form stocks.

Stock
is a store of materials that is held in an organisation, and is formed whenever materials are not used at the time they become available

---

- **Stocks** are stores of materials that are held in an organisation.

- They are formed whenever materials are not used at the time they become available – and whenever there are breaks in the smooth flow of materials.

All organisations hold stocks of some kind, whether it is a shop that stocks goods for customers to look at, a chef with stocks of ingredients in the pantry, a market research company with stocks of information in a database, or a bank with stocks of cash held in reserve. An inventory is a list of things held in stock (but there is some confusion and people often use it to mean the actual stock).

Inventory
a list of things held in stock (or sometimes the stock itself)

Chapter 9 looked at ways of controlling the flow of materials, and the underlying assumption was that stocks are a waste of resources that should be eliminated, or at least minimised. So you might get the impression that every organisation is getting rid of its stocks and moving as fast as it can to JIT and 'stockless' operations. There has certainly been a long-term trend in this direction. In 1998 the Institute of Grocery Distribution[1] found that stock levels were falling by as much as 8.5% a year, while the Institute of Logistics[2] found that UK companies, 'managed to almost halve the stockholding requirements since the 1995 survey'. Government figures[3–5] give a broader picture, and the ratio of aggregate stock to gross domestic product (GDP) gives an interesting comparison of performance over time. Figure 11.1 shows the value of aggregate stock held in the UK as a percentage of GDP from 1949 to 1998.[6]

As you can see, there has been a steady fall in stock levels, and this has continued to the present. Superimposed on the underlying trend are some short-term fluctuations. For instance, from the 1940s and into the early 1950s there was a rapid decline in stocks as the economy returned to normal after the Second World War; and there was instability around 1973 when oil prices suddenly rose and caused widespread economic disruption.

The steady fall in stocks suggests better management, but other factors are also having effects, such as the changing structure of industry, the move towards services, international competition, economic cycles, inflation, changing GDP, currency value and increasing mobility. Inventories clearly respond to such external influences, and you can see this in, for example, business cycles. A business cycle starts with industry being over-optimistic about the future – they expect sales to rise and increase production to meet this higher demand. Stocks build up as sales lag behind production, and at some point industry loses confidence

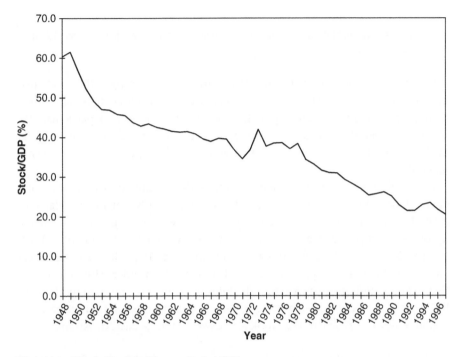

Figure 11.1   Historical trend for UK aggregate stock/GDP

and cuts back on production to use the excess stocks. This causes a decline in the economy, which only picks up again when stocks are lower and production is not meeting current demand. It is relatively easy to change stock levels, and much easier than adjusting production levels, so they tend to fluctuate more than the business cycle itself.

Every organisation holds stocks, even those offering intangible services – but manufacturers hold particularly large amounts. In the UK, manufacturing industry contributes less than 20% of the GNP, but it holds 40% of the stocks. At the same time, the amount of stock held by manufacturers has fallen much faster than in other sectors of industry, suggesting that they have been at the forefront of stock reduction – and also that they are in the best position to reduce stocks.

Not all organisations can eliminate, or even reduce, their stocks. For instance, retailers need stocks of items for their customers to look at, and they often find that bigger stocks give higher sales. Wholesalers have to react quickly to replace items that customers buy, which generally needs stocks near the end of supply chains. Farmers grow hay in the summer, and then store it to feed their animals in the winter; a distillery stores barrels of whisky for at least three years before selling it; a library buys books and keeps them in stock until someone borrows them; Fort Knox keeps the USA's strategic reserve of gold. These organisations do not want to eliminate stocks, but they want to control them properly – and they do this by efficient stock control. This function is known by several names, particularly inventory control, or inventory management.

Stock control
another term for inventory management

Inventory management
is responsible for the control of stock levels within an organisation

Inventory control
another term for inventory management

> • **Inventory management** is responsible for the control of stock levels within an organisation.

In Chapter 9 we described material requirements planning (MRP) and just-in-time (JIT) as dependent demand systems for controlling materials. These automatically define ordering policies and set stock levels. In particular, JIT places an order through a kanban when operations are ready to start work; MRP schedules an order needed to meet production specified in the master schedule.

The alternative approach assumes independent demand, where the total demand for an item is made up of lots of separate demands that are not related to each other. For instance, the overall demand for bread in a supermarket is made up of lots of demands from separate customers who act independently. With independent demand systems there is no obvious ordering policy, and managers have to decide when to place orders and how much to order. This is a part of their work in designing short-term schedules. A number of standard models can help with these ordering decisions, generally by finding the best balance between various costs. In particular, they look for answers to three basic questions.

1. **What items should we stock?** No item, however cheap, should be stocked unless the benefits outweigh the costs. So organisations should never add unnecessary, new items to stock, and they should make regular searches to remove obsolete or dead items.

2. **When should we place an order?** This depends on the inventory control system used, type of demand (high or low, steady or erratic, known exactly or estimated), value of the item, lead time between placing an order and receiving it into stock, supplier reliability, and a number of other factors.

3. **How much should we order?** Large, infrequent orders give high average stock levels, but low costs for transport and administering orders: small, frequent orders give low average stocks, but high costs for transport and administering orders.

The first of these questions is a matter of good housekeeping, simply avoiding stock that is not needed. The rest of the chapter looks for answers to the other two questions.

Stock as a buffer

As so many people consider stocks to be a waste of resources, we should ask why all organisations still hold them. The answer is that they provide an essential buffer between supply and demand. Both the supply of materials and demand can be variable and uncertain, and stocks give a cushion between them.

Imagine the food delivered to a supermarket. This comes in large quantities – perhaps a truckload a day – but it is sold in much smaller quantities to individual customers throughout the day. There is clearly a mismatch between supply and demand, and stocks are needed to give a cushion between them. Stocks held on the shelves and in storerooms allow the supermarket to continue working efficiently, even when delivery vehicles are delayed, or there is unexpectedly high demand from customers.

- The main **purpose of stocks** is to give a buffer between supply and demand.
- They allow operations to continue smoothly through variable and uncertain supply and/or demand.

We can be a bit more specific and list the following reasons for holding stocks:

- to act as a buffer between different parts of the supply chain
- to allow for demands that are larger than expected, or at unexpected times
- to allow for deliveries that are delayed or too small
- to take advantage of price discounts on large orders
- to allow the purchase of items when the price is low and expected to rise
- to allow the purchase of items that are going out of production or are difficult to find
- to allow for seasonal operations
- to make full loads and reduce transport costs
- to provide cover for emergencies
- to generate profit when inflation is high.

LOGISTICS IN PRACTICE – STOCK HOLDINGS

Tesco

Tesco is the largest food retailer in UK, where it has 21% of the market. It also has growing international operations and has diversified into non-food items. Their annual report for 2007 showed:

Total sales	£46.6 billion
Number of stores	2672
Total sales area	55.2 million square feet
Stocks	£1.93 billion

IBM

For many years IBM has been a leader in the computer industry, where they have moved progressively from hardware and into services and software. Their financial report to 2007 showed a revenue of $91.4 billion, 356,000 employees – and stock of $2.81 billion.

LOGISTICS IN PRACTICE – STOCK HOLDINGS   (CONTINUED)

Shell

Shell is a global group of energy and petrochemical companies. They work in more than 130 countries and employ 108,000 people. In the year to 2007 their revenue was $320 billion, giving a net income of $26 billion – and stocks of $23.2 billion.

L.T. Francis

L.T. Francis is a manufacturer of pre-cast concrete fittings for the building trade. Their 2008 annual report showed sales of £16 million and total stocks £2.6 million.

These organisations all hold large stocks. In Tesco the stock is around 4% of sales, in IBM about 3% in total, in Shell it is 7% for the full year, and in L.T. Francis it is 16%. Many organisations have very high stocks, and it is not unusual for this to reach 25% of annual sales.

Question

- Should all organisations aim at reducing their stocks?

(*Sources*: Company annual reports and websites www.tesco.com, www.shell.com and www.ibm.com)

Types of stock

Just about everything is held as stock somewhere, whether it is raw materials in a factory, finished goods in a shop or tins of baked beans in your pantry. We can classify these stocks (illustrated in Figure 11.2) as:

- **raw materials** – the materials, parts and components that have been delivered to an organisation, but are not yet being used
- **work in progress** – materials that have started, but not yet finished their journey through the organisation's operations
- **finished goods** – goods that have finished the process and are waiting to be shipped out to customers.

Nationally, there are roughly equal amounts of raw materials, work in progress and finished goods stored. But this is a fairly arbitrary classification, as one company's finished goods are another company's raw materials. Some organisations (notably retailers and wholesalers) have stocks of finished goods only, while others (like manufacturers) have all three types in different proportions. Some items do not fall easily into these categories, so we can define two other types:

- **spare parts** for machinery, equipment, and so on
- **consumables** such as oil, fuel, paper, and so on.

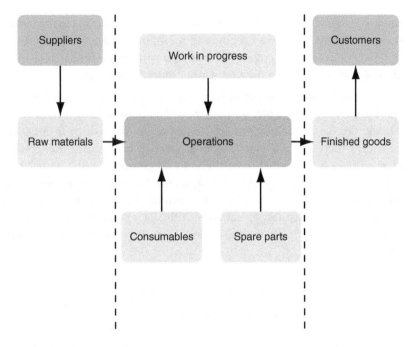

Figure 11.2 Classification of stock

Costs of carrying stock

The usual approach with independent demand has managers analysing the inventory system and looking for ordering policies that minimise the total cost. A rule of thumb says that the total cost of holding stock is around 25% of its value a year. You might think that minimising this cost is the same as minimising the stock – but this is not necessarily true. If a shop holds no stock at all, it certainly has no inventory costs – but it also has no sales and effectively incurs another cost of losing customers. Then a reasonable option is to balance the costs of holding stock and making sales, with the costs of having no stock and losing sales. Before going into more detail, we should look at the different costs of stock. These are usually divided into four types.

1. **Unit cost:** the price of an item charged by the supplier, or the cost to the organisation of acquiring one unit of the item. It may be fairly easy to find this by looking at quotations or recent invoices from suppliers, but it is more difficult when several suppliers offer slightly different products, or offer different purchase conditions. If a company makes the item itself, it may be difficult to get a reliable production cost or set a transfer price.

2. **Reorder cost:** the cost of placing a repeat order for an item. This might include allowances for preparing an order, correspondence, delivery, insurance, receiving, unloading, checking, testing, use of equipment and follow-up. Sometimes

a range of other costs can be included, such as quality control, sorting, repackaging, movement of received goods, and so on. In practice, the best estimate for a reorder cost often comes from dividing the total annual cost of the purchasing department by the number of orders it sends out.

3. **Holding cost:** the cost of holding one unit of an item in stock for a unit period of time – for example, the cost to Air France of holding a spare engine in stock for a year. The obvious cost is tied-up money, which is either borrowed (in which case there are interest payments) or it is cash that could be put to other uses (in which case there are opportunity costs). Other holding costs are for storage space (warehouse rent, financing, taxes, equipment, building maintenance, etc.), risks (deterioration, damage, loss, obsolescence, etc.) and services (insurance, handling, utilities, special treatment such as refrigeration, administration, etc.). These costs vary widely, but a guideline might have:

	Percentage of unit cost per year
Cost of money	8–15
Storage space	2–5
Loss and obsolescence	4–6
Handling	1–2
Administration	1–2
Insurance	1–5
Total	17–35

4. **Shortage cost:** occurs when an item is needed but it cannot be supplied from stock. In the simplest case a retailer loses direct profit from a sale. But the effects of shortages are usually much wider and include lost goodwill, loss of reputation, and loss of potential future sales. Shortages of raw materials for production can cause disruption, rescheduling of production, re-timing of maintenance periods, and laying off employees. Shortage costs might also include payments for positive action to remedy the shortage, such as expediting orders, sending out emergency orders, paying for special deliveries, storing partly finished goods, or using more expensive suppliers.

It can be difficult to get reliable figures for any inventory costs, but shortage costs cause particular problems. These can include so many intangible factors – such as lost goodwill – that it is difficult to agree a reasonable value. Most organisations take the view that shortages are expensive, so it is generally better to avoid them. In other words, they are willing to pay the relatively lower costs of carrying stock to avoid the relatively higher costs of shortages. Unfortunately, this defensive approach tends to increase the amount of stock, particularly when there is uncertainty.

WORKED EXAMPLE

Janet Long is a purchasing clerk at Overton Travel Group. She earns £16,000 a year, with other employment costs of £3000, and has a budget of £6200 for telephone, communications, stationery and postage. In a typical month Janet places 100 orders. When goods arrive there is an inspection that costs about £15 an order. The cost of borrowing money is 9%, the obsolescence rate is 5% and insurance and other costs average 4%. How can Overton estimate their reorder and holding costs?

Answer

The total number of orders a year is 12 × 100 = 1200 orders.

- The reorder cost includes all costs that occur for an order. These are:

  ○ salary = £16,000/1200 = £13.33 per order

  ○ employment costs = £3000/1200 = £2.50 per order

  ○ expenses = £6200/1200 = £5.17 per order

  ○ inspection = £15 per order

Adding these together gives the reorder cost of 13.33 + 2.50 + 5.17 + 15 = £36 per order.

- Holding costs include all costs that occur for holding stock. These are:

  ○ borrowing = 9%

  ○ obsolescence = 5%

  ○ insurance and taxes = 4%

Adding these together gives the holding cost of 9 + 5 + 4 = 18% of stock value a year.

Changing value over time

At first sight, the value of something held in stock seems to remain constant over time – you paid €40 for a component, so this is its value. But it is easy to see that the value really changes. If you have a stock of newspapers, they have no value when the next edition arrives; food gets out of date – and conversely a tank of oil might rise in price; and inflation might increase the cost of materials. A particular problem here is obsolescence, which refers to stock that has been kept in storage so long that it has little or no value. You can imagine this with spare parts for equipment that has been replaced, or food that is past its sell-by date. There is a general trend for products to have shorter life cycles – and a corresponding increase in the risks of obsolescence.

Managers clearly want to avoid obsolescence, and the way to do this is not to keep materials for long periods, but to keep them moving as fast as possible. The rate of movement is usually measured in terms of turnover, where:

Stock turnover

(annual amount spent on stock)/(Average value of stock held)

$$\text{Stock turnover} = \frac{\text{Annual amount spent on stock}}{\text{Average value of stock held}}$$

If a company spends \$120,000 a year on stock, and the average value held is \$20,000, its stock turnover is 120,000/20,000 = 6. This means that an average item is replaced six times a year and each unit stays on the shelf for 1/6 of a year, or two months.

If the value of an item changes over time, this raises questions about the value of stock held. A company must know this, as stock forms part of the assets that are recorded in its accounts. Is the stock worth the amount you actually paid for it, the amount you would have to pay to replace it, the amount you can sell it for, or some other value? In practice, there are several accounting conventions, with the most common based on the amount actually paid. Variations on this are:

- **Actual cost** – when it is possible to identify each unit remaining in stock and the amount paid for it. This works with small numbers of expensive items, such as cars and antiques, but most stocks have larger numbers of identical units.

- **FIFO** – first-in-first-out assumes that stock is sold in the order it was bought, so the remaining stock consists of the most recent purchases.

- **LIFO** – last-in-first-out assumes that the latest stock is used first, so the remainder is valued at earlier acquisition costs.

- **Replacement cost** – this is the full cost of replacing units at the current price.

- **Average cost** – this finds the average cost over some period.

WORKED EXAMPLE

Each month Johnson Kline Ltd bought the following numbers of an item. In July it had 8 units in stock. What was the value of this stock?

Month	Jan	Feb	Mar	Apr	May	Jun
Number bought	6	4	5	8	3	2
Unit price	21	19	18	22	24	26

Answer

There is no right answer to this, as it depends on the conventions that the company chooses.

- Actual cost. For this, the company would have to record the cost paid for each unit, and identify the units actually remaining. There is not enough information for this.

- FIFO assumes that the remaining units are the last that were bought, and the cost of the last eight units is $(2 \times 26) + (3 \times 24) + (3 \times 22) = 190$.

- LIFO assumes that the first units bought are still in stock, and the cost of these first eight units is $(6 \times 21) + (2 \times 19) = 164$.
- Current replacement cost is 26, giving a value of $(8 \times 26) = 208$.
- The average cost over, say, the last three months is $(22 + 24 + 26)/3 = 24$, giving a value of $(8 \times 24) = 192$.

Economic order quantity

The economic order quantity (EOQ) is the optimal size for an order in a simple inventory system. This analysis for this was done early in the last century[7-9] and it remains the best way of controlling many stocks with independent demand. It is flexible and easy to use, and gives good guidelines for a wide range of circumstances.

Economic order quantity
the optimal size for an order in a simple inventory system

EOQ
economic order quantity

Imagine a single item that is held in stock to meet a constant demand of D per unit time. Assume that we know the unit cost (U), reorder cost (R) and holding cost (H), but the shortage cost is so high that no shortages are allowed and all demands must be met. The item is bought in batches from a supplier who delivers after a constant lead time. We want to calculate the best order quantity, Q. There is no point in carrying spare stock, so we time orders to arrive just as existing stock runs out. Then we get a series of **stock cycles**, where the stock level follows the saw-tooth pattern shown in Figure 11.3.

At some point an order of size Q arrives. This is used at a constant rate, D, until no stock is left. We can find the total cost in each period of time by adding the four components of cost – unit, reorder, holding and shortage.

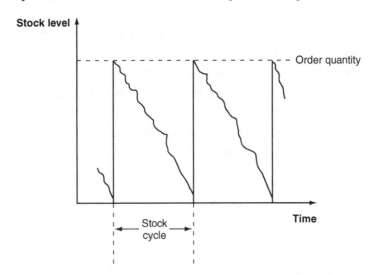

Figure 11.3   The repeated pattern of stock cycles

- No shortages are allowed, so we can ignore this component.
- The number of units bought each period is D, so multiplying this by U gives the unit cost component, UD.
- The average stock level is $Q/2$, so multiplying this by H gives the holding cost component, $HQ/2$.
- The average number of orders in each period is D/Q, and multiplying this by R gives the reorder cost component, RD/Q.

Adding the cost components gives:

$$\text{Cost per period} = \text{unit cost component} + \text{reorder cost component}$$
$$+ \text{holding cost component}$$
$$= UD + RD/Q + HQ/2$$

The unit cost component does not vary with the order size, but if we plot the other two components separately against Q we get the results shown in Figure 11.4.[10]

In this graph you can see that:

- The reorder cost component falls as the order size increases (confirming that larger orders give fewer orders and lower reorder cost components).
- The holding cost component rises linearly with order size (confirming that larger orders give higher stock levels and higher holding costs components).
- Large, infrequent orders give high holding cost component and low reorder cost component.
- Small, frequent orders give low holding cost component and high reorder cost component.
- Adding the two cost components gives a total cost curve that is an asymmetric 'U' shape with a distinct minimum.
- This minimum variable cost identifies the optimal order size.
- The minimum cost occurs when the holding cost component equals the reorder cost component, or $RD/Q = HQ/2$.

We can use this last observation to calculate the economic order quantity, as rearranging the equation gives the standard result:

$$\bullet \quad \text{Economic order quantity} = \sqrt{\frac{2RD}{H}}$$

where D = demand per unit time
R = reorder cost
H = holding cost per unit time

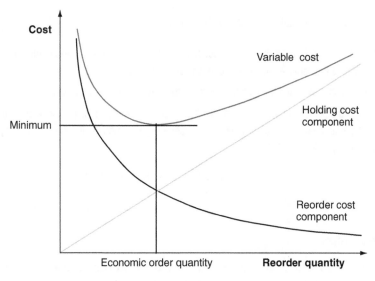

Figure 11.4 The economic order quantity

WORKED EXAMPLE

John Pritchard buys stationery for Penwynn Motors. The demand for printed forms is constant at 20 boxes a month. Each box of forms costs £50, the cost of processing an order and arranging delivery is £60, and the holding cost is £18 per box per year. What can you say about the stock?

Answer:

Listing the values we know in consistent units:

$D = 20 \times 12 = 240$ units a year
$U = £50$ a box
$R = £60$ an order
$H = £18$ per box per year.

- Substituting these values into the economic order quantity gives:

$$Q = \sqrt{\frac{2RD}{H}} = \sqrt{\frac{2 \times 60 \times 240}{18}} = 40 \text{ units}$$

So John should always order 40 boxes at a time.

- Then the cost is:

$$C = \text{unit cost component} + \text{reorder cost component}$$
$$+ \text{holding cost component} = UD + RD/Q + HQ/2$$
$$= 50 \times 240 + 60 \times 240/40 + 18 \times 40/2$$
$$= 12000 + 360 + 360$$
$$= £12{,}720 \text{ a year}$$

> WORKED EXAMPLE　　(CONTINUED)
>
> - Of this total cost, £12,000 is the unit cost component that is fixed regardless of the order size, and £720 is the variable cost from orders and stock holding.
> - John buys 40 boxes at a time, so the average stock level is 40/2 = 20 boxes.
> - Buying 40 boxes at a time and using 20 boxes a month means that the stock cycle is two months long, meaning that John places an order every two months. In general, the length of the stock cycle is $T = Q/D$:
>
> $$T = Q/D = 40/240 = 1/6 \text{ years or 2 months.}$$

Timing of orders

When an organisation buys materials, there is a **lead time** between placing the order and having the materials arrive in stock. This is the time taken to prepare an order, send it to the supplier, allow the supplier to make or assemble the materials and prepare them for shipment, ship the goods back to the customer, allow the customer to receive and check the materials and put them into stock. Depending on circumstances, this lead time can vary between a few minutes and months or even years.

Suppose the lead time, L, is constant. To make sure that a delivery arrives just as stock is running out, we have to place an order a time L earlier. The easiest way of finding this point is to monitor the amount of stock remaining and place an order when there is just enough to last the lead time. With constant demand, D, this means that we place an order when the stock level falls to LD, and this point is called the reorder level or ROL (illustrated in Figure 11.5).

Reorder level
stock level when it is time to place another order

ROL
reorder level

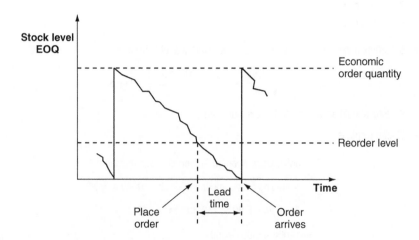

Figure 11.5　Using a reorder level to time orders

- Reorder level = lead-time demand = lead time × demand
- $ROL = LD$

In practice, inventory control systems keep a continuous record of the stock on hand, updating this with every transaction and sending a message when it is time to place an order. Ordinarily, this message is sent to a purchasing department; with e-procurement the message is sent directly to the supplier.

WORKED EXAMPLE

Demand for an item is constant at 20 units a week, the reorder cost is £125 per order and holding cost is £2 per unit per week. If suppliers guarantee delivery within two weeks what is the best ordering policy for the item?

Answer

Listing the variables in consistent units:

$D = 20$ units a week
$R = £125$ per order
$H = £2$ per unit per week
$L = 2$ weeks

Substituting these gives the economic order quantity:

$$Q = \sqrt{\frac{2RD}{H}} = \sqrt{\frac{2 \times 125 \times 20}{2}} = 50 \text{ units}$$

Reorder level = lead time × demand = $LD = 2 \times 20 = 40$ units

The best policy is to place an order for 50 units whenever stock falls to 40 units.

This calculation for the reorder level works well provided the lead time is shorter than the stock cycle. In the last worked example the lead time was two weeks and the stock cycle was 50/20 = 2.5 weeks. But suppose the lead time is raised to three weeks, and the reorder level becomes:

Reorder level = lead time × demand = $LD = 3 \times 20 = 60$ units

The problem is that the stock level never actually rises to 60 units, but varies between 0 and 50 units. To get round this we have to recognise that the calculated reorder level refers to both stock on hand and stock on order. So when it is time to place an order the stock on hand must equal the calculated reorder level minus

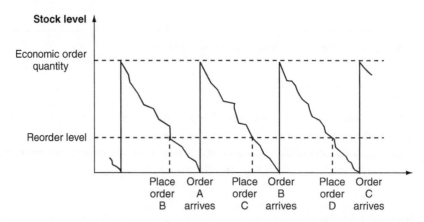

Figure 11.6　Order patterns when the lead time is longer than a stock cycle

any outstanding stock on order. In the example above, the order quantity is 50 units, so a lead time of three weeks would have one order of 50 units outstanding when it is time to place another order:

$$\text{Reorder level} = \text{lead-time demand} - \text{stock on order}$$

$$= LD - Q = 3 \times 20 - 50 = 10 \text{ units}$$

An order for 50 units should be placed whenever actual stock falls to 10 units. Because the lead time is longer than the stock cycle, there will always be at least one order outstanding, as shown in Figure 11.6.

Sensitivity analysis

A common problem is that the economic order quantity is an awkward size. For instance, it might suggest that a garden centre orders 88.3 wheelbarrows. The centre could round this to 88 barrows, but might prefer to order 90 or even 100. So does this rounding have much effect on overall costs? In practice, the total cost curve is always shallow around the economic order quantity, which means that costs rise slowly. If we order between 64% and 156% of the economic order quantity, the variable costs will still be within 10% of the minimum (as shown in Figure 11.7); if we order between 54% and 186% of the economic order quantity, the variable cost will be within 20% of the minimum. This is one reason why the EOQ analysis is so widely used. Although the calculation is based on a series of assumptions and approximations, costs rises slowly around the EOQ and it is a good guideline in many different circumstances.

Logistics managers are often under pressure to become more flexible, and one way of doing this is to have small, frequent deliveries. But to reduce the size of the economic order quantity, they have to lower the reorder cost. (In principle, they could raise the holding cost, but this would not be a sensible move.) The economic order quantity is proportional to the square root of the reorder cost, so

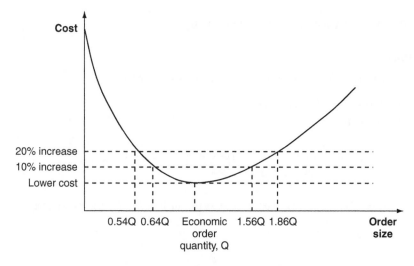

Figure 11.7   The variable cost rises slowly around the economic order quantity

to halve the EOQ, manages would have to reduce the reorder cost to a quarter. This could be unrealistic, so managers might simply choose to work with orders that are smaller than the EOQ, and accept that costs are only a bit (hopefully) higher than optimal.

If they actually set about reducing the reorder cost, a practical way is to combine orders for different materials. Combining orders, say, four orders to a single wholesaler might effectively reduce the reorder cost by a quarter – and halve order size. This works when transport and other fixed costs form most of the reorder cost, but is less effective when administration costs are dominant. It also reinforces the move towards using fewer suppliers.

WORKED EXAMPLE

Cheng Tau Hang notices that demand for one of his company's products is constant at 500 units a month. Unit cost is $100 and shortage costs are known to be very high. The purchasing department sends out an average of 3000 orders a year, and their total operating costs are $180,000. Any stocks have financing charges of 13%, warehouse charges of 8% and other overheads of 9% a year. The lead time is constant at one week.

a. What is Cheng's best ordering policy for the product?

b. What is the reorder level?

c. What is the reorder level if the lead time increases to three weeks?

d. What range of order size keeps variable costs within 10% of optimal?

e. What is the variable cost if orders are placed for 200 units at a time?

WORKED EXAMPLE   (CONTINUED)

Answer

Listing the values we know and making sure the units are consistent:

$D = 500 \times 12 = 6000$ units a year
$U = \$100$ a unit

$$R = \frac{\text{annual cost of purchasing department}}{\text{number of orders a year}} = \frac{180,000}{3000} = \$60 \text{ an order}$$

$H = (13\% + 8\% + 9\%)$of unit cost per year $= (0.3) \times U = \$30$ per unit per year

$L = 1$ week

(a) We find the best ordering policy by substituting these values into the equations:

- order quantity,

$$Q = \sqrt{\frac{2RD}{H}} = \sqrt{\frac{2 \times 60 \times 6000}{30}} = 154.9 \text{ units}$$

- cycle length, $T = Q/D = 154.9/6000 = 0.026$ years or 1.3 weeks
- variable cost a year $= RD/Q + HQ/2 = 60 \times 6000/154.9 + 30 \times 154.9/2 = \$4647$ a year
- total cost a year $= UD +$ variable cost $= 100 \times 6000 + 4647 = \$604,647$ a year

(b) The lead time is less than the stock cycle, so:

$$\text{Reorder level} = LD = 1 \times 6000/52 = 115.4 \text{ units}$$

The optimal policy is to order 154.9 units whenever stock falls to 115.4 units.

(c) If the lead time increases to three weeks, there will be two orders outstanding when it is time to place another. Then:

$$\text{Reorder level} = \text{lead time} \times \text{demand} - \text{stock on order}$$

$$= LD - 2Q = 3 \times 6000/52 - 2 \times 154.9 = 36.4 \text{ units.}$$

(d) To keep variable costs within 10% of optimal, the quantity ordered can vary between 64% and 156% of the economic order quantity. That is:

0.64×154.9 units to 1.56×154.9 units
or 99.1 units to 241.6 units.

(e) If orders are placed for 200 units:

$$\text{variable costs a year} = RD/Q + HQ/2 = 60 \times 6000/200 + 30 \times 200/2$$

$$= \$4800 \text{ a year}$$

Weaknesses of the EOQ

The economic order quantity has been around for a long time and it is still the basis of most inventory systems for independent demand. Among its advantages are that it:

- is easy to understand and use
- gives good guidelines for order size
- finds other values such as costs and cycle lengths
- is easy to implement and automate
- encourages stability
- is easy to extend, allowing for different circumstances.

On the other hand, there are a number of weaknesses, as it:

- takes a simplified view of inventory systems
- assumes demand is known and constant
- assumes all costs are known and fixed
- assumes a constant lead time and no uncertainty in supplies
- gives awkward order sizes
- assumes each item is independent of others
- does not encourage improvement, in the way that JIT does.

We can overcome some of these problems by developing more complicated models, and in the next section take one step in this direction.

LOGISTICS IN PRACTICE–MONTAGUE ELECTRICAL ENGINEERING

Montague Electrical Engineering is an electric motor manufacturer based in Toronto, and is part of a larger international corporation. In 2006 Robert Hellier, the operations manager, read the monthly inventory report and found that annual sales were steady at $21 million, but stocks had jumped from $4.4 million to $5.2 million.

All stocks seemed to have risen, but he considered – almost at random – the stocks of part number XCT45/07, which is a 3 cm diameter bearing. Montague used around 200 of these a week, at a cost of $11 each. They bought batches of 2500 units and the average stock was over 2000 units.

It was clear to Robert that the company bought parts through regular, agreed orders – and without any regard for the costs of stocks. Production liked this arrangement as they always had the materials they needed; procurement was easy, as the company placed routine orders with their usual suppliers; and transport was easy as suppliers organised a regular delivery. The only people who seemed less pleased were in the warehouse, where they had to deal with an increasing amount of stock, and Robert, who was responsible for the finances.

> LOGISTICS IN PRACTICE – MONTAGUE ELECTRICAL
> ENGINEERING   (CONTINUED)
>
> Montague's accountant calculated the cost of holding stock as 30% a year, with each order costing $40 to administer. Based on these figures Robert did some simple calculations and changed some purchasing policies. For instance, the orders for XCT45/07 were reduced to 500, with a target of getting this down to 200 units, with an average stock level of 200. One year after starting his investigations, Robert had reduced stocks to $3.8 million, customer service had improved, emergency orders were virtually eliminated and Montague were saving almost $5 million a year.
>
> **Question**
>
> - Do you think it likely that companies often use convenient orders, rather than calculate optimal – or even good – policies?
>
> (*Source*: Robert Hellier. (2007) Progress with Independent demand, Western Operations Group, Vancouver)

Uncertain demand and safety stock

The economic order quantity model assumes that demand is constant and known exactly. In practice it can vary widely and unpredictably. For instance, a company selling a new DVD does not know in advance how many copies will sell, or how sales will vary over time. When the variation is small, the EOQ model still gives useful results – but as the variation increases its results get worse. You can see why this happens from the reorder level. An order is placed when stock falls to the reorder level, which is calculated as the average lead-time demand. But when the actual demand in the lead time is above average, stock will run out before the next delivery arrives. By definition, demand is above average half the time, so this means that there are shortages in half the stock cycles. Conversely, demand is below average half the time, so there will be unused stock at the end of the other half of stock cycles.

The shortages give most concern, as few managers would be pleased by a system that only met the demands of half their customers. A way around this is to hold extra stocks – above the expected needs – to add a margin of safety. Then organisations increase their holding costs by a small amount, to avoid the higher shortage costs. These safety stocks are used when the normal working stock runs out. They have no effect on the reorder quantity – which is still defined by the EOQ – but do effect the time when an order is placed (shown in Figure 11.8). In particular, the reorder level is raised by the amount of the safety stock to give:

Safety stocks – stock beyond expected needs which is kept to add a margin of safety

> - reorder level = lead-time demand + safety stock = LD + safety stock

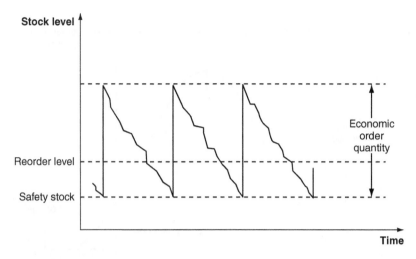

Figure 11.8 Safety stock raises the average stock level

Higher safety stocks give a greater cushion against unexpectedly high demand and reduce shortages – but they also increase holding costs. So managers have to balance the costs of holding safety stock with the cost of shortages. Unfortunately, shortage costs are so difficult to find that they are usually little more than guesses. An alternative approach relies on managers' judgement to set a service level, which measures the likelihood that a demand can be met from stock. An organisation typically gives a service level of 95%, which means that it meets 95% of orders from stock – and accepts that 5% of orders cannot be met. The service level needs a positive decision by managers, based on their experience, objectives, competition, and knowledge of customer expectations.

Service level the likelihood that a demand can be met from stock

There are really several ways of defining service level, but we will take it as the probability of not running out of stock within a stock cycle. This is the **cycle-service level**. Now suppose that demand for an item is normally distributed with a mean of D per unit time and standard deviation of σ. When the lead time is constant at L, the lead-time demand is normally distributed with mean of LD, variance of $\sigma^2 L$ and standard deviation of $\sigma\sqrt{L}$. We get this result from the fact that variances can be added, and when:

then
- demand in a single period has mean D and variance σ^2,
- demand in two periods has mean $2D$ and variance $2\sigma^2$,
- demand in three periods has mean $3D$ and variance $3\sigma^2$,

and
- demand in L periods has mean LD and variance $L\sigma^2$.

The size of the safety stock depends on the service level that managers set (as shown in Figure 11.9). To be specific, when lead-time demand is normally distributed the safety stock is:

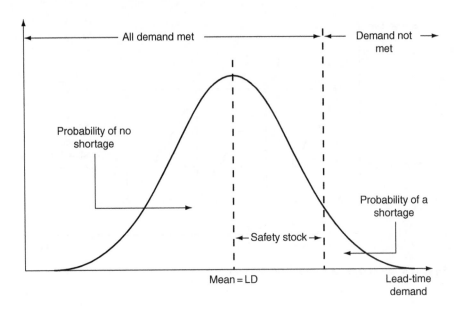

Figure 11.9   Safety stock for Normally distributed demand

• **Safety stock** $= Z \times$ standard deviation of lead-time demand $= Z\sigma\sqrt{L}$

Where: Z is the number of standard deviations away from the mean.

Then we can use any statistical package or tables to find the probability of running out of stock with any specific safety stock. To give some examples:

• $Z = 1$ gives a stock-out in 15.9% of stock cycles,

• $Z = 2$ gives stock-outs in 2.3% of stock cycles,

• $Z = 3$ gives stock outs in 0.1% of stock cycles.

When demand varies widely, the standard deviation of lead-time demand is high – and very high safety stocks are needed to give a service level anywhere close to 100%. Managers usually choose service levels that reflect the importance of each item, so very important items might have levels around 99%, while less important ones are 95% or even lower.

WORKED EXAMPLE

Associated Kitchen Furnishings runs a retail shop to sell a range of kitchen cabinets. The demand for cabinets is normally distributed with a mean of 200 units a week and a standard deviation of 40 units. The reorder cost, including delivery, is £200, holding cost is £6 per unit per year and lead time is fixed at three weeks. Describe an ordering policy that gives the shop a 95% cycle-service level. What is the cost of holding the safety stock in this case? How much does the cost rise if the service level is set at 97%?

Answer

Listing the values we know:

D = 200 units a week = 10,400 units a year
σ = 40 units
R = £200 an order
H = £6 per unit per year
L = 3 weeks.

○ Substituting these values gives:

- $Q = \sqrt{(2RD/H)} = \sqrt{(2 \times 200 \times 200 \times 52/6)} = 833$ (to the nearest integer)
- Reorder level = LD + safety stock = 600 + safety stock

○ For a 95% service level Z = 1.64 standard deviations from the mean. Then:

- safety stock = $Z\sigma\sqrt{L}$ = 1.64 × 40 × $\sqrt{3}$ = 114 (to the nearest integer)
- The best policy is to order 833 units whenever stock falls to 600 + 114 = 714 units.
- On average orders will arrive when there are 114 units – the safety stock – left.
- The cost of holding the safety stock is:

$$= \text{safety stock} \times \text{holding cost} = 114 \times 6 = £684 \text{ a year.}$$

○ For a 97% service level, Z is 1.88 (found from a standard package or tables) and:

- safety stock = $Z\sigma\sqrt{L}$ = 1.88 × 40 × $\sqrt{3}$ = 130
- The cost of holding this is:

$$= \text{safety stock} \times \text{holding cost} = 130 \times 6 = £780 \text{ a year.}$$

LOGISTICS IN PRACTICE – WIESIEK TEKNIKA

Wiesiek Teknika (WT) markets a range of diagnostic equipment for clinical laboratories and blood banks. They are the Polish branch of a Dutch parent company, and have been working for more than 25 years. A summary of their activities includes:

- marketing equipment
- customising equipment to customer needs
- installing it in customers' premises
- training customers to use the equipment

LOGISTICS IN PRACTICE – WIESIEK TEKNIKA   (CONTINUED)

- maintaining a 24-hour help and advice desk

- preventive maintenance

- emergency repairs.

WT currently support 33 types of equipment, guaranteeing a repair within 48 hours. For this they need stocks of parts and consumables, and currently hold 22,000 items valued at Zł 1.6 million (based on internal transfer prices). These are ordered from the parent company with a normal lead time of 14 days, but rush orders can arrive in four days. Until 2006, the amount of stock was set by the parent company. WT recorded transactions and every month placed an order to replace the parts that had been used in the previous month. This system had a number of disadvantages, with:

- no attempt to minimise or reduce costs

- time-consuming procedures to check transaction records and prepare orders

- no check that all items held were actually needed

- no guarantee that stock levels were appropriate

- occasional shortages needing rush orders

- no records of stock performance

- stock levels rising by 60% in the previous four years.

In 2007 the parent company passed control of stocks to WT and encouraged them to review and improve their inventory management. WT looked at some standard packages, but decided to get tailored software from the company that had installed its information system. Using the same supplier had the advantages of:

- integrating the new system easily with existing systems

- using existing systems for some of the analyses

- giving a customised system for stock analyses

- building on WT's experience with current systems

- having a software supplier that has proved reliable and helpful

- giving lower development and operating costs.

The new system allowed managers to set appropriate service levels for all parts, and related purchases to actual use, forecast demand, and lead times. Key parts of the system allow easier data entry (using bar codes and RFIDs), analyses of demand (giving patterns, forecasts, customer service, etc.), order generation (automatically generating and transmitting orders to the parent company) and order tracking (checking progress or each order, timing, costs, etc.). Its benefits include lower stock levels, costs, time spent on administration, and shortages.

Question

- What do you think of WT's approach to managing its stocks?

(*Source*: Company reports)

Periodic review systems

The EOQ analysis defines a fixed quantity that is always ordered when stock falls to a certain level. A heating plant may order 25,000 litres of oil whenever the amount in the tank falls to 2500 litres. These systems need continuous monitoring of stocks to notice when they fall to the reorder levels, so they are best suited to low, irregular demand for relatively expensive items. An alternative periodic review system orders varying amounts at regular intervals (illustrated in Figure 11.10). For instance, at the end of each day a shop might order replacements for everything that was sold during the day. The operating cost of this system is generally lower and it is better suited to high, regular demand of low-value items.

When the demand is constant these two systems are the same, but differences appear when demand varies. We can show this by extending the last analysis, and looking at a periodic review system where demand is normally distributed. Then we are looking for answers to two questions. Firstly, how long

(a) Fixed order quantity

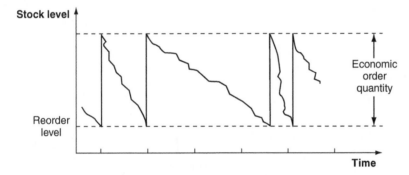

(b) Periodic review

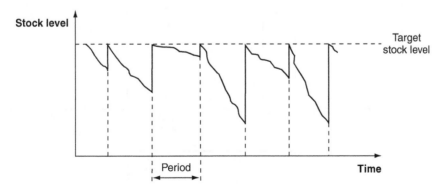

Figure 11.10 Comparison of fixed order quantity and periodic review systems

should the interval between orders be? This can be any convenient time, and organisations typically place orders at the end of every week, or every morning, or at the end of a month. If there is no obvious cycle they might aim for a certain number of orders a year, or some average order size. One approach is to calculate an economic order quantity, and then find the period that gives orders of about this size. This decision is largely a matter for management judgement.

Secondly, what is the **target stock level**? The system works by looking at the stock on hand when an order is due, and ordering an amount that brings this up to a target stock level.

$$\text{Order quantity} = \text{target stock level} - \text{stock on hand}$$

At the end of a month a company might have ten units remaining of an item with a target stock level of 40, so it orders 30 more units.

We can calculate the target stock level by extending our previous analyses. Suppose the lead time is constant at L. When an order is placed, the stock on hand plus this order must last until the next order arrives. As you can see from Figure 11.11, when placing an order at point A, managers have to make sure that there is enough stock to last until the next order arrives at B, which is $(T + L)$ away.

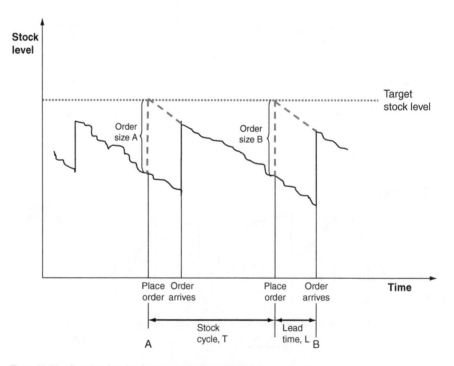

Figure 11.11   An order placed at A has to cover demand until B

Now we assume that the demand in each period is normally distributed with a mean D and variance σ, and that both the order period and lead time are fixed at T and L respectively. Then using the same arguments as before:

- demand over $(T + L)$ periods has mean $D(T + L)$
- the variance is $\sigma^2 (T + L)$
- standard deviation is $\sigma\sqrt{(T + L)}$.

Then we can define a safety stock as:

safety stock $= Z \times$ standard deviation of demand over $(T + L) = Z\sigma\sqrt{(T + L)}$

With:

- Target stock level $=$ mean demand over $(T + L) +$ safety stock $= D(T + L) + Z\sigma\sqrt{(T + L)}$

WORKED EXAMPLE

Demand for an item has a mean of 200 units a week and standard deviation of 40 units. Stock is checked every four weeks and lead time is constant at two weeks. Describe a policy that will give a 95% service level. If the holding cost is €20 per unit per week, what is the cost of the safety stock with this policy? What is the effect of a 98% service level?

Answer

Listing the values given in consistent units:

$D = 200$ units
$\sigma = 40$ units
$H = €20$ a unit a week
$T = 4$ weeks
$L = 2$ weeks
$(T + L) = 6$ weeks.

- For a 95% service level, Z is 1.64 (which you can find from a standard package or tables). Then:

  ○ safety stock $= Z\sigma\sqrt{(T + L)} = 1.64 \times 40 \times \sqrt{6} = 161$ (to the nearest integer)
  ○ target stock level $= D(T + L) +$ safety stock $= 200 \times 6 + 161 = 1361$.

  When it is time to place an order, the policy is to find the stock on hand, and place an order for:

  Order size $=$ target stock level $-$ stock on hand $= 1361 -$ stock on hand.

WORKED EXAMPLE   (CONTINUED)

For example, if there are 200 units in stock, you place an order for $1361 - 200 = 1161$ units.

- The safety stock is not normally used, so the cost of holding it is:

$$= \text{safety stock} \times \text{holding cost} = 161 \times 20 = \text{€}3220 \text{ a week.}$$

- If the service level is increased to 98%, $Z = 2.05$. Then:

  - safety stock $= Z\sigma\sqrt{(T + L)} = 2.05 \times 40 \times \sqrt{6} = 201$ units
  - target stock level $= D(T + L) + \text{safety stock} = 200 \times 6 + 201 = 1401$ units
  - cost of the safety stock $= \text{safety stock} \times \text{holding cost} = 201 \times 20 = \text{€}4020$ a week.

Supermarkets traditionally use periodic review, and every night the tills pass messages to suppliers to replenish products that were sold during the day. But the system becomes more responsive and reduces stock levels, if it sends messages more frequently, say, two or three times a day. Suppliers consolidate these orders and send deliveries as often as necessary. But why stop at two or three messages a day, when the tills can send messages every time they make a sale. This is the approach of **continuous replenishment**, which has reduced stocks in Tesco by 10%, while increasing availability by 1.5% and significantly increasing productivity.[11]

ABC analysis

Even the simplest and most automated inventory control system needs some effort to make it run smoothly. For some items, especially cheap ones, this effort is not worthwhile – so very few organisations include routine stationery or consumables in their automated systems. At the other end of the scale are very expensive items that need special care above the routine calculations. For instance, aircraft engines are very expensive, and airlines have to control their stocks of spare engines very carefully.

ABC analysis
puts items into categories that show their relative importance (typically the amount of effort worth spending on inventory control)

An ABC analysis puts items into categories that show the amount of effort worth spending on inventory control. This is a standard Pareto analysis or 'rule of 80/20', which suggests that 20% of inventory items need 80% of the attention, while the remaining 80% of items need only 20% of the attention. ABC analyses define:

- A items as expensive and needing special care
- B items as ordinary ones needing standard care
- C items as cheap and needing little care.

Typically an organisation might use an automated system to deal with all B items. The system might make some suggestions for A items, but decisions are made by

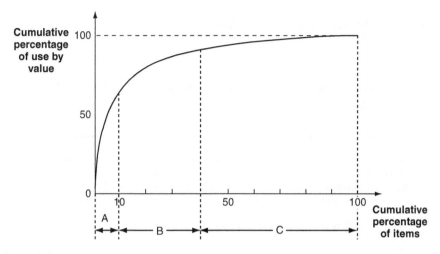

Figure 11.12 Typical results for an ABC analysis

managers after reviewing all the circumstances. C items might be excluded from the automatic system and controlled by ad hoc methods.

The categories are defined in terms of the value of annual demand, so an ABC analysis starts by calculating the annual use by value of each item. This means that it multiplies the number of units used in a year by the unit cost. Inevitably, a few expensive items account for a lot of use, while many cheap ones account for little. So listing the items in order of decreasing annual use by value, leaves A items at the top of the list, B items in the middle, and C items at the bottom. We might typically find:

Category	% of items	Cumulative % of items	% of use by value	Cumulative % of use by value
A	10	10	70	70
B	30	40	20	90
C	60	100	10	100

Figure 11.12 shows typical results of plotting the cumulative percentage of annual use against the cumulative percentage of items.

WORKED EXAMPLE

A small store has ten categories of product with the following costs and annual demands:

Product	P1	P2	P3	P4	P5	P6	P7	P8	P9	P0
Unit Cost (€)	1	20	10	20	50	10	50	5	20	100
Annual demand (00s)	2.5	50	20	66	15	6	10	5	1	50

Do an ABC analysis of these items. If resources for inventory control are limited, which items should be given least attention?

WORKED EXAMPLE   (CONTINUED)

Answer

The annual use of P1 in terms of value is $20 \times 250 = €5000$. Repeating this calculation for the other items gives:

Item	P1	P2	P3	P4	P5	P6	P7	P8	P9	P0
% of items	10	10	10	10	10	10	10	10	10	10
Annual use (€'000s)	5	50	40	330	15	30	5	10	10	5

Then sorting these into order of decreasing annual use:

Product	P4	P2	P3	P6	P5	P8	P9	P1	P7	P0
Cumulative % of items	10	20	30	40	50	60	70	80	90	100
Annual use (£'000s)	330	50	40	30	15	10	10	5	5	5
Cumulative annual use	330	380	420	450	465	475	485	490	495	500
Cumulative % annual use	66	76	84	90	93	95	97	98	99	100
Category	<-A-><————————-B——————-><——————————C————->									

The boundaries between categories of items are often unclear, but in this case P4 is clearly an A item, P2, P3 and P6 are B items and the rest are C items.

The C items account for only 10% of annual use by value. If resources are limited, these should be given least attention.

Although they are useful for focusing attention on important items, ABC analyses can be misleading, as the annual use by value of an item is often a poor measure of its importance. For instance, essential safety equipment must be available, even if it is never used; an assembly line can only keep going if all materials are available, even the cheapest; a medicine may be both cheap and rarely used, but patients hope that it is still available when they need it.

Vendor managed inventory

If an organisation is trying to reduce the amount of effort it puts into inventory control, one option is to outsource some activities. For instance, as a start, a company might outsource some of the information systems that control stocks. A more radical approach outsources the entire warehousing function (which we discuss in Chapter 12) so that a third party stores and manages all stock and makes sure that materials are available whenever needed. Between these two extremes are various alternatives for sharing responsibility, often with a third party managing the stocks without actually holding them. We have already mentioned another common arrangement of **vendor managed inventory**. You can imagine this in a department store, which holds stocks of, say, shoes. Then a supplier controls the stocks, and delivers new shoes when they are needed. The benefits of such arrangements are that the supplier can coordinate stocks over a wider area, use optimal inventory policies, organise transport more efficiently, increase integration in the supply chain, collect more information about demand patterns, and give a consistent customer service.[12] The drawbacks include more reliance on a single supplier, differing aims and objectives, unclear responsibility for some aspects of stock, the need for more sophisticated information systems, and less flexibility.

LOGISTICS IN PRACTICE – BHP AND NALCO/EXXON ENERGY CHEMICALS

Every day BHP offshore produces 70,000 barrels of oil and 300 million cubic feet of gas. Since 1995 they have had an alliance with Nalco/Exxon Energy Chemicals to supply speciality chemicals. In 1998 they looked for improvements to the supply chain, a key section of which is shown in Figure 11.13. This had several problems including:

- very large safety stocks
- poor order policies
- no single point of responsibility for stocks
- poor management practices
- barriers and delays to orders.

The companies decided to introduce a single inventory system, based on vendor management. Local operations gave up their stocks and relied on the supply from Nalco/Exxon, removing stages 2, 3, 4 and 6 from the supply chain in Figure 11.13. Although the companies already had a working alliance, this was a significant step. The new system was launched after a lot of preparation in 1999, and reduced costs by 28% – or $300,000 a year – with no reduction in customer service. There have also been numerous intangible benefits, such as the redeployment of scarce resources to a more profitable area.

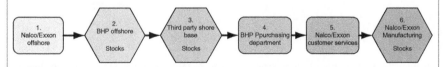

Figure 11.13   Original supply chain for Nalco/Exxon

Question

- What are the likely benefits of outsourcing inventory management?

(*Source*: Jones, A. (2001) Vendor managed inventory, Logistics and transport Focus, 3(5), 31–5)

Chapter review

- Stocks appear whenever materials stop moving through a supply chain. They are the materials that organisations keep in storage until they are needed.

- Every organisation holds stocks of some kind. Their main purpose is to allow for uncertainty and variation, giving a buffer between supply and demand. Although stocks are expensive, they perform a useful function. Organisations should look for ways of managing their stocks and not necessarily eliminating them.

- There are many types of stocks – classified as raw materials, work in progress, finished goods, spare parts and consumables.

- With independent demand managers have to make decisions about stocks. Many analyses can help with this, often finding the best balance between different costs.

- We can classify the costs of stocks as unit, reorder, holding and shortage. These are often surprisingly difficult to find.

- Independent demand inventory systems analyse the patterns of use and calculate optimal order patterns – typically an economic order quantity. This is the order size that minimises the total cost of a simple inventory system. The reorder level shows the times to place orders.

- The basic EOQ analysis can be extended in many ways. We illustrated one extension for variable demand, which added a safety stock to give a specified service level.

- An alternative approach to fixed order quantity systems uses a periodic review. This works by placing regular orders that bring stocks up to a target level.

- Inventory management always needs some amount of effort. ABC analyses give a reasonable way of allocating limited effort to different items. Another option is to outsource inventory management, perhaps using vendor managed inventory.

CASE STUDY – LENNOX WHOLESALE GROUP

Brisbane is the main city of Queensland, Australia. To the north are a series of coastal towns that are now growing very quickly. In the past, this remote area relied on general traders and direct deliveries from manufacturers for their supplies of pharmaceuticals and related products. But the growing population encouraged wholesalers to open, and in 1994 George Lennox opened a pharmaceutical distribution centre in Cairns to supply retail pharmacies, hospitals, dispensing doctors, residential homes and some other outlets. The company has now become the Lennox Wholesale Group (LWG) and is classified as a medium-sized private company. This is run efficiently and gives a good service to customers, through its three main activities of:

- order taking and processing

- stock holding and control

- delivery to customers.

To ensure his company's continuing success, George Lennox is always looking for improved performance. A short while ago he was concerned that the cost of deliveries to customers was rising. The distribution system has been reviewed occasionally as the company has grown, but it was essentially designed for a much smaller operation. George hired a management consultant to give advice on improving transport. The consultant suggested areas for improvement, and his final report suggested that the company look at its stock holding policies.

The stock control system was based on standard software provided by CyborgExceler seven years earlier. This had been updated and expanded twice, and still seemed to work well. But a close examination showed that stock levels had been drifting upwards for some time. The purchasing department explained that the company was successful because it had a reputation for reliability and service. A customer could e-mail, fax, telephone or post an order, and delivery would be guaranteed the next working day. Unfortunately, LWG had occasionally run out of stock and had let down customers (their own lead time from manufacturers averaged about a week). To make sure this happened rarely, the purchasing department had adopted a policy of keeping two weeks' demand in reserve stock, but for some reason this seemed to be drifting up to three weeks' demand.

The same ordering procedure was used for all items, and this was based on the average demand over the past five weeks. Then a reorder level was set as:

$$\text{Reorder level} = \text{Average demand} \times (\text{lead time} + \text{safety allowance}) \times \text{Factor}$$

'Factor' is a variable between 1 and 2 to give a subjective view of the item's importance and the supplier's reliability, and the safety allowance is a number arbitrarily set by purchasing staff.

Order quantities were really defined by the number of staff in the purchasing department. Three people worked there, each processing up to 120 orders a day. In 200 working days a year they processed 72,000 orders. As there were 8000 main items in stock, each item could only have an average of 9 orders a year. So each order was made big enough to last for six or seven weeks.

The system was largely automated, and nobody really checked its performance. Items were usually in stock when they were needed, so managers did not look at the details of the operations. Unit costs varied between one dollar and several hundred dollars, and no one had calculated the costs of stock holding or purchasing. As an experiment, George collected the following information about sales and order policy for a small sample of nine items.

	Item								
Week	1	2	3	4	5	6	7	8	9
1	53	284	252	27	145	1,235	567	121	987
2	64	301	260	32	208	1,098	664	87	777
3	82	251	189	23	177	987	548	223	743
4	41	333	221	22	195	1,154	602	304	680

CASE STUDY – LENNOX WHOLESALE GROUP   CONTINUED

Continued

Week	Item								
	1	2	3	4	5	6	7	8	9
5	73	276	232	27	211	1,559	530	76	634
6	18	259	195	30	179	1,209	650	377	655
7	40	242	217	31	205	993	612	156	598
8	53	310	225	23	187	1,313	608	198	603
9	52	311	186	28	156	1,405	596	94	621
10	21	336	265	23	182	1,009	637	355	564
11	67	258	245	25	171	985	555	187	559
12	50	277	212	28	169	1,237	589	209	519
13	22	263	224	31	210	1,119	601	304	485
Reorder level	302	1,220	1,050	160	1,120	6,100	2,520	900	4,400
Order quantity	450	2,000	1,500	245	1,450	7,900	4,500	1,950	6,400
Unit cost (A$)	45.25	10.20	8.75	32.60	12.25	6.50	28.50	36.00	4.20

Questions

- How well do you think the existing inventory control system works? What are its strengths and weaknesses?

- How could you improve the system?

- George Lennox is keen to make progress in this area. What would you advise him to do next?

Project – national stockholding

On a national scale, the amount of stock seems to be steadily falling. Collect some figures to confirm this observation. Do the figures vary for different countries? What are the main factors that affect national stockholdings?

National stocks are closely related to business cycles, and some people suggest that variations in stocks actually causing business cycles. In 1961 Klein and Popkin[13] suggested that controlling 75% of the variation in stock levels in the United States between the two world wars would have avoided all recessions. How do stocks have such marked effects on national economies? If wide variations are so damaging, why do governments not control the changes?

Problems

11.1 Sonya Mah records the following monthly purchases and sales of an item. Assuming she has no opening stock, what is the value of her stock at the end of the period? What are the profit and profit margin if each unit sold for €35?

Month	Number bought	Cost of each unit (€)	Number sold
October	110	22	73
November	60	26	71
December	70	30	49
January	50	28	53
February	80	24	37
March	40	32	71

11.2 The demand for an item is constant at 200 units a year. Unit cost is €50, cost of processing an order is €20 and holding cost is €10 per unit per year. What are the economic order quantity, corresponding cycle length and costs?

11.3 Jean Jeanie Ltd meet a steady demand for around 200 pairs of jeans a week, during their 48-week working year. They pay £40 a pair and the company aims at a return of 20% on capital invested. Annual storage costs are 5% of the value of goods stored. The purchasing department costs £32,000 a year and sends out an average of 1000 orders. What is the optimal order quantity for jeans, the best time between orders and the minimum cost of stocking them?

11.4 Demand for an item is steady at 40 units a week and the economic order quantity has been calculated at 150 units. What is the reorder level when the lead time is: (a) 1 week (b) 3 weeks (c) 5 weeks (d) 7 weeks?

11.5 Fenicci e Fantocca forecast demand for components to average 18 a day over a 200-day working year. Any shortages disrupt production and give very high costs. The holding cost for the component is $120 per unit per year, and the cost of placing an order is $240. Find the economic order quantity, the number of orders a year and the total annual cost of inventory when the interest rate is 20% a year.

11.6 A company advertises a 95% cycle-service level for all stock items. Stock is replenished from a single supplier who guarantees a lead time of 4 weeks. What reorder level should the company adopt for an item that has a normally distributed demand with a mean 1000 units a week and a standard deviation of 100 units? What is the reorder level for a 98% cycle-service level?

11.7 Wolfgang Heinz stocks an item with a unit cost of €80, reorder cost of €100 and holding cost of €2 a unit a week. Demand for the item has a mean of 100 a week with a standard deviation of 10. Lead time is constant at three weeks. Design an inventory policy for the item to give a service level of 95%. How would you change this to give a 90% service level? What are the costs of these two policies?

11.8 Describe a periodic review system with interval of two weeks for the company described in Problem 11.6.

11.9 A small store with ten categories of product and the following costs and annual demands:

Product	H1	P2	A3	X1	W2	P3	Z1	C2	C3	Z2
Unit Cost (Dm)	60	75	90	3	12	18	30	45	60	66
Annual demand (00s)	3	2	2	10	8	7	30	20	6	4

Do an ABC analysis of these items.

Discussion questions

11.1 Stock is always a waste of money. Do you think this is true?

11.2 What is a reasonable amount of stock for a manufacturer to hold?

11.3 What are the costs of holding stock? If these costs are really difficult to find, how reliable are the results from any kind of analysis?

11.4 What assumptions are made in the economic order quantity model? How realistic are they?

11.5 What effects do variability and uncertainty have on inventory control?

11.6 What should you consider when setting a service level? For instance, how can a hospital set a reasonable service level for its supplies of blood for transfusions?

11.7 We have discussed the control of stocks in terms of MRP, JIT and independent demand systems. When would you use each of these? Are there any other methods?

11.8 What features would you expect to see in an automated inventory control system? Look at some commercial packages and compare the features they offer.

11.9 Stocks are inevitable in all operations. Methods like JIT only transfer stocks from one part of the supply chain to another. Do you think this is true?

References

1. Institute of Grocery Distribution (1998) Retail distribution 1998, IGD, Herts.
2. Institute of Logistics (1998) European logistics; comparative survey, Institute of Logistics, Corby.
3. Office of National Statistics (2008) Annual abstract of statistics, HMSO, London.
4. Office for National Statistics (2008) UK economic accounts, HMSO, London.
5. Office of National Statistics (2008) Economic trends HMSO, London.
6. Waters, C.D.J. (2001) Inventory management, Chapter 12 in Handbook of logistics and supply chain management, Brewer, A.M., Button, K.J. and Hensher, D.A. (editors), Pergamon, London.
7. Harris, F. (1915) Operations and Cost, A. Shaw & Co., Chicago.
8. Raymond, F.E. (1931) Quantity and Economy in Manufacture, McGraw-Hill, Chicago.
9. Wilson, R.H. (1934) A Scientific Routine for Stock Control, Harvard Business Review, No. XIII.
10. Waters, D. (2003) Inventory Control and Management (2nd edition), John Wiley and Sons, Chichester.
11. Tesco plc (2001) Annual review and summary financial statement, Tesco, Cheshunt, Herts.
12. Herring, S. (2000) Inventory management into the 21st century, Logistics and Transport Focus, 2(7), 43–5.
13. Klein, L.R. and Popkin, J. (1961) An economic analysis of the post war relationship between inventory fluctuation and change in aggregate economic activity, in Inventory fluctuation and economic stabilization, the Joint Economic Committee, Washington, DC.

Further reading

Axsater, S. (2006) Inventory control, Springer-Verlag, New York.

Greene, J.H. (1997) Production and inventory control handbook (3rd edition), McGraw-Hill, New York.

Lewis, C.D. (1998) Demand forecasting and inventory control, John Wiley and Sons, Chichester

Silver, E.A., Pyke, D.F. and Peterson, R. (1998) Inventory Management and Production Planning and scheduling (3rd edition), John Wiley and Sons, New York.

Tersine, R.J. (1998) Principles of Inventory and Materials Management (3rd edition), Prentice-Hall, Englewood Cliffs, NJ.

Waters, C.D.J. (1998) A Practical Introduction to Management Science (2nd edition), Addison-Wesley Longman, Harlow.

Waters, C.D.J. (2003) Inventory Control and Management (2nd edition), John Wiley and Sons, Chichester.

12

WAREHOUSING AND MATERIAL HANDLING

Contents

LEARNING OBJECTIVES

After reading this chapter you should be able to:

- understand the need for warehouses and the role they play in supply chains

- describe the different activities within warehouses

- compare the benefits of private and public warehousing

- appreciate the importance of good warehouse layout

- discuss the factors that affect warehouse layout and operations

- review the different types of equipment used in warehouses

- discuss the use of packaging and the different forms it takes.

Purpose of warehouses

In Chapter 11 we considered questions about the management of stocks to find the best patterns for orders, amount to stock, and so on. In this chapter we are going to look at the way the stocks are actually stored.

Stocks occur at any point in the supply chain where the flow of materials is interrupted. Traditionally, it is kept in warehouses – and this gives a convenient label for any storage areas. In practice, there are many arrangements for storage, and 'warehouses' might be open areas where raw materials like coal, ores or vegetables are heaped; or sophisticated facilities that give the right conditions for frozen or delicate materials; or databases that hold stocks of information; or people who have a stock of skills; or tanks that store bulk liquids like oil; or almost any other that you can think of. Reflecting the different physical arrangements, people use different names for the stores, with the most common being **distribution centres** and **logistics centres.** Often distribution centres are described as storing finished goods on their way to final customers, while logistics centres store a wider mix of products at different points in a chain. Other names, such as depot and transit centre, suggest that they not only store materials but do some other jobs. To make things easy, we will use the general term 'warehouse' to cover all kinds of places where materials are stored.

Warehouse
any location where stocks of material are held on their journey through supply chains

---

- A **warehouse** is any location where stocks of material are held on their journey through supply chains.
- Warehouses take many forms and do other activities in addition to storage.

Karabus and Croza[1] say that a, 'product should never be warehoused or stored, but should continually be in movement, with the least possible number of handling steps'. This view reflects the common view that stocks should be minimised and preferably eliminated, but the reality is that warehouses remain an essential part of most supply chains. Olsen[2] comments that, 'We have seen the demise of warehousing predicted again and again, especially with the evolution of the philosophies of just-in-time, quick response, efficient consumer response, direct store delivery, and continuous flow distribution.' However, every organisation still keeps stocks of some kind, and as long as they keep stocks they will need warehouses to store them.

From an organisation's point of view, there are two main types of warehouse:

- those linked to upstream suppliers and dealing with the raw materials that are collected before operations
- those linked to downstream customers and dealing with finished goods during distribution to customers.

So a typical configuration has materials arriving from suppliers and put into a raw materials warehouse, moving through operations, and then put into a finished goods warehouse before being sent to customers. In addition, there are smaller stores of spare parts, consumables and work in progress (formed by products that are between operations).

Managers have the option of working without either both raw material or finished goods warehouses. They can do cost analyses, and a warehouse is only attractive when its operating costs are less than the savings it generates. For instance, a company should open a warehouse for distribution rather than deliver directly to customers when:

Cost of direct deliveries to running	<	cost of deliveries to finished goods warehouse	+	cost of running finished goods warehouse	+	cost of deliveries from warehouse to customers

The problem with this kind of analysis is getting reliable figures. For instance, the real costs of running a warehouse before it is opened can only be forecast, and changing demand patterns inevitably change them. Nonetheless, such calculations illustrated the basic principle of warehouses – breaking journeys and doing various activities at warehouses can both lower the overall cost of a supply chain and improve service.

Warehouses and logistics strategy

Warehouses are expensive and they need careful planning. We have already looked at some of the key decisions here. The logistics strategy sets the overall structure of the supply chain, including the role of warehouses; location decisions show where to open them; capacity plans show the number of warehouses to build and the size of each; inventory management gives the materials to store and amounts of stock. Now we look at some related decisions: What jobs should we do in the warehouses? Who should own them? What is the best layout? What equipment should we use to move materials? How do we measure performance?

As always, there is a hierarchy of decisions, with the logistics strategy leading to a series of tactical and operational decisions about the running of warehouses. For example, if the business strategy aims for high customer service, the logistics strategy will probably include more, smaller warehouses (assuming that warehouses located near to customers can give faster response and better service). So warehouses must contribute to the logistics strategy, and this means that managers analyse the strategies, design warehouses that will support them, and then run these warehouses as effectively as possible. One approach to this has the following steps:[3]

1. Analyse the logistics strategy – setting the context and finding what the warehouse has to achieve.
2. Examine current operations – to see the failings and how these can be overcome.

3. Design an outline supply chain structure – defining the best number and locations for warehouses.

4. Make detailed plans – finding the size of facilities, stock holdings, material handling equipment, systems to develop, people to employ, transport needs, and so on.

5. Get final approval – with senior managers agreeing the plans and funds.

6. Finalise building design – purchasing land, choosing contractors and building.

7. Finalise equipment design – choosing equipment, suppliers and purchasing.

8. Finalise systems design – designing the ordering, inventory control, billing, goods location, monitoring, and all other systems needed.

9. Fit out – installing all equipment, systems, staff and testing.

10. Open and receive stock – to test all systems, finish training and begin operations.

11. Sort out teething problems – to get things running smoothly.

12. Monitor and control – ensuring that everything works as planned, measuring performance, revising incentive schemes, and so on.

This is not a recipe, and the steps are not done in strict sequence, but it highlights some of the important decisions. To develop a new warehouse always takes time – perhaps several years in total – and all of the questions can be difficult. For instance, the basic question of size obviously depends on forecast throughput (as we saw with capacity planning in Chapter 8) but it also has to allow for practical details, such as:

- the number of products using the warehouse
- the type of demand for each product, how much it varies, average order size, and so on
- physical features of the products, particularly size and weight
- special storage conditions, such as climate control, packaging, and so on
- target customer service level
- lead times from suppliers and promised to customers
- economies of scale
- type of material handling equipment
- layout of storage and related facilities
- office space needed.

LOGISTICS IN PRACTICE – DANIEL WEST WHOLESALE

Daniel West Wholesale (DWW) is a privately owned wholesaler of frozen food and processed foods. It employs 82 people, receives goods from 49 suppliers, and delivers to 580 main customers in the North of England using a fleet of 29 vans. All its operations are based in a single warehouse in Gateshead.

DWW is successful in a highly competitive market, and they attribute their success to their outstanding customer service. This is judged by the five criteria of close personal relationships, flexibility to respond to individual needs, low prices enhanced by discounts, high stocks meeting 98% of orders off the shelf, and frequent deliveries, normally twice a day.

DWW's turnover is £42 million a year, with a gross margin of about 4.5%. All the costs are classified as acquisition (75%), storage (7%), distribution (4%) and others (14%).

Every morning the order-processing room in DWW checks orders that have been sent automatically by customer systems, e-mailed, faxed, or telephoned overnight. Then they contact customers who have not sent orders, asking if they want anything. These orders are consolidated into 'customer requirement lists', which are sent to the warehouse. The goods for each order are picked from the shelves, assembled, put into a delivery box, checked, and taken to a departure bay. At the departure bay the materials have final packing and promotional material added.

The customer requirement lists are used to design routes for the vans. The drivers collect the schedule of customers to be visited, pick up the boxes to be delivered, and load them into the van in the specified order. Then they set off on their deliveries, visiting an average of 20 customers, travelling 110 miles in a morning, and delivering £3000 worth of goods. This whole procedure is repeated on a slightly smaller scale in the afternoon.

DWW's inventory system records each transaction, and keeps a check on all stocks. At the end of each day, it checks for items that need replenishing, consolidates these into orders (based on supplier and delivery details), and automatically transmits them to suppliers. The orders are delivered at agreed times during the next working day.

Question

- This is clearly a finished goods warehouse. What would be different in a raw materials warehouse?

(*Source*: West, D. (2007) Report to shareholders, Newcastle-upon-Tyne)

Activities within a warehouse

The purpose of a warehouse is to support the broader logistics function by storing materials until they are needed, with a combination of low costs and high customer service. Specific aims might include:

- providing safe and secure storage at key points in a supply chain, keeping materials in good condition and with minimal damage

- efficiently doing the associated handling, moving, sorting and checking of materials
- keeping accurate records, processing information and transferring this as required by suppliers and customers
- adding value by doing other tasks that may be best performed in the warehouse, such as packing of finishing for postponement
- being flexible enough to deal with uncertainty, variations, special requirements, and so on.

These aims say what a warehouse might want to do – emphasising its core function as a store of goods – and now we can see how it achieves these. All warehouses do similar activities, essentially receiving deliveries from upstream suppliers, storing them until they are needed, and passing them on to downstream customers. We can add some details and get the following list of activities that are generally included in warehousing. You can imagine these as a sequence of jobs that are done as materials move through the warehouse operations. We are clearly giving a general picture here, and while some warehouses do not do all of the following activities, others do many more;

- meeting delivery vehicles from upstream suppliers and directing them to arrival bays
- identifying the materials delivered and matching them to orders
- unloading materials from vehicles, and checking their condition, quantity and quality
- sorting goods and forming convenient units for storage
- labelling storage units so they can be identified (generally with bar codes, magnetic strips or RFIDs)
- moving storage units to a bulk storage area
- holding them in stock until needed
- when necessary, removing storage units from bulk storage, breaking them into smaller parts and transferring them to a picking store
- when requested by customer orders, picking materials from this store, checking them and consolidating them into orders
- moving the orders to marshalling or consolidation areas
- checking, packing and packaging the orders
- moving the orders to departure bays, loading them onto delivery vehicles and dispatching them to customers
- controlling all communications and related systems, such as inventory control and accounting.

Moving beyond storage

Organisations are increasingly trying to move materials quickly though supply chains, without interrupting the flow or having them sit in stock. So the focus of warehouses has changed, moving away from long-term storage and towards giving convenient locations for a range of associated activities. For example, warehouses can be the best places for inspecting and sorting materials, packing and consolidating deliveries. They might also be used for finishing products, labelling, packaging, making products 'store ready' for retailers, other aspects of postponement, servicing vendor managed inventories, collection points for reverse logistics, and so on. The trend is clearly for warehouses to do more jobs, positively adding value. This is an important point, as warehouses have traditionally been seen as pure cost centres. By looking at their ability to reduce overall costs, add value – and generally increase utility – managers can see warehouses as an asset rather than a necessary overhead.

The broader role of warehouses has developed from their traditional jobs. For instance, they have always been the places where organisations do most sorting of materials. Transport is often divided into full-load and part-load operations, and you might hear of TL (truckload) and LTL (less than truckload) operators. Here part-loads are amounts that do not fill the transport used, so a part-load might be part of a container, some of a tanker of liquid, or less than a full van load. Managers prefer full-load operations because they are a lot easier to organise and give cheaper unit costs. This is the approach of containers, where the whole container moves on its journey through intermodal operators. Unfortunately, not all customers want full loads, and you can imagine them wanting several part-loads of different materials from different suppliers. The best way of organising this is to consolidate the part-loads into fewer full-loads. The practicalities are that the part-loads are delivered to a warehouse where they are sorted and consolidated into full loads, and are then transported in full-loads to the customer (as shown in Figure 12.1a). The extra cost of sorting and consolidation in the warehouse is more than recovered from the reduced cost of transport.

It may be difficult for a single company to consolidate loads in this way, but several companies working together could combine loads. More often, third parties organise the consolidation, and freight-forwarders do this for global logistics. Freight-forwarders might book a number of containers on a ship travelling between Hong Kong and Rotterdam, and then consolidate loads from a number of companies around Hong Kong who all want to ship relatively small amounts. The forwarders make their money by paying full-container rates, and charging somewhat more than this – but obviously less than small load rates.

Freight forwarders intermediaries who consolidate and organise freight movements

As well as moving parcels between transport, consolidation at warehouses can include other jobs. For example, a warehouse might receive bulk products, and then do the final packing, paperwork and packaging and send the finished product to customers. Wine and other liquids are often carried in bulk tankers, and are put into bottles (which would be expensive to transport) near their destinations.

(a) Consolidation

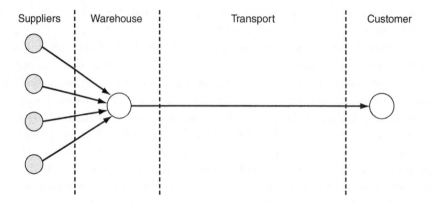

(b) Break-bulk

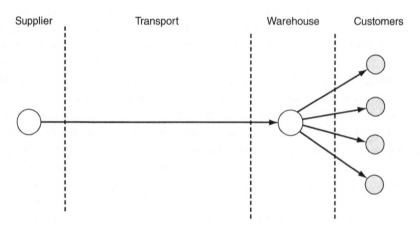

Figure 12.1 Using a warehouse to sort materials and reduce transport costs

Then the bottling plant is really 'breaking bulk' in an extension of the warehouse. A warehouse can do more jobs, including a limited amount of final assembly. A manufacturer might make the parts for a product in a number of factories in different locations, then arrange for all the parts to be sent to a warehouse, which assembles the final product and delivers it to customers. A warehouse might collect a keyboard from Brazil, software from the USA, a monitor from the UK, speakers from Taiwan, and a main box from Japan, assemble them into a boxed computer system and deliver them to customers. As we have already seen, this is the basis of postponement, where the final steps of production are left to the last possible moment. It also suggests that there is no rigid distinction between factories and warehouses, and that they are both part of the overall process of delivering products to final customers.

The opposite of consolidation occurs when warehouses **break-bulk** (shown in Figure 12.1b). Here a supplier sends all the deliveries for a particular area in a single load to a local warehouse. The warehouse breaks this load into the separate deliveries and passes them on to customers. Again, this brings the benefit of lower transport costs, which more than cover the extra handling. A long journey typically includes both consolidation at the start and then break-bulk at the end. A package may go through this handling several times when it moves between different legs of a long and complex journey.

With their declining role as long-term stores, an efficient way of organising warehouses avoids actually putting materials into storage at all. This gives cross-docking, where the arrival of materials at a warehouse is coordinated with their departures to customers. Materials are received at an arrivals area, and are transferred directly to the loading area, and immediately sent for delivery to customers. In practice, there might be some delay, but this is usually less than 24 hours. There may also be a limited amount of sorting and rearrangement of materials for orders. The result is a reduction of operating costs of up to 30%[4] and lower capital costs for warehouse that are much smaller and with limited storage facilities. The Director of Logistics at Oshawa Foods, estimates that 'cross-docking full pallets of product can save 60% of a company's direct labour costs in a warehouse'.[5] Because of the rapid turnaround needed in its products, the food industry uses cross-docking in, perhaps, three-quarters of supply chains.

Cross-docking
coordinates the supply and delivery of materials so that they arrive at a warehouse receiving area and are transferred straight away to the loading area, where they are put onto delivery vehicles

LOGISTICS IN PRACTICE – 25 CANADIAN FORCES SUPPLY DEPOT

25 Canadian Forces Supply Depot opened in Montreal in 1995, and is the largest military logistics centre in Canada. The 60,000-square metre warehouse replaced three earlier facilities in Montreal, Toronto and Moncton. Its aim is to, 'receive, warehouse and issue everything needed to support bases, stations, ships and service battalions across eastern Canada and United Nations peacekeeping units around the world'.

The warehouse receives new materials from commercial suppliers, together with returns from Canadian Forces units. When a truck arrives, the documents are checked and the vehicle is directed to one of 11 receiving docks. It is unloaded, bar codes on materials are scanned, and data is fed into the Warehouse Management Information System (WMIS). Materials are then put onto conveyors, where each unit is automatically weighed and measured. When everything has been checked, and details confirmed, the materials are officially 'received'. Then WMIS prints a bar code to identify each unit, and assigns a storage location. This location is set by the features of the unit, and is chosen to give the best use of storage space. A range of handling equipment delivers the unit to its storage location, using fixed, hand-held and vehicle-mounted scanners around the warehouse to track and control movements. WMIS is also linked to other Canadian Forces systems to keep track of ordering, stocks, invoicing and related information.

WMIS has four different types of storage location:

- Larger, palletised shipments are moved by fork-lift from the conveyor to one of six stacker cranes, which work in the high bay area. There are 18 aisles, 20 metres high, providing 140,000 locations for storage.

> ### LOGISTICS IN PRACTICE – 25 CANADIAN FORCES SUPPLY DEPOT (CONTINUED)
>
> - Smaller units are taken from the conveyor by a monorail system, which delivers them to the mid-rise stacks. Four monorail trains, each with 8 trolleys, move on a 400-m track and take units to delivery chutes. They are picked up by 10 wire-guided stock pickers, which work in the 37 aisles, 10 metres high, providing 600,000 storage locations.
>
> - Larger units are taken from a special arrivals dock to the bulk storage area, which has space 6 metres high for free-standing goods.
>
> - Hazardous materials are taken from a special arrivals dock to a separate area for special treatment.
>
> The warehouse cost about $32 million to build with a developer-lease arrangement, and savings from closing older facilities meant that the Canadian Forces recovered this within three years. The warehouse now stocks 330,000 items, of which 2000 are classified as hazardous.
>
> #### Question
>
> - Are the operations in this warehouse significantly different from those in commercial warehouses?
>
> (*Sources*: www.forces.gc.ca and Brooker, D. (1995) Forward march, Materials Management and Distribution, August, 19–21)

Options for ownership

The traditional view has each organisation running its own warehouses – each wants its materials nearby, so it stores them close to operations. Small organisations would find it prohibitively expensive to build their own warehouses, but we have made the point that these can be any storage areas rather than the huge buildings that you see by the side of motorways. Another option is to use facilities provided by specialised warehousing companies. This can benefit even large firms, so there is a choice between private and public warehouses.

Private warehouse
is run by an organisation for its own materials

A private warehouse is run by the organisation that owns the materials, and forms a part of its internal operations. The warehouse may actually be owned by the firm, but there are different arrangements for ownership and leasing. The key point is that the firm that owns the materials runs the warehouses as part of its core operations. This has the benefits of:

Public warehouse
provides services that anyone can use

- greater control over a central part of the supply chain
- closer integration of logistics activities
- facilities tailored to the organisation's needs, being in the right location, right size, fitting in with customer service, and so on
- easier communications with integrated systems throughout the organisation
- lower costs, without the profit needed by another organisation

- possible tax advantages and development grants
- enhanced corporate image, giving an impression of reliability and long-term dependability.

A public warehouse is run as an independent business, which makes money by charging users a fee. The provider might use spare capacity in its existing facilities, or for large operations it might build and run extra, dedicated facilities. There are many different arrangements and types of public warehouse, including bonded warehouses, cold stores, bulk storage, tankers, general purpose, cross-docking depots, and various speciality stores. The facilities available are so flexible that an organisation can get, within reason, any facilities it needs. There are also many arrangements for their use. At one extreme, a company might simply rent an area of empty space in a warehouse that it shares with other organisations. The company looks after all aspects of warehousing itself. At the other extreme, an organisation might contract out all its warehousing operations to a specialist third party. Then the organisation does none of its own warehousing, but specifies standards that the service provider must meet.

Organisations are increasingly concentrating on their core activities and contracting out some of their logistics, so it is not surprising that there is a trend towards public warehouses.[6,7] Firms are not limiting themselves to renting space in public warehouses, but they are also transferring the operations and responsibility to third parties. In Chapter 11 we mentioned vendor managed inventories, which keeps stock within an organisation but transfers responsibility for inventory management to the supplier. A more common arrangement outsources all warehousing, so that stocks are held and managed by a third party in public warehouses. When there is a long-term agreement or alliance between an organisation and the service provider this becomes **contract warehousing**.

The main benefits of public warehouses are that:

- flexible capacity can deal with changing demand, perhaps due to seasonality
- large capital investment is avoided, giving lower fixed costs and higher return on investment
- costs are directly related to the level of use
- it provides skills and experience that firms do not have internally
- it gives access to the latest technology, systems, equipment and practices
- it allows easy access to new markets and a wider geographical area
- it allows short-term tests to assess new methods and areas
- economies of scale are used to reduce unit transaction costs
- it consolidates work with other organisations to reduce unit costs
- it guarantees a high quality and efficient service

These benefits have to be balanced against the loss of control. There is also some question of cost. Public warehouses might be efficient and large enough to get economies of scale, but they also have to make a profit and – by definition – generate more income than their costs.

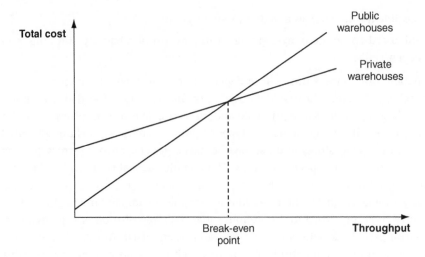

Figure 12.2   Break-even analysis for public/private warehouses

Choice of option

The choice between private and public warehousing ultimately depends on which can give the better service for the same (or lower) cost. This is often seen as a 'make-or-buy' decision, and is presented as a break-even analysis. Private warehouses have higher fixed costs but generally lower unit operating costs, while public warehouses have low fixed costs but higher variable costs, as shown in Figure 12.2.

This gives a very simple view, and there are really many other factors to consider, including the following.

- *Operating cost*. In different circumstances – and depending on throughput and financing arrangements – either private or public warehouses might give lower unit costs.

- *Capital costs*. Capital is always scarce, and even when private warehouses seem attractive it might be difficult to justify the heavy investment.

- *Customer service*. Organisations must have warehousing that gives acceptable customer service. Sometimes, they find it impossible to get a third-party operator who can meet all their requirements, and then private warehousing is the only option. Conversely, it may be impossible to provide a good enough service internally, and then public warehousing is the only option.

- *Control*. An organisation clearly has greater control over warehousing – and logistics in general – when it runs its own warehouses. Some organisations are not prepared to take the risk of handing over such key operations to outside companies.

- *Flexibility*. Private warehouses tend to have rigid structure and operations, making it difficult to make quick adjustments in response to changing conditions.

If there is a sudden peak in demand, they cannot increase the size of a warehouse for a few days, and then reduce it again when the peak is past. Public warehouses handle these adjustments, with peaks in demand from some companies being compensated by troughs in demand from others.

• *Management skills.* Managing a warehouse needs special skills, which are not readily available in even the biggest organisation. This gives a strong argument for public warehouses, as operators can provide management teams with the necessary specialist skills, knowledge and experience.

• *Recruitment and training.* Warehousing is labour intensive and has high employment costs. Many organisations finding it difficult to recruit and train with the necessary skills.

After considering the benefits of both private and public warehouses, a common arrangement uses some mixture of the two. An organisation uses private warehouses for basic, core needs and then tops this up with public warehousing as needed. A rough guideline suggests that a warehouse with enough capacity to meet peak demand will only work at full capacity for 75–85% of the time. Then a sensible option is to have private warehouse with enough capacity for this 75–85% of the time, and then use public warehouses for the rest. With such arrangements (illustrated in Figure 12.3) organisations can achieve occupancy rates of over 90%.[8]

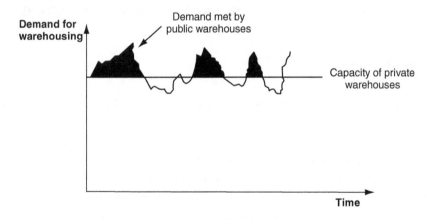

Figure 12.3 Meeting demand with a mixture of public and private warehouses

---

LOGISTICS IN PRACTICE – SOBCZYK-NOVAKOVSKI

Sobczyk-Novakovski provides a specialised logistics service in central and eastern Europe. They run a number of logistics centres, which ensure a smooth flow of materials. Most of these are large, private, general-purpose warehouses – but they also have a number of long-term contracts with major customers.

LOGISTICS IN PRACTICE – SOBCZYK-NOVAKOVSKI (CONTINUED)

They do an annual review of operations to see how the costs vary in different countries. In 2007 they found that warehousing added an average of 3.6% to selling price. The breakdown of this cost was:

- employment (wages, benefits, compensation, training etc.) 36%
- storage (rent, depreciation, interest, local, taxes, etc.) 22%
- material handling (fork-lift trucks, pallets, packaging, etc.) 12%
- utilities (electricity, heat, etc.) 8%
- communication and control (Internet, telephone, systems, etc.) 10%
- administration (management, insurance, security, etc.) 12%

In future surveys they hoped to be more specific and classify costs as:

- direct handling (employment, handling equipment, packaging, pallets, etc.)
- direct storage (building costs, storage equipment, utilities, interior maintenance, security, etc.)
- overheads (management, warehouse information system, exterior maintenance, etc.)

Question

- Is cost a major consideration in warehousing?

(*Source*: Scarborough, J. (2007) Costing a warehouse, Cost Management Conference, Prague)

Layout of facilities

An important decision in the design of a warehouse concerns the layout of its facilities.

Layout
describes the physical arrangement of storage racks, loading and unloading areas, equipment, offices, rooms, and all other facilities in a warehouse

> - Layout describes the physical arrangement of storage racks, loading and unloading areas, equipment, offices, rooms, and all other facilities in a warehouse.

The layout directly affects the efficiency of operations, as you can see in, say, a library. When you visit a library with a good layout it is easy to find the books you want, find somewhere to sit and read them, or check them out. In a library with a poor layout you spend a long time trying to find your way around, cannot find things that are in obscure places, move long distances, and generally waste time. If a warehouse keeps a frequently-used product a long way away from delivery and departure bays, it wastes time whenever the stock is used. Stevenson[9] summarises this by saying that, 'Layout decisions are important for three basic reasons: (1) they require substantial investments of both money and effort, (2) they involve long-term commitments ... (3) they have significant impact on the cost and efficiency of short term operations.'

People have different views on layout (which you see when an architect praises a building that you think is a mess), but there are some simple guidelines for warehouses. Apart from the normal requirements for any building to be safe, functional, energy efficient, durable, allow for long-term needs, and so on, a warehouse should:

- put everything on the same floor – as moving between floors is difficult and wastes time

- only use mezzanine floors for administration or some sorting

- separate arrival areas and departure areas to reduce congestion and avoid confusion

- plan the layout to give a smooth and easy flow of materials into, through and out of the warehouse

- simplify movements, eliminating or combining separate movements where possible

- make movements in straight lines

- use efficient and appropriate material handling equipment

- make storage as dense as possible, with the minimum space used for aisles

- have high-level storage to reduce the area, using all the height of the building

- have offices outside the main storage area, as space above them is wasted.

Notice that these guidelines emphasise the use all the available volume. The costs of running a warehouse are often proportional to the floor area that it cover, and they can be reduced by making the building taller. However, the extra height has to be properly used. Then it makes sense to judge performance not by turnover per square metre, but by turnover per cubic metre.

Within such general guidelines, we can now look in more detail at the layout. You can see the main principles of layout every time that you go into a supermarket. Then materials are delivered at the back of the supermarket, they are sorted and put on to shelves in the middle, customers pick items they want and take them away from the front. So the five basic elements in a warehouse (illustrated in Figure 12.4) are:

1. an arrival bay, or dock, where goods coming from suppliers are delivered, checked and sorted

2. a storage area, where the goods are kept as stock

3. a departure bay, or dock, where customers' orders are assembled and sent out

4. a material handling system, for moving goods around

5. an information system, which records the location of all goods, arrivals from suppliers, departures to customers, and other relevant information.

There are many variations on this basic pattern, designed to suit specific circumstances. Perhaps the most common version actually has two storage areas – a bulk

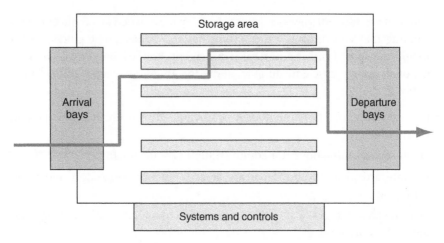

Figure 12.4   Basic layout of a warehouse

store and a picking store. When goods arrive, they are put into a bulk store, which is the main storage area. The packages in the bulk store are broken into individual units and moved to a smaller picking store that is used to assemble orders. When customers send an order, the items needed are 'picked' from the smaller, picking store and brought together in a consolidation area, before moving to the departure bays. When stocks in the picking store run low, they are replenished from the bulk store. This gives the flow of materials from arrival bays, bulk store, picking store, consolidation area to departure bays, as illustrated in Figure 12.5.

Supermarkets have this pattern, with a stockroom giving bulk storage, shelves in the shop as a picking store, the checkouts as departure bays, and so on. But supermarkets are not typical warehouses, as they have fundamentally different aims. Warehouses want the picking and movements to be as fast as possible, with goods moving efficiently to the exit without any delays. But supermarkets want

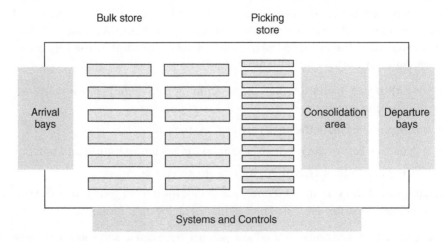

Figure 12.5   A common warehouse layout with two types of storage

their customers to pick goods slowly, and move around the whole store before heading towards the exit – as the longer customers remain in the shop the more they buy.

Variations on this theme include different types of store within the warehouse. For instance, big items are commonly held in different areas from small ones, simply so that bigger handling equipment can get around. Then big items are spread out so that fork-lift trucks can move freely, while small items are put on close-packed shelves so that people can reach them without moving far. Another distinction has weather-resistant goods, such as concrete pipes, left in the open, while delicate materials are kept in an expensive building. More specifically, products that need similar handling are put in the same area, such as frozen foods, liquids, dangerous chemicals and prescription drugs.

Types of racking

In most warehouses, materials are stored in some form of shelving or racking. This can take many forms, leading to three basic decisions:

1. What type of racking should be used?
2. What is the best layout for the racking?
3. Where should different items be stored on the racks?

The basic type of storage is an empty area of floor space, marked out in a grid to identify different locations. Bulky or heavy items are put into a location, probably by a fork-lift truck, with the grid reference used to locate it.

The more usual method of storage has shelving built in aisles, with materials typically on pallets. This gives a three-dimensional grid of locations – aisle, bay, level – with handling equipment moving down the aisles between locations. To minimise the amount of movements, storage has to be as dense as possible, which means having narrow aisles between high stacks. Smaller items are kept in some convenient type of bins, which are containers generally arranged in pigeonholes, so that materials are easy to find and remove. Flow racks can increase the density of storage by making the shelves much deeper. These are sloping shelves that are filled from the back, and as you remove a unit from the front, all the remaining units move forward. Other options for storage include horizontal carousels (bins on an oval track that rotate to bring materials to a picker), vertical carousels (shelves that rotate up and down to bring materials within reach), hanging racks for garments, silos and tanks for fluids, and a huge assortment of other arrangements.[10–12]

Layout of racks

The type of racking, and associated materials handling equipment, leads to the second question of how it should be laid out. In principle, there might be some optimal layout that minimises the amount of movement, but realistically the detailed layout is determined by the shape of the building, architect's views, height available, physical constraints, variability of demand, and so on. In particular, the layout depends on the type of goods being stored and the handling equipment used. If the goods are small and light, such as boxes of pills, they can be moved by hand, and the warehouse must have low shelving and be small enough to walk round. If the goods are large and heavy, such as engines, they need heavier handling equipment such as cranes and fork-lift trucks. Then the aisles must be big enough for these to manoeuvre. We return to this theme in the next section, but one approach to design:

- estimates demand for materials over the next few years
- translates this into forecast movements of materials into, through and out of the warehouse
- considers equipment for storing and handling these movements, and choose the best
- finds the space needed for storing and moving each item
- sees which materials should be in special areas (such as fast-moving materials nearer to transport bays, chilled goods in the same area, high-value goods in safe areas, etc.) and which should be far apart (such as foods far away from chemicals)
- designs a general layout for racking that combines all these spaces and handling areas
- adds details to give final plans.

This procedure also mentions the location of items within racks, which is an important factor in efficiency. Many costs of running a warehouse are fixed – such as rent, local taxes, utilities and depreciation. But a significant variable is related to the time needed to locate items and either add them to stock or remove them. This is directly determined by the details of the layout. When there are thousands of items in store, a small difference in the way they are arranged can give significantly different service and costs.

WORKED EXAMPLE

A small store has a rack with nine colours of paint in 5-litre tins. At one end of the rack is an issue area where the storekeeper works. Weekly demand for the paint is as follows.

Colour	Red	Blue	White	Black	Brown	Green	Yellow	Grey	Pink
Tins	150	210	1290	960	480	180	360	60	90

If all paint is stored in bins that are 5 m wide, design a layout for the rack. What is the best layout if the size of bins varies with the weekly demand?

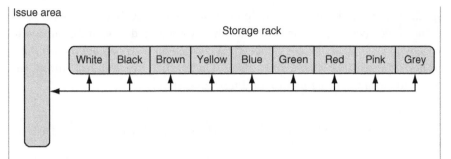

Figure 12.6   Layout of paint in the worked example

Answer

A reasonable aim is to minimise the distance walked by the storekeeper, assuming that each tin of paint needs a separate journey. The paint should be laid out so that colours with highest demand are nearest the issue area – and this has paint arranged in order white, black, brown, yellow, blue, green, red, pink and grey (illustrated in Figure 12.6). Assuming that tins come from the middle of bins, the total distance moved by the storekeeper is:

$$= 2 \times (2.5 \times 1290 + 7.5 \times 960 + 12.5 \times 480 + 17.5 \times 360 + 22.5 \times 210 + 27.5 \times 180$$

$$+ 32.5 \times 150 + 37.5 \times 90 + 42.5 \times 60)$$

$$= 86{,}400 \, \text{m}$$

This 86.4 km compares with 136.8 km when the paint is simply stored in the order given.

If the size of bin is proportional to the weekly demand, and assuming that paint is taken from the middle of the bins, the paint can be stored equally well in any order.

Turnaround time

Another aspect of warehouse efficiency concerns the speed with which it deals with vehicles at the arrival and departure bays. There are several measures of **turnaround time**, but the most common is the time taken between a vehicle arriving (either delivering materials or collecting them) and departing. Efficient transport operations need vehicles and drivers to spend as much time as possible actually moving, and as little time as possible sitting in warehouses being loaded and unloaded – or even worse, waiting to be loaded or unloaded. This is why airlines want passengers to embark and disembark quickly, so that the airline can get into the air quickly. It is also the reason why budget airline do not allocate seats, as passengers board more quickly when there is competition for the best seats.

It is not just transport companies that want a fast turnaround. Warehouses have limited dock space and want to serve as many vehicles as possible. So it is in everybody's interest to minimise the turnaround time. Three arrangements can help with this. Firstly, orders can be assembled and waiting to move on to a vehicle – when a vehicle arrives it is loaded quickly and moves on. Secondly, special loading and unloading equipment can be used, such as wheeled trolleys or roll cages (wire boxes on wheels, typically used to deliver milk cartons to supermarkets) – or rollers on vehicle floors. When all materials are put on these trolleys a lorry can be loaded and unloaded in less than five minutes. Thirdly, the bays can be laid out carefully to minimise congestion.

LOGISTICS IN PRACTICE – WAL-MART IN CORNWALL, ONTARIO

Wal-Mart operates 170 stores in Canada, where its logistics is managed by Tibbett & Britten. In 2000, they opened a new distribution centre in Cornwall, Ontario. This centre serves the 61 stores in eastern Canada, joining two other centres that serve the rest of the country. It also specialises in the supply of linen and shoes throughout Canada, as these need special inspections and finishing that are best centralised.

The Cornwall distribution centre covers 100,000 square metres and stocks 10,000 different items, with storage for 55,000 pallets and 10,000 cases.

An order management system analyses all demand met by the centre, forecasts future sales, and places orders with suppliers. These deliveries are received in 80 docks, with bar codes added to each pallet and case to allow automatic movement. Most goods arrive on pallets and are put onto conveyors for movement into storage. Nineteen docks are for articles that cannot use conveyors. There is some cross-docking, with items going from the receiving area to the departure docks in 15 minutes. Sixty high-volume products are kept near to conveyors, and stay in stock for less than a day. The average stay for remaining items is two weeks.

The centre breaks pallet loads into cases, with a throughput of 115,000 cases a day. Orders are automatically received from stores' point-of-sales systems, the cases are picked, put onto a conveyor and sent to the departure docks (automatically guided by bar codes). There are 79 departure docks, so one dock with its conveyor is used for each store. This makes sorting much easier. Some goods that cannot go on the conveyors are hand picked and moved by fork-lift. Then independent carriers, or one of the centre's small fleet of vehicles, deliver to stores, usually within 24 hours of ordering.

Question

- How is this very large warehouse different to smaller ones?

(*Source*: www.walmart.com and www.infochain,org; Daudelin, A. (2001) Supply chain management the Wal-Mart way, Supply chain and Logistics Journal, Spring)

Material handling

We have discussed the movement of materials into, through and out of a warehouse – and the details of this movement are generally described as **material handling**.

> • Material handling is concerned with the movement of materials for short distances generally within a warehouse, or between storage areas and transport.

Every time an item is moved it costs money, takes time, and gives an opportunity for damage or mistake. So efficient warehouses reduce the amount of movement to a minimum, and make the necessary movements as easy as possible. A reasonable set of aims for material handling includes:

• moving materials around a warehouse as required

• moving materials quickly, reducing the number and length of movements

• increasing storage density, by reducing the amount of wasted space

• reducing costs, by using efficient operations

• making few mistakes, with efficient material management systems.

To a large extent, these aims depend on the choice of handling equipment, as this affects the speed of movement, type of materials that can be moved, costs, layout, number of people employed, and so on. This handling equipment can range from something as simple as a supermarket basket, through to industrial robots and automated vehicles.

Imagine a store of, say, medicines, where each item is small and light. Material handling is done by hand, with little equipment except for trolleys and baskets. This gives the first level of technology, which is almost entirely manual. Another warehouse might store engineering equipment that is moved by fork-lift trucks or other tools. This gives a second level of technology, which is mechanised. Now imagine a warehouse where all movements are controlled by a central computer and hardly anything is done by hand. This gives a third level of technology, which is automated. These three levels of technology give warehouses with completely different characteristics.

Manual warehouses

This is probably the easiest arrangement to imagine, and is still one of the most common. Items are stored on shelves or in bins. People go round picking items from the shelves, and putting them into some sort of container for movement – like a supermarket trolley. There may be some aids, perhaps hand trucks for moving pallets, or carousels to bring materials to pickers but, essentially, people control all aspects of movements. You can get an idea of these operations by looking around a supermarket, which is very similar to a manual warehouse.

Manual warehouses only work if the items are small and light enough to lift – and then shelves must be low enough for people to reach and close together to reduce the distance they walk. The warehouse must be heated, well lit, and allow people to work safely and comfortably.

Manual systems have the benefit of low capital cost and all the other advantages of involving people in the operations, but they can only be used for certain types of materials as they have high unit handling costs.

Mechanised warehouses

Mechanised warehouses replace some of the muscle power of manual warehouses by machines. But the feature of mechanised systems is that these machines are still driven and operated by people. There is a huge range of mechanised equipment available,[10-12] but typical examples include:

- *fork-lift trucks* – by far the most widely used vehicle that you can see in almost any store, with estimates that they are used in up to 94% of companies.[13] They come in many different versions and are used to move pallets and equivalent loads for short distances. They are very manoeuvrable, flexible, and can be adapted for many jobs. On the other hand, they need space to work, and are fairly expensive to use.

- *reach trucks*, which are usually electrically powered and move pallets and similar loads up to higher storage racks. A driver controls the truck, which raises loads and places them in the racks. These trucks are quite small, slow, and with limited facilities, but they work well in confined spaces.

- *order-picking machines* are a variation on reach trucks, where the driver is lifted with the materials to pick, or deliver, at high locations.

- *cranes or turret trucks*, which is a general term to describe a family of vehicles that can lift materials up to very high storage racks. They work in confined spaces, often limited to a single aisle, so they allow high density with narrow aisles.

- *towlines* are continuous cables that pull trailers or similar vehicles around a fixed path, rather like ski lifts. They are useful for moving large numbers of packages to, say, a departure dock, but their operations are much less flexible than free moving equipment.

- *conveyors* are belts that materials are placed on and taken around a fixed path. They can move large quantities of goods, and you can see examples of conveyor belts moving items that range from iron ore to letters.

- *tractors or trains* are power units that pull a chains of trailers containing materials – and they work like small articulated lorries or tugs and barges.

- *carousels* have a series of bins going round a fixed track. At some point on the journey items are put into a bin, and the bins are emptied when they pass another chute or collection point. These are typically used for picking, where materials are added at the picking store and emptied at a packing area.

Different types of equipment needs different warehouse layout. For instance, conveyors and towlines need regular fixed routes, fork-lift trucks need wide aisles to manoeuvre, and cranes are most efficient with very high racks.

Automated warehouses

In a mechanised warehouse equipment is still controlled by people, but the essence of an automated warehouse is that the control is transferred to a computer. As usual, there are many forms of automation ranging from modest levels through to sophisticated complete systems. These do the usual standard activities of a warehouse, but have:

- storage areas that are accessed by automatic equipment – with narrow aisles and racks up to, say, 40 m tall to get a high density of materials and minimise the distances moved

- automated storage and retrieval equipment to find materials, and move them into and out of storage; these are typically high speed stacker cranes that can reach any point in the narrow aisles very quickly

- equipment to move materials around the warehouse; these are typically automated guided vehicles (AGVs) which are controlled through guide wires in the floor, but they might include conveyors, tractors, and a range of other equipment

- transfer equipment to move materials between the different types of equipment; these automatic loaders and unloaders might include industrial robots

- a warehouse management system to control operations, including transactions, stock locations, and all movements

Automated systems clearly need some way of tracking materials, and for many years the standard method has used bar codes. Then readers around a warehouse can monitor all the movement. Alternatives are available, such as magnetic strips, and the latest development is **radio frequency identification** (RFID). This is not a passive label, but is an active transmitter that responds to a reader. An RFID tag is essentially a semiconductor chip which stores information (about its current location, status, associated material, destination, customer, etc.) and when it receives a message from a scanner it responds by transmitting this information. This has the advantages of being readable at some distance without contact or being in line of sight, faster reading speeds, greater security, more information, and so on. On the down side, there are still problems with cost and agreeing standards.

The benefits of automation include faster movement, lower unit costs, fewer errors, higher productivity, greater throughput, improved space utilisation, less handling, better control of movements, support of EDI, improved stock records and better customer service.[14] An obvious point is that no people work in the storage areas, so there is no need for heat, light or other comforts the people need. On the other hand, some of the disadvantages of automation are the high capital costs, time needed for maintenance and repairs, inflexibility to deal with change, obsolescence, need to integrate systems, extra training, and so on.

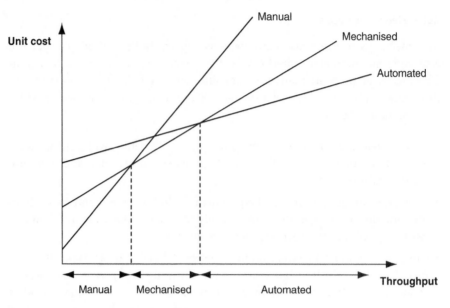

Figure 12.7 Unit costs for different level of automation

Because of the capital costs, higher levels of automation are usually limited to large warehouses with high throughput. Then warehouses for low throughput (like a shop) are usually manual, and those with medium throughput (like a food warehouse) are mechanised (as shown in Figure 12.7). In reality, throughput is only one factor in the choice of equipment, and other considerations are:

- physical characteristics of loads – size, weight, and so on
- number of loads to be moved – from receipts, internal movements for sorting, and then deliveries
- distance to be moved – from the size of the warehouse
- speed of movement required – how quickly the warehouse has to respond to demands, and so on.

LOGISTICS IN PRACTICE – HANDEMANN GROUP

Handemann Group run warehouse for distributing materials for their gas and electricity supply business in Austria and Germany. The warehouse is divided into a number of areas, shown in Figure 12.8.

- *Goods in*, 1200 square metres containing seven docks, and areas for checking, bulk breaking, re-packaging, quality assurance and returns.
- *Highbays*, 2400 square metres with eight aisles 45 metres long and 2 metres wide. Pallet racking is 14 metres high, with space for 3580 pallets weighing up to a tonne. This is the main storage for appliances and bulk materials.

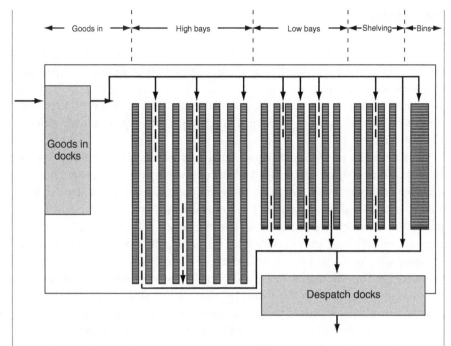

Figure 12.8   Outline layout of Handemann Group's warehouse

- *Lowbays* 1200 square metres with six aisles 35 metres long and 1.67 metres wide. Pallet racking is 8 metres high, providing space for 910 pallets weighing up to a tonne.

- *Shelving*, 600 square metres with three aisles 35 metres long and 1.5 metres wide. Shelves are 8 metres high, providing 8000 locations for packages of various sizes and weights up to 200 kg.

- *Bins*, 200 square metres, with one aisle giving 6000 locations for small, fast moving items.

- *Despatch area*, 800 square metres containing ten docks and areas for sorting, assembling deliveries.

The materials handling equipment can change according to current needs, but uses a variety of trucks to move people and/or materials along aisles and up storage racks. Typical configurations have 12 electric trucks (based on fork-lifts but of various designs), 10 hand operated trucks, 1 sweeper, 4 lorries for local deliveries.

Question

- What operations would you expect to see in Handemann's warehouse?

(*Source*: Company reports; Scarborough, J. (2008) Costing a warehouse, Cost Management Conference, Prague)

Packaging

Materials in most warehouses are not moved and stored as individual items, but are consolidated into 'unitized' loads. These are simply standard sized packages or containers that are used for all movements. This means that all handling equipment and movements can be designed around the standard packages, and operations are much more efficient than they would be parcels with different sizes and shapes.

The most common format for packaging uses pallets. These are the wooden trays that materials are put onto, and which evolved into a standard 1.2 m × 1 m format in the 1960s. Actually, there are many variations in the details of pallets, but they all work in the same general way. The other standard format is containers, which are the 20 or 40 foot metal boxes that are used to move a huge variety of goods around the world. A company might put small items into standard sized cardboard boxes, and combine these boxes into pallet loads that are moved by fork-lift trucks. These pallets can be assembled into container loads for transport anywhere in the world by road, rail or ship. Collecting together materials into these standard packages is called **unitisation** to form **unit loads**.

Although pallets and containers are the normal standards, firms can use any unit loads that fit into their operations. For instance, builders' merchants deliver aggregates in standard bags that hold about a tonne, and supermarkets put goods of different sizes into standard trolleys – or roll cages – that are simply wheeled on and off lorries.

Apart from the ease of movement, unitised loads can increase the density of storage. A company moving bicycles would have quite a low density as the handlebars and other bits stick out and prevent them being packed closely together. However, by removing the pedals, handlebars and saddles, and packing them separately, bicycles can be carefully packed into quite small standard crates, increasing load density and reducing freight charges.

Purpose of packaging

This example of the bicycle shows an obvious benefit of packaging, which is to form unitised loads that make material handling easier – which is the reason you put clothes into a suitcase when you go on holiday, rather than carrying everything separately. But there are other reasons for using proper packaging, such as protection from damage during transport, particularly for delicate items like china and electronics. Sometimes the packaging can protect goods from harsh environments, such as rain or sun; sometimes it is needed to separate materials that would contaminate each other, such as sugar and petrol; sometime it keeps the contents clean, such as foodstuffs and medicines. In general, packaging serves six basic functions as it:

- provides containers for moving items (such as tanks for liquids)
- gives conveniently sized load for movement – either combining small items or breaking up large ones

- identifies the products contained and gives information about it
- protects items while they are being moved through the supply chain
- gives unit loads to make handling easier
- assists in marketing, promoting the product, advertising and giving information to customers.

The type of packaging and its main purpose depends on the product. For instance, bars of chocolate use packaging to provide containers, and for marketing, while packaging for ice cream is more concerned with protection. There are also two types of packaging to consider. Firstly, the interior or **consumer packaging** is designed for the customer, and includes the marketing and promotional materials. This is the one that is brightly coloured and has cellophane and advertisements. Secondly, the exterior or **industrial packaging** that is designed to protect and make handling easier. This is the plain box or pallet that gives information to firms in the supply chain.

Packaging can be made from many different materials, but the consumer packaging tends towards bright plastic, while the industrial packaging tends towards dull cardboard. Some perfumes and alcoholic drinks come in very elaborate bottles that cost a lot more to produce than the contents. With expensive consumer goods this might be acceptable, but it would certainly not work with basic products such as milk or sugar. So we have to consider the design and materials of the packaging carefully. There are six main materials for packaging.

- *Glass* is easy to clean, reuse and recycle, but is fragile, relatively expensive and difficult to make.
- *Plastic* is light, strong and easy to clean, but can be expensive and difficult to make or reuse.
- *Cardboard* is light, cheap and can be recycled, but has little strength and poor durability.
- *Wood* is strong, durable, easy to use and can be reused, but it is heavy, bulky and difficult to clean.
- *Metal* is strong and durable, but it is heavy and expensive.

The choice of these, or other, materials depends largely on the type of products, movement and protection needed. This can be a difficult decision, balancing many factors. For instance, you would normally expect liquids to be delivered in some kind of plastic bottles, but this would give the wrong image for wine or spirits, which generally comes in glass bottles. Similarly, shrink-wrapped pallet loads give a lot of protection, but they would not be appreciated by JIT operations that want fast access to small quantities of parts.

Packaging waste

When you buy something, you might be surprised by the amount of packaging. Cakes and chocolates routinely have three layers of wrapping – sometimes you might find up to five layers. But remember that you only see the consumer wrapping, and probably two more layers of industrial wrapping have already been removed. There are growing concerns about the amount of packaging, its cost and disposal. There are abundant pressures to reduce the amount of packaging and its cost, based on the standard formula of 'reduce, reuse, recycle'. Some positive steps in this direction are to:

- reduce the total amount of packaging to the minimum necessary
- use lighter materials to reduce transport costs
- use more environmentally friendly packaging to reduce its impact, save money and improve the organisation's image
- replace disposable containers by reusable ones, as these reduce the amount of waste and save money
- plan package sizes carefully to give better utilisation of warehousing and transport
- use enough protective packaging to minimise damage and consequent waste.

Conventionally, industrial packaging is more likely to be reused and recycled than consumer packaging, because it is more robust, and can be collected from a few locations. Some companies, like ASDA, have ambitious plans that aim to eliminate all scrap, and move to complete recycling and reuse. Consumer packaging is more likely to be discarded. But there are increasing trends, led by companies like Body Shop, to have reusable containers. This is an important issue as there is increasing legislation, for instance in the EU, to limit the amount of packaging waste that companies can discard. Most countries have targets for reducing the amount of waste, starting with glass containers and moving on to metal containers (particularly aluminium cans) and then plastic and board containers. This is in line with the European Commission's priorities for waste reduction in batteries, tyres, vehicles and packaging,[15] and its overall target of increasing recycling to 50%. Such trends will ultimately lead to much less packaging that is simply discarded – and to the benefits of lower costs and a cleaner environment.[16] They also encourage the growth of reverse logistics – which move packaging and materials back though supply chains for reuse by upstream firms.

LOGISTICS IN PRACTICE – IKEA

IKEA is a company that continues to grow so quickly that it is difficult to keep up with its activities. In 2007 it had 260 stores visited by 583 million customers, sales of $21 billion – and distributed 191 million copies of its catalogues.

The company continuously looks for ways of improving its operations. During one investigation it found that some packages contained more air than products, and they could save transport costs by reducing the amount of empty space. Obvious moves here were to use flat packs for unassembled furniture, and vacuum packing bulky items like pillows. But IKEA use similar principles for other products. For instance, they sell massive numbers of GLIMMA (tealights), which are their third best-selling product in the UK. The original packaging held 100 candles in a plastic bag, and these bags were packed in large cardboard boxes that were moved on pallets. But this caused problems as the plastic bags were difficult to handle, product display was poor, and space utilisation was low.

The solution was to change the packaging – which needed new machinery to sort and pack the candles – but it gave packages that were easier to handle, faster to unpack and gave better displays. Crucially, it increased the number of packs on a pallet from 252 to 360 – thereby reducing the amount of packaging and number of pallet movements from 60,000 to 42,000 a year, saving more than 200 truck journeys, lowering costs, and reducing CO_2 emissions by 21%.

Question

- Can you find other examples where carefully designed packaging can improve logistics?

(*Sources*: www.guardian.co.uk and www.ikea.com)

Chapter review

- A warehouse is the general term for any place where materials are stored on their journey through a supply chain. Warehouses are needed for a variety of reasons, primarily reducing the overall costs of a supply chain while improving customer service.

- The traditional function of a warehouse is to store materials. This involves a series of activities from receiving materials from suppliers, through storage, and on to the preparation of deliveries to customers.

- The aim of moving materials more quickly through supply chains is changing the role of warehouses. Their role as long-term stores is declining, and they are increasingly seen as a convenient location for other jobs, such as consolidating part loads and postponement. They are developing value-adding activities, rather than being pure cost centres.

- An important consideration is the ownership of warehouses, with a choice between private and public warehouses. Each can give benefits, but the trend is towards specialist third-party providers with public warehouses.

- The layout of a warehouse describes the way that racks and handling areas are physically arranged. Good layout ensures a fast and efficient flow of materials, and there are guidelines for good layout.

- Although warehouses share common features, each is essentially unique. Within each warehouse the two main types of equipment are for storage and material handling. We can classify the levels of technology as manual, mechanised or automated.

- There are many different types of storage systems, racking arrangements, handling equipment, special facilities, and so on. The choice depends on factors like the throughput, and it largely determines the type of operations in a warehouse.

- Packaging is an important aspect of materials handling. It serves several purposes including protection, easing movement and passing on product information. Trends are clearly moving towards less packaging and reducing waste –which encourages reverse logistics.

CASE STUDY – VIA CENDOR

Hungary had a centrally planned economy for over 50 years, with most economic activity controlled by the government. By the 1990s, commercial and industrial organisations were inefficient, outdated and falling further behind competitors from other countries. Political and economic reforms started in the 1990s with the aim of transferring most commercial firms to the private sector. Transport had been tightly controlled, but was then substantially privatised and deregulated.

Janos Cendor was keen to take advantage of the new economic conditions, and started a trucking company. He needed a central depot and bought one – with all its facilities – when a newly privatised company was disposing of excess assets. Janos realised that this depot had problems, but planned on transforming it into a modern and competitive business. Initially, he had considerable problems. Competition from other new businesses was fierce, his facilities were decaying, his vehicles were falling apart, he was overstaffed, and working practices were outdated. In the past the depot had focused on trade with countries in the former Soviet bloc, and now had to look for other trading partners in the West – particularly other members of the expanded EU.

By 2000 Janos was making noticeable progress, and was profiting from the huge increase in Hungarian trade. Much of this was internal, but there was growing export and import business. He had modernised his depot, replaced vehicles and was making progress with staff. In early 2007 he was planning a new warehouse near to the Austrian border to import consumer goods and export agricultural produce. Janos wanted this new facility to play a key role in moving his company forward. It would be a flagship operation that would give a clear advantage over competitors.

The problem facing Janos is that, like everyone else, he does not know exactly what the future will hold. He read reports (for example Hurdock[17]), which suggested that warehouses of the future would concentrate on:

- better service to give complete customer satisfaction
- concentration of operations in fewer logistics centres

- reducing stocks by improved materials flow

- paperless electronic transactions

- flexibility, giving customised operations

- cross-docking

- third-party warehousing

- automation of material movements

- more skilled employees to manage new operations.

Despite his own entrepreneurial flair he did not know how such ideas would fit into the Hungarian context. He felt that ideas developed in the USA, western Europe and Japan might not be appropriate in Hungary.

Questions

- How have changing economic conditions in Hungary and other central European countries changed logistics in the region?

- If you were advising Janos on the facilities needed by his new warehouse, what would you suggest? What benefits would these new operations bring? Would these give a sustainable competitive advantage?

Project – warehouse options

Imagine that you have started a company to make some product – say a new type of ice cream for sale in super-markets. Your logistics system will include warehousing. How would you set about designing the type, number, size, location and facilities of the warehouse? Have a look around and see how companies actually handle this problem. Are there significant differences between the real companies and your model?

What equipment could you use in the warehouse? Do a survey of the types of vehicles and storage available from major suppliers.

Discussion questions

12.1 If the flow of materials is properly coordinated there is no need for stock and, therefore, no need for warehouses. When do you think that warehouses will disappear from the supply chain?

12.2 Warehouses used to be places where goods were stored, often for long periods, until they were needed. Has this role significantly changed over time?

12.3 There should be a clear distinction between factories which produce things and warehouses that store them. What do you think of this view?

12.4 What is cross-docking and when can you use it?

12.5 How would you measure the capacity of a warehouse, and why is it important?

12.6 What are the benefits of outsourcing warehousing operations? How can this be organised?

12.7 Why is the layout of a warehouse important? Supermarkets are really a type of warehouse, so the same factors are important. Is this true?

12.8 Automation always gives the most efficient warehouses, so everyone should move in this direction. When do you think all warehouses will be automated?

12.9 We are often told that packaging is a major problem for waste disposal. Why is there so much packaging, and how can the amount be reduced?

12.10 What is the point of reverse logistics?

12.11 Supermarkets sell fresh fruit on polystyrene trays wrapped in plastic film. They say that this protects the fruit and reduces waste. Some people say that the packaging is more wasteful. Who is right?

References

1. Karabus, A. and Croza, M. (1995) The keys to the kingdom, Materials Management and Distribution, May, 21–2.
2. Olsen, D.R. (1996) Warehousing trends for the next generation, Logistics Focus, 4(2), 6–8.
3. Waters, C.D.J. (2007) Warehouse strategy, Logistics Roundtable, London.
4. Whiteoak, P. (2004) Rethinking efficient replenishment in the grocery sector, in Logistics and retail management, Fernie, J. and Sparks, L. (editors), Kogan Page, London.
5. Robertson, R. (1996) On the move, Materials Management and Distribution, May, 56.
6. Anonymous (1999) The rise of the infomediary, The Economist, 351, 8215.
7. Hurdock, B. (2000) Ten 21st century warehouse trends, DSN Retailing Today, 39(15), 14.
8. Doerflinger, T.M., Gerharty, M. and Kerschner, E.M. (1999) The information revolution wars, Paine-Webber Newsletter, New York.
9. Stevenson, W.J. (1993), Production/operations management (4th edition), Irwin, Homewood, IL.
10. Linde (2008) Material handling facts and good truck guide, Linde Material Handling, Basingstoke, Hampshire and website at www.linde-mh.co.uk
11. Warehouse News Magazine Website at www.warehousenews.co.uk
12. Material Handling World Magazine Website at www.mhwmagazine.co.uk
13. McGillivray, R. and Saipe, A. (1996) Logging on, Materials management and Distribution, January, 19–23.
14. Greenwood, P.N. (1997) How will a warehouse management system benefit me?, Logistics Focus, 5(4), 10–13.
15. McIntyre, K. (2007) Delivering sustainability through supply chain management, in Global logistics (5th edition), Waters D. (editor), Kogan Page, London.
16. Pihl, A. (1997) Packagine re-use: how to meet legal obligations and cut costs, Logistics Focus, 5(3), 8–13.
17. Hurdock, B. (2000) Ten 21st century warehouse trends, DSN Retailing Today, 39(15), 14.

Further reading

Fernie, J. and Sparks, L. (editors) (2004) Logistics and retail management (2nd edition), Kogan Page, London.

Frazelle, E.H. (2002) World class warehousing and materials management, McGraw-Hill, New York.

Hensher, D.A. and Button, K.J. (editors) (2003) Handbook of transport and the environment, Elsevier, Amsterdam.

Mulcahy, D.E. (1993) Warehouse distribution and operations handbook, McGraw-Hill, New York.

Stock, J.R. (1998) Development and implementation of reverse logistics programs, Council of Logisics Management, Oak Ridge, IL.

Simchi-Levi, D., Kaminski, P. and Simchi-Levi, E. (1999) Designing and managing the supply chain, McGraw-Hill, New York.

13

TRANSPORT

Contents

LEARNING OBJECTIVES

After reading this chapter you should be able to:

- understand the importance of transport

- discuss the cost of transport and its impact

- describe and compare different modes of transport

- discuss the concept and use of intermodal transport

- consider alternative forms of transport ownership

- explain the types of services available for transport

- consider operational problems of transport, such as routing.

Features of transport

When people think about logistics, they often imagine lorries driving down a motorway. We know that logistics has a far wider meaning, but transport is certainly one of its main, and most visible, components. In Chapter 12 we discussed the role of material handling in moving materials within a facility. Here we look at transport, which is concerned with the movement of materials between facilities.

Transport
is responsible for the physical movement of materials between points in the supply chain

- Transport is responsible for the physical movement of materials between points in the supply chain.

Transport is at the heart of all logistics, moving materials between a series of suppliers and customers, adding what we described in Chapter 3 as place utility. As transport also takes time, we can say that it also affects time utility. Generally we assume that it is better to move products quickly through supply chains, meaning that time utility declines with increasing transit times.

Transport is so pervasive that we tend to take it for granted and not notice it – unless your car gets stuck behind a stream of lorries. But transport is a major industry. In the UK 1.6 million people out of a workforce of 28.5 million work in transport-related industries[1] – including 800,000 drivers. The 27 countries of the EU have more than 9 million people working in transport-related industries and move 4000 billion tonne-kilometres of freight a year.[2,3] In the USA 4 million

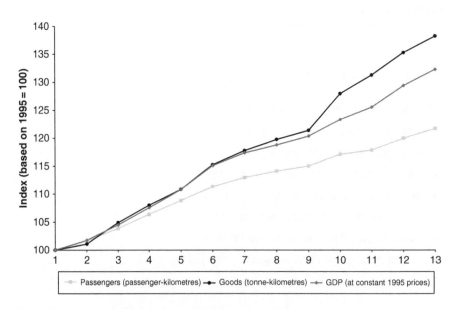

Figure 13.1 Index of growth in transport and GDP in the European Union

people work directly in transport contributing 3% of the GDP, with another 16 million working in related industries.[4]

You might think that e-commerce is affecting so many areas of logistics that fewer people are working in transport. But e-commerce is really part of the information system, and when you buy goods from a website you still need transport to deliver it. As people are buying more, the transport industry continues to grow – perhaps at 1–2% a year in the USA, 2–3% within Europe[5] and 10% in China and India. Figure 13.1 shows this growth within the EU. Here you can see that the GDP is growing in real terms, but the amount of goods moved (measured in tonne-kilometres) is growing at a slightly faster rate. Interestingly, the total amount of passenger transport (measured in passenger-kilometres) is growing at a somewhat slower pace, perhaps due to increasing car ownership.

LOGISTICS IN PRACTICE – THE EDDINGTON TRANSPORT STUDY

In 2005 the UK's Chancellor of the Exchequer and Secretary of State for Transport commissioned a study of the long-term links between transport and economic productivity. This became known as the Eddington Report, and its press release said,[6] 'Economic growth drives transport demand . . . Government and the private sector will need to show considerable foresight to deliver a transport system capable of supporting the continued success of the UK economy, able to continue to compete globally and meeting its environmental challenges.'

The report contained a number of key findings and recommendations, starting with:

1. A comprehensive and high-performance transport system is an important enabler of sustained economic prosperity.

2. In mature economies constraints imposed by transport networks are likely to limit productivity and competitiveness.

3. Transport networks support the success of urban areas by getting people to work, supporting productive labour markets and allowing businesses develop.

4. Transport corridors provide the arteries of domestic and international trade, boosting the competitiveness of imports and exports.

5. The transport industry contributes a significant amount of greenhouse gas emissions, and the environmental impacts of should be reflected in decision making.

6. Delays and unreliability in the transport network cost £7–8 billion a year.

7. The UK transport system supports 61 billion journeys a year, with over 75% of the population within a half-day truck journey of hubs in the West Midlands.

8. Travel demand is growing rapidly with economic growth and is densely concentrated on certain parts of the networks at certain times of day. This puts serious strain on parts of the system.

> **LOGISTICS IN PRACTICE – THE EDDINGTON TRANSPORT STUDY   (CONTINUED)**
>
> 9. The UK is already well connected, so the key challenge is to improve the performance of the existing network.
>
> 10. The priorities for long-term transport policy should be growing and congested urban areas and their catchments, key inter-urban corridors, and key international gateways are showing signs of increasing congestion and unreliability.
>
> 11. Transport projects can offer very high returns, even when environmental costs are included.
>
> 12. The economic case for targeted new infrastructure is strong and both the government and private sector should continue to invest in transport.
>
> 13. Transport projects should consider the full range of economic, environmental and social impacts.
>
> 14. The methods of delivering transport projects should change to meet new conditions, with the government focussing clearly on objectives and returns.
>
> **Question**
>
> - The Eddington Report emphasises the need for continuing investment in transport. Can you think of arguments for reducing it?
>
> (*Source*: Eddington, R. (2006) Transport's role in sustaining UK's productivity and competitiveness, HMSO, London)

Cost of transport

Transport is usually responsible for a major part of logistics costs, but this varies widely between different products. When you download software from a website the transport cost is very low – but if you want a load of industrial sand the transport cost forms a major part of the price.

When organisations use third-party transport companies to move goods, they pay a commercial rate or **tariff**. When they use their own transport fleet, they incur costs, but these should be lower than the commercial rates (or else they should switch to the third-party carriers). The rate is often quoted in dollars per kilogramme, but it depends on several factors including:

Rate
quoted transport cost for moving an item on a particular journey

- *features of the product* – its weight, size, density (defined as the ratio of weight over volume), value, ease of handling, special conditions needed (such as cold storage or security), 'stowability' (how easily it fits into standard containers and vehicles), liability (the chance of problems and who is responsible for the consequences), and so on

- *features of the journey* – such as the length, complexity, number of countries, difficulty of border crossings and geographical barriers

- *transport* – such as mode of transport, transfers between modes, routes, operators and return loads
- *market conditions* – value of the customer, competition among transport providers, imbalance of trade, seasonal variations in demand, government regulations, and so on.

This rate is a fundamental consideration for logistics, and affects whole patterns of trade. Imagine an item that costs $250 to make in Abletown while an efficient new plant in Bakertown can make it for $200. Clearly the maximum rate worth paying for transport from Bakertown to Abletown is $50. If the rate is actually $30, producers in Bakertown start exporting to Abletown – meaning that customers in Abletown pay less for the item, price sensitive demand rises, logistics companies expand to move the item, competition encourages producers in Abletown to reduce their costs, and some producers in Abletown diversify to other products that they can trade back to Bakertown. So trade rises and everyone seems happy. However, if the transport rate is $60, none of this happens and everyone seems to lose out.

You can see many example of this effect. For instance, the reason why trainers can be imported from Malaysia to Europe is that the transport cost is less than $0.40 a pair – which is far less that the difference in production costs. Similarly, Singapore can make electronic equipment very efficiently and export, say, televisions to Europe with transport costs of $10 a set. Even bulky items are freely traded, and it costs less than $3 to transport a tonne of iron ore from Brazil to Sweden, $0.20 for a bottle of whisky from Scotland to Japan, and $9 a tone of grain from the USA to Europe.[7,8]

The real cost of transport has fallen in recent years, as increasing efficiency has more than offset rising prices. For instance, container ships are moving more than 14,000 TEUs (20-foot equivalent units – equivalent to a standard 20-foot container), each which of which can hold up to 25 tonnes of goods. But over shorter journeys there is concern that rising prices of fuel, vehicles and drivers are making transport more expensive. For instance, in 2002 the price of a barrel of crude oil dropped to $20 – by 2008 it had risen to more than $130. This changing balance of costs means that the cost of importing food to the UK is small in comparison to the costs of moving it around the country – which is one reason why the country is increasingly dependent of imported food, currently amounting to 12.2 million tonnes a year.[9]

Relatively cheap long-distance transport allows firms to extend their supply chains over longer distances, and also change their shape. For instance, it becomes possible to cover a wider area from a single facility – and an organisation might replace a string of national warehouses by a single logistics centre that delivers materials to any destination in Europe. Many companies followed Nike's lead when it changed from 25 warehouses in Europe to a single pan-European distribution centre in Belgium. Transport costs remained constant, with inbound transport costing falling slightly and outbound transport costs rising slightly – but there were huge savings in warehousing and inventory costs.[10]

One problem with transport rates is that users have little influence in setting them. In principle, an organisation negotiates freely with a transport company and agrees an acceptable rate. The transport industry is very competitive, and when an organisation cannot negotiate a good rate, it has the option of running its own transport. However, there are two faults with this view. The first is that transport is seen as a nationally important industry, and many areas still have state-owned or heavily regulated industries. There has been a considerable move towards privatisation and deregulation, but in many areas it is still run as a state monopoly, or privately owned but without the freedom to compete effectively. The second problem is that transport companies often quote fixed terms. For example, shipping conferences quote agreed rates between destinations, while cartels of transport operators use industry agreed rates. Nonetheless, users are getting more choice, and they can make a series of decisions about the mode of transport, routes, service suppliers, and so on.

LOGISTICS IN PRACTICE – LINIE AQUAVIT

Aquavit ('water of life') is a popular drink in Scandinavia, where it is distilled several times from potatoes or grain, and flavoured with caraway, anise, coriander and lemon peel. A particularly popular version is distilled in Norway under the name 'Linie Aquavit' which is about 47⁰ proof. An essential part of its production is maturation. However distillers arrange this in an interesting way – hinted at by the name, where 'linie' means 'line' in general and the equator in particular. The drink gets its distinctive flavour and mellow colour by maturing in oak barrels during a 19-week journey to Australia and back, during which it crosses the equator twice. Apparently, the variation in temperature and humidity and the constant motion of the ship give exactly the right conditions. This unusual process was discovered in 1805 when Jorgen Lysholm took some barrels of aquavit to Indonesia, but returned to Norway with five barrels that did not sell. There the owners found that the taste had been smoothed and enhanced. Now more than a thousand barrels of Linie are maturing in ships at any time.

Doubtless, the process could be replicated in a warehouse, which would be cheaper and less risky – but the legend and maturing process have become an essential part of the product. Keeping the authenticity of the process adds value, and it is interesting to read on every bottle the dates of the spirit's journey and the ship it travelled on.

Question

• Can you find examples of other interesting journeys for products?

(*Sources*: www.linie-aquavit.com; www.aquavit.com; www.bbc.co.uk)

Mode of transport

Mode of transport
the type of transport, either road, rail, air, water or pipeline

The Mode of transport describes the type of transport used. There are basically five options – road, rail, air, water or pipeline. Each mode has different characteristics, and the best depends on the type of goods to be moved, locations, distance, value and a whole range of other things. Sometimes there is a real choice of mode, such as moving natural gas by tanker or pipeline, or the choice of road, rail or air between Rome and Geneva. But often there is little real choice. If you want to move grain from Australia to India, you use shipping; if you want to move gas from the Gulf of Mexico to Dallas, you use a pipeline; if you run an express parcel service across the Atlantic, you use air freight.

The standard mode of transport in most regions of the world is by road, and this accounts for more than 70% of freight moved within the EU (measured by tonne-kilometre).[2,3] For heavy loads moved over a longer distance, the main competitor is rail, which accounts for 15% of movements. Where there are suitable rivers, canals, or seaports, water transport can be used for heavy goods, and this accounts for almost 10% of movement. For light, high-value loads over long distances, the competitor is air freight, but weight limits means that this accounts for less than 1% of movements. This leaves about 4% of movements by pipeline – primarily oil and gas. Imports and exports are more likely to be moved long distances by sea, and Figure 13.2 shows the total transport effort of European countries by mode. All modes have risen over time, with most of this increase due to road and water transport, which clearly remain dominant.

Although there is some variation, most countries follow a similar pattern. For instance, Figure 13.3 shows the amount transported by mode for the UK. Here there are few inland waterways, so the amount moved by water is lower. On the other hand the substantial oil and gas industry moves more by pipeline.

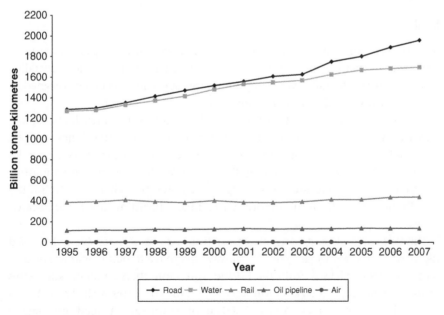

Figure 13.2 Transport by different modes by EU countries

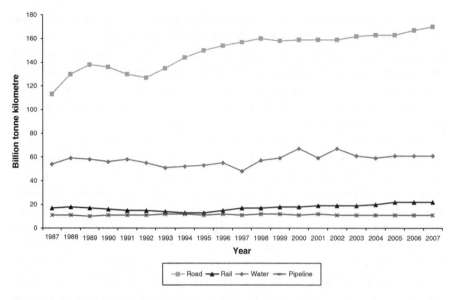

Figure 13.3   Trends in UK transport by mode

Some journeys use more than one mode of transport, and you can imagine a package being taken by road from Luxembourg to Amsterdam, then by air to New York, then by train to Chicago, and finally by road to its destination. In the following section we see that transfers between modes are becoming easier, and intermodal journeys are becoming more common.

Road

Road is clearly the most widely used mode of transport and it appears in virtually every supply chain. Most road transport involves lorries driving along metalled roads, but it can include everything from large specialised vehicles designed to carry very heavy loads through to donkeys.

The main benefit of road transport is its flexibility, as it can reach almost any location. Although the maximum speed on roads is limited, the ability to give a door-to-door (or customer-to-customer) service avoids transfers to other modes and can give shorter overall journey times. You can see this effect on a journey between, say, Paris and Brussels – the plane is faster, but when you add on the travel times to and from the airports, check-in and boarding, it is faster to catch a bus.

The flexibility of road transport comes from its use of extensive public road networks that already exist – unlike railways that have to build, or at least maintain, their own tracks. Within the EU there are more than 5 million kilometres of road, including 62,000 km of motorway.[2,3] This compares with the USA's 6.5 million kilometres of roads and 195,000 km of motorway.[4] As roads can handle many more vehicles than rails, their timetables are more flexible, and they can go on journeys at short notice and with little planning.

A huge variety of road vehicles can transport almost any load, but the most common are as follows:

- *Delivery vans* are the small delivery vehicles which can carry a tonne or two in a sealed body. Smaller vans are based on car designs, while larger ones – such as Luton Box vans – are like small removal lorries.

- *Flat-bed lorries* are basic, rigid lorries with two or three axles, and a flat platform. Materials are stacked and tied on to the platform, or small sides are added.

- *Box bodied lorries* are like the flat beds, except they have enclosed bodies to give more protection to their loads. Traditionally, access to the interior was through doors at the back, but the 1970s Boalloy added curtain siding to give easier access from the sides.

- *Articulated lorries* are more manoeuvrable than rigid ones, so they can be bigger – up to the legal weight limit, which is typically 40 tonnes. There are several variations on articulated lorries, usually with a two- or three-axle truck and a two- or three-axle trailer. These form the standard heavy goods vehicles that deliver materials through most supply chains.

- *Lorry and trailer* combine a rigid lorry pulling a two axle trailer. This gives greater capacity than an articulated lorry, but maintains some of their manoeuvrability.

Many other formats have been tried. For example, in Sweden, articulated lorries pull trailers, giving two or even three point of articulation. In Alberta, Canada, two trailers are used to move loads over the Rockies. In Australia 'land trains' have four or five trailers to move through the outback. The limits are generally set by national laws, which can restrict length, weight, width, and other features of the vehicle. Within the EU the normal weight limit is around 40 tonnes, meaning that a lorry can carry loads of 20–30 tonnes. In exceptional circumstances, very large loads can be carried, such as the 1000-tonne loads that are moved for oil companies in the Arctic.

Road transport is not without its problems, including rising costs of equipment and fuel, shortages of skilled drivers, regulations on driver hours, restricted access to cities and sensitive areas, limits on exhaust emissions, traffic congestion, driving empty on return trips, and so on. The result is that road transport can be relatively expensive – despite intense competition from the large number of operators – so it is generally used for shorter distances. The average length of a truck journey in Europe is around 350 km. Beyond this it becomes more economical to use rail for heavy goods and air for light ones.

Alongside the freight movements are a huge number of passenger movements. These range from people on foot, through horses, bicycles, motor cycles, buses and cars. In most of the world, private cars are dominant, with the EU's 230 million cars moving 5000 billion passenger-kilometres travelled (83% of the total) and 7500 billion passenger-kilometres in the USA (86% of the total). This is rising steadily as increasing prosperity allows more people to buy cars, but there are consequent problems with congestion and pollution. Governments are trying to combat these, with measures that include rising fuel taxes, congestion charges for city centres and busy roads, limited access either to areas or at specified times. Buses move 500 billion passenger-kilometres in the EU (230 billion passenger-kilometres in the USA), and although these are promoted as more environmentally friendly alternatives to cars, their use has remained remarkably stable.

Rail

Railways are most commonly used for heavy and bulky loads over long journeys. In Europe the average rail journey for freight is 1600 km.[9] Again this varies between countries, and in a smaller country like the UK the average journey by rail is 180 km, and 95 km by road.[1]

Railways are almost invariably public carriers (giving a service to all other organisations) rather than private carriers (carrying goods for one organisation). This public service is often considered so important that it is run by the state. Even when the rail service is not nationalised, there are usually so few operators that they have a virtual monopoly. For instance, in the USA road transport has around 40,000 public carriers and 600,000 private fleets – but a relative handful of rail operators.

The main reason for the limited number of operators stems from the huge investment needed for tracks, rolling stock and terminals. A trucking company can start a service between, say, Berlin and Zagreb by renting a truck and using public roads; a rail operator has to build its tracks and terminals and buy the trains before it can start work. The French TGV track to Marseilles cost $3.5 billion, while in the UK a high-speed line from London to the Channel Tunnel cost almost £6 billion. Of course, costs can be reduced by sharing facilities with several train operators using commonly owned tracks, or tracks owned by another company.

We noted that there are 5 million kilometres of road in the EU, and for comparison there are about 220,000 km of railways. There are 62,000 km of motorway, but less than 6000 km of high-speed rails.

Once the rail track is built it has the advantages of very high capacity, low unit costs, maintaining a consistent service, reasonably high speed, and causing less pollution than road transport. The low unit costs mean that it can be used for moving large volumes of relatively low-priced materials, such as coal and minerals. Then a rule of thumb says that rail transport is more common upstream in the supply chain and road transport is more common downstream. The high capacity is another factor that discourages competition, as a track built by one firm between two points will generally have enough capacity to meet all demand, and it is unviable for a competitor to open a parallel line. For instance, there is only one rail line under the English Channel, and as this has enough capacity to meet demand for the foreseeable future it is unlikely that a competitor will open a second tunnel.

Apart from their regular timetabled services, trains can provide other kinds of operations – including merry-go-round services (where a train continually moves between two locations, such as a port and a factory), full train services (where customers hire an entire train), full wagon load attached to scheduled services, container transport, or shared wagons on scheduled services. Despite these options, the main problem with rail is its inflexibility. All train services have to be timetabled in advance, so that they can fit on the same tracks, and the regular services leave little opportunity for last minute or emergency deliveries. So journeys are at fixed times – and they are clearly along prescribed routes, offering a terminal-to-terminal service rather than the more flexible customer-to-customer service of roads.

Of course, rail terminals have facilities to link with other modes – particularly road. As most customers are some distance from rail terminals, they have to transfer goods to road at both ends of the journey – and this inevitably increases cost and journey time. Another intermodal option has rail delivering to sea transport at major ports.

Overall, rail transport can be a very effective option for certain types of operation, and then it is worth a firm choosing a location near to a terminal – and occasionally it is worth building special facilities. For instance, it might be cheaper for a power station to build a special rail line to a coal mine, rather than to use deliveries by road.

Passenger rail services have an interesting past, as they were often the first means of allowing people to travel longer distances. However, their use lost out to the more flexible private cars and they went into a long period of decline. More recently there has been some increase, due to commuting routes to city centres, the introduction of high-speed lines to compete with airlines, subsidised fares, and a series of government pressures. However, their use remains at 450 billion passenger-kilometres within the EU (just over 8% of all passenger travel) compared with 22 billion passenger-kilometres in the USA (2% of passenger travel).

LOGISTICS IN PRACTICE – DIRFT

The Channel Tunnel has provided efficient rail links between the UK and European destinations. This – along with rising prices and congestion on roads – has encouraged companies to move their freight from heavy goods vehicles to the train. Daventry International Rail Freight Terminal (DIRFT) realised that this would create a demand for a centralised logistics, away from the expensive south-east of England and near to major population centres. Daventry in Northamptonshire has good connections to rail and road, and is within a 4.5 hour drive of 85% of the UK's towns and cities.

In 1994 construction started on the Railport by the side of both the M1 Motorway and the West Coast Main Line railway. The first facilities opened in 1997, operated by Tibbett & Britten and by 2004 this had expanded to 0.23 million square metres. The key feature was the state-of-the-art

LOGISTICS IN PRACTICE – DIRFT   (CONTINUED)

intermodal facility that could unload three 750-metre trains simultaneously. EWS runs 35 trains from the Channel Tunnel each week, largely from Germany, France and Italy. Upgrading of the West Coast Main Line would make rail movements even more efficient.

The site has attracted major customers, such as Eddie Stobart, Royal Mail, Tesco, Mothercare, Excel, . Demand is strong and by 2007 another 0.13 million square metres were being developed. DIRFT 2 is being added on an adjacent site, with planning permission for almost 0.2 million square metres, most of which has dedicated rail connections. The Strategic Rail Authority encourages such developments. But not everyone supports this kind of development, which is turning 200 hectares of green fields into industrial estates.

Question

- What are the attractions of a major inland rail terminal?

(*Sources*: Jones, J. (2001) Success is not enough, Logistics and Transport Focus, 3(6), 32–5; Strategic Rail Authority (2001) A strategic agenda, HMSO, London; www.dirft.com)

Water

Both rail and road transport have the obvious limitation of only being used on land. Most supply chains use shipping to cross the oceans at some point, and over 90% of world trade is moved by sea. You can see the importance of shipping to a country like the UK, where 95% of freight arrives or leaves by ship, shipping is the fifth largest service sector exporter, the City of London insures 25% of the world's marine risk, the marine and repair business is one of the largest in Europe, there are 300 ports around the coast, and the surrounding waters are among the busiest in the world.[11]

There are basically three types of water transport – inland waterways (rivers and canals), coastal shipping (moving materials from one port to another along the coast) and ocean transport (to cross the major seas).

Obviously, all water transport depends on geography – and the access of customers and suppliers to waterways. Even when there is potential access, water transport needs expensive port facilities and then, like rail, it is limited to terminal-to-terminal routes with intermodal facilities at each end.

Localised inland shipping depends on the availability of smaller scale waterways and facilities. Within the EU are 42,000 km of canals, rivers and lakes that are used for freight transport. Some countries have well developed river and canal systems that move a lot of freight. You might think that these are limited to small loads – perhaps narrow boats and barges moving slowly through green fields. But ocean-going ships can travel surprisingly long distances, and the Mississippi is navigable to Minneapolis more than 2500 km from the Gulf of Mexico. Similarly, the St Lawrence Seaway and Great Lakes route is navigable for several thousand kilometres, gives access to central areas of Canada and the USA, and makes Chicago a major port in the Prairies. In Europe a lot of freight moves on the Rhine, Danube, Elbe and Rhone rivers.

Some countries are fortunate to have a coastline (or major river system) that can support sea transport. Particularly well-sited locations provide international facilities and cities such as Rotterdam, Hong Kong and New York have developed huge ports. The world's 20 biggest ports handle over half of all world trade.[12] As well as shipping products to their local markets, these act as transhipment hubs for transferring loads to smaller ships for other markets.

Most water transport involves large vessels travelling through the world's shipping lanes, and many types of ship have been designed to meet specific needs:

- *General cargo ships* are the standard design, with large holds that carry any type of cargo. Most of these are loaded by crane, although some have side doors that allow vehicles to drive on and off. Many ports around the world do not have facilities to handle more specialised ships, so these general-purpose vessels are very widely used.
- *Bulk carriers* carry large quantities of cheap bulk materials in large holds, such as grain or ores.
- *Tankers* carry any liquid, but by far the biggest movements are oil and natural gas.
- *Container ships* are specially designed to carry standard containers and their capacity is rated in TEUs (20-foot equivalent units) or FEU (40-foot equivalent units). A typical container ship is up to 5000 TEUs, with the biggest around 14,000.
- *Ferries* are usually RO-RO (roll-on-roll-off) vessels that carry road vehicles over relatively short distances. However, there are some longer RO-RO routes between, say, Europe and America.
- *Barges* are towed behind ocean going tugs. These are used for shorter routes where sea conditions are fairly reliable, such as between USA and Puerto Rico. They have the advantage of being cheaper to run than normal ships.
- *Combination ships*. Many ships are designed for special purposes, often combining different kinds of operation. Examples of such combination ships are the RO-RO/container ships that carry vehicles imported to the USA and return with bulk grain to Japan, and the oil-bulk vessels that carry oil from the Middle East and return carrying ores. One useful combination is passenger/container, as the passengers ensure priority treatment in ports.

The following table shows the composition of the world's shipping fleet, giving the number of registered ships of each type and the total weights.[13]

Economies of scale mean that ships are built as big as possible. Oil takers evolved into 'super tankers' and 'very large crude carriers'. The Knock Nevis (formerly the Jahre Viking) was retired in 2007, but was 485 metres long, 69 metres wide and weighed 565,000 tonnes. In the same way, container ships have

Type	Number	Weight (million tonnes)
Oil tankers	7,863	353.5
Chemical tankers	1,354	9.9
Liquid gas tankers	1,184	24.2
Bulk carriers	6,494	333.6
Ore/bulk/oil carriers	137	8.1
Container ships	3,514	111.7
General cargo	16,544	97.4
RO–RO Passenger ferries	2,330	4.0
Other Passenger ferries	1,492	1.7
Cruise ships	269	

increased in size from the 4000-TEU Neptune Garnet in 1980 to 'ultra large container ships'. The Emma Maersk is 397 metres long, can carry 14,000 TEUs with a total weight around 157,000 tonnes, and current plans move progressively up to 18,000 TEU. But these big ships have problems as their routes become increasingly restricted. To a large extent, this is because of the port facilities they need, which means they can only use a few of the world's biggest ports. But their routes are also restricted as they cannot use the two main canals (Panama and Suez) and are progressively restricted in other areas, such as the Malacca Straight canal and English Channel. For instance, in 2005 the Hanjin Boston at 8000 TEUs made its maiden voyage to Long Beach, but at 77,000 tonnes the ship is 42.5 metres wide, which is 9 metres wider than the Panama Canal. However, its unit fuel costs and emissions are 20% less than smaller vessels.[14]

The main drawback with water transport is its inflexibility, being limited to appropriate ports. So journeys from suppliers to customers inevitably need a change of mode, even if they are close to ports. For instance, in St Austell, UK, the china clay works are very close to specialised ports in Fowey, but clay still has to be moved to the quayside. The other problem with shipping is that it is relatively slow, and needs time to consolidate loads and transfer them at ports. However, these transfers can be very efficient, and then coastal shipping can compete with road transport for even relatively short distances.[15]

An interesting aspect of shipping is the continued existence of Conference services. This means that all carriers in a given area agree to charge a common price and regulate the frequency of their service. The justification for this cartel is that it guarantees a more regular service than would otherwise be available. However, people increasingly question the idea of price fixing and non-Conference lines now offer deep discounts.

Water has a limited role in passenger transport that is largely confined to short-haul ferries and holiday cruises.

Air

The low unit costs mean that water transport is the standard mode for international transport – but sometimes it is too slow. For instance, if you run a factory in Argentina and a critical machine breaks down, you do not want the spare part to be put on the next scheduled ship from Japan, which will arrive in five weeks' time. Then the only feasible alternative is air transport. However, it is rare for the speed of delivery to be so much more important than the cost – and air freight is limited to small amounts of expensive materials, such as jewellery, pharmaceuticals, flowers, and documents. Although air freight continues to grow, it only accounts for 1% of all freight movement.

There are three main types of operation for air freight. The first uses scheduled passenger services, where major airlines use the cargo space that is not needed for baggage. The second is a cargo service, where operators run cargo planes on regular schedules. These are public carriers, moving goods for any customers. The third type has charter operations, where a whole aircraft is hired for a particular delivery.

Airlines offer terminal-to-terminal movements and they rely on road transport for the initial movement from supplier to airport, and the final movement from airport to customer. Many facilities have grown around airports for organising these moves, but the transfers take time especially with increased concerns about security. It often takes longer to get through the security checks than to make the flights, and this considerably reduces the benefits of air travel.

There are some specialised freight airlines – such as DHL, FedEx and UPS – but passengers account for almost all airline business. This passenger business continues to grow quickly, with low fare carriers (Ryanair, Virgin Express, Go, easyJet, buzz, etc.) accounting for more of the market.[16] With passenger flights almost doubling in the past ten years, there are 28 European airports that handle more than 10 million passengers a year (six in Germany, 4 in Spain and the UK, 2 in France and Italy). Atlanta International airport is the world's busiest, handling 90 million passengers a year, followed by O'Hare International in Chicago (76 million), Heathrow, London (68 million) and Tokyo (67 million).[17]

Pipeline

The main users of pipelines are oil and gas – together with the utilities of water and sewage – where they form the only feasible method of transport and distribution. They can also be used for some other movements such as pulverised coal in oil, and clay slurries.

In the EU there are about 35,000 km of oil pipeline handling 135 billion tonne-kilometres a year (about 5% of the total). The USA moves more through its long pipelines in Alaska at 835 billion tonne-kilometres.

Pipelines have the advantage of moving large quantities over long distances, working continuously without a break, with very low operating costs, reliably with very few accidents or breakdowns, largely unaffected by environmental conditions, and with small workforces. On the other hand, they have the disadvantages of being slow (typically moving at less than 10 km per hour), inflexible (only transporting between fixed points), vulnerable to attack in politically unstable areas, and only carrying certain types of fluid. In addition, there is the huge initial investment of building dedicated pipelines.

Choice of mode

Sometimes the choice of transport mode seems obvious. When you want to move heavy items between Singapore and Brisbane you use shipping; to move gas from Siberia to Germany you use a pipeline; for moving vegetables from a farm to the local market you use road transport. Sometimes the choice is not so clear, but managers still tend to go for the easiest option and put materials on lorries without much thought for the alternatives. In practice, the choice of mode depends on a variety of factors, including:

- availability of facilities – which determines the modes that are realistically available
- nature of materials to move – their weight, volume, and so on
- nature of the journey – such as the distance, physical barriers, location of supplier and customer
- value of materials – expensive items raise inventory costs and encourage faster modes
- importance – even low-value items that would hold up operations need fast, reliable transport
- transit times – as operations that have to react quickly cannot wait for critical supplies using slow transport
- reliability – with consistent delivery often being more important than transit time
- cost and flexibility to negotiate rates
- reputation and stability of carriers
- security, loss and damage
- schedules and frequency of delivery.

Transport costs are often a relatively small part of overall costs, so organisations that routinely use the cheapest mode may be losing out in some other way. An early analysis by Lewis et al.[18] found that air freight can actually save money, as it moves materials through the supply chain so quickly that organisations need fewer warehouses. So the choice is not always obvious. A rule of thumb says that the cheapest modes of transport are the least flexible, so managers have to balance different factors. The following table ranks some features, where 1 is the best performer and 5 is the worst. Obviously this only gives a general guide, and there is a lot of variability.

	Rail	Road	Air	Water	Pipeline
Cost	3	4	5	1	2
Speed	3	2	1	4	5
Capacity	3	4	5	1	2
Distance moved	4	5	2	1	3
Flexibility	2	1	3	4	5
Volume/weight limits	3	4	5	1	2
Accessibility	2	1	3	4	5
Reliability	2	4	5	3	1
Value of goods	3	2	1	5	4
Competition	4	1	2	3	5

LOGISTICS IN PRACTICE – ALBERTA COALMINES

Canada's largest coalmines are in the western province of Alberta. Unfortunately, most of the demand for coal comes from power stations in the population centres of southern Ontario over 3000 km away.

The main competitors for coal in power stations are oil, gas, nuclear power and hydroelectricity. Coal is currently a popular choice as oil and gas are expensive, nuclear power has questions about long-term safety, and there is limited capacity for hydroelectricity. Alberta coal also has low sulphur content, which reduces the need for expensive flue-gas emission control equipment. There are, however, obvious problems with transport.

About 3 million tonnes of coal is shipped each year from Alberta to Ontario, with transport costs around $45 a tonne. The coal industry looks for ways of reducing this, and the alternatives considered are summarised below (see Figure 13.4).

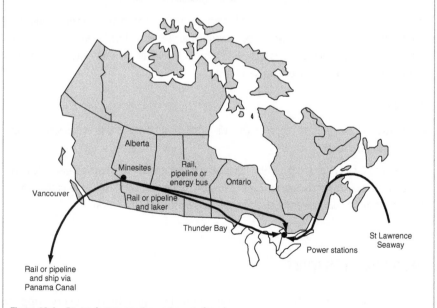

Figure 13.4   Routes for transporting coal across Canada

- *Rail and ship.* This is the current practice, with coal transported by rail from the mine to a terminal on the Great Lakes (usually Thunder Bay) and then by ship to a lakeside power station.

- *Direct rail*, moving coal by rail from the mine directly to a stockpile at power stations. This avoids the transfer to a ship, but replaces a sea journey by a considerably longer rail journey.

- *High efficiency rail.* These use newly designed rail cars that increase maximum loads and reduce unit costs. With appropriate investment, high efficiency trains can replace conventional trains in either of the first two options.

- *West Coast ports and Panama Canal.* This carries coal by train to a West Coast port such as Vancouver, transfers it to ship for the journey down through the Panama Canal and back through the St Lawrence Seaway to power stations in Ontario.

- *Coal/oil agglomeration – eastbound.* Alberta is a major oil producer and the transport of oil and coal can be combined. This would crush the coal at the mine and mix it with crude oil to be pumped through a pipeline either directly to the power stations, or to a port on the Great Lakes. At the destination the slurry is separated, with coal sent to the power stations and oil sent to markets in Eastern Canada and the USA.

- *Coal/oil agglomeration – westbound.* This is similar to the previous option, except that the slurry is piped to Vancouver for separation. The coal is put on to ships for the Panama Canal and St Lawrence Seaway, while the oil is sent to markets in Western Canada and the USA.

- *Energy bus* avoids the movement of coal by generating electricity near to the mines and using an inter-provincial electricity grid to send it for distribution in Ontario.

Analysing all the costs showed that a high efficiency rail service from the mine to Thunder Bay, followed by ship to the power station gives the lowest cost. This is marginally cheaper than the current arrangement, but is unlikely to happen because of the extra capital investment. Realistically, the current arrangements seem best.

Question

- Can you find examples of supply chains where the most obvious mode of transport is not necessarily the best?

(*Sources*: Ash, L and Waters, C.D.J. (1991) Simulating the transport of coal across Canada, Journal of the Operational Research Society, 42(3), 195–204; Richmond, E.A. (2007) The cost of coal, Presentation to the Coal Research Establishment, Johannesburg, South Africa)

Intermodal transport

Road transport is the only mode with enough flexibility to visit every supplier and customer, so the other modes typically transfer loads to road for both ends of their journeys. The obvious point is that organisations do not have to use a single mode for an entire journey. For long journeys the best option is to break a journey into distinct stages and use the best mode for each stage. Then if you move materials from, say, Lanchow in central China to Warsaw in Poland, you might start by putting the goods on a lorry, transferring them to rail for the journey across China to Shanghai, then onto a ship to Rotterdam, then back onto rail to cross Europe to Warsaw, and then lorry for local delivery. Journeys that use several modes of transport are called intermodal.

- Intermodal transport refers to journeys that involve more than one mode of transport.

- The best mode is used for each part of the journey, with transfers at appropriate points.

Intermodal transport uses different modes of transport for each part of a journey

The aim of intermodal transport is to combine the benefits of several separate modes, but avoid the disadvantages of each; perhaps combining the low cost of shipping with the flexibility of road, or getting the speed of air with the cost of road. But the problem is that each transfer between modes needs extra handling, causing delays and adding costs. You notice this effect when you transfer between a bus and train, or between a car and plane – where you always have an annoyingly long wait at the interchange. Intermodal transport only works if this transfer can be done quickly and cheaply, giving a virtually seamless journey. The best way of achieving this is to use modular or unitised loads – which means that all materials are put into standard containers, and all equipment at the transfer point is designed to deal efficiently with these. In practice, this means that as much as possible is moved in 'containers' – the ubiquitous metal box that is 20 feet long and 8 feet wide and high. This size has become somewhat restricting and it is commonly replaced by a 40-foot box. Even this can be limiting, and the Hudson's Bay Company, for example, uses 53-foot containers on the trip from Vancouver to Montreal, reducing costs by 10–15%.[19] Other sized containers are used, but this raises the obvious point that if more sizes are used they lose the benefit of standardisation.

Before containers, ships spent about 60% of their time laid up in port for loading and unloading,[20] and this was a slow, time-consuming manual process, with each item individually identified and loaded or unloaded from the ship. Even in the most advanced ports, this was surprisingly labour intensive. Then containers were introduced in 1956 for moving goods between New York and Houston, and they have transformed ideas about transport. Modern container ships can turn around in a few hours – and where it used to take three weeks to turn around a conventional ship, a container ship reduces this to one day. Over 70% of freight shipped now use containers[21] and these move between huge container ports around the world. These are built as big as possible to get economies of scale, and they have sophisticated facilities that largely automate movements – effectively replacing labour intensive operations by capital intensive ones. But the high capital costs mean that container terminals are not available in all parts of the world, and general cargo ships are still common.

Container ports ports with facilities for dealing with containerised, intermodal transport

Of course, container ports are only one link in the chain, and the containers are then moved onto trains, lorries or other ships for the next steps in their journey. These might be to final customers, or to container terminals for transfer to the next leg of the journey, or maybe to warehouses that break-bulk, allowing individual packages to continue their journeys.

Benefits of containers

Putting materials into standard, sealed and robust containers eliminates the need to handle items individually, and the whole container moves from source to destination. This brings considerable benefits, including:[22]

- simplified transport and flow of goods
- easier and faster handling, which can be automated
- genuine door-to-door service
- shorter lead times for delivery
- relatively secure loads with less loss due to damage, misplacement and pilferage
- reduced packing costs as containers protect the contents
- lower insurance costs
- separation of incompatible goods
- use of less congested routes
- improved transport, encouraging more trade.

Land bridges
have materials crossing land on what is essentially a sea journey

Intermodal operations allow many types of operation that would otherwise be impossible. For instance, they allow land bridges, which occur when materials cross land on what is essentially a sea journey. The best-known examples are in the USA, when materials from Asia cross the Pacific to the West coast of America, and then travel by rail to ports on the East coast, before continuing their sea journey to Europe. Two main routes are the 'long bridge' in the north between Seattle and Baltimore, and the 'short bridge' in the south between Long Beach and New Orleans.

Piggy-back
has a lorry, or usually just the trailer, driven onto a train for fast movement over a longer distance

Another form of intermodal transport is Piggy-back, where a lorry – or usually just the trailer – is driven onto a train for fast movement over a longer distance. You can see this in the Channel Tunnel, where cars and lorries are driven onto a train for this part of their journey.

LOGISTICS IN PRACTICE – SOUTHAMPTON CONTAINER TERMINALS

Because of the high capital cost and economies of scale, a relatively small number of major container ports are scattered around the world. Even in the USA, where there is ample funding to build terminals, three ports – Long Beach, Los Angeles and New York – account for almost half of all imports and exports. Southampton is one of the UK's busiest deepwater ports, and continues to expand. In 2001 it covered 73 hectares and by 2007 had expanded to 87 hectares, most of which is covered by container stacks with a capacity of 2 million TEUs.

On the ship-side, the port is 4 km from the main international shipping lane around the south coast of England. The main access channel and berths are dredged to a depth of 15 metres, allowing the biggest ships to enter, and the port's 'double tide' allows access for 80% of the time. There is a continuous quay 1350 metres long that can handle 4 ships at the same time. The port schedules 18 ships a week (usually in the range 5000 TEUs to 9600 TEUs) and eight smaller, feeder vessels.

Along the quays are 11 ship-to-shore gantry cranes for unloading container ships. An important factor for these unloading cranes is their reach, as they have to reach over containers stacked on the deck to lift ones beyond. The Southampton cranes have reaches up to 20 containers wide and can lift up to 60 tonnes – with a floating crane for heavy lifts with a capacity of 200 tonnes.

On the land-side, straddle carriers move containers between the quay and the stack. There are 90 of these with a capacity of 50 tonnes, 5 sprinter carriers – and a fleet of other vehicles. The stacking yard sorts containers and keeps them, usually in stacks 3 or 4 high, until they are sent inland or delivered to a ship at the quay. Throughput is fast, as it is in everyone's interest for the containers to spend a minimum time in these stacks.

The port is 2 km from the motorway network, and trucks make this journey within 5 minutes. The major centres of Birmingham and Cardiff are around 200 km away. Multi-line sidings allow fast rail connections, and Freightliner runs a main service of 13 trains a day that connect to major destinations in the UK.

Question

- What are the other major ports and terminals within the EU?

(*Source*: Company reports and website www.sct.uk.com)

Ownership of transport

In the last chapter we looked at the ownership of warehouses, where firms have the choice of using privately owned, public, or a combination of the two. With transport we meet the same decision. Is it better for an organisation to run its own transport fleet, to use a specialist, public transport company, or a combination of the two? With transport the more common terms are in-house or own account transport compared with third-party transport.

Own account or third-party transport

Own account transport means that an organisation uses its own transport fleet to move materials, and does not offer a service to other organisations. The most common form of private transport has large companies running their own fleets

In-house transport
transport run by an organisation to move its own materials

Own account transport
transport run by an organisation to move its own materials

Third-party transport
outsources transport to specialised transport operators

of lorries – but the same principles apply to running fleets of ships or planes. Own account transport has the advantages of common aims, flexibility, shared systems, greater control, closer integration of logistics and easier communications. Transport can also be tailored to the organisation's needs, with the best type of vehicles, fleet size, delivery schedule, customer service, and so on.

Clearly, an organisation should only use in-house transport when it is cheaper than a third-party carrier. The implication is that own account transport must be as efficient as a specialist transport company, or else it will be too expensive. However, the calculation is not always this clear. Sometimes own account transport can benefit from the reduced pressure for it to make a profit, tax advantages, and development grants – and its capital costs can be reduced by renting, hiring, hire purchase or leasing facilities. It can also have less tangible benefits, such as the marketing benefits of vehicles painted in identifiable livery, less stringent government regulations, and an impression of reliability and long-term dependability.

Third-party carriers are specialist transport companies that offer their services to other organisations. The advantage of this arrangement is that the organisation is free to concentrate on its core activities – while the transport company uses its size, skills and expertise to give better services and lower costs. The transport company can also give more efficient operations by, for example, reducing the number of journeys by consolidating smaller loads from different clients into larger ones, or coordinating journeys to give backhauls (where delivery vehicles are loaded with other materials for the return journey, rather than returning empty).

Common carriers
companies that move materials on a one-off basis whenever asked by another organisation

Most third-party transport is provided by common carriers. These are companies like TNT and Excel Logistics that move materials on a one-off basis whenever asked by another organisation. If you want to send a package to Australia, you would use a common carrier, such as UPS's parcel service.

Contract carrier
common carrier with a long-term contract to provide transport for a customer

Another option has an organisation forming a long-term relationship with a contract carrier. The contract carrier then takes over some, or all, of the organisation's transport for an extended period. For example, Schenker is a contract carrier when it moves all the materials needed by Roche Diagnostics in the USA. Contract carriers offer many types of service, ranging from an occasional parcel delivery through to running a large, dedicated fleet for a customer. It is worth noting that when you see a lorry painted in a firm's livery, it does not necessarily mean that the firm actually owns or runs the vehicle. It is more likely to be a contract carrier that is looking after the transport in exchange for a fee.

Choice of ownership

In the last chapter we discussed the choice between private or public warehouses – and exactly the same considerations apply to the choice between own account or third-party transport. Then the main considerations are:

- *operating cost* – and the lowest unit costs
- *capital costs* – and the investment needed
- *customer service* – which must reach an acceptable standard
- *control* – and the amount to be retained
- *flexibility* – and the response to changing conditions
- *management skills* – and their availability
- *recruitment and training* – of people to work in the fleet.

Again in common with warehousing, an increasing number of organisations are choosing to reduce their fleets and form alliances with contract suppliers. A common alternative is to use a mixture of own account transport and third-party carriers – typically using in-house transport with enough capacity for the main operations and using a third party for any additional requirements.

To be viable, the cost of third-party services must fall between two limits. The lower limit comes from the operating costs of the transport company, and is the cost of providing the service; the upper limit is set by the customer, and is the maximum value they put on the service. In reality, this upper limit is likely to be the customer's cost of providing the service with in-house transport.

Related services

When an organisation decides to run some of its own transport, it can call on many other firms to provide supporting services. These firms provide the special skills and expertise that are not usually available within a single company. Some of these firms actually move materials. For example, parcel delivery services are so efficient that it is rarely worth an organisation using its own transport. Other firms do not move materials but provide related services. These might be general, such as management consultants and software companies that tailor packages for transport, or they may be specific transport services, such as freight forwarders and shipping agents. We can use this distinction – intermediaries that actually move materials through some part of their journey, and firms that offer specific transport services – to give a feel for the type of services.

Intermediaries that move materials

- *Common carriers*. We have already seen that these are companies that give a transport service to any customer – usually a one-off delivery using common facilities.
- *Contract carriers*. These take over some, or all, of an organisation's transport over an extended time. There are many arrangements for contract carriers, but they typically involve dedicated facilities set aside exclusively for one organisation.

- *Intermodal carriers.* Traditionally carriers have concentrated on one type of transport, such as shipping lines or road haulers. With the growth of intermodal transport, many companies offer integrated services that cover different modes – so they might run both road and air freight, or a combination of road and rail transport.

- *Terminal services.* When materials switch from one mode of transport to another, or move between different operators, the transfers are done at ports, airports, terminals, container bases or warehouses. Typically, a transport company delivers a container to a terminal, and there the terminal operator unloads it, stores it, keeps track of movements, and loads it onto outgoing transport. The terminal operator might also provide related services, such as sorting goods, breaking-bulk for local delivery, and concentrating goods for onward movement. In this context you might hear of demurrage. Terminals earn money from their throughput, which they want to be as fast as possible. Any goods that are not collected as soon as they are ready take up space and get in the way of other operations. So terminal operators charge demurrage – which is a penalty for late collection and subsequent storage – to encourage companies to collect their materials promptly.

Demurrage
a charge at terminals for storage of goods

- *Export packers.* Specialist companies can pack materials before they are shipped. This service has three advantages. The first is the obvious one of making sure that goods are adequately protected for their journey – including handling and climatic variations. The second ensures that available space is used efficiently – perhaps putting as much as possible into a container. The third ensures that packages conform to international requirements, and avoids sorting and repacking to meet local regulations.

- *Postal services.* These are the traditional national mail services – such as the UK's Royal Mail, America's US Postal Service, and La Poste in France. These are often state owned, but many have become privatised, or private competitors have emerged. They normally concentrate on letters or small parcels.

- *Small parcel carriers.* These are similar to postal services, but concentrate on very fast deliveries of small packages. Companies such as FedEx, DHL, TNT and UPS have integrated networks that deliver to almost any location in the world, offering high customer service and generally guaranteeing next-day delivery. This service, partly encouraged by e-business and just-in-time operations, is increasing by more than 10% a year.

Intermediaries that help administer movements

- *Freight forwarders.* One problem with third-party carriers is the expense of moving smaller loads, when transport increasingly works with unitised loads and standard packages. For instance, you may want to move a third of a container of goods from Germany to Japan. Your first option is to leave empty space in the container – but then you pay to move a whole container and only use part of it.

An alternative is to use a freight forwarder. These are people who collect part loads, and consolidate them into full loads travelling between the same points. So a freight forwarder will find other companies that each want to move part of a container from Germany to Japan, and it will combine the loads to fill a container. This reduces unit costs and gives faster delivery. Freight forwarders take responsibility for the movement, including all the administration, documentation, chartering space on vessels, customs clearance, insurance, expediting, arranging further transportation, and so on.

- *Brokers*. A broker acts as an intermediary between customers and carriers. Effectively, they look at the goods to be moved, see what transport is available, and then find the best routes and negotiate conditions with carriers. There are several variations on this theme, with specialised brokers who assist with particular parts of the journey. For instance, customs house brokers prepare the documents needed for customs clearance and facilitate the movement of materials through customs and across international borders. Notice that brokers really offer advice, so they have a more distant relationship than freight forwarders.

- *Agents*. These are usually local people who represent, say, shipping companies. They provide a local presence and act as intermediaries between distant carriers and local customers, exchanging information, making arrangements, sorting out problems, and so on.

- *Export management companies*. If a company want to sell products in international markets, but lacks experience, it can use an export management company (EMS) to supply the expertise. This is a local company that essentially finds customers for their client's products, and then makes arrangements for the delivery. The EMS has a continuing contract with its client that typically gives exclusive distribution rights in a specified area, and it may take ownership of the goods or sell them on commission. EMS generally specialise in certain types of product where they have local market knowledge, but they can expand their activities and become general trading companies. Large Japanese trading companies – the sogo shosha – consolidate all aspects of overseas trade in one body, and this is often given as a reason for their exporting success.

Many transport services really help with the routine administration. This may seem simple, but bureaucracy is often overwhelming, and in some parts of the world it can take several days to sort out all the details needed for a lorry to pass through an international border. At the heart of the administration is a document called a bill of lading, which provides all the information a carrier needs for a journey – including a description of the goods, ownership, transport details and terms of trade. This is the key document that accompanies goods on their journey and acts as a receipt when they are delivered. Unfortunately, transport can generate a lot more paperwork and in 1984 Schary[23] reported that a single international shipment typically needed 46 documents and 360 copies, and in extreme cases this could rise to 158 documents and 690 copies. EDI has

Bill of lading
provides all the information a carrier needs for a journey

reduced this considerably, and there have been moves towards standardisation, deregulation, and free trade areas – but there can still be a daunting amount of paperwork.

OPERATIONS IN PRACTICE – EDDIE STOBART

In the 1950s Eddie Stobart established an agricultural contracting business in Cumberland. In the 1970s this developed into a transport and distribution company, and in 2006 it bought Carlisle Airport and formed Stobart Air, and founded Stobart Rail. The company was acquired by WA International in 2007 and formed the Stobart Group. Now Eddie Stobart is one of UK's largest logistics companies, with a turnover of £170 million an year. To support this they have 2000 employees, a fleet of 950 trucks, 1500 trailers, a port, 27 depots at strategic locations in Europe, and 0.26 million square metres of warehousing.

The company's strength is being 'customer focused and offering flexible solutions to suit our customers' unique requirements' and 'offering customers a one-stop solution for all their storage and distribution needs'.

One of Stobart's major customers is Crown Holdings Inc., which is a leader in metal packaging technology, employing 24,000 people in 42 countries. Stobart provide transport services, involving more than fifty 44-tonne trucks constantly working for Crown and driving millions of miles a year. They achieve the service level of 99% on-time deliveries demanded by Crown's just-in-time operations. The utilisation of the fleet is high, as vehicles deliver raw materials and then return with finished goods. Stobart also provide warehouse services of 50,000 square metres – equivalent to 120,000 pallets.

Question

• What are the benefits of this service arrangement to both Crown and Stobart?

(*Source*: Company reports and website at www.eddiestobart.co.uk)

Productivity issues

When managers have decided on the longer-term issues of transport ownership, mode, suppliers, and so on, there is always a string of tactical and operational questions. How many vehicles do they need, what type and size, do they need special features, what routes should they use, what customers and loads are assigned to each vehicle, what are the best schedules, and so on. For instance, they may decide to use third-party transport, but then have to go through all the stages of selecting the best. This involves the usual steps of supplier selection that we discussed in Chapter 10.

A common problem for all transport operators is how to increase the productivity – or general efficiency – of their fleet. We discuss this in Chapter 14, but it is worth mentioning the scale of the problem for transport. A survey by McKinnon[24] in 2002 identified major potential savings from reducing fuel consumption to save up to 19% of fuel costs, increasing the capacity utilisation from its average of 69%, reducing the amount of empty running from the average of 19%, and increasing the amount of time that vehicles spend on the road above the average of 28%. Along the same lines Key3 Partners[25] suggest that of the 28.5 billion kilometres driven by the UK's trucks every year, 2.2 billion are completely wasted – translating to 50,000 truck journeys every day. They estimate that every transport company can reduce the distances travelled by 5–20%.

Routing vehicles

An obvious way of reducing distances travelled is to design more efficient routes for vehicles. This problem appears in many different forms, but it is based on a delivery vehicle finding the shortest route around a set of customers. There are usually different kinds of constraints on the journey, including the distance the vehicle can travel, the time available, the speed it can travel, space and weight limits, the times at which customers accept deliveries, and so on. Unfortunately, we saw in Chapter 9 that such scheduling problems are surprisingly difficult to solve, because there are so many possible routes to consider. We mentioned that a driver who has to visit ten customers has to choose the best route from the 3,628,800 possible routes. Standard software is available for such routing problems – and the problems have become considerably easier since the introduction of global positioning systems, roadside traffic monitors, satellite navigation, in-cab computers, and all the other improvements to technology and communications. However, to solve a routing problem managers still have to use one of the methods described in Chapters 8 and 9:

1. haggling and negotiating
2. intuitive or heuristic methods
3. adjusting previous plans
4. spreadsheets
5. graphical methods
6. simulation
7. expert systems and artificial intelligence
8. mathematical programming and other mathematical models.

Routing problems have traditionally been solved by using intuitive methods, where scheduler study maps and use their knowledge of local conditions to give reasonable routes. People are good at recognising patterns and this often gives reasonably efficient solutions. You can see how this might work in the following very simple example.

WORKED EXAMPLE

A depot has map coordinates of (120,90) and has to make deliveries to 12 customers at the following locations. What is the best route?

Customer	x-coordinate	y-coordinate
1	100	110
2	120	130
3	220	150
4	180	210
5	140	170
6	130	180
7	170	80
8	160	170
9	180	130
10	80	50
11	100	60
12	140	80

Answer

Real routing problems can have hundreds or thousands of locations to visit, and huge numbers of complicating factors. This very simple problem has 12 customers – giving 479,001,600 possible routes that we have to evaluate. Standard software gave the solution shown in Figure 13.5, and you can check that this really is the shortest route.

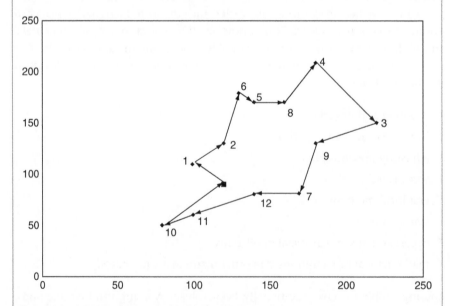

Figure 13.5   Solution to the worked example's routing problem

Chapter review

- Transport is responsible for the movement of materials between the facilities in a supply chain. It makes all the physical movement of goods between suppliers and customers.

- Levels of world trade are increasing, and there is a continuing growth in transport. Relatively low costs mean that transport is growing faster than gross domestic products. The industry plays a major role in national economies in terms of both employment and income.

- The five modes of transport are road, rail, air, water and pipeline. Each of these has different features – ranging from fast, expensive air travel to cheap, bulk transport on ocean ships. Each mode is best in different circumstances, and the final choice needs a compromise between different factors.

- Road transport is the only mode with enough flexibility to visit every supplier and customer location, and is included in virtually every supply chain.

- In practice, the best option is often intermodal transport, using a different mode for each part of the journey. This relies of efficient transfers between modes – often at container terminals or ports – with the aim of creating a seamless journey.

- Organisations have a choice between owning their own transport, using third-party carriers, or some combination of the two. The best alternative depends on a number of factors, but there is a clear trend towards outsourced transport.

- Many companies offer specialised support services for transport. The two basic kinds are those that actually move goods for some part of the journey, and those that offer advice and help with the administration.

- Many operational problems relate to transport, with managers particularly interested in raising performance. A common problem concerns the routing of vehicles, and this is surprisingly difficult to solve.

CASE STUDY – MOUNT ISA MINES

Mount Isa Mines is one of the world's great metal mines. Its main operations are at Mount Isa, in Queensland, Australia, where it mines adjacent deposits of copper and silver-lead-zinc ores. Production levels change with world demand and prices, but in a typical year 7 million tonnes of ore are mined to give 150,000 tonnes each of copper and lead (containing silver) and 200,000 tonnes of zinc.

Mount Isa has serious transport problems. It produces huge quantities of ore in a remote area of the Australian outback, while the main demand for finished metals is in the industrialised areas of the world, particularly Europe. The problem is to process the ores and move them to final markets as cheaply as possible.

CASE STUDY – MOUNT ISA MINES   (CONTINUED)

You can see the scope of the problem from an outline of the journey for copper. This starts with underground explosions to break up the ore body. The broken ore is collected by front-end loaders and put onto ore trains that carry it to underground crushers. The crushed ore is then hoisted to the surface and stored in crude ore bins, with a capacity of 60,000 tonnes. A conveyor moves ore from these bins to another crusher, where it is reduced to about 10 mm, and passed to fine ore bins. The ore then goes to a rod and ball crusher for fine grinding, and is pumped to a floatation process, which produces a concentrate of about 25% copper. This concentrate is passed to smelters that roast it to remove some of the sulphur, smelt the roast product to remove iron and silica and leave a copper matte, and oxidise the matte in a converter to remove more sulphur. The result at this stage is impure copper. This is sent to a casting furnace to remove most of the remaining impurities, and cast the copper into 300-kg ingots.

These operations are all carried out at the mine site, so there are two main logistics problems. The first moves huge quantities of materials from the mine to world markets, and the second moves materials needed by the mine, smelters and other operations into the remote site.

The copper ingots are taken by train to Townsville, 800 km away on the coast, for electrolytic refining that removes any remaining impurities and gives almost completely pure copper. These facilities have a capacity of over 150,000 tonnes a year. At this point the copper is cast into its final form, of cake, bars, rods and wire. These are driven to the port of Townsville where they are shipped around the world.

Copper is only one of Mount Isa's products, and it has similar transport problems with lead and zinc. It also mines coal and gold, has organised its transport operations into a separate company, generates electricity and supplies water for the city of Mount Isa, and is involved in a wide range of mining and associated ventures.

Questions

- How important do you think transport is for the operations at Mount Isa?
- What alternatives are there for transport? What are the current arrangements and how might they be improved?
- Can you find other mining companies that have similar transport problems?

Project – Toorvik Transport Consultants

Imagine that you have recently started work for Toorvik Transport Consultants, and are tackling your first study for a major customer. This customer buys electronic games from Japan, Singapore and Taiwan and imports them to Scandinavia. Now it is considering replacing some of the increasingly expensive games from Japan with cheaper models from China. How would you set about finding the different options for transporting these games? How would you compare these options? What specific problems do you think your customer will have with transport?

Discussion questions

13.1 'Transport is becoming less important, as e-commerce is replacing flows of goods by flows of information.' Do you think this is true?

13.2 What types of technology are used in transport? How do you expect this to change in the future?

13.3 For most operations road is the only realistic mode of transport. If this is true, why do so many people disapprove of heavy lorries?

13.4 How can you choose between the different available transport modes? Are there any noticeable trends in the choice?

13.5 Why have containers made such an impact on transport?

13.6 Many areas of the world say that they need more ports, with up-to-date facilities. Is there any evidence to support this view?

13.7 There has been a significant move away from in-house transport and towards contract providers. Why?

13.8 An organisation with weak transport management suffers by giving worse performance than competitors; one with strong transport management suffers by diverting talent away from core activities. What do you think of this argument?

13.9 If you want to move a load of materials from Europe to Australia, who can you ask for help?

13.10 What kind of operational problems are there with running fleets of transport?

References

1. Department for Transport (2007) Transport statistics Great Britain, The Stationery Office, London.
2. Directorate-General Energy and transport (2008) Energy and transport in figures, European Commission, Brussels.
3. website at www.ec.europa.eu.
4. U.S. Department of Transport (2007) National transportation statistics, Washington, DC.
5. European Union Road Federation (2007) European road statistics, ERF, Brussels.
6. Eddington, R. (2006) Transport's role in sustaining UK's productivity and competitiveness, Presentation at the Commonwealth Club, London.
7. Eurostat (2007) Transport statistics, European Commission, Brussels.
8. website at www.eurostat.ec.europa.eu.
9. Pretty, J.N., Lang, T., Morison, J. and Ball, A.S. (2005) Food miles and farm costs, Food Policy 30(1), 1–20.
10. Ashford, M. and Porter, K. (1995) Exploiting the open frontiers of Europe, Logistics Focus, 3(8), 2–6.
11. Cochran, I. (1999) UK shipping, Logistics and Transport Focus, 1(2), 22–5.
12. Karundawala, G. (2000) World trade, Presentation at the eighth annual Chartered Institute for Transport's Sri Lanka conference, Colombo.
13. ISL (2007) Shipping statistics yearbook, Institute for Shipping Economics and Logistics, Bremen.
14. Anon. (2005) 8,000-TEU Hanjin Boston arrives at Port of Long Beach, CILT World, 12, (Sept/Oct) 3.
15. Anon. (2001) UK marine motorways study, Logistics and Transport Focus, 3(4), 39.
16. Lewis, C. (2000) Fortune favours the brash, Logistics and transport Focus, 2(4), 26–8.
17. ACI (2008) World Report, Airports Council International, Geneva and website at www.aci.aero.
18. Lewis, H.T., Culliton, J.W. and Steel, J.D. (1956) The role of air freight in physical distribution, Harvard Business School, Boston, MA.
19. Anon. (1995) The Bay unveils new container strategy, Materials Management and Distribution, December, 11.
20. Union Internationale Rail Route (2001) Transport statistics, UIRR, Brussels.
21. Grainger, A. (2000) Globalisation – implications for supply chains, Logistics and Transport Focus, 2(2), 46–7.
22. Waters, C.D.J. and Soman, S.B. (1990) Containerised freight trasnsport in developing countries, Canadian Journal of Development Studies, 9(2), 297–310.
23. Schary, P. (1984) Logistics decisions, Dryden Press, New York.
24. McKinnon, A. (2002) Key performance indicators for the food supply chain, Department for Transport, London.
25. Anon. (2005) UK truckers waste 2.2 billion kms every year, CILT World, 12, 10 (Sept/Oct) (from www.key3partners.com).

Further reading

Balluch, I. (2004) Transport logistics, Winning Communications, Dubai.

Bamford, C. (2001) Transport Economics, Heinemann, London.

Emmett, S. (2006) Logistics freight transport, Liverpool Academic Press, Liverpool.

Fawcett, P. (2000) Managing passenger logistics, Kogan Page, London.

Gunther, H. and Kim, K.H. (2004) Container terminals and automated transport systems, Springer, Berlin.

Hensher, D. (2001) Transport – an economic and management perspective, Oxford University Press.

Leinbach, T.R. and Capineri, C. (editors) (2007) Globalised freight transport, Edward Elgar Publishing, Cheltenham, Gloucestershire.

Lowe, D. (2007) The transport manager's and operator's handbook, Kogan Page, London.

MEASURING AND IMPROVING PERFORMANCE

Contents

LEARNING OBJECTIVES

After reading this chapter you should be able to:

- appreciate the importance of measuring performance
- use some general measure of performance on supply chains
- use a range of specific measures for supply chain performance
- discuss the best measures and their use
- use benchmarking
- analyse the operations in a supply chain
- use different charts to describe operations
- discuss different approaches to improving logistics.

General measures of performance

We have continually made the point that a supply chain should be efficient. Although we have not explained explicitly what we mean by 'efficient', we have assumed that it means some combination of fast deliveries, low costs, high customer service, no waste, and so on. Now we should look at this in more detail and consider exactly what we mean by an efficient supply chain, and how managers can make their logistics more efficient.

These questions come in the context of supply chains that are not fixed, but continue to evolve. Logistics managers are continually looking for ways to improve their operations, and for this they have to answer four questions:

1. *What do we want our supply chain to be doing in the future?* – giving clear aims and objectives, setting goals that are demanding but achievable.

2. *What are we doing now?* – with a logistics audit to analyse current methods and practices, measuring actual performance.

3. *What is the best way to get there?* – looking at ways to move from current operations to better ones.

4. *How do we know that we are making progress?* – measuring performance, comparing actual results with expectations.

We know from Chapter 3 that the answer to the first question comes from an organisation's strategy, which defines the course of logistics into the future. We also know that the answer to question 2 comes from a logistics audit. In this chapter we are going to concentrate on the other two questions, but will also look again at ways of describing current operations.

Performance measures

We start by considering the fourth question, which asks how managers know that they are making progress – and the answer is that they measure performance and make sure that it is improving. This seems an obvious statement, but it is really quite complicated. The first point is an assumption that measuring performance serves a useful purpose. This seems reasonable as virtually every other aspect of management performance is measured, so there is no reason why logistics should be excluded. Without measures of performance, managers do not know how well they are meeting objectives, which areas need improvement, where limited funds should be invested, or how changes have affected operations. In the same way, they cannot compare current performance with historical performance, competitors, or other parts of the firm. So measuring performance is an essential part of every function, and an old maxim says, 'What you can't measure, you can't manage.' However, we have to be careful here, as measures are not answers in themselves, but they only give one set of information that managers can use when they actually make their decisions.

The next assumption is that there are appropriate measures of logistics performance. Again, there always seem to be things to measure, and with logistics there is actually a huge number of possible measures. The problem is not finding a measure but choosing the most appropriate from those available. This does not mean that every important factor can be measured, and many key issues are essentially qualitative. For instance, we talk about customer relations and use some surrogate measures, but there are no real measures. Deming[1] warns of such things when describing, 'management by use only of visible figures, with little consideration of figures that are unknown or unknowable' in his list of seven deadly management diseases. This raises the question of what are the most important measures of logistics.

The key point about measures is that we are not looking at some numbers for the pleasure of it, but want them to serve a useful purpose. This means that we are also not using measures just because they are easy to find or show us in a good light. So a call centre might measure the cost of answering a call, but that is not necessarily a good measure if their aim is to solve customer problems. A better measure would be the extent to which customer problems are solved, but this is much more difficult to measure. Cualkin[2] warns of this effect by saying, 'What gets measured, matters. Measures set up incentives that drive people's behaviour,' The argument is that when something is measured people work in a way that gets a good result for the measure, even when this bears no relation to their real aims.

We conclude that managers should measure logistics performance, that measures are available, and they should choose the most appropriate. Now we should consider the options. Here, we can classify two types of measure – general measures that can be used for different functions, and specific measures for logistics. We start by reviewing some general measures, and in the next section look at more specific ones.

Financial measures

Many general measure of performance concern finances, such as the return on assets, payback period, or contribution to profits. The basic financial measure is profit, which is the difference between revenue and costs. This seems straightforward – but remember that any financial data depends on accounting conventions and does not necessarily give an objective view. Another problem is that absolute measures do not really say much, as a profit of a million pound would be wonderful for Jane's Hairdressers, but a disaster for Microsoft. To get around this, financial measures are often reported as ratios, such as:

- *Profit margin* – which is the profit before tax and interest as a percentage of sales:

$$\text{Profit margin} = \frac{\text{profit before tax and interest}}{\text{sales}}$$

- *Return on assets (ROA)* – profit as a percentage of the organisation's assets:

$$\text{Return on assets} = \frac{\text{profit before interest and tax}}{\text{fixed assets + current assets}}$$

This is arguably the most comprehensive measure of business performance, and we saw in Chapter 1 that logistics can affect this in several ways.

- *Acid test* – the ratio of liquid assets and liabilities:

$$\text{Acid test} = \frac{\text{liquid assets (cash and readily saleable assets)}}{\text{current liabilities}}$$

Financial measures are popular, as they are easy to find, sound convincing, give a broad view, and allow comparisons. But they also have weaknesses as they concentrate on past rather than current performance, are slow to respond to changes, rely on accounting conventions, and do not record important aspects of logistics. Financial performance can show that something is wrong, but it does not show what is wrong or how to correct it. This is like a doctor finding that you have a fever – it shows that something is wrong, but does not show how to get better.

Financial measures also assume that firms know their logistics costs reliably, but this is not always true. Accounting conventions describe costs in ways that are not aligned to logistics, so 'fixed costs', for instance, include a range of costs that are directly attributed to logistics and a range of others that are not; and the cost of logistics depends on the way that overheads and administrative charges are allocated. In principle, we can say that:

$$\text{Total cost of logistics} = \text{Transport costs} + \text{Warehousing costs} + \text{Inventory costs} \\ + \text{Information costs} + \text{Purchasing costs} + \text{Other costs}$$

But the reality is that finding a total cost for logistics is far more difficult that it appears.

Even when managers cannot find logistics costs exactly, they can often use surrogate measures. For instance, they can use a system of standard or nominal costs that should be incurred if everything is working normally, and if actual costs are higher than this it means that something is going wrong and needs investigation. Reducing costs (either real or surrogate) is a common theme for managers. They do not necessarily look for the lowest cost, but for a balance that best achieves their aims. For instance, building another warehouse will inevitably increase some logistics costs, but it is an attractive option when it lowers other costs or improves other measures of performance. The point is that logistics costs do not occur in isolation, and changes to the supply chain affect a broad set of functions. Imagine a company that decides to import materials from a distance supplier because it can negotiate a lower price. But if there is any problem with material, such as slightly more variation in quality, this cost is not picked up by logistics but by manufacturing, quality management, or customer service.

So financial measures give useful information, but they should be viewed in conjunction with more specific measures for logistics. In the same way, we can use some other general measures like capacity and utilisation, but they should be viewed alongside specific measures for logistics.

LOGISTICS IN PRACTICE – KEYSTONE-GUNTERBACH

Keystone-Gunterbach offers a range of transport and warehousing services around Berlin. For several years the major shareholders felt that the company was under-performing, and in 2005 they appointed a new Chief Executive, with an explicit goal of improving results. The Chief Executive started a restructuring and cost-cutting exercise, and by 2006 could report some progress. The annual report showed that the company's performance was now generally comparable with competitors. The following table shows an extract of some key indicators.

Performance indicator	Value	Change in year
Return on capital	12.4%	+2.4%
Return on assets	6.1%	+2.0%
Pre-tax margin	3.3%	+0.1%
Return on shareholders' funds	21.2%	+6.5%
Equity gearing	28.9%	−4.2%
Debt gearing	43.7%	−6.3%
Interest cover	2.5 times	−0.2
Current ratio	1.27 times	−0.3

At the annual meeting three shareholders who had worked for the original Gunterbach transport company asked for some clarification. They felt that the company's long-term survival depended on its being competitive. They could see the financial performance, but did not know how well the company was running its core logistics operations.

In practice, their concerns were well founded as the company was having trouble with competition in the developing markets of central Europe. They tried to compete on the quality of their service and being responsive to customer needs – but delivery times were actually getting longer, there were increasing problems with reliability, lack of investment meant that their systems were becoming outdated, and customer satisfaction was declining. Increasingly, new competitors were introducing new ideas, and the company was not responding quickly enough. In the fourth quarter of 2007 their business fell by 15% and they appointed a new Chief Executive.

Question

- What do the financial figures given in the annual report mean? How relevant are they to logistics?

(*Source*: Company annual reports)

Capacity and utilisation

In Chapter 8 we defined the capacity of a supply chain as the maximum amount that can move through it in a specified time. This is a basic measure of supply chain performance. Each part of a supply chain has a different capacity, and the overall capacity is set by the bottleneck. It might seem strange to describe capacity as a measure of performance, rather than a fixed value or constraint on the throughput, but there are two answers to this. Firstly, we can say that the capacity depends on the way that resources are used. Two organisations can use identical resources in different ways, and get different throughputs. Then the capacity gives a direct measure of performance and management skills. Secondly, we have already pointed out that capacity is not fixed, but varies over time. At the start of the day a team of people might be able to move 500 cases an hour; at the end of the day the same team are tired and can only move 400 cases an hour. The operations are exactly the same and have the same designed capacity, but the effective capacity has declined.

Remember that the designed capacity is the maximum possible throughput in ideal conditions; effective capacity is what we can actually achieve over the long term; actual throughput shows what we actually achieved. The designed capacity of Ellison's call centre is 1000 telephone calls an hour. They can achieve this for a short period, but after taking into account different types of calls, staff schedules, holidays, faults with equipment and other factors the effective capacity is 850 calls an hour. In one typical hour Ellison actually handled 710 calls. This shows that they were working below capacity and have not fully used their resources.

Utilisation
shows the proportion of designed capacity that is actually used

Utilisation shows the proportion of designed capacity that is actually used. Suppose you have a vehicle fleet that is designed to deliver 100 tonnes of materials

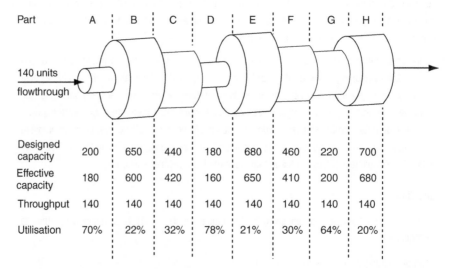

Part	A	B	C	D	E	F	G	H
Designed capacity	200	650	440	180	680	460	220	700
Effective capacity	180	600	420	160	650	410	200	680
Throughput	140	140	140	140	140	140	140	140
Utilisation	70%	22%	32%	78%	21%	30%	64%	20%

Figure 14.1 Varying capacity and utilisation along a supply chain

a week. This is its designed capacity. If the fleet only delivers 60 tonnes in one week:

$$\text{Utilisation} = \frac{\text{amount of capacity used}}{\text{designed capacity}} = \frac{60}{100} = 0.6 \text{ or } 60\%$$

We know that the designed capacity of a supply chain varies along its length, so it also has different utilisations. Then you might find that a transport fleet is under-utilised, while the warehouse it is delivering to is working flat out. Figure 14.1 illustrates some typical calculations for this. Here the capacity along part of a supply chain varies between 180 units and 700, and when the throughput is 140 units the utilisation varies between 20 and 78%. The bottleneck is the part with the smallest capacity, which is section D. If managers want to increase throughput to more than 180 units they will have to increase the capacity of this section.

OPERATIONS IN PRACTICE – YING-CHIA KOW ASSOCIATES

In July 2007, Ying-Chia Kow Associates had ten people organising 1000 specialised insurance policies for dangerous goods movements. In theory they could process 1250 policies a month but breaks, interruptions, holidays, schedules and other factors limited this to about 1150. The direct costs of this operation were $230,000.

Demand for the service was growing, and in September the company did a small reorganisation. After this they employed eleven people, who could deal with a maximum of 1600 policies a month, but with a more realistic limit of 1300. They were a little disappointed to find that in the following month they only processed 1200 policies, with direct costs of $312,000. Some measures of this performance are shown in the following table.

	Before reorganisation	After reorganisation
Number of policies processed per person	1000/10 = 100	1200/11 = 109
Direct costs per policy	230,000/1000 = $230	313,000/1200 = $260
Designed capacity	1250	1600
Effective capacity	1150	1300
Utilisation	1000/1250 = 80%	1200/1600 = 75%

As you can see, even these simple measures have to be interpreted with some care. Ying-Chia Kow's reorganisation increased the number of policies processed per person, but they also increased the direct costs per policy. The capacity has risen, but the utilisation has declined. Whether performance has improved, or not, depends on the objectives of the company.

Question

- Is it usual for some measures of performance to improve while others decline?

(*Source*: Company reports)

Productivity

Productivity is one of the most widely used measures of performance. Unfortunately, people often confuse its meaning, assuming that it is the amount of work done by each person. There are really several kinds of productivity. The broadest picture comes from total productivity, which relates throughput of a supply chain to the amount of resources used.

Total productivity
total throughput/total
resources used

$$\text{Total productivity} = \frac{\text{total throughput}}{\text{total resources used}}$$

Unfortunately, this definition has a number of drawbacks. Throughput and resources must use consistent units, so they are normally translated into units of currency. Then the result depends on the accounting conventions used (for assigning overheads, etc.), and we no longer have an objective measure. Another problem is finding values for all the inputs and outputs. This is particularly difficult for intangible inputs (such as sunlight, the legal system and economic stability) and outputs (such as pollution, product image and reputation). Of course, we could say that we are only interested in the important factors – but then someone has to decide which these are, and we have again lost our objectivity.

Because of these practical difficulties, virtually no one uses total productivity, preferring to use partial productivity, or **single factor productivity**. This measures the throughput of a supply chain to the amount of one resource used.

Partial productivity
total throughput/units of a
single resource used

$$\text{Partial productivity} = \frac{\text{total throughput}}{\text{units of a single resource used}}$$

The four most common types of partial productivity relate the throughput to four types of resource:

- *equipment productivity* – such as the number of customer visits per van, pallets moved per forklift truck, or miles flown per aeroplane
- *labour productivity* – such as the number of deliveries per driver, tonnes moved per shift, or orders shipped per hour worked
- *capital productivity* – such as the amount stored for each dollar of investment, deliveries per unit of capital, or throughput per pound invested in equipment

- *energy productivity* – such as the number of deliveries per litre of fuel, amount stored per kilowatt-hour of electricity, or the value added for each pound spent on energy.

Productivity is a very useful measure of performance – but if you hear someone talking about it you have to look very carefully at what they mean.

WORKED EXAMPLE

The van der Perlitz Corporation runs a number of warehouses in Southern Africa. Over the past two years they collected data about logistics, using standard units for throughput and converting values into South African Rand.

	2006	2007
weight of materials moved	1,000	1,200
selling price	R100	R100
raw materials used	5,100 kg	5,800 kg
cost of raw materials	R20,500	R25,500
hours worked	4,300	4,500
direct labour costs	R52,000	R58,000
energy used	10,000 kWh	14,000 kWh
energy cost	R1,000	R1,500
other costs	R10,000	R10,000

How can you describe the productivity?

Answer

From the information given we can use several measures of productivity.

- The total productivity in 2006 was:

$$\frac{\text{total value of throughput}}{\text{total value of resources used}} = \frac{100 \times 1000}{20,500 + 52,000 + 1,000 + 10,000}$$

$$= 1.2$$

By 2007 this had risen to:

$$\frac{\text{total value of throughput}}{\text{total value of resources used}} = \frac{100 \times 1200}{25,500 + 58,000 + 1,500 + 10,000}$$

$$= 1.26 \text{(which is a rise of 5\%).}$$

- Units of throughput per kilogramme of raw material in 2006 was 1000/5100 = 0.196. In 2007 it was 1200/5800 = 0.207 which is a rise of 5%

WORKED EXAMPLE   (CONTINUED)

- Some other measures are:

	2006	2007	Percentage increase
total productivity	1.20	1.26	5
units/kg of raw material	0.196	0.207	5.6
units/R of raw material	0.049	0.047	−4.1
units/hour	0.233	0.267	14.6
units/R of labour	0.019	0.021	10.5
units/kWh	0.100	0.086	−14.0
units/R of energy	1.000	0.800	−20

In general, labour productivity has risen, raw materials productivity has stayed about the same, and energy productivity has fallen.

Specific measures of logistics

As well as the general measures mentioned above, there are many specific measures of logistics performance. For instance, some common measures of transport performance include:

- product availability
- reliability of delivery
- total travel time and distance
- delivery cost
- prices and discounts offered
- information available
- order location and tracking
- orders received on time
- mistakes in deliveries
- customer satisfaction
- flexibility and customisation
- frequency of delivery service
- loss and damage
- availability of special equipment
- helpfulness of drivers
- handling of queries
- time to load and unload
- total weight moved
- number of errors in deliveries
- areas covered
- size and capacity of vehicles
- skills of drivers
- utilisation of vehicles
- advance warning of supply problems
- convenient delivery size
- consistency of service
- errors in processing and administration
- additional services provided.

Although we describe these as 'measures', some are clearly more difficult to quantify than others. We might say that '95% of orders were delivered on time', but it is much more difficult to measure customer satisfaction, or the helpfulness of drivers. Nonetheless, these may all be important, so we can benefit by assigning numerical values. Sometimes we can use surrogate measures, perhaps measuring customer satisfaction by the number of complaints received. More often we use notional scales, typically asking customers to rate some factor on a scale of one to five. But remember that when we use these methods to judge 'customer satisfaction', 'staff morale', 'management leadership', or any other intangible concept, we are trying to give numerical values to essentially non-quantifiable factors and should treat the results with caution.

LOGISTIC IN PRACTICE – MICROCOM.COM

MicroCom.com is a supplier and wholesaler of computer systems, communications devices and electronic accessories. Its main logistics centre is in New York, but in 2007 it opened other centres in Charleston and Chicago. The company expects to grow quickly over the next few years.

Although MicroCom.com runs its own logistics centres, it uses contract transport to distribute orders to customers. It continually monitors the performance of these transport companies using a scoring model. For this, MicroCom.com identifies important performance criteria and assigns each a weight. Then it gives each transport company a score (out of 100) to measure its performance in the criteria, and multiplying the weight by the score gives an idea of performance. It can use these to identify areas where performance is acceptable, and those that need improvement. Figure 14.2 suggests some of the criteria used in the scoring model.

	A	B	C	D	E	F
1			Weight	Score	Rating	Comments
2	Services					
3		Appropriate services				
4		Meeting requirements				
5	Coverage					
6		Required geographical area				
7	Schedule					
8		Pick-ups at scheduled times				
9		Deliveries at scheduled times				
10	Transit time					
11		Overall time				
12		Consistency of transit time				
13	Costs					
14		Rates				
15		Discounts				
16	Systems					
17		EDI				

Figure 14.2 Outline transport evaluation report for MicroCom.Com

LOGISTIC IN PRACTICE – MICROCOM.COM   (CONTINUED)

	A	B	C	D	E	F
18		Compatability				
19		Level of integration				
20		Accuracy of transactions				
21	Tracing					
22		Barcode or RFID				
23		Global positioning				
24		Real-time reporting				
25	Equipment					
26		Suitable types available				
27		Amounts				
28		Condition				
29	Drivers					
30		Reliability				
31		Customer acceptance				
32		Attitude				
33	Damage					
34		Amount				
35		Insurance				
36		Claims administration				
37		Fast settlement				
38	Management					
39		Skills				
40		Attitude				
41		Integrity				
42		Settlement of complaints				
43		Problem solving				
44	Finances					
45		Stability				
46	Special requirements					
47		Meet rush orders				
48		Deal with unusual circumstances				

Figure 14.2   Continued

(*Source*: Richmond, E. (2007) Efficiency and cost, Richmond, Parkes and Wright, London)

Performance of warehouses

Warehouses operations have a different range of performance measures, often related to the rate of stock turnover or utilisation of space. A basic measure is the **throughput**, which is generally taken as the value of items issued in some period. Many other measures are based on the value of stock held, but there is an obvious problem as this can vary quite widely over time. So these measures use an average or typical value for stock. Taking a single product, the average amount of stock is around halfway between the minimum and maximum levels. To find the average value of stock for the product, we multiply this average level by the unit value. Adding this for all products gives an average total inventory value.

$$\text{Average total inventory value} = \sum (\text{minimum stock} + \text{maximum stock})/2 \times \text{unit value}$$

This is really a notional value as there is no point at which the average amount of every product is actually in store – the average stocks are estimates, as are the unit costs (which we discussed in Chapter 11). Nonetheless, managers can track this value over time and look for trends, and if it rises steadily over time there might be some cause for concern. More useful measures relate the amount of stock to the demand. Then managers can measure the number of weeks' supply held in stock.

$$\text{Weeks' supply in stock} = \frac{\text{average total inventory value}}{\text{average weekly throughput}}$$

Ideally this should be as low as possible, suggesting that stocks are kept to a minimum. But when supply or demand varies widely or is uncertain, then a manufacturers may hold, say, ten weeks' supply or more. On the other hand, companies using just-in-time operations might only hold a few hours' supply.

A slightly different view measures the **stock turnover**, or **turn**. This shows how quickly materials move through the supply chain.

$$\text{Stock turnover} = \frac{\text{annual throughput}}{\text{average total inventory value}}$$

If the annual throughput of a warehouse is $1 million and the average total inventory value is $200,000, the turnover is 5. This means that materials are replaced an average of five times a year, and the average stock level is 1/5 years or 10 weeks' supply.

Other common measures of warehouse performance include:

- average stock value
- changes in stock value
- utilisation of storage area and volume
- proportion of orders met from stock
- proportion of demand met from stock
- weeks of stock held
- stock turnover
- order cycle time

- number of orders processed
- cost of each stock transaction
- time taken to prepare each shipment
- customer services

- errors in order picking
- damage and loss
- special storage facilities
- amount of product substitution

WORKED EXAMPLE

DL's warehouse received 3150 orders last month, and shipped out 2980 with a total value of €11.9 million. During this month the warehouse employed 75 people, had operating costs of €1.2 million. What measures of performance can you get from these figures?

Answer

The warehouse received 3150 orders but only shipped 2980 (or 94.6% of them) suggesting that they created a backlog of 170 (or 5.4%) unfilled orders. This alone should cause concern. Other measures are:

- average shipment value = 11,900,000/2980 = €3993
- estimated value of unshipped orders = 170 × 3993 = €0.68 million
- shipments per person = 2980/75 = 39.7
- value shipped per person = €11,900,000/75 = €158,666
- cost per shipment = 1,200,000/2980 = €403
- cost per person = 1,200,000/75 = €16,000
- warehouse costs as a percentage of value = 1.2/11.9 × 100 = 10.08%

LOGISTICS IN PRACTICE – AIR CARGO WORLD SURVEYS

Air Cargo World run surveys to compare the freight service given by various airports and airlines. They base this survey on a number of different measures of performance, including:

- **For airports**
    - **performance:** fulfils contractual agreements, dependable, prompt and courteous service, associated services such as ground handling
    - **value:** competitive rates, rates appropriate to service level, value added
    - **facilities:** for planes, loading facilities, warehousing, facilities for perishable goods, access to road and other transport
    - **regulatory:** customs, security, free trade zones.
- **For airlines**
    - **performance:** fulfils contractual agreements, dependable, meets scheduled delivery times

- **customer service:** knowledgeable sales force, problems solved promptly and courteously, efficient handling of claims

- **value:** competitive rates, rates appropriate to service level, value added

- **information technology:** tracking and tracing systems, use of Internet and e-commerce.

Question

- What other measures of performance would be useful for airline and airport freight services?

(*Source*: Air Cargo World Online (2006) Air cargo excellence survey, www.aircargoworld.com, 12 September 2007)

Balancing different measures

The lists of measures for transport and warehouses are obviously not complete, and in different circumstances many others could be important. Now we could make similar lists for other functions of logistics. For example, managers might measure performance of procurement by the cost per transaction, cost as a percentage of purchase value, time to submit orders, value of materials bought, discounts achieved, number of transaction per person, number of errors, proportion of automatic orders, and so on.

There is clearly no shortage of measures, but we might ask about the ones that are actually used. A survey by Harrison and New[3] found that 80% of organisations use some formal measures for supply chain performance – but this means that 20% of their respondents did no assessment at all (as shown in the following table).

Means of assessing supply chain performance	Percentage of companies
No formal means	20
Limited formal means	29
Some formal means	39
Extensive formal means	12

In 1989 a small survey of office furniture manufacturers by Sterling and Lambert[4] found that the most important aspects of performance were ability to meet delivery date, error-free orders, competitive prices, advance notice of delays, price discounts, value for money, availability of information. By 1993 Ferreira[5] found that the ten most common measures are quality, lead time, order fulfilment (which measures the proportion of orders that are delivered as expected), on-time delivery, responsiveness to demand, technical support, warranty and service, consolidation of deliveries, payment terms and ordering systems. Some of these seem difficult to measure, but a more interesting point is that none explicitly refers to cost. It seems that logistics cost is not really a major concern – a view that was supported in 2002 by Harrison and New[3] who found the most common measures of performance are customer delivery performance (86%), inventory turn (76%), supplier performance (66%), days of inventory (57%), order fulfilment (54%), lead time (52%), customer returns (52%), and supplier costs (48%). Less than half of companies reported using cost as a measure of performance – a finding that has been reported in other surveys.[6]

An obvious problem with so many diverse measures is that they give different – and often conflicting – views. When a truck is driven faster than usual, the miles per hour go up, but the miles per litre of fuel go down; when a shop is renovated. its sales per square metre go up, but its sales per pound invested go down; increasing the amount of automation in a warehouse gives higher labour productivity but lower capital productivity. To get a reasonable picture of logistics we have to take a balanced view of measures. This means that we have to decide which measures are important and the weight to give to each. For this we have to remember that measuring performance is not an end in itself, but it gives information about how well a supply chain is achieving its goals. When a goal is to have a very fast flow of materials through the chain, managers measure the speed of movement to see if this is being achieved – and maybe they put relatively less emphasis on, say, productivity. When a goal is to reduce costs to a minimum, managers measure different aspects of cost, but may not be so worried about equipment utilisation. Although this seems fairly obvious, managers often use inappropriate measures because they are easiest to find, support their preconceived views, have always been used in the past, or show managers in the best light. Consequently, you can find warehouses overfilled with goods because management pay is set by the amount of investment they control, rushed service because people are judged by the number of clients they speak to and not the quality of their service, double-booked seats because airlines are judged by seat occupancy, speeding trucks because drivers are judged by the number of deliveries they make in a day.

To give a reasonable view of logistics, a measure must:

- relate to the objectives of the supply chain
- focus on significant factors, rather than unimportant ones
- be measurable
- be objective
- look at current performance, not historical trends
- allow comparisons over time and with other organisations
- be easy to understand by everyone concerned
- be difficult to manipulate, avoiding false values
- be useful in other analyses.

LOGISTICS IN PRACTICE – DELIVERING FROZEN FOOD

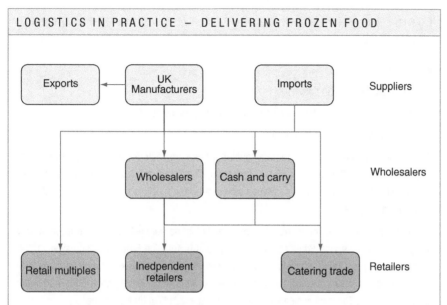

Figure 14.3   Structure of the UK frozen food industry

Figure 14.3 outlines the structure of the UK frozen food industry. An important feature is the dominant role of the retail multiples, where the three largest supermarket chains buy directly from several hundred manufacturers and importers and sell a third of all food.

A problem, which is common for many industries, is that suppliers and retailers use different criteria to judge performance. The main requirements of suppliers' logistics are summarised as:

- allowing them to focus on core operations of processing and manufacturing
- standard distribution through a single contractor
- automated order processing
- integrated stock management system
- single stockholding point near to production
- low production and distribution costs
- long lead times and production runs.

On the other hand, retailers' requirements from logistics include:

- no stock-outs in shops and displays
- small, frequent, reliable deliveries
- deliveries made at any requested time
- short lead times
- linked systems based on efficient customer response
- direct movement of goods arriving on to display

LOGISTICS IN PRACTICE – DELIVERING FROZEN FOOD (CONTINUED)

- lower stock in stores

- no errors or damage in deliveries

- influence in the supply chain aiming at lower distribution costs

- opportunities to backhaul returnables.

There is broad agreement about requirements, but there are some areas where the two groups judge success in different ways. For example, suppliers want third-party contractors to take responsibility for logistics, while supermarkets want a more positive role and greater influence over costs and operations.

One area where manufacturers and retailers agree is that delivery vehicles should move quickly and give a reliable service. When the Cold Storage and Distribution Federation[7] surveyed 11,900 journeys, delivering 206,000 pallets of food and covering 1.16 million km, they found that 25% were delayed. The main causes of the delays were problems at the delivery point (31%) and traffic congestion (23%). This survey also found that trucks spent 21% of their time idle.

Activity of trucks	Percentage of time
Running on the road	35
Idle (empty and stationary)	21
Loading/unloading	16
Waiting for loading or departure	12
Maintenance and repair	6
Delayed on the road	6
Delayed while loaded	4

Question

- Does the fact that different members of a supply chain have different aims cause any problems?

(*Sources*: McKinnon, A. (2000) Measuring the efficiency of road freight transport operations, Logistics and Transport Focus, 2(8), 26–27; Lindfield, G. (1998) Logistics Focus, 6(1), 2–8; Van Hook, G. (2007) Frozen food delivery, Transport Reports, UCLA, Los Angeles, CA)

Comparing performance

Measures of performance are not an end in themselves, but they help logistics managers make decisions. In particular, they can be used to:

- see how well objectives are being achieved

- compare the current performance of logistics with performance in the past

- make comparisons of logistics with other organisations

- compare the performance of different parts of the supply chain
- make decisions about investments and proposed changes
- measure the effects of changes to the supply chain
- help with other internal functions, such as wage negotiations
- highlight areas that need improving.

You can see that several of these involve comparisons – because absolute measures often have little real meaning. If you know that a shop has annual sales of €1.8 million, this does not really tell you much – it would be excellent for a local convenience store but a disaster for a supermarket chain. But if you knew that sales were €1200 per square metre, this would be much more use as you could compare it with other shops, years and targets. There are four ways you can make such comparisons:

1. *Absolute standards* – which give the best performance that can ever be achieved. This is an ideal performance that operations might aspire to – such as the target of zero defects in quality.

2. *Target performance* – which is a more realistic target that is agreed by managers, who want to set tough, but attainable, goals. The absolute standard for the number of customer complaints received each week is zero, but a more realistic target might be four.

3. *Historical standards* – which give the performance that was actually achieved in the past. As managers are always looking for improvement, this is really the worst performance that they should accept.

4. *Competitors' standards* – which looks at the performance achieved by competitors. This is the lowest level of performance that an organisation must achieve to remain competitive. FedEx deliver packages 'absolutely, positively overnight' so other delivery services must achieve this standard to compete. This is the basis of benchmarking.

Benchmarking
comparing an organisation's performance with the best in the industry, and learning from their experience

Benchmarking

Some ways of making comparisons are very informal, such as warehouse managers visiting other companies and looking for ideas they can use. Benchmarking gives a more formal approach. It says that there is no point in comparing performance with some random competitor, so managers should look for the industry's best performers and get ideas from them. A standard six-step procedure (shown in Figure 14.4) starts with managers recognising the need to improve logistics. Then they define the most appropriate measures of performance, identify the leading competitor in the industry, and examine their logistics to see how they achieve this superior performance. The next step is to redesign their own supply chains and implement their results. To be blunt, managers use benchmarking to find ideas for logistics that they can copy or adapt.

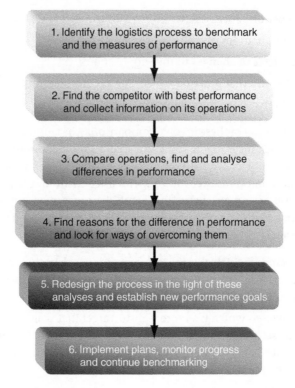

Figure 14.4   Steps in benchmarking

The easiest way to organise benchmarking is not to use a competitor, but for one division of a company to compare its operations with another division. Although this gives a limited view, it avoids the obvious problems with getting access to information, ensuring cooperation and commercial sensitivity. You might assume that a company with superior performance would be reluctant to give details of its operations to a competitor, but in practice it can be fairly easy to get the information. Fears that passing on such details will be damaging are largely groundless. Everyone knows how FedEx delivers parcels, how Wal-Mart runs supermarkets, and how Amazon sells books – and despite the fact that competitors routinely use their operations for benchmarks, they are still industry leaders. Organisations in the same industry share information when they can all benefit from the results, as even the best performers can learn things to make them even better. When Sainsbury's benchmarked the operations at their depot in Buntingford, they contacted 45 companies who had agreed to take part in the exercise. More than half returned useful information, and Sainsbury's made follow-up visits to ten particularly useful operations.[8]

Of course, it is sometimes difficult to find or get information from a direct competitor, but managers can still get useful results from organisations in other industries. BP is not a direct competitor of Tate & Lyle, but they both run fleets of tankers and may learn from each other's transport operations. Sometimes firms can learn from completely different types of operation, in the way that train operators can find improvements from airlines or other companies that are not involved in transport but give high customer service, such as supermarkets.

LOGISTICS IN PRACTICE – KEY PERFORMANCE INDICATORS FOR THE FOOD SUPPLY CHAIN

In 2002 detailed records were made of the movement over a 48-hour period of 53 transport fleets working in UK food supply chains. This survey gave a huge amount of information about transport, including hourly records of the activities of 3500 vehicles, making 6000 journeys, delivering 221,000 pallets and travelling 1.5 million kilometres.

To give a broad view of performance, the survey focused on the following five measures. The first three of these generally relate to vehicle utilisation, while the last two relate to productivity and control.

1. **Vehicle fill** – giving the utilisation of vehicle capacity, measured by weight, pallet numbers and average pallet height. Traditional analyses only consider weight, but with many low-density products deck area or volume are likely to be more important. The majority of loads are unitised on pallets or in roll cages, so utilisation is the ratio of the actual number of units carried to the maximum number that could have been carried.

2. **Empty running** – the distance a vehicle travels empty (but excluding the return movement of empty packaging or handling equipment where this prevented the collection of a backload.

3. **Vehicle time utilisation** – to record an hourly view of the dominant activity of the vehicle, classified as running on the road, stationary during the driver's rest periods, loading or unloading, loaded and awaiting departure, delayed, undergoing maintenance or repair, and empty and stationary.

4. **Deviations from schedule** – recording significant delays. These were due to a problem at the collection point, a problem at the delivery point, company actions, traffic congestion, equipment breakdown, or lack of a driver.

5. **Fuel consumption** – giving the fuel efficiency in terms of litres per kilometre. This was calculated as an average annual value for the fleet rather than a spot value for the two days of the survey.

Analyses of these figures give a wealth of information, and in particular they allow comparisons with industry standards. For instance, if the fleets with below average fuel consumption raised their performance to the industry average, they would save 5% of fuel costs a year – and if they improved performance to the average of the top third of companies they could save 19%. Capacity utilisation (measured by volume) varied widely from 50% to more than 85%. Raising the utilisation of all fleets to the average of 69% would give significant savings. The amount of empty running ranged from almost nothing to more than 40%, with a mean of 19%. This largely depends on the types of journey, but can be a source of major savings. Vehicles only spent 28% of their time running on the road. Traffic congestion was the largest single source of hold-ups, but 71% of journeys went smoothly with no significant delay.

Question

- What incentives do transport managers have to improve the performance of their fleets?

(*Source*: McKinnon, A. (2002) Key performance indicators for the food supply chain, Department for Transport, London)

Analysing a supply chain

Suppose that you benchmark a competitor's purchasing system, and find that it is 10% cheaper than yours. Now you have to look at the details of their operations, see exactly how they work, and where they make the savings. In other words, you need some way of describing the detailed operations of the supply chain. The easiest way of doing this is with a diagram, which is generally referred to as a process chart.

Process chart
a diagram used for
analysing a process

Process chart

There are several types of process chart, but they all start by breaking down a process into distinct activities and showing the relationships between them. For example, the main activities in the process for submitting a purchase order might be:

1. receive a request to purchase materials
2. check departmental budgets and get clearance to make the purchase
3. form a short list of possible suppliers and send a request for quotations
4. examine the quotations returned and pick the best
5. discuss, negotiate and finalise terms and conditions
6. issue a purchase order for the materials
7. do any necessary follow-up and expediting
8. arrange payment of the supplier's invoice.

We can use this ordered list of activities for several purposes. In the next chapter we see how to use it for analysing risks; we could also use it to analyse costs, value added, timing, or several other factors; here we use it for analysing performance. Although the ordered list is useful, it is often easier to see patterns in some kind of diagram. The easiest is a flow chart (illustrated in Figure 14.5).

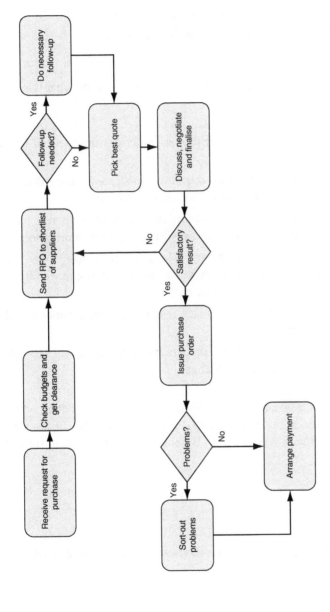

Figure 14.5 A flow chart for the process of making a purchase

This chart gives one view of the process, but it does not give many details. A better approach starts by classifying all the activities as:

- *operation* – where something is actually done
- *movement* – where products are moved
- *storage* – where products are put away until they are needed
- *delay* – where products wait for something to happen
- *inspection* – to test the quality.

Then we can track a series of activities and describe exactly what happens with the following six steps:[9, 10]

Step 1. List all the activities in their proper sequence from the start through to the finish.

Step 2. Classify each activity as an operation, movement, inspection, delay or storage. Find the time taken and distance moved.

Step 3. Summarise the activities by adding the number of activities, total times, rate of doing each activity, and any other relevant information.

Step 4. Critically analyse each activity, asking questions like, 'Why is it done this way?', 'Can we eliminate this activity?', 'How can we improve this activity?', 'Can we combine activities?'

Step 5. Now revise the process, to give fewer activities, shorter times, less distance travelled, and so on.

Step 6. Check the new procedures, prepare the organisation for changes, train staff, and implement the changes.

The first three steps give a detailed description of current activities, with steps 1 and 2 usually done by observation, and step 3 by calculation. The last three steps look for improvements. We can show the start of this procedure in the following example.

WORKED EXAMPLE

Draw a chart of the process involved when a lorry makes a delivery to a supermarket.

Answer

Details of the process, and particularly the time, vary considerably. Figure 14.6 shows the start of a chart from one supermarket. When this chart is completed with as much detail as we need (from steps 1 to 3 of the procedure), we can start looking for improvements (in steps 4 to 6). Why, for example, do we have to move 100 metres to put goods into storage – can we reduce this somehow? Why does it take 30 minutes to put goods on to the shelves – can we do this faster?

Process chart

Number	Description	Operation	Move	Store	Delay	Inspect	Time	Distance	Comment
1	Get details of deliver	X					10		
2	Unload lorry	X					45		
3	Check goods					X	25		
4	Move to storage		X				15	100	
5	Store			X			450		
6	Take from store	X					15		
7	Move to consolidation		X				10	75	
8	Wait for check				X		20		
9	Check goods					X	15		
10	Move to shelves		X				12	110	
11	Put onto shelves	X					30		
	Totals						647	285	

Figure 14.6 Part of a Process chart for delivering at a supermarket

Precedence diagram

Another format for describing the operations in a supply chain uses a **precedence diagram**. This consists of a network of circles (representing activities) and arrows (representing the relationships between them). Suppose a very simple operation has two activities – A and B, and A must finish before B can start. We can represent the activities by two circles and the relationship by an arrow, as shown in Figure 14.7. Then we can extend this method to more complex supply chains, as illustrated in the following example.

Figure 14.7 Precedence diagram for activity B following activity A

WORKED EXAMPLE

A supply chain has eleven activities with the precedence shown in the following table. Draw a precedence diagram of the chain.

Activity	Must be done after
1. receive an order	–
2. confirm order and negotiate conditions	1

WORKED EXAMPLE   (CONTINUED)

Activity	Must be done after
3. check financial arrangements, etc.	1
4. check all items are in stock	2, 3
5. pick the items from stock	4
6. order replacement items	4
7. issue payment details and invoice	4
8. complete any work needed to the items	5
9. update all transaction records	6, 7
10. prepare the order for shipping	8, 9
11. deliver to the customer	10

Answer

Activity 1 can be done right at the start. When this is finished, both activities 2 and 3 can start. Activity 4 can be done after both activities 2 and 3, and so on. Continuing with this logic gives the diagram shown in Figure 14.8. When we have drawn this network, we can start looking for improvements.

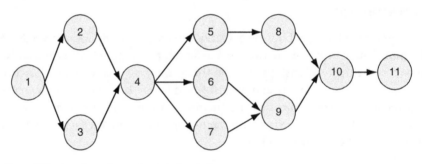

Figure 14.8   Precedence diagram for worked example

Multiple activity chart

It is often useful to see what each person or piece of equipment is doing at any time, and a useful format for this is a **multiple activity chart**. This is essentially a table with a timescale down one side, all the participants listed along the top, and the time each participant works on the process blocked off in the body. By following each activity we can look at the pattern of work to identify bottlenecks and idle periods.

WORKED EXAMPLE

One operator is currently assigned to each of three packing machines. The machines work a cycle with 6 minutes for loading, 6 minutes of operating and 4 minutes for unloading. An operator is needed for the loading and unloading, but the machines can work without any supervision. The warehouse manager plans to make savings by using two people to operate the three machines. Draw a multiple activity chart to see if this is feasible.

Answer

Figure 14.9 shows a multiple activity chart for three machines and two operators, assuming all people and machines are idle at the start, and we follow the process in two-minute time slots for the first half hour.

Multiple activity chart

Time	Operator 1	Operator 2	Machine A	Machine B	Machine C
2	Load A	Load B	Load	Load	
4	Load A	Load B	Load	Load	
6	Load A	Load B	Load	Load	
8	Load C		Operate	Operate	Load
10	Load C		Operate	Operate	Load
12	Load C		Operate	Operate	Load
14	Unload A	Unload B	Unload	Unload	Operate
16	Unload A	Unload B	Unload	Unload	Operate
18	Load A	Load B	Load	Load	Operate
20	Load A	Load B	Load	Load	
22	Load A	Load B	Load	Load	
24		Unload C	Operate	Operate	Unload
26		Unload C	Operate	Operate	Unload
28		Load C	Operate	Operate	Load
30	Unload A	Load C	Unload		Load
Totals	**24**	**24**	**30**	**28**	**20**

Figure 14.9   Multiple activity chart for worked example

The process starts with operators 1 and 2 loading machines A and B respectively. These machines start working, while operator 1 loads machine C. The operators unload machines A and B as soon as they are finished, and then they reload the machines. Machine C has to wait to be unloaded until an operator is free. At the end of half an hour both operators have been idle for 6 minutes, and the three machines have been idle for 0, 2 and 10 minutes. Most of this idle time was needed to get things going at the start of the day, so it looks as if the new arrangement will work. We could confirm this by following the activities for a longer period.

Improving performance

Measures of performance tell managers when they need to improve operations, and analysing a supply chain with some form of chart highlights the areas for improvement. Now they have to actually make changes and get things working better. We should emphasise right away that the old-fashioned idea of 'getting people to work harder' has very little to do with improving performance. A hard-working person with a spade is far less productive than a lazy person with a bulldozer. About 85% of performance is set by the system that is designed by management; only 15% is under the control of individual employees. If things are going well, it is largely because the managers are doing a good job: if things are going badly, it is probably the managers who are to blame. So when we talk about improvement, we really mean that managers are introducing better methods.

However, this assumes that managers are convinced that their operations really need improving. They may measure performance and analyse operations, but still not be convinced that there are better ways of doing things. Unfortunately, the reality is that they would almost certainly be mistaken. You can look around anywhere and see things that could be done better – poor road layouts, enquiry desks with long queues, late deliveries, products that are too expensive, poorly trained staff, long waits for appointments, unhelpful service, and so on. Managers could easily improve these operations, but often seem happy to continue with their old, inefficient methods. There are many explanations for this. Sometimes they have tried to improve things in the past, failed, become disillusioned and do not want to repeat similar experiences. More often there is no incentive for them to change, or they lack authority to push through reforms. They may not have the time for the necessary investigation, or not see the need, or not like change, or not know how to improve things, or think that changes would be too expensive and difficult to implement, or claim that they cannot measure performance.

But the reality is that managers work with continually changing conditions and they must always look for improvements. Products, competitors, costs, markets, locations, infrastructure, employees, customers, the economy, the business environment, company objectives, technology, shareholders, and just about everything else changes over time. If managers do not respond to these changes, their organisations get left behind by more flexible competitors. The argument is that competitors are always trying to get an advantage by improving their own supply chains – and this means that every organisation has to keep improving just to stay in the same place. So the main benefits of better logistics include:

- long-term survival
- improved competitiveness and growth
- lower costs
- increased profits, wages, real income, and so on
- better job security and staff involvement
- better use of available skills

- less waste of resources
- realistic targets for improving performance
- monitoring improving performance
- allowing comparisons between operations
- measures of management competence.

In 1991 a survey by Byrne and Markham[11] found that 72% of firms improved logistics to gain a competitive advantage, 66% to reduce operating costs, 60% because there was a perceived need to improve, 51% because there was a broader improvement initiative, 31% because it was required by customers, and 31% to maintain parity with competitors. These finding show that most improvement is fuelled to get ahead of – or at least remain comparable with – competitors.

The context of continuous change means that organisations need a commitment to improvement – accepting that change is inevitable, necessary and beneficial. So managers should develop a culture that welcomes and encourages improvement. But a supportive culture does not necessarily generate new ideas, and firms still need some way of actually finding ways to improve it.

Finding improvements

Robert Townsend observed that,[12] 'All organisations are at least 50% waste – waste people, waste effort, waste space and waste time.' Beesley[13-15] goes further and says that, 'In typical UK manufacturing supply chains at least 95% of the process time is accounted as non-value adding.' Such observations – and our own experience – suggest that it should be fairly easy to find improvements. In practice, an obvious starting place is simply to ask people most closely involved for their suggestions. When it is done properly this is a highly successful approach, and suggestion schemes are at the centre of most improvement programmes. But it does have problems as people may be reluctant to suggest improvements, or they may be so closely involved with the details of their job that they do not notice better options. If they find improvements, there is also the unpleasant suggestion that they have been doing things badly and wasting their time in the past. A more pressing problem is that people who know how to make improvements do not have the authority to make the changes themselves, and are never asked for their opinion by those who could change things.

Another option is to look at specific areas where improvements can generally be made. For instance, guidelines would suggest eliminating mistakes, doing more value adding activities, using websites, using third parties for non-core business, reducing stock levels, and so on. Wheatley[16] used this checklist approach to suggest reducing the number of participants in logistics (number of suppliers, etc.), eliminating activities and resources that do not add value, using EDI, focusing on customer needs, using the Internet, and collaborating with partners. In the same way, Toyota identified six areas that caused most concern:[17]

- **quality** – that is too poor to satisfy customers
- **production level** – making products, or having capacity, that is not currently needed.
- **processing** – having unnecessary, too complicated or time-consuming operations
- **waiting** – for operations to start or finish, for materials, for repairs, and so on
- **movement** – with products making unnecessary, long, or inconvenient movements during operations
- **stock** – too much stock that need storing and raises costs.

We can add to these, transport over too-long distances, over-buying, excessive overheads, waste of human resources, low utilisation of facilities, and so on.[18] These specific suggestions can be expanded into broader themes, such as quality management, high technology, lean operations, human resources, alliances, and so on. Sordy[19] recommends the five themes for improving logistics:

1. *balance* – giving a smooth flow of materials
2. *location* – with all operations in the best positions
3. *minimising* – using the least amount of handling, distance travelled and cost
4. *simplifying* – making everything as simple as possible
5. *Communicating* – as a good information flow results in a good material flow.

Introducing broad management themes to focus thinking can bring enormous benefits. For instance, in the 1990s many companies adopted TQM as a theme for improvement, and they often reported major success. However, their successes (along with those from companies adopting other foci) generally seemed to come from their focus on improvement rather than their adoption of a specific theme. It was the fact that they were positively looking for improvement that was successful, rather than their use of any specific theme.

Procedure for improvement

So far we have mentioned performance measures and analysing processes to find areas for improvement – then suggestion schemes, common areas with poor performance and more general themes to identify specific improvements. But we could combine these into a general approach to improvement. We have already mentioned one structure in Chapter 4 when we described a plan-do-check-act cycle. This has a team of people whose job is to go around and positively search for things that could be done better, using the following cycle:

- **plan** – looking at the existing logistics, collecting information, discussing alternatives and suggesting a plan for improvement
- **do** – where the plan is implemented, and data is collected on performance
- **check** – which analyses the performance data to see if the expected improvements actually appeared
- **act** – if there are real improvements the new procedures are made permanent, but if there are no improvements, lessons are learnt and the new procedures are not adopted.

The team is continuously looking for improvements, and at this point they return to the beginning of the cycle, and start looking for more improvements.

This cycle gives a good starting point, but a more detailed approach has the following steps.

1. Make everyone aware that changes are needed to the supply chain, describing the reasons, alternatives and likely effects.
2. Examine current operations, identify their aims, measure performance, see how well the aims are achieved, and identify problems and weaknesses.
3. Use benchmarking and other comparisons to identify potential improvements.
4. Identify specific areas for improvement.
5. Design better operations using the knowledge, skills and experience of everyone concerned.
6. Discuss the proposals widely and get people committed to the new methods.
7. Design a detailed plan for implementing the improvements and anticipating likely problems rather than waiting for them to happen.
8. Make any necessary changes to the supply chain's structure, systems, facilities, and so on; give appropriate training to everyone, setting realistic goals and showing how these can be achieved.
9. At a specific point, implement the changes.
10. Monitor progress and control the results, giving support and encouragement, discussing progress, problems, adjustments, and so on.
11. Remain committed to the new methods while they are giving improvements, but accept that they are only temporary, and continually look for further improvements.

This seems a rather formal list, but it is based on simple principles – analysing where we want to go and how we can get there. In reality, most improvements are relatively minor adjustments to existing operations. So we are normally talking about iterative, continuous improvement, rather than more radical approaches like reengineering (which we described in Chapter 4). Then a stream of relatively minor changes to the supply chain can easily be absorbed, cause few disruptions, and create no major problems. They also build a momentum for improvement, and make sure that logistics are always getting better. Remember, though, that the incremental approach has its critics who say that continually tinkering with the supply chain is counter-productive – and they recommend a more radical approach like business process reengineering.

LOGISTICS IN PRACTICE – HEBBLETHWAITE TRANSPORT

George Hebblethwaite runs a small warehouse and transport company distributing a range of camping equipment in northern Britain. He was keen to improve company performance and collected the following data on costs for transport and warehousing.

(a) Transport fleet operations

Fixed costs		Variable costs	
Wages	35%	Fuel	54%
Depreciation	27%	Maintenance	19%
Management	22%	Tyres	24%
Insurance	12%	Oil	5%
Licenses	4%		

George easily identified the areas where he could look for improvements. He got paid for moving vehicles, but his costs were largely fixed – so his first study looked for improvements in the activities for which he got no pay. Specifically, he looked for improvements in the loading, unloading and idle times (as trucks spend an average of 58% of their time idle.[20] The other area he focused on was vehicle routes. Variable costs generally rise with distance travelled, though they are also affected by traffic conditions, urban routes and hills that reduce speed and increase fuel consumption.

(b) Warehouse operations

Wages	58%
Buildings	23%
Equipment	19%

The cost of wages in the warehouse was particularly high, so George analysed people's activities and found the proportion of their time that they spent doing certain activities.

Total time		Of picking time	
Receiving materials	18%	Travel	58%
Putting on shelves	11%	Picking	31%
Picking	39%	Checking	8%
Despatching	23%	Other	3%
Other	9%		

Picking was clearly most time consuming, and then more than half of the picking time was spent moving around. George felt that this was another place with large potential savings.

Question

• How can the company systematically set about improving its operations?

(*Source*: Company reports; Hebblethwaite, G. (2007) Process improvement, Operations Management Forum, Leeds)

Chapter review

• Managers in every organisation must measure their logistics performance. Without these measures managers have no idea how good their operations are, whether they are meeting objectives, how they compare with competitors, how performance has changed over time, and so on.

• There are a huge number of possible measures for the performance of a supply chain. Many of these are indirect or general, such as those that consider finances, capacity, utilisation and productivity. These can be useful, but managers should look at them in conjunction with more direct measures of logistics.

• There are also many measures specific to logistics, such as those that measure transport and warehouse performance. These often give conflicting views and managers have to take a balanced view to get an overall picture.

• Absolute measures of performance do not necessarily give useful results, so managers tend to use ratios and comparisons. This is the basis of benchmarking, which compares an organisation's logistics with the best performance in the industry.

• Measures of performance show when operations need improving. To actually make the improvements we need to analyse the details of operations. Several types of diagram can help with this. They use a variety of formats, but each essentially divides the work into distinct activities and shows the relationships between them.

- Managers must continually improve their logistics to remain competitive. There are several ways that they can approach improvements (based on the measures of performance and analyses of operations). They may collect suggestions, look at common problem areas or use some theme to focus ideas.
- We combined these ideas into a general approach to logistics improvement.

CASE STUDY – ED'S DRIVE THROUGH BOTTLE SHOP

Ed's Drive Through Bottle Shop sells alcoholic drinks in Brisbane, Australia. The prices are low and the 'drive through' shop is busy. Customers accept some delays to get cheap drinks, but at busy periods the manager saw that he was losing customers.

The basic plan of the shop has a single line of cars driving past a service window (customers can park and visit the shop as normal, but relatively few do this). The obvious way of reducing the delays is to have more service windows working in parallel, but the site is rather long and narrow, so this is difficult.

The manager decided to try a number of improvements, such as dividing the service into several parts. He found the distributions of times for various operations, and then used a spreadsheet to consider a number of options. Figure 14.10 gives an idea of his approach. For this he put three servers in series. The first server, A, took the customer's order, the second, B, looked after the bill and payment, and the third, C, delivered the goods. Then he followed ten customers through the process and noted the timing. After repeating this a number of times, he found that he did not need to actually follow customers, but could use the spreadsheet to generate a set of typical times.

Customer	A			B			C		
	Join queue	Start service	Leave	Join queue	Start service	Leave	Join queue	Start service	Leave
1	8.45	8.47	8.51	8.52	8.55	8.60	8.61	8.62	8.64
2	8.45	8.51	8.53	8.53	8.60	9.01	9.02	9.04	9.07
3	8.58	8.58	9.01	9.02	9.07	9.09	9.10	9.10	9.13
4									
5									
6									
7									
8									
9									
10									

Analysis			
Number of customers	10		
Time in queue A	2.10	Service time A	2.50
Time in queue B	2.30	Service time B	2.10
Time in queue C	1.20	Service time C	2.40
Time in queues	6.00	Time being served	7.40
		Time in system	15.20

Figure 14.10   Part of a simulation for Ed's drive through bottle shop

Behind the shop is an area of bulk storage. Most orders are delivered by eight wholesalers, who generally make one delivery a week. Sometimes stocks run low, and the manager arranges a special delivery. Another twenty smaller suppliers deliver special goods or make special deliveries when there are problems. To make administration easy, the manager always uses a standard order for each supplier. Every week he takes the standard orders, adjusts them if there has been any unusual demand, and prepares for special events such as local football matches. Then he e-mails the order to suppliers, and the invoice is delivered with the goods.

Questions

- How do you think the manager can measure the performance of the shop?
- What information can he get from his spreadsheet?
- How can he describe the details of the operations and where should he start looking for improvements?

Project – Quality of logistics

Take a critical look around and see if you can find examples of poor logistics. You might find, for example, that a train is cancelled, a bus arrives at the wrong time, goods are delivered after the promised time, a shop runs out of a product that you want, a town centre is poorly laid out, and so on. How would you analyse the operations and show that they need improvement? What would you do to improve these operations? Why do you think that no one has already made these improvements?

Problems

14.1   In two consecutive years a warehouse had the following characteristics.

	Year 1	Year 2
Weight of materials moved	5,000 tonnes	6,500 tonnes
Number of orders satisfied	1,650	1,820
Number of stockouts	87	53
Average value stocked	£254,000	£287,000
Cost of administration	£60,000	£76,000
Hours worked	12,000	15,000
Direct costs	£115,000	£173,000
Energy used	20,000 kWh	24,000 kWh
Energy cost	£2,000	£3,000

What can you say about its performance?

14.2   A warehouse received 4250 orders last month, and shipped out 4375 with a total value of $12.7 million. During this month the warehouse employed 70 people, each working for 38 hours a week, with operating costs of €0.95 million. What measures of performance can you get from these figures?

14.3   The activities in an insurance broker can be described by the following table. Draw a precedence diagram of the process.

Activity	Must be done after
1	–
2	1
3	1
4	1
5	2, 3
6	4
7	2
8	5
9	6
10	7, 8
11	9, 10

14.4   Quality inspectors in a company take random sample of materials arriving from suppliers. An inspection involves three separate tests, each of which uses a different type of machine. There are two machines of each type. Each test takes six minutes for assessment, followed by four minutes for fine adjustment. There are three inspectors working in the area. Draw a process chart for the inspection area. How many units can be inspected each hour?

Discussion questions

14.1   'What you can't measure you can't manage.' To what extent do you think this is true of logistics?

14.2   Managers can be tempted to use the easiest measures of performance, or those that show them in the best light. What are the consequences of this? Can you give examples of problems this creates?

14.3   Logistics is a service, and managers should always look to provide it at the lowest costs. Everything else is simply mistaken. Do you think this is true?

14.4   What are the most appropriate direct and indirect measures of performance for a supply chain?

14.5   Performance measures can give conflicting views – changes that improve some measures, make others worse. How can you decide whether the overall effect is beneficial?

14.6   Is it easy to find improvements in any supply chain? If it is, why have the managers not already made the improvements?

14.7   Why would a successful company give away its commercial secrets to another firm that is benchmarking and trying to become more competitive?

14.8   What is the point of drawing some kind of chart to describe a logistics process?

14.9   Continuous improvement is not really useful as it just tinkers with existing operations and does not look for significant gains. So why do managers still use it?

References

1. Deming, E. (1986) Out of the crisis, MIT Press, Cambridge, MA.
2. Cualkin, S. (2008) The rule is simple: be careful what you measure, <u>The Observer</u>, 10 February.
3. Harrison, A. and New, C. (2002) The role of coherent supply chain strategy and performance management in achieving competitive advantage, Journal of the Operational research Society, 53(3), 263–271.
4. Sterling, J.U. and Lambert, D.M. (1989) Customer service research, International Journal of Physical Distribution and Materials Management, 19(2), 19.
5. Ferreira, J.A. (1993) Re-engineering the materials and procurement function, APICS – The Performance Advantage, October, 48–53.

6. Lennox, R.B. (1995) Customer service reigns supreme, Materials Management and Distribution, January, 17–19.

7. Cold Storage and Distribution Federation (2000) Key performance indicators, Bracknell.

8. Chaplen, A. and Wignall, J. (1997) Sainsbury's checks out benchmarking, Logistics Focus, 5(9), 13–14.

9. Waters, D. (2001) Operations management (2nd edition), Financial Times, Prentice Hall, Harlow, Essex.

10. Brunt, D. (1999) Value stream mapping tools, Logistics Focus, 7(2), 24–31.

11. Byrne, P.M. and Markham, W.J. (1991) Improving quality and productivity in the logistics process, Council of Logistics Management, Oak Brook, IL.

12. Townsend, R. (1970) Up the organisation, Coronet Books, London.

13. Beesley, A. (1995) Time compression – new source of competitiveness in the supply chain, Logistics Focus, 3(5), 24–25.

14. Beesley, A. (1995) Time compression tools, Logistics Focus, 3(7), 17–20.

15. Beesley, A. (2007) Time compression in the supply chain, in Waters D. (editor), Global logistics (5th edition), Kogan Page, London.

16. Wheatley, M. (1998) Seven secrets of effective supply chains, Management Today, June, 78–87.

17. Monden, Y. (1983) Toyota production system, Industrial Engineering and Management Press, Norcross, GA.

18. Emmett, S. (2000) Improving freight transport and warehouse operations, Logistics and Transport Focus, 2(2), 30–34.

19. Sordy, S. (1997) Do you have any principles, Logistics Focus, 5(8), 19.

20. McKinnon, A. (1999) The effect of traffic congestion on the efficiency of logistical operations, International Journal of Logistics Research and Applications, 2(2).

Further reading

Anderson, B. (2007) Business process improvement toolbox (2nd edition), American Society for Quality,

Armistead, C. and Roland, P. (1996) Managing business processes: BPR and beyond, John Wiley and Sons, Chichester.

O'Connell, J., Pyke, J. and Whitehead, R. (2006) Mastering your organisation's processes, Cambridge University Press, Cambridge

Rummler G.A. and Brache A.P. (1995) Improving performance (2nd edition), Jossey-Bass, Hoboken, NJ.

Rummler, G.A. and Harman, P. (2003) Business process change, Morgan Kaufmann, San Francisco, CA.

Sharpe, A. and McDermott, P. (2001) Workflow modelling, Artech House, Norwood, MA.

SUPPLY CHAIN RISK

Contents

LEARNING OBJECTIVES

After reading this chapter you should be able to:

- discuss the nature of risks to a supply chain

- understand the role of risk management and describe its activities

- identify and analyse risks to a supply chain

- review possible responses to risk

- show how new logistics methods increase supply chain risk

- describe a way of introducing risk management.

Defining risk

Everyone is familiar with risk, which we generally consider in terms of unpleasant things that might happen. In the context of supply chains, managers face the risk that a delivery is delayed, fuel prices increase, a project goes over-budget, a truck has an accident, a warehouse is destroyed by fire, and so on.

Risk
the threat of an event that might disrupt normal flows of materials or stop things happening as planned

> - Risk to a supply chain is any threat of an event that might disrupt normal flows of materials or stop things happening as planned.

To be pedantic, risk is the chance that an event might happen – it is not the event itself. So when we say there is a risk that a delivery will be delayed, the risk is the chance of a delay and not the delay itself.

Risks occur because we can never know exactly what will happen in the future. We can use the best forecasts and do every possible analysis, but there is always uncertainty about future events. It is this uncertainty that brings risks. Alberta Highways can do everything possible to build a new road on schedule, but an unexpected snowstorm can cause delays; Mitsubishi can carefully arrange a delivery of cars to Copenhagen, only to find their journey interrupted by industrial action; Dell can schedule its production of computers, and find that a typhoon in Taiwan hits the supply of chips.

As you can see, risks come in many different forms. They can appear at any point in a supply chain from initial suppliers through to final customers; they can interrupt the supply of materials or the demand for products; they can cause a suddenly peak in demand, or collapses; they can range in scope from a minor delay through to a natural disaster; their effects can range from the short term and lasting only a few minutes through to permanent damage; their effects might be localised in one part of a supply chain, or passed on to threaten the whole chain. With this almost limitless variety of risks, we can identify two basic kinds of risk to a supply chain – external and internal risks.

- **External risks** come from outside the supply chain, such as earthquakes, hurricanes, industrial action, wars, terrorist attacks, outbreaks of disease, price rises, problems with trading partners, shortage of raw materials, crime, financial irregularities, and so on.

  Supply chains are inherently risky. They move materials through a series of organisations, each with different operations, aims, cultures and structures, dispersed around the world, and working in widely different conditions. And they move through regional instability, war zones, changing government policies, new trading regimes, inhospitable climates, and every other problem that you can imagine.

  When you hear about something going wrong with a supply chain, it is usually the dramatic effects of external risks – such as the 1995 earthquake in

Kobe, the 1999 earthquake in Taiwan, the 2004 tsunami in the Indian Ocean, or Hurricane Katrina in New Orleans in 2005. Each of these is certainly a major one-off incident – but when you add together all of the one-off incidents they form an ever-present background of external risk. We can illustrate this by the earthquake that damaged the Japanese city of Kobe. This was widely reported, because of the amount of damage – and because of concerns that a significant part of the world's electronics industry that was sited nearby. This earthquake was officially 'strong', registering 6.9 on the Richter scale – but there are 1100 earthquakes of this size around the world each year. These are so common that we might consider them as posing a significant risk.

The key feature of these external risks is that they are outside managers' control. So managers cannot change the risk, but they can design operations that work as efficiently as possible within a risky environment. For instance, there is a continuing risk of hurricanes hitting the South-west coast of America. Managers cannot alter this risk, but they can design operations to reduce its effects, perhaps by having secure buildings, closing during the hurricane season, or simply moving to another location.

- **Internal risks** appear in normal supply chain operations, such as late deliveries, excess stock, poor forecasts, financial risks, minor accidents, human error, faults in information technology systems, and so on. These internal risks are generally less dramatic, but more widespread in their effects. They are also the risks that operations managers can control – such as delays and breakdowns – and there are traditional ways of dealing with them. For instance, risks from suppliers can be avoided by multiple sourcing, and when problems occur with one supplier it is easy to switch orders to another. Similarly, risks to the flow of materials are reduced by holding stocks throughout the supply chain to insulate the flows from unexpected variations. But using stocks to reduce the effects of risk illustrates a common problem. We know that stocks are expensive and there are clear incentives to reduce or even eliminate them. Then the initial balance seems to be between high stocks (which give low risk of disruption, but high costs) and low stocks (which give high risk of disruption and low costs). But you can see that there are other types of risk associated with high stock – such as obsolescence, deterioration, tied-up money, uncertain future demand, damage during storage, and so on. So higher stocks increase some risks while reducing others, and managers have the more complex problem of balancing different types of risk and the associated costs.

In reality, most risks are fairly minor and have limited consequences. For instance, congestion on a motorway might make a delivery an hour late; although this is unfortunate, in the big scheme of things it is rarely a catastrophe. On the other hand, risks occasionally have serious consequences, such as Toyota closing 20 of its 40 assembly lines for six weeks following a fire at a valve supplier, at an estimated cost of $40 million a day.[1]

LOGISTICS IN PRACTICE – TELEFON AB L. M. ERICSSON

On 17 March 2000 there were thunderstorms in New Mexico, and lightning hit an electric power line. This caused a surge in power, which started a small fire in Philips' chip-making factory in Albuquerque. The automatic sprinkler system put this out within ten minutes and fire damage to the building was slight. Unfortunately, thousands of chips that were being processed were destroyed. But more importantly, the sprinklers caused water damage throughout the factory and smoke particles got into the sterile area, contaminating millions of chips held in stock.

Four thousand miles away, Ericsson was Sweden's largest company with an annual revenue $30 billion, 30% of which came from mobile telephones. For many years, Ericsson had worked on the efficiency of its supply chains, and single sourcing was a key element in its drive towards lower costs and faster deliveries. Now the Philips plant was its sole source of many radio frequency chips, including those used in an important new product.

At first, Philips thought that the plant would return to normal working within a week, so Ericsson were not too concerned when they heard about the fire. However, it soon became clear that there was more extensive damage. Philips actually shut the factory completely for three weeks, it took six months for production to return to half the previous level, and some equipment took years to replace. Ericsson had no alternative suppliers, and at a time of booming sales they were short of millions of chips.

In 2001 Ericsson said that the drastic reductions in production and sales caused by the fire cost them more than $400 million. When this figure was published, their share price fell by 14% in a few hours. For a variety of reasons – including the consequences of the fire – Ericsson's mobile phone division lost $1.7 billion that year. They decided to withdraw from handset production and now outsource manufacturing to Flextronics International. They also changed their approach to procurement, moving away from single sourcing and ensuring that there are always back-up suppliers.

Question

• Can you find other examples of risky events causing such severe damage?

(*Sources:* Latour, A. (2001) Trial by fire, Wall Street Journal, 29 January; Norman A. and Jansson U. (2004) Ericsson's proactive supply chain risk management, International Journal of Physical Distribution and Logistics Management, 34(5), 434–56)

Risk management

Risk management
the process for systematically identifying, analysing and responding to risks throughout an organisation

Ericsson's experience shows how vulnerable a major corporation can be to relatively small events. It also emphasises the need for careful risk management – which means the identification of risks and procedures for dealing with them. This is defined as risk management.

> • **Risk management** is the process for systematically identifying, analysing and responding to risks throughout an organisation.

Risk management is not a new idea, and it is the standard work of insurance companies and banks, but in recent years risk management has expanded from its traditional home in finance. It is becoming a broader function that is now considered an intrinsic part of management. As Handy[2] says, 'Risk management is not a separate activity from management, it is management.'

The main reason for this growth of risk management is the perception that business is becoming more risky. The Economist Intelligence Unit[3] found that, 'Many companies perceive a rise in the number and severity of the risks they face.' This is an interesting point, as there may, or may not, be a real change, but managers perceive them as increasing. The risk of flooding in most areas remains more or less constant, but when you see the consequences of a severe flood it is difficult not to become worried.

The three core elements of risk management (shown in Figure 15.1) are:

1. **Identify risks to the supply chain**. This examines the supply chain, defining the separate activities and their relationships, and systematically studying these to find areas of risk.

2. **Analyse the risks**. After identifying the risks, the next step is to consider their potential impact. This impact depends on two factors – the probability that a risky event may occur, and the severity of the consequences when it does occur. Managers can prioritise risks according to their impact and decide where to concentrate resources. Clearly they should focus on risks with the highest impact, but they should consider other factors, such as the likelihood that they can actually reduce the impact.

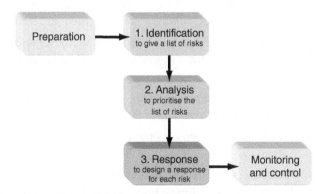

Figure 15.1 Three steps in supply chain risk management

3. **Design appropriate responses to the risk.** Here managers know the serious-ness of risks and consider different ways of dealing with them. There are many types of response, but three common ones are prevention (to reduce the prob-ability of a risky event occurring), mitigation (to reduce the consequences), or response (waiting to evaluate actual events before deciding on a response).

Identifying risks

We have suggested that risks are either external or internal, but there are other ways of classifying them. A common one describes three types of risk to the related flows of materials, money and information. A more detailed list suggests the following risks to a supply chain:

- *strategic* – arising from strategic decisions made within organisations that directly increase the risk
- *natural* – arising from unforeseen natural events such as extreme weather, lightning, earthquakes, flood, landslides or outbreaks of diseases
- *political* – such as government instability, new legislation, regulations, policies, permits, treaties, customs barriers, conflicts, wars
- *economic* – from the broad economic environment, including interest rates, inflation, currency exchange rates, taxes, growth
- *physical* – risks to buildings and facilities, such as traffic accidents, equipment failure, congestion, or limited capacity
- *supply* – all issues with the movement of materials into an organisation, includ-ing sources, supply market conditions, constraints, limited availability, supplier reliability, lead times, material costs, delays
- *market* – all aspects of customer demand, such as level of demand, variability, alternative products, competition, patterns of change
- *transport* – for all movements of materials, including risks to the infrastructure, vehicles, facilities, loads
- *products* – risks arising from product features, including technology used, innovation, product mix, range, volumes, materials used and standardisation
- *operations* – arising from the nature of activities in the organisation, type of process, complexity, technology, special conditions, after sales service, and so on
- *financial* – all money transactions including payments, prices, costs, sourcing of funds, profit, and general financial performance
- *information* – including the availability of data, data transfer, accuracy, reliability, security of systems
- *organisation* – arising from the way the organisations works, including its structure, disputes, types of interactions, subcontractors, communication flows, culture

- *management* – and risks arising from their knowledge, skills, experience, decisions, real aims, and so on
- *planning* – risks from the design and execution of plans for operations, including mismatch between supply and demand, inadequate detail, missed constraints, poor forecasting, lack of synchronisation
- *human* – from all the complex interactions between people, including working requirements, aims, culture, human errors, industrial action
- *technical* – and new technology in processes, communications, new products, process designs, reliability
- *criminal* – arising from all illegal activities, such as theft, fraud, bribery, vandalism, terrorism
- *safety* – to people and facilities, including accidents, hazardous substances, fire
- *environment* – such as pollution, use of resources, traffic, regulations
- *local permits* – usually administered by local governments and including planning permissions, land use, local policies, grants, and so on.

This is a daunting list – especially as it is by no means exhaustive. Thankfully, managers do not have to identify every possible risk to a supply chain, but only those that are likely to have the greatest impact. For instance, there may be a risk that a transport company cannot deliver a package – but when an alternative company can deliver it, this risk will have no impact at all. So managers have to compile a register of the most significant risks, and for this they have to:

1. define the operations within a supply chain
2. divide this into a series of distinct, related activities
3. systematically consider the details of each activity
4. identify the risks in each activity and their main features
5. describe the most significant risks in a register.

You can see that the first three steps analyse the activities, giving an ordered list. This is the start of the procedure we described in Chapter 14 for drawing a process chart, so managers can use the results for at least two purposes, looking for improvements and identifying risks. In practice, this list is a useful tool that can be used for purposes ranging from costing through to managing relationships.

Generally the most difficult stage is number 4, which actually identifies the risks. There is no formal procedure for doing this, and it relies largely on knowledge and experience. Managers can use their personal knowledge, interview people who are most familiar with the operations, use group meetings to discuss risk, a Delphi analysis, or any other feasible means to get a register of significant risks. Rather than starting from scratch, a common approach is to look at the risks identified by other organisations, or to use guidelines published by trade associations, government departments, consultants and journals.

Analysing risks

Having prepared a register of the most significant risks, the next stage is to analyse them more carefully, give each a priority, and identify the most pressing. This analysis is based on two factors:

1. the likelihood of a risky event occurring

2. the consequences when the event does occur.

From these two factors we can calculate an expected value for each risk.

Expected value
= probability of
event × consequence

- expected value of an event = **probability × consequence**

When there is a 20% chance that a delivery is delayed, and any delay costs £12,000:

$$\text{expected value of a delay} = 0.2 \times 12,000 = £2400$$

If something is repeated many times, the expected value gives the average consequence. If there is a chance of 0.1 that a daily delivery is delayed, and each delay costs €200, then the expected value of $0.1 \times 200 - €20$ is the average daily cost.

The expected value is useful for showing the relative importance of risks, and we can use it to rank them in order of priority. However, it can be misleading and you have to be careful to interpret it properly. The expected value shows the average result over the long term, and not the cost each time. With the delayed truck, there is a 90% chance of no delay and no cost. The actual cost is usually nothing, and it is occasionally €200 – but it is never really €20.

Another problem is finding values, or even reliably estimates, for either the probability of risky events or their consequences. How can you really find the probability that a truck will be delayed, or that a major supplier will go bankrupt, or that there will be an earthquake next month? If these risky events were to occur, how can you find a convincing cost? Many people suggest that the probabilities of such risky events and value of consequences can never be more than informed guesses. In which case it may not be worth doing such detailed calculations, but we can make some simplifications. For instance, rather than using a specific value for a probability, we can classify the likelihood as:

- *very unlikely* – an event that might happen, but so rarely that most people will never meet it

- *rare* – an occasional event which people might expect to meet once or twice in their working lives

- *occasional* – an event that occurs sometimes, with people meeting it sporadically throughout their working lives

- *frequent* – an event that occurs regularly, with people commonly meeting it
- *very likely* – an event that occurs often, with people meeting it continuously and accepting it as normal.

In the same way, rather than putting a precise value on the outcome we might describe its impact as:

- *negligible* – an insignificant effect on the working of the supply chain
- *minor* – causing some inconvenience with minor disruptions, delays and increased costs to some parts of the chain, but most functions are unaffected
- *moderate* – causing some disruption to parts of the supply chain, but the main functions continue to meet requirements
- *serious* – major disruptions to the essential operations of the supply chain, causing serious delays and high cost of recovery
- *critical* – failure of the whole supply chain for an extended time, with major cost and effort needed for recovery
- *catastrophic* – causing complete and unrecoverable failure of the supply chain and possibly whole organisations.

Managers should clearly give highest priority to the most significant risks – which are those with the combination of highest probability and greatest consequence. Risks that have a low probability are unlikely to occur, so managers can pay them less attention, even when the consequences are severe. Risks that have minor consequences do not need much attention, even when they have a high probability of occurring. The least important risks have low probabilities and minor consequences, so managers can virtually ignore them.

In Chapter 11 we described an ABC, or Pareto, analysis for stock, and we can do the same thing here to describe different categories of risk. In particular, we can say that 20% of the risks cause 80% of concerns, while the remaining 80% of risks cause only 20% of concerns. Then we can classify risks as:

- *A risks*, the most severe that need special attention
- *B risks*, the medium ones that need normal attention
- *C risks*, the low ones that need little attention.

And we might typically find the following pattern:

Category	Percentage of risks	Cumulative percentage of risks	Percentage of concerns	Cumulative percentage of concerns
A	10	10	70	70
B	20	30	20	90
C	70	100	10	100

Potential consequence						
		Negligible	Minor	Moderate	Serious	Critical	Catastrophic

Probability	Very high	B	B	A	A	A	A
	High	B	B	B	B	A	A
	Medium	C	B	B	B	A	A
	Low	C	C	B	B	A	A
	Very low	C	C	C	B	B	A

Figure 15.2 The structure of a probability-impact matrix

Probability-impact matrix
table showing a Pareto analysis for the relative importance of risks

A more formal presentation of the relative risks is a probability-impact matrix. This is a table with the rows showing the probability categories, the columns showing categories of consequences. A description of risks is put in the body of the table, where they are categorised as A, B or C. Figure 15.2 shows the general layout of a probability-impact matrix, and we can put descriptions in the appropriate cells. For instance, if we felt that the probability of an earthquake are very low but the consequences are critical, we can put this in the appropriate cell, noting that this risk is category B. If the three descriptions of A, B and C are insufficient, we can add others to help the prioritising.

Dealing with risk

Now we have different categories of risk, and can concentrate on the most important. We want to design an effective response to these that will allow the supply chain to continue working normally, or with minimum disruption.

In the same way that there is a very large number of possible risks, there is also a very large number of possible responses. The most common are:

1. *Ignore or accept the risk* – which means that the likelihood of the risk occurring is small and its consequences are minor, so that managers can ignore it. Effectively, the option of doing nothing is better than the option of actually doing anything.

2. *Reduce the probability of the risk* – taking actions to reduce the chance that a risky event occurs. For instance, being attacked by pirates is a surprisingly high risk for cargo ships in some parts of the world; a way of reducing the risk is to use other routes that avoid the most dangerous areas.

3. *Reduce or limit the consequences* – so that when the risky event occurs it is less harmful. For example, car seat belts do not necessarily reduce the probability of an accident, but they reduce the effects on people involved.

4. *Transfer, share or deflect the risk* – moves some or all of the risk from one organisation in the supply chain to another that is more able or willing to handle it. The standard way of organising this is to take out insurance, and transfer risk to the insurance company.

5. *Make contingency plans* – which means that managers take no immediate action, but they plan what to do if a risky event actually occurs (often referred to as 'plan B'). For example, a company might normally use low-cost road transport, but if there is a sudden emergency order they have a contingency plan of using higher-cost air freight.

6. *Adapt to it* – accept that a risky event is inevitable and try to adapt operations to fit in to the new circumstances. For example, when there is a risk that demand for a product might fall, managers adjust their operations so that they would still be profitable with the lower demand.

7. *Oppose a change* – when managers get prior notice that an event is going to happen, such as a government announcing that it will introduce new regulations at some point in the future, they can actively resist the change and try to prevent it happening.

8. *Move to another environment* – which admits that some events are so risky that an organisation cannot work with them. Then the only feasible options are to close down, or reorganise and move to another market or industry that does not have the risk.

LOGISTIC IN PRACTICE – CONTAINERS LOST AT SEA

It is difficult to get exact figures, but somewhere between 2000 and 10,000 containers are lost over the side of ships each year. At any particular time, there are probably around 6 million boxes in transit, so the probability that any one will be lost is very small. It is unclear whether this risk is increasing or not. On the one hand, there have been continuing improvements in the methods of securing containers to decks, and monitoring their positions and safety. On the other hand, growing international trade means that more containers are being moved, and ship designs are leaving them more exposed to the weather and seas.

The number of containers lost may be small – but the few that are lost can cause significant damage to their owners, risks to the environment if they sink or their contents are washed ashore, and risk to other shipping if they float. Rough weather and waves break open the boxes and there are many stories of lost containers spreading their contents around the world. In 1990 Nike lost 80,000 pairs of tennis shoes from a container ship in the Pacific, and there were still reports of them being washed ashore more than ten years later (ten years is about the maximum time that trainers will float in the ocean). In 1997 three containers with 5 million pieces of Lego fell overboard in the Atlantic when M/V Tokio Express ran into a storm. These are expected to drift north into the Arctic Ocean and then through the North-east Passage before turning south, where they are expected to come ashore on beaches in Alaska by 2012 and in Washington by 2020.

LOGISTIC IN PRACTICE – CONTAINERS LOST AT SEA (CONTINUED)

Less common are reports of ships being damaged by hitting partly submerged containers. An empty container weighs between two and four tonnes, and is generally weatherproof rather than watertight, so it soon fills with water and sinks. However, a full container might have trapped air or light contents, and float for some time. Roughly speaking a sealed 20-foot container would have to weigh more than 16 tonnes before it begins to sink, and weight restrictions should keep it below this. So sealed containers should float – but in reality they usually fill with water and sink. If the seals are in poor condition this will happen quickly, but if the seals are good a light container might remain afloat for more than six months.

Question

- Can you find other examples of unexpected risks to transport?

Increasing risk to the supply chain

The nature of supply chains and their complexity make them particularly vulnerable to different kinds of risk. Historically, logistics managers have been aware of the risks, but have paid little attention to the formalities of risk management. In 2002, Christopher et al.[4] reported that, 'it appears from the available literature that the implementation of risk management in supply chains is still in its infancy'. Partly as a result of this lack of attention, levels of risk have tended to drift upwards. Perhaps this is the reason that Hendricks and Singhal[5] were able to notice a significant increase in both the number and costliness of supply chain disruptions.

Risks have not spontaneously increased, but they have been positively encouraged by the efforts of managers to make their supply chains more efficient by simultaneously raising customer service and lowering costs. In effect, managers have put so much effort into supply chain improvement – where they have made a lot of progress – that they have not noticed that they are unwittingly raising levels of risk. We can illustrate this effect with stocks. Managers increasingly believe that stocks are an expensive waste of resources, so they have spent years introducing methods to lower, and preferably eliminate, all stocks. But stocks often serve a genuine purpose, giving a buffer between variable and uncertain supply and demand. Without this cushion, supply chains become more vulnerable to unforeseen events, and even a small disturbance that would have been absorbed by stocks can now cause severe disruptions.

The worrying problem with new methods increasing risk is not that managers have taken a positive decision to work with higher levels of risk, but that they have simply not considered the risks and included them in their calculations. To be fair, managers usually do include risk in their decisions, but they take a superficial view. For instance, managers claim that lower stocks actually reduce risk as there is less chance of unsold stock, obsolescence, damage, deterioration, and all the other risks of accumulated stock. This is undoubtedly true, but we know that lower stocks increase other risks, notably shortages and poor service. So managers should really be taking a more balanced view.

A survey by Jüttner[6] found that factors likely to increase supply chain vulnerability are globalisation (reported by 52% of managers), reducing stock levels (51%), smaller supply base (38%), and outsourcing (30%). In practice, almost all new innovations to logistics increase risk in some way. It may not be clear how this happens, so we should review some of the key effects.

Integration of supply chains

Greater integration of the supply is one of the key themes of supply chain improvement. The argument is that a change in any one part of a supply chain inevitably affects other parts, so it is best to take a coordinated view of the whole. This integration starts with internal merging of associated functions and moves to external coordination of activities along the chain.

The arguments are convincing, so it seems that the move towards greater integration is inevitable, but this is not always the best model, and neither integration nor arm's-length relationships is intrinsically best. It is often better to have elements of both, in the way that Dell has strong single-supplier relationships with Intel for its processors and Microsoft for operating systems, but more distant relations with vendors of other components.

From a risk perspective, the benefits of integration can be summarised as lower risk, achieved through transparency, allowing one part of a supply chain can see what is happening in other parts. This is achieved when all members share information and work together. A manufacturer can monitor sales at retailers and plan production from actual sales rather than forecasts, and raw materials suppliers can see manufacturer's production schedules and use these to plan their own operations. The result is less uncertainty, and lower risks.

But extensive integration is an ideal rather than a reality. One reason is that each member of the chain has to search for individual benefits, even when these come at the expense of their trading partners. Then one member might raise prices to increase its own profits, but perhaps at the risk of lower demand for all of the chain – and another firm might reduce its own risk from high stocks by transferring them to other organisations through vendor-managed inventory. The underlying dilemma is that supply chain partners rely on each other and must work together, but they can only gain by making a profit from each other.

In 1997, Szymankiewicz[7] noted that, 'In the grocery sector ECR is often regarded as an established way of doing business . . . [but] overall there is more talk than action.' And by 2003 Poirier and Quinn[8] noted that most organisations were still working on internal integration and, although they were moving towards external integration, only 10% had made any significant progress.

Christopher et al.[4] found that, 'upstream and downstream visibility was poor' and, 'all interviewees agreed that end-to-end management of an organisation's complex and unstable supply chain network, (particularly upstream into the supplier base), would be an improbable if not impossible task'.

We can conclude that external integration reduces some risks (say, from surprise actions of trading partners) but the pressures are not strong enough for firms to make much real progress in this direction. Possibly they realise that integration actually increases other risks, such as those inherent to sharing information. When information is distributed more widely, there is a greater threat to its security, and greater chance that it is passed on to unwanted bodies.

No amount of cooperation can overcome the underlying reality that each member of a supply chain can only make a profit by paying less for materials bought from one partner, and charging more for materials sold to another partner. Transparency might highlight inconsistencies in the chain, perhaps where one member seems to be gaining a disproportionate share of the benefits. The concept of shared benefits is unconvincing when a dominant organisation decides to flex its muscles and attract more benefit to itself at the expense of smaller, more vulnerable partners.

A basic principle of integration is that firms develop long-term relationships with suppliers, working largely – or even exclusively – with small numbers of the best. We saw in Chapter 10 that single sourcing has many advantages, but it can also cause difficulties, particularly when the sole source hits problems. We gave the example of Land Rover, which hit problems when its sole supplier of chassis frames went out of business. This is a fairly common story, as you can guess from the following examples.

LOGISTICS IN PRACTICE – PROBLEMS WITH SINGLE SOURCING

1. British Airways reduced its operating costs by outsourcing virtually all catering. Its in-flight meals at Heathrow are now provided by Gate Gourmet. This company has its headquarters in Switzerland, and generates an annual turnover approaching $2 billion by producing more than half a million meals a day for major airlines. But in 2005 the company had a dispute with staff over working conditions at Heathrow, and it sacked a number of people – variously reported to be between 350 and 600. BA lost its sole source of in-flight meals at Heathrow, and its problems increased when 650 of its own ground staff – who had close associations with Gate Gourmet staff, including many family members – staged a four-day sympathy strike. Such secondary strikes had been unknown in the UK for decades and were technically illegal. But the results for BA were hundreds of cancelled flights, 70,000 stranded passengers, and additional costs of £40 million.

2. In 1999 General Motors spun off its component-making units to form Delphi Corporation. This remained its sole supplier for many parts, with business amounting to $30 billion a year. But Delphi could not compete with increasingly efficient competitors, and its problems were compounded by GM's falling sales. In 2006 it went bankrupt and GM risked losing its only supplier

of a wide range of parts. US Law allows (Chapter 11) bankruptcy, where a corporation can continue trading while it reorganises and looks for ways of settling its debts. Delphi went down this route, but its survival plans included cutting 23,000 jobs, closing 25 plants, cutting employee benefits – and renegotiating contracts for parts with GM, and passing some of its employee pension liabilities back to GM.

Question

- Can you find other examples of increasing risk from single sourcing?

(*Source*: Waters, D. (2007) Supply chain risk management, Kogan Page, London)

Cost reduction

When managers improve logistics, they often mean reducing costs, perhaps following a strategy of cost leadership or leanness. The benefits of leanness are obvious, as it reduces the waste of resources, gives lower prices and more competitive products, reduces costs and gives higher profit margins. But more efficient operations invariably come with increased risk. We can illustrate this with just-in-time operations (JIT), which are at the heart of leanness. As we saw in Chapter 9, JIT reduces waste by making sure that activities are done at exactly the time they are needed. They are not done too early (as this would waste resources that are waiting to be used), nor too late (as this would cause delays and reduce service). The result is efficient flows of materials, no stocks of work in progress – and lower risks from waste, interruptions, delays, obsolescence, loss, and so on. But the real picture is more complicated, as JIT removes slack from operations and makes them vulnerable to the slightest hiccup. If there is even a small delay, breakdown, accident, surge in demand, new product, or any change, there is no cushion and the whole supply chain comes to a halt. So the real picture is that JIT significantly increases risks to the supply chain.

Agile logistics

Lean logistics can be criticised for putting too much emphasis on costs, and removing the flexibility to deal with unexpected events. An alternative agile strategy puts more emphasis on customer satisfaction by responding quickly to changing conditions. People often argue that agility is becoming more important, as product cycles are getting shorter, market requirements change quickly, and demand is becoming more volatile. So agility is essential for satisfying more demanding customers, who are looking for more choice, better products, lower prices, shorter lead times, and better value – and can use websites to access suppliers in any part of the world, giving a transparent market where they can compare products, deals and conditions.

But agility brings its own risks, such as its need for spare capacity that allow flexible operations. This spare capacity reduces productivity and increases costs, so there is more risk that customers who are primarily interested in low prices move to other suppliers.

E-business

Electronic trading, under the general umbrella of e-business, has transformed the way that many organisations buy and sell their products. It does not just improve purchasing, but allows completely new types of logistics with the emphasis moved away from physical materials to information. For instance, organisations that traditionally held stocks to allow for uncertain demand can now wait until they know actual demand and then use agile operations to meet it quickly – effectively 'replacing inventory with information'.

But as usual the news is not entirely good, as logistics has come to rely on a complex network of integrated systems. When any one of these develops a glitch, it is not just inconvenient, but it can bring the whole supply chain to a standstill. A new virus entering one computer can quickly travel to all the connected systems throughout the supply chain. So systems in the supply chains are as vulnerable as the weakest links, and this is particularly worrying when it comes to the security of, say, related banking systems. The reliance on new – perhaps only partially tested systems – introduces new types of risk, as demonstrated by the Y2K 'millennium bug'.

LOGISTICS IN PRACTICE – THE MILLENNIUM BUG

In the 1990s it was widely thought that computer BIOS (basic input output system) were only programmed to deal with dates up to 1999. The story grew that when their internal clocks clicked up to the year 2000 they would not be able to cope and there would be widespread disruption of computer systems. Most organisations were aware of this and took action to check that their systems were 'Y2K compliant', but it was difficult to guarantee that networked systems would continue work.

In practice, most firms thought that their own systems were all right, but they feared problems with their suppliers' systems or others in the supply chain. If anything did go wrong, the problems would appear during a holiday period when few people were around to solve them. Faced with the perceived risk, organisations took steps to mitigate their effects, typically holding extra stocks. But these stocks had knock-on effects that included the following:

- Pressure was put on limited warehousing space.
- The cost of pre-emptive purchases strained cash flows.
- Financial pressure increased as customers looked for extended credit to cover their own financial difficulties.
- The strain on finances increased the risk of business failures.
- Pre-emptive purchases were interpreted as genuinely increasing demand, with demand amplification in upstream suppliers.

- Rising demand gave an apparent boom in some industries in 1999, followed by a recession in 2000 as excess stocks were used.
- Customers transferred business from smaller suppliers to larger ones who they considered more able to cope with any problems.
- Customers moved from suppliers in developing countries to those in industrialised countries who might be more able to cope with problems.

In practice, very few problems actually appeared with the millennium bug. Systems were perfectly able to deal with the new date, and more harm was done by actions taken to avoid problems than by the problems themselves.

Question

- More harm often seems to be done in trying to avoid a risk than in accepting that it might happen. Why is this?

Globalisation

Globalisation is one of the major trends in logistics. It brings obvious benefits, but there are also risks in extended journeys around the world. The general view is that longer, more complicated journeys have inherently higher risks. Three obvious sources of risk with globalisation are:

1. Risks from working in a region that is less familiar and more distant from the organisation's usual operations. These include reduced control over remote sites, cultural differences, variable levels of skills, language problems, legal systems, political instability, unstable economic conditions, changing costs, rapidly changing conditions, different levels of commitment to quality, and so on.

2. Risks of moving materials over longer distances. These include the inherent risks of extended journeys, crossing international borders, meeting different cultures, extended lead times, more stock in transit, more handling, the need for bigger order quantities, greater chance of loss, obsolescence of products with short life-cycles, and so on.

3. Unexpected barriers to trade, such as:

    (a) product design limiting demand, with different regions demanding different types of product, a product not lending itself to global operations, or customers simply not liking them

    (b) practical difficulties making it impossible to meet demand, owing to protectionist government policies, problems at national frontiers, inadequate infrastructure, missing technical skills, or other cultural and economic differences.

Another source of risk comes with centralisation, as firms moving to new locations normally look for the economies of scale from large, centralised facilities. In practice, such moves rarely go as smoothly as hoped, and the resulting facilities tend to be less flexible and more vulnerable to change. There is also the risk that the relative transport and manufacturing costs will change, reducing the cost advantages of concentration.

Outsourcing

We know that outsourced, or third-party, logistics has a number of advantages – among them is the passing on of some risks to the service providers. For instance, as well as getting rewards, a third-party transport provider also accepts some of the risks associated with transport.

But, again, a decrease in some risks comes at the cost of increases to others, particularly loss of control and too much reliance on a single partner. Outsourcing also needs an organisation to switch to new types of operations – thereby replacing a set of relatively familiar and well-known risks by new ones that are less clearly understood. One surprising risk is that outsourcing does not work as well as expected,[9, 10] typically not delivering the required service level, or the expected reductions in cost, or the savings in internal time and effort. This gives increased risk of poor performance, more complex chains, uncontrollable costs, 'price creep', unsatisfactory working relationships, and so on. Another less obvious risk appears when a service provider has problems with one supply chain and moves resources away from other customers to solve it – so that one supply chain becomes susceptible to problems in a completely different chain.

Growth of risk management

Governments have a long tradition of emergency planning for, say, terrorist attacks, riots, wars and natural disasters. But this is less clear in business, where companies tend to assume that they will not be hit by a major disaster. At first sight, this laissez-faire attitude makes sense. Why should they put effort into planning for events that will probably never happen? But you could ask the same thing about insurance. Why do you take out fire insurance when your house is very unlikely to burn down? The answer is the same – some events may be very unlikely, but when they do occur the consequences are catastrophic. If you do not have fire insurance and your house burns down, you face bankruptcy; if a company is hit by an unforeseen crisis, it may not have the resources to continue. Unfortunately, there are many examples of this actually happening. The Enron Corporation was widely praised as a model of good management – before its dramatic collapse due to accounting irregularities. This collapse also took along the auditors, Arthur Andersen, who had been considered one of the world's leading firms of accountants. WorldCom followed in the USA, along with

Barings Bank and Energis in the UK, the Dutch retailer Royal Ahold, the Italian dairy conglomerate Parmalat Finanziaria, and a host of other major names.

When the effects of risk were apparent in even the biggest company, managers came under growing pressure to improve corporate governance and, in particular, identify and manage risks. These produced a series of reports and legislation, such as the Turnbull report in the UK,[11] adjustments to the German commercial code and in 2002 the Sarbanes-Oxley Act in the USA. These Acts generally require chief executives and financial directors to make specific statements about risk in their annual reports, and disclose all significant risks to corporate well-being. In particular, good corporate governance requires that companies use a formal approach to risk management, and as a minimum this should:

- protect the interests of stakeholders
- ensure that senior managers properly discharge their duties of risk management
- safeguard the continuing operations of the organisation by developing appropriate systems for risk management
- use formal procedures to identify and analyse the threats from risk
- have processes in place for dealing with risky events that actually occur, and mitigating their effects
- monitor, review and control the whole risk management effort
- ensure the company's compliance with laws and regulations.

Growing concern over supply chain risk

A dominant feature of supply chains is that all members are linked together, and a risk to one is automatically transferred to all other members. For instance, when one key supplier goes out of business, it is not just their immediate customers who are affected, but all other members of the chain. When a manufacturer stops production, all the upstream tiers of suppliers are affected back to the original suppliers. You can see the way that supply chain risks ripple around the world with the 2003 outbreak of SARS, or bird flu. This was largely contained to southern China and Hong Kong, but restrictions on travel disrupted business operations as far away as Toronto and London. Similarly, in 2005 hurricanes Katrina and Rita both hit oil refineries in the Gulf of Mexico, but the consequent fears of fuel shortages raised prices around the world.

In the past few years organisations have started making some progress in the area, perhaps motivated by the terrorist attack on New York's World Trade Center – now universally known as '9/11'. Suddenly it became clear that a single event can have catastrophic consequences. Although relatively few organisations were directly effected by the attack, the raised awareness and new security at US borders had widespread effects.

Clearly the main risks to supply chains do not come from terrorist attacks, but from the broad range of unforeseen events that might affect them.[12] All supply chains face risks of many different kinds, and the flow of materials is much more likely to be disrupted by an unreliable supplier. Managers can control many of these risks, and the key point is that they should not wait to see what damaging events occur, and then start thinking about their response. Instead, they should be proactive, identifying potential risks and planning their responses in advance. Then they are prepared and can take immediate action when an unexpected event actually occurs.

This seems a reasonable view, but despite growing concern over supply chain risk management, Christopher et al.[4] reported that, 'Little research has been undertaken into supply chain vulnerabilities' and, 'Awareness of the subject is poor.' This is changing, but progress is slow and most organisations have made little real progress.

Steps to introduce risk management

When organisations want to introduce risk management, they need some kind of formal plan. We have listed the three core considerations as identifying risks, analysing them and designing ways of dealing with them. We can add some details to this, and suggest a general approach to introducing supply chain risk management in the following nine stages.

1. *Consider risk within the organisation*
   Risk management in a supply chain generally starts with one organisation taking a lead and transferring their knowledge and requirements to more of the chain. So the first step is to make sure that senior managers within the lead organisation are committed and have defined broad policies for risk, that a risk management team has been appointed, necessary systems have been installed, that there are smooth information flows, and so on. In other words, there has been some progress on risk management within their organisation. Now the aim is to formalise this and spread the effort to other members of the supply chain.

2. *Take a strategic view*
   In common with all major initiatives, supply chain risk management needs commitment from senior managers who are aware of the issues and can allocate the resources. It is a strategic initiative that can have widespread effects on an organisation and the way that it is run.

3. *Understand the concept of supply chain risk*
   Before they can successfully plan for risk along a supply chain, managers must clearly understand what they are studying. In other words they must understand the concept of risk, as well as the members, roles, links, interactions,

objectives, forces, dynamics, power, and all other elements that form the complex web of a supply chain.

4. *Consider risk in the design*

   The principle here is that managers should explicitly include the effects of risk in their decisions. If they ignore risk, they will focus on leanness, efficiency or some other goals that inadvertently increase vulnerability. The best design needs a balance between resilience and normal measures of efficiency.

5. *The chain is only as strong as its weakest link*

   Disruption at any point in a supply chain causes problems for the whole chain, so managers have to identify risks throughout the chain to find the weakest parts. This is difficult, but there is little point in managers building a resilient chain in the areas they control, if adjacent areas are still vulnerable.

6. *Look for collaboration*

   The sharing of ideas, methods and information is a core part of supply chain management. This is the only way that members of the chain can identify mutual risks and design effective ways of dealing with them, gaining synergies from the collaboration.

7. *Prevention is better than cure*

   The principle here is that it is always better to avoid harm rather than look for compensation after it has occurred. So we can characterise the best options for dealing with a risk, in descending order of preference, as trying to prevent a harmful event from happening, then reducing the consequences if it does happen, and finally seeking redress for damage after it has happened.

8. *Create agility*

   Risk is based on uncertainty, which exists in all operations. So despite our best plans we are always susceptible to unforeseeable events, and must have the flexibility to deal with them. There are many ways of increasing agility, such as spare capacity, back-up systems, stocks of finished goods, holding cash reserves, postponement, short lead times, modular processes, and so on.

9. *Have emergency procedures*

   When a risky event occurs, flexible operations can avoid its worst effects and continue to work normally. But sometimes the effects are too severe for even the most flexible operations to deal with. For instance, if a delivery of materials is delayed, flexible operations will allow normal working to continue.

Using this approach will give a resilient supply chain whose features allow it to withstand risk. For instance, it is likely to be shorter and simpler, but with parallel paths, so that a problem in any one path can be avoided by going around another route. Contrary to the demands of leanness, it is also likely to involve higher stocks and spare capacity to give a buffer against problems. As in all aspects of logistics, the overall design will be a compromise. In this case, managers have to decide how much attention they will give to the relatively few risks, rather than their normal operations.

LOGISTICS IN PRACTICE – SUDAN RED 1

Food safety has a very high priority with most governments. Strict regulation and rigorous testing mean that most of us face little risk from the food we buy, and new technologies and improving methods for ensuring safety generally mean that this risk is declining. However, some practices are increasing the risk, such as sourcing in regions with less rigorous attitudes towards food safety, longer supply chains that move food around the world, and untried technology.

Sudan red 1 is an industrial dye that has been banned as a food colourant throughout the EU since 2003. However, in 2005 it was found in a batch of chilli powder being used by Premier Foods in the UK to manufacture Worcester sauce. There was an immediate scare over Premier Foods' products – and any other product that contained red dye – so 500 products were taken off store shelves. This was an essential move, as shops clearly cannot sell food containing an illegal substance – or run the risk of selling food that might possibly contain it.

In reality, no products were actually contaminated, and no one bought any product containing Sudan red 1.

On the positive side, an average supermarket stocks 50,000 food items, so even 500 is a relatively small number. The case also showed that risk management procedures moved very quickly to prevent any harm. The UK government alerted food agencies in European countries and the European Commission's rapid alert system and, within minutes, retailers' information systems were updated, blacklisting affected products, and immediately preventing further sales. It also issued automatic press releases, along with television and radio warnings. Within the food industry integrated systems distributed information, alerting firms by e-mail, EDI, and phone calls.

Question

- Do you think that risk management systems are always as efficient as they were in this example?

(*Source*: Corbett, K. (2005) Red scare, Checkout, July)

Chapter review

- In the context of supply chains, risks appear whenever unexpected events might disrupt the flow of materials. Because we can never know exactly what will happen in the future, there are always risks in logistics.
- The nature and complexity of supply chains makes them particularly vulnerable to risk. Some of these risks are external to the chain and outside managers' control; others are internal and under managers' control.

- Risks can cause a lot of damage to an organisation, so they should be properly managed. Risk management involves three stages to identify risks, analyse them and plan responses.

- Risk identification considers the risks to each activity and compiles a register of the most significant. Risk analysis finds their likelihood and impact, and then categorises them using expected values of some form of Pareto analysis. There are many forms of appropriate response, which range from doing nothing through to closing down operations.

- Historically, logistics managers have paid little attention to risk. As a result, levels of supply chain risk have tended to drift upwards.

- A more worrying trend has managers designing more efficient supply chains by removing all the slack – and inadvertently increasing the risks. We illustrated this effect with current trends in the supply chain of integration, cost reduction, flexibility, e-business, and so on.

- It is easy to see the effects of risky events. This has encouraged a growing concern about supply chain risk management. Despite this growing interest, progress is slow and most organisations have made little real headway. We outlined a general procedure for introducing risk management.

Project – effects of risk

You can find many examples of businesses that have suffered when they have been hit by unexpected events. Some of these are well-known examples of financial irregularities or market problems. Others are more directly linked to risks in the supply chain.

Find some examples of organisations that have been affected by supply chain risks and discuss the type of risk, its effects, what managers did to counteract the risks, and what they could have done differently.

CASE STUDY – BUSINESS CONTINUITY MANAGEMENT

Business continuity management – often referred to a crisis management – consists of the procedures that an organisation develops to help it continue functioning through any kind of disaster. It is a general plan, which is not restricted to a specific kind of risk. For instance, a transport might have a plan to help it continue working if it cannot get fuel. The reason it cannot get fuel does not matter, but its continuity plan is only concerned with avoiding disruption to operations.

The UK's Department of Trade and Industry,[13] in association with the Business Continuity Institute and the Disaster Recovery Institute International, summarises the business continuity management process. This is phrased in terms of a 10-point plan for running a project to implement business continuity management.

CASE STUDY – BUSINESS CONTINUITY MANAGEMENT (CONTINUED)

1. *Project initiation and management.* Identify a business continuity manager, get support and sponsorship from senior managers, establish a management structure.

2. *Risk evaluation and control.* Do a risk assessment and identify procedures for reducing and mitigating risk.

3. *Business impact analysis.* Identify critical business processes, assess the impact of their loss, consider the interdependencies between operations.

4. *Developing business continuity strategies.* Consider both recovery and risk reduction, set timetables for business recovery, consider related strategies and support for operations.

5. *Emergency response and operations.* Establish a crisis management process for responding to emergencies, ensure that all team members are aware of their responsibilities.

6. *Developing and implementing business continuity plans.* Design business continuity plans to support the strategy, ensure their ownership and management.

7. *Awareness and training plans.* Make sure that all staff are aware of business continuity management and that this is promoted as an ongoing initiative, train recovery teams in their roles and responsibilities, ensure that IT and other specialist groups are aware of their responses and can provide the necessary support.

8. *Maintaining and exercising business continuity plans.* Assign responsibilities for maintaining the plans, ensure that they are regularly maintained and tested, update the plans to reflect changes in business operations.

9. *Public relations and crisis coordination.* Include both internal and external communications in the business continuity plans, ensure that procedures are in place to keep all stakeholders informed of the current status.

10. *Coordination with public authorities.* Inform local authorities and emergency services about the plans, ensure that procedures and policies comply with statutes and regulations.

Questions

- What exactly is 'business continuity management'? How does it differ from standard risk management?

- What would be the advantages to an organisation of introducing business continuity management?

- How might an organisation introduce business continuity, and what problems might it meet?

Discussion questions

15.1 Risks are nasty things that damage a supply chain. Is this true?

15.2 Is it fair to say that logistics managers have traditionally paid little attention to supply chain risk?

15.3 Almost by definition, risks are rare events. So why should managers spend their time worrying about the slight chance that some obscure event will actually happen, when they could spend their time worrying about the ordinary things that almost certainly will happen?

15.4 What are the main risks facing a supply chain?

15.5 Do managers have to consider every risk to the supply chain? If not, which ones should they concentrate on?

15.6 How would you interpret the expected value of an event? What alternative measures are there?

15.7 Managers rarely have any control of the serious risks facing their supply chains, and there is little they can do to influence conditions. So why should they bother with risk management?

15.8 It seems that almost every new development in logistics increases the level of risk. Is this a fair statement?

15.9 Why is risk management seen as an increasingly important issue?

References

1. Nelson, D., Mayo, R. and Moody, P. (1998) Powered by Honda: developing excellence in the global enterprise, John Wiley and Sons, New York.
2. Handy, C. (1999) Beyond certainty, Harvard Business School Press, Boston, MA.
3. Economist Intelligence Unit (2001) Enterprise Risk Management, implementing new solutions.
4. Christopher, M. et al. (2002), Supply chain vulnerability: final report on behalf of DTLR, DTI and Home Office, School of Management, Cranfield University.
5. Hendricks, K.B. and Singhal, V.R. (2003) The effect of supply chain glitches on shareholder wealth, Journal of Operation Management, 21(5), 501–23.
6. Jüttner, U. (2005) Supply chain risk management, International Journal of Logistics Management, 16(1), 120–41.
7. Szymankiewicz, J. (1997) Efficient customer response – supply chain management for the new millennium? Logistics Focus, 5(9), 16–22.
8. Poirier, C.C. and Quinn, F.J. (2003) A survey of supply chain progress, Supply Chain Management Review, September/October.
9. Richards, G. (2006) Client satisfaction with 3PL suppliers, Burman Group, London.
10. Manktelow, B. (2006) Why does outsourcing not deliver? Logistics and Transport Focus, 8(9), 42–5.
11. Turnbull (1999) Internal control, The Institute of Chartered Accountants in England and Wales, London.
12. Sheffi, Y. (2002) Supply chain management under threat of international terrorism, International Journal of Logistics Management, 12(2), 1–11.
13. Department of Trade and Industry (2006) Information security: understanding business continuity management, The Stationery Office, London.

Further reading

Brindley, C. (editor) (2004) Supply chain risk, Ashgate, Aldershot.

Waters, D. (2007) Supply chain risk management, Kogan Page, London.

GLOSSARY

Throughout the text key terms have been tinted. The definition of these terms is included in the following glossary:

3PL	third-party logistics
ABC analysis	puts items into categories that show their relative importance (typically the amount of effort worth spending on inventory control)
Aggregate plans	tactical decisions that give summarised plans for related activities, typically by month at each location
Agile logistics	a flexible approach, which aims at customer satisfaction
B2B	trade that is business-to-business
B2C	trade that is business-to-customer
Backward integration	when an organisation owns a lot of the upstream operations in a supply chain
Benchmarking	comparing an organisation's performance with the best in the industry, and learning from their experience
Bill of lading	provides all the information a carrier needs for a journey
Bottleneck	the part of a supply chain that limits throughput because it has the smallest individual capacity
Bottom-up emergence	assumes that senior managers do not design a strategy in a single step, but that it emerges over time from the actions of managers lower down the organisation
(Supply chain) breadth	is the number of parallel routes that materials can flow through, or the number of organisations in each tier
Business process reengineering	the fundamental redesign of business processes to achieve dramatic improvements
Capacity	of a supply chain is its maximum throughput in a given time
Centre of gravity	the centre of supply and demand defined as the point (X_0, Y_0), where $X_0 = \sum XW / \sum W$ and $Y_0 = \sum YW / \sum W$
Change manager	generates enthusiasm for change within an organisation
Collaborative planning, forecasting and replenishment	has organisations in a supply chain cooperating and jointly planning key activities
Common carriers	companies that move materials on a one-off basis whenever asked by another organisation
Container ports	ports with facilities for dealing with containerised, intermodal transport

Continuous improvement	a series of small adjustments to give iterative improvements
Contract carrier	common carrier with a long-term contract to provide transport for a customer
Covering problem	finds the location with the best maximum delivery lead time
CPFR	collaborative planning, forecasting and replenishment
CRM	Customer relationship management
Cross-docking	coordinates the supply and delivery of materials so that they arrive at a warehouse receiving area and are transferred straight away to the loading area, where they are put onto delivery vehicles
Customer focus	means that organisations have a strategy that includes an emphasis on customer satisfaction
Customer relationship management	covers all aspects of the ways that companies manage their relationships with downstream customers
Customer satisfaction	depends on logistics meeting, and preferably exceeding, customer expectations
Customer service	a measure (or set of measures) that show how well logistics is performing
Dependent demand	means that demand for different products (or from different customers) are somehow related
Demand management	adjusts demand to match available capacity
Demurrage	a charge at terminals for storage of goods
Designed capacity	the maximum possible throughput in ideal conditions
Distribution requirements planning	uses the MRP approach to plan logistics
Downstream	after an organisation and moving materials outwards to final customers
Drop-shipping	has wholesalers keeping no stocks themselves, but coordinating the movement of materials directly from upstream suppliers to downstream customers
DRP	distribution requirements planning
Economic order quantity	the optimal size for an order in a simple inventory system
ECR	efficient customer response
EDI	Electronic data interchange
Effective capacity	the maximum realistic throughput in normal conditions
Efficient consumer response	connects operations in the supply chain, so that materials are pulled through tiers of suppliers
EFT	Electronic fund transfer
Electronic Data Interchange	uses standard formats to allow remote computers to exchange data without going through any intermediaries
Electronic fund transfer	automatically transfers money between bank accounts
Electronic point-of-sales	system for automatically recording and transmitting information about sales from cash terminals
Enterprise resource planning	extends the MRP approach to other organisations in the supply chain
Environmental scan	analyses the business environment in which the logistics work
EOQ	economic order quantity
EPOS	electronic point of sales
e-purchasing	purchasing products using the Internet
e-procurement	purchasing products using the Internet
ERP	enterprise resource planning
Expected value	= probability of event × consequence

Facilities location	finds the best geographic locations for different elements in a supply chain
Factory gate pricing	has a single organisation, often a major retailer, taking responsibility for delivering products from the factory gate through to the final customer
Feasible set approach	where there are only a small number of feasible sites so that managers have to compare and choose the best
(Strategic) Focus	an aspect of performance that an organisation's strategy concentrates on
Forward integration	when an organisation owns a lot of the downstream operations in a supply chain
Forward logistics	makes deliveries out to customers
Freight forwarders	intermediaries who consolidate and organise freight movements
Global companies	see the world as a single market
Implementation	translates strategic plans into positive actions
Inbound or inward logistics	move materials into an organisation from suppliers
Independent demand	means that demand from one customer is not related to demand from any other customer
Infinite set approach	uses geometric arguments to find the best location, assuming that there are no restrictions on site availability
In-house transport	transport run by an organisation to move its own materials
Integrating logistics	has all the related activities of logistics working together as a single function
Intermodal transport	has different modes of transport used for each part of a journey
International companies	have facilities in different countries, but they are centred on one home country
International logistics	occur when supply chains cross national frontiers
Item coding	gives every item a unique identifying tag so that its movements can be traced
Inventory	a list of things held in stock (or sometimes the stock itself)
Inventory control	another term for inventory management
Inventory management	is responsible for the control of stock levels within an organisation
Joint venture	where two (usually) companies put up funds to start a third company with shared ownership
Just-in-time (JIT)	organises all activities to occur at exactly the time they are needed
Kaizen	continuous improvement
Kanban	card that control the flow of materials through JIT operations
Land bridges	have materials crossing land on what is essentially a sea journey
Layout	describes the physical arrangement of storage racks, loading and unloading areas, equipment, offices, rooms, and all other facilities in a warehouse
Lead time	the total time between ordering materials and having them delivered and available for use
Lean logistics	an approach that aims to remove all waste from supply chains
(Supply chain) length	is the number of tiers, or intermediaries, that materials flow through between source and destination

Learning curve	which shows that the more often you repeat something, the easier it becomes and the faster you can do it
Logistics	the function responsible for all aspects of the movement and storage of materials on their journey from original suppliers through to final customers
Logistics audit	systematic collection of information about existing logistics activities, procedures, costs, resources, utilisation, performance, and all other relevant details
Logistics infrastructure	consists of the organisational structure and the systems, human resources, culture and resources to support it
Logistics' mission	states the underlying long-term aims for the supply chain
Logistics strategy	consists of all the long-term goals, plans, policies, culture, resources, decisions and actions that relate to the management of an organisation's supply chains
Manufacturing resources planning	is an integrated system for synchronising functions within an organisation by connecting the schedules back to the master schedule
Mass customisation	a production method that combines the benefits of mass production with the flexibility of customised products
Master schedules	tactical plans that give schedules for each activity, typically by week
Material requirements planning	uses the master schedule and other relevant information to plan the supply of materials
Materials	anything that is moved into, through, or out of an organisation
Materials management	controls the movement of materials within an organisation
Mode of transport	the type of transport, either road, rail, air, water or pipeline
MRP	material requirements planning
MRP II	manufacturing resources planning
Multinational companies	form a more loosely linked, largely independent set of companies working in different geographical regions
National companies	only work within their home market
Operations	all the activities that create an organisation's products
Outbound or outward logistics	move materials from an organisation out to customers
Outsourcing	has organisations concentrating on their core operations and outsourcing peripheral activities to third parties
Own account transport	transport run by an organisation to move its own materials
Ownership utility	value added by having products delivered to the right people
Partial productivity	total throughput/units of a single resource used
Physical distribution	a general term for the activities that deliver finished goods to customers
Piggy-back	has a lorry, or usually just the trailer, driven onto a train for fast movement over a longer distance
Place utility	value added by having products available at the place they are needed
Plan-do-check-act cycle	approach to finding continuous improvements
Postponement	moves almost-finished products into the distribution system, and delays final modifications or customisation until the last possible moment
Private warehouse	is run by an organisation for its own materials
Probability-impact matrix	table showing a Pareto analysis for the relative importance of risks

Procurement	is responsible for acquiring all the materials needed by an organisation
Process chart	a diagram used for analysing a process
Product	the combination of goods and services that an organisation supplies to its customers
Product package	view of a product as a complex mixture of goods and services, including logistics
Public warehouse	provides services that anyone can use
Purchase orders	initiate the actual flow of materials from a vendor to a purchaser
Purchasing	is the function responsible for buying all the materials needed by an organisation
Quick response	a form of efficient customer response that links organisations to pull materials through supply chains
Radio frequency identification	an active transmitter used for identifying items
Rate	quoted transport cost for moving an item on a particular journey
Rectilinear distance	between two points is the difference in x coordinates plus the difference in y coordinates
Reorder level	stock level when it is time to place another order
Resource requirements planning	a standard approach to matching available resources to forecast demand
Reverse logistics	returns materials back to an organisation after they have been delivered to customers
RFID	radio frequency identification
Risk	the threat of an event that might disrupt normal flows of materials or stop things happening as planned
Risk management	the process for systematically identifying, analysing and responding to risks throughout an organisation
ROL	reorder level.
Safety stock	stock beyond expected needs which is kept to add a margin of safety
Scheduling rules	simple rules, which experience suggests give reasonable results for scheduling problems
Scoring model	assigns a range of factors, weighted scores to compare locations
Service level	the likelihood that a demand can be met from stock
Short-term schedules	operational plans that show detailed timetables for all jobs and resources, typically by day
Single median problem	finds the location with the shortest average travel distance to a set of customers
Single sourcing	has an organisation acquiring each material, or related materials, from only a single supplier
SRM	Supplier relationship management
Stock	is a store of materials that is held in an organisation, and is formed whenever materials are not used at the time they become available
Stock control	another term for inventory management
Stock turnover	(annual amount spent on stock)/(Average value of stock held)
Strategic fit	means that there is a good balance between higher strategies, organisational strengths and external environment
Strategy	sets the long-term direction of an organisation
Supplier rating	has a customer monitoring the performance of a supplier

Supply chain	consists of the series of activities and organisations that materials move through on their journey from initial suppliers to final customers
Supply chain management	an alternative name for logistics
Supplier relationship management	covers all aspects of the ways that companies manage their relationships with upstream suppliers
Supply management	adjusts available capacity to match known demand
SWOT analysis	analyses internal strengths and weaknesses, and external opportunities and threats
Third-party logistics	outsources logistics to specialised third-party providers
Third-party transport	outsources transport to specialised transport operators
Time compression	a strategy based on the reduction of the time taken for activities in the supply chain, largely by removing things that add no value
Time utility	value added by having products available at the time they are needed
Top-down design	has senior managers designing a logistics strategy and then passing it down to lower levels for implementation
Total logistics cost	total cost of all logistics activities
Total productivity	total throughput/total resources used
Transport	is responsible for the physical movement of materials between points in the supply chain
Upstream	in front of an organisation and moving materials inwards from original suppliers
Utilisation	shows the proportion of designed capacity that is actually used
Utility	a measure of added value
Value density	the ratio of a product's value to its weight or size
Vendor managed inventory	has suppliers managing both their own stocks and those held further down the supply chain
Vendor rating	has a customer monitoring the performance of a vendor
Vertical integration	the amount of a supply chain that is owned by one organisation
Visibility	has shared information to allow one organisation to see what is happening in other parts of the supply chain
Warehouse	any location where stocks of material are held on their journey through supply chains

INDEX